1979 YEARBOOK

EVENTS OF 1978

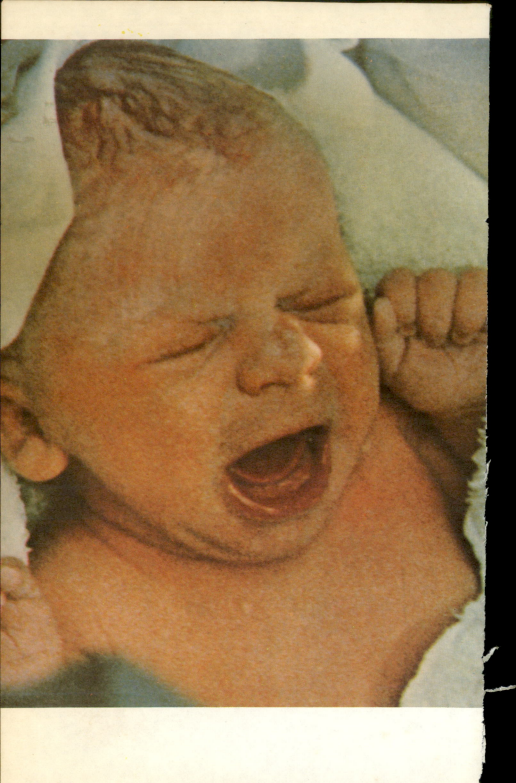

FUNK & WAGNALLS NEW ENCYCLOPEDIA 1979 YEARBOOK

LEON L. BRAM
Vice-President and
Editorial Director

ALBERT BENNETT
Editor

Funk & Wagnalls, Inc., New York

Frontispiece:
**July 25, 1978: Louise Joy Brown, the first child to have been
conceived outside the mother's body, greets the press.**

TABLE OF CONTENTS

MEMBERS OF THE STAFF

FOREWORD TO THE EVENTS OF 1978 YEARBOOK

Unpredictable—that is probably the most accurate adjective for 1978.

Several of the year's least predictable events came in threes: a triple crown winner in horse racing, a heavyweight boxing championship won for the third time, three Americans crossing the Atlantic in a balloon, and three churchmen wearing the robes of the Roman Catholic pope. Certainly the birth of a baby conceived outside its mother's womb was a surprise to most people, if not to the scientific fraternity. And who could have foreseen the tragedies of the year—a mass death in the jungles of Guyana, the assassinations of the mayor and a county supervisor of San Francisco, and the murder of Italy's foremost statesman. The long-hoped-for Arab-Israeli peace agreement seemed a virtual certainty in September; but negotiations soon broke down. In December came a startling announcement: the forthcoming exchange of diplomats between the United States and the People's Republic of China.

These events, indeed all the happenings of the unpredictable year that is now history, are chronicled in the following pages. We are also pleased to present, preceding our record of the year, a series of essays that provide background information on some widely divergent subjects, each a prime topic of conversation during 1978. The first, written by the director of a Nobel Prize-winning organization, discusses the past and the present of the dramatic struggle for human rights. In the second essay a distinguished science reporter tells why his job is such a difficult one in these days of cloning, test-tube babies, and flying saucers. And finally, a U.S. Senator offers a description of the joys and the benefits of running—not for office, but for exercise.

THE EDITORS

HUMAN RIGHTS

by Martin Ennals

Human rights became an increasingly prominent
issue in world affairs during 1978—a year of political
trials, executions, assassinations, and the continuing
detention of hundreds of thousands for their political
or religious beliefs. Nor was freedom of expression
the only human right under attack. Freedom from
hunger, disease, illiteracy, and economic deprivation
was no closer for millions suffering under the
continuing impact of widespread underdevelopment
and social injustice. Ironically, 1978 was also the
thirtieth anniversary of the Universal Declaration of
Human Rights, adopted by the General Assembly of
the United Nations in December, 1948. The
declaration establishes the principle that all
individuals are entitled to economic, social, and
cultural rights (freedom from want) and to civil and
political rights (freedom from fear).

Speaking on the occasion of the award of the
Nobel Peace Prize for 1977 to Amnesty International,
Mümtaz Soysal, vice-chairman of the organization's
International Executive Committee, underlined the
indivisibility of human rights. "The freedom of the
human mind and the welfare of the human being are
inextricably linked," he argued. ". . . The right to
education and the right of freedom of information
and public debate on official policies are necessary to
secure full public participation in the process of
social and economic development."

But public debate on official policies carried with it
high risks in numerous countries in 1978. Much
international publicity surrounded the Moscow trial
of Yuri Orlov in May. At the time of his arrest Orlov,
a physicist, was chairman of the unofficial Helsinki
Monitoring Group. This group, composed of private
Soviet citizens, was established in mid-1976 to collect
and publicize facts regarding Soviet compliance with
the human-rights obligations set forth in the Final
Act of the 1975 Conference on Security and

Martin Ennals has been
Secretary General of Amnesty
International since 1968. An
Englishman trained as an
economist, he served as
General Secretary of the British
Council for Civil Liberties from
1960 to 1966. In 1968 he
resigned from a post on the
National Committee for
Commonwealth Immigrants to
protest the British government's
restrictive immigration policies.
Amnesty International, founded
in 1961, is a worldwide human-
rights organization based in
London. It works for the release
of all men and women
detained anywhere for their
beliefs, color, ethnic origin, sex,
religion, or language, provided
that they neither used nor
advocated violence.
Independent of all
governments and ideologies, it
is financed by its membership
and by private contributions
from all over the world. A
recent contributor was the
Nobel Foundation, which
awarded Amnesty International
the 1977 Nobel Peace Prize.

Cooperation in Europe—the so-called Helsinki
Agreement.

Orlov was convicted of "anti-Soviet agitation and
propaganda" and sentenced to the maximum term
applicable, seven years' strict-regime imprisonment
and five years' exile. He was one of at least 160 Soviet
citizens sentenced to terms of imprisonment, exile,
or banishment for exercise of their human rights in
the period between the formation of the Helsinki
Monitoring Group and the date of his own trial. At
least another fifty to sixty people had been confined
to psychiatric hospitals for political reasons in the
same period.

Such cases and the struggle for human rights
which they embody have a long history. Human-
rights issues are seen by some as central to the
evolution of world culture. The concept of basic
obligations which people should respect in their
relations with one another and the need for
protection against discrimination and abuse of
authority have emerged with their own traditions in
different cultures and societies.

In 1948 the U.N. adopted the Universal Declaration
of Human Rights in the belief that "recognition of
the inherent dignity and of the equal and inalienable
rights of all members of the human family is the
foundation of freedom, justice, and peace in the
world." The thirty articles of the declaration provide
that everyone has the right to life, liberty, and
security of person; to equality before the law without
discrimination; to a fair and public trial; and to be

presumed innocent before proven guilty. Everyone is
assured freedom of movement; freedom of thought,
conscience, and religion; freedom of opinion and
expression; and freedom of peaceful assembly. No
one shall be held in slavery; no one shall be
subjected to torture or to cruel, inhuman, or
degrading treatment or punishment; no one shall be
subjected to arbitrary arrest, detention, or exile.
Everyone has the right to a nationality, to marry, to
own property, to take part in the government of his
or her country, to work, to receive equal pay for
equal work, to receive just and favorable

*Out of the book burnings, forced resettlements,
penal abuses, and devastation of World War II
came the modern movement to define and protect
human rights.*

remuneration, to enjoy rest and leisure, and to have an adequate standard of living and education.

The Universal Declaration of Human Rights is only one of a number of important international human-rights documents. Between 1951 and 1978 the U.N. General Assembly adopted more than fifteen conventions, covenants, and declarations dealing with human rights, ranging from the outlawing of genocide to the elimination of all forms of discrimination. The International Covenant on Economic, Social and Cultural Rights and the International Covenant on Civil and Political Rights, in force since early 1976, are legally binding upon every nation that signs them (almost fifty by 1978).

But practical implementation still remains the Achilles heel of the quest for human rights. One of the crucial tests of protection of human rights is the effectiveness of the actual mechanisms for investigating alleged violations of these rights and for ensuring that such violations cease. Within the U.N. itself, the main protection mechanism is the Commission on Human Rights. This body consists of thirty-two members appointed by the Economic and Social Council of the U.N. However, the members function as representatives of governments—a limitation which many observers believe inhibits the commission from functioning free from political pressures. The cases referred to the commission are scrutinized—normally in closed proceedings—and further investigations may be made and a report submitted to the Economic and Social Council. There are still no effective sanctions to enforce any recommendations, but the publicity that accompanies the case can be an effective form of pressure on the government at fault.

In 1978 the commission considered allegations of substantial human-rights violations in fourteen countries. Chile, the Israeli-occupied territories, Rhodesia, and South Africa were already on the agenda. In addition, the commission dealt confidentially with submissions on Bolivia, Equatorial Guinea, Ethiopia, Indonesia, the Republic of Korea, Malawi, Paraguay, Uganda, and Uruguay. Under the commission's procedures, the decisions taken by it on these nine cases remain undisclosed. At the same session the commission publicly considered the human-rights situation in Cambodia, where large-

Freedom from hunger and freedom to learn are two basic human rights and needs. The Universal Declaration of Human Rights, adopted by the United Nations in 1948, established the principle that such cultural rights are as important as political ones, and often more urgently in need of defense.

scale killings had been reported by refugees since the change of government in April, 1975.

Important human-rights protection mechanisms exist at regional levels as well. The Council of Europe has both a European Commission of Human Rights and a European Court of Human Rights. The Organization of American States (OAS) has an Inter-American Commission on Human Rights.

In early 1978 the European Court of Human Rights ruled that the interrogation methods used against suspected terrorists by the United Kingdom in Northern Ireland in 1971 constituted a violation of Article 3 of the European Convention on Human Rights, which states: "No one shall be subjected to torture or to cruel, inhuman or degrading treatment or punishment." This was the culmination of a lengthy investigative and judicial procedure in which the European Commission of Human Rights had investigated complaints brought forward by the Republic of Ireland. At one point the commission interviewed victims of the interrogation techniques

13

The right to leisure—provided for by the United Nations Universal Declaration of Human Rights—is enjoyed by a picnicking family.

at special hearings held, for security reasons, at an isolated air base in Stavanger, Norway.

Such instances of determined action by governments and intergovernmental institutions to deal with human-rights violations are rare. There has been a tremendous amount of lip service paid to human rights, but in fact the actual observance of those rights is increasingly threatened. It is common, for example, for a country's laws and practices to contravene international human-rights standards. By law, a person may be subjected to prolonged detention without charge or trial. Retroactive legislation may introduce penalties for membership in previously legal associations. Some countries have splendid constitutional guarantees for human rights which are deliberately flouted by the political administration. Or laws providing equal rights for minorities or a more equitable distribution of land and resources may, in practice, be totally ignored.

Numerous voluntary, nongovernmental organizations have been formed to mobilize international public opinion in an effort to close the gap between international declarations on human rights and the reality of appalling violations of those

When troops are deployed to impose order and search for weapons and explosives, as in Northern Ireland during the sectarian violence of the early 1970's, civil rights are often curbed or denied. So is the fundamental right to freedom from fear.

rights. Their main strength lies in playing the role of watchdog: tirelessly exposing to public view the international hypocrisy about human rights. Amnesty International is one such organization. It opposes torture and execution in all cases. It seeks fair and prompt trials for all political prisoners. In the case of prisoners of conscience—individuals imprisoned anywhere for their political or religious beliefs or for their race, color, sex, language, or ethnic origin, who have neither used nor advocated violence—it works for their immediate and unconditional release.

The rights which the Amnesty International movement tries to defend are based on only four of the thirty articles of the Universal Declaration of Human Rights. These are the provisions against torture and other cruel, inhuman, or degrading treatment or punishment; against arbitrary arrest, detention, and exile; for freedom of thought, conscience, and religion; and for freedom of opinion and expression. Nevertheless, even using this limited yardstick, the measure of respect for human rights in the world today gives cause for grave concern.

In 1978 Amnesty International was active on behalf of more than 5000 cases of known or possible prisoners of conscience in at least seventy-five countries throughout the world. For each known prisoner, the organization estimated that there might

Freedom of assembly, here exercised by a crowd in Hyde Park, London, is among the rights specified by the Universal Declaration of Human Rights.

The history of human rights is one of documents. Right: The Babylonian king Hammurabi promulgated the earliest known code of legal rights and penalties in the 18th century B.C. Bottom left: King John of England was forced to yield rights to his nobles in the Magna Charta, signed in 1215. Bottom right: Tourists examine the U.S. Constitution and Bill of Rights in Washington, D.C. Opposite page, left: A painting depicts the drafting in 1864 of the first Geneva Convention, which laid down rules for the treatment of wounded prisoners of war and for the protection of medical personnel. Right: The Helsinki Conference of 1975 brought together the leaders of thirty-five nations. The conferees signed a "final act" document pledging respect for freedom of travel, emigration, and information.

16

be another fifty or one hundred who were unknown.
Thus, there exists a large, worldwide,
unacknowledged population of prisoners of
conscience held in secret interrogation centers, in
overcrowded prisons, in labor camps, on isolated
islands.

Large numbers have been held without charge or
trial—in many cases for more than a decade. In
Indonesia alone tens of thousands of political
prisoners are believed to remain in detention. The
vast majority are persons arrested after the abortive
coup attempt of 1965 who were deemed dangerous
to society but against whom there was no evidence
on which to bring them to trial. Many of the
Indonesian prisoners, and others like them in
countries where imprisonment is not subject to
judicial review, were simply victims of circumstance.
They include people picked up on the streets
without means of identifying themselves and unable
to defend themselves against political charges;
women whose sons and daughters were being sought
by the army; women who were arrested together
with their husbands or sons for no reason other than
their family ties.

Take the case of one uneducated and apolitical
Indonesian woman in her mid-30's. She was doing
domestic work or selling in markets at the time of
the attempted coup and was apparently picked up by
the military authorities simply because she failed to

17

The work of advancing human rights has been shared by politicians, philanthropists, and propagandists. A single book, Uncle Tom's Cabin (the title page of the first edition is shown above), may have furnished the moral impetus for the abolition of slavery in the U.S. A best-seller in the 1850's, the novel brought fame to its author, Harriet Beecher Stowe (above).

produce an identity card. Arrested in the late 1960's, she was still in detention in Bukit Duri prison as 1978 ended.

Apparently in response to sustained international concern on this issue, the Indonesian government commenced a release program in late 1977. It reported that a first batch of 10,000 political prisoners would be released in December, 1977. Some of these releases were observed by foreign diplomats and journalists invited for the occasion to special ceremonies at one of the prison camps. The release of a further 4000 was announced midway through 1978. Many thousands more remained in detention.

Elsewhere, the use of national security legislation has frequently resulted in similar abuses. In numerous countries laws have been enacted to provide for administrative detention of individuals. This detention is not subject to normal legal procedures such as a hearing before an independent judge in open court with full rights of defense. Under the powers granted by laws known variously as the preservation of public security act or internal security act, individuals may be imprisoned indefinitely without being notified of the reason for their arrest, without an appearance in a court of law, and with no right of appeal against their detention. For three prisoners of conscience in Singapore (to take only one instance), 1978 marked their fifteenth year of detention without trial. Said Zahari (Singapore's leading poet), Ho Toon Chin (a trade unionist), and Lim Hock Siew (a former official of the opposition *Barisan Sosialis* Party) were among more than one hundred people rounded up in February, 1963, in a massive swoop code-named Operation Cold Store. On a more massive scale, the declaration of martial law or states of emergency in various countries has suspended all legal and constitutional safeguards designed to protect citizens against arbitrary arrest and ill treatment in detention.

In May, 1978, constitutional guarantees were suspended and a state of emergency decreed in Peru in response to widespread disturbances protesting austerity measures that doubled public transport fares and raised basic food prices by 80 percent. Over 3000 people, mostly trade unionists, were detained. Arrested political and trade union leaders were flown to the El Sepa penal colony in the Amazon jungle

where they remained in total isolation. Seventeen
journalists, trade unionists, and political leaders were
ordered into exile. Thirteen of them were flown to
Argentina where they were confined in military
barracks until granted asylum in other countries.
Most of the 3000 detainees were released within two
months.

The effects of martial law were still being felt in
the Philippines in 1978. Originally decreed in 1972
and still in force, martial law suspended the writ of
habeas corpus, thereby canceling any effective
judicial review of the arrest and detention of any
Filipino. Amnesty International continued to receive
evidence of torture of prisoners seized under martial-
law regulations. An Amnesty International mission
that visited the country in 1975 and interviewed
political prisoners reported: "The Republic of the
Philippines has been transformed from a country
with a remarkable constitutional tradition to a system
where star chamber methods have been used on a
wide scale to literally torture evidence into
existence."

The use of "reeducation" camps in Laos and
Vietnam also presented the problem of large-scale
detention taking place outside accepted judicial

19

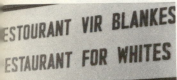

Apartheid—racial separation—remains part of the legal and social fabric of the Republic of South Africa. Spectators at a horse-racing club (above) and travelers in an airport waiting room (below) are segregated according to race.

procedures. Nguyen Duc Hanh, for example, was the subject of an Amnesty International appeal in early 1978. He had been sent, along with an estimated one million others, for reeducation in August, 1975. Although many of these were "reeducated" for three to four days, Dr. Hanh, former head of the human microbiology and immunology department of the Pasteur Institute in Saigon, remained in detention for nearly three years. He was reportedly in poor health and suffering from malnutrition. It was not known what charges had been brought against him and the length of his reeducation appeared to be indeterminate. Following the Amnesty International appeal, Dr. Hanh was reported released in mid-1978.

Two broad categories of human-rights violations can be defined, although elements of each may overlap. One category occurs where various aspects of national life make political imprisonment virtually inevitable. It may be due, for example, to the social system, or to the constitution and national legislation, or to the legal machinery and police apparatus. It may be that large-scale political imprisonment has been institutionalized over a long period of time. This kind of situation prevailed in Spain under Generalissimo Francisco Franco. It still exists in different forms in Indonesia, South Africa, and the Soviet Union—to mention only three examples.

The second broad category of violations occurs in

countries where the primary right to life and security of person is in the balance. There, torture has become a state institution, secret arrest either by the state or paramilitary groups is common, and political murders and executions are carried out either officially or by paramilitary groups acting with impunity. Such countries included, in 1978, Argentina, El Salvador, Equatorial Guinea, Ethiopia, Guatemala, Uganda, and Uruguay.

Human-rights organizations—in capitalist, Communist, and Third World countries—generally attracted more attention and support in 1978. In some instances, though, human-rights activists found *themselves* among the victims of arbitrary arrest, political imprisonment, disappearance, and torture. Their determination to persevere, however, was evident and perhaps best expressed by the words of an anonymous political prisoner writing from jail: "Ideas are not extinguishable by force but only by better ideas. To persecute ideas is a basic violation of human rights and is the oldest form of human tyranny since the beginning of organized society. I am confident that ideas will triumph over human tyranny in the end. . . ."

Controversial human-rights issues of 1978 involved three groups widely considered oppressed, underrepresented, or persecuted. Upper left: New Yorkers rally in support of Soviet Jews denied freedom of religion and emigration. Lower left: A march for the rights of homosexuals, who have suffered discrimination in housing, public accommodations, and employment. Right: Women, unique in being an oppressed majority, assert their claim to full legal, economic, and social equality with men.

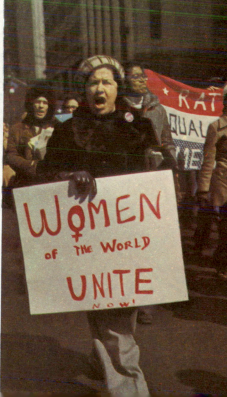

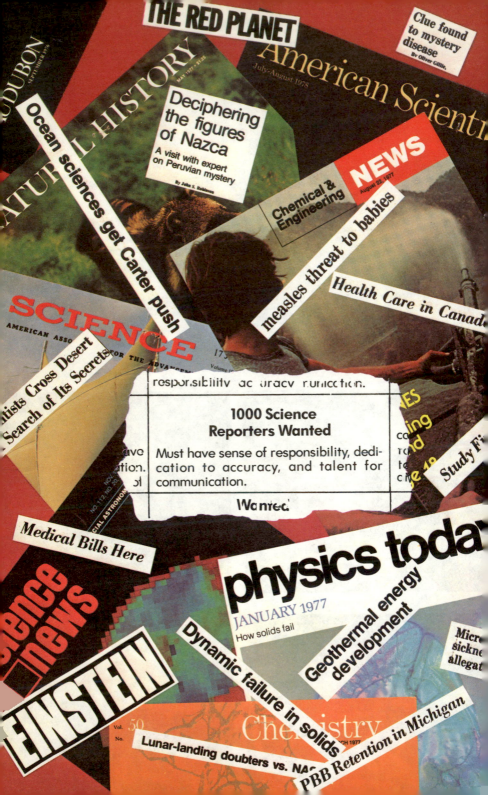

The late William L. Laurence rode the plane carrying the atomic bomb to its Japanese target in 1945. He was a science writer. Isaac Asimov's name has become a household word through the 200 science books he has written. Alton Blakeslee, just retired as science writer for the Associated Press, has written words read by more people than any other science writer. He is the second of three generations of science reporters. Jules Bergman's face on ABC News has become as familiar as Lassie's.

These are only the front-runners of about a thousand men and women who form a bucket brigade for science and technology in this country; they sample the stream of research, discovery, and invention and bring bucketfuls of information to the public. They work on newspapers and magazines, and in television and radio. They write books. They are public information officers for universities, hospitals, drug companies, and other science-based industries. You will find their work wherever you find science written or talked about.

Yet as a science writer myself, I have a doubt. Why is it, I ask, that so many people in this, the 20th century, are duped by horoscopes, false claims of extrasensory perception (ESP), fake cancer cures, and reports of flying saucers from other worlds? Why, indeed, have millions turned their heads to such arrant nonsense and turned up their noses at the findings and methods of science?

Astrology appears harmless, until I read that high government officials have their horoscopes cast before making a decision. And while stories of flying saucers may make exciting science-fiction movies, belief in such unidentified flying objects (UFOs) as real can poison public confidence in real science. And fake cancer cures? They can kill. I expect to hear of such superstitious beliefs in former times. But now? In this age of the triumph of science and technology?

If I face the question head on, I have to record a failure for myself and my science-writing colleagues. We have failed to convey the essence of science—that knowledge comes from objective measurements, tested and retested, and that one tested fact is worth a thousand opinions. Today, vast numbers of the public reject these ideas of science. Their thinking is

by Earl Ubell

Earl Ubell, seen delivering a report on camera, is health and science editor for WCBS-TV News in New York City. He moved to television in 1966 after twenty-three years on the staff of the New York Herald Tribune. The recipient of many awards for science reporting, he is a member and past president of the National Association of Science Writers.

still medieval. They say, "Science be damned. I know better."

Nothing could be more dangerous for the United States and for the world than such archaic thinking. Science and technology have brought this planet to the threshold of a true golden age of health, adequate food supplies, and a lifting of the spirit as we begin to understand nature, our society, and ourselves. Medieval thinking can dash our chances of cashing in on the benefits of science. Our government officials, fearful of a public distrustful of science, will make decisions that ignore tested research. That has already happened.

What an awesome responsibility for science writers: to bring to the public the findings, ideas, and methods of science! And further, to do it in such a way that the public joins in the scientific enterprise with enthusiasm and, because scientists are human and fallible, with skepticism.

Fortunately, our failure is laced with some success. Scientists are still held in high esteem, right up there with U.S. Supreme Court justices. Surveys show that a majority of the public still believe in the scientist's right to research. And thanks to the communications explosion—from printing to broadcasting and computers—more human beings know more about the findings of science than ever before in history. People do crave scientific evidence to guide them to the right medical treatment or the safest automobile

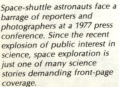

Space-shuttle astronauts face a barrage of reporters and photographers at a 1977 press conference. Since the recent explosion of public interest in science, space exploration is just one of many science stories demanding front-page coverage.

tire or the cleanest air. Such information, although still hard to get, is spreading.

Confidence in science stems from its obvious benefits: smooth-running automobiles, glorious color television, easy-to-get, nutritious food, durable and inexpensive clothing, medicines that cure once-fatal diseases, fast and cheap jet travel, and a myriad of products that the kings of France would have ransomed with gold. Even the less practical achievements of science and technology bring gasps of appreciation: landing men on the moon, uncovering ancient royal tombs, measuring the multitrillion-mile depth of the universe, and smashing atoms to examine their innards and tease out the nature of the universal atomic glue.

In the face of all that, a substantial minority—perhaps one person in three—damns science and technology, preferring what is believed to be an older, simpler way. Alas, the good old days were hardly ever good: the average age at death was thirty-five; filth was everywhere; water was suspect; only the rich had an assured food supply; only 5 percent of the population could read and write. And it is the present vocal minority looking backward that can ruin our chances.

Wadsworth Likely, executive director of the National Association of Science Writers, believes that it is the responsibility of the science writer to give the public some idea of the general progress of science. If that could be achieved, confidence in science would rise. To do it, science writers cover nearly every facet of science, medicine, and

Famous scientists and science interpreters have helped to present important and complex new information to the public. Albert Einstein (left)—familiar, humane, but mostly incomprehensible—was everyone's idea of the theoretical scientist. Veteran science editor Walter Sullivan (middle) patiently explains the findings of Einstein and his successors to readers of the New York Times. ABC News Science Editor Jules Bergman (right), shown describing the 1975 U.S.-Soviet space linkup, is one of a new breed of television reporters who must be brief, clear, and interesting to watch.

technology. Some, like Barbara Seaman and T George Harris, specialize in psychology and behavior. Many are medical experts, medicine being by far the most popular field. A few, like Walter Sullivan, Gloria Lubkin, and Irving Bengelsdorf, talk easily with physicists, astronomers, and mathematicians. Of course, Isaac Asimov is an expert in everything. His knowledge is truly encyclopedic. (He also writes encyclopedias.)

Most science writers see their responsibility in a simple but powerful way: cover the news of science. Victor Cohn, science writer for the Washington *Post,* says: "Our function is to report the news; not to comment on it, not to say what it means. Analysis may be important; but the news comes first." Cohn, more than most writers, understands the political uses to which science information can be put. He knows that such data are often hidden by people

A current concern of science reporters is the possibility of creating human life artificially. Above: The subject has inspired fascination since the days of the medieval alchemist. Right: Protesters at a science symposium illustrate their fears of "genetic engineering." Below: An artist offers a fanciful conception of cloning, a genetic duplication of a single organism.

who would be embarrassed by its publication. So he looks for news that people do not want published. It greases the wheels of democratic debate.

Cohn tells the story of Gio B. Gori, a leading scientist at the National Cancer Institute, who introduced the idea of the "tolerable cigarette" in 1978. Such a cigarette has so low a level of poisonous chemicals that it would be impossible to detect any increased risk of dying among its smokers. At first, Gori's ideas were distributed as an Associated Press feature intended for the back pages. Cohn spotted it and Gori's "tolerable cigarette" became page-one news.

Gori's bosses were aghast. Their boss, Joseph A. Califano, Jr., secretary of Health, Education, and Welfare, had launched a grand anti-smoking campaign because "cigarettes are hazardous to your health." Although Gori never said the low-tar cigarette was safe, the *idea* of a "tolerable cigarette" could scuttle the war on smoking. The argument continued throughout the year. Cohn had stirred the debate.

On the other hand, Frank Field, science editor of WNBC-TV, New York, takes as his duty NOT to report some items. He makes sure that whatever information he broadcasts has passed strong scientific tests. Bad science can shake the public's confidence.

In 1978 a press conference was called in New York City to trumpet the creation of cystic fibrosis in an animal. If the method were effective, it could help scientists find a cure or a preventative for this terrible lung disease. "The scientific evidence for the finding was weak," Field says. "I checked with other researchers and the production of the disease in one animal (if it really was cystic fibrosis) means nothing unless it can be produced regularly. I dropped it."

Such rigorous standards can land Field in hot water with his superiors. If other reporters, not so exacting, publish the item, Field's news director may ask: "How come you missed that great story?" Field hopes that those who broadcast or publish poor science will be found out. Many of them have. And Field has flourished.

George Alexander, science editor of the Los

Lenticular clouds form shapes resembling flying saucers over a Brazilian city. "Unidentified flying objects" may often be mistaken sightings of natural phenomena. Such scientific facts, says author Ubell, must be asserted against the "arrant nonsense" of horoscopes and occultism.

Science fact or science fantasy? Accurate reporting can help keep the two separate. Upper left: Orson Welles directs a 1938 radio adaptation of H. G. Wells's War of the Worlds, a story of an invasion from Mars that thousands of frightened listeners mistook as real. Upper right: A 1975 photograph taken 80 feet beneath the surface of Loch Ness, Scotland, seems to show the legendary monster known as Nessie. Lower left: The Cardiff Giant, a stone sculpture widely exhibited during the early 20th century as the petrified remains of an actual giant. Lower right: Fake prehistoric jawbone of the Piltdown Man, found in England in 1912. At first accepted and acclaimed by archeologists, the bone, actually from an orangutan, was later discovered to be a hoax.

Angeles *Times*, sees himself "as a step-down transformer for the 220-volt research in laboratories to the 110 volts necessary for the ordinary user." Alexander dips into the stream of science and comes up not only with important but with interesting news. He reports extensively on archeology and anthropology, two subjects hardly likely to revolutionize our lives. In 1977 Alexander reported work indicating that the Pueblo Indians of the 12th century worsened a drought by overcutting their trees. The research suggests that "natives" do not necessarily treat their environment better than moderns.

In all his work Alexander reflects the stated feelings of Albert Einstein, the preeminent scientific genius of the 20th century: "It is of great importance that the general public be given an opportunity to experience consciously and intelligently the efforts and results of scientific research. It is not sufficient that each new result be taken up, elaborated, and applied by a few specialists in the field. Restricting the body of knowledge to a small group deadens the philosophical spirit of a people and leads to spiritual poverty."

Dennis Flanagan, editor of a highly regarded periodical, *The Scientific American*, agrees fundamentally with the Einstein thesis. He sees his job as being aware of the main currents in science and technology and putting them before his readers. Like Alexander, he includes the interesting along with the important, and like Field he discards "scientific" garbage. He has yet to publish an article on ESP. Flanagan also reaches out for social issues raised by science and technology. Readers of *The Scientific American* can delve into nuclear warfare, racial discrimination, medical-care costs, and missilery, to name but a few of the issues discussed in its pages.

Most science reporters agree that research and engineering that touch the core of society need special attention, especially now that science reaches down to the deepest levels of our population. My brother, Robert Ubell, is editor of *The Sciences,* the magazine of the New York Academy of Sciences; most of each issue deals with the impact of science on society.

Consider just some of the present-day controversies: test-tube babies, genetic engineering, soft-energy versus hard-energy, atomic-energy plants, air pollution, auto safety, food additives, medical-care funding, computer information storage—the list goes on and on and on.

In 1978 the birth of Louise Brown in England generated a full-scale debate. She was the first human being born of an egg fertilized outside the mother's womb. Her birth raised issues in ethics, religion, economics, science, and medicine that captured the imagination of the whole world. Science writers had to deal with such questions as: Was it ethical for the English scientists to risk a malformed baby by impregnating a woman with an egg that may have been injured by their technique? What are the positions of major religions concerning such a birth? Will the process lead to cloning—that is, the production of human beings from the cells of other human beings so as to create duplicates of the donors of the cells? Should society's limited medical resources be diverted to produce more children?

As a social issue the birth of Louise Brown pales

The spiritualist medium, the crystal-ball gazer, the palm reader, the amusement-park handwriting expert, and the tea-leaf interpreter all exploit man's need to probe the mysteries of life, character, and death. Their continuing popularity, writes Ubell, is a sign that science writers are failing to convey respect for tested facts.

Scientific fact was pitted against religious belief in a well-reported controversy that started with biologist Charles Darwin (top) and his supporter Thomas H. Huxley, seen in 19th-century caricatures. Above right: The controversy made headlines with the debates of Clarence Darrow (left) and William Jennings Bryan at the 1925 "monkey trial" in Dayton, Tenn.

before the problem of the world's future energy resources. The argument is split between those at one extreme who see atomic power as forming the backbone of our energy supply and those at the other extreme who advocate power produced in dollops locally by the sun, wind, and tides. For science reporters the problem is tough: the technical issues are highly mathematical and rely on information about which there is much disagreement and secrecy. The debate does not lend itself to entertaining writing. But our future depends on the choice of the correct path.

In such controversies we often see symptoms of medieval thinking. Naively, many people want the answer to come down from those in authority. In feudal times the king decreed the answer. Now, we hope, science provides information; through our government we act on that information. But today there are those who yield to government the exclusive right to give us the answer. Many in government gladly arrogate to themselves that right. Knowing that information is power, they try to keep data secret, often in the name of national security. Yet, scientists know that there are no scientific secrets; what one scientist discovers, another will soon.

Walter Sullivan, science editor of the New York *Times,* found himself on the horns of a fascinating science-versus-secrecy dilemma in 1958. In secret, a scientist had proposed that the U.S. launch rockets 300 miles above the earth and there explode atomic bombs. High above the earth in near-vacuum, the earth's magnetism would trap electrified particles generated by the explosions. Nature had already trapped such particles at higher altitudes—particles shot out from the sun. For the military, artificial belts of electrified particles might shield radar. For the scientists, the experiment could verify important aspects of magnetic theory.

Hanson W. Baldwin, then military editor of the *Times,* learned of the proposed experiment and informed Sullivan. In checking the story Sullivan alerted the Department of Defense that the *Times* knew the secret. The military pleaded with Baldwin and Sullivan to keep it quiet. They did. Three bombs were exploded in August and September of 1958. The reporters did not publish their story until March, 1959. Sullivan says that they kept the secret for three reasons. At first, they were told that if they published the story the experiment would not be done because it would stir up diplomatic trouble. After the explosions, they were told that the U.S. would have a military advantage if the secret were kept. Finally, they were warned that if the story got out it would upset delicate negotiations with the Soviet Union over a treaty to ban atomic testing in the atmosphere.

Now, twenty years later, Sullivan says he would do the same thing again, although he admits that times have changed. Reporters today are less willing to keep government secrets. They have learned that officials often try to hide their mistakes under the "secret" label.

Stuart H. Loory, now managing editor of the

Is nuclear power a safe alternative to oil and other fuel sources? Demonstrators in New Hampshire (left) and California (right) disagree, as do nuclear physicists and technicians. Science writers must present with great care the mass of complex data and conflicting opinion on this crucial question of public policy.

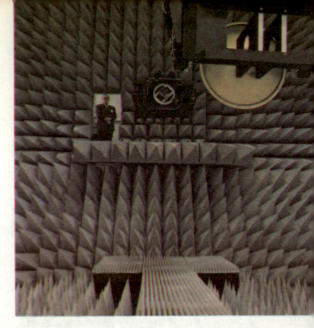

Some of the more technical scientific subjects lack apparent connection with everyday life and tax the science reporter's ability to explain vividly and simply. An anechoic chamber, a room for testing sound equipment that eliminates all echoed vibrations, is such a challenging subject.

Chicago *Sun-Times,* is a former science writer who says that the people's right to know comes first. "It turned out that the Soviet Union knew all about the rocket-bomb project," says Loory. "Their instruments had picked up many of the magnetic and electric effects. So who was being kept in the dark? The Russians? No. The American people. And why? Because somebody was afraid he had made a political mistake."

"In the 1950's, I can understand why Sullivan kept quiet. The cold war was at its peak. All of us wanted to do what we could to help our government. We didn't realize we weren't really helping. Today, I don't think there is a reporter who would keep that project secret more than five minutes."

Scientists themselves do not believe in secrecy. They want to share their discoveries with the world. It is an old tradition. Today scientists are under great pressure from government, from industry, and even from fellow scientists to keep certain secrets and not engage in certain experiments.

Right now the hottest issue in scientific news is "recombinant DNA." In the last ten years geneticists have learned how to alter the chemistry of heredity in bacteria and plants by "recombinant" techniques. Leaving the complexities aside, the fear is that such alterations could create a bacterium or a virus that would produce a plant, animal, or human disease that is deadly and unstoppable. Scientists themselves have asked their fellows to eschew certain genetic experiments because of the danger. Federal guidelines have been established. In Cambridge, Mass., the local government fought the construction of a laboratory for such tests.

In the thick of the battle, science writers have explained and analyzed. And they continue to do so because the problem has not yet gone away. Never have scientists been so insistent that the issues be accurately portrayed. And science writers do see accuracy as one of their heaviest responsibilities.

Barbara Culliton, who writes for the news section of *Science*, the magazine of the American Association for the Advancement of Science, adds another burden to our shoulders. "We also have a responsibility not to be boring," Culliton says, "whether we write for a special audience like that of *Science* or for the mass public watching television." I find this duty the most pressing of all. If I am not interesting or entertaining, I am not read. If I am not read, I do not communicate. If an audience does not watch my television broadcast, I do not communicate. And if I do not communicate, I am nothing.

Other recent science stories are full of life and immediate interest. Entomologist Cathy Brugger, who helped discover the overwintering grounds of the Monarch butterfly, sits surrounded by them in the mountains north of Mexico City. Science writers must deal impartially with noiseless rooms (opposite page) and butterfly havens.

RUNNING
for
the Senate

by William Proxmire

Sen. William Proxmire of Wisconsin is conceded by political friend and foe alike to be among the hardest-working and most effective members of Congress. A liberal Democrat with a grudge against waste in government, he first entered the Senate in 1957; he became chairman of the Senate Banking Committee in 1975; he has not missed a Senate roll call since 1966. Trim and youthful at 62, Proxmire practices the physical fitness that he preaches—even during a snowfall. After the morning exercise he describes here, he puts in a ten-hour day and walks briskly home.

My daily run to work begins at 7:00 A.M. after twenty minutes of calisthenics and warm-up. The first couple of hundred yards are always easy: flat, then downhill. As the blocks pass I feel more relaxed and rested. I begin to think about what's going on today in the Senate. A hearing is scheduled with Federal Reserve Chairman G. William Miller, where we'll discuss Federal Reserve System membership and the proper rate of monetary growth. Press coverage is always heavy at this sort of hearing, and I hope to use the allotted two hours to cut into the heart of these issues.

It is fashionable these days to be in shape. Joggers and bicyclers decorate our roads, and tennis is a national passion. It has been estimated that 38,500,000 adult Americans participate in swimming, 34,700,000 play tennis, and 27,200,000 are regular bowlers. According to a Gallup Poll conducted in 1978, 25,000,000 Americans—roughly 11 percent of the population—run or jog regularly. A large number of these are more than casual about their exercise: an estimated 60,000 Americans ran the grueling, 26.2-mile marathon in 1978. In 1966 there were only about 1500 marathoners. Roughly 400 marathons have sprouted up around the country. *Running Times* magazine estimates that 1,600,000 Americans compete in road races of all lengths, excluding organized college and high-school competition.

This trend toward fitness is encouraging, but I suspect that most Americans are doing more reading and TV-watching than running. The New York *Times* cites a recent poll in Chicago that showed that "although 40 percent (of a random sample of adults) said they were overweight, only a quarter said they were trying to do something about it; 85 percent realized the importance of exercise, but only 32 percent followed an exercise program; and all acknowledged the health risk of cigarettes, but 42 percent smoked." The President's Council on Physical Fitness estimates that 43 percent of all adult Americans do not exercise at all. Ten to 30 percent of all Americans weigh at least 30 percent more than their ideal body weight. Heart disease—a frightening epidemic in this century—is just one of the consequences.

We live in a society in which people are deliberately unhealthy. How else can one describe a population which chooses, against expert advice, to smoke, drink to excess, ingest toxic substances, shun exercise, and overeat? A people that relies on booze for a pickup, on cigarettes or a tranquilizer for relaxation, on aspirin to relieve tension, on sleeping pills to sleep—such a people is not only physically sick but bound to be sad and depressed.

The obvious reason for our physical decline is that as our civilization has become more mechanized we use our bodies less, and our health and well-being suffer accordingly. It used to be that in the course of routine daily activity we unthinkingly worked our bodies into shape. But where once we walked from place to place, we now ride. Jobs that once required muscle now are performed by machine. Today even typical manual workers lead a far softer life, with little physical activity. They ride to work and sit most of the day in a crane or a truck. Yet they are manual workers, viewed by our society as people who use their muscles. Of course, some hard hats and other blue-collar workers still do difficult physical work, but far fewer than in the past. In spite of—or perhaps because of—our exceptionally high standard of living, we Americans are too fat, too soft, lazy, and prone to alcoholism and other forms of drug abuse.

This dichotomy—the physical fitness movement on the one hand and the widespread disregard for health on the other—indicates that the conditioning gospel is not getting through to everyone. Polls indicate that the people who exercise tend to be young, affluent, and well-educated. But millions of our citizens either do not realize the importance of

Following pages: Author Proxmire's morning run to the Senate takes him through contrasting sections of Washington, D.C. Clockwise from upper left: Cleveland Park, Proxmire's own neighborhood; the National Zoo; Connecticut Avenue; DuPont Circle, hangout of chess players; Massachusetts Avenue; Union Station; the U.S. Capitol building seen from Lafayette Park; and the Dirksen office building, where Proxmire showers, dresses, and sets to work.

Daily physical labor, as depicted in Thomas Hart Benton's 1938 oil painting "Cradling Wheat" (left), used to keep people fit. In a modern office, however, workers rarely exert themselves.

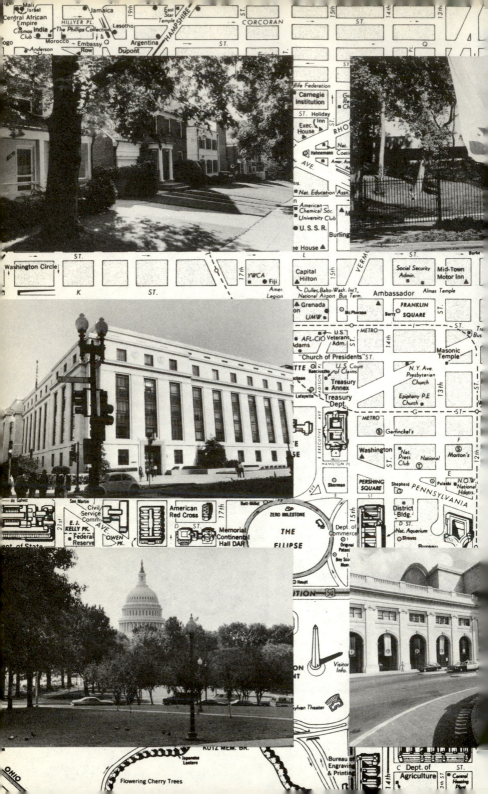

The three most popular forms of exercise in the U.S. in 1978: swimming (38,500,000 adult participants), tennis (34,700,000), and bowling (27,200,000).

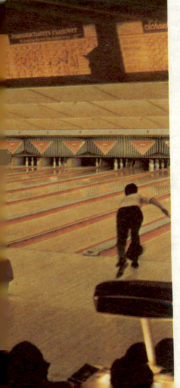

good health habits or else choose to ignore the overwhelming evidence in their favor.

My 7.5-minutes-per-mile pace and my thoughts are interrupted as I approach the upgrade near the National Zoo. Only a long-distance runner appreciates what it means to run up a hill. It can be an uncomfortable if not painful test of will. Coming at the beginning of a run, it is psychologically even tougher, but I keep on.

Exercise is difficult. It requires determination, dedication, and discipline. But it is indispensable to our good health, and combined with a careful program of diet, avoidance of drugs, and relaxation, daily exercise is the solution I recommend for keeping healthy and fit.

I exercise by running to work every day. Others may find another form of exercise easier to fit into their schedules, but the important point is to make exercise a *daily* part of our lives. Build your strength and endurance slowly, bit by bit. Too much exercise too soon causes muscles to rebel and may do bodily damage. Unfortunately, once the body is well conditioned it requires regular exercise to stay that way. Give up habitual training for a short months and you are as weak and flabby as if you had never started. Thus physical fitness must be a way of life. What makes it easier is developing an exercise habit. Exercise every day, not every other day or when you feel like it. Some people have the will or motivation to exercise three or four days a week. Most do not. Unless exercise is a daily habit, it is too easy to give up.

Choice of an exercise routine depends on an individual's tastes, schedule, and motivation, but anyone who wants to can fit exercise into his or her routine. Some people run before or after work or during their lunch hour. Others enjoy swimming, bicycling, tennis, or handball—all of which are beneficial when sustained for a reasonable period of time. Walking or bicycling at least part of the way to work or school, doing errands on foot rather than driving, climbing stairs instead of using the elevator—all these things can help. Walking is by far the most popular form of exercise in the United States, and it can be the most fun. Many combine this activity with a special interest such as bird-watching, plant study, photography, or sightseeing. To be effective as a conditioner, however, walking must be done briskly—at a rate of 3 mph or more. This speed will provide the benefits of "aerobic" conditioning, as described in Kenneth H. Cooper's book *Aerobics*.

For healthy individuals to condition their body they must increase their pulse rate through strenuous exercise from an average of 70 beats per minute at rest to 120 beats per minute or more for at least ten minutes. They should do this at least three or four days a week. Activities that lead to aerobic conditioning include swimming, running, jogging, fast walking, bicycling, skating, basketball, cross-country skiing, rowing, rope-skipping, and competitive singles tennis. Sports that call for periods of inactivity, such as baseball, bowling, and golf, are not so helpful.

While exercise is a new gospel that has not reached all sectors of the population, we have nearly all been well enough educated to understand the need for a healthy, balanced diet of fruits, vegetables,

grains, dairy products, meats, and fish. *Moderation* is the key to healthful eating, and there is no substitute for will power. Overweight is not only unsightly; it is a serious threat to our health.

The dangers of smoking and many drugs, including alcohol, have been well documented. We don't need these substances, and indeed, our bodies tell us so. Hangovers and chronic coughs should convince the most stubborn of us of the pernicious effects of alcohol and cigarettes.

Substitute the exercise habit for the cigarette habit. Consider that the first few cigarettes we try taste terrible, and the smoke makes us cough and choke. But we persist. After a while we enjoy smoking, and eventually it becomes such a part of our lives that we light up without even thinking about it. So should it be with exercise.

Getting in shape and staying there are not easy tasks. It is important to admit this fact from the outset of any training program. Dieting, as millions of Americans know, is very tough, and regular, strenuous exercise may be even more difficult. While physical activity brings with it some moments of exhilaration, it is 90 percent steady, relentless plodding along. Muscles ache, the lungs burn, and the psyche rebels at such self-inflicted torture. Only after a period of regular exercise do we begin to see the satisfying results that make our efforts worthwhile.

Soon I am heading downhill again. The sudden effortlessness makes me think of something said by the late Robert M. Hutchins, former president of the University of Chicago. "I never run when I can walk," boasted Dr. Hutchins. "I never walk when I can stand still. I never stand still when I can sit down. I never sit when I can lie down. Whenever I feel the urge to exercise I lie down until it goes away." The good doctor didn't know what he was missing.

There is a tendency on the part of observers of the conditioning craze to scoff at "fitness freaks." I must admit that it looks strange for a 62-year-old U.S. Senator to run down a crowded sidewalk in shorts or sweatpants. But the benefits to be derived from such activity outweigh any personal embarrassment.

When talk at dinner parties turns to shin splints and the relative merits of running-shoe manufacturers, you can be sure that a discussion of the metaphysical side of running will soon follow. The exhilaration that comes during a long run has been likened to certain states of religious ecstasy. Many runners claim to have experienced visions on the road, and others find in running the key to life's mysteries.

I don't go that far. But I have discovered a long list of benefits—physical and mental—which result from running and other forms of exercise. One of the immediately noticeable effects of fitness is an improvement in appearance, for the essence of good looks is good health. Your figure becomes leaner, stronger, and more attractive, your posture improves, and your skin becomes clearer. As you look better you feel better. You can literally exercise your way out of listlessness, boredom, and anxiety. The distraction that exercise brings, the time it allows for emotions to cool down, and the general sense of well-being it engenders make for good medicine. Tension headaches disappear, and you will uncover a calmer, more pleasant personality as you become more relaxed. You can also eat more without gaining weight, since exercise burns up calories. Most runners also find that running moderates their appetites and reduces their intake of carbohydrates.

The relationship between a healthy body and a healthy mind has not been lost upon hundreds of U.S. corporations, which now provide organized fitness programs for their employees. These businesses find that good physical conditioning leads to clearer thinking and better productivity. It also reduces time lost from work and the cost of employee health insurance.

There is convincing evidence that exercise may prevent or delay the progression of heart disease. It has been shown that long-term fitness increases cardiovascular efficiency, lowers cholesterol and triglycerides (fats in the blood which lead to heart attacks), lowers blood pressure, and increases glucose tolerance. The net effect of these changes is a reduced rate of heart attacks.

My route continues down Connecticut Avenue past fashionable shops and restaurants. Many regular bus riders and cab drivers recognize me and wave or yell out encouragement. A policeman lobbying for a pay raise follows me for several blocks.

People can get good exercise in the course of their daily activities by simply using their feet. Opposite page: Boston children walk to school and a New York City businessman bicycles to work. Above: Effective exercise, rarely taken—using the stairs instead of the escalator.

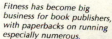

Fitness has become big business for book publishers, with paperbacks on running especially numerous.

It is distressing to note the tendency among modern Americans to look to the government to solve all of their problems—health included. Many of those who clamor for national health insurance seem to believe that such a program would inevitably, almost magically, result in long and healthy lifetimes. Others feel certain that imminent advances in health technology will guarantee good health: just take a pill every day and you'll never be sick.

While I share a strong faith in American technology, I recognize that this country is based on individual freedom and responsibility, and it is the individual who will determine the level of his or her own health. The government has no right to meddle with your body or your life-style. We tried that with Prohibition, and it didn't work. If we are going to continue as a strong and proud nation, we must all individually look hard at our health habits. The U.S. government has tripled spending on health research over the last few years, but we still find people dying before their time simply because they refused to exercise good judgment and self-discipline in their personal habits.

The national health bill for 1978 hovered around $200 billion. Experts estimate, however, that individual efforts to prevent illness could cut health-care costs by one half. The field of preventive

Left: A jogger experiences the strain of a long run. Right: A stress test measures the body's capacity to withstand such strenuous exercise. These tests are recommended prior to beginning any exercise program for those who are over thirty or badly out of shape.

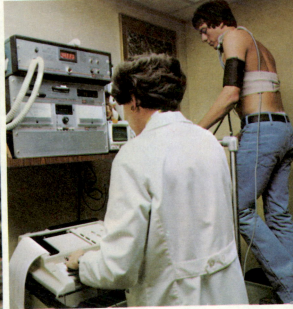

medicine is relatively new and underfunded and conclusions are open to debate, but there is growing agreement that preventive medicine (good health habits) is far more important to our well-being than any medical treatment, since it leads to prevention of diseases for which there sometimes is no cure.

A start has been made toward improving our preventive medicine. During the period from 1968 through 1977, deaths from cardiovascular diseases have dropped by about 2 percent a year. Apparently, this dramatic reduction is the result of deliberate changes in smoking, eating, and exercise habits and to the expanded national efforts to detect and treat high blood pressure.

At DuPont Circle—hangout for folksingers and chess players—I turn onto Massachusetts Avenue, site of many of the city's embassies. The avenue changes character as I near Capitol Hill, becoming a poor, black residential area.

It is a truism that as we get older our health deteriorates, we have less strength, less stamina, and less energy. Indeed, we are almost all in worse shape at 40 than we were at 30, and even worse at 50 and 60. But I state flatly that this need not be so. With proper care our bodies can be *better* in later life than in our youth.

Consider my own case. I can vividly recall trying to run at a steady speed for more than a mile and to swim for more than 50 yards when I was in college. I was in better physical condition than most students, but I simply couldn't do it. And I can remember the extreme fatigue that would stay with me for three or four days after I'd had only five or six hours of sleep for a night or two.

At the age of 62, after a dozen years of hard,

Two groups of Miss America contestants, from 1921 (left) and 1978, pose in Atlantic City, N.J. Modern styles of dress—and undress—call for a lean, physically fit appearance. Lifestyles, too, have changed to favor the active and youthful.

prolonged exercise and a deliberately limited diet, I find that I have far greater endurance than I did in high school or college. I'm sure, for instance, that I would not have been able to run 5 miles when I was in college without being tired. Now it's no problem. I can swim half a mile without difficulty, and when I get only three or four hours of sleep at night, I still feel vigorous and rested. Altogether, I am in far better shape than when I was younger.

In my opinion youth is highly overrated. For most people it is a time of anxiety and ignorance, a time when many of life's pleasures go unappreciated. At 40, 50, 60, or older we can have the health, vitality, and attractiveness of youth—in tandem with the maturity and wisdom that give fuller meaning to the world around us.

Physical conditioning at any age will always require a struggle. But consider another important by-product. In addition to the physical rewards there is a psychic challenge and reward as well. Call it determination or guts or drive, the good distance swimmer or runner has the capacity to go out and face the pain of prolonged exertion and overcome it. Long-distance swimming or running develops the psyche that way. The will that brings the distance athlete through his or her physical ordeal also gives strength to stay with a detailed, complex problem that must be patiently and painfully broken down and analyzed.

I feel that self-discipline of this kind is the way to freedom—freedom from self-destructive habits. Some people might disagree and argue that spending so much time, energy, and effort on physical conditioning takes away one's freedom. But we are

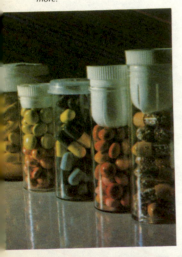

Drugs, junk food, and alcohol are modern evils that might be less of a problem, says author Proxmire, if people exercised more.

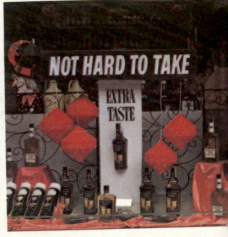

The national weakness for nonparticipatory sports is well observed in this drawing by Geo. Price, ©1956 by The New Yorker Magazine, Inc.

not truly free unless we can control our own behavior. By accepting responsibility for ourselves we gain a sense that we are free to be the people we want to be. We don't always admit it, but freedom always implies discipline.

Union Station, surrounded by dozens of state flags, is soon before me, and to my right I can see the Capitol dome. A short two blocks through landscaped parks, and I enter the Dirksen office building. I shower, dress, and prepare for the long day ahead—relaxed and refreshed. The 4.7-mile run has actually left me with more energy than when I began.

This is how, where, and why I run. There are other times and places. There are other forms of exercise. Every American should find a time and place to suit him or her. There is no excuse for a reasonably healthy person to avoid a program of physical conditioning. The benefits are better health, longer life, improved appearance, an exuberant sense of well-being, and strengthened self-discipline—the same kind of discipline that, when applied to political matters, will make us a better and stronger nation.

Following page: A lone runner pursues freedom—exuberant, restful, and natural.

1979 YEARBOOK

EVENTS OF 1978

CHRONOLOGY FOR 1978

JAN. 6

JAN. 6

JAN. 13

JANUARY

1 • An Air India jet plane explodes and crashes into the sea shortly after taking off from Bombay. All 213 people aboard were killed.

6 • President Jimmy Carter returns to the United States, ending a nine-day, seven-country tour. Since Jan. 1 he had visited Iran, India, Saudi Arabia, Egypt, France, and Belgium. (He began the trip in Poland in December, 1977.)
• U.S. Secretary of State Cyrus R. Vance officially returns the Crown of St. Stephen to Hungary. The symbol of Hungarian sovereignty and unity had been in American hands for thirty-two years.

11 • Two Soviet cosmonauts dock their Soyuz 27 and join two other cosmonauts aboard the Salyut 6 space station. This was the first linkup of a spacecraft with an already manned space station in the history of spaceflight.

13 • Hubert H. Humphrey, U.S. Senator (D, Minn.) and former Vice-President of the U.S., dies at the age of 66.

24 • A Soviet satellite, equipped with a nuclear reactor, reenters the earth's atmosphere and disintegrates over northwestern Canada. (On Jan. 30 it was announced that a mildly radioactive metal object had been retrieved and identified as debris from the satellite.)

26 • At least 100 people die as a blizzard, described as perhaps the worst in history, strikes the Great Lakes, the Ohio Valley, and the Middle West.

FEBRUARY

6-7 • A record-breaking snowstorm strikes the Atlantic coastal states, from Maine to Delaware.

9 • The nomination of William H. Webster, a federal appellate judge from St. Louis, to serve as director of the Federal Bureau of Investigation is confirmed by the U.S. Senate.

In his eighth professional fight, Leon Spinks, • 15
24, becomes the heavyweight boxing champion of the world. He defeated 36-year-old
Muhammad Ali in a fifteen-round, split-deci-
sion battle in Las Vegas. (See Sept. 15.)

Egyptian commandos attack a jetliner at the • 19
Larnaca (Cyprus) airport in a successful attempt to free 11 hostages held by Palestinian
terrorists aboard a Cyprus Airways DC-8. In the
battle between the Egyptians and members of
the Cypriot National Guard, 15 Egyptians were
reportedly killed.

MARCH

The nomination of G. William Miller to serve • 3
as chairman of the Federal Reserve Board is
approved by the U.S. Senate with only one dis-
senting vote.

Announcement is made of the reappointment • 5
of Hua Kuo-feng as chairman of the Chinese
Communist Party. The National People's Congress also named Yeh Chien-ying as chairman
of its Standing Committee, or honorary head
of state. Teng Hsiao-ping, regarded as the most
powerful man in China, retained his post as
first deputy premier.

In Belgrade, the Conference on Security and • 9
Cooperation in Europe ends its five-month
session, having adopted a compromise summary document containing no mention of human rights. The conference was convened to

FEB. 9

FEB. 15

MARCH 3

MARCH 5

53

MARCH 17

MARCH 21

MARCH 21

review progress on the accords signed at Helsinki, Finland, in 1975.

11 • Palestinian terrorists seize a tour bus on the highway between Haifa and Tel Aviv, Israel. The vehicle exploded during an exchange of gunfire with police, and 37 Israelis and 9 Palestinian terrorists were killed.

14-15 • Israeli land, sea, and air forces invade southern Lebanon. By March 20 they had occupied all of the country below the Litani River.

16 • Aldo Moro, former premier of Italy, is kidnapped by members of the left-wing Red Brigades terrorist guerrilla organization.
• The U.S. Senate passes, by a vote of 68-32, the first of two Panama Canal treaties.

17 • A Liberian-registered, American-owned tanker, the *Amoco Cadiz,* runs aground off the northern coast of France. Eventually it split up, spilling almost 1,600,000 bbl of oil on the shores of Brittany.

21 • A provisional Rhodesian government is formed as three moderate black leaders are sworn in as co-leaders with Prime Minister Ian Smith.
• Israeli Defense Minister Ezer Weizman orders a cease-fire in Lebanon.

24 • Announcement is made of the acceptance by a majority of the 160,000 members of the United Mine Workers of a contract that will end their 109-day strike. On March 6 the Taft-Hartley Act had been invoked at the request of President Carter.

28 • The Japanese government announces that the opening of Tokyo's new international airport at Narita has been indefinitely postponed. Two days earlier, radical students had occupied the airport's control tower and destroyed valuable equipment.

APRIL

---

3 • President Carter ends a seven-day tour of four Third World nations. He visited Venezuela, Brazil, Nigeria, and Liberia.

6 • A law amending the Age Discrimination in Employment Act is signed by President Carter. Effective Jan. 1, 1979, the mandatory retirement

age was raised to 70 for private industry. For most federal workers compulsory retirement was eliminated altogether as of Sept. 30, 1978.

The former acting director of the FBI, L. Patrick ● **10** Gray 3rd, and two former FBI executives are charged by a federal grand jury with conspiracy to deprive U.S. citizens of their rights.

United Nations and State Department spokesmen announce the defection of Arkady N. Shevchenko. As under secretary-general for political and security council affairs, he was the highest ranked Soviet official at the U.N. Secretariat. On April 26 he announced his resignation and his intention to remain in the U.S.

In compliance with a U.N. Security Council ● **11** regulation approved March 19, Israeli forces begin to withdraw from southern Lebanon. They were to be replaced by units of the U.N. Interim Force in Lebanon, known as UNIFIL.

The Senate, by a vote of 68–32, approves a sec- ● **18** ond Panama Canal treaty. By the terms of the treaty, the canal would be turned over to Panama on Dec. 31, 1999.

An off-course Korean Air Lines Boeing 707 jet- ● **20** liner is forced down by a Soviet interceptor in Soviet territory, about 280 mi. south of Murmansk. On April 23 an American plane and several other vehicles picked up 106 survivors and 2 dead passengers and took them to Helsinki, Finland; the pilot and navigator were held in the U.S.S.R. until April 29.

President Carter announces his plan to reduce ● **21** by two thirds the number of members of the U.S. armed forces scheduled to be withdrawn from South Korea during 1978.

The Supreme Court of the U.S. reveals its de- ● **24** nial of an appeal for a review of the conviction of newspaper heiress Patricia Hearst on a charge of bank robbery.

In Willow Island, W.Va., scaffolding erected ● **27** inside the cooling tower of a power plant collapses. All fifty-one men working on the scaffolding were killed.

A military coup headed by Lt. Gen. Abdul Qa- ● dir ousts the government of Afghanistan during a battle lasting several hours. President Mohammad Daud Khan was reportedly killed during the fighting. On April 30 a Marxist

APRIL 20

APRIL 27

55

APRIL 30

MAY 7

MAY 19

Revolutionary Council was proclaimed, headed by a civilian president, Noor Mohammad Taraki.

30 • Naomi Uemura, 37, a Japanese explorer, becomes the first person to reach the North Pole alone by dogsled.

MAY
---

7 • Prime Minister Menachem Begin of Israel ends an eight-day, coast-to-coast visit to the U.S. He addressed a crowd of several thousand assembled in New York City's Central Park to celebrate his nation's 30th birthday.

8 • In San Francisco a California District Court of Appeals orders a new trial for Juan Corona, convicted in 1972 of the murders of twenty-five farm workers. The unanimous opinion of three judges was that the defendant had been inadequately represented by his lawyer.
  • David Berkowitz pleads guilty to six charges of murder in the so-called Son of Sam case.

9 • The body of Aldo Moro, former premier of Italy who was kidnapped fifty-four days earlier, is found in Rome. He had been assassinated the previous day.

15 • The U.S. Senate votes (54–44) not to thwart the Carter administration's plan to sell jet fighter planes to Israel, Egypt, and Saudi Arabia. A total of 200 planes were scheduled to change hands in the package deal.

19 • French and Belgian forces are ordered into Kolwezi, Zaire, to protect and rescue foreigners trapped by insurgent forces. The bodies of forty-four Europeans, reportedly shot by the rebels, were found. (On May 25, French forces began to withdraw from Kolwezi; Belgian troops had already departed.)

20 • Peru is placed under martial law after a week of rioting and sabotage. (On May 22 a general strike began, and a curfew was imposed in the cities of Lima and Callao.)

21 • After five years of struggle against leftist opponents, Narita airport near Tokyo, Japan, opens. More than 14,000 policemen were on duty.
  • Voters in Egypt give President Anwar el-Sadat

56

an overwhelming mandate (98.29 percent) to continue his repressive measures, aimed at "protecting the home front and social peace."

JUNE

In a California referendum, Proposition 13, an • **6** initiative designed to reduce property taxes by as much as 60 percent beginning July 1, passes by a 2–1 margin.

In Annapolis, Md., President Carter tells the • **7** graduating class of the U.S. Naval Academy that the U.S. is prepared to confront the Soviet Union should the U.S.S.R. choose confrontation rather than cooperation.

MAY 21

Spencer W. Kimball, president of the Church • **9** of Jesus Christ of Latter-day Saints, announces in Salt Lake City that as a result of a revelation given the Mormon Church's leaders, black men would no longer be excluded from the priesthood.

Affirmed, ridden by Steve Cauthen, wins the • **10** Belmont and thus becomes the eleventh horse to win racing's triple crown. The 3-year-old colt had previously won the Kentucky Derby (May 6) and the Preakness (May 20).

JUNE 10

Israeli military forces complete their with- • **13** drawal from southern Lebanon. But the final strip of occupied territory was turned over to Lebanese Christian forces rather than to U.N. troops.

JUNE 15

Faced with charges of corruption, President • **15** Giovanni Leone of Italy resigns.
King Hussein of Jordan marries an American, • Elizabeth Halaby, and proclaims her Queen Noor al-Hussein.

Two treaties, under which control of the • **16** Panama Canal eventually will pass from the U.S. to Panama, are formally concluded. The leaders of the two nations, Jimmy Carter and Brig. Gen. Omar Torrijos Herrera, signed the ratified documents in the city of Panamá.

In Peru's first nationwide elections in eleven • **18** years, the largest bloc of seats in the constituent assembly is won by a moderate leftist party, the American Popular Revolutionary Alliance.

JUNE 23

JUNE 28

22 • A much-publicized and litigated march, scheduled for June 25 by the National Socialist Party of America in the predominantly Jewish Chicago suburb of Skokie, is called off. The Nazi leader, Frank Collin, said he had achieved his purpose: "to restore our free speech."

23 • In Turin, Italy, 29 members of the Red Brigades terrorist organization are sentenced to up to fifteen years in prison; 16 others are acquitted. Charges against one of the terrorists had been dropped earlier in the fifteen-week trial.

24 • Ahmed Hussein al-Ghashmi, chairman of the Military Command Council of the Yemen Arab Republic, is assassinated, allegedly by a bomb exploded by an envoy from the People's Democratic Republic of Yemen.

26 • Salem Rubayi Ali, chairman of the Presidential Council of the People's Democratic Republic of Yemen, is ousted and reportedly executed in a coup.

28 • The U.S. Supreme Court issues two split decisions in the case of Allan P. Bakke, a 38-year-old white man denied admission to the University of California Medical College at Davis. One decision (5–4) affirmed the constitutionality of college admissions programs favoring minorities; the other (also 5–4) directed that Bakke be admitted to the medical school in the fall.
• Reporters from all over the world descend upon Monte Carlo to cover the wedding of Princess Caroline of Monaco and Philippe Junot, a French commoner. (A civil ceremony was held on June 28, a religious ceremony on June 29.)

JULY

5 • The head of state of Ghana, Gen. Ignatius K. Acheampong, resigns. He was succeeded as chairman of the Supreme Military Council by Lt. Gen. Fred W.K. Akuffo.

7 • The Solomons, a 900-mi. island chain in the Pacific Ocean northeast of Australia, become independent after eighty-five years of British rule.

8 • Alessandro Pertini, an 81-year-old Socialist, is elected president of Italy.

An estimated 100,000 demonstrators march in • **9**
Washington, D.C., in support of an extension
of the March 22, 1979, deadline for ratification
of the so-called Equal Rights Amendment to
the U.S. Constitution.

In Mauritania, a bloodless military coup led by • **10**
the army chief of staff, Col. Moustapha Ould
Mohamed Saleck, deposes the president, Moktar Ould Daddah.

Hundreds of campers are seriously injured and • **11**
at least 180 die as a truck carrying liquid gas
explodes at a beach on the Mediterranean Sea
near Tarragona, Spain.

Leaders of the world's seven foremost indus- • **17**
trial democracies—the U.S., West Germany,
Great Britain, Japan, Italy, France, and Canada—end a two-day economic summit in
Bonn, West Germany.

President Carter announces that he has ac- • **20**
cepted the resignation of Peter G. Bourne. The
psychiatrist, chief adviser to the President on
drugs and narcotics, had prescribed a sedative
for one of his assistants who was using a fictitious name.

In Oldham and District General Hospital in • **25**
Lancashire, England, Lesley Brown gives birth
to the first baby conceived outside the mother's body. The child, a girl (later named Louise
Joy Brown), weighed 5 lb. 12 oz.

AUGUST

The House of Representatives votes 208–205 to • **1**
lift the arms embargo against Turkey. The Senate passed a similar resolution on July 25.
Margaret (Midge) Costanza resigns as an •
assistant to President Carter after several
months of clashing with other top Presidential
aides.
Christina Onassis, Greek shipping tycoon, is •
married in Moscow to Sergei Kauzov, a former
Soviet merchant marine official.

Robert P. Whalen, New York State health com- • **2**
missioner, recommends evacuation of the
Love Canal area of Niagara Falls. On Aug. 7,
President Carter declares it a disaster area because of contamination from buried chemicals.

JULY 9

JULY 25

TEST-TUBE BABY GIRL

Daily Mail

First test-tube baby is born
and medical history made as
a mother's dream comes true

IT'S A GIRL

AUG. 2

LOVE CANAL RECIPE:
1. MIX 82 CHEMICALS
2. PLACE IN CANAL FOR
   25 YRS.
YIELD: SICKNESS + DEATH

AUG. 17
AUG. 26

SEPT. 1

6 ● Paul VI, 263rd pope of the Roman Catholic Church, dies at the age of 80 in his summer residence at Castel Gandolfo.

7 ● President Juan Alberto Melgar Castro of Honduras is overthrown in a bloodless coup. Gen. Policarpo Paz García of the army was the leader of the military junta that took over the Honduran government.

8 ● A policeman is killed and 18 persons, including 12 policemen and firemen, are injured in Philadelphia. The officers were attempting to evict a self-styled revolutionary group known as MOVE from a barricaded house.

16 ● Antonio Guzmán is inaugurated as president of the Dominican Republic. The first peaceful transfer of power in Dominican history came after three months of heated dispute over the conduct and results of the May 16 election.

17 ● The first successful crossing of the Atlantic Ocean in a balloon is completed as three Americans (Ben Abruzzo, Max Anderson, and Larry Newman) touch down in a wheat field near Paris. The historic crossing began in Presque Isle, Maine, on Aug. 11.

18 ● Police and firemen in Memphis end a strike that began Aug. 10. National Guardsmen had been called in to take over police and fire-protection duties and an 8 P.M.–6 A.M. curfew was imposed.

22 ● The U.S. Senate votes (67–32) to approve a proposed constitutional amendment granting the District of Columbia full voting representation in Congress. The House of Representatives had approved the measure (289–127) on March 2.
   ● Jomo Kenyatta, the leading figure in Kenya's struggle for independence and its president since 1964, dies. He was succeeded by Vice-President Daniel Arap Moi. (Moi was elected president on Oct. 10.)

26 ● Albino Luciani, patriarch of Venice, is elected pope of the Roman Catholic Church. The new pope, who took the name John Paul I, was formally installed Sept. 3.

SEPTEMBER

1 ● Communist Chinese leader Hua Kuo-feng

ends a sixteen-day trip abroad, during which he visited Rumania, Yugoslavia, and Iran.

Muhammad Ali defeats world champion • 15 heavyweight boxer Leon Spinks in a fifteen-round fight in New Orleans. Ali thus became the first heavyweight prizefighter to win the crown three times. (See Feb. 15.)

At least 25,000 persons die as an earthquake • 16 strikes northeastern Iran.

At the White House, President Carter joins Is- • 17 raeli Prime Minister Menachem Begin and Egyptian President Anwar el-Sadat in signing two documents governing a peace settlement. The settlement had been hammered out in summit meetings held at Camp David, Md., beginning Sept. 6.

John Vorster, prime minister of South Africa • 20 since 1966, resigns. Pieter W. Botha, former defense minister, became prime minister Sept. 28; Vorster was named president Sept. 29.

A midair collision between a Pacific Southwest • 25 Airlines jetliner and a single engine training plane takes at least 150 lives. The accident, which occurred over San Diego, was the worst midair collision in U.S. aviation history.

Pope John Paul I dies on the thirty-fourth day • 28 of his reign.

A federal grand jury in Baltimore indicts eigh- • 29 teen individuals as a result of a probe of the General Services Administration of the U.S. government.

Tuvalu, formerly known as the Ellice Islands, • 30 becomes the world's smallest independent country. The South Pacific nation and its 6500 citizens had formerly been under the British flag.

SEPT. 15

SEPT. 17

SEPT. 25

OCTOBER

In Calcutta a baby girl is born to Bela Agarwal • 3 and her husband Pravat. The child, named Durga, was the second human baby to have been conceived outside the mother's body. (See July 25.)

The U.S. Senate votes (60–36) to approve an • 6 extension of the ratification deadline for the

OCT. 16

OCT. 23
NOV. 2

so-called Equal Rights Amendment. The extension to June 30, 1982, had been approved by the House of Representatives (233–189) on Aug. 15.

13 • Ola Ullsten, leader of the minority Liberal Party, is named prime minister of Sweden.

16 • Karol Wojtyła, archbishop of Cracow, is elected pope of the Roman Catholic Church and assumes the name of John Paul II. The Polish prelate, the first non-Italian pope in 456 years, was officially installed Oct. 22.

17 • World chess champion Anatoly Karpov of the U.S.S.R. retains his title when challenger Viktor Korchnoi, a Soviet defector resident in Switzerland, resigns in the thirty-second game of their match. The two had begun playing July 18 in Baguio, the Philippines.

23 • Documents formally implementing a treaty of peace and friendship between Japan and the People's Republic of China are exchanged in Tokyo.

24 • In a nationally televised speech President Carter unveils an anti-inflation plan that calls for voluntary wage-price controls. On Oct. 25 he named Alfred Kahn, chairman of the Civil Aeronautics Board, to head the new drive against inflation.

30 • Two Soviet citizens, former U.N. employees, are sentenced in U.S. District Court in Newark, N.J., to fifty years each in prison. The two were convicted of trying to buy U.S. military secrets.
  • Ugandan troops invade 18 mi. within Tanzania, occupying territory west of Lake Victoria. Contradictory reports on the continuation or cessation of hostilities continued to be issued for several weeks.

NOVEMBER

2 • Soviet cosmonauts Vladimir Kovalenok and Aleksandr Ivanchenkov land safely in Kazakhstan. They had established a new space endurance record of 139 days 15 hr.
  • At midnight, the Caribbean island of Dominica becomes an independent nation, after 173 years of British control.

5 • Prime Minister Jaafar Sharif-Emami of Iran resigns as rioters continue to rampage through

Tehran after two months of martial law in major cities. On Nov. 6, Shah Mohammed Riza Pahlavi put the nation under military rule.

A chartered DC-8 jetliner crashes outside the ● 15 airport at Colombo, Ceylon. Of the 259 persons aboard, at least 183 (all Muslim pilgrims returning from Mecca) died.

U.S. Rep. Leo J. Ryan (D, Calif.) and four others ● 18 are slain in an ambush at a remote airstrip near the religious settlement of Jonestown, Guyana. Shortly thereafter, 911 members of the colony, including the leader, Reverend Jim Jones, died, most of them voluntarily.

President Fidel Castro of Cuba pledges to re- ● 21 lease some 3000 prisoners, at a rate of 400 per month, to the U.S.

NOV. 18

NOV. 27

About 200 Vietnamese refugees drown when ● 22 their fishing boat capsizes at Kuala Trengganu, Malaysia.

George Moscone, mayor of San Francisco, and ● 27 Harvey Milk, a county supervisor, are shot to death. The alleged assailant was Dan White, a recently resigned supervisor who was reportedly seeking reinstatement.
Prime Minister Takeo Fukuda of Japan resigns ● in favor of Masayoshi Ohira. Ohira had won a primary election to head the ruling Liberal-Democratic Party.

DECEMBER

Luis Herrera Campíns, candidate of the oppo- ● 3 sition Social Christian Party, is elected president of Venezuela.

DEC. 8

Spanish voters overwhelmingly endorse a new ● 6 democratic constitution. The abstention rate, however, was 32.3 percent.

Golda Meir, prime minister of Israel from 1969 ● 8 to 1974, dies in Jerusalem at the age of 80.

Seven men, masked and armed, steal $3,000,- ● 11 000 in U.S. cash and foreign currency and jewelry worth an estimated $2,000,000 from a Lufthansa cargo facility at Kennedy International Airport in New York City.

In a nationwide television broadcast President ● 15 Carter announces the establishment of diplo-

DEC. 15

matic relations with the People's Republic of China, effective Jan. 1, 1979.

17 • The Organization of Petroleum Exporting Countries announces a 14.5 percent rise in the price of petroleum, to be effected in stages by the end of 1979.

19 • The Indian parliament expels Indira Gandhi and sends her to jail for the remainder of the parliamentary session (she was released Dec. 26). She was punished for authoritarian acts late in her term as prime minister.
  • A power blackout strikes France and parts of Switzerland. Power was restored to about three fourths of the blackout area after two hours.

DEC. 19

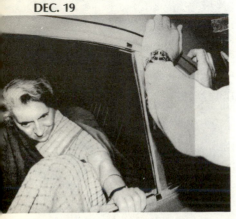

27 • After remaining in a coma for forty days, Houari Boumédienne, president of Algeria since 1965, dies in Algiers. Rabah Bitat, chairman of the Popular National Assembly, was named interim president.

29 • The shah of Iran names an opposition leader, Shahpur Bakhtiar, to form a civilian cabinet, amid rumors that the shah is planning to leave the country or turn over power to a regency council.

30 • The House Select Committee on Assassinations concludes that the assassination of President John F. Kennedy was "probably . . . a result of a conspiracy" and that "there is a likelihood" that the assassination of Martin Luther King, Jr., was "a result of a conspiracy."

A

ACCIDENTS AND DISASTERS. The following were among the notable accidents and disasters of 1978.

Jan. 1, India: All 213 people aboard are killed when an Air India Boeing 747 explodes in flight and crashes into the Arabian Sea after departing from Bombay. This was India's worst air accident and the world's third most disastrous to date.

Jan. 28, Missouri: Sixteen people die in a fire that destroys the Coates House hotel in Kansas City.

Feb. 11, Canada: Forty people are killed when a Pacific Western Airlines plane crashes during a landing attempt at Cranbrook, British Columbia.

Feb. 24, Tennessee: Twelve people are killed and 50 injured when a derailed railroad tank car laden with liquid propane gas explodes in Waverly.

Feb. 25, Argentina: At least 37 people are killed and 120 injured when a train collides with a truck and is derailed at a crossing about 70 km (45 mi.) north of Santa Fe.

Feb. 26, Florida: After a sabotage-caused derailment of 47 railroad cars and 5 locomotives near Youngstown, 8 people die and 67 are injured when a tank car involved in the incident spills chlorine gas, which spreads over cars on a nearby highway.

March 3, Venezuela: All 47 persons aboard are killed when an airliner crashes into the Caribbean Sea shortly after takeoff from Caracas.

March 16, Bulgaria: All 73 persons aboard are killed when a Bulgarian airliner crashes after takeoff from Sofia.

April 15, Italy: A train collision kills 45 people and injures about 200 others 30 km (19 mi.) south of Bologna.

April 16, India: Between 400 and 500 people are killed by a tornado that flattens six villages in the state of Orissa. About 100 others are killed by a tornado in a West Bengal village.

April 27, West Virginia: Fifty-one workers are killed when scaffolding on which they are working at a height of 52 m (170 ft.) collapses; the power plant cooling tower was under construction at Willow Island, St. Marys.

June 10, Sweden: Fire in a hotel in Borås kills 20 teenagers and injures more than 55 during a high school graduation celebration.

June 20, Greece: An earthquake measuring 6.5 on the Richter scale kills at least 47 people and injures 150 in the Thessaloníki area.

July 11, Spain: More than 180 people are killed and many badly injured when a tank truck laden with propylene overturns and explodes at a campsite 193 km (120 mi.) southwest of Barcelona. The victims are nearly all vacationers,

s wing afire, a jetliner with 35 persons aboard plunges oward the ground Sept. 25. he passenger plane collided with a Cessna at 3000 ft., then rashed in a residential neighorhood of San Diego. At east 150 persons were killed the worst midair collision U.S. history.

ACCIDENTS AND DISASTERS

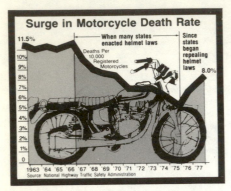

Surge in Motorcycle Death Rate

When many states enacted helmet laws — Since states began repealing helmet laws

Deaths Per 10,000 Registered Motorcycles

11.5% ... 8.0%

1963 '64 '65 '66 '67 '68 '69 '70 '71 '72 '73 '74 '75 '76 '77
Source: National Highway Traffic Safety Administration

Reprinted from issue of Sept. 4, 1978, of "U.S. News & World Report." © 1978, U.S. News & World Report, Inc.

many of them children and most of them from Belgium, France, and West Germany.

July 17, Egypt: At least 56 people are killed when a Cairo bus crashes into the Nile River.

Aug. 4, Canada: Forty-one people are dead after a bus carrying handicapped people runs off the road into Lac d'Argent 80 km (50 mi.) southeast of Montréal.

Aug. 20, Iran: A theater fire in Abadan, set by extremists, kills 430 persons, most of them children. The sole exit had been locked as an anti-terrorist precaution, trapping the victims.

Sept. 16, Iran: At least 25,000 people are killed in northeast Iran in an earthquake measuring 7.7 on the Richter scale. Nearly all the buildings in the ancient, mud-brick city of Tabas are demolished, killing 11,000 of the town's 12,000 to 13,000 residents.

Sept. 19, India: Government officials report a total of more than 1200 deaths in northern India as a result of three months of monsoon floods.

Sept. 25, California: At least 150 people are killed in a midair collision between a jetliner and a training plane over San Diego. All 135 persons aboard the airliner and both people in the trainer are killed. In addition, at least 13 people on the ground are killed by falling wreckage.

Oct. 20, Maryland: Eleven crew members of the U.S. Coast Guard cutter *Cuyahoga* are drowned when the vessel sinks after being rammed by the Argentine freighter *Santa Cruz II* in Chesapeake Bay.

Oct. 27, the Philippines: Typhoon Rita strikes Luzon and causes more than 314 deaths.

Nov. 15, Ceylon: At least 183 people are killed when an Icelandic jetliner chartered to return Indonesian pilgrims from Mecca crashes near the airport at Colombo as the pilot attempts an instrument landing in heavy rain.

Nov. 19, India: The crash of an Indian air force transport plane near Leh airport in Kashmir kills all 77 persons aboard plus 1 person on the ground.

Nov. 24, Ceylon: A hurricane causes deaths estimated at more than 150 and is reported to leave hundreds of thousands of people homeless.

Dec. 9, Mississippi: Fifteen middle-aged and elderly residents die at the Ellisville State School for the mentally retarded, and 16 are injured by smoke and heat caused by a fire.

Dec. 21, Spain: A locomotive making test runs crashes into a school bus at Salamanca, killing 27 children and 1 adult. An investigation into the conduct of the bus driver was ordered by the government.

Dec. 28, Oregon: A United Airlines jet crashes short of the Portland airport, killing at least 10 and injuring more than 50 of the 185 passengers and crew. There was no explosion or fire in the crash, which led to speculation that the jetliner had run out of fuel.   L.A.S.

ADVERTISING. Lawyers made use of their new-found freedom to advertise in 1978, encouraging architects and other professionals to do likewise. Steep penalties for deceptive advertising, several major acquisitions, and the superselling of the film *Superman* also made news during the year.

Accounts and Mergers. Two newsworthy agency events were the capture of a "hot" airline account by N. W. Ayer ABH International and the largest agency acquisition in history by Interpublic.

Ayer, the industry's oldest agency, took over not only Pan Am's $20,000,000 domestic account but also the airline's international advertising. Ayer won out against three other bidders by affiliating—within one month—with agencies in Australia, Brazil, Japan, and other countries. Only a few weeks earlier, Ayer had captured the $20,000,000 Seven-Up account and a $55,000,000 U.S. Army ad campaign.

In November, Interpublic joined with SSC&B to create an amalgam of agencies with unprecedented total billings. Interpublic (including McCann-Erickson) was already the largest communications company of its kind in the world, serving General Motors, Coca-Cola, and Exxon. SSC&B, a front-running package-goods agency, is a major house for Lever Brothers and a minority owner of Lintas, a worldwide advertising company. American Brands, Johnson & Johnson, Bristol-Myers, and Sterling Drug headed the list of SSC&B's accounts.

Ads by Professionals. The U.S. Supreme Court ruling in 1977 that lawyers could not be prevented from advertising their fees paved the way for the first use of television commercials by a law firm in

66

Polishing the President's Image

Public perception of "weak and vacillating" White House leadership sent Jimmy Carter's Gallup Poll rating skidding to 39 percent in April. With an eye toward reversing that trend, Atlanta advertising executive Gerald Rafshoon, 44, was added to the Presidential staff in May as assistant for communications. An old friend and associate (he created the Carter campaign commercials in 1976), Rafshoon oversaw the public activities of the President, the Presidential staff, and the cabinet as well. Press reports describing the adman as a behind-the-scenes Svengali seemed overdrawn, but he was clearly one of the President's most trusted and influential advisers on a variety of public policies.

Gerald Rafshoon of Atlanta and Washington, D.C.

1978. In November the Nationwide Law Firm made history by airing on four New York City channels a total of fifty-three thirty-second spots that gave viewers a toll-free phone number to call. Altman-Stoller Weiss was the agency responsible.

Architects and eyeglass retailers also broke through long-standing bans against advertising. On May 24, the American Institute of Architects voted to permit "dignified" print ads but prohibited photographs and television ads. That same day, the Federal Trade Commission (FTC) ended restrictions on the advertising of prices for eyeglasses and contact lenses. Advertised, competitive prices may save consumers $400,000,000 annually in the forty-three states where price advertising had been restricted or prohibited.

Corrective Advertising. Questionable product claims cost some accounts dearly in 1978. The STP Corp. was fined $500,000, the largest such penalty ever imposed by the FTC, for making false claims about its automobile engine additive. The Supreme Court refused to review FTC and lower-court decisions requiring the manufacturers of Listerine mouthwash to "correct" the false claims made for the germicide. Warner-Lambert Co. was ordered to pay $10,000,000 for new ads bearing this statement: "Contrary to prior advertising, Listerine will not help prevent colds or sore throats or lessen their severity." Similarly, American Home Products had to amend its Anacin copy to read, "Anacin is not a tension reliever"—an interim ruling by the FTC that would cost the company $24,000,000 in new ads.

Wallpaper was only one of nearly 1000 items licensed by Warner Communications to promote its Superman movie. Other spin-offs included "S"-shirts, dolls, lunch boxes, record albums, books, costumes—they even had plans for an electronic pinball game.

The Taylor Wine Co. uncorked a controversy
over taste tests with its $1,500,000 comparative
campaign devised by Kenyon & Eckhardt. Rivals
could not swallow Taylor's boast of "three firsts
and a second" against other name—and named—
brands. K&E launched the television and print
campaign on behalf of Taylor California Cellars, a
line of premium wines selling for 10 to 30 percent
more than the wines they were compared with.

Consumers took special interest in a year-end
brouhaha over Anheuser-Busch's new malt-based
Chelsea beverage, introduced to test markets with
the coy slogan "The Not-So-Soft Drink." The gin-
ger-flavored drink, which had an alcoholic content of less than 0.5 percent, was packaged like
beer but could be bought by children like any soft
drink. Civic backlash in Virginia forced the manufacturer to alter both its product and its advertising.

Wary of the boom in celebrity endorsements,
the FTC indicated that stardom would not exempt
endorsers from responsibility for determining the
truth of what they are paid to say. In one well-
publicized case, singer Pat Boone agreed to pay
possible restitution for untruthful claims he had
made in print and on television on behalf of
Acne-Statin, a skin treatment.

Superman and Supersell. The $40,000,000 motion
picture Superman hardly took the public by surprise. By the time the movie opened in December, Warner Communications had sponsored an
estimated 6,500,000 television, radio, trailer, and
print "messages," 12,000 floor displays, and a
swarm of spin-off paraphernalia ranging from
"S"-shirts to more than a half-dozen Superman
paperbacks. Encouraged by the $400,000,000 in
ancillary income earned by Star Wars, Warner li-

censed some one hundred manufacturers to advertise and market nearly 1000 red-white-and-
blue products. Frankfurt Communications, which
began work on the film's "low-key" marketing
strategies two years ago, is a subsidiary of Kenyon
& Eckhardt; Grey Advertising handled the media
buying.

Obituaries. Deaths during 1978 included those of
agency founder Raymond Rubicam (see OBITUAR-
IES); Russian-born hotel executive and promoter
Serge Obolensky (Sept. 29 at 87); and Polish-born
publicist Benjamin Sonnenberg, who represented
many corporations and celebrities (Sept. 18 at 77).

See RADIO AND TELEVISION BROADCASTING. D.G.

AFGHANISTAN. Afghanistan's careful balancing
act between East and West ended in 1978 with a
leftist coup, tilting the country toward the Soviet
orbit and sending tremors throughout the region.
On April 27, as President Mohammad Daud's government moved to quell disorders following the
assassination of a Communist trade union leader,
army and air force units rose in revolt under the
leadership of Lt. Gen. Abdul Qadir. Daud and his
family were slain, and in a day of bloody fighting
the rebels gained complete control of Kabul, the
capital city.

On April 30 a new Revolutionary Council was
proclaimed. Heading the council was a civilian,
Noor Mohammad Taraki, the chairman of the
People's Democratic Party of Afghanistan (PDPA).
Taraki was also named prime minister, and Qadir
became minister of defense. In a mildly worded
statement to the press, Taraki denied that the
PDPA was Communist, affirmed Afghanistan's de-
votion to Islam, and asked for the friendship of all
nations.

During the next few months, there were signs
of increasing friction between the PDPA's two
main factions—Khalq, of which Taraki was a
member, and Parcham. In July, Babrak Karmal, the
leading figure in Parcham and a hard-line Marxist,
was removed from his posts as deputy prime minister and vice-president of the Revolutionary
Council; he was subsequently arrested. On Aug.
17, Radio Kabul announced that Lt. Gen. Qadir,
also a Parcham adherent, had been arrested while
attempting a coup.

The elimination of Karmal and Qadir left Taraki
and Hafizullah Amin (the newly appointed minister of foreign affairs, vice-president of the Revolutionary Council, and deputy prime minister) as
the two most powerful men in the country.
Toward the end of 1978, Taraki's public statements became more overtly Marxist, and Soviet
advisers were increasingly evident at all levels of
government and military affairs.

See STATISTICS OF THE WORLD. W.J.G.

AFRICA

Warriors from Cuba, the Soviet Union, France, and Belgium joined the native warriors of Africa during the year, as the arbitrary borders established by colonial powers were besieged and tested. Newly won freedom brought chaos to some countries; for others, freedom was still just a future dream.

Military intervention from abroad proved to be one of the most dominant and divisive issues facing Africa in 1978. The threat of foreign intervention brought more African heads of state to the fifteenth annual meeting of the Organization of African Unity (OAU) than at any time since the organization was founded; thirty-four such leaders converged upon Khartoum in July. OAU member states were deeply divided, however; all that they could agree on was that each of them had the right to ask any country in the world for help.

Military Intervention. The problem of foreign military intervention, with either men or munitions, had resurfaced in Africa in the mid-1970's, after having been forgotten for a decade. Following the turmoil of independence in Zaire and the reunification of its breakaway Katanga (Shaba) region in 1963, the United States and the U.S.S.R. focused their diplomatic attentions elsewhere, and Africa entered a period of benign neglect.

In the 1970's, as African nationalist movements began to challenge white settlers for control of southern Africa—Angola, Mozambique, Rhodesia, South-West Africa (Namibia), and South Africa itself—they encountered stiffening white military resistance and hesitation from the Western powers, which felt both ties of kinship to the area's white settlers and a need to protect massive investments. And as the West hesitated, African nationalists turned increasingly to the Soviet Union and its Eastern European allies, to Cuba, and to the People's Republic of China for arms and training. For example, the nationalist guerrillas who forced the Portuguese to withdraw from Angola and Mozambique were equipped mainly with Soviet and Czech arms. And in the Horn of Africa, Somali frustration over a territorial dispute with Ethiopia led to an infusion of Soviet arms in exchange for a naval base on the Red Sea. While the Chinese as well as the Soviets and their allies were supporting the "progressive" regimes and liberation movements of Africa, France intervened to support "conservative" or client governments in Gabon, Chad, and Upper Volta; and

small French forces were also garrisoned in other countries.

Massive foreign military intervention came in 1975, during the Angolan civil war. Battling against groups supported by South Africa and clandestinely by the U.S. Central Intelligence Agency, the leftist Popular Movement for the Liberation of Angola (MPLA) called for help from Cuba. More than 15,000 Cuban troops and technicians saw duty in Angola before MPLA control of the government was secure. Although the West condemned the intervention and the U.S. declared that it would not establish diplomatic relations with Angola until Cuban forces were substantially reduced, the MPLA continued during 1978 to rely upon Cuban troops to bolster the forces fighting its guerrilla enemies. The MPLA also claimed that the Cuban forces helped to provide a shield against South African military incursions.

Cuban forces also proved invaluable in 1978 in supporting the Soviet intervention in the Ethiopian-Somali war. When the Somalis attacked Ethiopia in 1977, the Soviet Union attempted to restrain them; the Soviets were rebuffed—their naval base was closed and they were forced to withdraw from the country. Shifting their allegiance, the Soviets organized massive shipments of arms as well as the transfer of some 17,000 Cuban troops and 1500 Soviet advisers to Ethiopia. This intervention permitted the Ethiopian government forces, first, to contain the Somali attack, and, early in 1978, to defeat the Somalis and regain their lost territory (although there were reports of renewed fighting late in the year). When the Ethiopians attacked their longtime foes in Eritrea, however, the Cubans refused to allow their forces to take part. But Soviet arms allowed the Ethiopian government troops to regain most of the urban centers that had been taken by the Eritrean rebels in 1977 and to force the secessionists to fall back on guerrilla tactics once again.

The presence of Soviet arms and technicians and Cuban ground troops in Ethiopia brought

President Fidel Castro of Cuba visits Ethiopian strongman Lt. Col. Mengistu Haile Mariam in September. Cuban military support helped the Ethiopian regime to achieve major victories over Somali and Eritrean rebels in 1978.

outcries from Sudan, Egypt, and the conservative Arab states of the Red Sea and the Persian Gulf. In Africa generally, however, Soviet and Cuban intervention in Angola and Ethiopia was applauded. In the case of Angola, intervention was seen as aid to a true independence movement—the other movements were tainted by South African support—and, in Ethiopia, it was viewed as a defense of existing national borders. Given the artificial nature of most national boundaries in Africa (most were established by colonial powers), local governments are extremely reluctant to allow any changes. They fear that an unending process of fragmentation of their young nations might get started and that border wars might go on indefinitely. In southern Africa, the governments providing sanctuaries and support for the black nationalist movements in Rhodesia, South-West Africa, and South Africa increasingly have felt compelled to explore the offers of Soviet and Cuban aid. Mozambique, Angola, and Zambia have all claimed incursions by South African as well as Rhodesian forces, and the Western powers have been slow to prevent these attacks or provide help. Nevertheless, the threat of Soviet and Cuban

intervention in southern Africa appears to have motivated the U.S. and Great Britain to continue their initiatives to reach settlements in Rhodesia and South-West Africa. They also appear to have forced the governments of South Africa and, to a lesser degree, Rhodesia to be more receptive to these proposals.

African distrust and distaste for foreign military interventions clearly have been eroded in recent years. So too has the principle of inviolable boundaries. The Ethiopian-Somali war was primarily a struggle over possession of the Ogaden, a region of Ethiopia inhabited by Somali tribesmen. Continued Libyan support of Muslim guerrillas in Chad was inspired partly by religious sentiments and partly by claims to territory in northern Chad. Angolan support of or acquiescence in invasions of Zaire's Shaba region in 1977 and 1978 was largely a response to Zairian aid to guerrilla movements seeking to overthrow the MPLA government or dismember the country. Certainly the most blatant violation of the principle was the 1978 Ugandan attack on Tanzania, the details of which remained unclear as the year ended.

Internal Dissension. Much of the other news from Africa in 1978 pointed to the severe difficulties African central governments have encountered as the slogans of independence and unity gave way to the realities of economic, religious, and regional differences. In February the central govern-

ment of Chad negotiated a cease-fire with Froli-
nat, the Chad National Liberation Front, one of
the northern, Muslim factions in revolt. The
cease-fire called for a government of national
unity, but in April heavy fighting erupted, and
French intervention with ground troops and aircraft was necessary to maintain the southern,
Christian government. At year's end, fighting was
continuing, but the central government under
President Félix Malloum no longer appeared
threatened.

Following a general strike and riots in January,
the Tunisian government declared a state of
emergency. A number of labor leaders were arrested, and the government declared that an attempt had been made to engineer a coup d'etat
against ailing President Habib Bourguiba. In Mali,
the cabinet and top administration were changed
in February, following an alleged conspiracy to
topple the head of state, Col. Moussa Traoré. Libya's Col. Muammar el-Qaddafi narrowly escaped
an assassination plot in March, and a number of
air force officers were arrested soon afterward. In
mid-May the government of the Comoro Islands
was overthrown in a bloodless military coup engineered with the aid of white mercenaries. President Ali Soilih, who was killed two weeks later,
allegedly while attempting to escape, was replaced by Ahmed Abdallah as president and Mohammed Ahmed as premier, but the influence of
the French leader of the mercenaries, said to be
one of the most hated men in Africa, remained
strong. (Abdallah himself had been ousted by Soilih in a 1975 coup.) The government of Mauritania's President Moktar Ould Daddah was overthrown in July in a bloodless coup. A military

The First Family of the U.S. visits Nigeria on March 31:
Amy Carter attracts the attention of an official's daughter,
her father the President beams, and First Lady Rosalynn
Carter accepts a bouquet.

government under Lt. Col. Moustapha Ould Mohamed Saleck took power, pledging to find a solution to the ongoing war which pitted Mauritania
and Morocco against Saharan nationalists, known
as the Polisario Front.

Peaceful Transition. On the other side of the ledger, peaceful elections in February resulted in the
reelection of Senegal's President Léopold Sédar

Surrounded by cabinet members, Jomo Kenyatta's two
wives, Mama Ngina (in black dress) and Grace Wahu,
attend his funeral in Nairobi in August. The Kenyan leader's successor, President Daniel Arap Moi, is at right.

Water brought by truck is distributed among the people of Tatki, Senegal, in June. The exceptionally arid western part of the Sahel region was faced with its worst drought in many years.

Somali soldiers hold the front against Ethiopian forces on Feb. 20. Within weeks the Somalis were driven out of the Ogaden by an Ethiopian army that had the help of troops from the Soviet Union and Cuba.

Senghor. In 1977 Senghor had ended the ban on political activity and allowed the formation of three opposition parties. This pressure-valve device proved popular, and his Socialist Party won 83 of the 100 seats in the Senegalese National Assembly. Elections were also held in February in Sudan; these pointed to the success of President Gaafar al-Nimeiry's program of national reconciliation. A number of figures who had earlier opposed al-Nimeiry were given posts in the government or in the country's political structure. In Upper Volta elections were held in April and May, resulting in a return to civilian rule. Gen. Sangoulé Lamizana, who had served as president under the military government, was elected president of the new republic. Opposition parties

won a substantial share of the seats in the National Assembly. In Sierra Leone in a June referendum, more than 2,000,000 voters turned out in favor of a new constitution and a one-party state. The long-feared death of Kenya's President Jomo Kenyatta occurred in August, but the transition to a new civilian government took place peacefully as Daniel Arap Moi replaced the venerable Kikuyu leader. In Zambia, President Kenneth D. Kaunda was returned to office in December elections. Algerian President Houari Boumédienne died Dec. 27 after a long illness, and the machinery for choosing a successor went into operation.

See also ARAB LEAGUE; MIDDLE EAST; and individual articles on many of the countries mentioned.   J.T.S.

AGRICULTURE. World farm production, helped by generally favorable weather, again set records in 1978. Some trouble spots developed, including locust infestations in parts of East Africa, grasshopper infestations in the western United States, flood damage on the Indian subcontinent, and drought in some other areas. Grain stocks rose again, boosted by near-record harvests in the Soviet Union and record crops of feed grains in the U.S. Despite pressure on cash grain prices because of the huge grain supplies, U.S. farm income rebounded sharply from 1977.

Farm Production. Extremely wet weather early in the year reduced some vegetable and fruit crops in the West but ended that region's drought and restored water supplies. The weather also delayed spring planting of corn and soybeans in the Middle West but turned favorable through the summer, allowing almost optimum growing conditions for the crops. In the fall, farmers harvested yields of about one hundred bushels of corn per acre, a new record. The wheat harvest was down 12 percent from the previous year, largely because of government programs mandating farmers to take land out of production in order to qualify for federal price supports.

Overall crop production dropped slightly from the record level of 1977. Record harvests of corn (6.8 billion bu.) and soybeans (1.8 billion bu.) were the main increases. Wheat and cotton registered the steepest declines, and sorghum production was down 12 percent. But the overall total of grain (337,000,000 metric tons), counting leftover supplies from previous crops, was up sharply from the 1977 level (250,000,000 metric tons).

Strengthened by brisk grain exports and a rising demand for grain as livestock feed, farm prices rose steadily for nine consecutive months from late 1977 through mid-1978, before dropping sea-

sonally in the summer. For all of the year, farm prices averaged about 13 percent above 1977. This meant a significant rise in net farm income to about $24 billion ($8800 per farm) in 1978 from $20.6 billion ($7600 per farm) in 1977, still well below the record of $33.3 billion in 1973.

Livestock. After a four-year slump, cattle prices rose dramatically in 1978, despite a slight decline in the summer. For the year, cattle prices averaged about 50¢ a pound, compared to about 34¢ in 1977, as total beef production dropped 4 percent. Hog producers increased output only about 2 percent, much less than the higher pork prices and abundant feed supplies had led experts to expect. Pork prices for the year averaged about 47¢ per pound, 7¢ more than the 1977 average.

Cattlemen were angered by U.S. President Jimmy Carter's action in June to ease the pressure on retail meat prices by allowing about 200,000,000 lb. more foreign beef to enter the U.S. This decision raised the 1978 beef import quota to 1.5 billion lb., about 7 percent of U.S. domestic consumption. The National Cattlemen's Association mounted a major legislative drive to change the law so that in the future a President could not arbitrarily raise quotas in such cases. The Carter administration did not object to the "countercyclical" formula proposed by the cattlemen—a

A medicinal bath helps protect cattle from scabies, a skin infection that plagued many herds in 1978.

Since the world's supply of timber is finite, the search is on for easily grown fibers that can be converted into paper. One promising material is kenaf, an exotic plant that is being grown experimentally in Illinois by the U.S. Department of Agriculture, in association with the American Newspaper Publishers Association.

A laser-guided land leveler at work in Yuma Valley, Ariz. This system, devised by the Laserplane Corp., can be used for leveling, grading, and surveying, and is especially valuable when preparing fields for surface drainage and irrigation in areas where water is scarce.

mechanism that would allow more foreign beef to enter the U.S. when domestic production is declining and less when it is rising—but did object to limiting the President's options.

Farm Legislation. Under intense pressure from protesting farmers, Congress devised emergency legislation to boost price supports for major crops but then modified it under threat of a Presidential veto. Carter did go along with new authority to raise cotton support prices slightly and to boost

subsidies for wheat producers through higher target prices.

Wheat loan rates were raised from $2.25 to $2.35 per bushel, and the target price from $2.90 a bushel in 1977 to $3.40 for the 1978 crop. Corn loan rates remained at $2.00 a bushel, but the target was raised from $2.00 to $2.10.

Congress revised federal agricultural credit programs with a new $4 billion plan to help farmers refinance debts. It also wrote new legislation requiring foreigners to notify the U.S. government of all lands they own or buy. The measure was designed to alleviate the fears of some Americans that foreigners were taking over U.S. farmland.

New legislation that would have raised price supports for domestic cane and beet sugar failed to pass Congress, but the Carter administration announced it would boost price supports anyway. The Administration also pledged to take further action, if necessary, to raise import levies to help reduce the importation of cheaper foreign sugar.

Farm Exports. U.S. farm exports continued their record pace, totaling nearly $27 billion in the marketing year that ended Sept. 30, up from $24 billion the previous year. Total volume also set a record at about 117,000,000 metric tons, compared with the previous high of 102,000,000 metric tons in fiscal 1977. Exports were boosted by orders for almost 15,000,000 tons of wheat and corn from the Soviet Union, an increase from 6,100,000 tons in the 1976–77 marketing year. The People's Republic of China, after a four-year absence in the U.S. grain market, bought wheat and corn totaling more than 4,000,000 tons during 1977–78. The major exports overall were wheat, corn, soybeans, cotton, rice, and tobacco.

World Agriculture. World grain production was up approximately 5 percent in 1978, about matching the record of more than 1.1 billion metric tons produced in 1976. Stocks projected for mid-1979 should total about 175,000,000 metric tons, the most left over at the end of a global marketing year since 1970. Larger crops in Europe, the huge U.S. feed grain harvest, and the record production estimated for the Soviet Union (about 230,000,000 metric tons) were major contributors to the bumper crop for 1978.   D.K.

ALABAMA. *See* STATISTICS OF THE WORLD.

ALASKA. *See* STATISTICS OF THE WORLD.

ALBANIA. Albania lost its only ally in 1978. On July 7, the People's Republic of China informed the Albanian government that it was cutting off all economic and technical aid. In subsequent public

Entomologists believed that the boll weevil had no effective biological control agent—until Winfield Sterling of Texas A. & M. University disclosed that the fire ant, a common pest in the South, has a voracious appetite for cotton worms and weevils. A cotton boll is the scene for this battle between a weevil and a platoon of fire ants.

announcements, China said its help to the Balkan nation had amounted to $5 billion over twenty-four years and blamed Albanian leaders for the break. The Chinese noted that Albania had consistently criticized their internal policies and their increasing ties with the West. Albania responded with a harsh letter accusing the Chinese Communist Party of wavering in its stand against the Soviet Union and of straying from the path of true Marxism-Leninism.

The Sino-Albanian break was not unexpected; bilateral relations had been souring for several years. Nonetheless, Albania was left more isolated from the world than ever. In a policy switch that may signal a search for new allies, Albanian Communist leader Enver Hoxha began to speak of Greece and Turkey with unprecedented warmth.

Apparently hoping to bolster domestic support, Hoxha indicated that he might relax his stern internal policies. During a tour of southern Albania in March, he showed sympathy toward the public's desire for more consumer goods. "A woman, among other things, longs for a pretty and tastefully made blouse," Hoxha declared in an unusually solicitous speech.

See STATISTICS OF THE WORLD.   F.W.

On Dec. 27, following the announcement of the death of President Houari Boumédienne, thousands of mourners gather outside the Palace of the People in Algiers. Their chant: "Boumédienne lives."

ALBERTA. *See* STATISTICS OF THE WORLD.

ALGERIA. The lingering illness and death of President Houari Boumédienne, the nation's iron-willed leader for thirteen years and the architect of its "socialist revolution," overshadowed all other events in Algeria during 1978.

Boumédienne's Illness. The death of Boumédienne on Dec. 27 ended a three-month medical saga. He spent a month in the U.S.S.R., but Soviet doctors apparently failed to diagnose his condition, which eventually turned out to be Waldenstrom's disease, a rare malady that attacks blood cells and bone marrow. On Nov. 18, after his return to Algiers, Boumédienne sank into a coma. Dr. Jan Waldenstrom of Sweden, discoverer of the disease, and doctors from the United States, the Soviet Union, China, France, Great Britain, Cuba, Denmark, and Tunisia all flew to Algiers to attend Boumédienne. Despite all their efforts, Boumédienne never regained consciousness. Since his early personal history was cloaked in mystery, his age at death was variously estimated at from 46 to 53; *see* OBITUARIES.

Political Legacy. Boumédienne had seized power in 1965, just three years after Algeria had gained its independence from France. During his thirteen years as president, Boumédienne raised Algeria from a largely agricultural nation to one of the more developed countries of the Third World, in part because of large amounts of assistance from

the Soviet Union. But as a radical socialist, Boumédienne also pursued a fiercely independent and pragmatic foreign policy. At the time of his death, the U.S. was Algeria's largest trading partner, taking a quarter of its natural gas exports and more than half of its oil.

The New Government. After Boumédienne's death, the Algerian government named Rabah Bitat, chairman of the Popular National Assembly, to serve as interim president for up to forty-five days. The Algerian constitution does not allow the speaker of the assembly to run for president, however. Boumédienne's successor will be nominated by a special congress of Algeria's one political party, the National Liberation Front, and then popularly elected. A member of the eight-man Council of the Revolution, Col. Mohammed Salah Yahiaoui, was regarded as the most likely of several possible choices. (The council is the remnant of the junta that headed the 1965 coup.)

Economic Developments. The most critical economic development of 1978 for Algeria was the U.S. Department of Energy's announcement Dec. 18 that it was voiding a 1976 commercial contract calling for export to the U.S. of Algerian liquefied natural gas worth about $500,000,000 a year for twenty years. It was apparent that some of this loss, however, would be offset by the 14.5 percent price increase that was announced by OPEC (the Organization of Petroleum Exporting Countries; q.v.) on Dec. 17.

Foreign Affairs. The death of Boumédienne was expected to diminish at least temporarily the leading role Algeria had played in Third World affairs. Boumédienne had backed the Polisario guerrilla movement, fighting Morocco and Mauritania for possession of the former Spanish Sahara, and Morocco's King Hassan II voiced optimism that Algeria might in the future lessen its support for the Polisario. Other Arab leaders felt the new government might also decrease the support Boumédienne had provided for the Palestine Liberation Organization; Algeria was one of the four "steadfastness and confrontation" states that had severed all relations with Egypt after the September Camp David agreement between Israel and Egypt.

See STATISTICS OF THE WORLD. *See also* AFRICA; ARAB LEAGUE; and MIDDLE EAST.   M.R.B.

ANGOLA. The government of Angolan President Agostinho Neto continued to be beset by internal and external opposition during 1978. Early in the year the governing MPLA Party of Labor (formerly the Popular Movement for the Liberation of Angola) purged itself of ideological dissidents, some of whom had supported the abortive May, 1977, coup d'etat.

Efforts to stamp out the guerrilla opposition in

Late in the year Angolan foreign policy took a surprising westward turn. The avowedly Marxist president, Agostinho Neto (right), even welcomed U.S. Sen. George S. McGovern (D, S.Dak.) to Luanda on Dec. 18.

Angola's northern, eastern, and southern provinces were less successful. Encouraged by the withdrawal of Cuban forces bound for Ethiopia, guerrilla activity increased in the northwestern exclave of Cabinda as well as in the south. A government offensive, spearheaded by Cuban troops, against the National Union for the Total Independence of Angola (UNITA) was unsuccessful in the south in April. A new offensive in June proved equally unsuccessful, but the effort was renewed in October.

In May, South African troops penetrated some 250 km (150 mi.) into Angola to destroy bases and training camps of the South-West African People's Organization (SWAPO), the principal threat to South Africa's plans for Namibia (South-West Africa, q.v.), which remained under South African administration in 1978. This "flagrant violation" of Angola's sovereignty was condemned in the United Nations Security Council. Despite accusations of Angolan support of anti-Mobutu rebels in Shaba region, both Neto and President Mobutu Sese Seko of Zaire appeared to be making a serious attempt to mend relations between the two countries. An abortive Shaba invasion was repelled with the aid of French and Belgian troops in May, and on June 10 Angola announced that the rebels would be given asylum but would be disarmed. In July the two countries agreed to reopen the Benguela Railway (it was finally opened Nov. 5) and to establish diplomatic relations; in

ANTHROPOLOGY

Elders of the Haya tribe of Tanzania contemplate a replica of the smelting furnace that their ancestors used to make carbon steel 1500 years ago.

August Neto and Mobutu met and agreed to establish a commission to monitor security along their borders; in October they met again to reach a formal accord on air, sea, and rail traffic.

Efforts to improve Angolan relations with the United States were less successful. Although Angola appeared eager to diversify its sources of technical and financial support and the U.S. sought Angolan help in stabilizing the Mobutu government and achieving independence for Namibia, the U.S. continued to insist that full diplomatic relations were dependent upon a substantial Cuban military withdrawal from Angola. In December Neto dismissed his prime minister and other cabinet officials believed to be ideologically inflexible. He also apologized for past mistakes and, in talks with U.S. Sen. George McGovern (D, S.Dak.), sought U.S. aid and investment.

See STATISTICS OF THE WORLD.   J.T.S.

ANTHROPOLOGY. In 1978 anthropologists working in Africa and South America reported several important discoveries.

Prehistoric Footprints. In February, Mary B. Leakey, the renowned British discoverer (in 1975) of the oldest extant human fossils, announced yet another dramatic find: the oldest-known footprints of humanity's early ancestors.

Discovered in Laetolil, Tanzania, 48 km (30 mi.) from Olduvai Gorge, the site of her 1975 find, the tracks were embedded in what had been an old watering hole that had been buried under ash from a nearby volcano. Each of the five footprints was 15 cm (6 in.) long and 11.4 cm (4½ in.) wide. The tracks had been made 3,500,000 years before by a hominid, a humanlike creature about 1.2 m

(4 ft.) tall, with an extremely wide foot. From the arrangement of the imprints, it appeared that the creature, unlike its human descendants, moved slowly and took short steps, each step probably no longer than the length of its foot. The Leakey team also found tracks of various animals, including elephants, rhinoceroses, antelopes, and giraffes, as well as those of such extinct creatures as the saber-toothed cat. And among the other curiosities found at the prehistoric water hole were the tracks of a knuckle-walking primate, possibly an ancestor of the great apes.

Early African Technology. Two of the year's other discoveries drastically revised scientific opinion about early technology in Africa.

Anthropologists had always assumed that iron smelting in sub-Saharan Africa during the Early Iron Age (1200–500 B.C.) depended on the process that the Europeans used during that period, namely, the cold-blast bloomery process. This process required a great deal of fuel to smelt the ore and produced a low-carbon iron that was soft and weak. In 1978, however, two Brown University scientists, anthropologist Peter Schmidt and metallurgist Donald H. Avery, found evidence that some Iron Age Africans had used a smelting technology far more advanced than that of their European counterparts and that the iron produced by this technology was almost as hard and strong as today's high-grade steel.

While studying the Haya people of Tanzania, an agricultural tribe on the western shore of Lake Victoria, Schmidt and Avery discovered that the tribal elders knew how to produce a high-grade iron using a fuel-efficient furnace. Assuming that the Haya's blacksmithing expertise was part of an ancient tribal tradition, the scientists made excavations on the western shore of Lake Victoria and unearthed the remains of similar furnaces dating back at least 1500 years. So it became obvious that during the Early Iron Age tribes of sub-Saharan Africa had an iron-smelting technology superior to any used by their European contemporaries.

Still more of the cultural complexity of African prehistory was revealed when anthropologists discovered what they believed to be an astronomical monument, located near Lake Turkana in northwestern Kenya. Such monuments, like Great Britain's Stonehenge, had previously been found only in Europe and North America.

As described in 1978 by B. M. Lynch and L. H. Robbins of Michigan State University, the structure consisted of nineteen stone columns with an average height of 48 cm (19 in.), arranged in a manner that appeared to be nonrandom; these columns were found to date back to 300 B.C. Since tribesmen of that area use a calendar based on the rising of seven stars and constellations, Lynch and Robbins wondered if their discovery might not be an astronomical monument related to a similar calendar. They did indeed find that the rising points for the same seven stars and constellations, as they appeared in 300 B.C., could be located by sighting along the nineteen columns.

El Jobo Hunters. In June, 1978, the discovery of the oldest example of a big-game hunting culture in the New World was announced. Until then, it had been thought that the Clovis hunters, named for the area near present-day Clovis, N.Mex., where their tools were first located, were the New World's original hunters of giant mammals.

A team of Canadian, Argentine, and Venezuelan anthropologists working on the El Jobo complex at the Taima-taima dig in Venezuela had recently recovered not only the remains of a mastodon (an extinct mammal similar in size to the elephant) but also the stone tools used to kill it. Carbon-dating of a piece of wood found near the site was concluded in 1978; it established that the animal had been killed at least 13,000 years previously—1500 years before the oldest-known Clovis hunting expedition. The scientists concluded from this evidence that the El Jobo and Clovis technologies for making tools capable of killing big game had evolved separately and that both methodologies must have been based on simpler technologies in use in the New World even earlier.

An astronomical monument discovered in northwestern Kenya by Michigan State University anthropologists B. M. Lynch and L. H. Robbins. The megaliths, 19 in. tall, were aligned to coincide with certain stars and constellations about 2300 years ago to form a complex calendar.

The Piltdown Hoax Reexamined. Evidence was provided late in 1978 that the so-called Piltdown man—a "missing link" that had been unearthed in 1912 in the English town of Piltdown—had actually been created by a jealous geology professor, William Sollas, to discredit his highly esteemed colleague, Sir Arthur Smith Woodward. Just before his death in February, 1978, James Douglas, who had worked with both scientists, made a tape recording in which he stated that Sollas had buried a chemically aged human cranium and ape jawbone in the soon-to-be-famous gravel pit at Piltdown. Sollas's hated colleague Smith Woodward, keeper of geology at the British Museum, had then viewed the "fossils" and lent his considerable authority to their authenticity. The hoax was exposed in 1953, but until the playing of Douglas's tape, it had been thought that one Charles Dawson, an amateur fossil hunter who "discovered" the cranium and jawbone, was the sole perpetrator.

A Death. Margaret Mead, the renowned American cultural anthropologist, died during the year; *see* OBITUARIES.   G.B.K.

ARAB LEAGUE. For much of 1978, members of the Arab League split on a number of issues along traditional radical versus conservative lines. But in November the one issue that had united the Arab world in the past—Israel—once again pulled radicals and moderates together, as they voiced their opposition to Egypt's plan to sign a peace treaty with the Jewish state.

Arab-Israeli Issues. Egypt was not invited to the Nov. 1–5 summit conference in Baghdad. Leaders of the other twenty Arab League member nations and the Palestine Liberation Organization (PLO) secretly approved a ten-year, $3.5 billion plan to strengthen the states other than Egypt that border Israel. Their intention was to compensate for the presumed lack of Egyptian participation in any future military confrontation with Israel.

Conference sources said $1.85 billion of the fund would go to Syria, $1.2 billion to Jordan, $400,000,000 to the PLO, and $50,000,000 to forces working in the Israeli-occupied West Bank, Gaza Strip, and Golan Heights.

The war chest was made up of pledges of $1 billion from Saudi Arabia, $500,000,000 each from Libya and Iraq, and smaller amounts from the other Arab oil-exporting countries. The money was scheduled to be paid in installments due three times yearly. Given the disappointing performance of Arab states in meeting pledges made at previous summits, the question of how much would ultimately be raised remained open.

Nevertheless, Yasir Arafat, leader of the PLO, hailed the results of the Baghdad summit as a "magnificent victory," and it was clear that the strong measures voted against Egypt in fact represented a triumph for Arab radicals.

In addition to the military fund, the Arab leaders also agreed on a number of other punitive measures against Egypt that were to take effect automatically upon the signing of a peace treaty with Israel. These were to include suspension of Egyptian membership in the Arab League; transfer of Arab League headquarters out of Cairo; and inclusion of any Egyptian companies that deal

Palestinians demonstrate outside a Paris mosque on Aug. 5. Two PLO representatives had been killed at Arab League headquarters in the French capital two days earlier, in one of several terrorist acts committed by antagonistic factions within the PLO during 1978.

with Israel on the list of firms subject to the Arab League boycott.

Despite the stiff measures adopted at Baghdad, however, moderates clearly had some impact on the summit decisions. For one thing, the Arab rulers did not adopt a hard-line proposal that would have called on all Arab states to sever diplomatic relations with Cairo. There was also no indication that Saudi Arabia had agreed to suggestions that it cut off the $1 billion to $2 billion annual subsidy that it has provided to prop up Egypt's sagging economy.

Lebanon. At the conclusion of the summit, the Arab leaders decided that their foreign ministers would meet within three months to discuss the reconstruction of war-ravaged Lebanon. Previously, on Oct. 26, the Arab League had agreed to extend the mandate of its peacekeeping force in Lebanon for an additional six months. Syria had provided the bulk of the 30,000 members of the Arab peace force, which was set up in 1976 to supervise a truce in the Lebanese civil war. The funding of the peace force continued in 1978 to be largely provided by Saudi Arabia.

The rare unanimity of the Arab states attending the summit conference in Baghdad was all the more unusual in view of the Arab League's inability earlier in the year to pull feuding factions together to oppose the Israeli invasion of southern Lebanon. In March, the secretary-general of the Arab League, Mahmoud Riad, sent out invitations to an Arab summit conference on the Lebanon question, but the response was so unenthusiastic that the idea was quickly allowed to die.

Yemen. The splits between rival factions in the Arab League were also evident in July, when an emergency session of Arab League foreign ministers condemned the People's Democratic Republic of Yemen (South Yemen) for the murder of the president of the Yemen Arab Republic (North Yemen). While the 15 Arab states attending the July meeting imposed unprecedented sanctions on South Yemen's Marxist rulers—including a halt to all economic, technical, and cultural assistance to that country—5 Arab League members that more or less shared South Yemen's radical, pro-Soviet alignment boycotted the meeting. Libya, Syria, Iraq, Algeria, and the PLO did not attend. South Yemen opted not to appear in its own defense, and Djibouti stayed away, probably because it is situated across the Red Sea from South Yemen.

The Arab League's freeze on diplomatic and political relations with South Yemen was believed to be the strongest such action by any regional grouping against a member since the Organization of American States severed relations with Cuba in 1964.

Dissension among Palestinians. Before the November summit, the PLO was torn by terrorist actions resulting from enmity between hard-line pro-Iraqi factions and groups which seemed more willing to compromise on the Arab-Israeli dispute. In one such episode, two PLO officials were killed Aug. 3 at the Paris offices of the Arab League. Ten days later a nine-story building belonging to a Palestinian organization was demolished by a bomb in Beirut, Lebanon, killing perhaps 200 persons.

See also MIDDLE EAST; PALESTINE LIBERATION ORGANIZATION; and articles on individual countries mentioned.   M.R.B.

ARCHEOLOGY. The year 1978 was a bonanza year for archeologists in both the Old and New Worlds.

Aztecs in Mexico City. The dramatic discovery early in 1978 of a 500-year-old Aztec pyramid only one block away from the presidential palace in Mexico City sparked both elation and controversy. A magnificent 10-ton circular monolith bearing the image of Coyolxauhqui, the Aztec moon goddess, together with jade and turquoise ornaments, obsidian, and other ancient artifacts, was found just inches below a construction site on one of the city's main streets. The entire base of what is believed to have been the greatest of all Aztec pyramids was also discovered, bringing a halt to construction and endangering choice real estate in the immediate vicinity.

Although the ongoing excavations fascinated tourists and sidewalk superintendents, residents of the neighborhood were less than pleased with the demolition of their homes, and historians bemoaned the possible loss of valuable Spanish colonial buildings. Once local resistance is overcome, however, and all the archeological treasures have been excavated, Mexican cultural authorities plan to convert the area into an open-air museum. (*See* illustration at MEXICO.)

Eyes on Easter Island. Because of discoveries made in early June, 1978, it is now believed that the famous Easter Island megaliths—monumental sculptures of human heads with abstract bodies—were originally inlaid with naturalistic eyes made of white coral with red volcanic lava irises. Working at Anakena Beach on the island's northern coast, Sergio Rapu, an island native and the director of the island's archeological museum, found one complete and four fragmentary eyes. (The actual site of the discovery was a buried statue platform known as Ahu Nau Nau.) The single intact eye fit perfectly into the empty eye socket of one of the stone sculptures. And the iris of the eye, which measures about 13 cm (5 in.) in diameter, was carved from the same red lava that had been

An excavator holds what is believed to be an eye from one of the famous beetle-browed statues of Easter Island. Fashioned from red volcanic lava and white coral, the "eye" fits perfectly into the sculptured socket of one of the massive religious monuments.

used for the topknots or hats of the great stone monuments. It has been suggested that the eyes were knocked out during a revolt against the cult that constructed the hundreds of sculptures that adorn the island, probably in the 16th century.

This vaulted tunnel leads to a stadium used for ancient Panhellenic games. Built by Greek architects 2300 years ago, it predates any vault built by the Romans, who, until this discovery, were credited as the inventors of the arch.

Pre-Roman Arch. In the history of architecture the Romans have always been given credit for inventing the arch and its cousin the vault, a structure of masonry that employs the arch in the construction of ceilings and roofs. In September, however, American archeologists working in Neméa, Greece, unearthed a vaulted tunnel that clearly indicates the Greeks used the arch long before the Romans.

Stephen G. Miller and his colleagues at the Uni-

versity of California at Berkeley reported that graffiti found on the wall of the tunnel included the name of Telestas, a Greek boxer known to have competed at Olympia during the 4th century B.C. Pottery shards found at the site also date back to the 4th century. Thus it became evident that the Greeks, and not the Romans, were the first constructors of arches in the Western world.

Mycenaean Palace Unearthed. In November scientists digging into a hill on the Greek island of Páros unearthed the remains of a provincial Mycenaean palace dating back to the 12th century B.C. The site, at Koukounaries, contained buildings that formed a complex covering a rocky plateau 46 m (50 yd.) wide by 27 m (30 yd.) deep. Fortified by a massive stone wall that once stood 4.5 m (15 ft.) high, the palace was destroyed by a fire during a siege that took place in the Bronze Age, more than 3000 years ago. Ancestors of the classical Greeks, the Mycenaeans were a warlike people who usurped the power and wealth of Minoan Crete during the second millennium B.C. and were constantly engaged in defending their preeminence at sea. The director of the dig, Demetrius Schilardi of the University of Ottawa, in Canada, expressed hope that further exploration of the site might shed more light on a turbulent and little-known period of Mycenaean history.

Solstice Marker in Chaco Canyon. In June a team of artists and scientists studying rock art created a thousand years ago by North American Pueblo Indians announced that some of that art may have been part of a sophisticated system of astronomy.

Anna Sofaer, a Washington, D.C., artist with a deep interest in Indian petroglyphs, or rock art,

joined her scientist colleagues, Volker Zinser and Rolf Sinclair, in making a remarkable discovery at Fajada Butte, a promontory in Chaco Canyon in northeastern New Mexico. They noted that three rocks situated in front of the sandstone wall of the butte bent sunlight in such a way that at noon of the summer solstice (June 22) a dagger of light passed through the exact center of a spiral carved into the wall. The scientists speculated that the Indians who had inhabited the canyon from 950 to 1150 A.D. had built this accurate sundial or clock to help them predict the occurrence of the summer solstice; June 22 was an important day not only in their planting schedule but also in their religious calendar. Archeologists learned from this discovery that these New World Indians had a more complicated system of astronomical observation than had previously been assumed. (*See* illustration at ASTRONOMY.)

Deaths. Two eminent British archeologists, Dame Kathleen Mary Kenyon and Sir Max Mallowan, died in August; *see* OBITUARIES.   B.R.

ARCHITECTURE AND CITY PLANNING. Architecture in 1978 was in the full flood of the postmodernist reaction against the stark, functional glass boxes of the international style. Rejecting the mechanistic, purist principles that have dominated architectural thinking since World War II, the versatile Philip Johnson and such younger iconoclastic architects as Robert Venturi of Philadelphia, Charles Moore of the University of Cali-

The East Building of the National Gallery of Art in Washington, D.C., was designed by I. M. Pei in the form of two triangles to fit a trapezoidal site. The larger one has three towers surrounding a skylit court.

fornia at Los Angeles, Cesar Pelli of the Yale School of Architecture, and Hugh Hardy of Hardy, Holzman, Pfeiffer Associates called for a more eclectic approach. They valued individual imagination, ornament, color, historical allusions, and popular appeal.

New Building. A monument in the classic tradition of the international style is the East Building of the National Gallery of Art in Washington, D.C., designed by I. M. Pei & Partners and completed in 1978. Disciplined and rational in concept and meticulous in craftsmanship, its design also shows ingenuity and sensitivity in its adjustment to the trapezoidal site, the adjacent neoclassical main building, and the needs of a museum. It consists of two unequal triangles of reinforced concrete sheathed with pink marble. The large one has a tower at each point, linked by a skylit court, and galleries of varied shapes and sizes to accommodate different works of art. The small one was planned to contain a library and space for study.

The Illinois Regional Library for the Blind and Physically Handicapped was designed by Stanley Tigerman. The Chicago building has a long window at wheelchair eye level and an undulating service counter to guide the blind.

O House in Thy Flight!

The company spokesman said it had never happened before, but that did not give the client much comfort. Charles Topping had contracted to have his five-room house moved five miles through the streets of Attleboro, Mass., in May. When he arrived at his new homesite, expecting to walk right in and make himself at home, he was astonished to find that the back door faced the street and the front door opened onto the back yard. The house was on the right lot, but the movers had set it down backward.

A fine 1978 example of the postmodernist movement is the Illinois Regional Library for the Blind and Physically Handicapped in Chicago, designed by Stanley Tigerman. Shaped like an irregular triangle on its triangular plot, it has one brilliant yellow and red wall, which the partially sighted can see. A long, undulating window on the long wall allows people in wheelchairs to look out. Curved and dipped Formica book counters help the blind to find their way, and the floor is of nonskid Pirelli rubber tile.

Also innovative was the Boettcher Concert Hall in Denver, which was inaugurated during the year—the first indoor surround concert hall in the United States. Hardy, Holzman, Pfeiffer Associates designed it so that 592 of the 2700 seats are in back of the stage with the rest on the sides and in front. Acoustician Christopher Jaffe's plans included a canopy of 106 large disks and a moat under the stage, which make up for the lack of a rear wall to throw the sound forward.

An illustration of the new interest in historical motifs is Charles Moore's 1978 work, the Piazza d'Italia. This huge tiered plaza in downtown New Orleans includes a fountain that rises from one end of a long stone map of Italy and cascades past fragments of walls and colonnades designed in the ancient Roman style.

In other recent structures, glass panes no longer form neat, dull boxes but surprising, irregular geometric shapes. Johnson-Burgee Architects arranged them into two tall trapezoids for Pennzoil Place in Houston. Cesar Pelli massed blue-tinted panes in a heavy, looming structure two football fields long for his Pacific Design Center in Los Angeles. Pelli also created a plum-painted, glass-filled steel frame, triangular in silhouette, to protect landscaped trees and plants in his Winter

Garden in Niagara Falls, N.Y. Newer houses also show great variety, ranging from the smooth white and glass surfaces of a Long Island (N.Y.) house by Charles Gwathmey, pointing back to Le Corbusier, to the corrugated metal and raw plywood of the "minimal" California dwellings designed by Frank Gehrey.

Buildings in Progress or Proposed. When they are completed, three buildings by Johnson-Burgee will be further evidence of the postmodernist trend. The Garden Grove (Calif.) Community Church, being built for the popular evangelist Robert Schuller, is a multi-faceted, steel-pipe framework sheathed in glass. Their Dade County Cultural Center in Miami, Fla., is to be a series of white stucco and coral-rock buildings with red tiled roofs in the local Spanish style. And for the American Telephone and Telegraph Co. (AT&T) headquarters in New York City the architects have proposed a pink granite and glass tower with a delicate Renaissance-style facade at the bottom and a broken pediment, such as is usually found on neoclassical doorways or furniture, at the top. The Johnson-Burgee plans also include a glass-covered interior plaza.

More glass—over a park and an arcade—is to be a feature of the New York City headquarters of the International Business Machines Corp., which will be built on the next block from the new AT&T building. The structure has been designed by Edward Larrabee Barnes as a towering five-sided prism of gray-green granite and glass that will not block the sun from the park. Also in the new mode is Three First National in Chicago, a fifty-seven-story skyscraper covered with bay windows, being built by Skidmore, Owings and Merrill. Unusually innovative was Kevin Roche's concept for Union Carbide Corp. headquarters in Danbury, Conn. It consists of a central-core parking lot surrounded by offices arranged in lacelike projections so that each enjoys a rural view.

Urban Renewal. The first elements of Dallas' 50-acre downtown development, called Reunion, were completed in 1978. The Dallas Hyatt Regency Hotel, by Victor Chu of Welton Becket Associates, is thirty stories of mirrored glass forming twelve blocks of varying heights, grouped, as is usual with Hyatt hotels, around an interior court. Rounded, glass-walled elevators whisk guests up and down, and a multistoried window affords a

Boettcher Concert Hall in the Denver Center for the Performing Arts, designed by Hardy, Holzman, Pfeiffer Associates. It is the first indoor concert hall in the U.S. in which the audience surrounds the performers.

ARCHITECTURE AND CITY PLANNING

dramatic view of the nearby freeway. Near the hotel rises Reunion Tower, a fifty-story structure composed of four concrete poles topped by a geodesically framed sphere that contains a revolving restaurant. The tower, spectacularly lit at night, is a striking addition to the Dallas skyline.

Other cities continued existing renewal schemes or planned new ones during the year. Toronto, for example, was well into its 14.5-acre development, Eaton Centre, designed by Bregman & Hamann and Zeidler Partnership. Already completed were the curvilinear mirrored office tower, Number One Dundas, and the nine-story Eaton's Department Store. Partly finished was a domed gallery running between four buildings, with retail shops on the first three levels and offices and parking space overhead. The complex also contains Holy Trinity Church and the old City Hall.

Chicago's urban renewal continued with two dozen skyscrapers planned or under construction. Detroit was adding two buildings to its highly successful Renaissance Center, initiated by Henry Ford 2nd, and was planning to develop New Center as a residential and office complex around the

The modern, glass-domed shopping gallery of Eaton Centre in Toronto. Reminiscent of the 19th-century Galleria in Milan, it accommodates shops on three stories, with space for offices and parking above them.

General Motors Corp. headquarters. Boston, home of the highly praised Quincy Market renovation, also planned to develop its Copley Square. Washington, D.C., had begun work on a new complex of shops, offices, and hotels, including a restored Willard Hotel, to replace a squalid section of Pennsylvania Avenue. Baltimore's plans for downtown renewal included offices and a park, already completed, and a convention center, subway, and waterfront shopping plaza. On its outskirts the city was building a middle-class residential neighborhood designed by the Israeli-Canadian architect Moshe Safdie. In both Washington and Baltimore, middle-income couples were buying once good, now decayed row houses in poor neighborhoods and restoring them. Sociologists were concerned, however, since the consequent rise in land values threatened to displace poorer residents.

A successful example of urban restoration was the new City Hall of Rochester, N.Y. Architects Handler and Grasso managed a skillful preservation of the towered brownstone structure, which dates from 1891, with its interior colonnaded court in the heavy Richardsonian Romanesque style; they installed modern elevators and mechanical systems, and a modest three-story addition—all for less money than a new building would have cost.

A law to preserve 400 historical buildings in New York City, including Grand Central Terminal, was declared constitutional by the U.S. Supreme Court in the spring. The decision equated landmark preservation with zoning, which meant that the city did not have to compensate the owner, as would have been necessary if the land had been taken over. The decision was deplored by real estate interests eager to build new, more profitable structures, but was believed to be of aid to preservationists everywhere.

On the other hand, New York City's Westway project, a plan to build a six-lane superhighway and park to replace the defunct West Side Highway, was still in dispute. It had become a political hot potato: The mayor and governor approved it as bringing more jobs and business to the city; the Board of Estimate and most environmentalists were opposed on the grounds that greatly increased traffic would pollute the air, a smaller highway would suffice for traffic and do less damage to the area, and a similar sum spent rebuilding the old highway and revamping mass transit would ultimately provide more jobs.

See also TRANSPORTATION: *Mass Transit.*

People. Philip Johnson received the American Institute of Architects' Gold Medal for 1978. The internationally known American architect Edward

Interior of the City Hall of Rochester, N.Y., built in 1891 in heavy Romanesque style. Renovation, completed in 1978, restored a long-unused colonnaded court, refinished the wood paneling, and added a new wing in the rear.

Durell Stone died during the year; *see* OBITUARIES. Among the other notable architects who died were Lorimer Rich, designer of the Tomb of the Unknown Soldier in the National Cemetery in Arlington, Va. (June 2 at 86); and Lloyd Wright, eldest son of Frank Lloyd Wright and a respected designer of houses in California (May 31 at 88).   S.C.W.

ARGENTINA. Long-standing rivalry in their claims to three barren but strategic islands at the tip of South America brought Argentina and Chile threateningly close to war in 1978.

Foreign Affairs. In 1977 a British-sponsored arbitration panel had awarded the disputed islands of Picton, Lennox, and Nueva in the Beagle Channel off the extreme southern tip of the South American continent to Chile. Argentina objected because Chile consequently was able to claim a 200-mi. offshore zone in the South Atlantic, believed to have valuable gas and oil deposits. The presidents of Argentina and Chile conferred in January, 1978; successive talks by commissioners ended unsuccessfully on Nov. 2. Meanwhile both countries mobilized troops. Argentina staged naval maneuvers in the channel and held an air raid drill in Buenos Aires. Finally, on Nov. 8, Argentina accepted Chile's proposal to seek a mediator in the dispute. After further wrangling, both countries accepted Pope John Paul II's offer to mediate. Cardinal Antonio Samorè, appointed to act for the pope on Dec. 23, spent the rest of the year shuttling between the two countries seeking a solution.

Domestic Affairs. President Jorge Rafael Videla, head of the military government that had ruled Argentina since the 1976 overthrow of President Isabel Martínez de Perón, resigned as commander in chief of the army on Aug. 1. The ruling three-

Ecstatic soccer fans raise team captain Daniel Passarella to their shoulders as Argentina celebrates its first World Cup championship. Star goalie Ubaldo Fillol (aloft, right) helped gain the final victory over the Netherlands in tumultuous River Plate stadium, Buenos Aires, on June 25.

man military junta then selected Videla to continue as president until 1981. In November Videla reorganized his cabinet; it included only one member who was a military officer on active duty. Although the president had mentioned the possibility of future political dialogue in Argentina, political parties were still banned at the end of the year. Censorship had been reduced, but strikes by labor unions remained outlawed.

As a result of strict government measures, the leftist terrorist groups that had bedeviled Argentina for a decade had largely been eliminated by the end of 1978. The ranks of the Marxist People's Revolutionary Army were virtually decimated, and the Montoneros were down to an estimated 200 active guerrillas. In response to pressure from the United States, the government released several hundred political prisoners in April, and in October agreed to allow the Organization of American States to investigate alleged Argentine violations of human rights. Nevertheless, by U.S. estimate there were still 12,000 to 17,000 political prisoners in Argentina; and kidnappings, arrests, and rightist terrorism continued.

The Economy. The highest inflation rate in the world, estimated at 150 percent for 1978, continued to stalk Argentina. The cost of living rose 178 percent between Jan. 1 and Nov. 1, 1978. But the national treasury, bankrupt in 1976, reportedly

Possession of three tiny islands in the Beagle Channel off Tierra del Fuego—and maritime rights in the surrounding waters—are the subjects of long-standing dispute between Argentina and Chile that almost erupted into war in 1978.

had $6 billion in reserves, and beef and grain production were at all-time highs. The government announced plans to construct an experimental plutonium reprocessing plant, to be completed in the early 1980's.

See STATISTICS OF THE WORLD.   J.N.G.

ARIZONA. See STATISTICS OF THE WORLD.

ARKANSAS. See STATISTICS OF THE WORLD.

ART. New museum additions and acquisitions, striking exhibitions, and high market prices dominated the news of the art world in 1978.

Museums. In June the National Gallery of Art in Washington, D.C., opened its new East Building, designed by I. M. Pei in the shape of two unequal triangles to occupy a difficult trapezoid of land on the Mall. Modern in feeling yet in keeping with the neoclassical style of the National Gallery, the finely crafted building received wide critical praise. Most of the more than $94,000,000 cost was met by Paul Mellon, the late Ailsa Mellon Bruce, and the Andrew W. Mellon Foundation, all instrumental in the development of the National Gallery since its founding in 1937. See ARCHITECTURE AND CITY PLANNING.

In late September the Metropolitan Museum of Art in New York City unveiled its newest treasure, the 1st-century B.C. Nubian Temple of Dendur, enshrined in a new, glass-walled addition to the neoclassical museum building. The small, golden sandstone temple and its pylon gateway, both covered with well-preserved reliefs, were constructed by the Roman Emperor Augustus to commemorate a Nubian chieftain's two drowned sons. The temple was awarded to the United States in 1965 by the Egyptian government in recognition of a $16,000,000 U.S. contribution to save architecture in danger of being flooded by the Aswân High Dam. The gray granite wing with one sloping, glass-sheathed side and a broad reflecting pool was designed by Kevin Roche, John Dinkeloo and Associates to protect the temple and suggest its original setting on the Nile River.

Exhibitions. Several exhibitions were planned to show off the flexible display space in the National Gallery's East Building. "Aspects of Twentieth-Century Art" dealt with Picasso and cubism, Matisse cutouts and "Jazz," and other European painting and sculpture. "American Art at Mid-Century: The Subjects of the Artist" offered an in-depth look at thematic series by seven abstract expressionists, including Willem de Kooning's "Women," Mark Rothko's late color panels, and David Smith's welded-metal "Voltri."

The Temple of Dendur, built in Nubia approximately 2000 years ago and reconstructed at the Metropolitan Museum in New York City. In 1978, in a pavilion that suggested the original Nile River site, the temple was put on display.

A portrait of a man and his wife in the traveling exhibit "Pompeii, A.D. 79," seen at the Boston Museum of Fine Arts in the spring. The fresco shows late Egyptian stylistic influence as well as Roman fashions of the 1st century A.D.

From earlier eras were architectural drawings by the 18th-century Italian Giovanni Battista Piranesi and the impressive "Splendor of Dresden." The Dresden exhibit, jointly organized by the National Gallery, the Metropolitan, and the Fine Arts Museums of San Francisco, offered viewers a rare look at more than 700 objects from eight state collections in Dresden, East Germany. Collected by the rulers of Saxony, the works included armor, jeweled and enameled objects, Meissen and oriental porcelain, old-master paintings and engravings, and examples of 20th-century German expressionism.

The Boston Museum of Fine Arts presented "Pompeii, A.D. 79," a picture of life in a rich Roman resort town destroyed by a volcanic eruption. Crowds admired mosaics, sculpture, small frescoes, household objects, and a photographically recreated Hall of the Mysteries. The exhibit, which came from London and Copenhagen and was scheduled to tour Chicago, Dallas, and New York City, rivaled in popularity the 1977 "Treasures of Tutankhamun" exhibition, which wound up 1978 at the Metropolitan.

The European origins of American abstract expressionism were explored in an exhibition at the Whitney Museum in New York City in October. Two important abstract expressionists were given retrospectives—Jackson Pollock, by the Yale University Art Gallery in New Haven, Conn., and Mark Rothko, by the Guggenheim Museum in New York City. A forerunner of expressionism, the late 19th-century Norwegian Edvard Munch, was the subject of a large retrospective at the National Gallery.

Discoveries, Damage, and Theft. The most important art discovery of the year was made in Mexico City when construction workers unearthed a massive circular monolith with reliefs of the Aztec moon goddess and, later, the base of the greatest of all Aztec pyramids. (*See* ARCHEOLOGY; *see also* illustration at MEXICO.) Another remarkable find was a carved ivory plaque brought to Sotheby Parke Bernet in London, which turned out to be an early 9th-century product of one of Charlemagne's court workshops. Considered one of the finest of forty similar surviving Carolingian ivories, it was valued at $250,000 to $500,000.

A discovery of a different order, based on a technical study by British art experts Leslie Parris and Ian Fleming-Williams, was that many oil sketches and drawings attributed to the great 19th-century English landscapist John Constable

"Near Stoke-by-Nayland," a painting in the Tate Gallery in London, is one of several works formerly attributed to 19th-century English landscapist John Constable. In 1978, as the result of technical studies by British art experts, they were credited to his son Lionel.

are really the work of his son Lionel. Since all of Constable's five children painted, the attribution of other minor works could also be challenged.

Five important art collections suffered damages during the year. A bomb exploded in the palace

"The Jolly Flatboatmen, No. 2" by frontier painter George Caleb Bingham. The oil, dating from around 1848, was sold at Sotheby Parke Bernet in Los Angeles to the Hirschl & Adler Galleries in New York City, for $980,000, an auction record for American art.

George Segal's sculpture of Abraham and Isaac, "In Memory of May 4, 1970, Kent State," was rejected by the university as too violent to be an appropriate commemoration of the shooting of four students. It was later accepted by Princeton University.

of Versailles in late June, damaging several rooms filled with Napoleonic-era art works (*see* illustration at FRANCE). In December, two Breton nationists were sentenced to fifteen years in prison for the bombing. In Amsterdam in April a Dutch artist released from a mental hospital slashed a Van Gogh self-portrait, valued at $1,500,000, in the Vincent van Gogh State Museum. Another Van Gogh, in the Amsterdam Municipal Museum, had been attacked earlier in the month. Also in April, a vandal slashed to bits a 17th-century French canvas by Nicolas Poussin in London's National Gallery. In Rio de Janeiro in July an accidental fire in the Museum of Modern Art destroyed nearly 1000 art works. They included paintings by Picasso, Miró, and Klee and almost the entire oeuvre of the late Uruguayan painter Joaquin Torres García.

There were also several serious thefts. In April Rubens's "Three Graces" and nine other works vanished from the Palazzo Pitti in Florence. And in late December, thieves stole a Rembrandt portrait and three other 17th-century Dutch works from the M. H. De Young Memorial Museum in San Francisco, while the Art Institute of Chicago lost three valuable Cézannes.

The Art Market. The year 1978 was a monumental one for art auctions. The June sale of Baron Robert von Hirsch's estate through Sotheby Parke Bernet in London brought $34,100,000, far outstripping the $10,300,000 fetched by the 1977 Mentmore auction of Rothschild possessions, billed then as "the sale of the century." For seventy years Von Hirsch, a leather manufacturer who left Germany for Basel, Switzerland, before World War II, had amassed outstanding examples of master paintings and drawings, sculpture, ivories, porcelains, enamels, glass, and furniture dating from the 12th to the 20th century. Since many of the treasures were of German origin, government-subsidized West German museums accounted for almost two thirds of the total sum bid. A rare watercolor by Albrecht Dürer brought $1,177,600, and two 12th-century German enamel and copper gilt ornaments went for more than $2,000,000 each, making them the costliest art objects, other than paintings, ever sold. American museums bought a 15th-century Sienese altarpiece (the Norton Simon Foundation in Pasadena, Calif.) and a Rembrandt drawing (the Cleveland Museum of Art).

The art market also flourished in North America. The London firm of Christie, Manson & Woods International, which opened a house in New York City, sold a Gutenberg Bible for $2,000,-000, the highest auction price ever paid in New York, except for a Rembrandt painting sold in 1961. A Sotheby Parke Bernet auction in Los Angeles set a new high for an American work when 19th-century genre painter George Caleb Bingham's "The Jolly Flatboatmen, No. 2" went for $980,000. A painting by the 19th-century realist Thomas Eakins, sold for $265,000, set a world record for an American portrait.

Deaths. In 1978 the art world mourned the deaths of painters Giorgio de Chirico, Duncan Grant, and Richard Lindner; illustrator Norman Rockwell; critic Harold Rosenberg; and collector John D. Rockefeller 3rd; *see* OBITUARIES. Among other artists who died in 1978 were the Italian-born Harry Bertoia, sculptor and designer of furniture in direct metal (Nov. 6 at 63); the Greek-born cubist George Constant (Aug. 13 at 86); the poetic representational painter Edwin W. Dickinson (Dec. 2 at 87); and the expressivist colorist Abraham Rattner (Feb. 14 at 82). Other deceased art world figures were French art dealer Germain Seligman (March 27 at 85) and art historian John Shapley (Sept. 8 at 88). H.T.H.

ASTRONOMY. In 1978 astronomers peered farther into space with more sensitive telescopes and solved more of the mysteries of the cosmos. The solar system itself disclosed some well-kept secrets during the year. Scientists found a moon in orbit around Pluto; they also found three asteroids near the earth, bringing to twenty-six the number of asteroids known to have orbits within that of the earth; *see* EARTH AND PLANETARY SCIENCES.

Black Holes. Although the burned-out collapsed stars known as black holes are so dense that even light cannot escape their extreme gravity, they can be located by their gravitational effects on neighboring stars. Before 1978, astrophysicists had found only one black hole, Cygnus X-I; their research in 1978, however, brought the total number to four.

In April astronomers working at Hale Observatories on Mt. Palomar in California and at the Kitt Peak National Observatory in Arizona reported their joint discovery of an incredibly large black

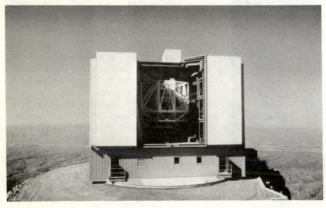

With six reflecting telescopes to gather light from distant celestial objects and direct it toward a common focus, the steel-framed Multiple-Mirror Telescope is here revealed in all its complexity. Situated atop Arizona's Mt. Hopkins, the MMT was scheduled to be fully operative early in 1979.

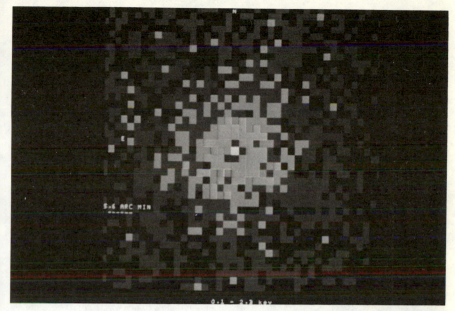

S-6 ARC MIN

0.1 - 2.0 keV

An X-ray intensity representation of a halo around M-87, an elliptical galaxy in the constellation Virgo. This image—covering an area about 1,000,000 light-years in diameter—was recorded from a rocket carrying an X-ray telescope that had been designed by Paul Gorenstein of the Harvard-Smithsonian Center for Astrophysics.

hole in the constellation Virgo. Using their 4 m (157 in.) telescope, the Kitt Peak observers had found that stars on the periphery of an elliptical galaxy in Virgo were revolving at such high speeds that only an extremely massive object at the core of the galaxy could exert the gravity needed to accelerate them thus. Not having the kind of telescope needed to observe the core, the Kitt Peak astronomers asked their Mt. Palomar colleagues to make further observations. When the Mt. Palomar 5 m (200 in.) telescope focused on the center of the galaxy, known as Messier 87 (M-87), they found a bright point of light; but it came from an object too small to account for the gravitational effects. Scientists at both observatories had to conclude that a black body 5 billion times more massive than the sun must exist at the core of M-87.

April also brought the discovery of another black hole, but one with only 100,000,000 times more material than the sun. Radio astronomers from the California Institute of Technology claimed they had located the hole at the core of a galaxy, NGC 6251. The astronomers reached this conclusion after their telescopes picked up the image of what appeared to be a "cosmic blowtorch" 750,000 light-years long at the center of NGC 6251. (A light-year is the distance that light travels in a year at the rate of 186,000 mi. per second.) They theorized that this "blowtorch" was a stream of gas being drawn from stars at one side of the galaxy toward the center, and their calculations indicated that only a massive black hole could provide the gravitational force needed to produce the stream.

While the two discoveries of black holes in April were made from ground observations, the next one was made by a satellite telescope. In June, Copernicus, an X-ray satellite launched in 1972 by the National Aeronautics and Space Administration (NASA), gave scientists a glimpse of what may be a black hole in the constellation Scorpio. Employing a telescope sensitive to X rays (radiation that cannot fully penetrate the earth's atmosphere), the high-orbiting observatory had detected such rays being drawn away from a star in the constellation. Since there were no other celestial objects nearby, the observing astronomers concluded that the radiation was being deflected by a previously unknown black hole, one with a mass of only a few suns.

Finally, evidence mounted during the year to support the theory that these massive stellar corpses are the binding force of many galaxies.

About 1000 years ago Pueblo Indians carved a spiral into the walls of Chaco Canyon, N.Mex. Each year at noon on the summer solstice (June 22), sunlight passes through the space between three slabs of rock and falls on the exact center of the spiral. The slabs and the spiral apparently constitute a crude but accurate astronomical clock.

Telescopes and Observatories. The second of three unmanned High Energy Astronomy Observatories (designated HEAO 2) was launched by NASA on Nov. 13. Like its predecessor, HEAO 1 (launched in 1977), HEAO 2 will use X-ray sensitive telescopes capable of observing pulsars, quasars, and black holes. Unlike HEAO 1, however, the new observatory carries instruments that focus in on, rather than scan, these mysterious cosmic bodies.

The Multiple-Mirror Telescope (MMT) atop Mt. Hopkins in Arizona was given its final test in November. Five years in building, it consists of six telescopes arrayed in a circle and directing their light toward a common focus, producing a single image. Its most unusual feature is an internal laser tracking system that enables all six telescopes to track the same object across the sky with an incredible degree of accuracy. Astronomers hoped to see it in full operation soon.   D.D.

AUSTRALIA. Prime Minister Malcolm Fraser of Australia rode into 1978 on a tide of success. His

Liberal-National Party coalition had won national elections in December, 1977, by a hefty margin. The nation's inflation rate had dropped from 14 percent in 1976 to 7.9 percent for fiscal year 1978, due to Fraser's conservative economic policies. Nonetheless, Fraser was faced with a legion of problems, both political and economic.

Politics and the Economy. Australia's 1975 constitutional crisis still festered as a political issue. The Labour Party resented former Governor-General Sir John Kerr's actions in dismissing Labourite Prime Minister Gough Whitlam, calling Fraser to the premiership, and scheduling parliamentary elections that Fraser then won. In February, 1978, when Fraser appointed the controversial Kerr to the post of Australian representative to the United Nations Educational, Scientific, and Cultural Organization, Labour mounted a noisy attack on the decision. Kerr resigned his appointment in March.

Unemployment was at a postwar record high of 445,300, or 7.2 percent, in January. Even so, when the government presented its program to parliament in February, it emphasized its intention of further cutting inflation, regardless of the cost in unemployed workers. One of Fraser's motives in maintaining this stance was to attract new foreign investment. For the same reason, Treasurer John Howard announced in June that the administration planned a significant relaxation of rules governing local operations of foreign companies.

In August the government presented its 1978–79 budget proposals. Again it chose deflation over higher employment. To reduce inflation to 5 percent by mid-1979, Howard proposed to prune public medical services, to increase income taxes by 1.5 percent, and to impose steep tax increases on gasoline, tobacco, and alcoholic beverages. The budget was sharply attacked by Labour

Principal Export: "Cocosnuts"

In the Indian Ocean about 1600 mi. west of Australia lie the Cocos Islands, twenty-four tiny dots on the map that were settled in the 1820's by Malay laborers hired by a Scottish sea captain named Clunies-Ross. In 1886, Queen Victoria gave the Clunies-Ross family perpetual sovereignty over the islands; they had ruled as feudal lords ever since—until 1978, when John Clunies-Ross (also known as Ross V of the Cocos) sold his domain for $7,000,000. At the same time the purchaser, the Australian government, acquired 625 new citizens, 26.04 per island.

Uranium mining was a major issue in Australia in 1978. Here, Peter Garton of the Northern Territory environmental council studies the soil at Rum Jungle, where a uranium mine ceased operations in 1964, to determine what long-range effects such mining can have if precautions are not taken.

spokesmen in parliament, and at one of Fraser's public appearances later in the year, some Australian citizens hurled eggs and paint bombs at the prime minister.

As the year advanced, Fraser's popularity within his own party began to fade. Early in 1978 a key Fraser adviser, Sen. Reginald Withers, was accused of improper actions in influencing the redrawing of election district boundaries in Queensland. In early August Fraser removed Withers from his cabinet post as minister for administrative services. The prime minister's decision did not sit well with his party's members of parliament, and his control over the party appeared to suffer from his handling of the case.

In the state election held Oct. 1 in New South Wales, the Labour Party won 60 percent of the vote and gained control of the upper house for the first time in twenty years. This result was thought to be an indication of declining national support for the Fraser government, since federal economic policies had been a major issue in the election.

Foreign Affairs. Fraser pursued an active foreign policy. In February he played host in Sydney to the first Asian and Pacific regional conference of Commonwealth heads of government. It was Fraser's hope that Australia might assume a position of leadership among the Commonwealth nations of the region. Little concrete action resulted from the meeting, but observers credited Fraser with initiating a promising new regional lobby.

Australian leaders continued to complain about international trade restrictions during the year. In meetings with ministers of European Economic Community nations, Fraser government spokesmen pressed for more permissive import policies toward Australian cereals, dairy products, and beef. Requests for freer trade were also made during conferences between Australian and Japanese government representatives. In October, however, the government imposed controls on mineral exports, claiming that buyers were forcing settlements on sellers in a depressed international market for iron ore and coal.

Unlike Whitlam's Labour government, Fraser's Liberal-National coalition endeavored to maintain warm ties with the United States. In May the prime minister played host to U.S. Vice-President Walter F. Mondale. The two officials agreed on a variety of issues, among them the danger of Soviet activism in Africa and the need for an American presence in Asia. According to reports, however, a chill fell over the bilateral talks when Fraser began

New South Wales official John M. Wallace points out the sights of Sydney harbor to Chip and Caron Carter, including the opera house in the background. U.S. President Jimmy Carter's son and daughter-in-law made an official Australian-American week visit in May, several months before the young couple separated.

to criticize U.S. economic plans and to recommend deflation as a policy for the administration of President Jimmy Carter. "We do not intend to solve the problems of inflation by massive unemployment," Mondale is said to have told Fraser.

Australia reached a notable accord with the Finnish government in July. It agreed to sell uranium to Finland in return for Finnish assurance that the material would be used only for peaceful purposes. The treaty was expected to serve as a prototype for agreements with other uranium buyers.

A Death. Sir Robert Menzies, 83, died in Melbourne on May 14. Founder of the Liberal Party,

he served as Australia's prime minister from 1939 to 1941 and from 1949 until his retirement in 1966; see OBITUARIES.

See STATISTICS OF THE WORLD.   F.W.

AUSTRIA. The government of Socialist Chancellor Bruno Kreisky was under severe political strain in Austria during 1978, as the major political parties marshaled their forces for the 1979 general election. In July an illustrated monthly of the conservative People's Party accused Finance Minister Hannes Androsch, Kreisky's heir apparent, of indirectly profiting from his political office by holding the controlling share in a prospering tax consultancy business. Critics charged that it was improper for him to combine high public office with business activity in a related field.

Though Androsch denied any wrongdoing, a chill developed between him and Kreisky. After months of discussion the two finally reached a compromise in December. It was agreed that Androsch might retain his position as Kreisky's deputy if he agreed to transfer his business to control by a trustee.

In addition to the Androsch controversy, the Socialist government became embroiled in a running battle over nuclear power policy. The country's first nuclear power plant had been scheduled to go into operation at Zwentendorf in 1976. Environmentalists mounted an increasingly noisy campaign against the installation and managed to delay its inauguration. After attempting unsuccessfully to reach an all-party compromise, Kreisky agreed to hold a nonbinding referendum on whether or not to utilize Zwentendorf. The People's Party urged a no vote, the Socialists asked for a yes, and Kreisky indicated he might resign if the referendum went against government wishes. When the vote was held on Nov. 5, the antinuclear forces won by a hair (half a percentage point). Kreisky ultimately decided not to step down, but the vote was a severe blow to his government. In addition, experts predicted, Austria would have to spend tens of millions of dollars more each year for imported energy.

See STATISTICS OF THE WORLD.   F.W.

B

BAHAMAS. See STATISTICS OF THE WORLD.
BAHRAIN. See STATISTICS OF THE WORLD.
BANGLADESH. With its economic recovery progressing and law and order fairly well restored,

Bangladesh was able to hold national elections during 1978.
Political Affairs. During the early months of 1978, political activity remained closely restricted under

During 1978 some 150,000 Muslims fled persecution in Buddhist Burma by crossing the border into Bangladesh. Burma agreed to take them all back, but many of the refugees preferred to stay in predominantly Muslim Bangladesh.

martial law (in effect since 1975). On April 21, however, President Ziaur Rahman, the chief administrator of martial law, announced that free and impartial presidential elections would be held on June 3. Parliamentary elections, originally scheduled to be held before the end of 1978, were postponed.

Offering himself as a presidential candidate, Gen. Zia (the name by which Ziaur Rahman is commonly known) organized a coalition of diverse political parties and conducted a very active campaign. His principal opponents, the Awami League (followers of the late Sheikh Mujibur Rahman), also campaigned vigorously. While Gen. Zia took a stand favoring a strong presidency, the Awami candidate, Gen. M.A.G. Osmani, argued for a parliamentary democracy with a strong prime minister at the helm. The results were a resounding endorsement of Gen. Zia, who won 77 percent of the vote. Gen. Osmani took 20 percent, and other candidates 3 percent.

The Economy. For the fourth consecutive year, Bangladesh had a good grain harvest, although output still fell short of need. Exports profited from strong world demand for jute, jute products, and tea. However, prices for imports—mainly raw materials and food grains—also continued to rise, leaving a huge trade gap to be covered by foreign aid. Government economic planning continued to stress the development of agriculture and cot-

tage industries, the spread of literacy, and the promotion of family planning.

Foreign Relations. For the most part, Bangladesh enjoyed excellent relations with other countries. Relations with Burma, however, were roiled by the expulsion of "illegal" settlers of Muslim Bangladeshi origin from that predominantly Buddhist country. By early June, some 150,000 refugees had crossed into Bangladesh, creating an immense relief problem. On July 9, negotiators for the two nations agreed on a plan to return all the refugees to Burma (q.v.).

See STATISTICS OF THE WORLD.   W.J.G.

BARBADOS. See STATISTICS OF THE WORLD.

BEHAVIORAL SCIENCES. Advances in our knowledge of brain chemistry and of primate communication and gains in our understanding of lethal childhood ailments and of schizophrenia were at the forefront of behavioral science research in 1978.

Brain Chemicals. It is becoming more evident that the chemistry of the brain—more critically, the relative concentrations of brain chemicals—plays an important role in a number of emotional states. In the first reported study of its kind with

Sherman (left) responds to Austin's request for food. Researchers at Yerkes Regional Primate Research Center in Georgia taught the two young chimps to associate different foods with different geometric symbols embossed on keyboards in their cages. They are the first nonhuman primates to communicate with each other through the use of symbols.

human beings, National Institute of Mental Health (NIMH) researchers found evidence that the mental state that accompanies "human aggression . . . may have a biological component to it." The component appears to involve the crucial balance of two or three key chemical transmitters in the brain, Frederick K. Goodwin of the NIMH reported at the annual meeting of the American Psychiatric Association in May.

In their study of twenty-six U.S. Navy enlisted men, the researchers found that those with high aggression scores (measured by a ten-item scale) had uncommonly high levels of the transmitter norepinephrine in their brain. And those who were least aggressive almost invariably had extremely high levels of serotonin, another chemical involved in electrical transmission between certain brain cells. Previous animal studies had indicated that aggression might also be linked to a third substance, dopamine; Goodwin's work confirmed no such connection.

In nonrelated experiments with rats, investigators at Hunter College and Albert Einstein College of Medicine in New York City reported preliminary evidence that the mechanism for narcotic addiction may occur in specific brain areas. In a study presented at the Eastern Psychological Asso-

ciation meeting in April, the researchers said they significantly decreased opiate withdrawal symptoms in the animals by electrically stimulating one of two brain areas—the mid portion of the dorsal thalamus in the central brain and the periaqueductal gray matter in the upper brain stem. "This might suggest that certain aspects of [narcotic] tolerance and dependence might involve modulation of certain brain areas," said Eliot L. Gardner of Einstein College, who conducted the experiments with Diane Avallone of Hunter College.

Chimpanzees and Gorillas. It was a banner year for primates. For reportedly the first time ever, two chimpanzees—4½-year-old Sherman and 3½-year-old Austin—communicated with each other through symbolic language taught by humans. (Previously, chimps had shown they could communicate in sign language with humans.) In a project at the Yerkes Regional Primate Research Center in Georgia, Sherman and Austin talked—mostly asking each other for specific types of food—by using a computerized keyboard embossed with geometric symbols representing individual foods.

In yet another first, a 140 lb. lowland gorilla named Koko became the world's first talking gorilla. Trained by Stanford University graduate student Francine ("Penny") Patterson, Koko mastered 375 hand signals, thereby refuting previous implications that gorillas were not as bright as chimps. In fact, Koko was given the standard Stanford-Binet IQ Test and scored between 85 and 95.

And in a somewhat less comforting advance toward humankind, naturalist Jane Goodall's chimps in Tanzania began displaying tendencies toward murder. Brutal, calculated killings—for no apparent survival-related reasons—were perpetrated by members of one chimp tribe upon another. Goodall termed it "the gradual extermination of a social group by a stronger neighboring group. Now we know there is strong similarity to humans."

Sudden Infant Death. Each year, some 10,000 babies succumb to Sudden Infant Death Syndrome (SIDS) or "crib death"—a label usually applied by doctors who have little or no idea what actually killed these apparently healthy 2- to 4-month-olds in their sleep. In 1978, however, results from extensive research at Brown University indicated a number of these infants may have suffered from a subtle form of learning disability. Brown psychologist Lewis P. Lipsitt reported his results suggest the presence of a minor flaw in the developmental process in which totally biological, protective reflexes present at birth—such as the ability to regain breathing after a short period of apnea, or breathing stoppage—evolve into learned, voluntary responses. When combined with a number of other physical and behavioral factors, this disability might be responsible for some incidents of crib death, according to Lipsitt, who stresses the idea is still in the theory stage.

Diagnosing and Treating Schizophrenia. Some critics of psychiatry have long asserted that terms such as "schizophrenia" are overused in diagnosing patients. In the August *American Journal of Psychiatry*, University of Chicago Medical School psychiatrists Michael Alan Taylor and Richard Abrams analyzed admissions to a university psychiatric inpatient facility in a suburban-rural area in New York State. Using "more rigorous . . . reliable" criteria to define the disorder, the researchers determined that hospital officials diagnosed five times more persons as schizophrenics than actually fit into that category. Misdiagnosis, they added, carries the risk of using potentially dangerous drugs on the wrong patients, and the psychiatrists called for more stringent diagnostic procedures in the United States.

One school of researchers has suggested, however, that once schizophrenia has been truly diagnosed, it may be alleviated by periodic use of hemodialysis—the same technique used to cleanse the blood of patients suffering from kidney disease. Robert Cade of the University of Florida and Herbert Wagemaker of the University of Louisville reported encouraging rates of success with dialysis, which they said had enabled some chronically disabled schizophrenics to resume relatively normal lives. The researchers said they had found signs of an abnormal brain compound, called leucine-endorphin, in the filtered remains of the subjects' blood. They said it is too early to be certain, but the substance may contribute significantly to the development of schizophrenia.

J.P.G.

BELGIUM. Serious domestic and international problems beset Belgium during 1978, producing a government crisis in midyear and eventually bringing about the resignation of Premier Léo

In 1978, University of Pennsylvania psychologists H. A. Sackeim, R. C. Gur, and M. C. Saucy tested their theory that emotions are more strongly expressed by the right side of the brain—and the left side of the body. Confirmation came through the use of composite photographs. In the center, a man expresses disgust. At the left is a composite of the left side of his face; at the right, a right-side composite.

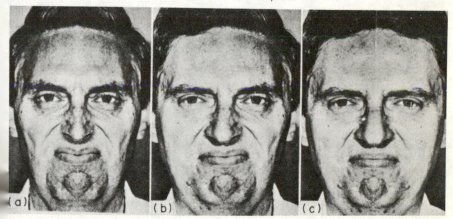

(a)   (b)   (c)

Tindemans, the leader of the Flemish-dominated Christian Social Party.

The three French-speaking parties warned Tindemans early in January that they would quit his coalition unless he immediately put into effect the concessions he had agreed to under the devolution compromise (which provides for Belgium to become a federated state with two communities—French and Flemish—and three economic and political regions). The immediate problem was eased on Jan. 17: The coalition parties reached an agreement on a program under which the federated state would become a reality in the mid-1980's.

A problem that could not be solved by compromise was that of unemployment. The job situation in Belgium remained critical, with 7.4 percent of the work force unemployed in January. Also, a bitter international dispute had been building up in Zaire, the former Belgian Congo. In May civil war trapped more than 2500 Europeans in the Zairian mining town of Kolwezi. About 1750 Belgian troops were flown to Africa on May 18 to rescue them. Some 800 French troops were airlifted to Kolwezi on May 19 and about 700 Belgian troops were dropped there the next day. On May 22, after the trapped Europeans had all gone, the Belgian troops also left. Tindemans had suggested on May 19, however, that the French part of the action had been undertaken in an attempt to replace Belgium, which has investments worth $1 billion in Zaire. The Belgians, in turn, were criticized for delays that cost the lives of many Europeans. The devolution, unemployment, and Zaire situations—in addition to labor unrest, financial difficulties in the steel and textile industries, and a budget dispute—produced such tension within the coalition that Tindemans submitted his resignation on June 15.

The five-day cabinet crisis that followed was accompanied by fevered negotiations. These talks ended in a compromise on June 19 that permitted the Tindemans coalition to remain in office, and King Baudouin formally rejected Tindemans's resignation.

On Oct. 11 the Tindemans government resigned again, because the four parties of the coalition could not agree on the degree of autonomy that would be granted to the three regions under devolution. This time the king accepted Tindemans's resignation; nine days later he swore in a caretaker government with the French-speaking Paul Vanden Boeynants, a Christian Socialist like Tindemans, as premier.

An election was held on Dec. 17, but no significant changes in party strength resulted. Vanden Boeynants, saying that the election had solved nothing, resigned the next day, and the new parliament was faced with the old problems of forming a coalition and resolving the constitutional issues.

See STATISTICS OF THE WORLD.   L.A.S.

BENIN, PEOPLE'S REPUBLIC OF. See STATISTICS OF THE WORLD (Dahomey).

BHUTAN. See STATISTICS OF THE WORLD.

BOLIVIA. A brief military coup on July 21 gave Bolivia its 188th government in 153 years of independence. On Nov. 24, a little over four months later, another bloodless coup occurred, and army commander Gen. David Padilla Arancibia succeeded Air Force Gen. Juan Pereda Asbún as head of the Bolivian government.

On July 9, at the urging of the United States, Boliva held its first general election in twelve years. Pereda, candidate of the rightist military government, was declared winner by a narrow 50.1 percent, based on 80 percent of the count. His more liberal opponent, former President Hernán Siles Zuazo, came in second with about 40 percent of the vote. Military leaders, noting that Siles was supported by Communists, had campaigned vigorously against him. However, a widespread outcry of fraud arose and the electoral court nullified the election. Finally Pereda, demanding recognition of his victory and citing the danger of communism, launched a revolt, which, unresisted, quickly brought him to power. He installed a largely civilian cabinet and promised a reform government much like that of his predecessor as president, Hugo Banzer Suárez. (An army general, Suárez had won office in a military coup in 1971.)

Pereda said he would hold an election in 1980 but would not be a candidate. As a result, the U.S., which had suspended military aid in protest against his election, restored its payments. Pereda's civilian cabinet resigned in late October, to be replaced on Nov. 6 by a cabinet dominated by military men. The second coup of the year occurred eighteen days later. The new Padilla government, army dominated, promised that elections would be held on July 1, 1979.

The Bolivian economy expanded slightly during the year, chiefly in the mining sector. The increase in the gross domestic product was estimated at 6.4 percent.

See STATISTICS OF THE WORLD.   J.N.G.

BOPHUTHATSWANA. See STATISTICS OF THE WORLD.

BOTSWANA. See STATISTICS OF THE WORLD.

BRAZIL. On Oct. 15, 1978, despite the growing public clamor for a return to civilian rule in Brazil, the electoral college chose retired Army Gen. João Baptista da Figueiredo, candidate of the military

Brazil's president-elect, Gen. João Baptista da Figueiredo, is joined by his wife as they celebrate his Oct. 15 victory. Figueiredo was the handpicked candidate of the retiring President Ernesto Geisel.

government, to be the next president. He was scheduled to take office on March 15, 1979.

Domestic Politics. Handpicked by the incumbent president, Ernesto Geisel, in January, the little-known Figueiredo had been Geisel's director of national intelligence. Geisel's party, the National Alliance for Renovation (ARENA), dominated the electoral college, which is made up of the members of both houses of congress and delegates from the state legislatures; moreover, after the election, there were allegations that the Figueiredo supporters had been bribed.

Many Brazilians were dissatisfied. With the September repeal of a number of repressive measures, including the Institutional Act No. 5, which had granted the president dictatorial powers, some feared that Figueiredo's promises to encourage a greater degree of democracy would lead to political instability. On the other hand, others thought that Figueiredo would not be democratic enough; they felt that after four military presidents, it was time for a change. They also wanted direct elections and they distrusted the intentions of Figueiredo, who had declared in April that he had not yet defined his concept of democracy. The future president had also proclaimed that liberalism was dead, that full democracy did not exist anywhere, and that any form of democracy adopted by Brazil would be, in President Geisel's term, "relative."

Many of Figueiredo's opponents had backed another retired general, Euler Bentes Monteiro, the candidate of the only other legal party, the center-left Brazilian Democratic Movement (MDB). Bentes, who did not enter the presidential race until the last minute, campaigned hard, denouncing the electoral procedure as undemocratic, urging an early return to civilian rule, and demanding more government attention to social reform. Voting for national and state legislatures in 1977 had suggested to many observers that the MDB was Brazil's strongest party, but because of ARENA control of the electoral college, Figueiredo won 355 votes to Bentes's 226. Congressional elections held on Nov. 15 resulted in gains for the MDB. Pending recounts, the Opposition won 191–193 of the 420 seats. The outcome was seen as a rebuke to the military leadership.

Foreign Affairs. Tension in Brazil's relations with the United States had been mounting for some time because of the Latin American country's alleged infractions of human rights and because of its long-standing agreement to purchase atomic reactors from West Germany. The U.S. opposed the West German agreement on the grounds that

101

Brazil gained a huge paper factory in 1978. Built in Japan by U.S. billionaire Daniel K. Ludwig, it was towed on a barge along the Amazon River to an inland site on a jungle-locked tributary.

it would enable Brazil, which had not signed the nuclear-arms limitation treaty, to make enriched uranium of weapons grade. The visit of U.S. President Jimmy Carter to Brazil in March eased tensions somewhat. But Geisel had already made clear, on a five-day visit to West Germany just prior to his meeting with Carter, that there was scant likelihood of any change in Brazil's determination to acquire sophisticated nuclear technology. In May, Geisel turned down Carter's invitation to visit him in the U.S.

The Economy. After three years of recession, Brazil's economy showed some resilience in 1978. According to government statistics, Brazil had the strongest economy in Latin America, although inflation was running at 40 percent annually and the national debt had reached $40 billion. And in August it was announced that severe late winter frosts had caused the loss of more than 30 percent of the 1979 coffee crop. (Brazil is the world's foremost exporter of coffee.) Although Brazil had exported hardly any soybeans before 1971, by 1978 it had become the world's second largest exporter of that crop. Brazil also continued to be a major exporter of iron ore, bauxite, copper, nickel, and scores of other minerals. But Brazil's real economic problem was its lack of oil. It was the world's largest oil importer in 1977, able to produce no more than 10 percent of its consumption. In 1978, Petrobrás, the state oil monopoly, entered into several new joint ventures with Middle Eastern oil-producing countries; it also invested more than $200,000,000 in the search for oil at home.

Although strikes were illegal, the government looked the other way when hard-pressed auto workers in São Paulo left their jobs in May to demand higher wages and lower costs. Doctors, teachers, and some other workers also staged strikes throughout the summer.

See STATISTICS OF THE WORLD.   J.N.G.
BRITISH COLUMBIA. *See* STATISTICS OF THE WORLD.
BULGARIA. Unlike other Soviet-bloc nations, Bulgaria seemed until 1978 to be spared the problem of an organized human-rights movement. In April, however, an Austrian newspaper, *Die Presse,* published the text of "Declaration '78," a document that appeared to be the Bulgarian version of the human-rights manifestos produced elsewhere in Eastern Europe in recent years. The declaration demanded civil liberties for Bulgarians, as well as improved pensions and living standards. Western observers considered the document authentic but knew nothing of the identity of its authors or the extent of public support for them.

In its official 1977 economic report, published in February, 1978, the government of Communist Party leader Todor Zhivkov admitted to serious economic failures. Industrial production and labor productivity fell short of expectations and farm production declined 6.3 percent compared with 1976. Following a national Communist Party conference in April, two deputy premiers and the agriculture minister were relieved of their jobs.

Bulgaria made a notable gesture to the West during June, presumably with Soviet approval. After arresting four terrorists wanted by West Germany, Bulgarian officials promptly turned the fugitives over to Bonn police. Relations with Great Britain were strained by a bizarre episode in September, when a Bulgarian defector, Georgi Markov, died of poisoning after being stabbed in the leg on a London street by a man wielding an umbrella.

Georgi Markov (above), a Bulgarian defector, was walking on a London street in early September when he felt a stabbing pain in his thigh. A few days later he was dead—murdered by a poisonous pellet injected into his body by the point of an umbrella. The incident was one of several attacks on Bulgarian émigrés during 1978.

The Bulgarian government continued to develop ties with neighboring Greece and Turkey. Zhivkov played host to Turkish Premier Bülent Ecevit in May and to Greek Premier Constantine Karamanlis in July. In addition, Shah Mohammed Riza Pahlavi of Iran visited Bulgaria during May.

Bulgaria continued to quarrel with Yugoslavia over the Macedonians, a minority in both Communist nations. Bulgaria's claim that resident Macedonians were Bulgarians, and not members of a separate ethnic group, was seen by Yugoslavia as an indirect claim on traditionally Macedonian territory within its own borders.

See STATISTICS OF THE WORLD.   F.W.

BURMA. In 1978, sixteen years after he overthrew civilian rule, Gen. Ne Win appeared to be firmly in control of the Burmese government. But the country was in deep political and economic trouble, and most analysts doubted that Ne Win's "Burmese way to socialism" would survive when the strongman—67 years old and ailing—passed from the scene.

Politics. The Burmese Communist Party, which claimed to have as many as 20,000 guerrilla fighters in the field, strengthened its cooperation with the strongest tribal groups, chiefly the Shans and the Kachins, during the year. The Communists, abetted by nearly thirty tribal rebellions scattered through Burma's jungle and highland, continued to tie up the 150,000-man Burmese army. Fortunately for the Rangoon government, however, many of the tribal groups seemed more interested in smuggling and drug-running than in fighting for local autonomy.

Despite these challenges, Ne Win retained the backing of the army. On March 2, in a State Council vote that was purely a formality, he was re-elected chairman of the council and president of the republic.

Refugees. Beginning in February, Muslims in the western state of Arakan fled by the tens of thousands across the border into Bangladesh (q.v.). The exodus was touched off when the government launched Operation Dragon—ostensibly a routine check on illegal Muslim immigration into Arakan. The operation, however, was carried out by the Burmese army and local Buddhist militants with extreme brutality. Whole towns of Burmese Muslims emptied, as their inhabitants made the arduous trek across the border. After at least 150,000 Muslims had fled the country, the Rangoon government finally agreed to take the refugees back and ensure their safety. At the end of the year, however, the vast majority of the refugees remained in squalid camps in Bangladesh, fearful of returning to Burma.

The Economy. The government-run, nationalized sectors of the economy continued to stagnate under crushing bureaucracy and near-zero economic growth, as they had throughout the 1970's. Once the world's leading rice exporter, Burma had little to sell abroad in 1978, and the country thus faced serious shortages in foreign exchange. As in the past, much of the country's economic activity was conducted on the black market.

Foreign Policy. Chinese Deputy Premier Teng Hsiao-ping visited Burma in January on his first foreign trip since his reinstatement in 1977. In the summer, Ne Win dispatched a military delegation to Peking in an effort to get China to halt its aid to Burma's Communists. The success of the mission was doubtful, and there was some speculation that Burma might end its policy of strict nonalignment and adopt a slight westward tilt. On Nov. 14, however, Teng paid another visit to Burma as part of a ten-day tour of four non-Communist Southeast Asian nations (the three other countries were Thailand, Malaysia, and Singapore).

See STATISTICS OF THE WORLD.   R.J.C.

BURUNDI. See STATISTICS OF THE WORLD.

C

CABINET, UNITED STATES. On Jan. 19, 1978, in his first State of the Union message, U.S. President Jimmy Carter told the nation that it was time to create a "separate department of education." The formal proposal for such a department was presented to Congress on April 14. Under the plan, the new secretary of education would take over 164 existing educational programs with a staff of 23,325 employees and an annual budget of $17.5 billion. Most of these programs would be taken from the Department of Health, Education, and Welfare, but other programs would also be included, such as the child nutrition programs of the Department of Agriculture, the Indian education programs of the Department of the Interior, and the schools for overseas dependents operated by the Department of Defense. The Senate approved the proposal on Sept. 28, but the House of Representatives did not act on it before adjourning in October.

The Attorney General. On July 6, Griffin Bell became the first U.S. attorney general to be held in contempt of court for refusing to release information. He had been ordered to turn over files of Federal Bureau of Investigation informants who had penetrated the Socialist Workers Party, which was suing the FBI for $40,000,000. Bell argued that releasing the files would impair "the nation's ability to protect itself against enemies, foreign and domestic," but Federal District Court Judge Thomas P. Griesa of New York City found him in contempt. Bell appealed; a three-judge federal appeals court heard the case on Nov. 15 but reserved judgment at that time.

Membership. President Carter made no changes in his cabinet or cabinet-level advisers during 1978. Cabinet-level officers—those who occupy high executive positions but do not have cabinet rank—included Andrew Young, U.S. ambassador to the United Nations; Zbigniew Brzezinski, special assistant to the President for national security affairs; James T. McIntyre, director of the Office of Management and Budget; and Charles L. Schultze, chairman of the Council of Economic Advisers.

The executive departments, the years of their establishment, and their heads during 1978 follow:

Hoping to improve U.S.-U.S.S.R. trade relations, Commerce Secretary Juanita Kreps and Treasury Secretary W. Michael Blumenthal (second from left) join U.S. Ambassador Malcolm Toon in negotiations with Soviet officials in Moscow on Dec. 6.

Department of State, 1789: Secretary, Cyrus R. Vance.

Department of the Treasury, 1789: Secretary, W. Michael Blumenthal.

Department of the Interior, 1849: Secretary, Cecil D. Andrus.

Department of Agriculture, 1862: Secretary, Bob Bergland.

Department of Justice, 1870: Attorney General, Griffin B. Bell.

Department of Commerce, 1913: Secretary, Juanita M. Kreps.

Department of Labor, 1913: Secretary, F. Ray Marshall.

Department of Defense, 1949: Secretary, Harold Brown.

Department of Health, Education, and Welfare, 1953: Secretary, Joseph A. Califano, Jr.

Department of Housing and Urban Development, 1965: Secretary, Patricia Roberts Harris.

Department of Transportation, 1966: Secretary, Brock Adams.

Department of Energy, 1977: Secretary, James R. Schlesinger.

See biographies of many of the above at PEOPLE IN THE NEWS. L.A.S.

CALIFORNIA. *See* STATISTICS OF THE WORLD.

CAMBODIA, officially known as DEMOCRATIC KAMPUCHEA. In 1978, three years after they gained power, a small group of Communist fanatics continued to rule Cambodia by terror. In April, U.S. President Jimmy Carter called Cambodia "the worst violator of human rights in the world today."

Politics. Overall authority in Cambodia was exercised by a shadowy body called the *Angka*—"the organization." Premier Pol Pot still appeared to be the country's top leader, but his government's control of the country seemed shaky. Cambodian officials even admitted what had been charged by neighboring Vietnam: that numerous coups, assassinations, and uprisings had been attempted since 1975. Elements within the army, the administration, and the Communist Party itself took part in the incidents. Possibly to rally support, the regime arranged for the public reappearance of Prince Norodom Sihanouk, the former head of state, at a banquet with government leaders in October.

The New Society. Earlier in the year, a group of Yugoslav journalists, the first Europeans allowed an extended look at Communist Cambodia, were given a tightly supervised tour of the country. They confirmed reports that Cambodia had reverted to a near-primitive condition. It was, they said, a country where no schools existed above the rudimentary level, no books were published,

no money was allowed, and children were taught to spy on their parents. The Yugoslavs reported that the entire population had been organized into work groups, with almost everyone, including children, forced to labor up to sixteen hours a day in the fields. Besides tending the rice crop, which was said to be a good one in 1978, the workers built or repaired irrigation canals and dams.

Cambodians who complained of the harsh life were brutally punished—often by execution. Some reports indicated that, far from tapering off, the executions had actually increased during 1978. The victims of this latest purge were the wives and children of former soldiers, dissident members of the Communist Party, and anyone thought to have too much formal education.

According to a British government study released in September, "many hundreds of thousands" of people have died in Communist Cambodia as the result of brutality, execution, and disease and debility brought on by mass evacuation of the cities. To escape the horror, thousands of Cambodians braved land mines and the bullets of border guards to flee to Thailand during the year.

Conflict with Vietnam. Fighting flared sporadically along the ill-defined border with Vietnam. In mid-June, Vietnamese troops launched an offensive, thrusting 30 mi. into Cambodia; however, this attack fizzled out with the onset of the rainy season. But at the end of the year, Vietnam concentrated large numbers of troops along the border, and some analysts predicted a dry-season offensive aimed at bringing down the Cambodian government. Lending support for this view was Hanoi's announcement in December that a Kampuchean United Front for National Salvation had been formed in the areas of Cambodia that had been "liberated" by Vietnamese forces.

Foreign Policy. Fearful of Vietnam's intentions, the Cambodian government took its case to the outside world in 1978. Vice-Premier Ieng Sary visited the United Nations, Europe, and many countries in Asia to denounce Vietnamese aggression. He even went so far as to invite U.N. Secretary-General Kurt Waldheim to visit Cambodia to assess the human rights situation there.

The Cambodian-Vietnamese conflict was potentially explosive, since the People's Republic of China backed Cambodia and the Soviet Union supported Vietnam. The United States, though it condemned the brutality in Cambodia, took no sides in the conflict between the two Communist states.

See STATISTICS OF THE WORLD. R.J.C.

CAMEROON. *See* STATISTICS OF THE WORLD.

CANADA. The year 1978 was not a happy one for Canada. The economy lagged badly and regionalism—not only in Québec but in the English-speaking provinces as well—posed a growing challenge to the federal government in Ottawa. Moreover, the personal leadership of Pierre Elliott Trudeau, the country's prime minister for a decade, was called into serious doubt, even within his own Liberal Party.

National Politics. Early in the year, it was fully expected that Trudeau would call a national election, either in the spring or in the fall. The prime minister's five-year term of office would not end until July, 1979, but elections customarily have been called at least every four years. With the polls showing the Liberals lagging behind the Progressive Conservatives, however, Trudeau decided on Sept. 15 to postpone balloting until the spring of 1979.

In October, Trudeau suffered a stinging setback when the Liberals won only two of fifteen parliamentary by-elections. The opposition Progressive Conservatives won 10 of the seats, 5 of them from Liberal incumbents in crucial Ontario Province. Trudeau's Liberals retained an 8-seat majority in the 264-seat House of Commons, but the crushing by-election defeat made it seem unlikely that the

party could win a national election in the near future. Some Liberals openly stated that Trudeau should step aside as party leader and prime minister to let someone else guide the party into the elections. On Dec. 7, Trudeau secured the required formal approval of Elizabeth II for the appointment of Edward R. Schreyer, a member of the left-wing New Democratic Party and a former premier of Manitoba, as Canada's next governor-general, to take office in January, 1979.

The Québec Question. Canada's only French-speaking province had become the center of a national crisis on Nov. 15, 1976, when the pro-independence Parti Québécois led by René Lévesque was unexpectedly voted into power. Lévesque vowed to hold a referendum in the spring of 1979 on his party's proposal for sovereignty. The position placed him on a direct collision course with Trudeau, a determined opponent of Québec independence.

In January, 1978, Trudeau even hinted that the federal government would not shrink from using force to prevent an "illegal" declaration of independence by Québec. He later warned that an independent Québec, if it came into being, would be treated like any other foreign country in economic matters and therefore suffer in terms of trade and employment. A poll announced in June showed that more than half of Québec's citizens would vote against independence and only a third would vote for it.

In September, Lévesque postponed the independence referendum until late 1979, or even

Canadian Prime Minister Pierre Elliott Trudeau (left) had problems in 1978—with regionalists, the economy, and his cabinet. Here he greets Francis Fox, his former solicitor general, on Feb. 25 in Ottawa. Fox had resigned his cabinet post a month earlier when it became known that he had forged a hospital admission document.

106

The scene: a Montréal unemployment office. More than 8 percent of Canadian workers were unemployed—or sans-travail—during 1978; the country's economy was in bad shape in any language.

1980. Then, in October, the Parti Québécois leader made a sharp tactical change. Instead of a referendum asking for the authority to separate, Lévesque said he would ask only for the authority to negotiate the terms of a separation with Canada. Under his new plan, Lévesque hoped to work out an ill-defined economic association with Canada, to include a common currency, a joint central bank, and some sort of common market. Then, if all went well, he would go back to Québec's voters and ask for the right to separate. It appeared that Lévesque might stand a better chance of winning a referendum with this strategy, but it was unlikely that Trudeau or any other national leader would cooperate in such a scheme.

Western Regionalism. Québec was not the only dissatisfied province. The far western provinces, meekly subservient to Ottawa in the past, grew increasingly aware of the political muscle bestowed on them by their newfound riches in oil, gas, and potash. During 1978, they made plain their anger over federal policies they considered discriminatory. They pointed out that Ottawa taxed their oil exports but not mineral exports from Ontario. They also complained about having to buy expensive, heavily protected clothes and textiles from Québec and Ontario, while their own products were available in the east at what they considered to be unfairly low prices. The dissatisfaction was not, however, purely economic. The mood in the west, and in other parts of the country, was one of alienation from Ottawa, a feeling that the federal government cared little about regional interests.

Constitutional Reform. In response to the various regional pressures, Trudeau announced some long-awaited proposals for a new Canadian constitution. The new charter, which would replace

the British North America Act of 1867, would include a bill of rights guaranteeing the linguistic rights of minorities—particularly the French-speaking population of Québec. The new constitution would also give the provincial governments a stronger voice in choosing the members of the Supreme Court and the Senate. The latter body, whose members are now appointed by the

A group of "boat people," refugees from Vietnam, arrive in Montréal on Nov. 25. They had spent several weeks on board the freighter Hai Hong in Malaysia, waiting to find a country that would let them in. Canada was the first Western nation to accept Vietnamese refugees.

prime minister, would be called the House of the Federation.

As outlined by Trudeau in a series of meetings with the provincial prime ministers, the proposals clearly were intended to mollify the regionalists. But Lévesque sneered at the attempt to head off Québec independence, and a limited agreement reached by the provincial premiers and Ottawa in November was considered fragile and unlikely to hold up.

The Economy. In April the government began to phase out the wage and price control program it had instituted in October, 1975. Critics had charged that it dampened business confidence and failed to halt inflation. Over the year, inflation ran at over 8 percent, and there were other signs of economic malaise. More than 8 percent of the work force was unemployed, the highest figure since before World War II. The Canadian dollar continued to decline on the international exchange markets, falling at one point to less than 85¢ in U.S. currency and losing even more ground against other currencies. As the economy faltered, Canadians began to shed some of their antipathy to large-scale U.S. investment in the country and sought closer economic ties with their southern neighbor.

On Nov. 24, Trudeau made several shifts in his cabinet in an effort to promote industrial development. At the same time he created the Board of Economic Development Ministers to coordinate government policies affecting economic growth.

Two major strikes created further problems for the economy. Air Canada's ground service workers shut down the airline for ten days in August and September, and the postal workers had a bitter confrontation with the government in October. The 23,000 postal workers went out on strike Oct. 16; two days later the government pushed through legislation requiring them to return to work. They ignored it for a week, however, until the government threatened mass firings and brought criminal charges against union officials. The dispute was then placed in the hands of a conciliator-arbitrator.

Foreign Policy. Relations with the United States continued to occupy a major part of Canadian foreign policy. Aside from a minor dispute over fishing rights, with each side banning the other's fishing boats from its waters while a new fisheries treaty was being negotiated, ties between the two countries were stronger than they had been in a decade. Trudeau and President Jimmy Carter seemed to have developed a strong personal rapport. Moreover, Washington was pleased with Canada's decision to strengthen its military posture, a matter of considerable importance to the

North American Air Defense Command. In November, U.S. Secretary of State Cyrus R. Vance visited Ottawa, and, after talks with Trudeau, set Dec. 31 as the deadline for settling the fisheries dispute. Negotiations between the two countries, however, continued into 1979.

See STATISTICS OF THE WORLD.   R.J.C.

CANAL ZONE. See STATISTICS OF THE WORLD.

CAPE VERDE. See STATISTICS OF THE WORLD.

CENTRAL AFRICAN EMPIRE. See STATISTICS OF THE WORLD.

CEYLON, officially the REPUBLIC OF SRI LANKA. Ceylon abandoned its thirty-year-old British-style parliamentary form of government and switched to a French-style system with a strong presidency as of Feb. 4, 1978. On that date, Prime Minister Junius R. Jayewardene, whose United National Party (UNP) had pushed the necessary constitutional changes through the National Assembly, resigned his office and was sworn in for a six-year term as president, with full executive powers. His second-in-command in the UNP, Ranasinghe Premadasa, succeeded him as prime minister. The Opposition, led by former Prime Minister Sirimavo R.D. Bandaranaike, strongly protested President Jayewardene's sweeping new authority, but was powerless to prevent the changeover.

In an effort to combat widespread bribery and corruption, President Jayewardene called upon all UNP members of the National Assembly to submit declarations of personal assets and liabilities. Similar statements were required from chairmen and directors of state corporations and from board members of all local authorities. Anticorruption measures were also strengthened in the civil service. On Aug. 1 a presidential commission commenced a formal inquiry into charges of abuse of power, corruption, fraud, and nepotism under the administration of the former prime minister, Sirimavo Bandaranaike; her party had been voted out of office in 1977 after seventeen years in power.

See STATISTICS OF THE WORLD.   W.J.G.

CHAD. See STATISTICS OF THE WORLD; see also AFRICA; LIBYA.

CHEMISTRY. The year 1978 saw advances in such areas of chemical research as organic and inorganic synthesis and the breakdown of biodegradable and toxic substances.

A Major Advance in Organic Synthesis. Gibberellins are hormones produced by many species of plants to stimulate the growth of stems and leaves and to facilitate pollen germination. Although the chemical structures of these forty or so plant growth substances have been known for the past twenty years, chemists had not been able to synthesize any of them because of the complexity of

A scanning electromicrograph of a crystal of (SN)$_x$, a synthetic polymer made from long chains of alternately arranged sulfur and nitrogen atoms. The newly produced material has both the flexibility of plastic and the electrical conducting properties of metal. By making subtle changes in its composition, scientists can vary the electrical conductivity of (SN)$_x$, polymeric sulfur nitride, by an astonishing twelve orders of magnitude—from insulator to semiconductor to metal.

their molecular structures. During 1978, however, Harvard University chemist Elias J. Corey managed to create in the laboratory an important member of the gibberellin family, gibberellic acid, ending one of the longest quests in synthetic organic chemistry.

Working with Rick L. Danheiser of the Massachusetts Institute of Technology, Corey achieved this synthesis in a manner different from that used by most other organic chemists. Instead of starting with a simple molecule and building upon it to get the desired structure, Corey began with the target molecule and traced possible synthetic routes backward. Using this approach, which is known as antithetic analysis, the chemist synthesized during the year not only gibberellic acid, but also another naturally occurring substance with an equally complicated molecular structure—erythronolide B, an important precursor of the antibiotic erythromycin. Corey, who had synthesized hormonelike prostaglandins some years before, expressed optimism that more and more chemically complicated naturally occurring substances would be synthesized by chemists using the antithetic analysis process.

Hemoglobinlike Inorganic Molecules. In December, C. A. McAuliffe, a chemist at the Manchester Institute of Science and Technology in England, made public his discovery of compounds that mimic the respiratory proteins in their ability to absorb and release oxygen. Called "the only true

analogs to date" of the blood oxygenator hemoglobin and the muscle oxygenator myoglobin, these compounds, which are complexes of phosphine (PH$_3$) and manganese, can bind reversibly with oxygen under normal temperatures and pressures—a trait not found in other synthetic compounds. McAuliffe and his co-workers learned also that by making substitutions in some of the phosphate groups in the complex they could produce a series of compounds in which each member has a different gas-scavenging property. For instance, by replacing a hydrogen atom in the phosphate group with a bromine atom, the chemists created a molecule able to scavenge oxygen more effectively than the old unsubstituted molecule.

McAuliffe said he foresees the use of the discrete properties of the individual members of this new family of complexes in many industrial processes. For instance, one family member might be able to absorb sulfur dioxide, a pollutant from stack gases of coal-fired furnaces. An oxygen-scavenging member could be utilized to remove minute traces of oxygen—which constitute an impurity—from the inert gas streams used to produce microelectronic circuitry. The same compound could be used to produce 99.9995 percent nitrogen—a degree of purity difficult to achieve by existing techniques.

Although other mimics of hemoglobin have been produced, they needed special conditions, such as low temperatures and high pressures, to make them effective in industrial applications. Phosphinomanganese compounds, on the other hand, are effective at normal temperature and pressure. Furthermore, they can undergo thousands of gas-uptake and -release cycles in the solid state and in solution without appreciable deterioration. Such stable and energy-efficient compounds make them attractive alternatives to the gas-scavenging compounds and processes now used by industry.

Safety of Biodegradable Pesticides Questioned. Since scientists made the discovery that the widely used pesticide DDT persists in the environment for long periods of time and is hazardous to animal, and possibly human, health, they have been synthesizing substitute pesticides that either disintegrate into short-lived, harmless substances or are metabolized by soil microorganisms. In 1978, however, a chemist at the University of Wisconsin reported that some of the waste products of these pesticide-ingesting microbes can also pose a threat to human health.

At the 1978 national meeting of the American Chemical Society, held in September, M. T. Stephen Hsia disclosed that fungi and microorganisms acting upon propanil, a safe chemical used to control grass weeds, were found to generate 3,4,3',4'-tetrachloroazobenzene (TCAB), a chemical structurally similar to dioxin, the most toxic synthetic chemical known. Hsia also disclosed that when he subjected this dioxinlike compound to a series of screening tests he found that it not only changed the character of proteins in cultured rat cells, but also caused genetic mutations in bacteria—a strong indication that TCAB is a potential cancer-causing agent. Although definitive tests to determine its carcinogenicity in mammals had yet to be conducted, Hsia expressed his strong suspicion that TCAB might indeed cause cancer in humans. The most significant aspect of Hsia's report, however, was his warning to chemists that the breakdown products of other so-called harmless, biodegradable pesticides may present health hazards that are as great as, if not greater than, the hazards of TCAB.

Microwave Detoxification. In 1978, after having received persistent complaints about deteriorating health from residents of Love Canal, N.Y., a small Niagara Falls community once occupied by a chemical company, health authorities tested the area for the presence of toxic wastes. When they found that the people of Love Canal were being poisoned by chemicals that had been disposed of thirty years ago, industrial chemists were once again faced with the almost insoluble problem of how to dispose safely of hard-to-degrade toxic chemicals. See ENVIRONMENT.

Hope was offered to industrial chemists in March, however, when scientists at Lockheed Palo Alto (Calif.) Research Laboratory reported that the complete breakdown of such toxic substances can be accomplished by exposing them to microwave radiation. According to Lockheed's Lionel J. Bailin and Barry L. Hertzler, when microwave (2450 megahertz) radiation was emitted into a two-liter reactor containing waste material suspended in oxygen, all the chemicals were degraded to harmless and simple substances. The scientists added that the two-liter reactor can degrade as much as 7 lb. of waste per hour—providing an inexpensive and efficient means for chemical companies and industrial chemicals users to dispose of toxic wastes.   M.J.C.

CHESS. Chess gained international attention in 1978 for the first time in six years, owing to a highly controversial world championship match between Anatoly Karpov of the Soviet Union and Viktor Korchnoi, a Soviet defector resident in Switzerland.

Karpov Retains His Crown. Karpov, who had won the world championship from the American Bobby Fischer by default in 1975, successfully de-

fended his title in the year's major event, a marathon 32-game match in Baguio, the Philippines. Karpov, 27, defeated Korchnoi, 47, by a score of 6 wins to 5, with 21 draws.

The match was punctuated by political and personal bitterness arising out of Korchnoi's 1976 defection to Western Europe from his native Leningrad. During the match, which began in mid-July, Korchnoi accused Soviet officials of holding his wife and son hostage by denying them exit visas. Both players also exchanged numerous charges of cheating, and at different points threatened to forfeit the contest in protest.

Karpov earned the $450,000 winner's share by taking an early 4–1 lead and then fending off Korchnoi's comeback attempt in the final two weeks of play. The Soviet champion's victory meant that he would not be required to risk his title again until 1981.

Eliminations. The championship match closely resembled another contest: the final elimination match that ended in January with Korchnoi's 10½–7½ victory over former champion Boris Spassky. The winter match, also marked by charges of cheating and by an unsuccessful comeback effort, was held to determine who would play Karpov later in the year.

Korchnoi held a commanding lead at the start of the match but was unnerved by Spassky's habit of considering his next move from an adjoining room with a demonstration board, rather than at the board of play. At one point, Spassky won four games in a row, but he later lost the initiative and the match.

A Comeback for Fischer? Bobby Fischer, who had lived in seclusion in Pasadena, Calif., since losing the world title in 1975, began negotiations with Yugoslav chess officials for his return to competitive play. In October the Yugoslav officials said that Fischer had agreed to play Svetozar Gligoric in March, 1979. But several details remained to be worked out. After winning his championship match, Karpov also indicated his eagerness for a match with Fischer.

Other Matches. The world women's champion was ousted when 17-year-old Maya Chiburdanidze defeated fellow Soviet Georgian Nona Gaprindashvili in a 15-game match by a score of 8½–6½ in September. Gaprindashvili, 37, had held the world women's title since 1962.

Controversy extended to U.S. competition when defending champion Walter Browne walked out of the national invitational championship in June after forfeiting his first game in a dispute over lighting. Lubomir Kavalek, a U.S. resident since the 1968 Soviet invasion of his native Czechoslovakia, won the tournament with a 10–4 score. Kavalek and second-prize winner James Tarjan thereby qualified for the 1979 zonal tournaments that lead to the 1981 world championship match.

The biggest upset of the year came in August when Joseph Bradford, a little-known master from Absecon, N.J., won the U.S. Open championship in Phoenix out of a field of 500 players.   A.S.

CHILDREN'S LITERATURE. *See* LITERATURE.

CHILE. In 1978 the military government of Chile was beset by continuing charges of civil rights violations as well as by fears that border disputes might erupt into a three-front war.

Foreign Affairs. Chile worried that Argentina, Bolivia, and Peru (qq.v.) might simultaneously use force to uphold long-standing claims to land that Chile considered its own. Bolivia and Peru still disputed Chile's victory in the War of the Pacific (1879–83). Bolivia, which broke diplomatic relations with Chile in March, insisted that it would regain a corridor to the sea in 1979. Such a corridor would probably be on land Chile had taken from Peru.

Even more threatening was the dispute with Argentina over three barren islands in the Beagle Channel at Tierra del Fuego, possession of which would allow the owner to claim a 200 mi. offshore economic zone believed to be rich in gas, oil, and fish. Chile had been awarded the islands by an international tribunal in 1977, but Argentina rejected the settlement. Both sides mobilized in 1978; they also agreed to look for a new mediator. On Dec. 23, Pope John Paul II appointed Cardinal Antonio Samorè as his emissary to mediate the dispute. The cardinal spent the rest of the year shuttling between the two countries.

In addition, Chile was confronted by the United States, which in September requested the extradition of three Chilean officers charged with the 1976 assassination in Washington, D.C., of Orlando Letelier. (Letelier was ambassador to the U.S. from the government of Salvador Allende Gossens, the Marxist president of Chile who was deposed in 1973.) One of the suspects, Gen. Manuel Contreras Sepúlveda, had been head of the Chilean secret police and was said to be a close friend and adviser of President Augusto Pinochet Ugarte. The other two accused were also associated with the secret police. The Chilean government, which denied implication in the case, accused the U.S. of using it as a means of unseating Pinochet. It seemed likely at the end of the year that months would pass before the Chilean authorities would reach a decision on the case. *See* UNITED STATES OF AMERICA.

Domestic Affairs. In March, in a slight relaxation of government control, Pinochet lifted the state of

siege that had been imposed during the military coup against Allende in 1973; other restraints, however, remained in effect. In April the government granted amnesty to violators of the siege laws. Although it refused to admit the existence of some 1500 political prisoners claimed by Amnesty International, the London-based civil rights organization, it allowed the United Nations to investigate alleged violations of human rights. Also in April Pinochet formed a new cabinet with a civilian majority and announced a new charter that would move Chile closer to civilian rule.

Beginning in May there were a number of antigovernment labor and student demonstrations and many hunger strikes—the first since 1973. In July Air Force Gen. Gustavo Leigh Guzmán, who had openly criticized Pinochet's long-term personal rule, was removed from the military junta and his command. Nineteen other air force generals who supported Leigh were forced into retirement or resigned.

Aided by foreign banks, the Chilean economy improved slightly in 1978. Inflation was down to about 50 percent from its dizzying height of 1000 percent in 1973. Agricultural production declined, but noncopper products, once only 15 percent of total exports, nearly equaled copper products in value.

See STATISTICS OF THE WORLD.   J.N.G.

CHINA, PEOPLE'S REPUBLIC OF. China's leaders charted bold new plans for their nation's political and economic future in 1978. Internationally, a historic peace treaty with Japan and the long-awaited normalization of relations with the United States climaxed a year of mounting tensions with the Soviet Union and border clashes with Vietnam.

Politics. The major political event of 1978 was the fifth meeting of the National People's Congress (China's legislature) in Peking from Feb. 26 to March 5. The congress made appointments to top government posts, continuing the trend toward moderation and pragmatism in political leadership which had been evident since late 1976. Communist Party Chairman Hua Kuo-feng was reappointed premier. Marshal Yeh Chien-ying, formerly minister of defense, was named chairman of the congress's Standing Committee, a ceremonial post equivalent to head of state. Teng Hsiao-ping, who is believed by Western observers to wield power second only to Hua, retained his post as first deputy premier. Teng's political allies figured prominently on the list of thirteen deputy premiers and thirty-seven ministers of the State Council named by the congress.

The congress adopted a new national constitution which replaced the constitution of 1975 and

CHINA, PEOPLE'S REPUBLIC OF

Chinese Deputy Premier Teng Hsiao-ping (left) with Japanese Prime Minister Takeo Fukuda. Teng flew to Tokyo in October to confer with Fukuda and to attend ratification ceremonies for the Sino-Japanese peace treaty.

returned to many of the principles of the 1954 charter. The right to defense counsel during trial was restored, as was the people's right to lodge complaints against officials. Ethnic minorities were guaranteed the right to preserve or reform their own ways. The National People's Congress was reaffirmed as the highest organ of state power; unlike the earlier constitutions, the new document did not state that the congress was subordinate to the Communist Party. The office of the procurator (public prosecutor) was reestablished, a move apparently designed to combat lawbreaking and indiscipline.

In the wake of the congress, the government continued its campaign against radicals allied with the so-called Gang of Four (who included Chairman Mao Tse-tung's widow, Chiang Ch'ing). In June it was disclosed that more than 100,000 purge victims were being rehabilitated; many of them had been arrested during the antirightist campaign of 1957 and the Cultural Revolution of the late 1960's. Official attacks on radicalism were more frequent during the summer and fall, including thinly veiled criticism of Mao himself for failing to promote democracy in the party and even for supporting the Gang of Four.

The Economy. Premier Hua's report to the National People's Congress revealed that the econ-

omy had suffered badly from disruptions between 1974 and 1976. The new constitution included a ten-year development plan (1976–85) calling for an average annual increase of 4–5 percent in farm output and 10 percent in industrial production. Steel production would be increased from 22,000,000 tons in 1977 to 60,000,000 in 1985, and the grain harvest from 272,000,000 to 440,000,000 tons over the same period. Some 120 new industrial projects were announced; see CONSTRUCTION. Reorganization of the economy into regional units and the use of wage incentives, particularly in the agricultural sector, were also sanctioned.

Less than a month after the economic plan was announced, the State Scientific and Technical Commission made public an eight-year program to improve scientific and technological development. Among the fields to be emphasized was petrochemical technology, the importance of which was underscored by the disclosure in May that major new deposits of oil and natural gas had been located in the South China Sea.

The economic record for the first half of 1978 was impressive. Industrial production was reported up 24 percent over the first half of 1977, while steel increased 67 percent, petroleum 11 percent, coal 19 percent, and electricity 17 percent during the same period. All sectors of light industry also gained.

Foreign trade volume for 1977 was up 12 percent over 1976, with exports exceeding imports by a substantial margin. Oil figured prominently in the export trade. On Feb. 16, in a move designed to bolster foreign trade, China signed an eight-year, $20 billion trade pact with Japan, exchanging Japanese industrial technology for Chinese coal and oil. Trade with the U.S. increased sharply from $374,000,000 in 1977 to an estimated $1 billion in 1978, with American exports accounting for about 70 percent of the total.

Foreign Affairs. On Dec. 15, in a move which caught the world by surprise, China and the U.S. announced that they would resume formal diplomatic relations on Jan. 1, 1979. The U.S. agreed to withdraw recognition from the Republic of China (Taiwan), terminate the U.S.-Taiwan Defense Pact within a year, and pull all U.S. forces off the island. While the Chinese made no explicit promise not to employ force in retaking Taiwan—a matter which they regard as a domestic problem—they did not object to the continuation of U.S. economic and cultural ties with the island, or even to the shipment of U.S. arms to Taiwan under existing contracts.

Events earlier in 1978 made it clear that China was far more concerned with events along its borders with Vietnam and the U.S.S.R. than with the

Taiwan problem. In April, Chinese and Vietnamese forces clashed on China's southern border. The long-standing border dispute between the two Communist neighbors was aggravated by charges that Hanoi had recently begun enforcing discriminatory commercial regulations aimed at the ethnic Chinese business community in Ho Chi Minh City (formerly Saigon). Hanoi accused Peking of siding with Cambodia (q.v.) in its frontier war with Vietnam. In May, as ethnic Chinese refugees streamed northward across the border, China reduced its economic and technical aid to Vietnam. Throughout the summer and fall, the two sides haggled over procedures for the repatriation of the ethnic Chinese, but could reach no agreement.

The official Chinese press charged that the root of the trouble was the rapid growth of Soviet influence in Vietnam. China accused the Russians of feeding Vietnamese ambitions for regional hegemony and of attempting to extend the Soviet presence in Southeast Asia.

Peking stepped up its diplomatic offensive against the Soviets in late summer when Premier Hua made an unprecedented trip to Rumania, Yugoslavia, and Iran. During the trip, which lasted from Aug. 16 to Sept. 1, Hua launched sharp propaganda attacks on Moscow. The visits reestablished a Chinese foothold in Eastern Europe following the severance of relations with Albania (q.v.) earlier in the year.

Another example of diplomatic fence mending was the ratification, on Oct. 23, of the historic Japan-China Peace Treaty, a ten-year pact which binds the two nations to settle all disputes peace-

Passengers disembark in Canton, China, after traveling by hovercraft from Hong Kong. Ferry service between the two cities resumed in November for the first time since 1949, when the Communists took over the mainland.

fully. Both nations pledged to oppose hegemony in Asia by any country. Moscow viewed the new treaty apprehensively, fearing a Chinese-Japanese alliance against the Kremlin.

A Death. Deaths during 1978 included that of Lo Jui-ching (Aug. 3 at 72). He was a former minister of public security who was purged during the late 1960's but rehabilitated in 1975.

See STATISTICS OF THE WORLD.   T.L.K.

CHINA, REPUBLIC OF. See TAIWAN.

CIVIL RIGHTS AND CIVIL LIBERTIES. In 1978 the ability of the United States to alter the human rights policies of other nations was sharply tested. At home the principle of affirmative action to help disadvantaged minorities was upheld, but "reverse discrimination" against Whites continued to be an issue, and minorities feared that economic concerns would produce a lessened commitment to the securing of their basic rights. In the Southwest the growing population of Mexican-Americans demanded review of cases of alleged police brutality. And in many localities across the nation, the question of homosexual rights was put to the voters, with mixed results.

International Human Rights. In July world attention was focused on trials of dissidents in the Soviet Union, the most prominent being that of Anatoly Shcharansky, who was convicted of high treason. The Soviet crackdown on dissenters touched off a storm of international protest. The insistence of the U.S. on publicizing human rights violations—"the soul of our foreign policy," according to President Jimmy Carter—put strains on U.S.-Soviet relations, but apparently bore some fruit, since Jewish emigration from the U.S.S.R. was allowed to increase during 1978.

There was increasing criticism, however, of the selectivity of the U.S. human rights policy. Rather than withholding aid from specific countries with alleged human rights violations, such as Nicaragua, South Korea, and Paraguay, Congress voted for a percentage reduction in foreign military assistance.

Soviet-bloc nations and groups such as the British-based human rights organization Amnesty International accused the U.S. itself of detaining political prisoners. They cited the Wilmington Ten, a group of civil rights activists who had been found guilty in 1972 of fire-bombing a grocery store during racial disturbances in Wilmington, N.C. In 1978 the U.S. Justice Department filed a court brief in support of the activists' contention that they had been denied a fair trial.

The Bakke Case. The most significant civil rights action of the year was the U.S. Supreme Court's June ruling in the "reverse discrimination" lawsuit brought by Allan P. Bakke. Bakke, a 38-year-old

A Ku Klux Klansman and a black citizen go their own way on Main Street, Tupelo, Miss., in June. Klansmen and a civil rights group, the United League of North Mississippi, were gathering for rival marches that took place without major violence.

white engineer, challenged the special admissions program of the medical school of the University of California at Davis, claiming that the reservation of sixteen places for minority students unlawfully denied him admission. The Supreme Court declared the special admissions program unlawful and Bakke was ordered admitted to medical school, but the principle of giving special consideration to minorities in school admission policies was upheld. (See EDUCATION.) The Bakke decision left unanswered many questions about the permissible limits of affirmative action. One such question was addressed in a July ruling that upheld a legal decree requiring the American Telephone and Telegraph Co. to hire more Blacks and women. In this case the Court unanimously approved an affirmative action program even though it conflicted with union seniority systems. Further clarification was expected from the Court in 1979 decisions.

The Carter Administration. The Administration received mixed reviews for its civil rights efforts. Although President Carter was considered more sensitive to civil rights concerns than former Presidents Richard M. Nixon or Gerald R. Ford, he still proved more conservative than civil rights activists had anticipated.

On the positive side, Carter took what he called "the single most important action to improve civil rights in the past decade," by reorganizing and consolidating federal efforts against discrimination in hiring and promotions. The Equal Employment Opportunity Commission became the point agency for ensuring evenhanded practices among public and private employers, and the Labor Department became the central authority for ensuring that all federal contractors comply with antidiscrimination laws. The reorganization plan was generally praised by civil rights and women's groups, who felt that a better coordinated federal effort against discrimination would result.

Facing an issue that had caused consternation among civil liberties groups, Carter supported and signed legislation passed in October outlawing most warrantless government searches and wiretaps conducted in the U.S. for national security purposes.

The Administration also supported the congressional effort to write charters specifying the functions and scope of the Federal Bureau of Investigation and the Central Intelligence Agency (CIA).

Of Mice and Censors

The cartoon mouse was obviously not responsible for the words that were put in his mouth by the advertising men. But they got him banned from television in South Africa in June. The state-owned South African Broadcasting Co. apparently felt that a line in a commercial for a Walt Disney film was sacrilegious. "Where possible," they said in their admonition to the film company, "the phrase 'Holy Mackerel!' should be avoided." The Disney mouse's response to being censored was not recorded, but we hope that it wasn't "Holy Mackerel!" since the South Africans said that such "repetition could create a negative reaction."

quiring employers to include pregnancy disability in comprehensive health insurance plans, although the abortion procedure was largely excluded.

U.S. Rights Groups. It was a year of fragmentation and disappointment among the major civil rights and civil liberties groups, which suffered from increased costs and reduced public support. At the sixty-ninth annual convention of the National Association for the Advancement of Colored People in July, Executive Director Benjamin L. Hooks expressed the sentiment of many black leaders that Whites would use the Bakke decision to backslide on civil rights commitments.

Speaking for the Black Leadership Forum, a coalition of sixteen civil rights, political, and business organizations, National Urban League President Vernon E. Jordan, Jr., warned in December of urban unrest if Blacks and other minorities had to bear the burden of the Administration's infla-

And in another action praised by civil rights groups, the Justice Department recommended passage of a law prohibiting surprise police raids on newsrooms. Such raids were authorized in a May decision of the U.S. Supreme Court.

On the negative side, the Administration prosecuted former CIA operative Frank Snepp for breaching his contractual obligation to submit a book manuscript for prepublication review. The action, which deprived Snepp of royalties due him for a book he wrote critical of CIA tactics in South Vietnam, was regarded by civil liberties groups as a major infringement on the free speech rights of government employees.

In assessing the Administration's overall civil rights record after eighteen months, the Leadership Conference on Civil Rights stated: "President Carter has made little use of the moral influence of his office to further public understanding of continuing denials of opportunity and to rally public support for effective civil rights enforcement."

Congress. Civil rights issues, on the whole, were not prominent in Congress in 1978. In August the Senate passed a constitutional amendment giving full voting representation to the District of Columbia. In September the Senate and House of Representatives defeated amendments that would have restricted federal funds used for busing. In October proponents of the Equal Rights Amendment won a major victory when Congress agreed to allow thirty-nine additional months for its ratification; see WOMEN. On another divisive women's issue, Congress maintained the status quo on abortion, banning most federally funded abortions for poor women. A bill was also passed re-

Comedian George Carlin talks to newsmen in Los Angeles after the U.S. Supreme Court ruled on July 3 that the Federal Communications Commission could restrict the broadcast of "patently offensive" language. A recorded Carlin routine about "seven dirty words" was the catalyst in the case.

CIVIL RIGHTS AND CIVIL LIBERTIES

tion-fighting effort. Carter responded by canceling a proposed $2 billion budget cutback in federal job-funding and other social welfare programs.

The American Civil Liberties Union (ACLU) began to mend its internal disagreements and recoup its financial losses caused by its unpopular defense of the National Socialist Party's right to hold a rally in Skokie, Ill. After ACLU lawyers finally gained court approval for the gathering, Nazi leaders switched their location to Marquette Park in Chicago. The rally, held July 9, attracted about twenty-five Nazis and several thousand onlookers, some of whom exchanged insults and punches.

Other Court Decisions. In the delicate balance between freedom of the press and a defendant's right to a fair trial, courts continued to favor defendants. In the most prominent clash between First and Sixth Amendment rights, the New York *Times* was fined $285,000 and reporter Myron A. Farber spent forty days in jail for refusing to turn over voluminous notes subpoenaed during the murder trial of a New Jersey surgeon, Mario E. Jascalevich; *see* CRIME AND LAW ENFORCEMENT. The Supreme Court refused to review Farber's contempt conviction. It also ruled against press rights in June when it ruled that newsmen need not be given special access to jails and other government facilities.

In an obscenity case, the Court upheld the government's right to ban "patently offensive" words on radio. The majority opinion argued for greater restraints on broadcasters' freedom of speech than on print journalists'. The High Court also reversed a 1961 decision and made cities liable for civil rights violations.

Homosexual Rights. Homosexual or gay rights advocates in California adopted low-key, broad-based tactics to defeat a proposition in the November election that would have prohibited avowed homosexuals from teaching in public schools. Also in November, voters in Seattle

turned back an attempt to repeal a law forbidding discrimination based on sexual preference. But in the spring, gay rights ordinances had been repealed by voters in St. Paul, Minn., Eugene, Oreg., and Wichita, Kans. And in Dade County, Fla., where voters had rejected gay rights in a bitter 1977 contest, a broad equal-opportunity measure was defeated in November. At year's end, thirty-nine municipalities had gay rights ordinances, including a strong one passed by the Berkeley, Calif. city council that imposed cash penalties on offenders.

The military slightly softened its view toward homosexuals in 1978. Veterans dismissed for homosexuality could now apply for retroactive honorable discharges. And a federal court of appeals ruled in December that homosexuality alone, without "some reasoned explanation," was insufficient grounds for dismissal from the armed services.

Mexican-Americans. A growing minority, Americans of Mexican descent, voiced demands for equal rights and equal treatment under the law. Hispanic leaders alleged that an "epidemic" of police brutality was depriving Mexican-Americans of their civil rights throughout the Southwest. Several cases prompted requests for federal prosecution of offenders handed light sentences in lower courts. In one of the most publicized of these cases, the Justice Department announced in July that it would not prosecute Dallas police officer Darrell Cain, who had been sentenced to five years for the 1973 murder of a 12-year-old Mexican-American burglary suspect.   D.Ca.

COIN COLLECTING, *or* NUMISMATICS. The production of a new dollar coin and legislation authorizing the United States Treasury to mint small gold medallions were the stories exciting coin collectors in 1978.

Susan B. Anthony Dollar. On Oct. 10, U.S. President Jimmy Carter signed the Susan B. Anthony Dollar Act of 1978. Treasury and mint officials expressed hope that the new coin would reduce de-

New dollar coins bearing on the obverse the likeness of U.S. suffragist leader Susan B. Anthony (1820–1906) will enter circulation in July, 1979. The design on the reverse symbolizes the Apollo 11 lunar landing.

mand for $1 bills, currently the largest single product of the Bureau of Engraving and Printing. Although the new dollar coin will be more expensive to produce than its paper counterpart, its lifetime in circulation is estimated at twenty years—as against the mere eighteen months a normal dollar bill survives. Should the public accept the new coin, the U.S. government could save as much as $30,000,000 in annual production costs.

In authorizing the new coin, Congress made the first size reduction in U.S. coinage since the large cent was replaced in 1857. The biggest deterrent to circulation of the current Eisenhower dollar had been its large size (38.1 mm, or 1½ in.) and weight (22.68 g, nearly an ounce). In contrast, the Anthony dollar will be only 26.5 mm (less than 1¼ in.) in diameter—slightly larger than the quarter—and will weigh only 8.1 g (about ¼ oz.).

The design of the coin caused considerable controversy. Its reverse will be identical to that of the Eisenhower dollar; but for the obverse, mint officials had originally supported a personification of Liberty, who had appeared on all earlier dollar coins except for the Eisenhower dollar. However, feminists and others argued that since all other U.S. coins portray distinguished men of history, any female appearing on a coin should also be an actual historical figure. Susan B. Anthony, the 19th-century suffragist, was the final choice.

Plans called for the new coin to be struck as soon as galvanos—large master sculptures from which dies are duplicated—could be prepared. The coin will be stockpiled until July, 1979, when it will be released for general circulation.

Gold Medallions. Starting Oct. 1, 1979, the U.S. Treasury is authorized to begin minting small gold medallions to honor famous American artists, writers, and performers. Two new medallions are to be issued annually between 1980 and 1984; the first set, scheduled for sale in 1980, will honor painter Grant Wood and contralto Marian Anderson. Each medallion will have either one ounce or one-half ounce of gold. The intent of Congress, in authorizing the series, was not only to commemorate outstanding artists but also to enable the average American to purchase gold as a possible hedge against inflation. W.E.M.

COLOMBIA. After twenty years of coalition rule, in which Liberals and Conservatives had alternately held power in Colombia, a hotly contested election on June 4, 1978, resulted in the narrow victory of the Liberal presidential candidate, Julio César Turbay Ayala.

The coalition, known as the National Front, had given Colombia a degree of stability rare in Latin America. But it had also alienated a large segment of the population; fewer than 40 percent of the electorate voted in June. Turbay and his Conservative opponent, Belisario Betancur Cuartas, had waged a bitter campaign of mutual denunciation. Turbay was charged with trafficking in drugs, and the incumbent government, which sent troops to patrol the streets during the election, was accused of fraud and mismanagement and of illegally influencing the election. Both sides claimed victory, until a recount showed a slim margin of 140,000 votes for Turbay. The new president, who took office in August beneath a cloud of suspicion and public disaffection, did promise to include Conservatives in his cabinet.

Turbay also faced continuing crime and violence through the months that followed, including bombings, three dozen political kidnappings, labor unrest, and nearly 50,000 unsolved robberies in Bogotá alone. Much of the violence appeared to be the work of leftist guerrilla groups. Another source of potential trouble for the new government was soaring inflation, despite the increase in the exports of coffee and other products.

See STATISTICS OF THE WORLD. J.N.G.

COLORADO. *See* STATISTICS OF THE WORLD.

COMMONWEALTH OF NATIONS. The curiously diverse membership of the Commonwealth of Nations grew to thirty-nine in 1978 with the addition to its ranks of three newly independent countries. Throughout the year, the Commonwealth's major concerns were economic.

At the opening ceremonies of the 1978 Commonwealth Games, held in Edmonton, Canada, in August, members of the home team wave their Stetsons in a salute to Queen Elizabeth II, as Prince Philip waves back.

COMMONWEALTH OF NATIONS

Conferences. A meeting of ministers from thirty-two Commonwealth countries was held in London in April. The major item on the agenda was a proposed common fund to stabilize the price of raw materials. At earlier international conferences, the industrialized nations had agreed with the developing world that such a fund was necessary. But at London, a wide divergence of opinion emerged on how it should operate.

The industrialized countries, including Great Britain itself, wanted the financing of the fund to come from commodity associations and borrowings from the capital market supported by government guarantees. However, the developing countries, by and large, thought the fund should be financed by commodity associations and government subscription. The industrialized nations called for "realism" about the size and nature of the fund. They contended that it should not duplicate the operations of existing institutions such as the World Bank, and they disputed the Third World view that the fund should finance measures other than the stockpiling of buffer supplies of commodities. These complex issues were not resolved, but all sides agreed that negotiations on the common fund should continue at the earliest possible time in other international forums.

The 1978 meeting of Commonwealth finance ministers was held in Montréal in September. Among other things, the developing countries complained of the slow pace of progress on the common fund and the decline—on the basis of percentage of gross national product—of economic aid from the industrialized nations. Ministers from the developed Commonwealth countries agreed to work for a reversal of this trend. Both sides agreed that the World Bank's capital resources should be increased substantially and that the bank should increase its lending to the developing world.

The first regional meeting of Commonwealth nations took place in Sydney, Australia, in February. Leaders of twelve nations of the Asian and Pacific region met for four days and discussed such matters as international cooperation to improve the world economic order. Prime Minister Malcolm Fraser of Australia hoped that the conference would issue a statement critical of the restrictive trade policies of the European Community, but the other leaders were unwilling to do so. Some of them, however, took advantage of the occasion to criticize Australia's trade barriers.

New Members. Three British dependencies gained their independence during the year—the Solomon Islands, Tuvalu, and Dominica—and all three opted to join the Commonwealth.

A 900-mi.-long archipelago in the Western Pa-

cific, the Solomon Islands—the scene of bitter fighting between the United States and Japan during World War II—became independent on July 7. Prince Richard, Duke of Gloucester, represented Queen Elizabeth II at the ceremonies. About 90 percent of the population of nearly 200,000 are Melanesians; the chief resources of the islands are fish, timber, copra, and minerals. The Solomons, a British protectorate since 1893, chose to become a constitutional monarchy, with the queen as head of state. Named to serve as prime minister was Peter Kenilorea, and as governor-general, Baddeley Devesi. The Solomons became the 150th member of the United Nations on Sept. 19.

At a constitutional conference in London in February, it was agreed that Tuvalu—formerly the Ellice Islands—would become independent during 1978. Although its name means "cluster of eight," Tuvalu is made up of nine islands, 10 sq. mi. of land scattered across 500,000 sq.mi. in the southwest Pacific. The population numbers about 6500, almost entirely of Polynesian origin. They attain a reasonable standard of living by intensive exploitation of the sea and by sending their young men abroad to work and to return some of their earnings. On Sept. 30, Tuvalu became a constitutional monarchy, with Queen Elizabeth as its monarch and Toalipi Lauti as its prime minister. The queen's sister, Princess Margaret, was to represent her at the independence ceremony but became ill with a fever and was evacuated by a military plane.

On Nov. 2, Dominica—the largest of the Windward Islands in the eastern Caribbean—became an independent republic governed by a democratically elected parliament and a premier, Patrick John. The population of 80,000, chiefly of African or mixed European-African extraction, is largely Roman Catholic and speaks a French patois. Economically, the tiny new country will be dependent on the export of bananas and citrus fruit, as well as on substantial British aid. Dominica joined the U.N. on Dec. 18, 1978.

On Dec. 7, Great Britain agreed to grant independence to the Gilbert Islands, a Pacific neighbor of Tuvalu. The Gilberts are to take the name Kiribati when they become independent in July, 1979. In addition, a series of British Associated States in the Caribbean were expected to become independent in 1979 or soon thereafter. These include St. Lucia, St. Vincent, Antigua, and St. Kitts–Nevis.　　　　　　　　　　　R.J.C.

COMMUNICATIONS. In 1978 technological developments in telecommunications enhanced the telephone network, promised to speed up mail service, and added new options to the family television set and to earth satellites. The boundary

Technicians at Bell Laboratories demonstrate the Electronic Blackboard, which transmits handwritten messages for display on video monitors at distant locations. The key to the system is a pressure-sensitive chalkboard that transforms handwriting into a series of digital pulses for transmission over ordinary telephone lines.

between transmitting information and processing it in a computer became ever vaguer, and the whole way in which the United States regulates the communications industry came up for review. Many of these developments stemmed from the rapid evolution of semiconductor devices—a technology in which complex circuits are built into tiny packages, digital systems often replace analog systems, and electronic signals are strings of on-and-off pulses instead of continuously varying waveforms.

Telephones. One beneficiary of semiconductors is the telephone, which is becoming more convenient both to make and to use. For example, Bell Canada is trying out what it calls the E Phone, in which a mere 12 integrated circuits replace 120 electrical and electromechanical parts in the standard push-button phone. The E Phone uses digital signals not only to reproduce the caller's voice more faithfully but also to store telephone numbers in memory circuits and dial them automatically when requested. If the field test is successful, Bell Canada plans to phase out its standard push-button phone.

In telephone central offices the large digital switches that route calls to the right destination are also improving. In New York City the American Telephone and Telegraph Co. (AT&T) installed a new model called Electronic Switching System No. 4, which switches calls into and from the complicated international network faster and in greater volume than its predecessors.

Digital technology is also bringing new services into the home. Systems introduced during 1978

enable the standard television set to receive special video transmissions such as stock-market reports, foreign-language lessons, and adult-education courses. Viewers may obtain this information directly over the television set as a service. Alternatively, they may hook up the television set to a telephone, so that the set serves merely as a display device for the telephone information.

They're Harder to Remember, Too

The Manhattan telephone directory appeared in the fall, right on schedule. But in the 1978–79 book there was a difference: no letters at all, just numbers. Ma Bell had decided to complete her institution of what she called an "all-digit information system." All well and good, but this does raise some questions. Will the John O'Hara novel henceforth be known as *28-8*, rather than *Butterfield 8*? And what of the Glenn Miller recording of "Pennsylvania 6-5000"? Who wants to jitterbug to "736-5000"?

COMMUNICATIONS

Electronic Mail. The possibility of sending people letters, photographs, or drawings by means of electronics has been discussed for a long time. The basic technique involves converting each document into strings of digital pulses, transmitting these by telephone or satellite to their destination, and then reconverting them to their original format. Western Union Telegraph Co. gave a big boost to this idea in 1978 by starting up a system for electronically transmitting bills and other computer-generated mass mailings to central post offices. Delivery to the final destination takes two days at most. The U.S. Postal Service began similar experiments.

An even bigger development in this area was AT&T's proposal for an Advanced Communications Service to serve the "office of the future." Just about all the information-generating equipment in a typical business office would be accommodated by special telephone connections, so that any one office system could "talk" to similarly equipped systems in other offices. The Bell System would use the present telephone network to implement the service. Many objections were immediately raised by those who felt that such a business lay outside Bell's already privileged monopoly position.

Regulatory Matters. While arguments raged over what AT&T and other communications companies should or should not be doing, the very law that has governed U.S. communications policy since 1934 was under attack. The revised Communications Act of 1978 proposed sweeping legislative changes and attacked the structure of AT&T, particularly its ownership of a manufacturing subsidiary, Western Electric Co. The bill also proposed to reorganize the Federal Communications Commission (FCC), the government body responsible for regulating and controlling the communications industry. The year was spent in negotiations and hearings on the detailed provisions of the bill, but no new law resulted.

Another important regulatory matter involved preparations for the 1979 World Administrative Radio Conference. Such a conference is held once every twenty years to decide which countries and communications services get what portion of the broadcast spectrum for their exclusive use during the following two decades. The 1979 meeting promised to be the scene of much controversy between the emerging and the developed nations over just what constitutes each bloc's fair share of that most finite of resources—operating frequencies.

Satellites. Satellites advanced rapidly in 1978. Again, digital technology was the watchword, as designers of both commercial and military satellites rushed to exploit the new integrated semiconductor circuits. The National Aeronautics and Space Administration, for one, began to study designs for satellites that would do more than act as big amplifiers in the sky. The new versions would also make computerlike decisions on how to handle messages and where to send them. Such "smart" satellites were expected to be very common in the near future.

International Business Machines Corp. and its partners, Comsat General Corp. and the Aetna Insurance Co., continued their efforts to get satellites ready for their joint business venture, Satellite Business System (SBS). Geared to use by large companies for their internal communications, the SBS service would employ a roof antenna to receive satellite transmissions. The work was expected to bear fruit in 1980.

Another likely competitor in the office communications market is Xerox Corp. The communications network proposed by Xerox in 1978 uses both satellite and microwave radio transmissions. Messages would be relayed from an office electronic terminal to a relatively inexpensive rooftop microwave antenna, and then beamed by microwave radio to a multisubscriber collection antenna. Only then would the information be sent to an earth station for satellite transmission to a distant earth station, where the message-handling process would be reversed. One problem with the proposed system is that the microwave portion of the spectrum that Xerox wants to use is not at present allocated for such purposes, and the FCC must first give its permission.

Integrated Optics. In principle, integrated optical circuits can convey signals from place to place much faster, over many more frequencies simultaneously, and no more expensively than electronic circuits. They are particularly efficient when combined with transmission lines made of optical fibers—long glass or plastic fibers that transmit light much as copper wire transmits electricity. In practice, however, transmitters and receivers of optical frequencies are still hard to design. Nevertheless, in 1978 both Bell Laboratories in the U.S. and Nippon Electric Co. in Japan produced various components that brought optical "radios" much closer to reality. Nippon's filters and other devices use glass rods and lenses, whereas Bell's system deposits layers of materials on a base to create filters, switches, and amplifiers.

Fiber Optics. So many advances were made in fiber-optic technology in 1978 that no area of electronics now seems likely to escape its impact. Fiber-optic cables and circuits began to appear in industrial-control processes, computers, closed-circuit television, telephone networks, and ships and planes. Fiber-optic links were also used to connect the antenna of a satellite ground station to a color television distribution system, and to illuminate a car's instrument panel from a single light source. The military was especially interested because fiber-optic devices resist electronic eavesdropping and cannot be jammed.

The great advantage of fiber optics for direct transmissions became obvious when the Nippon Telegraph and Telephone Public Corp. announced the successful test of a practical communications system linking two points 53 km (33 mi.) apart by a single fiber-optic cable without intermediate amplifiers. Such a length is unheard of in conventional electronics, and Nippon Telegraph expects to reach even greater distances.

Finally, in a move that was expected by many (but not so soon), Bell Laboratories introduced a telephone totally powered by light energy. The light comes through a fiber-optic cable from the central office to the telephone. To achieve this breakthrough, Bell scientists had to redesign some of the internal parts of the telephone. Their achievement, although still in the research stage, removed a major stumbling block from the use of the telephone as a home or office link to all kinds of communications services. Standard telephones, hooked up by copper wire, can only handle a limited range of frequencies without special techniques. In the new fiber-optic cable phone, this limitation is removed because the fiber can handle all the frequencies needed for applications in the foreseeable future.

See also RADIO AND TELEVISION BROADCASTING. H.H.

COMMUNISM. The Communist world was pulled and tugged in diverse directions in 1978.

Internal Changes. The most remarkable evolution in any Communist nation took place in the People's Republic of China. Following the death of Mao Tse-tung and the purge of the radical "Gang of Four" in 1976, China's new leaders had embarked on an ambitious program of national development. At a meeting of the National People's Congress in late February and early March, Premier Hua Kuo-feng stressed that "four modernizations"—industrial, agricultural, scientific-technological, and military—were the country's main goal.

To achieve modernization by the year 2000, the Communist Party dropped many of Mao's egalitarian policies. Elite schools were established. Promising youths were permitted to enter college without service in the countryside, and school examinations were emphasized. In factories and on communes, managers restored bonuses and material incentives in order to encourage harder work. There were signs of a loosening of China's system of stern internal controls. Equally important, China deemphasized self-reliance as a national policy and actively sought help from foreign governments, businessmen, and technicians.

Shifting Relationships. The Albanian government was thoroughly disenchanted with China's new course. Albania kept up a steady drumroll of criticism about China, until Chinese patience finally gave out. In July, Peking announced it was suspending further aid to Albania, which had been a longtime ally.

In Asia, two Communist neighbors became in-

Marksmen guard Cambodia's border with Vietnam during the summer. China sided with Cambodia and the Soviet Union backed Vietnam in the conflict between these two Communist nations of Southeast Asia.

creasingly bitter rivals. After its hard-won victory in 1975, Vietnam's Communist regime was intent on remaining independent of pressure from neighboring China. The Hanoi government also hoped to dominate Cambodia, which looked to China for support. At the same time, Vietnam wove ever-closer ties with the Soviet Union. The two nations signed a friendship treaty in November that was virtually a military alliance. Many Western observers believed that the military conflict between Vietnam and Cambodia was thus becoming a "proxy war" between the Soviet Union and China.

Vietnam's warm relationship with the Russians only worsened the Sino-Soviet dispute. Chinese journals repeatedly blasted the Soviet Union for seeking "hegemony" in Asia. The Soviets replied in kind. Ill feelings between the two countries ran so high that in May there was a military incident along the Sino-Soviet border.

China, meanwhile, worked at cementing friendships in the Soviets' own backyard. The Chinese exchanged numerous delegations with both Yugoslavia and Rumania. In May, Rumanian President Nicolae Ceauşescu made a state visit to Peking. This was followed in August by Hua Kuo-feng's journey to Rumania and Yugoslavia. Hua's trip marked the first time a Chinese Communist head of state had ever visited Eastern Europe, and the Soviet government was openly disturbed.

Nor did the Chinese neglect the major non-Communist powers. China and Japan ratified a historic peace treaty in October, and the United States and China announced on Dec. 15 their agreement to normalize relations at the beginning of 1979.

The Soviet Bloc. Although Russian-dominated Eastern Europe remained quiet in 1978, there were signs of strain. Ten years after the Soviet invasion of Czechoslovakia, citizens of that nation remained sullen over the Russian presence. The election of a Polish Roman Catholic pope in October caused a groundswell of nationalist—and religious—feeling in Poland.

Rumania persisted in its role as Warsaw Pact maverick. At a summit conference held in Moscow in November, President Ceauşescu resisted Soviet demands for higher military spending. Ceauşescu also refused to go along with Soviet efforts to transform the Warsaw Pact into an alliance aimed in part against China.

Eurocommunism. The Communist parties of France, Italy, and Spain pressed their efforts to develop a "Eurocommunism" free of Soviet interference and to compete in Western Europe's political arenas. Their successes were limited in 1978. France's Communist Party waged an unsuccess-

ful campaign in a March national election. Originally committed to working with the Socialist Party, the Communists began to attack their ally when it became clear that they would be the junior—not senior—partner of the team. As a result of this infighting, the two French leftist parties lost the parliamentary elections to a Center-Right coalition.

The Italian Communist Party was hurt by the kidnapping of former Christian Democrat Premier Aldo Moro by Red Brigades terrorists in March. As part of a power-sharing accord with the ruling Christian Democrats, the Communists had agreed there would be no government compromise with the terrorists. When Moro was murdered by his abductors, both the efficacy of government policy and the wisdom of the Communists' commitment to it were questioned by the party's supporters.

At a congress in April, the Spanish Communist Party dropped the descriptive word "Leninist" from its label. The Spanish leftists thereby hoped to make the point that their party was democratic. Despite that move, public backing for the Spanish Communist Party remained small.

See articles on individual countries mentioned; see also COUNCIL FOR MUTUAL ECONOMIC ASSISTANCE; WARSAW TREATY ORGANIZATION.   F.W.

COMORO ISLANDS. See STATISTICS OF THE WORLD. See also AFRICA.

CONGO, REPUBLIC OF, in full PEOPLE'S REPUBLIC OF THE CONGO. Dire economic conditions, made worse by a stagnant export rate and worldwide inflation, continued to occupy the Congo's military government in 1978. After issuing a warning in May of the dangerous state of the Congolese economy, President Joachim Yhombi Opango imposed drastic economic cutbacks. First, government expenditures for salaries and student grants were reduced by 23 percent, and a tax was imposed on gasoline used for purposes of tourism. Then in June, Yhombi Opango announced a "national solidarity fund": anyone earning more than $120 a month would be required to contribute 20 percent of his income to the fund; anyone earning less was to contribute 10 percent. These and other measures taken earlier were designed to transfer income from expatriates and the privileged classes and provide funds for rural development. These innovations, as well as his efforts to reduce corruption and inefficiency in the government, won Yhombi Opango considerable popular support. They also helped him survive an August attempt by former officials to overthrow his reform government.

In February the new government executed ten persons convicted of participating in the March 1977, assassination of President Marien Ngouabi

Former Vice-President Hubert H. Humphrey died in January; his wife Muriel succeeded him as U.S. Senator from Minnesota. Here on Feb. 5, the day she took the oath of office, are (left to right) Vice-President Walter Mondale, Mrs. Humphrey, Sen. Wendell Anderson (D, Minn.), majority leader Robert Byrd (D, W.Va.), and minority leader Howard Baker (R, Tenn.).

And in April the curfew imposed after Ngouabi's death was lifted.

See STATISTICS OF THE WORLD. J.T.S.

CONGRESS OF THE UNITED STATES. The 1978 session of the 95th Congress began slowly and ended with a rush of moderate legislation emerging from sometimes bitter compromise. No far-reaching measures were passed. Most observers agreed that special interest groups had a stronger influence than ever and that broader national interests rarely found a voice.

Membership. When the session convened on Jan. 19, the Democrats held 287 seats in the House of Representatives and the Republicans 146, with 2 vacancies. In the Senate, Democrats maintained a 60–38 edge; two vacancies arose a week before convening with the deaths of Hubert H. Humphrey (D, Minn.) and Lee Metcalf (D, Mont.). At adjournment on Oct. 15, the House lineup stood at 285 Democrats, 146 Republicans, and 4 vacancies. In the Senate, 62 Democrats faced 38 Republicans. Both parties retained their leaders from the previous session; see DEMOCRATIC PARTY; REPUBLICAN PARTY.

Legislation. The longest-debated measure of the year, the five-part energy bill, passed both houses in a hastily assembled compromise in the last hours of the session. It imposed new taxes on fuel-wasting cars; provided for the gradual lifting of federal price controls on natural gas; offered tax credits for home insulation; and promoted the conversion of large industries from oil usage to coal. Another eleventh-hour compromise produced an $18.7 billion tax-reduction bill that omitted many reforms proposed earlier by President Jimmy Carter.

Also in October, Congress passed an ethics bill requiring all high-ranking federal employees, including congressmen and Supreme Court justices, to make annual public disclosures of their income. Another measure allowed airlines to alter routes and fares without federal approval. A civil-service reform bill, part of Carter's plan to streamline the federal bureaucracy, provided for salary incentives and more efficient means of hiring and firing. The deadline for the ratification of the Equal Rights Amendment was extended from March, 1979, to June, 1982. Another proposed constitutional amendment, passed in August and sent to the state legislatures for ratification, would give the District of Columbia the same representation as a state in Congress.

Four bills passed by Congress were vetoed by President Carter. In September the House upheld Carter's veto of a $37 billion weapons authorization bill which included a $2 billion nuclear aircraft carrier, and in October Carter courted Republican support to sustain his veto of a $10.2 billion public works, or "pork barrel," bill; see PRESIDENT OF THE UNITED STATES.

Social issues made few appearances on the 1978

Seven rabbis journeyed from New York City to Washington, D.C., in May, to handcuff themselves to a White House fence. They were protesting the sale of American jet fighters to Egypt and Saudi Arabia. The package deal—which included arms for Israel—had been approved by the Senate in a 54–44 vote.

to furnish up to $1.65 billion in federal loan guarantees for New York City.

Among the year's legislative failures were welfare reform and national health insurance, both tabled by the Administration in a midyear trimming of legislative goals. Congress did not go along with Carter-sponsored measures that would have provided for congressional campaign financing, hospital-cost containment, labor-law reform, a consumer affairs agency, and a new federal department of education.

Foreign Policy. The Carter administration achieved its clearest congressional successes in the field of foreign affairs. After two months of debate, the Senate ratified two treaties in March and April turning over control of the Panama Canal to Panama by the year 2000 and guaranteeing the canal's neutrality thereafter. In May, Congress was persuaded to approve a package sale of U.S. military aircraft to Israel, Egypt, and Saudi Arabia. And in August the embargo on U.S. arms sales to Turkey was lifted at the insistence of the Administration.

The New Congress. U.S. voters elected a new, 96th Congress on Nov. 7. The Republicans picked up a net gain of 3 Senate seats and 11 House seats, thus cutting the Democratic majorities in the forthcoming Congress to 59–41 in the Senate and 277–158 in the House. The 96th Congress, equipped with a mandate for budget cutting to ease inflation, was expected to be slightly more conservative than its predecessor.

See also CRIME AND LAW ENFORCEMENT: *Assassination Probes, Accused Congressmen;* ELECTIONS.

W.M.H.

agenda. A ban on most federally funded abortions, repeating the hotly debated wording of a 1977 ban, was attached to two appropriations bills passed by the House but not by the Senate. The mandatory retirement age for most U.S. workers was raised from 65 to 70. In July, Congress agreed

95th CONGRESS, 2nd SESSION (Jan. 19–Oct. 15, 1978)

Senators	Term Expires
ALABAMA	
John J. Sparkman (D)	1979
Maryon Pittman Allen (D)[1]	1979
ALASKA	
Ted Stevens (R)	1979
Mike Gravel (D)	1981
ARIZONA	
Barry Goldwater (R)	1981
Dennis DeConcini (D)	1983
ARKANSAS	
Kaneaster Hodges, Jr. (D)	1979
Dale Bumpers (D)	1981
CALIFORNIA	
Alan Cranston (D)	1981
S. I. Hayakawa (R)	1983
COLORADO	
Floyd K. Haskell (D)	1979
Gary Hart (D)	1981
CONNECTICUT	
Abraham Ribicoff (D)	1981
Lowell P. Weicker (R)	1983
DELAWARE	
William V. Roth (R)	1983
Joseph R. Biden (D)	1979

Senators	Term Expires
FLORIDA	
Lawton Chiles (D)	1983
Richard Stone (D)	1981
GEORGIA	
Herman E. Talmadge (D)	1981
Sam Nunn (D)	1979
HAWAII	
Daniel K. Inouye (D)	1981
Spark M. Matsunaga (D)	1983
IDAHO	
Frank Church (D)	1981
James A. McClure (R)	1979
ILLINOIS	
Charles H. Percy (R)	1979
Adlai E. Stevenson 3rd (D)	1981
INDIANA	
Birch Bayh (D)	1981
Richard G. Lugar (R)	1983
IOWA	
Dick Clark (D)	1979
John C. Culver (D)	1981
KANSAS	
James B. Pearson (R)	1979
Bob Dole (R)	1981

Senators	Term Expires
KENTUCKY	
Walter Huddleston (D)	1979
Wendell H. Ford (D)	1981
LOUISIANA	
Russell B. Long (D)	1981
J. B. Johnston (D)	1979
MAINE	
Edmund S. Muskie (D)	1983
William D. Hathaway (D)	1979
MARYLAND	
Charles Mathias (R)	1981
Paul S. Sarbanes (D)	1983
MASSACHUSETTS	
Edward M. Kennedy (D)	1983
Edward W. Brooke (R)	1979
MICHIGAN	
Robert P. Griffin (R)	1979
Donald W. Riegle, Jr. (D)	1983
MINNESOTA	
Muriel Humphrey (D)[2]	1979
Wendell R. Anderson (D)	1979
MISSISSIPPI	
James O. Eastland (D)	1979
John C. Stennis (D)	1983

MISSOURI
Thomas Eagleton (D)..........1981
John C. Danforth (R)..........1983
MONTANA
Paul Hatfield (D)[3]..........1979
John Melcher (D)..........1983
NEBRASKA
Carl T. Curtis (R)..........1979
Edward Zorinsky (D)..........1983
NEVADA
Howard W. Cannon (D)..........1983
Paul Laxalt (R)..............1981
NEW HAMPSHIRE
Thomas J. McIntyre (D)........1979
John A. Durkin (D)..........1981
NEW JERSEY
Clifford P. Case (R)..........1979
Harrison Williams (D)..........1983
NEW MEXICO
Pete V. Domenici (R)..........1979
Harrison H. Schmitt (R)..........1983
NEW YORK
Jacob K. Javits (R)..........1981
Daniel P. Moynihan (D)........1983
NORTH CAROLINA
Jesse A. Helms (R)..........1979
Robert Morgan (D)..........1981
NORTH DAKOTA
Milton R. Young (R)..........1981
Quentin N. Burdick (D)........1983
OHIO
John Glenn (D)..............1981
Howard M. Metzenbaum (D)....1983
OKLAHOMA
Henry L. Bellmon (R)..........1981
Dewey F. Bartlett (R)..........1979
OREGON
Mark O. Hatfield (R)..........1979
Bob Packwood (R)..........1981
PENNSYLVANIA
Richard Schweiker (R)..........1981
H. John Heinz 3rd (R)........1983
RHODE ISLAND
Claiborne Pell (D)..........1979
John H. Chafee (R)..........1983
SOUTH CAROLINA
Strom Thurmond (R)..........1979
Ernest F. Hollings (D)..........1981
SOUTH DAKOTA
George McGovern (D)........1981
James Abourezk (D)..........1979
TENNESSEE
Howard H. Baker (R)..........1979
James R. Sasser (D)..........1983
TEXAS
John G. Tower (R)..........1979
Lloyd M. Bentsen (D)..........1983
UTAH
Jake Garn (R)................1981
Orrin G. Hatch (R)..........1983
VERMONT
Robert T. Stafford (R)..........1983
Patrick J. Leahy (D)..........1981
VIRGINIA
Harry F. Byrd, Jr. (I)..........1983
William Lloyd Scott (R)........1979
WASHINGTON
Warren Magnuson (D)..........1981
Henry M. Jackson (D)..........1983
WEST VIRGINIA
Jennings Randolph (D)........1979
Robert C. Byrd (D)..........1983
WISCONSIN
William Proxmire (D)..........1983
Gaylord Nelson (D)..........1981
WYOMING
Clifford P. Hansen (R)..........1979
Malcolm Wallop (R)..........1983

Representatives

ALABAMA
1. Jack Edwards (R)
2. William L. Dickinson (R)
3. Bill Nichols (D)
4. Tom Bevill (D)
5. Ronnie G. Flippo (D)
6. John Buchanan (R)
7. Walter Flowers (D)
ALASKA
At large: Donald E. Young (R)
ARIZONA
1. John J. Rhodes (R)
2. Morris K. Udall (D)
3. Bob Stump (D)
4. Eldon D. Rudd (R)
ARKANSAS
1. Bill Alexander (D)
2. James G. Tucker, Jr. (D)
3. John P. Hammerschmidt (R)
4. Ray Thornton (D)
CALIFORNIA
1. Harold T. Johnson (D)
2. Don H. Clausen (R)
3. John E. Moss (D)
4. Robert L. Leggett (D)
5. John Burton (D)
6. Phillip Burton (D)
7. George Miller (D)
8. Ronald V. Dellums (D)
9. Fortney H. (Pete) Stark (D)
10. Don Edwards (D)
11. Leo J. Ryan (D)[4]
12. Paul N. (Pete) McCloskey, Jr. (R)
13. Norman Y. Mineta (D)
14. John J. McFall (D)
15. B. F. Sisk (D)
16. Leon E. Panetta (D)
17. John Krebs (D)
18. William M. Ketchum (R)[5]
19. Robert J. Lagomarsino (R)
20. Barry Goldwater, Jr. (R)
21. James C. Corman (D)
22. Carlos J. Moorhead (R)
23. Anthony C. Beilenson (D)
24. Henry A. Waxman (D)
25. Edward R. Roybal (D)
26. John Rousselot (R)
27. Robert K. Dornan (R)
28. Yvonne Brathwaite Burke (D)
29. Augustus F. (Gus) Hawkins (D)
30. George E. Danielson (D)
31. Charles H. Wilson (D)
32. Glenn M. Anderson (D)
33. Del Clawson (R)
34. Mark W. Hannaford (D)
35. Jim Lloyd (D)
36. George E. Brown, Jr. (D)
37. Shirley N. Pettis (R)
38. Jerry M. Patterson (D)
39. Charles E. Wiggins (R)
40. Robert E. Badham (R)
41. Bob Wilson (R)
42. Lionel Van Deerlin (D)
43. Clair W. Burgener (R)
COLORADO
1. Patricia Schroeder (D)
2. Timothy E. Wirth (D)
3. Frank E. Evans (D)
4. James P. (Jim) Johnson (R)
5. William L. Armstrong (R)
CONNECTICUT
1. William R. Cotter (D)
2. Christopher J. Dodd (D)
3. Robert N. Giaimo (D)
4. Stewart B. McKinney (R)
5. Ronald A. Sarasin (R)
6. Toby Moffett (D)

DELAWARE
At large: Thomas B. Evans, Jr. (R)
FLORIDA
1. Robert L.F. Sikes (D)
2. Don Fuqua (D)
3. Charles E. Bennett (D)
4. Bill Chappell, Jr. (D)
5. Richard Kelly (R)
6. C. W. Bill Young (R)
7. Sam M. Gibbons (D)
8. Andrew P. Ireland (D)
9. Louis Frey, Jr. (R)
10. L. A. (Skip) Bafalis (R)
11. Paul G. Rogers (D)
12. J. Herbert Burke (R)
13. William Lehman (D)
14. Claude D. Pepper (D)
15. Dante B. Fascell (D)
GEORGIA
1. Bo Ginn (D)
2. Dawson Mathis (D)
3. Jack Brinkley (D)
4. Elliott H. Levitas (D)
5. Wyche F. Fowler, Jr. (D)
6. John J. Flynt, Jr. (D)
7. Larry McDonald (D)
8. Billy Lee Evans (D)
9. Edgar L. Jenkins (D)
10. D. Douglas Barnard, Jr. (D)
HAWAII
1. Cecil Heftel (D)
2. Daniel K. Akaka (D)
IDAHO
1. Steven D. Symms (R)
2. George Hansen (R)
ILLINOIS
1. Ralph H. Metcalfe (D)[6]
2. Morgan F. Murphy (D)
3. Martin A. Russo (D)
4. Edward J. Derwinski (R)
5. John G. Fary (D)
6. Henry J. Hyde (R)
7. Cardiss Collins (D)
8. Dan Rostenkowski (D)
9. Sidney R. Yates (D)
10. Abner J. Mikva (D)
11. Frank Annunzio (D)
12. Philip M. Crane (R)
13. Robert McClory (R)
14. John N. Erlenborn (R)
15. Thomas J. Corcoran (R)
16. John B. Anderson (R)
17. George M. O'Brien (R)
18. Robert H. Michel (R)
19. Thomas F. Railsback (R)
20. Paul Findley (R)
21. Edward R. Madigan (R)
22. George E. Shipley (D)
23. Melvin Price (D)
24. Paul Simon (D)
INDIANA
1. Adam Benjamin, Jr. (D)
2. Floyd J. Fithian (D)
3. John Brademas (D)
4. J. Danforth Quayle (R)
5. Elwood Hillis (R)
6. David W. Evans (D)
7. John T. Myers (R)
8. David L. Cornwell (D)
9. Lee H. Hamilton (D)
10. Philip R. Sharp (D)
11. Andrew Jacobs, Jr. (D)
IOWA
1. James A.S. Leach (R)
2. Michael T. Blouin (D)
3. Charles E. Grassley (R)
4. Neal Smith (D)
5. Tom Harkin (D)
6. Berkley Bedell (D)
KANSAS
1. Keith G. Sebelius (R)

2. Martha Keyes (D)
3. Larry Winn, Jr. (R)
4. Daniel R. Glickman (D)
5. Joe Skubitz (R)

KENTUCKY
1. Carroll Hubbard, Jr. (D)
2. William H. Natcher (D)
3. Romano L. Mazzoli (D)
4. M. G. (Gene) Snyder (R)
5. Tim Lee Carter (R)
6. John Breckinridge (D)
7. Carl D. Perkins (D)

LOUISIANA
1. Robert L. Livingston, Jr. (R)
2. Corinne C. (Lindy) Boggs (D)
3. David C. Treen (R)
4. Joe D. Waggonner, Jr. (D)
5. Jerry Huckaby (D)
6. W. Henson Moore (R)
7. John B. Breaux (D)
8. Gillis W. Long (D)

MAINE
1. David F. Emery (R)
2. William S. Cohen (R)

MARYLAND
1. Robert E. Bauman (R)
2. Clarence D. Long (D)
3. Barbara A. Mikulski (D)
4. Marjorie S. Holt (R)
5. Gladys Noon Spellman (D)
6. Goodloe E. Byron (D)[7]
7. Parren J. Mitchell (D)
8. Newton I. Steers, Jr. (R)

MASSACHUSETTS
1. Silvio O. Conte (R)
2. Edward P. Boland (D)
3. Joseph D. Early (D)
4. Robert F. Drinan (D)
5. Paul E. Tsongas (D)
6. Michael J. Harrington (D)
7. Edward J. Markey (D)
8. Thomas P. O'Neill, Jr. (D)
9. John Joseph Moakley (D)
10. Margaret M. Heckler (R)
11. James A. Burke (D)
12. Gerry E. Studds (D)

MICHIGAN
1. John Conyers, Jr. (D)
2. Carl D. Pursell (R)
3. Garry E. Brown (R)
4. David A. Stockman (R)
5. Harold S. Sawyer (R)
6. Bob Carr (D)
7. Dale E. Kildee (D)
8. Bob Traxler (D)
9. Guy Vander Jagt (R)
10. Elford A. Cederberg (R)
11. Philip E. Ruppe (R)
12. David E. Bonior (D)
13. Charles C. Diggs, Jr. (D)
14. Lucien N. Nedzi (D)
15. William D. Ford (D)
16. John D. Dingell (D)
17. William M. Brodhead (D)
18. James J. Blanchard (D)
19. William S. Broomfield (R)

MINNESOTA
1. Albert H. Quie (R)
2. Tom Hagedorn (R)
3. Bill Frenzel (R)
4. Bruce F. Vento (D)
5. Donald M. Fraser (D)
6. Richard Nolan (D)
7. Arlan Stangeland (R)
8. James L. Oberstar (D)

MISSISSIPPI
1. Jamie L. Whitten (D)
2. David R. Bowen (D)
3. G. V. (Sonny) Montgomery (D)
4. Thad Cochran (R)
5. Trent Lott (R)

MISSOURI
1. William L. Clay (D)
2. Robert A. Young (D)
3. Richard A. Gephardt (D)
4. Ike Skelton (D)
5. Richard Bolling (D)
6. E. Thomas Coleman (R)
7. Gene Taylor (R)
8. Richard H. Ichord (D)
9. Harold L. Volkmer (D)
10. Bill D. Burlison (D)

MONTANA
1. Max Baucus (D)
2. Ron Marlenee (R)

NEBRASKA
1. Charles Thone (R)
2. John J. Cavanaugh (D)
3. Virginia Smith (R)

NEVADA
At large: Jim Santini (D)

NEW HAMPSHIRE
1. Norman E. D'Amours (D)
2. James C. Cleveland (R)

NEW JERSEY
1. James J. Florio (D)
2. William J. Hughes (D)
3. James J. Howard (D)
4. Frank Thompson, Jr. (D)
5. Millicent Fenwick (R)
6. Edwin B. Forsythe (R)
7. Andrew Maguire (D)
8. Robert A. Roe (D)
9. Harold C. Hollenbeck (R)
10. Peter W. Rodino, Jr. (D)
11. Joseph G. Minish (D)
12. Matthew J. Rinaldo (R)
13. Helen S. Meyner (D)
14. Joseph A. LeFante (D)
15. Edward J. Patten (D)

NEW MEXICO
1. Manuel Lujan, Jr. (R)
2. Harold Runnels (D)

NEW YORK
1. Otis G. Pike (D)
2. Thomas J. Downey (D)
3. Jerome A. Ambro (D)
4. Norman F. Lent (R)
5. John W. Wydler (R)
6. Lester L. Wolff (D)
7. Joseph P. Addabbo (D)
8. Benjamin S. Rosenthal (D)
9. James J. Delaney (D)
10. Mario Biaggi (D)
11. James H. Scheuer (D)
12. Shirley Chisholm (D)
13. Stephen J. Solarz (D)
14. Frederick W. Richmond (D)
15. Leo C. Zeferetti (D)
16. Elizabeth Holtzman (D)
17. John M. Murphy (D)
18. S. William Green (R)
19. Charles B. Rangel (D)
20. Theodore S. Weiss (D)
21. Robert Garcia (D)
22. Jonathan B. Bingham (D)
23. Bruce F. Caputo (R)
24. Richard L. Ottinger (D)
25. Hamilton Fish, Jr. (R)
26. Benjamin A. Gilman (R)
27. Matthew F. McHugh (D)
28. Samuel S. Stratton (D)
29. Edward W. Pattison (D)
30. Robert C. McEwen (R)
31. Donald J. Mitchell (R)
32. James M. Hanley (D)
33. William F. Walsh (R)
34. Frank Horton (R)
35. Barber B. Conable, Jr. (R)
36. John J. LaFalce (D)
37. Henry J. Nowak (D)
38. Jack Kemp (R)

39. Stanley N. Lundine (D)

NORTH CAROLINA
1. Walter B. Jones (D)
2. L. H. Fountain (D)
3. Charles O. Whitley, Sr. (D)
4. Ike F. Andrews (D)
5. Stephen L. Neal (D)
6. Richardson Preyer (D)
7. Charles Rose (D)
8. W. G. (Bill) Hefner (D)
9. James G. Martin (R)
10. James T. Broyhill (R)
11. V. Lamar Gudger (D)

NORTH DAKOTA
At large: Mark Andrews (R)

OHIO
1. Willis D. Gradison, Jr. (R)
2. Thomas A. Luken (D)
3. Charles W. Whalen, Jr. (R)
4. Tennyson Guyer (R)
5. Delbert L. Latta (R)
6. William H. Harsha (R)
7. Clarence J. Brown (R)
8. Thomas N. Kindness (R)
9. Thomas L. Ashley (D)
10. Clarence E. Miller (R)
11. J. William Stanton (R)
12. Samuel L. Devine (R)
13. Donald J. Pease (D)
14. John F. Seiberling (D)
15. Chalmers P. Wylie (R)
16. Ralph S. Regula (R)
17. John M. Ashbrook (R)
18. Douglas Applegate (D)
19. Charles J. Carney (D)
20. Mary Rose Oakar (D)
21. Louis Stokes (D)
22. Charles A. Vanik (D)
23. Ronald M. Mottl (D)

OKLAHOMA
1. James R. Jones (D)
2. Theodore M. Risenhoover (D)
3. Wesley W. Watkins (D)
4. Tom Steed (D)
5. Mickey Edwards (R)
6. Glenn English (D)

OREGON
1. Les AuCoin (D)
2. Al Ullman (D)
3. Robert Duncan (D)
4. James Weaver (D)

PENNSYLVANIA
1. Michael O. Myers (D)
2. Robert N.C. Nix (D)
3. Raymond F. Lederer (D)
4. Joshua Eilberg (D)
5. Richard T. Schulze (R)
6. Gus Yatron (D)
7. Robert W. Edgar (D)
8. Peter H. Kostmayer (D)
9. E. G. (Bud) Shuster (R)
10. Joseph M. McDade (R)
11. Daniel J. Flood (D)
12. John P. Murtha (D)
13. Lawrence Coughlin (R)
14. William S. Moorhead (D)
15. Fred B. Rooney (D)
16. Robert S. Walker (R)
17. Allen E. Ertel (D)
18. Doug Walgren (D)
19. William F. Goodling (R)
20. Joseph M. Gaydos (D)
21. John H. Dent (D)
22. Austin J. Murphy (D)
23. Joseph S. Ammerman (D)
24. Marc L. Marks (R)
25. Gary A. Myers (R)

RHODE ISLAND
1. Fernand J. St Germain (D)
2. Edward P. Beard (D)

SOUTH CAROLINA
1. Mendel J. Davis (D)
2. Floyd Spence (R)
3. Butler Derrick (D)
4. James R. Mann (D)
5. Kenneth L. Holland (D)
6. John W. Jenrette, Jr. (D)

SOUTH DAKOTA
1. Larry Pressler (R)
2. James Abdnor (R)

TENNESSEE
1. James H. Quillen (R)
2. John J. Duncan (R)
3. Marilyn Lloyd (D)
4. Albert Gore, Jr. (D)
5. Clifford Allen (D)[6]
6. Robin L. Beard (R)
7. Ed Jones (D)
8. Harold E. Ford (D)

TEXAS
1. Sam B. Hall, Jr. (D)
2. Charles Wilson (D)
3. James M. Collins (R)
4. Ray Roberts (D)
5. James A. Mattox (D)
6. Olin E. Teague (D)
7. Bill Archer (R)
8. Bob Eckhardt (D)

9. Jack Brooks (D)
10. J. J. (Jake) Pickle (D)
11. W. R. Poage (D)
12. James C. Wright, Jr. (D)
13. Jack Hightower (D)
14. John Young (D)
15. E. (Kika) de la Garza (D)
16. Richard C. White (D)
17. Omar Burleson (D)
18. Barbara Jordan (D)
19. George H. Mahon (D)
20. Henry B. Gonzalez (D)
21. Robert (Bob) Krueger (D)
22. Bob Gammage (D)
23. Abraham Kazen, Jr. (D)
24. Dale Milford (D)

UTAH
1. K. Gunn McKay (D)
2. Dan Marriott (R)

VERMONT
At large: James M. Jeffords (R)

VIRGINIA
1. Paul S. Trible, Jr. (R)
2. G. William Whitehurst (R)
3. David E. Satterfield 3rd (D)
4. Robert W. Daniel, Jr. (R)
5. W. C. (Dan) Daniel (D)
6. M. Caldwell Butler (R)
7. J. Kenneth Robinson (R)

8. Herbert E. Harris 2nd (D)
9. William C. Wampler (R)
10. Joseph L. Fisher (D)

WASHINGTON
1. Joel Pritchard (R)
2. Lloyd Meeds (D)
3. Don Bonker (D)
4. Mike McCormack (D)
5. Thomas S. Foley (D)
6. Norman D. Dicks (D)
7. John E. Cunningham (R)

WEST VIRGINIA
1. Robert H. Mollohan (D)
2. Harley O. Staggers (D)
3. John Slack (D)
4. Nick Joe Rahall 2nd (D)

WISCONSIN
1. Les Aspin (D)
2. Robert W. Kastenmeier (D)
3. Alvin Baldus (D)
4. Clement J. Zablocki (D)
5. Henry S. Reuss (D)
6. William A. Steiger (R)[9]
7. David R. Obey (D)
8. Robert J. Cornell (D)
9. Robert W. Kasten, Jr. (R)

WYOMING
At large: Teno Roncalio (D)

[1] Appointed June 8 to succeed her husband, James B. Allen, who died June 1.
[2] Appointed Jan. 25 to succeed her husband, Hubert H. Humphrey, who died Jan. 13.
[3] Appointed Jan. 22 to succeed Lee Metcalf, who died Jan. 12.
[4] Died Nov. 18.
[5] Died June 24.
[6] Died Oct. 10.
[7] Died Oct. 11.
[8] Died June 18.
[9] Died Dec. 4.

CONNECTICUT. *See* STATISTICS OF THE WORLD.

CONSTRUCTION. The U.S. construction industry had a good year in 1978, with total bidding volume up 14 percent from 1977, reaching $52.7 billion. But contractors were able to keep only part of the gain, because of rising costs and continued inflation. Building costs alone were up about 7 percent in 1978.

By the end of the year, contractors sensed a new industry slowdown, with demand for houses reduced by inflated prices and higher interest rates on home mortgage loans. The combined impact of reduced funding for public works projects and the new wage-price guidelines announced by U.S. President Jimmy Carter in October was expected to dampen construction starts and potential profits still further.

Construction Failures. The biggest construction tragedy of 1978, a year which saw many deaths from building accidents, was the collapse on April 27 of the scaffolding on a cooling tower project in Willow Island, W.Va. Fifty-one workers were killed. Separate investigations by the Occupational Safety and Health Administration (OSHA) and the National Bureau of Standards had not determined a single definite cause for the mishap by the end of the year, but lax safety procedures were thought to have been at least partly respon-

sible. OSHA itself had been criticized for not reinspecting the construction site after a March, 1977, inspection report had warned that improper use of the scaffolding might have "disastrous consequences."

Taxes. U.S. contractors and American construction workers on foreign sites had both good and bad tax news in 1978. The 10 percent investment tax credit was made permanent and extended to include rehabilitation of existing plant construction, which should mean increased projects for contractors in 1979. Moreover, U.S. construction workers and managers living abroad finally received some tax relief. In a revision of Internal Revenue Code Section 411, they were allowed to deduct housing, education, home leave, moving, and other costs from their gross income, and to claim an additional $5000 deduction in certain hardship posts, such as the Middle East; alternatively, they were permitted a total $20,000 exclusion from income. On the other hand, certain other tax concessions were dropped.

Tax credits for up to $2150 were allocated to contractors who build new homes using natural gas and solar heat and hot water. The reason for the program, implemented by Energy Secretary James R. Schlesinger, was that 60 percent of all new U.S. homes were still being built all-electric,

CONSTRUCTION

The cooling tower on Willow Island, St. Marys, W.Va., where fifty-one construction workers lost their lives on April 27. The tower was about one-third complete when its interior scaffolding collapsed. Safety violations were blamed for the disaster.

which the Administration considered a wasteful use of energy resources.

Materials. Cement shortages plagued contractors toward the end of 1978. As early as September, some cities began to reserve the use of concrete only for foundations, halting paving and many other projects. The shortage was most severe in the Midwest. Some cement masons in that area were reportedly working only 50 percent of the time.

A new material that can be used in paving instead of cement was developed by Nippon Kokan of Japan. Called Super Slag, the substance is made from steel mill furnace slag and slaked lime, and is said to increase in strength after paving takes place.

A new polystyrene foam construction material was also developed in 1978. If tests prove positive, the low-cost product will be used to stabilize

earth-fill structures such as berms, embankments, and dams.

International Competition. South Korean contractors continued to take work away from American and European firms. The main factor in the South Koreans' success is the use of low-cost labor. Among the contracts won by the South Koreans in 1978 was a $7 billion highway project tendered by Saudi Arabia. The South Koreans were winning half of all contracts on which they bid in the Middle East, according to *World Construction* magazine.

New Projects. Contractors from South Korea and almost every other major country geared up to compete for the multitude of new projects that China announced in 1978, although it seemed likely that the Chinese would mainly buy technology. Among the 120 new projects planned were steel mills, metals plants, oil and gas fields, and power stations. In August the Chinese made public a plan to build factories to make modular construction elements—a program that would greatly accelerate the building of domestic industrial properties.

Among new U.S. projects, especially noteworthy was a plan to relieve traffic congestion in downtown Detroit. The Urban Mass Transporta-

Constructing this giant (91 m/300 ft.) distillation tower for the Exxon Chemical Co. took remarkable skill. But it took even greater ingenuity—plus two crawler transporters, thousands of tons of timber mats, and a huge crane—to move the tower from the Baytown (Texas) docks and lift it into position.

was defeated in the House of Representatives on Feb. 8, the year saw vigorous action on consumer issues by existing government agencies, including the Food and Drug Administration (FDA) and the National Highway Traffic Safety Administration (NHTSA). U.S. President Jimmy Carter showed his continuing commitment to consumer protection by a series of administrative actions.

Presidential Actions. President Carter stepped up his efforts to promote consumer interests in all federally sponsored programs. In April he ordered his special assistant for consumer affairs, Esther Peterson, to advise him of the impact on consumers of all policies proposed or implemented by the executive branch. The President broadened Peterson's role in August by increasing her staff and also placing her in charge of the U.S. Office of Consumer Affairs, a branch of the Department of Health, Education, and Welfare.

In June, Carter appointed Susan B. King to head the beleaguered Consumer Product Safety Commission in hopes that she would take a more activist stance than her predecessors. The commission has been bombarded with criticism from both Congress and consumer activists for its slowness in developing enforceable product safety standards.

Traffic Safety. Recalls of defective automobiles

The National Westminster Tower nears completion in October. Located in London's Bishopsgate district, it is the tallest building in Great Britain and was awarded a prize by the European Convention of Structural Steelworkers as "a scheme of outstanding merit."

ion Administration awarded the city $1,200,000 to study the possibility of building a 2.3-mi.-long one-way loop route to move people around the inner-city area.

Skateboard parks offered U.S. contractors increased work in 1978. Modular, precast concrete segments were most often used to transform abandoned factories and warehouses into activity centers for the estimated 3,000,000 American skateboarders.

Other important new development projects announced during 1978 include one for Harlem, in New York City. This scheme, with an initial cost of $40,000,000, will be financed by a Middle Eastern corporation, Prudential International Commodities, Inc., of Beirut, Lebanon. The project is said to represent the first major foreign investment in the American black community. R.W.S.

CONSUMER EDUCATION AND PROTECTION. Consumer activists scored modest gains in 1978. Although a bill to consolidate U.S. consumer services into a federal Office of Consumer Protection

Maria Johnston of San Francisco shows her defective Firestone 500 steel-belted radial tire to U.S. Rep. John Moss (D, Calif.), who conducted hearings on the matter in May. Later in the year, Firestone agreed to exchange millions of the radials for the newer 721 model.

CONSUMER EDUCATION AND PROTECTION

What's in a name? That was the question puzzling Gloria Marsden of Waltham, Mass.—and millions of other consumers—in 1978 when U.S. supermarkets began offering "no-frills" products that sold for much less than brand-name merchandise.

were announced throughout 1978. In August the Cadillac Motor Car Division of General Motors (GM) reported that owners of nearly 400,000 1977 and 1978 DeVille and Fleetwood models would receive special heat shields to prevent ashtray fires that had already caused more than a dozen minor injuries. Later in the year, GM announced the recall of all 320,000 of its 1976 and 1977 Chevrolet Chevettes to strengthen weak rear-end fuel tanks. In a similar action, GM offered to correct potential lubrication problems in the front-wheel bearings of some 130,000 1975 subcompacts built by its Chevrolet, Oldsmobile, and Buick divisions.

In June the Ford Motor Co. agreed to fix 1,500,-000 Pintos and Mercury Bobcats, after testing by the NHTSA found that their fuel tanks were not strong enough to withstand even minor rear-end collisions. Ford ran into further trouble with the NHTSA when the agency's studies showed that the C-6 and FMX automatic transmissions in more than 9,000,000 Ford cars and trucks could jump from the park position into reverse. Drivers of such vehicles were advised to put the transmission stick firmly in park before leaving the car.

By far the most extensive action taken by the NHTSA concerned an estimated 9,000,000 Firestone 500 steel-belted radial tires, which the agency found defective. After a long and rancorous dispute with consumer groups and with NHTSA chief Joan Claybrook, the Firestone Tire & Rubber Co. agreed to recall the tires and exchange them, free of charge, for the newer 721 model.

The NHTSA stepped in to defend the Chrysler

Corp. against charges that its Dodge Omni and Plymouth Horizon had a serious handling defect. In the July, 1978, issue of the magazine *Consumer Reports,* the Consumers Union (CU) rated both cars "not acceptable" because of directional instability at high speeds. The federal agency did not dispute the CU's test data; instead, the NHTSA concurred with Chrysler in arguing that the tests themselves were irrelevant to actual driving conditions.

Foods. The food industry suffered a setback when the FDA further restricted the use of nitrites to preserve processed meats, such as hot dogs and bacon. Digestive products of nitrites have for several years been suspected of causing cancer. The FDA did not seek an outright ban on nitrites, preferring instead to use the new restrictions as a way of stimulating meat processors to develop a safer preservative, one which would prevent botulism but which would be free of dangerous side effects.

Saccharin, found in a 1975 Canadian study to promote the growth of bladder tumors in rats, was dealt a severe blow in November by the prestigious National Academy of Sciences. In a report of tests conducted by the academy, the artificial sweetener was said not only to produce cancer but also to offer few health benefits. One curious finding of the study was that dieters who use the artificial sweetener instead of sugar in order to reduce their caloric intake may develop stronger appetites for sugar than those who do not use saccharin at all.

Pharmaceuticals. Consumers were promised some relief from the soaring cost of medical care when the FDA initiated a broad campaign to lower the cost of pharmaceutical drugs. In June the FDA agreed to aid the implementation of a New York State law, enacted in April, that requires pharmacists to fill prescriptions with generic drugs (instead of the more expensive brand-name ones) if requested to do so by a doctor. The agency was to review the quality of generic drugs offered for sale in the state. If the results of the study were favorable, they would be publicized by the FDA to help convince doctors as well as the general public of the economic advantages of using generics.

While waging war against rising drug prices, the regulatory agency was also trying to stimulate the development of new and more effective drugs. One approach the FDA said it might take involves decreasing the number of years a drug company would be allowed exclusive rights to market a drug it has patented. To stay competitive, the manufacturer would be forced to develop in five years (instead of the present seventeen) a mo

130

effective medical equivalent of the same compound. The agency proposed to lengthen from 180 to 360 the number of days it is given to review the benefits and hazards of a new pharmaceutical.

The FDA also issued to drug companies a set of recommended practices for manufacturing pharmaceuticals. One noteworthy recommendation was that all prescription drugs carry expiration dates.   T.V.S.

COSTA RICA. In a presidential election on Feb. 5, 1978, Rodrigo Carazo Odio, leader of the opposition coalition Unity Party, ousted Luis Alberto Monge, candidate of the National Liberation Party (PLN), which had ruled Costa Rica for the last eight years. Contributing to the victory of Carazo, a businessman and former member of the PLN, were his charges of government waste and corruption and well-timed news of scandals. Monge was at a disadvantage because many voters thought it was time for a change in party and because, until the last moment, he was opposed within the PLN by its key leader, former national president José Figueres Ferrer.

The new president promised to reform the government but also stated that he would continue its policy of aid to the poor. He said he would maintain peaceful relations with Nicaragua, which had charged Costa Rica with aiding guerrillas in attacks against the Nicaraguan government. Carazo dealt firmly with the fugitive financier Robert Vesco, who had lived in Costa Rica for six years to avoid facing charges in the United States of stealing $224,000,000 from a mutual fund that he controlled. Declaring that Costa Rica would cease to be a haven for fugitives from justice, the president refused reentry to Vesco in May, when the financier was away from Costa Rica, and his application for Costa Rican citizenship was turned down.

See STATISTICS OF THE WORLD.   J.N.G.

COUNCIL FOR MUTUAL ECONOMIC ASSISTANCE, known as COMECON, a Soviet-dominated, Communist counterpart of Western European organizations aimed at achieving economic unity.

COMECON held its annual council meeting for 1978 in Bucharest, Rumania, in late June. The most noteworthy decision taken by council members was the admission of Vietnam as a full partner—COMECON's tenth. It was in the Soviet interest to include Vietnam in COMECON, for the Russians were attempting to develop close ties with the Vietnamese, thus precluding any warm relationship between Vietnam and China; see COMMUNISM. However, news leaks from the Bucharest session indicated that Eastern European members of COMECON were not eager to accept Vietnam.

The council was already extending development aid to two member states, Cuba and the Mongolian People's Republic; the Eastern European nations knew that war-torn, underdeveloped Vietnam was bound to be a further drain on COMECON resources. In the end, however, the Soviets prevailed, and Vietnam was admitted by unanimous vote.

In a speech to the council, Soviet Premier Aleksei Kosygin called for closer cooperation in long-term planning and urged that COMECON move more rapidly toward overall economic integration. There were discussions on how to develop natural resources, especially energy-producing ones. Three long-term cooperative programs were approved at the Bucharest session.

Rumania reportedly held firm against Soviet proposals for changing voting procedures within the organization. The Russians had wanted to abolish the so-called unity rule, which requires that no important decision be taken without the consent of all COMECON members.   F.W.

CRIME AND LAW ENFORCEMENT. In the first half of 1978 the overall rate of reported crimes in the United States dipped slightly, although violent crime continued to rise. Late in the year, two major incidents occurred: a series of murders and mass suicides in Guyana (q.v.) and the assassinations of the mayor and a county supervisor in San Francisco (see UNITED STATES OF AMERICA). And one of the most infamous crimes of the year occurred in Rome, where former Italian Premier Aldo Moro was kidnapped and murdered by members of the terrorist Red Brigades; see ITALY.

The Crime Rate. Reports of serious crimes, on a slight downward trend since early in 1977, continued to decline in the first half of 1978. The total number of reported offenses dropped 2 percent when compared with the same period of 1977. Both burglary and motor vehicle theft declined 1 percent. Violent crimes, however, increased 1 percent during the six-month period; reported rapes were up 5 percent and aggravated assaults rose 3 percent.

The trend toward stiffer penalties and less opportunity for parole for violent criminals continued in 1978. A major revision of the federal criminal code, establishing fixed terms of imprisonment and restricting parole, was passed by the U.S. Senate in January but became stalled in the House. Thirty-three states had laws providing for capital punishment, although none imposed it. In New York State, where one death penalty law was struck down by a state appeals court (the U.S. Supreme Court let the decision stand) and another was vetoed by Gov. Hugh L. Carey, the legislature overwhelmingly passed a

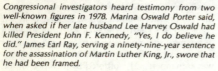

Congressional investigators heard testimony from two well-known figures in 1978. Marina Oswald Porter said, when asked if her late husband Lee Harvey Oswald had killed President John F. Kennedy, "Yes, I do believe he did." James Earl Ray, serving a ninety-nine-year sentence for the assassination of Martin Luther King, Jr., swore that he had been framed.

bill in July increasing criminal penalties. The new law provided for the trying of murder suspects as young as 13 in adult courts; such defendants would be subject to life sentences. Behind this new harshness in law enforcement were the beliefs that rehabilitation of criminals had been ineffective and that society's right to protection outweighed the criminal's right to a second chance.

The FBI and the Justice Department. The year began on a hopeful note for the Federal Bureau of Investigation (FBI). William H. Webster, a federal court judge from St. Louis, was appointed to succeed Clarence M. Kelley as director of the FBI. But despite the new leadership, ghosts from the 1960's and early 1970's, when illegal methods were used to suppress political dissidents, rose to haunt the nation's top law-enforcement agencies.

In April former acting FBI director L. Patrick Gray 3rd and two other former FBI executives were indicted for ordering illegal break-ins and searches at the homes of antiwar activists in the early 1970's. The trial was expected to begin in

early 1979. The indictments came after a three-year investigation by the Justice Department. The names of sixty-eight other FBI agents were referred to Director Webster for administrative discipline. An assistant FBI director, J. Wallace LaPrade, was dismissed by Attorney General Griffin B. Bell in July, allegedly for not cooperating in the investigation.

Attorney General Bell himself was accused of contempt of court in July by U.S. District Court Judge Thomas G. Griesa. Bell had refused to turn over the files of eighteen FBI informants who had spied on the Socialist Workers Party. The party was suing the government for $40,000,000 for disrupting its activities. The contempt order against Bell was stayed the day after it was issued, pending an appeal of the case that was still unresolved at year's end.

Assassination Probes. In the U.S. House of Representatives the Select Committee on Assassinations wound up their two-year-long probes of the murders of President John F. Kennedy and Martin Luther King, Jr. In the Kennedy case, acoustical studies of a recording made accidentally by a Dallas policeman indicated to the investigators that another gunman besides Lee Harvey Oswald had fired at the President. Evidence presented in September by forensic doctors, ballistic experts, and eyewitnesses tended to support the finding that

132

Oswald had fired the fatal shots. Finally, the committee concluded that Kennedy "was probably assassinated as a result of a conspiracy."

In the King case, the committee found no evidence that the civil rights leader was not shot by his convicted killer, James Earl Ray, who was serving a ninety-nine-year sentence for the 1968 murder. But it heard evidence that Ray might have been motivated by an offer of money for King's death made by two Missouri businessmen. The committee concluded that "there is a likelihood" of conspiracy in the case.

Accused Congressmen. An investigation of South Korean influence-buying among U.S. congressmen resulted in several indictments and formal reprimands. Former Rep. Richard T. Hanna (D, Calif.) was sentenced in April to from 6 to 30 months in prison for conspiracy in connection with the scandal. Hanna admitted having accepted bribes from South Korean businessman Park Tong Sun to further Park's interests. Former Rep. Otto E. Passman (D, La.) was indicted on similar charges. Park himself, testifying before the House ethics committee in February in return for a promise of immunity, denied that he was a South Korean agent. Three sitting congressmen were accused by the ethics committee of receiving campaign contributions illegally from Park. Reps. John J. McFall (D, Calif.), Charles H. Wilson (D, Calif.), and Edward R. Roybal (D, Calif.) were formally reprimanded by the House.

Other investigations exposed alleged financial wrongdoing by Rep. Daniel J. Flood (D, Pa.), who was indicted in September for lying about earlier

charges of bribery and again in October for bribery and conspiracy; Rep. Charles C. Diggs, Jr. (D, Mich.), convicted in October of mail fraud and sentenced to three years in prison; and Rep. Joshua Eilberg (D, Pa.), indicted in October for accepting unlawful fees. The Senate Select Committee on Ethics voted in December to undertake a full-scale investigation of certain activities of Sen. Herman E. Talmadge (D, Ga.), including his office expenses, campaign funds, taxes, and gifts. Sen. Edward W. Brooke (R, Mass.) was defeated for reelection in November, apparently because of questions concerning his financial dealings.

The Hearst Case. Patricia Hearst, the newspaper heiress who was kidnapped by terrorists in 1974 and convicted in 1976 of robbing a San Francisco bank with her abductors, lost her appeal to the U.S. Supreme Court and returned to prison in May to serve the rest of a seven-year sentence. But public sympathy for her increased. Many newspaper editors, columnists, and politicians joined in a campaign to have her released before her parole date of July, 1979.

In August the revolutionaries William and Emily Harris pleaded guilty to kidnapping Patricia Hearst, who had been prepared to testify against them. The Harrises were sentenced to from ten years to life in prison.

The Son of Sam. David Berkowitz, the 25-year-old former postal clerk accused of shooting six young people to death in New York City in 1976 and 1977, pleaded guilty to murder in May. The Son of Sam, as he referred to himself in notes written during his rampage, had earlier been judged men-

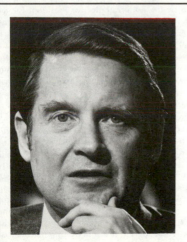

A Judge Takes Over the FBI
Party affiliation was no consideration in the Carter administration's choice of Federal Appeals Court Judge William H. Webster as the new director of the Federal Bureau of Investigation: Webster, 54, is a lifelong Republican. In February he took command of a demoralized agency whose image was tarnished by revelations of past transgressions. In his years on the bench the Missouri-born Webster, a graduate of Amherst College and Washington University Law School in St. Louis, came to be known as a cautious but fairminded jurist. In December he announced his intention to dismiss two FBI supervisors allegedly involved in illegal break-ins in the early 1970's—proving that the lot of an FBI director is not always a happy one.

FBI Director William Webster.

tally competent to stand trial in a ruling disputed by his lawyers. In June he was sentenced to from twenty-five years to life for each of the six slayings.

The Jascalevich-Farber Case. A New Jersey murder case tried during the year raised the issue of a reporter's right to protect confidential sources. Mario E. Jascalevich, an Argentine-born surgeon, was tried on charges that he gave three patients lethal injections of the muscle relaxant curare at a hospital in Oradell, N.J., in 1965 and 1966. The charges were partly derived from information unearthed by Myron A. Farber, a reporter for the New York *Times*. When Jascalevich's lawyer subpoenaed Farber's notes, insisting that his client's right to a fair trial was at stake, the journalist refused to turn them over. Farber persisted in his refusal and was jailed for contempt in July. After a trial of eight months, Jascalevich was acquitted on Oct. 24; on the same day, Farber was released after two confinements totaling forty days. His fines, amounting to $285,000, were paid by the *Times*. See CIVIL RIGHTS AND CIVIL LIBERTIES; PUBLISHING.

Other Murder Cases. San Francisco Mayor George Moscone and County Supervisor Harvey Milk were shot to death on Nov. 27; *see* UNITED STATES OF AMERICA.

In a sensational Texas case, millionaire industrialist T. Cullen Davis, who was acquitted of the murder of his stepdaughter and accused of attempting to murder his wife in 1977, was once again charged with attempted murder in 1978. The intended victim was Judge Joe H. Eidson, Jr., who presided over Davis's divorce. Davis allegedly paid a middleman to kill Judge Eidson and fourteen other personal enemies. But the middleman, fearing for his own life, went to the FBI instead. A trial on the new charges began in November.

In Philadelphia on Aug. 8 a policeman was killed in a shoot-out started by members of a small, predominantly black radical group known as MOVE. In May the group had agreed to leave their dilapidated, unsanitary house within three months. When they failed to do so, the police moved in. One policeman was killed, twelve adult members of MOVE were charged with murder, and their house was leveled.

In Los Angeles a series of killings of derelicts and drifters began in October and claimed ten victims in five weeks. Police had a description of the "Skid Row stabber," as the perpetrator was dubbed by the media, but they did not have sufficient evidence to hold a suspect; two potential witnesses had disappeared.

In Illinois, John Wayne Gacy was charged with murder on Dec. 21. Gacy allegedly told investigators that he had killed thirty-two young men and had then either buried their bodies under his home in a Chicago suburb or thrown them in a nearby river. By year's end the Cook County prosecutor had connected thirty deaths with the 36-year-old contractor's case.

There was a grisly epilogue to an earlier murder case. Patrick Kearney, who was convicted in 1977 of killing three young homosexual drifters in Los Angeles, pleaded guilty in February to an additional eighteen similar murders. And a new trial was ordered for Juan Corona, convicted in 1972 of the murder of twenty-five farm workers found in shallow graves the previous year. The California appeals court ruled that Corona's attorney had conducted an inadequate defense.

Other Incidents. At year's end only one figure in the 1972 Watergate burglary and the ensuing cover-up by the administration of President Richard M. Nixon remained in prison: former Attorney General John N. Mitchell. Former Nixon adviser John D. Ehrlichman was released in April, and former Nixon chief of staff H. R. Haldeman went free in December; each had served eighteen months.

The body of motion picture actor Charlie Chaplin, who died in 1977, was stolen from a Swiss cemetery in March. Two months later it was recovered, buried in a cornfield 10 miles away. The two confessed thieves, who had sought a ransom for the body, were sentenced in December. The originator of the plan, a Pole, was sentenced to four and a half years in prison, and his Bulgarian accomplice received an eighteen-month suspended sentence.

In what the FBI said was the largest cash robbery in history, seven bandits stole more than $5,000,000 in currency and jewelry from a Lufthansa cargo depot at Kennedy International Airport, New York City, on Dec. 11.　　　W.M.H

President Fidel Castro of Cuba (right) decided in 1978 to allow the emigration of thousands of political prisoners. He met frequently with delegations of Cuban exiles, as here in Havana on Nov. 21.

CUBA. The primary goal of Cuba's foreign policy in 1978 was to achieve leadership among the Third World (or developing) countries. To implement this policy, the Cuban presence in Africa was considerably strengthened.

Foreign Affairs. Western intelligence sources estimated that during 1978 close to 45,000 Cubans (including 7000 nonmilitary personnel) were posted in thirteen African countries. Much of President Fidel Castro's attention was focused on Ethiopia (q.v.). In February and March Cuban soldiers tipped the balance in favor of the Ethiopian government in its struggle to repulse Somali invaders of the Ogaden desert. In April a "grateful" Lt. Col. Mengistu Haile Mariam, the Ethiopian strongman, visited Cuba. By July, Castro was withdrawing Cuban troops from Ethiopia, not wanting to support the government in its war against the rebellious province of Eritrea. Castro himself visited Ethiopia in September to celebrate the fourth anniversary of the overthrow of the late Emperor Haile Selassie I.

The second major Cuban presence in Africa was in Angola (q.v.). Since 1975 Cuban soldiers had been supporting the dominant Marxist-oriented MPLA Party of Labor against the opposition National Union for the Total Independence of Angola (UNITA). Less successful than in Ethiopia, the Cubans in Angola found themselves mired in a difficult situation: The MPLA controlled the cities and highways; UNITA and other groups controlled the countryside. It was also reported that Cubans in Angola had trained the guerrillas who invaded Shaba (Katanga) region in Zaire (q.v.) in May. And Cubans in Zambia and Mozambique aided Rhodesian guerrillas.

According to President Julius Nyerere of Tanzania, Cuban forces were in Africa at the request of the African leaders. President Castro regarded Cuba's African concerns as normal. He stated in a speech in Havana on July 25 that "Cuba is not only a Latin American nation but an Afro-American nation."

While winning friends in the Third World countries, Castro was also trying to improve relations with the United States, in spite of U.S. objections to Cuba's African involvement. In August he announced the unexpected and unsolicited release of hundreds of Cuban political prisoners, who were to be permitted to go to the U.S.; the first group of forty-six arrived in Miami in October. In late November Castro increased the number of planned releases to 3000, to be accomplished at a rate of 400 per month. The U.S. promised to review the tedious process by which such released prisoners are admitted. On Dec. 9, Castro agreed to a program to reunite families; it would grant visitors' visas to Cuba to his political enemies. In addition, eighteen U.S. mayors conferred with a group of Cuban mayors in Havana in June, and the members of the official U.S. interest section in Havana were negotiating with Cuban officials on such matters as fishing rights and air agreements.

Domestic Affairs. In 1978 the Cuban economy continued to be strongly supported by the Soviet Union, at an estimated cost to the Soviets of $2,500,000 per day. Agricultural output improved, as Cuba harvested a record 7,400,000 tons of sugar, a 29 percent increase over the 1977 crop and the second largest in the country's history. Food rationing was continued, but the government began a variety of new public-works projects.

See STATISTICS OF THE WORLD.   J.N.G.

CYPRUS. The year 1978 provided no relaxation for the most pressing problem in Cyprus—the long-standing antagonism between the island's Greek and Turkish communities, which have been under separate regimes since the Turkish invasion of 1974.

Government. Spyros Kyprianou, caretaker president of Cyprus and head of the Greek Cypriot community, won a full five-year term as president by default as the opposition failed to nominate an opposing candidate by Jan. 26.

Necat Konuk resigned on March 24 as premier

At Larnaca airport in Cyprus, two Palestinian terrorists who killed an Egyptian editor and then hijacked an airliner are surrounded by their captors after their surrender Feb. 19. Meanwhile, a battle occurred when Egyptian commandos attempted a rescue operation.

of the "Turkish Federated State of Cyprus," which has been recognized by no country other than Turkey. Konuk's departure was reported to have been prompted by serious economic difficulties in the Turkish-controlled area. Osman Örek was chosen on April 22 to replace him as premier.

Negotiations. Greek and Turkish Cypriots held negotiations in Vienna in April with United Nations Secretary-General Kurt Waldheim mediating. Turkish Cypriot negotiators proposed the creation of two separate states linked by a weak central government. Kyprianou, rejecting the Turkish plan, told Waldheim on April 19 that its purpose was to partition Cyprus permanently.

In November the United States proposed a twelve-point plan for a federal state with two regions. It was thought that the lifting of the U.S. embargo on arms shipments to Turkey, approved by Congress in August, might have removed an obstacle to serious negotiations.

Terrorists Strike. In February Cyprus was the scene of a terrorist action that ended in the death of 15 Egyptian commandos and a rupture in relations between Cyprus and Egypt. The incident began on Feb. 18 in the lobby of a Nicosia hotel, where two Palestinian terrorists (Samir Mohammed Khadar and Zayed Hussein Ahmed al-Ali) shot to death Yousef el-Sebai, the editor of Egypt's leading newspaper. The gunmen then seized 30 hostages, most of them delegates to a conference of the Afro-Asian People's Solidarity Organization.

President Kyprianou headed a team that negotiated with the terrorists for a plane to fly them to another country. The plane took off from Larnaca airport with the terrorists and 11 of the hostages. It returned the next day—at least eight countries had refused to let it land; Djibouti allowed it to land only long enough to refuel.

An Egyptian transport plane with a commando force aboard landed at Larnaca shortly after the terrorists' plane returned. About two hours later

the Egyptian commandos left their plane and headed toward the terrorists' plane in a rescue attempt. Cypriot troops, however, fired on the Egyptians, killing 15 of them. The terrorists then freed their hostages and surrendered.

Egypt suspended diplomatic relations with Cyprus on Feb. 20 and cut relations entirely two days later. In November Kyprianou commuted the terrorists' death sentences a day before their scheduled hanging; no one had been executed in Cyprus since the mid-1960's. But Cypriot-Egyptian relations were not improved by the president's action.

See STATISTICS OF THE WORLD. L.A.S.

CZECHOSLOVAKIA. August 20, 1978, marked the 10th anniversary of the Soviet invasion that put an end to liberal reform in Czechoslovakia. The regime of President Gustáv Husák used this occasion to proclaim that Soviet armed intervention in 1968 had been necessary to stop an impending "counterrevolution." Meanwhile, Czechoslovakia's small human-rights movement, Charter 77, issued a document denouncing the invasion as illegal. Authorities flooded Prague with police and security men to prevent any demonstrations, but in fact, the anniversary was ignored by most Czechoslovak citizens.

Husák, who had been installed by the Soviets, remained in charge of the Communist Party, but he was under constant challenge from Communist Party Secretary Vasil Bilak, a neo-Stalinist. Rumors of party infighting became so widespread that Husák was forced to deny them publicly during a speech in February. Three months later, he received warm backing from Soviet President Leonid Brezhnev when the Russian leader paid an official visit to Prague. Significantly, however, Brezhnev awarded a high Soviet citation to Bilak as well as to Husák.

The Soviet government emphasized the closeness of Czechoslovak-Russian ties in a unique way before the Brezhnev visit. In March a Czech cosmonaut, Capt. Vladimir Remek, became the first non-Soviet citizen to join the crew of a Russian spacecraft. He journeyed aboard a Soviet-launched Soyuz 28 on an eight-day mission; *see* SPACE EXPLORATION.

The economy made only slow gains. Productivity remained low, and the country's industrial plant was becoming increasingly obsolete. According to reports in Prague, high-level debate took place within the Communist Party on the question of whether to enlist the aid of some of the 1968 reform leaders to help get the economy moving. Hundreds of thousands of former Communist Party members from that era, including former party leader Alexander Dubček, remained politically ostracized and confined to menial jobs.

Czechoslovakia's only notable foreign-affairs overture was a Husák visit to West Germany. The West Germans had for years been Czechoslovakia's foremost trade partners in the capitalist world, and Husák's April trip was meant to give new impetus to their relationship.

See STATISTICS OF THE WORLD.

D

DAHOMEY. *See* STATISTICS OF THE WORLD.

DANCE. The events that took place in the dance world in 1978 were memorable more for novelty than for artistic achievement. The seasons of the two major ballet companies in the United States were sparked by the debuts of famous dancers. Two companies from Communist countries made their first U.S. appearances. The boom in dance, no longer a new phenomenon in 1978, was officially recognized by the federal government, which proclaimed National Dance Week, beginning April 24, and issued four 13¢ dance stamps.

U.S. Ballet Companies. George Balanchine produced two masterful new ballets, *Ballo della Regina* and *Kammermusik No. 2*, in January for his New York City Ballet. Balanchine's towering reputation as a choreographer lured Mikhail Baryshnikov, star of American Ballet Theatre (ABT) since shortly after his defection from the Soviet Kirov Ballet in 1974, to join the New York City company.

Baryshnikov's switch caught the fancy of the dance public, who speculated on the dancer's ability to absorb the intricacies of Balanchine's choreography and on the company's ability to absorb a stellar performer into its no-star organization. Audiences flocked to the City Ballet's July season in Saratoga Springs, N.Y., where Baryshnikov first appeared with it, and virtually bought out the New York State Theater even before the City Ballet opened its winter season in mid-November. The Soviet defector, eager to try new roles, appeared with great critical success in the "Rubies" section of *Jewels*, *Harlequinade*, and *Orpheus*, all by Balanchine, and in Jerome Robbins's *Afternoon of a Faun* and *Dances at a Gathering*.

Recovering from Baryshnikov's departure, ABT acquired Anthony Dowell, on leave from Great Britain's Royal Ballet. He first appeared with ABT at the Metropolitan Opera House in New York City, partnering Natalia Makarova in *Giselle*. He

Lynda Meyer and Vane Vest perform a pas de deux from Romeo and Juliet, choreographed for the San Francisco Ballet by Michael Smuin. In 1978, after a thirteen-year absence, the West Coast company was warmly received in New York City.

DANCE

Hungarian-born dancer Ivan Nagy partners Cynthia Gregory in La Bayadère. *Their pas de deux was part of a gala September performance honoring Nagy on his retirement from American Ballet Theatre.*

made his debut as an actor in October, narrating the Gertrude Stein text for the Joffrey Ballet's production of Frederick Ashton's *A Wedding Bouquet.* Dowell's presence with ABT was all the more important because the company lost three principal male dancers: Ivan Nagy retired after a gala performance in September, Ted Kivitt joined the Pennsylvania Ballet, and John Prinz left to teach.

The San Francisco Ballet and the Los Angeles Ballet spread their wings in transcontinental tours. The San Francisco troupe concluded its tour in November in New York City, where its first visit in thirteen years was a great success. The Los Angeles company's tour, which included Florida, was the first in its four-year history.

Visiting Dance Companies. An improvement in relations between the U.S. and Cuba and the People's Republic of China brought dance companies from both Communist countries to America. The political implications, however, seemed to be more exciting than the aesthetic achievement. The Ballet Nacional de Cuba, founded by Alicia Alonso in 1948, appeared in Washington, D.C., and New York City in June. Its repertory ranged from the classics to contemporary Spanish and Cuban works. Audiences were impressed by the verve, training, and dramatic sense of the younger dancers in such works as *Giselle,* and especially by the technique of Alonso, still a star in her fifties. Spanish flamenco dancer Antonio Gades's choreography of *Blood Wedding* was outstanding. But some observers deemed many of the original Cuban works, incorporating folk music and dance, amateurish.

The Performing Arts Company from the People's Republic of China was created specifically for its U.S. summer tour to New York City; Wolf Trap Farm, Va.; Minneapolis; Berkeley; and Los

Angeles. They presented a potpourri of Chinese performing arts, including excerpts from Peking Opera, folk songs and dances, and a portion of the Chinese revolutionary ballet *Red Detachment of Women.* Although the virtuosity of acrobats from the Peking Opera thrilled audiences, some found the program superficial and awkwardly Westernized.

Summer engagements of the London Festival Ballet in New York City and Washington, D.C., aroused interest because the company had not performed in the U.S. since 1955. Owing to the presence of guest artist Rudolf Nureyev, who danced at every performance in either his own *Romeo and Juliet* or the rarely revived *Schéhérazade* of Michel Fokine, the Festival Ballet's own personality and style were obscured; the Nureyev glamour quotient remained high. The Berlin Opera Ballet, making its first New York City appearance in July, suffered similarly by dancing in the shadow of former Soviet stars Valery Panov and his wife Galina. The couple danced at every performance, often in ballets choreographed by Va-

"Rich Kids' Rag," originally choreographed by Bob Fosse for the musical Little Me *in 1962, was reconstructed and performed on Broadway in 1978 by the American Dance Machine. The company, organized in 1974, is dedicated to the preservation of choreography from American musicals.*

lery Panov himself. Such heavy reliance on box-office attractions by both the British and the West German companies reflected the growing commercial attitude of financially pressed ballet impresarios.

Modern Dance. Of smaller box-office potential, modern dance has found it easier to withstand pressure to glamorize. In 1978, however, the Martha Graham company underwent the glare of publicity when it performed at the Metropolitan Opera House in New York City in June. Its appearance at the Met, which had never before had a modern dance season, presumably marked Graham's ultimate triumph as a choreographer.

Other modern dance groups toured; some celebrated anniversaries. The Paul Taylor company visited the Soviet Union in the fall. Merce Cunningham and his troupe spent five weeks at colleges in Massachusetts; his radiant *Fractions* was premiered in Boston in February. For its December season in New York City, Alvin Ailey's company marked its 20th anniversary by inviting former members to recreate roles they had made famous. His backup troupe, however, suffered one death (that of 17-year-old Judi DeJean) and several injuries in a bus accident in October. The Connecticut Dance Theatre commemorated the 50th anniversary of the Doris Humphrey–Charles Weidman company by dancing Humphrey masterpieces in New England towns in October. The Arizona State University Dance Theatre introduced Humphrey works to the Southwest.

The American Dance Festival, a summer mecca of modern dance, shifted from its customary New London, Conn., location to Duke University in Durham, N.C. It also changed its financial operation, working for the first time under a planned deficit.

Deaths. Deaths in the ballet world in 1978 included those of Tamara Karsavina, former ballerina with the Maryinsky Ballet and Diaghilev's Ballets Russes (*see* OBITUARIES); Katharine Litz, sa-

tirical dancer and choreographer (Dec. 19 at 66); Ludmilla Schollar, teacher and former Maryinsky Ballet soloist (July 10 at 90); and Yuri Slonimsky, Soviet ballet historian and critic (April 23 at 76).   N.T.G.

DELAWARE. *See* STATISTICS OF THE WORLD.

DEMOCRATIC PARTY. In 1978 the Democrats used their heavy majorities in Congress to push through modified parts of President Jimmy Carter's legislative program. The President, stung by criticism of his political competence, became more accommodating and effective in dealing with Congress and took a more active role in party fund-raising and campaigning. Democrats maintained their large majorities in the November congressional elections, and late-year legislative

Two Massachusetts Democrats, Rep. Paul Tsongas and Sen. Edward Kennedy, chat at a fund-raising dinner in Boston on Oct. 23. Kennedy gave Tsongas considerable support in his successful effort to defeat incumbent Republican Sen. Edward Brooke.

Douglas A. Fraser, president of the United Auto Workers, speaks at a press conference held Oct. 18 in Detroit to publicize a new "labor-liberal" alliance formed to lobby the Democratic Party. Joining him were (from left) Rafe Pomerance, Friends of the Earth; Benjamin Hooks, NAACP; Eleanor Smeal, National Organization for Women; and Cesar Chavez, United Farm Workers.

A Senate Baron Steps Down
He was courtly, conservative, and a symbol of resistance to civil rights legislation. But Mississippi's James O. Eastland, 73, a U.S. Senator for half his life, allowed as to how he was growing weary and chose not to run for a seventh elected term. First appointed to fill out an unexpired term in 1941, "Big Jim" was president pro tem of the Senate and part of an "Old Guard" of Southern Democrats whose seniority, accumulated through successive reelections, assured them the chairmanships of key committees. Scheduled to replace Eastland as chairman of the Judiciary Committee: liberal Massachusetts Sen. Edward M. Kennedy who, it was noted, was only 9 years old when Eastland first went to Washington.

Sen. James O. Eastland (D, Miss.).

and foreign policy successes rescued Carter's sagging popularity. But in case of further slips, California Gov. Edmund G. (Jerry) Brown, Jr., and Massachusetts Sen. Edward M. Kennedy, potential Democratic candidates for 1980, were waiting in the wings.

The President and Congress. When Congress convened in January, Democratic leaders from the previous session were renamed. Speaker of the House was Thomas P. O'Neill, Jr. (D, Mass.), the President's closest legislative ally. But both O'Neill and House majority leader James C. Wright, Jr. (D, Texas), often expressed impatience with Carter's political inexperience during the year. Relations with Senate majority leader Robert C. Byrd (D, W.Va.) were also strained at times, although Carter said of him, "You couldn't ask for a better man to work with."

Congressional Democrats, who enjoyed nearly two-to-one majorities in both houses of Congress, seldom voted as a bloc behind the President. The Democrats held together to pass a watered-down version of Carter's energy program, but they withheld support from a union-backed labor-law reform bill and several other unsuccessful measures. In each legislative fight a new coalition, often including Republicans, had to be assembled by the leadership. Occasionally the leadership itself openly opposed the President. When he vetoed a $10.2 billion public-works bill that included funding for water projects he considered wasteful, the Democratic leaders combined to oppose this challenge to their pork barrel privileges. But the veto was sustained in a close House vote in October.

National Party Figures. One of the leading Democratic politicians of his time, Sen. Hubert H. Humphrey of Minnesota, died in January; *see* OBITUARIES. His funeral in Washington, D.C., was an occasion for bipartisan mourning and eulogy. The last major bill sponsored by him, the Humphrey-Hawkins full-employment bill, was passed by Congress in October in a form disappointing to his liberal supporters. It set goals for lowering unemployment and inflation but established no new programs to meet these goals. Sen. Lee Metcalf (D, Mont.) also died in January, and Sen. James B. Allen (D, Ala.) died in June.

Still the most popular Democrat of them all in most opinion polls, Sen. Edward M. Kennedy of Massachusetts denied that he was planning to challenge Carter for the Presidential nomination in 1980. But there were hints to the contrary. The Senator campaigned for his comprehensive national health-insurance plan with the vigor of a candidate and denounced a tax-cut bill acceptable to Carter as "the worst tax legislation . . . since the days of Calvin Coolidge."

Gov. Jerry Brown of California, a puzzling but popular figure who raised frugality and skepticism about government into a political creed, further strengthened his national prospects. After the June passage of Proposition 13, which drastically cut California property taxes, Brown got on the bandwagon and sponsored a $1 billion state income-tax reduction. He was easily reelected as governor in November.

Gov. George C. Wallace of Alabama, ineligible to run for a third consecutive term as governor, considered running for one of Alabama's Senate seats. But he decided against it, reportedly because of failing health. So Wallace, a power in national Democratic affairs for fifteen years, retired at year's end. Two other veteran Southern Democrats, Senators James O. Eastland of Mississippi and John J. Sparkman of Alabama, also retired in 1978.

Party Finances, Rules, and Strategy. At the January meeting of the Democratic National Committee (DNC), outgoing chairman Kenneth M. Curtis yielded the gavel to former Deputy Secretary of Agriculture John C. White. White, a Texan appointed by the President, was considered likely to be closer in outlook and obedience to the White House. Carter himself admitted having neglected the party during his busy first year in office and promised to assume command more directly in the future. Of serious importance was the large party debt, including $1,700,000 owed from the period before 1975. Plans were laid to continue paying it off gradually. To this end, the President was the featured speaker at five party fund-raising events during the year.

The DNC met again in June to adopt rules for the 1980 Presidential primaries and convention. Several of the measures that passed were expected to ease President Carter's renomination by making it harder for minor candidates to win delegates and thus keep the front-runner from amassing a majority.

Democratic campaign groups raised less than half as much money as the Republicans in 1978. But Democratic candidates, most of them incumbents, received greater contributions from business, labor, and other interest groups. At first, the DNC encouraged incumbents to avoid identification with the President in districts where he was unpopular. But after Carter's stock rose with his success in mediating a possible Egyptian-Israeli peace agreement in September, he was more welcome on the hustings. Carter campaigned hard in 6 states with close contests and visited 25 others briefly.

Election Results and Party Prospects. When the votes were all counted in November, it appeared that the party had suffered a net loss of 3 Senate seats and 11 House seats. Democratic congressional majorities were intact and still comfortable: 59 to 41 in the Senate and 277 to 158 in the House. The party lost more substantially in state executive and legislative contests. Republicans picked up 6 governorships, making the Democratic lead 32–18.

Diminished in numbers and heedful of the national mood of fiscal conservatism, the Democrats were not expected to press for major new legislation in 1979. In fact, a motion to oppose budget

cuts in current social programs was defeated by pro-Carter forces at the midterm party convention held in Memphis in December. Liberal Democrats, however, were preparing to reintroduce programs for welfare reform and national health insurance. Carter and party leaders were readying new energy conservation and inflation-fighting measures and planning for a difficult fight over Senate ratification of a possible new U.S.-Soviet arms limitation treaty.

See also CONGRESS OF THE UNITED STATES; ELECTIONS; PRESIDENT OF THE UNITED STATES.   W.M.H.

DENMARK. Inflation and unemployment continued to afflict the Danish economy, as Premier Anker Jørgensen managed to transform his minority Social Democratic government into a minority coalition during 1978.

Jørgensen's Social Democratic Party (SDP) made gains in municipal elections held on March 7, increasing its share of the local vote from the 32 percent of 1974 to more than 38 percent. It took nearly another six months for Jørgensen to win a relatively unpopular agreement for a government coalition of the SDP and the Liberal Party. Jørgensen remained as premier of the new minority government, which took office on Aug. 30.

A six-month freeze on prices and profits was immediately announced by the new government among a series of measures designed to deal with the nation's economic reverses. A wage freeze was not imposed directly. Instead, the government requested zero raises in the 1979 collective wage pacts.

When the new session of the *Folketing*, the Danish parliament, opened Oct. 3, Jørgensen proposed higher taxes on unearned income and consumption, while 10,000 workers demonstrated outside. Several strikes were called as well, because labor considered the Liberal part of the coalition too favorable toward business. Jørgensen also proposed that Denmark raise its foreign development aid to 0.7 percent of the gross national product; it would become the third nation in the world to meet this United Nations quota.

According to a newspaper study made public on Feb. 27, Danish hourly wages had risen by 80 percent between 1973 and 1977, forcing up the prices of Danish products in international markets and increasing Denmark's balance-of-payments deficits. In turn, Denmark's international borrowing rose, setting a $2.7 billion record in 1977, according to a March 14 report.

In a three-and-a-half-year trial, the longest in Danish history, the leader of the Progress Party was convicted of tax evasion. On Feb. 17, Mogens Glistrup, a tax lawyer who had formed the party in 1973 and had seen it become the second largest in the *Folketing,* was ordered to pay about $1,000,-000, of which 25 percent was his fine and the remainder was court costs and back taxes. Glistrup, whose party opposed income taxes and "big government," was charged with having evaded his own taxes since 1965; he had also counseled others to evade theirs.

On Nov. 17 the *Folketing* approved home rule for Greenland, which had been part of Denmark since 1953 and a colony before that. If the Greenlanders approve the proposal in a January, 1979, referendum, the island will rule itself, except for foreign policy and defense matters.

The death penalty was completely abolished in Denmark on April 29. The *Folketing* voted to end capital punishment during war for treason, desertion, or collaboration with the enemy.

Jens Otto Krag, the former prime minister (1962-68; 1971-72) credited with leading Denmark into the European Community, died at his summer home June 22 at the age of 63.

See STATISTICS OF THE WORLD.   L.A.S.

DISTRICT OF COLUMBIA. *See* STATISTICS OF THE WORLD.
DJIBOUTI, REPUBLIC OF. *See* STATISTICS OF THE WORLD.
DOMINICA. *See* STATISTICS OF THE WORLD. *See also* COMMONWEALTH OF NATIONS.
DOMINICAN REPUBLIC. *See* STATISTICS OF THE WORLD. *See also* WEST INDIES.

E

EARTH AND PLANETARY SCIENCES. With science's knowledge of extraterrestrial geologic processes being expanded by the National Aeronautics and Space Administration's exploration of the solar system, a new discipline—comparative planetary geology—appeared in 1978. By understanding the geological and climatological processes that have shaped the other planets, earth scientists are coming closer to understanding terrestrial evolution and development. The discovery of rare isotopes of argon on Venus, for instance, created considerable controversy during the year because it was contrary to existing theories of planetary formation. The discovery of a moon orbiting Pluto also changed existing theories of the dynamics of the solar system. In fact, scientists predict that as more and more data come in from the Venus and Jupiter missions, many geological and climatological theories may have to undergo drastic changes.

PLANETARY EXPLORATION

The year 1978 could be called "the year of the planets." With the success of the Pioneer-Venus mission, scientists obtained a wealth of information about the cloud-shrouded planet—so much information, in fact, that only after years of analysis will a clear picture of Venus emerge. Meanwhile, Voyager I and Voyager II continued their long journey to the outer planets of the solar system, providing planetologists with more and more data on far distant Jupiter and Saturn. The cold, lifeless planet Pluto also attracted a great deal of attention in 1978, when astronomers found a large moon revolving around it.

Pioneer-Venus Mission. Although Venus is earth's nearest planetary neighbor, the dense Venusian atmosphere had always kept earthbound observers, as well as flyby spacecraft, from obtaining accurate data on its geology and climate. Even when the Soviet Union successfully landed Veñera IX and Veñera X on the Venusian surface in 1975, their scientific probes had enough power to transmit data for only one hour each. This left unanswered many questions about the planet's atmosphere, shape, mass, surface characteristics, and magnetic field. In 1978 the U.S. National Aeronautics and Space Administration (NASA) set out to answer some of those questions by embarking on one of the most ambitious planetary explorations ever attempted, the Pioneer-Venus mission. This global study of the planet, scheduled to last eight months, employed two spacecraft equipped with a vast array of scientific instruments. By the end of December, both spacecraft, Pioneer-Venus I and Pioneer-Venus II, had provided planetologists with more data about Venus than had all previous Venusian missions.

Pioneer-Venus I, the first of the mission's spacecraft to reach Venus, was put into an elliptical orbit around the planet on Dec. 4, seven months after it was launched on a trajectory that took it halfway around the sun. Equipped with twelve scientific instruments and designed to circumnavigate the planet every 24 hours for a full Venusian day (243 earth days), Venus I immediately began collecting important data about the size, shape, and density of the planet. One instrument aboard Venus I, a telescope sensitive to ultraviolet

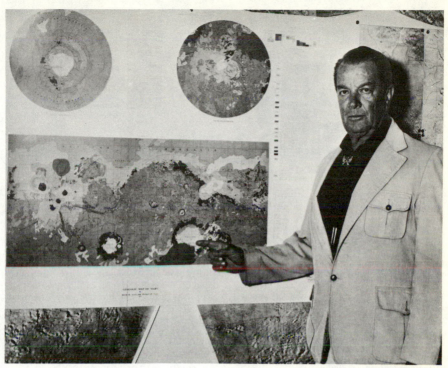

In July, David H. Scott of the U.S. Geological Survey unveils the first geologic map of the entire surface of Mars. It was assembled by Scott and his colleagues from photographs of the Martian terrain taken by Mariner IX in 1971–72.

rays, started measuring the vertical distribution of the cloud and haze particles that hover above the planet. A radar scanner provided images for what would eventually become the first topographic map of the Venusian surface. Another instrument began studies of the interaction between the Venusian atmosphere and the solar wind, the continuous stream of charged particles emitted by the sun. Still other instruments began measurements of Venus's mass and its gravitational and magnetic fields. Analyzing the data compiled from all these studies may take NASA scientists many months. At the end of December, agency spokesmen announced that the orbiter instruments were all functioning well and that the data were being analyzed as quickly as possible.

The second phase of the mission, an in-depth study of the Venusian atmosphere, began on Dec. 9, five days after the arrival of Venus I, when four probes belonging to Pioneer-Venus II plunged through the dense veil of gases that envelop the planet. The Venus II probes were transported from earth by a mother ship that was launched in August from Cape Canaveral. In November the probes were separated from the mother ship, and each probe aimed toward a different point in the Venusian atmosphere. The mother, also equipped with instruments, tagged close enough behind to serve as a relay station between the probes and earth. Scarcely a half hour after the fourth probe had hit the surface, the mother itself slammed into Venus's gaseous shroud, sampling the upper reaches of the planet's atmosphere before burning up from friction.

Although it will take many months to analyze the data transmitted by the Venus II probes, preliminary analysis indicated the presence of substances in the Venusian atmosphere that may change a widely accepted theory as to how the planets were formed. Astronomers believe that 4.5 billion years ago the solar system was a hot, swirling, dense, homogeneous cloud of matter that eventually condensed, forming the sun and the planets. As the planets cooled, volatile elements such as argon (which is believed to have existed

Keizo Yanai of the National Institute of Polar Research in Tokyo photographs a meteorite found on the ice near Mt. Baldr in Antarctica during a joint U.S.-Japanese expedition. More than 300 meteorites were recovered by the expedition (21 of them during one 2-hour period); one meteorite was identified as a rare achondrite.

in the primordial solar nebulus in the isotopic forms of argon-36 and argon-38) evaporated. Although some of these primordial isotopes can still be found on the planets in trace amounts, the predominant isotope is argon-40, a product of the radioactive decay of potassium-40. Data received from Venus II in December, however, showed that an abundance of the primordial isotopes— argon-36 and argon-40—still exist in the Venusian atmosphere. Unless further analysis finds a process that is currently producing these isotopes on Venus, scientists will be forced to develop a new theory of planetary evolution.

Pluto's Moon. Pluto, at a mean distance of 5.9 billion km (3.7 billion mi.) from the sun, was not discovered until 1930, when technological progress finally produced telescopes powerful enough to peer deep into space. Even in the most powerful contemporary telescope, Pluto, the solar system's most distant planet, had appeared as a single speck of light. In 1978, however, this speck was found to represent two celestial bodies so close together they appeared to be one.

On June 22, while examining photographs of Pluto taken with the U.S. Naval Observatory's 155 cm (61 in.) reflecting telescope at Flagstaff, Ariz., astronomer James W. Christy noticed that the planet seemed to bulge at the equator. He examined several other photographs, made numerous calculations, and concluded that Pluto's equatorial bulge was actually a moon, 800 km (500 mi.) in diameter, orbiting 19,300 km (12,000 mi.) above the planet. Christy dubbed the solar system's newly discovered moon "Charon," after the mythological boatman who ferried the dead across the river Styx to Hades, the underworld ruled by Pluto, the Greek god of the dead.

Before this discovery, astronomers had assumed that the planet was the same size and mass as the earth, and that irregularities in the orbits of Pluto's closest neighbors, Uranus and Neptune, were caused by the gravitational pull exerted by its large mass. However, from calculations made by Christy and his colleague Robert Harrington based on the size and orbit of Charon, Pluto appears to have an insufficient amount of mass (and, thus, gravitational pull) to exert appreciable force on its neighbor planets. So the inevitable question arose: If Pluto is not disturbing their orbits, what is? Scientists conjectured that there has to be another unidentified massive object in the solar system, perhaps even another planet.

Asteroid Discoveries. The discovery of three previously unknown asteroids with near-earth orbits received considerable attention during 1978. Once considered interplanetary litter, asteroids have come to be recognized as important clues to planetary origin and composition. In fact, through their analysis of the chemical composition of asteroids, planetologists on earth can infer much about the geologic characteristics of the other planetary members of the solar system.

The first two asteroid discoveries of 1978 were made in February by astronomer Hans-Emil Schuster of the European Southern Observatory in La Silla, Chile. Designated 1978 CA and 1978 DA, the two objects were found to have orbits that bring them very close to earth. In fact, the half-mile-wide 1978 CA, the larger of the two, was found to have an orbit very similar to that of earth, requiring only 435 days to circle the sun. The orbit of the somewhat smaller 1978 DA was found to be far more elongated, carrying it as close to the sun as earth and as far away as Jupiter. In March, when the orbits of the two asteroids brought them both close to earth, scientists around the world conducted thorough spectroscopic studies to determine their chemical make-up. It is hoped that these studies will shed some light on the origin of these interplanetary objects.

Seven months after the discovery of 1978 CA and 1978 DA, astronomers announced the discovery of still another near-earth asteroid. Called Ra-Shalom—a combination of the name of the Egyptian sun-god and the Hebrew word for peace—the asteroid was discovered by astronomer Eleanor Helin of the California Institute of Technology while the heads of government of Egypt, Israel, and the United States were meeting at Camp David, Md. With a diameter of 3 to 4 km (1.9 to 2.5 mi.), Ra-Shalom was found to rotate on its axis every 12 hours. Further studies revealed that it takes only nine months to revolve around the sun; thus Ra-Shalom makes its revolution in less time than any other asteroid. Although extensive studies of its composition had not been conducted before the end of 1978, scientists hoped that the proximity of Ra-Shalom to earth might facilitate the gathering of more conclusive data about asteroids in general.

GEOLOGY AND GEOPHYSICS

In 1978 three scientists at the University of Texas were able to predict the location and size of a massive earthquake, and a Smithsonian Institution geologist made a report that may change existing theories of rock formation.

An Earthquake Predicted. On Nov. 29 an earthquake with a magnitude of 7.9 on the Richter scale struck southern Mexico. Its epicenter was within a mile of where University of Texas scientists had predicted it would be. In 1977, by examining earthquake activity along a fault line that runs through Oaxaca state, geologists Masakazu Ohtake, Tosimatu Matumoto, and Gary V. Latham were able not only to predict that a quake would occur near the town of Puerto Angelo, but also to predict the quake's magnitude with remarkable accuracy.

The geologists' predictions were based on established geological principles. According to plate tectonic theory, a fault is a boundary between giant land masses that move in opposite directions past each other; this activity creates irregular tension along their common boundaries. Some masses may slip smoothly past one another, causing only minor tremors; others may lock, producing a major earthquake. To predict the earthquake at Puerto Angelo, the University of Texas geologists first surveyed those areas along the fault that had experienced quakes. From this study they learned that most of the area surrounding the fault had indeed experienced recent tremors—except for a 160 km (100 mi.) stretch near Puerto Angelo. They then calculated the amount of tension that had been released on either side of the

160 km area by the earlier tremors, and this enabled them to quantify the amount of tension that would be released in a possible quake around Puerto Angelo. The success of their prediction means that a new tool has been found for predicting major quakes.

A Geological Process Reevaluated. On Nov. 14 the Smithsonian Institution announced the results of its recently completed geological expedition into the southwestern desert region of Egypt—results that challenge basic assumptions about planetary geological processes.

Headed by Farouk El-Baz of the Center for Earth and Planetary Studies at the Smithsonian's National Air and Space Museum, the expedition studied the causes of erosion in a desert near Bir Tarfâwi, Egypt. They discovered that the various kinds of rocks found there had been textured by wind erosion. It had previously been assumed that rocks on earth—and other planets such as Mars—were pitted with holes because air pockets had formed as lava solidified. The expedition's

This spruce tree is part of a forest found 25 ft. (8 m) below the surface of a Michigan bog. Studies of the primordial woodland led Northern Michigan University scientists John D. Hughes and W. James Merry to conclude that it was buried by an advancing glacier 10,000 years ago. That is 2000 years after glaciation was believed to have taken place in the upper Great Lakes region.

findings, however, made it clear that the wind, not volcanic processes, was responsible for carving out the holes. The wind accomplishes this, according to the researchers, by creating a vortex around individual particles of stone on the surface of a rock. These particles are eventually dislodged, leaving small pits in which tiny grains of sand become trapped. Repeated gusting of wind grinds the sand into the rock, and the holes are enlarged. This finding could be important in understanding the geology of Mars, since the desert studied is similar in appearance to the Martian terrain photographed by NASA space expeditions.

CLIMATOLOGY

There is a frequently expressed fear that such technological advances as SST aircraft and modern aerosol products will deprive us of the ozone layer of the stratosphere, which protects us from dangerous cosmic radiation. But the industrial era appears to have increased the amount of ozone in the troposphere, or upper atmosphere, of the Northern Hemisphere. And the presence of ozone in significantly larger amounts than normal should have a warming effect on the climate of the Northern Hemisphere.

This startling fact was announced on June 6 during the American Chemical Society's Fourth Biennial Rocky Mountain Regional Meeting, held in Boulder, Colo. According to measurements taken by the authors of the report, Jack Fishman and Paul Crutzen of the National Center for Atmospheric Research in Boulder, the amount of ozone (O_3) in the upper atmosphere of the Northern Hemisphere is three times greater than that in the Southern Hemisphere. There is no acceptable meteorological explanation for this difference. According to existing theories, ozone originates in the stratosphere and is carried downward to the troposphere. If, as these theories further assert, ozone is "destroyed" as it comes in contact with the earth, ozone destruction in the industrialized Northern Hemisphere should be three times as large as that in the Southern Hemisphere. But this is not the case. The drastic difference in the ozone influx into the atmospheres of the two hemispheres is difficult to explain. Comparisons of seasonal variabilities, of the photochemistry of the lower stratosphere, and of cyclonic activity and intensity all yield no significant differences. Nor are tropical winds responsible. So the report theorizes that the larger amount of ozone in the north must have arisen from relatively slow but steady photochemical processes. These processes include the oxidation of carbon monoxide (CO), a major source of tropospheric ozone, and the oxidation of methane (CH_4); furthermore, the oxidation of nonmethane

hydrocarbons could contribute up to 50 percent as much ozone as the oxidation of CO. Because existing theories cannot account for this puzzling excess of ozone, the Fishman-Crutzen theory seems plausible to many observers. What does it all mean? It means that unless scientists can somehow control the buildup of ozone in the troposphere, weather patterns in the Northern Hemisphere could change drastically in the future.

OCEANOGRAPHY

In March marine geologists met at Arden House near Harriman, N.Y., in a conference organized by Columbia University's Lamont-Doherty Geological Laboratory. They were there to discuss the results of deep drilling in the Atlantic Ocean. Such drilling had been carried on for ten years at some 150 sites, and evidence gathered during these explorations confirmed the theory that the continents at one time were connected and had slowly drifted apart.

According to this theory the sea floor is constantly moving away from both sides of the ridges found in the middle of the Atlantic, carrying the continents with it. To prove the validity of the theory, geologists sampled cross sections of ocean

A striking image of the Baja California peninsula coast of Mexico (right), a chain of coastal islands (center), and the Pacific Ocean (left), obtained by a synthetic-aperture radar unit aboard Seasat A on July 7. The ill-fated ocean-monitoring satellite, launched by NASA on June 26, stopped transmitting a short time thereafter.

floor sediment and the sedimentary bedrock that lies below to determine if they had been created by volcanic activity. They studied the ancient processes that are still at work, deep volcanic forces tearing the ocean floor apart and pulling the continents away from one another, just as 150,000,000 to 200,000,000 years ago they pulled Africa away from North America and formed the Atlantic Ocean.

This process, it is believed, cracked the crusts of both Africa and North America, and as the lava welled up it formed great deposits of volcanic basalt. The lava left a "chemical imprint" of trace elements that varied from south to north. The volcanic deposits found along the East Coast of North America, from southern Appalachia to Nova Scotia, bear the same imprint as the lava that is still being deposited along the Mid-Atlantic ridge which bisects the Atlantic Ocean. Moreover, trace elements identical to those found in Connecticut have been seen in rock formations in Morocco on the African coast.

Geological samples from holes that are drilled along the flow lines further and further away from the ridge still show the same chemical imprint. This finding has given rise to many questions about the composition of the earth's mantle. Is it a homogenous mass, or is it heterogeneous in composition?

Through the use of a new technique for comparing the erupted volcanic material with the material from which the earth presumably was formed, evidence has been obtained from the Atlantic Ocean drilling sites that shows that the outer part of the earth's mantle, the source of the lava, has been depleted of elements that are present in the continental rock. This discovery lends weight to the theory, not yet proved, that the continents were formed out of substances that "boiled up" from the liquid upper mantle. And it also appears to contradict an alternative theory, which states that the crust, mantle, and inner core of the earth were all formed rapidly around 1.6 billion years ago. The boiling up process would have occurred continuously over some 4.6 billion years. J.T.D.

ECUADOR. After six years of military government, Ecuador moved during 1978 toward civilian rule, with the adoption of a new democratic constitution in January and a presidential election on July 16. Jaime Roldós, candidate of the workers' party, the Concentration of Popular Forces (CPF), won the largest number of votes but fell short of a majority. The government scheduled a runoff vote for September, but later it was postponed until April, 1979. There was some doubt, however, whether the government would permit a 1979 election. Roldós had been a stand-in for his father-in-law, CPF leader Assad Bucaram, a Lebanese who had been barred from running for the presidency when the government passed a new law requiring a candidate's parents to be native Ecuadorans. The military had seized power in 1972, apparently out of fear that the popular Bucaram would win that year's election.

The Ecuadoran economy, which showed a trade deficit in 1977, received another blow in 1978 with the discouraging news that its oil bonanza might be approaching an end. Lt. Col. Luis Jativa, manager of the state oil corporation, announced that recent explorations for the purpose of discovering new oil deposits had been unsuccessful and that the country's 1.5 billion bbl reserve, at the then current rate of consumption, would last only fifteen years.

See STATISTICS OF THE WORLD. J.N.G.

EDUCATION. It was the year of the Bakke decision: In 1978 the U.S. Supreme Court agreed that white applicant Allan P. Bakke had indeed been wrongly denied admission to a medical school, but the Court also decided that race could be considered in a university's admissions policy. The continuing public-school financial crunch centered in 1978 on Ohio. Congress debated but failed to enact a bill easing the burden on families paying college tuition, and the administration of U.S. President Jimmy Carter made good on its promise to propose a separate, cabinet-level department of education; Congress, however, was not persuaded. A new law requiring disabled students to have access to a free public education took effect in September. And Harvard College, in a decision that reflected the "back-to-basics" movement in American education, approved new, stiffer course requirements for undergraduates.

The Bakke Decision. The Supreme Court's decision in *Regents of the University of California vs. Allan P. Bakke* encompassed six opinions on three separate issues: whether the quota system at the University of California at Davis was discriminatory; whether Bakke should be admitted; and whether race was an acceptable criterion in the admissions process. A majority ruled "yes" on each of these questions. Justice Lewis F. Powell, Jr., who provided the critical vote that forged the decision, justified the consideration of race in admissions policies: "Race or ethnic background may be deemed a 'plus' in a particular applicant's file," he wrote. "An admissions program operated in this way is flexible enough to consider all pertinent elements of diversity." *See also* SUPREME COURT OF THE UNITED STATES.

Schools and the Taxpayers' Revolt. Across Amer-

EDUCATION

Hank Holley (left) and his father George Holley (center) discuss the Denver education system with CBS News correspondent Charles Collingwood. They appeared in August on a three-part CBS television report, "Is Anyone Out There Learning? A Report Card on Public Education." The program dramatized the widespread concern over the quality of education in the U.S.

ica, resistance to further increases in school taxes spread. But nowhere were citizens angrier than in Ohio. Residents throughout the state expressed their unwillingness to pay more for education by overwhelmingly rejecting school-tax levies. As a result, several school systems were unable to open their doors on time in the fall. In Cleveland it took an emergency state loan of $21,500,000 to enable

classes to continue in the spring, and another loan to get them started in September. Voters in the ailing city turned down tax levies in April and June by margins as high as three to one. The money issue was often linked to school desegregation; Dayton and Cleveland were under federal orders to integrate their schools, and strong opposition to the programs among Whites afraid of busing contributed to tax levy defeats.

School boards across the nation were caught between two opposing forces: inadequate tax revenues and increased salary demands by teachers. The result was more strikes than usual in 1978. Teachers in Cleveland, New Orleans, Seattle, and other cities in nine states walked out at the beginning of the school year in September, idling more than 420,000 students. Class hours and curricula were also affected by the financial crunch, perhaps most harshly in the Ohio systems of Dayton and Toledo, but also in Los Angeles, where summer programs were canceled.

The Los Angeles school system put into effect a court-ordered integration plan involving the busing of 85,000 elementary school pupils in September. Despite boycotts by some white parents, busing generally proceeded peacefully in Los Angeles, and in Wilmington, Del., as well.

Legislation. In the fall Congress passed an aid-to-education bill that extended existing federal programs and added others designed to improve the teaching of basic skills. But the great congressional education debate was over tuition tax credits, and it ended in failure when the House of Representatives and the Senate could not agree

---

The Bakke in the Bakke Case

Allan P. Bakke's personal characteristics include a shy, pleasant personality, blue eyes, and thinning blond hair. In 1972, at the age of 33, the Minneapolis-born Marine Corps veteran and father of two decided to switch his career from engineering to medicine. Denied a chance to compete for one of 16 places (in a medical school class of 100) at the University of California at Davis, Bakke sued and placed himself at the center of a trail-blazing "reverse discrimination" case. In June the U.S. Supreme Court ruled, 5 to 4, that while race may be considered in university admissions policies, specific racial quotas are to be barred. Vindicated after his tenacious six-year fight, Bakke's only comment on his first day at medical school in September was a laconic: "I'm glad to be here."

Medical student Allan P. Bakke.

on whether to provide credits for private elementary and secondary school tuition as well as college tuition.

Proponents of tuition tax credits argued that tax breaks would ease the burden on middle-class parents more effectively than assistance through bureaucratically administered loans and grants. Opponents, including President Carter, insisted that tax credits would unfairly benefit wealthy parents and expressed their concern that such a program could become extremely expensive. The prospect of tax breaks for private and parochial school students in elementary and secondary grades, which the House version of the bill proposed, also raised serious constitutional questions. The tuition tax-credit bill died in conference as Congress neared adjournment in October. But an Administration-sponsored substitute, the Middle Income Student Assistance Act, was passed and became law on Nov. 2. It extended a college-student aid program to middle-income families and removed altogether an income limit on another student loan program.

President Carter, following through on a campaign promise, proposed the creation of a separate, cabinet-level department of education. Such a department, he said, would bring together a host of education-based programs scattered among a variety of agencies. The proposal, endorsed by the National Education Association, was opposed by other groups arguing that the problems of contemporary education would not be solved by simply reshuffling the bureaucracy. A bill creating the new department was passed by the Senate but failed to pass in the House.

Education for the Handicapped. Guidelines for the 1975 Education for All Handicapped Children Act went into effect in September, 1978. The act mandated the opportunity for free, public educa-

The Shepherd and the Sheepskin

A New York State legislator went on the warpath during the year against degree mills (institutions that grant academic degrees for a fee). In September he produced evidence that a doctoral degree from Pacific College in Los Angeles would be awarded to 6-month-old Shanna Shiffman of Albany for the payment of $150. For $25, Shanna could have received a transcript of courses passed but not taken; $50 would have brought her an associate in arts degree. All this for a German shepherd dog who dropped out of the Tri-City Obedience School!

tion for the 3,700,000 American students identified as disabled. It also required that they be taught wherever possible alongside their non-handicapped peers, a practice called "mainstreaming." Teachers, parents, and children were expected to assist in devising curricula suited to each handicapped child's individual abilities.

Congress had appropriated $565,000,000 for mainstreaming programs during the school year 1978–79. But critics worried that such a far-reaching project could cost millions more at a time when all too many districts were underfinanced. Moreover, mainstreaming could also mean a staggering increase in paperwork and red tape. And some teachers feared that already crowded classrooms would prevent handicapped students from

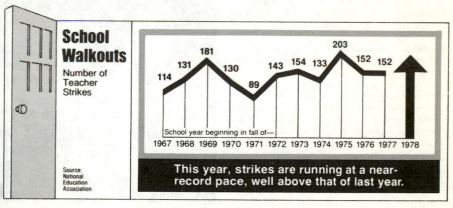

School Walkouts

Number of Teacher Strikes

114 131 181 130 89 143 154 133 203 152 152

School year beginning in fall of—
1967 1968 1969 1970 1971 1972 1973 1974 1975 1976 1977 1978

Source: National Education Association

This year, strikes are running at a near-record pace, well above that of last year.

EDUCATION

getting the extra attention they required. Supporters of the act suggested that such fears were unfounded. They pointed to statistics showing that 60 percent of all disabled students were already in regular classes. They also cited the success of mainstreaming in Massachusetts and other states. Whatever problems the act might raise, everyone agreed that its goals were both beneficial and necessary.

Harvard Curriculum Change. Changes in the undergraduate curriculum at Harvard University reflected a desire to endow all graduates with "basic literacy in major forms of intellectual discourse," in the words of the plan's architect, Dean Henry Rosovsky. It was the first major curriculum change at Harvard since 1945, when the university introduced its basic general education program, which required students to choose courses from the humanities, the social sciences, and the natural sciences, in addition to selecting a major field. But the pressures of the 1960's led to increasing flexibility in the requirements. The decline in the general education plan concerned Rosovsky, who wrote in 1974 that "at the moment, to be an educated man or woman doesn't mean anything." He appointed several committees to draw up a curriculum, which the faculty approved in May.

The new plan would require undergraduates to take from six to eight one-semester courses in five specific categories: literature and the arts; history; social and philosophical analysis; science and mathematics; and foreign languages and culture. The history requirement, for example, would consist of a course relating to the present day and one interpreting a major event, like the French Revolution. Students must also demonstrate competence in writing, a foreign language, and mathematics at the algebra level. Although there were grumbles from students and faculty about the plan, it was expected that other colleges and universities across the country would be watching closely as the new curriculum took effect in the fall of 1979.

Education Under Attack. Reexamination of the Harvard curriculum came at a time when education throughout the country was undergoing severe criticism. In a commencement address at Harvard in June, exiled Soviet author Aleksandr I. Solzhenitsyn implicitly denounced education along with the press, television, music, and other features of modern civilization; he said they had all contributed to the weakness and materialism of the West. Studies published in 1978 showed that more and more high school graduates were functional illiterates, unable to read signs or add up a bill. Average scores achieved by college-bound high school students in the Scholastic Aptitude Test continued a fourteen-year decline in the mathematics section of the test, although scores for the verbal section stabilized. One response to the general educational decline, the "back-to-basics" movement, was influencing federal school aid programs and curricula. In another response, required minimal competency tests were established in New York City high schools and elsewhere.   F.V.B.

EGYPT, ARAB REPUBLIC OF. The heady prospect of peace with Israel led many Egyptians to believe that their country's resources would finally be turned to dealing with Egypt's massive economic problems by the end of 1978. But at year's end, the peace treaty—which President Anwar el-Sadat had hoped to sign during the year—was still proving elusive, and several key details remained to be worked out.

The Peace Process. When President Sadat, Israeli Prime Minister Menachem Begin, and U.S. President Jimmy Carter agreed on a framework for a peacy treaty at Camp David, Md., in September, Egypt came closer to peace than it had been in thirty years. The Camp David summit reversed a spring and summer of bickering and recrimination in which the spirit engendered by Sadat's historic visit to Jerusalem in November, 1977, appeared to be vanishing. In presenting the Camp David accords to the National Assembly on Oct. 2, Sadat hailed them as the foundation for an overall Middle East peace. The pact, Sadat said,

Surviving Egyptian commandos are welcomed back from Cyprus on Feb. 21. In an abortive attempt to rescue a group of hostages held by Palestinian terrorists, fifteen Egyptian soldiers had rushed a Cypriot airliner without authorization. The commandos were shot down and diplomatic relations between the two countries were ruptured.

A Cairo office worker reads the Nov. 24 edition of the Egyptian newspaper al Ahram. On the front page was a draft text of the Egyptian-Israeli peace treaty, made public reportedly to demonstrate to the other Arab nations that Egypt was not negotiating a separate peace or abandoning its allies.

not only provided for the eventual return of all of the occupied Sinai to Egypt, but also called for an end to the Israeli military government of and the establishment of local autonomy in the Gaza Strip and on the West Bank of the Jordan River. "We are on the threshold of peace," Sadat declared. But hopes that the historic treaty would be signed by Dec. 17, the deadline agreed to in September, soon vanished. At the end of 1978, the document still had not been signed, and talks had broken down over two key articles in the treaty draft. First, Egypt was insisting on revision of Article 6, which would commit Cairo to consider its obligations under a peace pact with Israel as overriding any obligations in its 1951 collective security agreement with other Arab nations; second, the Arab country could not accept Article 4, which would establish permanent restrictions on Egyptian force levels in the Sinai. Egypt also wanted a timetable for the autonomy process in the West Bank and Gaza, but Israel was reluctant to accept such a "linkage" of the Egyptian-Israeli treaty with wider issues, since the Palestinians and Jordan would have to cooperate in a general agreement. And they had yet to show any interest in such participation.

Government. President Sadat received the backing of more than 98 percent of the voters in a May referendum; the result was considered a major vote of confidence. He dismantled the old Nasserite party, the Arab Socialist Union, and replaced it with his own organization, the National Democratic Party.

After the Camp David summit, Sadat decided that a new government would be necessary to lead Egypt into a new era of peace. So on Oct. 2 it was announced that Mustafa Khalil was being named prime minister to succeed Mamdouh Salem; Salem had held the post since April, 1975.

Khalil, a 58-year-old engineer who had been in and out of Egyptian cabinets since 1954, then named a new government in which only 11 of the 32 ministers were holdovers. The Ministry of War and War Production was renamed the Ministry of Defense and Military Production; and War Minister Mohammed Abdul Ghani Gamassi was succeeded by Defense Minister Lt. Gen. Kamal Hassan Ali. Ali, prior to his appointment, had been head of Egypt's Domestic Intelligence Service. Khalil also abolished the Ministry of Information, declaring that "state supervision of the information media has come to an end." He abolished the Ministry of Local Government, too, and said that more authority would be given to provincial governors and elected local councils. Khalil warned Egyptians against assuming that peace would automatically bring prosperity, but pledged to cut government expenses and improve public services.

Scandals and Plots. After Khalil took office the government moved swiftly to prosecute several politically sensitive corruption cases. Two former cabinet ministers and three former airline officials were indicted on charges of taking bribes and neglecting their duty in the purchase of four Boeing 707 jetliners—the case involved alleged payoffs by Boeing in the sale of the airliners to the Egyptian national airline in 1972. The prosecutor general also moved to revoke the parliamentary immunity of a former deputy prime minister, Ahmed Sultan Ismail, in anticipation of filing charges against him arising out of his tenure as minister of power. (He had been named in a Washington, D.C., court case as having been the recipient of a $322,000 bribe from the Westinghouse Corp. in connection with Egypt's purchase of a power plant.) Egyptian authorities announced Oct. 25 that sixteen members of a Communist secret organization had been formally charged with planning to overthrow President Sadat. The group, called "The Organization of the Egyptian Communist Party—Jan. 8," was reportedly formed in 1975. Officials said that the goal of the organization was to seize power by force and impose Communist rule in Egypt.

Military and Economic Affairs. The annual armed forces display, in which more than 200 planes flew low over massed troops and armor, demonstrated that Egypt continues to have the most powerful military force in the Arab world. But the show, held Oct. 6, also pointed up the equipment problems that plague the Egyptian armed forces, which are not able to obtain replacement parts for much of the equipment provided to them by the Soviet Union. The most advanced plane in the Egyptian air force, the Soviet Mig-23, did not take part in the 1978 display. Military sources said that none of Egypt's Mig-23s is operational. The arrival of the first of fifty F-5 jet interceptors that Egypt has ordered from the United States was also delayed, by a dispute over the price.

Egypt's overall economic position, however, continued to improve during 1978. Oil production was up to about 600,000 bbl per day—a level that made Egypt a net exporter of petroleum—and work continued on the widening and deepening of the Suez Canal. When that project is completed, supposedly in 1980, canal revenues are expected to double, to $1 billion annually. Egypt was also the beneficiary of a continued tourist boom during 1978. But at the same time international bankers and economists continued to bring pressure on Egypt to take tougher fiscal measures. The budget deficit for 1978 was estimated at $1.3 billion, and the trade deficit was expected to reach almost $2 billion. Egypt was expected to end 1978 with an estimated hard currency external debt of more than $13 billion—nearly equal to the country's gross national product. President Sadat declared in November that he felt there was "no other way" to deal with Egypt's accumulated economic problems than through a Middle East equivalent of the Marshall Plan. Sadat said he intended, after peace was achieved in the Middle East, to ask the U.S. to provide Egypt with $10–$15 billion in aid over a five-year period. He said he saw no other way he could simultaneously tackle the problems of overcrowding in Cairo; telephone, electric, and water systems that are always on the point of collapse; inadequate food production; and the need to industrialize. Sadat stated that a "Carter Plan" for Egypt, akin to the Marshall Plan following World War II, "will make miracles here like in Germany and Japan."

See STATISTICS OF THE WORLD. See also ARAB LEAGUE; MIDDLE EAST; and individual countries mentioned.   M.R.B.

ELECTIONS. The Democrats maintained their congressional majorities in the United States in the elections of 1978, losing fewer seats than usual for the party of a President two years into his term. But Republicans—especially conservative Republicans—posted significant gains in the Senate. The GOP also enhanced its future electoral prospects by winning major governorships and strengthening its position in state legislatures. A demand for tax and spending cuts and a suspicion of politicians were the chief concerns of 1978 voters. With local exceptions, voting in primaries was light, and only 38 percent of voting-age Americans turned out in November, the smallest number since World War II.

Primaries and Special Elections. Several of the primaries held to elect party senatorial and gubernatorial candidates resulted in upsets that signaled the middle-class "taxpayers' revolt" of 1978. Massachusetts voters turned out Gov. Michael S. Dukakis in favor of conservative challenger Edward J. King in the Democratic gubernatorial primary. In New Jersey, veteran Sen. Clifford P. Case lost the Republican primary to a former political director of the American Conservative Union, Jeffrey Bell. And in Minnesota, conservative businessman Robert E. Short defeated Rep. Donald M. Fraser for a chance to run as the Democratic nominee for the seat of the late Sen. Hubert H. Humphrey. King, Bell, and Short all campaigned to cut taxes drastically.

In Cleveland, 32-year-old Mayor Dennis J. Kucinich barely kept his office in a recall election in August.

In special elections held in February, Republicans picked up two seats in the House of Representatives. S. William Green and Robert Garcia won the seats vacated by Democrats Edward I. Koch, who resigned to take office as mayor of New York City, and Herman Badillo, whom Koch had appointed deputy mayor.

Senate Elections. Thirty-five of the 100 Senate seats—18 held by Democrats and 17 by Republicans—were up for election in November. Republicans picked up 8 formerly Democratic seats and lost 5, for a net gain of 3. The Democrat-Republican balance thus shifted from 62–38 to 59–41.

Among the 11 new Republican Senators-elect were 4 who unseated Democratic liberals. Conservative Roger Jepsen, with help from antiabortion and antigun-control groups, unseated Sen. Dick Clark of Iowa. Rep. William S. Cohen ousted Sen. William D. Hathaway of Maine. Conservative Gordon Humphrey, an airline pilot, defeated Sen. Thomas J. McIntyre of New Hampshire. And Rep.

William L. Armstrong ousted Sen. Floyd K. Haskell of Colorado. Two new Southerners also joined the Republican ranks. Rep. Thad Cochran defeated two opponents to become the first Republican Senator from Mississippi since Reconstruction. And Virginia's John W. Warner, a former secretary of the Navy, got campaign help from his wife, the actress Elizabeth Taylor, to edge Richmond lawyer Andrew P. Miller (D). Fate was also a factor in Warner's success. He had lost the Republican Senate primary to Richard D. Obenshain, but became the nominee when Obenshain was killed in an airplane crash in August.

The GOP scored gains in the midwestern and farm states. Republican candidates made a clean sweep of the Minnesota Democratic–Farmer–Labor Party, which had broken into factions. Attorney David Durenberger defeated Robert E. Short for Humphrey's old seat, and millionaire plywood salesman Rudy Boschwitz ousted Sen. Wendell R. Anderson. Sen. Charles H. Percy (R, Ill.) turned back a strong challenge from Chicago lawyer Alex R. Seith (D). In Kansas, Nancy Landon Kassebaum defeated former Rep. William R. Roy to become the first woman elected to the Senate since 1966. A political novice, Nancy Kassebaum counted heavily on middle-name recognition to win the Kansas race. She was the daughter of 1936 Republican Presidential nominee Alfred M. Landon. Two other women Senators, Muriel B. Humphrey of Minnesota and Maryon P. Allen of Alabama, both Democrats, were appointed to fill seats vacated by the deaths of their husbands in 1978. Muriel Humphrey did not run for reelection, and Maryon Allen was defeated in a primary runoff.

Nine freshman Democrats were elected. Among them were Rep. Paul E. Tsongas, who outpolled the Senate's only Black, Edward W. Brooke of Massachusetts, and former professional basketball player Bill Bradley, a New Jersey Democrat, who defeated Jeffrey Bell.

House Elections. Of the full 435 seats in the House

With a former governor of Georgia in the White House, successful gubernatorial candidates attracted increased attention in 1978. Among them were (clockwise from left) Dick Thornburgh (R), new governor of Pennsylvania; James Thompson (R), reelected in Illinois; Edward King (D), elected to his first term in Massachusetts; Ella Grasso (D), overwhelmingly reelected in Connecticut; and Jerry Brown (D), a big winner in his try for a second term in California. Both Brown and Thompson were frequently mentioned as possible Presidential timber.

A Troubled City, a Troubled Mayor
On election at age 31 as the youngest mayor of a major U.S. city, Dennis Kucinich promised to shake Cleveland out of its doldrums. And so he did during 1978, his first full year in office, though not exactly in the way expected. The brashly energetic mayor promptly alienated the city's business community and was at constant loggerheads with the city council. Police chief Richard Hongisto was hired away from San Francisco and then fired, after a public feud. A recall drive against Kucinich climaxed in August when he escaped ouster by a paper-thin margin of 236 votes out of more than 120,000 votes cast. His Honor's troubles, however, were far from over. In December, Cleveland failed to repay $15,500,000 in bank loans on schedule and became the first U.S. city to default since the Great Depression.

Mayor Dennis Kucinich of Cleveland.

of Representatives that were up for election, a record 58 seats were uncontested by their incumbents because of primary defeat, retirement, or death. Ninety-five percent of the running incumbents, including all prominent members, retained their offices. Republicans made a net gain of 11 seats; the Democrat-Republican balance thus shifted from 288-147 to 277-158.

Of the 19 defeated incumbents, 7 were so-called Watergate babies, first elected in the Democratic landslide of 1974. The total number of women in the House declined from 18 to 16. The number of black members remained unchanged at 16.

Governors. The Republicans won 9 governorships from the Democrats and lost only 3, for a net gain of 6. The Democrats still held a substantial 32-18

edge in governorships at year's end. Major Republican victories were scored in three states. In a bitter battle of Texas millionaires, Bill Clements defeated John L. Hill (D) by a slender margin. In Pennsylvania, former U.S. Assistant Attorney General Richard L. Thornburgh defeated former Pittsburgh Mayor Pete Flaherty (D). And in Wisconsin, a conservative college professor, Lee Sherman Dreyfus, upset Acting Gov. Martin J. Schreiber (D). Republican governors were also elected to replace Democrats in Minnesota, Nebraska, Nevada, Oregon, South Dakota, and Tennessee. Democrats succeeded Republicans in Kansas, New Hampshire, and South Carolina.

Democratic governors who won reelection included Hugh L. Carey of New York, who defeated state legislator Perry B. Duryea (R); Edmund G. Brown, Jr., of California, who exceeded his hoped-for million-vote margin over state Attorney General Evelle J. Younger (R); and Ella T. Grasso of Connecticut, who swamped Rep. Ronald A. Sarasin (R). Massachusetts remained Democratic as Edward J. King defeated state legislator Francis W. Hatch, Jr. (R). Florida elected Robert Graham (D), a state legislator who worked at one-hundred blue-collar jobs during his campaign, over businessman Jack M. Eckerd (R) to replace retiring Gov. Reubin Askew (D).

Among Republican governors winning reelection were James R. Thompson of Illinois, who won easily against State Comptroller Michael J. Bakalis (D); James A. Rhodes of Ohio, who narrowly defeated Lt. Gov. Richard F. Celeste (D); William G. Milliken of Michigan, who topped

Smile When You Pass That Resolution

Moriarty, N.Mex., has a population of 1300. In March an election was held for a vacancy on the city council. Two candidates ran; each of them won 99 votes. A runoff election would have strained the town's finances, so the candidates, electrician Bill Berry and farmer James Schwebach, agreed to settle the matter in a time-honored Western way: with a hand of stud. Schwebach's hand was king high, so a pair of nines won Berry a seat on the city council.

state legislator William B. Fitzgerald, Jr. (D); and Robert Ray of Iowa, who won a fifth term against state legislator Jerome Fitzgerald (D).

Achieving a goal set by the Republican National Committee, the GOP made large gains in state legislatures, winning about 275 seats and taking control of 13 legislative chambers from the Democrats. The lower chamber in Pennsylvania was also expected to shift to the Republicans, although several challenged elections and the death of a young legislator left the situation unresolved at year's end.

Referendums. California voters started a national trend in June by approving Proposition 13, a state constitutional amendment that restricted taxes on real property to 1 percent of its assessed value and limited increases in assessments to 2 percent a year. In effect, property taxes throughout the state were cut almost 60 percent, and local tax revenues were reduced by about $7 billion. By November, when a record 350 proposals appeared on ballots in 37 states, the tax revolt had spread widely. Alabama, Idaho, Massachusetts, Missouri, Nevada, North Dakota, South Dakota, and Texas passed Proposition 13-type limits on property or state income taxes. Voters in Maryland, Michigan, and Oregon rejected drastic tax-cut proposals, but one county in Michigan and two in Maryland did impose more moderate limitations. Arizona, Hawaii, and Illinois put limits on spending increases by state governments.

Other questions put to voters met generally negative or cautious responses. Philadelphia turned down a charter change that would have permitted Mayor Frank L. Rizzo to run for a third term. Labor scored a victory in Missouri, where a "right-to-work" law prohibiting mandatory union membership was defeated. In California voters turned down a ban on hiring homosexual teachers and another on smoking in enclosed public places. Pari-mutuel horse race betting was voted down in Virginia, jai alai betting was rejected in New Jersey, an equal rights amendment for women lost in Florida, and laws requiring deposits on beverage containers were defeated in Alaska and Nebraska. Voters approved restrictions on nuclear power plants in Montana and endorsed the death penalty for certain crimes in California and Oregon.   W.M.H.

EL SALVADOR. In 1978 tension mounted between the military government which has ruled El Salvador for the last forty-six years and the Popular Revolutionary Bloc (BPR), a three-year-old coalition of militant peasants, workers, and students. The bloc, encouraged by Roman Catholic clergy, demanded higher wages, lower rents, and other reforms. The government, fearing another mass

peasant uprising like that of 1932, was determined to suppress all discontent.

In March a clash between peasants and armed troops led to an eruption of small-scale rebellions, which the government put down with great severity. In mid-April protesting members of the BPR occupied the embassies of four foreign countries and the cathedral in San Salvador. The government then intensified its campaign against the BPR, resulting in another clash in September. An estimated 300 peasants were killed during the year. On the other hand, radical guerrilla groups continued to kidnap, bomb, and assassinate. A series of kidnappings of foreign executives in November and December, in the wake of the murder of a Japanese businessman, led to an exodus of foreigners. The few who remained adopted strong security measures. President Carlos Humberto Romero blamed the unrest on the Communists and the church. The Roman Catholic archbishop, Oscar Arnulfo Romero (no relation), in his turn denounced the government, not only in his sermons but also in a pastoral letter, for violating human rights.

See STATISTICS OF THE WORLD.   J.N.G.

ENERGY. After eighteen months of debate, the U.S. Congress on Oct. 15 passed a comprehensive energy program. Many observers noted that it was substantially weaker than what President Jimmy Carter had originally proposed on April 20, 1977, but it was nevertheless a program—the first comprehensive energy plan passed by Congress. Composed of separate bills on energy taxes, natural gas pricing, coal conversion, utility-rate reform, and general conservation, the program contained some landmark policies.

For example, it called for the eventual deregulation of natural gas prices, kept at what many said was an unnaturally low rate since 1954. It also mandated the conversion of large energy users, primarily industrial, from oil and natural gas to coal and gave tax credits for such conversion. Furthermore, by its utility-rate reform provisions, it encouraged individual states to set reduced rates for electricity use at off-peak hours and times of the year. According to one of the multitude of provisions in the new program, new cars getting less than 15 mpg would be taxed a $200 "gas guzzler" tax, starting in 1980. And tax credits would be allowed to homeowners who could recover 15 percent of the first $2000 for equipment designed to conserve energy.

The crude oil equalization tax, also proposed by President Carter and designed to allow domestic oil prices to be compatible with rising world oil prices, failed to pass Congress. Carter promised to include the provision in his second national en-

The Swain family of Hampton, Va.—Carol, Charles, Elaine, and Chuck—celebrate an anniversary in August. They had just completed a year's occupancy of a conventional house that had been equipped by NASA with an unconventional energy- and water-saving system. Total energy used during the year was less than 50 percent of what would have been used in an all-electric home; dollar savings amounted to $1200. Among the design features: improved insulation, solar collectors on the roof, and a water recycling system.

ergy plan, known as NEP-II, which he expected to send to Congress in the spring of 1979.

Nuclear Energy. Nuclear power continued to be a subject of considerable debate in 1978. At the end of the year, Commonwealth Edison ordered two nuclear steam supply systems and fuel fabrication services from Westinghouse; this was the only such order placed in 1978. Each unit will produce 1150 megawatts of electricity; the first is scheduled for completion in 1987 and the second in 1988.

On other fronts, however, there was even less activity. Several states put roadblocks in the way of nuclear power development. A committee of the California Assembly voted on April 13 not to exempt the Sundesert nuclear station, long a point of local controversy, from the state's nuclear safety laws. This action virtually doomed the plant, which was scheduled to house two 950 megawatt reactors.

On Aug. 17 the Wisconsin Public Service Commission told utility companies they could no longer spend planning money on nuclear power plants. Two already proposed plants were exempted from the ruling, which was to be in effect until uncertainties in nuclear fuel supplies and prices, waste disposal, and plant decommissioning plans and costs were dealt with.

Although Montana has no nuclear plants and no plans for one, the state voted 2 to 1 on Nov. 7 to impose strict standards on such installations. Montana became the sixth state (joining New York, Maine, Iowa, California, and Wisconsin) to have imposed strict standards on nuclear development.

The controversial Seabrook Nuclear Plant in southern New Hampshire continued to suffer its ups and downs. On June 30 the Nuclear Regulatory Commission ordered a suspension of construction, pending an evaluation of the cooling system and alternative sites. Although construction was ultimately allowed to continue, lowered demand estimates by several utilities involved in the project led them to attempt to withdraw, causing financial difficulties. At year's end, the ultimate construction of the project was somewhat in doubt.

There were nuclear power events overseas, too. In a close and surprising vote, Austrians voted on Nov. 5 not to allow the operation of a $530,000,-000 nuclear plant that had taken seven years to build (see Austria.). But in some parts of the world more rapid nuclear development was in order. The French, in particular, were extremely pleased with their "Phénix" sodium-cooled fast nuclear reactor and pushed for rapid expansion. And in Japan, four nuclear reactors, of the type manufactured by General Electric, continued the generation of electricity during an earthquake that measured 7.5 on the Richter scale at its epicenter. (The quake was one of the strongest in 1978, according to experts in Golden, Colo.)

Fusion energy received a boost when the Princeton University Large Torus achieved a record temperature for a tokamak-type machine. The event was considered significant since one of the main barriers to the successful commercial deployment of fusion power has been containment at the extraordinarily high temperatures at which the fusion reaction takes place. At Princeton a temperature of 60,000,000° C. was reached, well above the 44,000,000° C. needed for a substantial release of fusion energy. It was felt, however, that 100,000,000° C. would have to be reached before the machine could be considered successful. See PHYSICS.

Coal. The sixteen-week coal strike by the United Mine Workers of America in 1977-78, often marked by bitterness and violence, brought stocks of coal dangerously low. Mandatory curtailment of energy use was carried out in Ohio, Indiana, and Virginia. About 50 percent of coal production was affected.

The National Coal Policy Project—a group of academics, environmentalists, and industry representatives brought together to develop a consensus for the rules for the mining of coal—issued its detailed recommendations on May 23. But Interior Department officials predicted a three-month delay in the promulgation of permanent strip-mining regulations. After much controversy final regulations went into effect in mid-November.

Oil. At its annual meeting, held in Abu Dhabi in December, the Organization of Petroleum Exporting Countries (q.v.) decided to increase the price of oil by 14.5 percent by the end of 1979. Since the increase was to be in phases starting with a 5 percent increase effective Jan. 1, 1979, the average increase during 1979 would be 10 percent. The unexpected price rise (predictions before the event had been of a maximum increase of 10 percent) caused speculation about its impact on the U.S. inflation rate. U.S. Energy Secretary James R. Schlesinger estimated that it would add half a percentage point to the inflation rate and 3¢ per gallon to the price of gasoline.

In a widely followed estimate, the Exxon Corp. predicted world oil demand would shortly reach 148,000,000 bbl per day, representing a 65 percent increase over the 1976 demand of 90,000,000 bbl

per day. U.S. energy demand was expected to rise from its 1977 level of 38,000,000 bbl per day of oil equivalent to about 51,000,000 bbl per day in 1990. (This is significantly lower than historical growth trends; these estimates are based on a long-term growth rate of the world economy of 3.7 percent annually in real terms.) Oil would provide 48 percent of the world's energy requirements in 1990, down from 54 percent in 1976.

In a report issued in 1978, the American Petroleum Institute stated that 1977 was the most active drilling year since 1959. Preliminary figures showed that drilling in 1978 continued at about the same pace. On the other hand, successful wells were harder to come by—the number of successful oil wells drilled in the United States during the first half of 1978 declined 5.4 percent while the number of dry holes (unsuccessful wells) increased 11.4 percent.

A fire in the nation's Strategic Petroleum Reserve facility burned for six days before being extinguished on Sept. 27. Plagued with technical difficulties since its inception, the reserve (designed to be used in the event of another oil embargo) was able to store only 68,000,000 bbl by the end of 1978, instead of the planned 250,000,000 bbl.

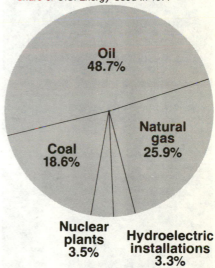

Fueling America
Share of U.S. Energy Used in 1977

Oil 48.7%

Natural gas 25.9%

Coal 18.6%

Nuclear plants 3.5%

Hydroelectric installations 3.3%

Source: U.S. Dept. of Energy

Diplomatic recognition of the People's Republic of China by the U.S., announced in December, should not only provide potential markets for the U.S. but also raises the possibility of new oil sources. Oil consultants and earth scientists predicted ultimate recovery of about 70 billion bbl of Chinese oil—40 billion from onshore wells and 30 billion from offshore wells. Major oil finds were also announced during the year in Mexico (q.v.).

Political and social unrest in Iran during the year, including a strike of oil-field workers, brought that nation's oil production down from its output of 6,500,000 bbl per day to a mere trickle, although by the end of 1978 the 700,000 bbl needed for daily domestic consumption were again being produced. The resulting gap for the world's oil importers was filled by an increase in the amount imported from countries other than Iran and by a drawing down of reserves. It was predicted that if the political turmoil were to con-

On Aug. 14 Texaco announced a "moderately encouraging" discovery of natural gas in the Baltimore Canyon area of the Atlantic Ocean, 100 mi. east of Atlantic City, N.J. Here the newly mined gas is being burned off prior to capping. In December, Mobil Corp., another of the eleven companies that had been drilling in the canyon, announced that it had abandoned its first well after tests had uncovered "no significant quantities" of either gas or oil.

tinue well into 1979, additional measures might have to be taken. The primary importers of oil from Iran are Japan, Israel, and the U.S.

Natural Gas. The proposed Alcan pipeline, designed to bring natural gas from Alaska to the U.S. and Canada, received a major boost in 1978 when the Canadian parliament approved the creation of a new federal agency to expedite its development. The only major stumbling blocks preventing construction of the pipeline were economic; a financial package, which should raise enough money to finance its building, was expected to be put together in 1979.

After the shortages and curtailments of the winter of 1977–78 the Federal Energy Regulatory Commission fortunately predicted a better supplied winter in 1978–79 for natural gas users. Primarily the result of switches away from natural gas to other fuels by industrial users, the predicted increased supply was also the result of higher prices in 1978. Many officials even predicted a surplus for 1978–79 and stated that industry should switch back to natural gas. In fact, Energy Secretary Schlesinger reversed the Department of Energy's previous position at the end of the year and stated that natural gas was in plentiful supply and should be viewed as a favored fuel, particularly since its use produced small environmental impact.

Solar Energy. The values of energy from the sun were celebrated on Sun Day, May 3, 1978. Events occurred from coast to coast, with thousands of people taking part in meetings and conferences. At the Solar Energy Research Institute in Colorado, President Carter announced a major policy review of the potential of solar energy. A report, sent to the President after seven months of study, stated that 20 percent of U.S. needs could be met by solar energy by the year 2000, assuming certain fairly aggressive federal actions were to be taken. The report recommended spending up to $47 billion between 1981 and 1985 for solar energy development. Previously, in a report issued on April 12, the Council on Environmental Quality had estimated that solar energy could meet 25 percent of U.S. energy needs by 2000 and as much as 50 percent by the year 2020.

The successful construction and operation of a novel solar electrical generating system was under way during 1978 in a new community college in Arkansas. When fully developed, the building will be one of the largest to obtain all of its energy from sunlight. The system will also provide space and hot water heating for the building, which has 52,000 sq. ft. The college's solar system will also include a large, advanced Iron Redox storage battery to provide electricity at night and during bad

"Gasahol" is a trademark held by the state of Nebraska. The fuel, which many users insist has increased their mileage as much as 20 percent, consists of 90 percent unleaded gasoline and 10 percent ethanol, or grain alcohol. In 1978 sixteen states from the farm belt and the Pacific northwest formed the National Gasohol Commission to promote use and production of the fuel.

weather. Trinity University of San Antonio, Texas, announced that it has saved almost $75,000 in one year with its large solar heating and air conditioning apparatus. A 352-ton absorption air conditioner, powered in part by 1608 concentrating solar collectors, began providing cooling, heating, and domestic hot water in December, 1977.

In another development, California Gov. Edmund G. Brown, Jr., signed into law on Sept. 25 a measure designed to spread the commercialization of energy from solar and wind sources. With several other bills previously signed into law, California thus became the most aggressive state in the nation in the development of solar energy. Effective Jan. 1, 1979, the State Energy Reserves Conservation and Development Commission must implement a state wind-energy program to speed commercialization of wind electric systems. Another law requires the Energy Commission to develop a plan for the maximum feasible solar energy implementation by the year 1990. A third newly enacted measure restricts the role of public utilities in the development of solar energy, while another law encourages energy surveys.

Also in 1978 the Tennessee Valley Authority offered twenty-year low-cost loans to 1000 Memphis residents to pay for the cost of installing solar water heating equipment. For an additional $3 or $4 per month (the loans are to be paid back at the rate of $13 per month) an electric backup unit for cloudy days would be installed. Current costs for heating water by electricity in Memphis were from $12 to $17 per month.

Conservation. Savings of up to 60 percent over conventional resistance heating were demonstrated in an Annual Cycle Energy Systems (ACES) concept tested by the Tennessee Valley Authority in conjunction with two federal departments—

Energy and Housing and Urban Development. The ACES concept uses the natural yearly weather cycle to provide heating, cooling, and hot water for residential or commercial buildings. Ice is formed in the winter as a heat pump draws heat from a storage tank under the building; the ice is preserved until summer, when it is recycled to provide cooling.

A special state commission reported on Aug. 15 that significant savings in energy could be accomplished in Massachusetts, as well as in the rest of New England, by the use of the process known as cogeneration, which uses the heat wasted in the production of electricity to heat and cool buildings. An investment of $240,000,000 in Massachusetts and $620,000,000 in other New England states in cogeneration could result in savings of $42,000,000 and $100,000,000, respectively, in fuel costs, according to the study.

Alternative Fuels. Missouri will have a $20,000,000 plant to turn corn and other farm products into alcohol for automotive use. On Sept. 25, 119 farmers established American Agri-Fuels (AAF), a cooperative, to build the facility. Alcohol, in quantities up to 10 percent, can be mixed with gasoline to form "Gasohol." Outlets in Illinois have been selling the mixture for several years, with some drivers reporting better performance. AAF proposed to produce the alcohol from the high-protein mash that is left over after grain has been processed.

Interest in the use of refuse as a potential fuel source increased during 1978. For example, drilling in a refuse landfill in Sun Valley, Calif., was scheduled to start in 1979 in a methane gas recovery project. Methane, the principal component of natural gas, can be produced from a variety of sources, including forestry waste, food processing waste, and commercial refuse landfills. It was ex-

ENVIRONMENT

pected that the Sun Valley project would provide enough fuel to generate 28,000,000 kw hours of electricity a year.

In Scotland, high sulfur coal (such as is found in large quantities in the Appalachian region of the U.S.) was successfully converted to pipeline quality gas (free of moisture and other impurities, such as sulfur dioxide formed from the sulfur in the coal) during a five-day test. The plant in Scotland is a forerunner of one slated to be built in Noble County, Ohio, to serve an estimated 100,000 residential customers.   A.M.

ENVIRONMENT. The effects and magnitude of man's assault on the environment were brought into sharper focus in 1978. But unlike the catastrophic grounding of the supertanker *Amoco Cadiz,* most of the year's major environmental issues developed slowly, subtly, and quietly.

Endangered Species. The Tecopa pupfish made news in 1978 when its name was struck from the U.S. Department of the Interior's endangered species list in July. The hardy 1.5-in.-long fish was the first listed animal to become extinct since the Endangered Species Act of 1973 came into effect.

The Socorro isopod (below), a tiny crustacean that developed while New Mexico was covered with seawater 130,000,000 years ago, joined the federal endangered species list in 1978. At right, Mike Hatch, the state official who discovered the rare isopod, peers into the drainage pond that is its only known habitat.

This pupfish, one of twelve known subspecies, sought out small pools and thermal springs in the Amargosa River near California's Death Valley. It could tolerate very salty water and temperatures approaching 42° C. (108° F.), but not the swift, barren river that resulted when the stream was rechanneled to build a bathhouse more than twenty years ago.

The Tecopa pupfish died quietly, but issues spawned by the threatened extinction of its Tennessee cousin—the snail darter—did not. As originally written, the Endangered Species Act prohibited any government-funded project that jeopardized an endangered species or its critical habitat. If and when an irresolvable conflict developed, the species was to win. In the first 5000 cases, no such conflict occurred. But the discovery of the snail darter—a 3-in.-long perch that could be found only in the Little Tennessee River, site of the nearly completed $119,000,000 Tellico Dam—changed all that.

The Tennessee Valley Authority (TVA), which began building the dam prior to the enactment of endangered-species legislation, challenged certain aspects of the law all the way to the U.S. Supreme Court. In June the Court ruled against the TVA (and for the snail darter), but the decision set off an intense public debate over the merits of the 1973 measure, which was due to expire at the end of September. Even earlier, Senators from Tennes-

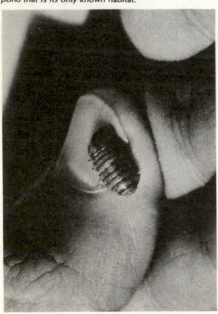

see and elsewhere had drafted an amendment that would permit the exemption of some public works projects if there was no reasonable and prudent alternative, if the project was of national or regional significance, or if the benefits of such an exemption "clearly outweighed" the benefits of conserving the species or its critical habitat. The decision on whether to override the act and exempt a particular project was left in the hands of a cabinet-level committee. In October this "override amendment" was passed by Congress (along with a measure allowing the TVA special consideration in this case) as part of the legislative package extending the Endangered Species Act.

Toxic Wastes. In August, New York State Health Commissioner Robert P. Whalen advised pregnant women and all children under 2 years of age to leave their homes in the Love Canal neighborhood of Niagara Falls. Whalen asserted that toxic wastes deposited in that area more than twenty-five years ago had created a health emergency in 1978, and he cited health statistics that showed a "significant excess" of reproductive problems. They included a relatively high miscarriage rate of 29.4 percent and a rate for birth defects exceeding 20 percent. Within a week, U.S. President Jimmy Carter had qualified the area for emergency relief assistance.

Love Canal residents first became alarmed by pungent fumes in 1976. Following heavy rains, a black liquid could sometimes be seen oozing from the soil or into basements. It appeared that a rising water table had leached out chemicals buried between 1930 and 1953, when the chemical dump was covered with earth and residential development began. As early as February, 1978, the Research Triangle Institute, under contract to the Environmental Protection Agency (EPA), had found 82 different compounds—including at least 10 known to cause cancer—in air samples taken from Love Canal homes.

The threat posed by toxic wastes was not confined to any single neighborhood or region. On Nov. 21 the EPA announced it had searched its files and found information indicating that an estimated 32,254 chemical dumps throughout the United States contained hazardous wastes in quantities that could prove harmful. Of these, the EPA claimed that some 638 probably represented a "significant" threat to public health. Still more disquieting was the agency's admission that it could identify only 103 of the actual sites, and that the larger numbers merely represented the "best professional estimate" the agency could hazard from what was known of past and present industrial disposal practices. Administrator Doug-

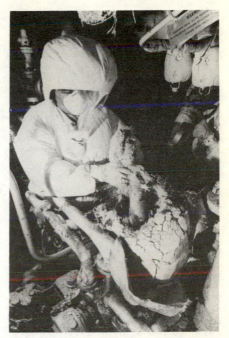

Beginning in 1978, workers in the Philadelphia Naval Shipyard were required to wear protective clothing when handling asbestos. The substance had long been suspected of causing cancer, but a special cancer-watch was declared when shipyard employees showed a high incidence of the disease.

las Costle noted that some 80 to 90 percent of the more than 30,000,000 tons of hazardous waste generated annually was being disposed of in ways which would not meet forthcoming EPA standards.

Radioactive wastes were a special concern. During the summer the Department of Energy announced that it would conduct radiological surveys of all sites where radioactive materials had formerly been handled. By November, some twenty-six sites with "enough radioactive contamination to warrant at least some cleanup" had been identified. All sites had been abandoned years ago by the former Atomic Energy Commission or its contractors. As at Love Canal, civilians now lived and worked at many of the sites. Preliminary estimates indicated that cleanup costs at each site would likely run into millions of dollars. But who would pay these cleanup costs was still in question by year's end.

The problem posed by mill-tailing wastes—residue from an early step in processing uranium

ENVIRONMENT

French cleanup workers fight the "black tide" of oil spilled by the wreck of the Amoco Cadiz. The supertanker broke up in March, dumping at least 67,000,000 gal. of oil off the Brittany coast.

ore—was covered in a measure signed into law by President Carter in late October. Under the law, twenty-two abandoned mill-tailing sites were made eligible for federal cleanup funds. Most of them are located in the West and are remnants of World War II weapons-development programs.

Alaska Lands. Despite an aggressive lobbying campaign by environmentalists, Congress was unable to resolve what has frequently been called the greatest conservation issue of the century: the Alaska lands debate. At issue was, first, how much of the state's majestic and pristine wilderness to set aside as national parks, wildlife refuges, and forests; and, second, whether such land should be permanently closed to commercial resource development, especially of mineral and energy resources.

The parcels under discussion, totaling about one quarter of the state, would have doubled the size of the national parks and refuge system. Nearly 110,000,000 acres of that land were protected from commercial development through mid-December under legislation enacted seven years earlier. But after new legislation failed to pass Congress, and with less than three weeks left until the seven-year protection period ended, President Carter invoked the Antiquities Act of 1906 to withdraw 56,000,000 acres for the creation of seventeen national monuments.

Protected areas included the remains of the Bering land bridge, the place where humans may first have entered the New World, and more than 110 gravel beach ridges which contain an archeological record of human habitation extending back 4000 years. Also protected was Admiralty Island, site of the nation's largest remaining virgin forest. Another monument embraces the Wrangell–St. Elias mountain range, containing the nation's largest group of peaks over 4500 m (15,000 ft.) and a glacier larger than the state of Rhode Island. Nor were living resources neglected: Many protected areas are sites where migrating waterfowl nest and where the bald eagle and brown bear roam.

Sport hunting was allowed on four of the monuments. Subsistence hunting by Indians and other rural Alaskans, such as the Eskimo, was permitted within all except the Kenai fjords, where there had been no current subsistence use. All the monuments were permanently closed to mineral leasing and mining.

Oil Spills. One of the worst oil spills in history took place in March, when the supertanker *Amoco Cadiz* smashed against the reefs off the north coast of France. The ship, which was carrying a full load at the time of the disaster, dumped at least 67,000,000 gal. of crude oil off the Brittany

Hail the First Antarctican

Environmentalists, fearful of the effect of overpopulation and dwindling natural resources, have long hoped for a population growth rate of zero throughout the world. So they were alarmed by the announcement that the birthrate in a single continent had recently skyrocketed 100 percent. The reason: On Jan. 7, 1978, Silvia Morello de Palma, wife of the chief of Argentina's southernmost outpost, gave birth to a son. Young Señor Palma was the first child ever born in Antarctica.

coast, polluting some 320 km (200 mi.) of coastline, half of it heavily.

The 3200 dead birds retrieved by French and American scientific study teams were estimated to be only 10 to 15 percent of the real kill. Several shellfish-breeding beds were destroyed and millions of dead or dying mollusks and other beach-dwelling animals littered the coastline for weeks. Oil penetrated shore and ocean sediments to depths of 23 in. and in concentrations averaging as high as 100 parts per million.

A University of Rhode Island conference in January showed just how difficult it is to assess the full impact of any particular oil spill. The conference reviewed the impact of the Dec. 5, 1976, grounding of the *Argo Merchant;* 7,500,000 gal. of crude oil were dumped by the tanker in what is still the largest oil spill in U.S. history. Within hours of the grounding, the first of what would ultimately number more than fifty research groups and government agencies began to assess the ecological damage. But because *Argo Merchant's* oil was quickly dispersed by stormy seas, the campaign was virtually fruitless. For example, a search for oil droplets suspended in water about the wreck site turned up a total of only one drop of oil. Contents of the stomachs of thirty-seven fish taken from the vicinity revealed only two fish that showed signs of ingesting oil that resembled the *Argo Merchant's*—and one of the two came from a spot believed to have been unaffected by the spill.   J.A.R.

EQUATORIAL GUINEA. *See* STATISTICS OF THE WORLD.

ETHIOPIA. Buttressed by some $800,000,000 worth of Soviet arms and 1500 Soviet advisers—in addition to an estimated 17,000 Cuban soldiers—the Ethiopians launched an all-out counteroffensive in January, 1978, to regain the Ogaden region. Somali forces, stalled since the previous November, were quickly overrun in the heavy fighting that followed. After the Soviets had given assurances that Ethiopia would not invade Somalia and after the fall of Jijiga, the key communications center, on March 5, Somalia announced its withdrawal from the Ogaden; and on March 24 Ethiopia announced that it had regained full control of the region.

Cuban troops were quickly redeployed in the rebellious province of Eritrea in March and April. On May 16, after stabilizing the besieged garrison at Asmara, the Ethiopians began their counteroffensive against the Eritrean secessionists. However, the Cuban forces, which had spearheaded the Ogaden offensive, were noticeably absent in the renewed fighting; a quarter of them had reportedly been withdrawn from Ethiopia by July. It was claimed that Cuba's President Fidel Castro had refused to allow them to take part in what he believed to be a strictly internal matter requiring a political solution. Although the offensive stalled in May, it was renewed in late June, and by August Ethiopian forces had broken the ten-month siege of Asmara and had regained a number of other towns. Eritrean secessionists regrouped, and in June the Eritrean Liberation Front and the Eritrean People's Liberation Front, which had merged in April, offered to negotiate. The central

Soviet and Cuban officers and advisers stand behind him as Ethiopian strongman Lt. Col. Mengistu Haile Mariam salutes his troops on March 8. It was a celebration of his country's victory over Somalia in the Ogaden.

government apparently rejected the offer. Faced with overwhelming Ethiopian material superiority, the Eritreans reverted to guerrilla tactics. Some pressure on the secessionist guerrillas was relieved by a renewal of guerrilla fighting in Ogaden, which was said to be growing at the end of the year; Ethiopian bombing raids on towns in Somalia were also reported. In both areas, however, the government remained in control of the major towns. In late November the government captured Keren, an Eritrean secessionist stronghold, and claimed victory, but the guerrillas said they would fight on.

Government efforts to root out domestic political opponents proved equally successful in 1978. The "red terror" campaign, which had led to the murder or execution of at least 1500 political opponents (2500–3000, according to Amnesty International), had proven effective by the summer, and attacks on government officials fell sharply. At the same time, however, the Soviets and Cubans appeared to be pressing Lt. Col. Mengistu Haile Mariam, head of the ruling military council, the Dirgue, to replace the military regime with a mass revolutionary party. In November, Mengistu traveled to Moscow to sign a treaty of friendship and cooperation with the Soviet Union.

While the government was concentrating on winning the wars in Eritrea and Ogaden and on rooting out its political opponents, the national economy continued to collapse. A locust plague broke out in the spring; by June it had affected approximately half of the country. Famine, considered worse than the disastrous 1973–74 famine, returned to Wallo and Tigre provinces, and, by year's end, United Nations officials estimated that some 1,500,000 Ethiopians were facing starvation.

See STATISTICS OF THE WORLD. J.T.S.

EUROPEAN COMMUNITIES, a supranational organization which includes the European Economic Community, the European Atomic Energy Community, and the European Coal and Steel Community. Because these communities share the same institutional framework, they are often called, collectively, the European Community (EC), or Common Market.

Membership. In 1978 the nine Common Market countries were Belgium, Denmark, France, Great Britain, Ireland, Italy, Luxembourg, the Netherlands, and West Germany. Greece, which applied for membership in 1976, will likely become the tenth EC partner. Observers expected negotiations on Greek entry to be completed in 1979, with full membership probable by 1981. Much less progress was reported on the applications of Spain and Portugal, both of which were submitted in 1977. Roy Jenkins, the Briton who heads the EC

Commission, an executive body, acknowledged in October the "moral right" of all three countries to join the Common Market. But Portugal's chronic economic woes and Spain's vast but underdeveloped agriculture (with its cheap prices posing a threat to French farmers) were stumbling blocks to membership for the two Iberian powers.

Only during the 1970's have Greece, Spain, and Portugal cast aside their right-wing dictatorships and opted for democratic government. With that fact in mind, the nine EC heads of state, meeting in Copenhagen in April, adopted a "Declaration of Democracy." The document states that "the maintenance of representative democracy and human rights in each member state are a central element of membership of the European Community." The purpose of the declaration was to ensure that the three prospective members would remain democracies before and after they joined the Common Market.

European Parliament. At their April meeting, the EC heads of state also agreed on a plan to hold direct elections for a European parliament on June 7–10, 1979. (Formerly, members of the European parliament were selected from their national legislatures.) The new body was to have 410 members, elected by voters in their respective countries.

It was still not clear, however, how broad the powers of the parliament would be. In November, French President Valéry Giscard d'Estaing warned that the parliament must not be allowed to expand its own powers, without the consent of EC member governments. Giscard's remarks were in keeping with traditional French opposition to the idea that the EC should become a European federation, with a strong central government.

Economic Policy. After prolonged negotiation, EC heads of state agreed in December on a common monetary policy—although not one to which all nine members could immediately subscribe. The heart of the new European Monetary System, effective Jan. 1, 1979, would be a complex "parity grid" which limits the extent to which the value of any member country's currency may rise above or fall below that of any other participant. Two countries whose currency values diverge beyond these limits are obliged to intervene on international money markets to bring their currencies back into alignment. The system also creates a European Currency Unit, based on a weighted average of all EC currencies, and establishes a $32.5 billion fund against which countries may borrow for purposes of monetary stabilization.

Six countries—Belgium, Denmark, France, Luxembourg, the Netherlands, and West Germany— joined the European Monetary System immediately. After some hesitation, Ireland and Italy also decided to join. But Great Britain, while agreeing to participate in the monetary-stabilization fund, declined to link the pound with the other EC currencies. The British reportedly feared that such linkage would make their weak economy vulnerable to the stronger EC economies, especially that of West Germany.

See articles on individual countries mentioned. G.H.

F

FASHION. Fashion turned around in 1978. At the beginning of the year it was "anything goes" or look like "Annie Hall." By the fall the fashion statement, influenced by European life-styles, was "dress up." The disco epidemic played a major role in clothing and life-styles. More and more boutiques, elegant restaurants, and disco nightclubs opened and became successful. The American consumer was ready to return to a measure of conformity and refinement. The average woman was tired of looking like a balloon, not even tied in the middle. Clothes became shapelier. Broader shoulders, straighter skirts, and waistlines appeared. "Dressing" not only for evening but for going to work was the key word. Influences from previous decades were felt on the fashion scene. The basic black cocktail dress, now worn with oversized jewelry, reappeared, accompanied by a foxtail scarf and a "smart" little hat with unusual trimmings and the ever-popular veil.

Fabrics and Colors. In fabrics, natural fibers, silk, cotton, and wool retained their status. Woven fabrics won over knits in all ready-to-wear categories in all price lines. The fluid knits remained important, however, in certain tops, dresses, and evening ensembles. Soft, textured fabrics continued to play a major part in the overall story. Jacquards, especially during the latter part of the year, became fashion news for day as well as evening.

In colors, neutral and muted colors remained important. Bright red, green, blue, and orange, however, made a strong showing, especially in tops. Observers predicted that for spring 1979 bright colors would be even more important in all clothing.

Sportswear. Sportswear continued to sell in all size ranges. Layered, oversized silhouettes were extremely popular at the beginning of the year, but by the end of the summer had lost much of their appeal. The slimmer skirt made news. The dirndl was pared down, and a straight slim skirt, almost always slashed at the side or front, was a fashion must. Pants became narrower, and some designers added a cuff. The full pants drawn tight at the ankle were frequently worn for day or after dark. Designer jeans acquired cachet, in versions offered by such names as Calvin Klein and Gloria Vanderbilt. Blouses were seen more often than shirts. Big and voluptuous, worn alone or over a

Right: Paris fashions displayed a new emphasis on hats and broader, padded shoulders in 1978. Shown here in a version from Laroche, the innovations had made their way to the U.S. by fall.

Far right: The 1977 film Saturday Night Fever, its disco dancing, and its star inspired new life-styles and the clothing to match. Like this model, many young men emulated the John Travolta look. His vested suit and open shirt became highly popular during 1978.

FASHION

Far left: Sheer fabrics and soft pleats mark this wedding dress in the style of Coco Chanel, from the spring collection of Philippe Guibourge. The model also wears the feminine high-heeled shoe that became popular in the U.S. during 1978.

Left: "Glamour returns to fashion" was the message carried by Ebony magazine's twenty-first annual tour of the U.S. Typical of the emphasis on black, slinky styles—and 1978's popular slit skirt—is this ensemble by John Bates, dubbed "Undone" by the designer.

sweater, another top, or with a vest, they were an integral part of dressing. Toward the latter part of the year, they too slimmed down and moved closer to the body. Femininity reentered, by way of the softer blazer and shorter, more fitted jacket, worn mainly with skirts. Sweaters, though big, were loose and lacy. The classic cardigan became a fashion item.

Active sportswear assumed a central role. Not only did bicycling, skiing, jogging, and tennis attract many more Americans, but new sports like racquet ball gained popularity. This of course necessitated the acquisition of new outfits appropriate to the sport. Running shorts retained their position as "the" shorts.

Dresses. Big, oversized, layered, and loose, the more cumbersome the dress the more it represented fashion. Sleeves were puffed, fuller, and wide. Shawls—single, double, or triple—were added. As the year progressed, however, dress manufacturers, influenced by sportswear, offered the two-piece ensemble in skirted dresses and in pants outfits as well. The most popular outfit featured an A-line tunic over pants. Styling began to narrow, and waistlines made their appearance. Belts or elasticized waistlines pushed aside the oversized garment. The collar line was reexamined, and the shawl collar became most popular. Necklines and hemlines were treated to more detail, and pleatings of all types were shown. Fabrics became softer and often sheerer, but combinations of fabrics were not forgotten.

Dancers' clothing gave the dress industry a helping hand. The body suit worn with a long or regulation-length wrap skirt was accepted by young and old. In soft knit fabrics it was slinky

and sexy. Worn for evening the dress moved with the body. Uneven and different hemlines added interest. Slimmed-down tunics were worn over narrow slit skirts or loose or very tight pants.

Coats and Suits. Early in 1978 coats were full, and the A-line coat was the winner. In fall, silhouettes narrowed, and the straight-line coat, mostly in solid colors, represented the newest fashion. The military influence became briefly apparent. During the latter part of the year, the long quilted coat, an outgrowth of the ever-popular ski jacket, arrived. It was not only great fashion but also utilitarian and warm. The skirted suit was accepted well by the consumer, particularly in the fall as narrower skirts replaced the full dirndl and the many variations of pleats. The shorter jacket with shawl collar or notched collar became the favorite.

Accessories. Belts for the newly emphasized waistline were a necessity. The Perry Ellis double-wrapped belt was seen everywhere. Belts went from very narrow, worn loose or fitted, to wide and cinched. They came in leather, rope, metal, fabric, and synthetics. Hats assumed new prominence. The pillbox, with or without veil, and the felt menswear look for women became popular. Still important were men's caps and knit hats with matching mufflers. For the disco crowd the sequined hat, often veiled, was a must. In jewelry, fine metals such as gold and sterling silver continued to adorn necks, arms, and ears. Dancing enthusiasts sported the flashy look of rhinestones. Handbags, except for basket weaves, added little to fashion news, but the shoe industry underwent a revolution. High heels, slim and narrow, were everywhere. They appeared on sandals, on strap-

166

ped pumps, and on high and ankle-length boots.
Menswear. For men "dressing" was as important a word as for women. For day, jeans and T-shirts were replaced by suits. Because suits were so expensive, however, dyed-to-match sport jackets and slacks became popular. Worn with shirts and ties, the look was tailored and conservative, and dress shirts and ties were widely sold. Men's toiletries had a banner year, especially in scents and skin products. Men wanted them, bought them, or received them as gifts.

Deaths. Among those prominent in fashion who died during 1978 were Charles James, innovative British-born designer of women's clothing, jewelry, and hats (Sept. 23 at 72); Barbara Cushing ("Babe") Paley, a frequent entry on the list of best-dressed women (July 6 at 63); Virginia Pope, a pioneer fashion editor for the New York *Times* (Jan. 16 at 92); Rose Marie Reid, the first to "construct" women's bathing suits (Dec. 18 at 66); and Sydney Wragge, designer and manufacturer of women's clothing (March 23 at 70).   M.H.

FIJI. *See* STATISTICS OF THE WORLD.

FINLAND. By early 1978 there were signs of improvement in Finland's economic situation. In 1977 the country had enjoyed its first trade surplus in a decade, according to figures made public on Jan. 30. The $50,000,000 surplus compared with a $1.1 billion trade deficit for 1976. The balance-of-payments deficit was reduced to $175,000,000 in 1977, a figure less than 1 percent of the gross national product.

Unemployment was reported to be declining from the total of 200,000, or 9 percent of the work force, reported on Jan. 30. Inflation was also said to be falling from the 13 percent average recorded in 1977.

In Finland's first presidential election in ten years, held Jan. 15–16, Urho Kekkonen won almost 84 percent of the vote for reelection to his fifth consecutive term. The 77-year-old Kekkonen, supported by the six largest parties in parliament, had called for a big vote to indicate mass support for his policy of ties with Western Europe and close relations with the Soviet Union. He was opposed by candidates of four small parties.

Helsinki was the site of a meeting held May 16–18 at which sixteen nations considered possible uses of their naval vessels during peacetime. Adm. Jorma Haapkylae of Finland acted as chairman of the meeting, which included naval leaders from the United States and the Soviet Union.

Acting Trade Minister Paul Paavela went to Australia in July to sign an agreement on safeguards for Australian uranium exports to Finland. Under the accord, Finland was authorized to buy Australian uranium for Finnish nuclear power plants. Finland already had one nuclear plant in operation, one nearly ready to be activated, and two under construction.

See STATISTICS OF THE WORLD.   L.A.S.

FISH AND FISHERIES. Throughout 1978 the U.S. fishing industry continued to feel the impact of the Fishery Conservation and Management Act of 1976, under which the United States had established a 200-mi. fishing zone on March 1, 1977.
Fishery Management Plans. Under the Fishery Conservation and Management Act, fisheries in the conservation zone are governed by eight Regional Fishery Management Councils. These councils were charged with management of all fisheries within their jurisdiction and were required to develop and implement Fishery Management Plans.

Dead dolphins litter the beaches of Iki Island in February, after Japanese fishermen had slaughtered about 1000 of the aquatic mammals. Environmentalists protested the killings, which the Japanese claimed were necessary in order to protect fishery resources.

FISH AND FISHERIES

Three plans implemented by the councils proved to be quite controversial. The Atlantic Groundfish Plan, prepared by the New England Council, dealt with cod, haddock, and yellowtail flounder—three species heavily fished by foreign fleets but now forbidden to them. In order to preserve supplies of cod and haddock spawned in 1975, the plan imposed quotas on American fishermen, resulting in the closure of several fisheries and a consequent storm of protest. Under pressure, a number of amendments were made to the plan, including a change that allows the fishing year to start Oct. 1. (This change was made in order to prevent a total shutdown of fisheries toward the end of 1978.)

A second plan, developed by the Mid-Atlantic Council, sought to preserve declining stocks of surf clams by severely restricting the harvest. This plan included a controversial moratorium on entry into the fishery.

A salmon plan prepared by the Pacific Council hit a major snag—the consequences of a 1974 ruling by Federal District Judge George H. Boldt concerning a treaty granting Indians in Washington State the right to fish "in common" with other citizens. The judge interpreted that language to mean that Indians were entitled to 50 percent of the salmon run. When state courts in Washington failed to accept this interpretation, the federal courts virtually took over the salmon fisheries in Puget Sound. Non-Indian fishermen were permitted very limited fishing time, leading to widespread law breaking and a few violent incidents.

Enforcement. Although the 200-mi. limit and Fishery Management Plans stirred controversy among U.S. fishermen, enforcement of the ban on unauthorized foreign vessels was easier than had been expected. The number of foreign vessels fishing in U.S. coastal waters declined by about one third, and few seizures were reported. Compliance improved steadily as an increasing number of American observers were assigned to foreign vessels.

Large Fish and Aquatic Mammals. A peculiarity of the 1976 law is that tuna were exempted from its provisions. As a result, Japanese long-liners harvested their customary 8000–9000 giant bluefin tuna (most in prespawning condition) from the Gulf of Mexico during the spring of 1978, although U.S. fishermen were limited to 3000 tuna under the international regulations to which the U.S. subscribes. The harvest of tuna by American vessels in the Pacific continued despite government restrictions on the bycatch of porpoises. Mortality of that mammal has been reduced by new fishing techniques.

Quotas set by the International Whaling Com-

mission in June are supposed to result in a reduction of the whale catch by 5 percent during 1979. Environmentalists had campaigned unsuccessfully for a ten-year moratorium on the killing of whales. The killing of 1000 dolphins off the Japanese island of Iki in February also aroused the concern of environmentalists, but this did not dissuade the Japanese government from allowing the slaughter of another 6000 dolphins later in 1978.

U.S.-Canada Dispute. Unable to reach agreement on reciprocal fishing rights, the U.S. and Canada on June 5 politely banned each other's vessels from disputed fishing areas. Canada banned U.S. commercial fishermen from its Atlantic and Pacific waters, while the U.S. extended its ban on Canadians to include the Great Lakes and sport as well as commercial fishing. Boardings were amicable, and no violent incidents were reported.

A.J.R.

FLORIDA. *See* STATISTICS OF THE WORLD.

FRANCE. The political highlight of 1978 in France was the close but decisive victory of the Center and Right parties over the challenging Socialist and Communist Union of the Left in the March parliamentary elections. The most notable developments in foreign policy concerned the People's Republic of China: the signing of a long-term trade agreement and the sale of advanced French weapons.

Political Affairs. In March, 85 percent of France's 26,000,000 voters flocked to the polls to elect a new National Assembly. The Center and Right parties beat the Left coalition of Socialists and Communists by a whisker, but the government of President Valéry Giscard d'Estaing was still able to count on 291 supporting deputies, as against 200 for the Opposition. The president's unusual intervention in the campaign, warning voters of the presumed perils of a leftist victory, together with the chronic disunity of the Union of the Left, largely accounted for the Center and Right success.

In the wake of this crucial election, Giscard's position was reinforced by the election of Jacques Chaban-Delmas as president of the National Assembly over Edgar Faure, the choice of right-wing Gaullist leader Jacques Chirac. Giscard made overtures to the defeated parties for their support but did not essentially change his cabinet or policies. Among the defeated leftists, not only were there bitter recriminations between Socialist François Mitterrand and Communist Georges Marchais, but there was also a rare display of strong public criticism by leading Communists of their party's leadership and its strategy. By October, however, leftists had defeated Giscard's candidates in five successive by-elections.

168

A general from the People's Republic of China checks out a rifle while shopping for arms in France. During 1978 the French negotiated extensive weapons sales to the Chinese, who are determined to modernize their huge military force.

Incidents of terrorism multiplied in France in 1978, although not on the same scale as in neighboring Italy. Most dramatically, Breton nationalists bombed the palace of Louis XIV at Versailles in June, extensively damaging several rooms and their contents. In Corsica, separatists set off numerous explosives and engaged in other violent acts to publicize their quest for independence from France. At the Iraqi embassy and elsewhere in Paris there were shootouts between feuding Arabs. And at Orly Airport on May 20, French security forces surveying El Al flights killed three Arab terrorists in a gun battle.

The Economy. The government instituted an unbending policy toward terrorism; this was paralleled by its austere approach to economic life. In 1978 the French economy exhibited some positive

Two paintings—"General Kléber" (left) and "Napoleon in Egypt"—were among the treasures damaged or destroyed when Breton nationalists bombed the palace at Versailles on June 26.

In Kolwezi, Zaire, French paratroopers conduct a house-to-house search for rebels on May 23. More than 800 French Foreign Legionnaires joined with Belgian troops to protect the European residents of this guerrilla-besieged Shaba region mining town.

tendencies—an improved balance of trade, a firmer franc, and a slightly increased rate of growth of the real gross national product—and some unfavorable trends, such as rising unemployment, a series of wildcat strikes, bankruptcy or serious weakness in such industries as textiles and steel, and a devastating spill of almost 1,600,-000 bbl of crude oil along the Brittany coast.

Toward the economy, Premier Raymond Barre, encouraged by the electoral defeat of the Left, pursued his earlier austerity program, with some modifications intended to create a freer market. A removal of long-standing price controls on consumer goods was accompanied by a curtailment of government spending and a lessening of subsidies to ailing, inefficient enterprises. The giant Boussac textile group, for example, was allowed to go bankrupt in May instead of being buttressed by state aid. On the other hand, in October the government moved to take control of steel production, pumping in $2.2 billion to modernize this key industry and make it more competitive in the world market.

Unemployment worsened during the year, increasing from 1,124,000 in May (5 percent) to about 1,500,000 by November. Youth and women continued to be the hardest hit, despite governmental emergency measures that included training programs and incentives to employers to hire representatives of those two segments of the work force. Further disgruntled by persisting inflation

and labor's loss in the March elections, French workers instituted many strikes during the summer and fall, interrupting truck production at Renault factories, garbage collection in Paris, and railway service throughout France.

The economy was dealt another blow on Dec. 19, when an electrical power failure affected most of the country for more than two hours. The blackout stranded rush-hour commuters in Paris and caused an estimated $1 billion in losses.

Three significant developments nevertheless promised to boost the French economy. In consortium with other European partners, the French continued building the world's first full-scale fast-breeder commercial power plant—the Super Phénix—on the Rhône River near Lyon. Also, through new contractual arrangements with the American Motors Corp., Renault was expected to gain wider distribution facilities in the United States. Another boon to the economy was the popularity of the Airbus, a jetliner manufactured by a European consortium in which France participated; these jetliners were sold to Eastern Airlines in the U.S. as well as to numerous other countries' lines; see TRANSPORTATION.

Foreign Affairs. French foreign relations were almost inseparably connected with French economic life in 1978. French officials and business representatives secured lucrative sales of French arms, industrial hardware, technology, and services. These ranged from a $226,500,000 contract for Soviet oil-field development to a $235,000,000 credit for Brazilian purchases of French industrial equipment, and a $140,000,000 highway project in Libya. Perhaps the most spectacular coup was a $350,000,000 sale of arms to China, with negotiations under way for a possible $2.7 billion sale, in spite of the objections of the Soviet Union, which did not want to see China's military strength increased. Finally, on Dec. 4, France and China signed a trade agreement for a potential $13.6 billion of exchanges through 1985.

The French also remained prominent in African affairs. In May, along with Belgian forces, French troops moved swiftly to rescue several thousand Europeans besieged in warfare in Zaire (q.v.; *see also* MILITARY AND NAVAL AFFAIRS). In Chad and Mauritania, too, French troops entered, in support of the existing regimes. In late May an estimated 24,000 French troops were stationed in Africa.

Giscard received a state visit from U.S. President Jimmy Carter in January, and, in July, joined him in Bonn, West Germany, at a meeting of the leading industrial powers to consider common economic problems.

See STATISTICS OF THE WORLD. D.J.H.

G

GABON. *See* STATISTICS OF THE WORLD.
GAMBIA, THE. *See* STATISTICS OF THE WORLD.
GEORGIA. *See* STATISTICS OF THE WORLD.
GERMAN DEMOCRATIC REPUBLIC, *or* **EAST GERMANY.** The Communist government of East Germany, led by Erich Honecker, was concerned in 1978 about public restiveness and continuing economic problems. Despite these difficulties, the nation stepped up its foreign-affairs activities in Africa, where it was acting as a surrogate for the Soviet Union.

Politics. In January the West German magazine *Der Spiegel* printed what it said was a protest document prepared by East German Communist Party dissidents. There was uncertainty about the authenticity of the unsigned manifesto, which criticized one-party rule and Soviet domination, but Western observers thought the document reflected the feelings of many discontented East Germans. The regime promptly denounced it, and Gen. Yevgeny Ivanovsky, the Soviet commander in East Germany, sternly warned citizens that anti-Soviet attitudes would not be tolerated.

To gain broader support, Honecker made unprecedented gestures to church leaders in March. He promised equality for every citizen, including those who practiced religion. That same month, a Protestant bishop was allowed to deliver a sermon on state-run television. In May, Protestants held a state-approved church festival in Saxony. Church and state leaders fell out, however, when the government proposed to begin military training for ninth and tenth graders. The courses were inaugurated in September, despite the clergy's objections.

The regime dealt harshly with dissenters. Writers who had protested the forced exile in 1976 of popular balladeer Wolf Biermann were pointedly excluded from an official Writers' Union congress in May. In August dissident Rudolf Bahro was sentenced to eight years' imprisonment for treason. An engineer and longtime Communist, Bahro had published materials criticizing the country's Moscow-style communism.

The Economy. Although East Germany continued to enjoy the highest living standard in Eastern Europe, the economy was under strain because of labor shortage, poor-quality production, high consumer expectations, and the rising cost of raw-materials imports. The government employed a variety of tactics to counter these problems. Honecker and other leaders continually urged workers to put extra effort into their work. To meet demands for consumer goods and to obtain hard currency, the regime maintained a chain of "intershops" where East Germans could pay for quality goods with Western money. That system only served to create friction between those who could somehow collect foreign currency—for example, from relatives in West Germany—and those who could not. East Germany's need for Western currency was largely responsible for a travel agreement reached with West Germany in November. Under the accord, West Germany was committed to pay more than $3 billion over a ten-year period; the major project involved a four-lane highway across East Germany from Berlin to Hamburg, West Germany.

At least one government program did meet with notable success. As a long-range solution to the labor shortage, the government offered incentives to couples having babies. As a result, East Germa-

171

ny's 1978 birthrate was higher than that of 1977.
Foreign Policy. East Germany's top priority in foreign affairs in 1978 was to maintain its close links
with the Soviet Union. In July, Honecker met with
Soviet President Leonid Brezhnev in the Crimea. It
was considered a sign of Soviet approval for the
Honecker regime that an East German, Lt. Col. Sigmund Jahn, was chosen to participate in a Soviet
spaceflight that was launched in late August; *see*
SPACE EXPLORATION.

With obvious encouragement from the Soviet
government, the East Germans increased their involvement in Africa. In Angola and Mozambique
they were active in organizing civil and security
police for national governments. East Germans
apparently helped orchestrate rebel attacks on
Zaire's Shaba region, and they reportedly aided
the Ethiopian government in fighting rebel forces.
In addition, they appeared to be aiding guerrillas
under Joshua Nkomo to mount attacks against the
Rhodesian government; *see* RHODESIA.

East Germany made a notable gesture to the
United States when a collection of more than 700

priceless art objects, grouped as "The Splendor of
Dresden," was shipped to the U.S. for exhibit beginning in June; *see* ART.

Deaths. The Honecker government suffered an
important personnel loss on March 6, when Werner Lamberz, 48, was killed in a helicopter crash
while on an official visit to Libya. Lamberz was the
youngest member of the Politburo and generally
regarded as one of the Communist Party's most
talented officials.

See STATISTICS OF THE WORLD.   F.W.

GERMANY, FEDERAL REPUBLIC OF, *or* **WEST
GERMANY.** The government of Social Democratic
Party leader and Chancellor Helmut Schmidt of
the Federal Republic of Germany suffered numerous setbacks early in the year. West Germany's
economic position remained strong, however, and
and Schmidt was personally popular with the German voters. By year's end, Schmidt appeared to
have regained firm political footing.

Politics. In late 1977 a West German newspaper
revealed that East German spies had gained access
to top-secret Western military documents. The affair reflected badly on the performance of
Schmidt's defense minister, Georg Leber. In January, 1978, Leber was forced to admit that the
home of a defense ministry secretary had illegally
been bugged by the government without his

*Soviet President Leonid Brezhnev (center), on a state visit
to West Germany May 7, has to support himself on his
foreign minister, Andrei Gromyko (left), in order to rise
from his seat. German Chancellor Helmut Schmidt is at
right.*

knowledge. Critics charged that Leber was incompetent.

Schmidt moved quickly to defuse the political crisis. In early February he reshuffled his cabinet. Leber resigned and was replaced by Finance Minister Hans Apel. New finance, research, education, development, and housing ministers were also appointed. The cabinet shake-up was the most important since Schmidt became chancellor in 1974.

Government efforts to combat terrorism proved to be a divisive political issue. Schmidt proposed legislation designed to make terrorist activity more difficult. Members of Schmidt's own Social Democratic Party feared that the bills would violate individual rights. After considerable compromise, antiterrorist legislation passed the *Bundestag*, the lower house of the West German parliament, in mid-February by one vote—the narrowest majority Schmidt had ever won. The laws were defeated in the upper house, the *Bundesrat*, in early April, but were repassed by the *Bundestag* a week later, giving police new power to search buildings and detain suspects.

Despite government wariness about terrorism, one of the country's most dangerous urban guerrillas escaped from a West German jail in late May. Two armed women forced prison guards to free Till Meyer, a man accused of kidnapping Christian Democrat politician Peter Lorenz in 1975. Meyer was captured in Bulgaria within a few weeks, however, and was returned to German custody.

Schmidt's government was shaken in June by several developments. West Germany's Free Democratic Party, the junior partner in Schmidt's coalition, suffered humiliating setbacks in two provincial elections. In the city-state of Hamburg and the state of Lower Saxony, the Free Democrats received less than 5 percent of the vote, thereby losing their representation in both provincial parliaments. Two days after the balloting, Interior Minister Werner Maihofer, a Free Democrat, had to tender his resignation to Schmidt. Maihofer had become the target of criticism for mishandling the 1977 search for kidnapped industrialist Hanns-Martin Schleyer.

The government looked forward to further state elections with apprehension. But the opposition Christian Democratic Union (CDU) was soon stung by a scandal. West German journals reported that Hans Filbinger, Christian Democrat premier of the state of Baden-Württemberg since 1966, had handed down death sentences as a naval judge during the Nazi era and had once personally supervised the punishment of a young German sailor. Filbinger, who was being men-

Convicted West German terrorist Till Meyer, seen here in a 1975 photograph, was on trial for political kidnapping and assassination when he escaped from Berlin's Moabit Prison May 27. Within a month he had been recaptured in Bulgaria and extradited to West Germany.

tioned as a possible candidate for the West German presidency during 1978, did not dispute the charge made against him but defended his past actions. A storm of protest ensued, and on Aug. 7, Filbinger stepped down as state governor of Baden-Württemberg.

The year's final state elections were held in Bavaria and Hesse during October. Bavarian conservative Franz Josef Strauss, head of the Christian Social Union (an ally of the CDU), led his party to a solid victory over the government parties. But in Hesse, a more important contest, the Social Democratic–Free Democratic coalition came out on top. On the basis of the Hesse results, political observers concluded that government popularity was on the upswing. Barring unforeseen events, Schmidt seemed assured of staying in office until the next mandatory national election in 1980.

The Economy. In his State of the Nation address in January, Schmidt emphasized that he intended to continue giving top priority to holding down inflation rather than to speeding economic growth. That policy led to public wrangling between West Germany and the United States. To help solve American problems with the declining dollar, the Carter administration hoped West Germany would stimulate its own economy. In February, U.S. Treasury Secretary W. Michael Blumen-

GERMANY, FEDERAL REPUBLIC OF

As the last Volkswagen beetle rolls off the assembly line Jan. 19, West German workers give it an affectionate send-off.

thal visited Bonn to press Schmidt for such a move; he met with no success.

The U.S. and West Germany partially resolved their differences in July, when President Jimmy Carter traveled to Bonn for a combined Western economic summit and state visit. In return for a Carter commitment to reduce American oil imports and to work for freer trade, Schmidt promised to introduce a stimulus program. Late in the month the West German chancellor announced a $6 billion package of tax cuts and measures for increased government spending on social programs and business investment. Parliament passed the program, increased to $7.8 billion, in November. A few days later it was disclosed that the U.S. Treasury planned to borrow over $1 billion worth of German marks in the market and use them to strengthen the dollar.

In the meantime, Schmidt and French President Valéry Giscard d'Estaing began to develop a plan for linking the currencies of the nine Common Market nations. The two leaders met in Aachen in September to hammer out the draft of their proposal. It was submitted to a Common Market summit in December with mixed results. Six of the nine member nations agreed to join and planned to exchange 20 percent of their gold and dollar reserves for a new currency called the European Currency Unit, or ECU. But Great Britain, Italy, and Ireland could not be convinced that such close cooperation was practicable so soon. **Foreign Affairs.** After numerous delays, Soviet President Leonid Brezhnev paid a formal visit to

West Germany in May. Brezhnev's aim was to air the Russian position on strategic-arms limitation and to cement long-term economic ties with the West Germans. Western diplomats were surprised by Brezhnev's evident bad health; at one point, he had to be helped to his feet. Even so, the Soviet leader negotiated a twenty-five-year economic-cooperation accord with Schmidt during his West German stay.

In May, Schmidt received Britain's Elizabeth II, and President Carter spent two days in West Germany in July. In addition to differences over economic policy, Carter and Schmidt failed to agree on the issue of the neutron bomb; see NORTH ATLANTIC TREATY ORGANIZATION. Talks between the two men put West German–American relations on a better footing. Bonn officials were especially pleased that Carter took time to visit West Berlin and pledge continuing American support for the city.

West Germany stepped up its diplomatic activity in Africa during the year. To repay the Somali government for its cooperation when a Lufthansa jet was hijacked to Mogadishu, the Somali capital, in October, 1977, Bonn granted a government loan to Somalia in January, 1978. During June, Schmidt made the first trip to black Africa ever undertaken by a West German leader. He conferred with Gen. Olusegun Obasanjo of Nigeria and President Kenneth Kaunda of Zambia in the evident hope of increasing West German exports and investment in the area.

Bonn signed a historic pact with Communist

174

East Germany in November. The two governments agreed to build a new highway linking Hamburg with West Berlin, which is surrounded by East German territory. *See* GERMAN DEMOCRATIC REPUBLIC.

A Death. Willy Messerschmitt, the German aircraft pioneer, died in September; *see* OBITUARIES.

See STATISTICS OF THE WORLD.   F.W.

GHANA. Gen. Ignatius K. Acheampong, head of Ghana's military government since 1972, was forced to resign on July 5, 1978. Increasingly autocratic in the face of civilian opposition to his plan for a so-called union government of military, police, and civilian representatives (with himself as elected head of state), Acheampong had submitted his plan in a March referendum; it narrowly won approval. With 43 percent of the electorate voting, the referendum carried 55.6 percent to 44.4 percent. Immediately afterward, opponents were arrested, with the government claiming that a general strike was being plotted. Professionals and students, who had led the 1977 strikes, rallied. Meanwhile, members of the Supreme Military Council (SMC) appeared disillusioned with Acheampong's failure to halt sharply rising consumer prices, government corruption, and a stagnant economy.

After he resigned, Acheampong was replaced by his deputy on the SMC, Lt. Gen. Fred W.K. Akuffo. Akuffo was sworn in as head of state on July 6. His first official act was to order the release of approximately forty political detainees. In the following months others were freed and political exiles were granted amnesty. Although Akuffo re-affirmed that the military leaders would turn the government over to elected civilians by July, 1979, civilian opponents remained suspicious of the military's objectives. And the new government appeared equally incapable of arresting the soaring food prices or increasing domestic production.

Kofi Abrefa Busia, who was Ghana's civilian head of state from 1969 until a military coup in 1972, died of a heart attack in London on Aug. 28 at the age of 65.

See STATISTICS OF THE WORLD.   J.T.S.

GREAT BRITAIN. The most surprising development in Great Britain in 1978 was the birth on July 25 of a baby girl conceived outside her mother's body. She was named Louise Joy Brown, and her birth was made possible by the pioneering work of two British doctors, Patrick Steptoe and Robert Edwards. *See* HEALTH AND MEDICINE; LIFE SCIENCES.

Politics and the Economy. Great Britain began 1978 in an upbeat mood. After enduring several years when their economy was plagued by a falling pound, double-digit inflation, and high unemployment, Britons were pleased to note a significant improvement in the financial picture. Substantial production at new North Sea oil wells was instrumental in turning the economy around. In addition, wage restraints imposed by the Labour government of Prime Minister James Callaghan had markedly reduced the rate of inflation.

The public appeared to give Callaghan high marks for improving Britain's economic outlook. His Labourites were short of a majority in Parliament, but the backing of the small Liberal Party—

The Rise and Fall of Jeremy Thorpe
He was a statesman and a wit, a tailored dandy, a rising star of Great Britain's Liberal Party who was touted as a potential prime minister. And then came a bizarre tale of sex and crime that left Jeremy Thorpe's political hopes in ruin and threatened to send him to prison for life. Allegations that he had had a homosexual relationship with a sometime male model, Norman Scott, surfaced in 1976 and forced him out of the party leadership. More devastating still, Thorpe and three associates were formally accused in August of hiring a gunman to kill Scott. The 49-year-old Thorpe, still a member of Parliament, denied all charges. But after a magistrate's hearing in December, Thorpe and his codefendants were ordered to stand trial for conspiracy to commit murder.

Jeremy Thorpe, MP.

The British Labour Party slogan proclaimed "Labour's Good for You." The Conservatives, led by Margaret Thatcher, seen here leaving a party conference with her husband on Oct. 11, apparently found an equally succinct rebuttal.

under the so-called Lib-Lab pact—kept Callaghan in power.

The opposition Conservatives were unable to mount a successful parliamentary offensive against the Labourites and trailed in national opinion polls. Late in January, Conservative leader Margaret Thatcher introduced a controversial new political issue in hopes of winning wider public support. Appealing to latent feelings of racism among Britain's blue-collar workers, Mrs. Thatcher told a television interviewer that Britain must be prepared to cut off nonwhite immigration or it would be "swamped by people with a different culture."

Mrs. Thatcher's remarks achieved some short-term gains. A hard-fought by-election at Ilford North in March, in which the Conservative candidate defeated his Labour opponent, represented a 7 percent swing to the Conservatives since the

general election of 1974. But Mrs. Thatcher also ran into a storm of protest. Labourites attacked her as a racist, and influential members of her own party, including former Prime Minister Edward Heath, were clearly disturbed by her tactics.

The Callaghan government, meanwhile, held to a steady course. In March it announced a long-range plan to use the massive profits from the sale of North Sea oil primarily for modernizing industry, but also for energy conservation, tax reduction, and improvement of essential public services. In April, Chancellor of the Exchequer Denis Healey presented an annual budget that called for modest tax cuts and limited stimulation for the economy. In the short run the government clearly intended to give priority to holding down inflation rather than to cutting unemployment, which was running at nearly 6 percent.

Trade union leaders, normally counted as Labour Party backers, denounced the government budget as too cautious. At the same time Liberal support for the Labourite administration began to erode. In two April by-elections the Liberals made a disastrous showing, and many party strategists concluded that the Lib-Lab pact was one reason for the Liberal decline. Party leader David Steel announced in May that the Liberals would end their accord with Labour when Parliament adjourned for its summer holiday.

Labour narrowly avoided defeat in the House of Commons in June. The vote came on a Conservative motion to halve the salary of Chancellor Healey as a slap at the government. Only after complicated bargaining with the Liberals (who abstained) and with a group of Welsh nationalists did Labour manage to squeak through, 287 votes to 282. In the weeks following, the Callaghan government completed work on two bills whose aim was to arouse support for Labour among Welsh and Scottish nationalists. The bills, known as devolution measures, granted limited home rule in matters like health and education. They were signed into law in late July, and are scheduled to go into effect in 1979 following referendums in Scotland and Wales.

The Liberal Party, meanwhile, was shaken by a stunning scandal. Former party leader Jeremy Thorpe, 49, was charged in August with conspiring to kill onetime male model Norman Scott. Thorpe promptly announced that he intended to retain his parliamentary seat and to run for reelection, adding to the Liberal Party's political problems. Thorpe's trial was still under way at the end of the year.

With the Liberals in disarray and no longer officially tied to Labour, the minority Callaghan government found itself in a ticklish spot. Most political pundits were convinced that Callaghan would call an autumn election to try to improve Labour's parliamentary position. But on Sept. 7, Callaghan pulled a surprise. In a brief television broadcast the prime minister announced that he had no intention of going to the polls just yet.

Callaghan had evidently concluded that Britain's economic situation would continue to improve and that Labour's chances would thus be better in 1979 than in late 1978. But he was playing a risky game. Inflation was down to 8 percent, but unions were increasingly restive about wage restraints. At the Ford Motor Co., 57,000 workers struck for nine weeks during the autumn and finally won a 17 percent pay raise—far above government-suggested guidelines. When Callaghan attempted to apply sanctions against Ford, he failed to get parliamentary backing.

Parliament reopened in early November, and the prime minister carefully avoided making controversial new legislative proposals. His government survived crucial test votes, but union demands in the wake of the Ford agreement and harassment by the Conservatives seemed certain to test Callaghan's political skills.

Northern Ireland. Sectarian violence in Ulster rose again in 1978 after having remained at a relatively low level in 1977. A series of bombings that began in January was reportedly a deliberate effort by the Irish Republican Army (IRA) to demonstrate that violence was not on the decline. The Provisional IRA claimed responsibility for the Feb. 17 firebombing of a Belfast restaurant, which took 12 lives and injured 30; this was the worst bombing since 1971. On Aug. 18 eight bombs exploded in West German towns that had British army bases. These bombs were the same kind used by the IRA, which was reportedly in contact with the German terrorist Red Army Faction. Other bombings, ambushes, and killings continued throughout the year in Northern Ireland. The terrorism spread to England on Dec. 17 when bombs exploded in Manchester, Liverpool, Coventry, Bristol, and Southampton, injuring nine persons. The Provisional IRA, believed to be responsible, had not set off bombs in England in almost two years.

Foreign Affairs. In 1978 the Callaghan government made an energetic effort, in conjunction with U.S. President Jimmy Carter, to head off possible racial

Life is a piece of cake for Prince Charles, heir to the British throne, as he celebrates his 30th birthday (Nov. 14).

war in southern Africa. Throughout the year, British Foreign Secretary David Owen devoted much of his time to developing proposals for possible political settlements in Rhodesia and South-West Africa (qq.v.).

In February, Britain joined the U.S. and three other Western nations in suggesting that free elections for an independent Namibia, as South-West Africa is known, be held under United Nations supervision. Namibia has been administered by the Republic of South Africa. After appearing initially to be receptive to the idea, South African Prime Minister John Vorster turned thumbs down; then in September he resigned his office. At year's end the Namibia issue was still unresolved.

An Anglo-American plan for Rhodesia was derailed in March when Rhodesian Prime Minister Ian Smith and three black leaders signed a political pact. Their so-called internal settlement did not include the black guerrilla Popular Front, and Owen and U.S. Secretary of State Cyrus Vance continued to press for an all-party solution to the Rhodesian political problem.

Two Communist leaders paid official visits to Britain in 1978: Yugoslavia's President Tito in March and Rumania's President Nicolae Ceauşescu in June. In May, Britain's Elizabeth II made a state visit to West Germany.

Two premiers confronted by a host of mutual problems—Constantine Karamanlis of Greece (right) and Bülent Ecevit of Turkey. They share a calm conversation at the White House in Washington, D.C., on May 30.

Three British territories became independent during 1978: the Solomon Islands in July, Tuvalu in October, and Dominica in November; *see* COMMONWEALTH OF NATIONS.

See STATISTICS OF THE WORLD. *See also* SOUTH AFRICA, REPUBLIC OF. F.W.

GREECE. Economic and foreign-relations problems continued to plague Greece during 1978. In the face of mounting inflation, workers won new wage increases but continued to demand additional raises. Little progress was made in efforts to negotiate solutions to the Greek-Turkish disputes. One bright note was the growing acceptance of Greece's application for membership in the European Community.

Domestic Affairs. The Greek trade deficit had risen from $3.33 billion in 1976 to $3.89 billion in 1977, it was reported on Feb. 6. The balance-of-payments deficit rose from $1.09 billion in 1976 to $1.24 billion in 1977. A budget totaling $6.94 billion for 1978 was presented to parliament on Feb. 16, an increase of 23.5 percent over the previous year. No tax increases were requested, however, since increased national and personal income was expected to produce sufficient revenues to cover the increase in expenditures.

The minimum wage was reported on Feb. 8 to have been increased by 22 percent to $10.50 daily for an unskilled worker. The award was made by a court of arbitration after employers and unions had reached a deadlock. A one-day strike was staged by workers in Athens on March 1 in demands for further raises, a five-day week, and reduced taxes.

Coordination Minister Constantine Mitsotakis, one of two new liberal ministers appointed by Premier Constantine Karamanlis in May, reported on June 18 that the inflation rate had increased from 12.8 percent in 1977 to about 15 percent in 1978. Mitsotakis said that, in order to reduce inflation and stabilize the economy, the government was taking steps to cut government spending by 15 to 20 percent and to reduce the public investments budget by 10 percent.

A law enacted on April 17 provided for mandatory death sentences as the penalty for terrorist actions resulting in loss of life.

Foreign Affairs. It was reported in January that the number of U.S. troops stationed in Greece had increased from 3300 to 3600 during 1977. Andreas Papandreou, leader of the opposition Panhellenic Socialist Movement, had demanded that all U.S. military installations in Greece be closed in retaliation for a decision to put Turkish generals in command of the North Atlantic Treaty Organization's southeastern forces. Although Greece had withdrawn from the integrated NATO command in 1974, U.S. officers had been in command of the predominantly Turkish forces remaining in the area.

At a summit conference in Paris Feb. 6–7, France and West Germany endorsed the proposed admittance of Greece to the European Community (EC). Premier Karamanlis visited Great Britain, Belgium, France, and West Germany between Jan. 25 and Feb. 1 to discuss the prospects of Greek entry into the EC. All four nations agreed to support Greece's admission.

Karamanlis and Turkish Premier Bülent Ecevit met in Montreux, Switzerland, March 10–11 to discuss the various Greek-Turkish disputes. They also met in Washington, D.C., during a NATO meeting in late May. The formal talks were resumed by foreign ministry officials of the two countries in Ankara July 4–6.

See STATISTICS OF THE WORLD. L.A.S.

GRENADA. *See* STATISTICS OF THE WORLD. *See also* ORGANIZATION OF AMERICAN STATES.

GUAM. *See* STATISTICS OF THE WORLD.

GUATEMALA. In a disputed election held March 5, 1978, Gen. Romeo Lucas García, candidate of the moderate military government, won the presidency of Guatemala by defeating Col. Enrique Peralta Azurdia, a former chief of state (1963–66), candidate of the extreme right National Liberation Movement (MLN). About 80 percent of the electorate, disillusioned by MLN fraud in the 1974 election and by the exclusion of leftist candidates, abstained or spoiled their ballots.

The election was very close, the two chief rivals each claiming victory and charging the opposi-

tion with fraud. Supporters of the MLN forcibly occupied the premises of the electoral council but were evicted. The Guatemalan Congress, which had chosen Lucas as the winner, refused the MLN request to annul the election. The bitter contest reflected a deepening split between the government and the MLN.

Violence plagued the new administration. In May landowners and soldiers clashed with peasant squatters in the northern village of Panzos. The peasants were demonstrating against the landowners' attempts to take over land where the government was to conduct a search for oil. The government blamed the resulting deaths of 38 to 114 peasants on incitement to riot by churchmen and Communists. Strife between rich and poor continued: The left-wing Guerrilla Army of the Poor killed soldiers and a general and seized two towns; right-wing guerrillas, backed by the government, committed some thirty political murders.

General strikes in February and October reportedly cost the Guatemalan economy $50,000,000. Nevertheless, owing largely to high coffee prices, the economy managed to grow by about 8 percent.

See STATISTICS OF THE WORLD. J.N.G.

GUINEA-BISSAU. *See* STATISTICS OF THE WORLD.

GUINEA, REPUBLIC OF. *See* STATISTICS OF THE WORLD.

GUYANA. The tragic deaths of more than 900 members of a religious cult in the jungles of Guyana drew the eyes of the world to the former British colony in 1978. At the same time the world became aware of the country's unfortunate economic plight.

Jonestown. In 1977 Jim Jones, an Indiana-born Protestant minister, and members of his California-based People's Temple moved to Guyana to establish an agricultural-religious commune, which they called Jonestown. In 1978 U.S. Rep. Leo J. Ryan (D, Calif.) went to Jonestown to investigate charges that Jones was depriving his followers of their civil rights. As Ryan and his group were preparing to leave on Nov. 18, he and four others were shot and killed, allegedly by followers of Jones. The mass deaths of the commune members, including Jones, came shortly thereafter. *See* RELIGION; UNITED STATES OF AMERICA.

Three separate legal proceedings were instituted by Guyanese officials. A preliminary inquiry into the deaths of Ryan and his four companions had reached no conclusion by the end of the year; one commune member, Larry Layton, stood accused in those deaths. Another commune member, Charles Beikman, was put on trial for the murder of a Jonestown representative and her three children in Georgetown, Guyana's capital. Finally, a coroner's jury declared Dec. 22 that Jones and "some person or persons unknown" murdered all but three of those who died at Jonestown.

Questions arose about relations between the commune and the Guyanese government. Observers noted that the Marxist, predominantly black government led by Prime Minister L.F.S. Burnham and his People's National Congress Party (PNC) since independence (1966) had welcomed Jones's socialist, multiracial commune. Leaders of the Opposition, the more strictly Communist People's Progressive Party (PPP), said that Jonestown seemed to be exempt from laws regulating imports and exports and the ownership of firearms. The Associated Press reported that the government had asked Jonestown residents, although they were U.S. citizens, to support it in a

July referendum. That referendum, which the PPP called a fraud, gave the PNC-dominated legislature the power to postpone elections and to revise the constitution almost at will.

The Economy. Guyana's economy, 80 percent nationalized, needed more than a new constitution. Based on agriculture, it had suffered a serious trade deficit in 1978, caused by heavy crop-destroying rains and a drastic fall in the price of sugar on the one hand and the high cost of imported oil on the other hand. The Guyanese also suffered from a food shortage, 14 percent inflation, an estimated 33 percent unemployment rate, and a high incidence of crime. The government, nevertheless, did obtain an $18,000,000 loan from the International Monetary Fund in August on condition that it meet several stringent economic requirements, including a reduction of its deficit.

See STATISTICS OF THE WORLD.   J.N.G.

The former British colony of Guyana was catapulted into the headlines in November. From deep in its tropical jungles, hundreds of bodies were flown across the Caribbean to the U.S. Most of the dead had participated in the establishment of Jonestown, a religious commune that vanished in a sudden orgy of suicide and murder. Reprinted from issue of Dec. 4, 1978, of "U.S. News & World Report." © 1978, U.S. News & World Report, Inc.

HAITI. *See* STATISTICS OF THE WORLD. *See also* WEST INDIES.

HAWAII. *See* STATISTICS OF THE WORLD. *See also* STATE LEGISLATIVE REVIEW.

HEALTH AND MEDICINE

The birth of an infant—Louise Joy Brown of Bristol, England—provided the medical headline of the year, for Louise was the first child to be conceived outside of her mother's body. And her story overshadowed all of the year's other dramatic developments, some of which involved such familiar and unfamiliar substances as asbestos and interferon.

During 1978 the government of the United States took steps to recognize mental health and alcohol and drug abuse as national problems requiring federal solutions. In his budget for 1978, President Jimmy Carter asked for substantial increases in appropriations for alcohol and drug research, and the President's Commission on Mental Health suggested that the federal government should alleviate overcrowding in state hospitals by creating a program based on community-centered mental health facilities. Plans for a national health insurance program, however, again got nowhere—although many observers remained optimistic that government-sponsored health insurance would eventually become a reality.

MEDICINE

During 1978 the death rate from heart disease and stroke continued to decline in the U.S. In fact, from 1970 to 1978 the decrease for heart disease alone amounted to 21 percent. During the same period the mortality rate from stroke went down 28 percent. The reasons for these decreases are not known with certainty, but it is likely that they stem from the American public's growing awareness of the dangers of smoking, overeating, and lack of exercise.

Louise Joy Brown and Friends. On July 25 in Oldham, England, medical history was made with the birth of a normal, healthy, 5 lb. 12 oz. girl named Louise Joy Brown. She was the first human being to have been conceived outside the womb. Her birth marked the culmination of years of painstaking research by two British medical men, gynecologist Patrick Steptoe and physiologist Robert Edwards, the well-known team who a few years before had won praise from reproductive scientists for their success in manipulating human eggs before and after fertilization.

Using techniques they had perfected from their earlier research, Steptoe and Edwards obtained an ovum from Lesley Brown, the child's mother, by first making an incision in her abdomen and then plucking the egg from one of her ovaries with a laparoscope, a device equipped with a viewer and a light. They placed the egg in a petri dish containing the sperm of Lesley's husband Gilbert Brown. Then they transferred the fertilized egg to a nutrient broth; after two-and-a-half days of growth, it was implanted in the womb of Lesley Brown. Except for a slight toxemia, or blood infection, which prompted delivery by Cesarean section nine days before full term, the pregnancy and birth were both normal.

Before they went to see Steptoe and Edwards, the Browns had little hope of having their own child. Although found to have no abnormalities in her uterus or ovaries, Lesley, like many other barren women, could not conceive because her Fallopian tubes (ducts that carry the eggs to the uterus) were blocked. With the success of the Steptoe-Edwards egg-manipulating technique, this blockage need no longer be regarded as an insurmountable barrier to parenthood. Many women previously considered infertile have been offered new hope that they will be able to bear children; in fact, it was reported that the births of several other infants conceived by the Steptoe-Edwards method of reproduction were expected in 1979.

On Oct. 3, two months after the birth of Louise Brown, Indian doctors announced the birth in Calcutta of the world's second so-called test-tube baby. The name of the baby, a 7-lb. girl, was at first not disclosed out of concern that the stigma of laboratory conception might jeopardize her future marriage prospects in India's conservative Hindu society. Later it was revealed that she was Durga Agarwal, daughter of Bela Agarwal and her husband Pravat. According to S. K. Bhattacharya, head of the three-doctor team who engineered her birth, the in vitro or "test-tube" method of fertilization had been utilized because, as in the case of Lesley Brown, the mother's Fallopian tubes were blocked. Other than revealing that the egg had been removed from the ovaries and kept in incubation for three-and-a-half days before it was

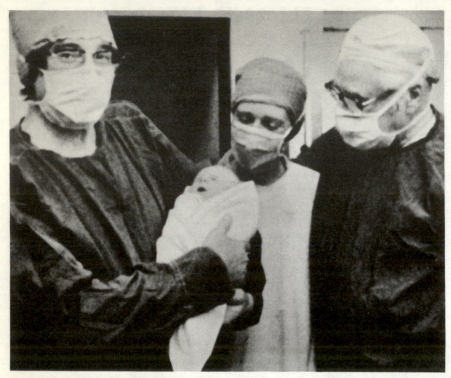

Louise Joy Brown, the first human being conceived outside the womb, is held by physiologist Robert Edwards; looking on is gynecologist Patrick Steptoe. The two doctors engineered Louise's birth, July 25 at Oldham General Hospital in England. In the center is the midwife who assisted at the delivery.

fertilized, the Indian physicians gave no details on the procedure they had used.

Coronary Artery Disease. For the past decade coronary bypass surgery has been considered one of the most effective treatments for coronary artery disease, a life-threatening condition in which the coronary arteries, the vessels that supply blood to the heart, are blocked by a buildup of fatty deposits. The surgery involves bypassing the clogged portion of the artery with a healthy section of vein transplanted from the patient's leg; an unobstructed conduit is thus provided through which blood can flow to the oxygen-starved heart. However, at the 1978 meeting of the American Heart Association, held in Dallas, a Canadian cardiologist presented grim statistics on the effectiveness of surgical intervention as a treatment for blocked arteries. Lucien Campeau, senior cardi-

ologist at the Montréal Heart Institute, reported that a large percentage of patients who had undergone bypass operations at the institute had not responded well. In fact, some had had a recurrence of angina pectoris, the severe chest pain that occurs when the heart is not getting enough oxygen. Campeau emphasized that the failure of the surgery should not have been a surprise, since the operation does not halt the progressive atherosclerosis (hardening of the arteries) that originally caused the blockage.

A less complicated and less expensive alternative to bypass surgery was developed in 1978 by Andreas Grüntzig of Switzerland and Richard C. Myers of San Francisco. Percutaneous transluminal coronary angioplasty, as the new procedure is called, takes only one hour to complete and involves the use of two simple tubes or catheters. The first tube, the guiding catheter, is inserted into a major artery of the leg or arm and gradually worked up into the diseased heart vessel. The other catheter, equipped at one end with a small inflatable balloon, is guided through the first catheter to the blockage, where the balloon is inflated. The balloon compresses the atherosclerotic plaque against the arterial wall, thus widening the narrowed vessel to normal size. Unlike bypass surgery, this method of treatment has had a high success rate, is not so costly, and does not entail possible medical complications. Cardiologists expressed optimism that this new nonsurgical procedure could be used in place of bypass surgery in as many as 10 to 15 percent of the diagnosed cases of coronary artery disease.

Smoking and Heart Disease. Research results made public in 1978 continued to implicate cigarette smoking as a major contributing factor in the development of heart disease. In April a team of researchers from Boston University Medical Center reported that women who smoke while taking oral contraceptives run a high risk of developing coronary problems. Earlier studies had proved that oral contraceptives alone can raise blood pressure and serum cholesterol levels, conditions that can lead to heart disease; the new study proved that these conditions are aggravated by cigarette smoking. Hershel Jick, author of the report, did point out, however, that these heart disease risk factors can be reversed if the patient discontinues the medication and gives up smoking.

Another Boston University study on the correlation between smoking and heart disease led to the conclusion that women who smoke are far more likely to have heart attacks than those who do not smoke. Dennis Sloane, a researcher involved in the study, reported in June that the probability of suffering a major heart attack is at least four times greater for women who smoke.

The effects of smoking on heart function in both men and women were disclosed in November by researcher Richard Naeye and his co-workers at the Milton S. Hershey College of Medicine in Pennsylvania. The scientists found that smoking accelerates a natural aging process involving the degeneration of small blood vessels in the heart and other organs. The muscles surrounding these small vessels are gradually replaced by fibrous, elastic tissue as we grow older—a process that normally begins at the age of 13 and proceeds very slowly throughout life. In smokers, however, this degeneration is so accelerated that it might give a 45-year-old smoker the heart of a 70-year-old nonsmoker.

The War Against Cancer. In August the American Cancer Society (ACS) announced that it would spend $2,000,000 for tests of the tumor-destroying capabilities of leukocyte interferon, a natural protein manufactured by the body. Earlier research had shown that white blood cells produced interferon a few hours after the onset of a viral infection. In order to prevent viruses from growing and multiplying, interferon interferes with their pro-

duction of the genetic material DNA and thus helps block cell division. In the course of their research on its antiviral properties, scientists found that interferon also inhibits the growth of cancerous tumors. Moreover, it has also shown a marked ability to slow down metastasis, or the spreading of cancer, because it is active in the bloodstream, the principal means by which cancer cells are transmitted to healthy tissue.

In previous cancer research the testing of interferon on human subjects had been limited by the meager supply and the high cost of this rare natural substance. The process of extracting even minute amounts of it from white blood cells is expensive and time-consuming, requiring large supplies of human blood, trained laboratory personnel, and advanced technology. With the ACS grant, however, researchers will be able to obtain enough interferon to conduct meaningful tests on human cancer victims. The ACS grant, the largest

Cardiologist Simon Stertzer of Lenox Hill Hospital in New York City displays an example of the balloon-tipped catheter that was introduced during the year for the treatment of some cases of coronary artery disease. By inserting the catheter into coronary blood vessels clogged by fatty deposits and inflating the balloon, a physician can relieve the severe pain associated with the disease.

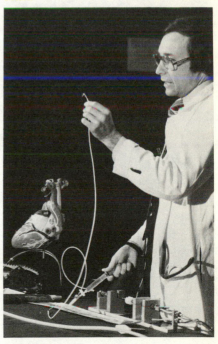

Future large-scale production of the hormone used for treating diabetes was made possible during 1978. Here the successful team of scientists, sponsored by Genentech, Inc., a research organization in San Francisco, explain how they produced human insulin at City of Hope National Medical Center in Los Angeles using the genetic apparatus of the intestinal bacterium E. coli.

in the organization's history for single-substance research, is a clear expression of confidence in the possibilities of interferon as an effective weapon against cancer.

Beginning late in the summer of 1978, the war against cancer spread to another front. Scientists under the auspices of the National Cancer Institute (NCI) of the National Institutes of Health began clinical trials of 13-*cis*-retinoic acid, an experimental drug that they hoped might eventually prove useful as an important cancer preventative. A synthetic analogue of vitamin A, the substance was to be administered over a six-month period to eighty-four volunteers who had previously been treated for cancer of the bladder. The NCI scientists are testing the effectiveness of the drug by monitoring these high-risk subjects for signs of any recurrence of their cancers. As explained by NCI scientist Michael Sporn, 13-*cis*-retinoic acid

belongs to a family of chemical compounds called retinoids, substances characterized by their ability to promote normal cell differentiation. Since abnormal cell differentiation is a common feature of malignancies, Sporn was hopeful that this particular retinoid might foster normal cell growth in cancer cells that might remain in the bodies of the volunteers. If the results of these tests of a vitamin A analogue are positive, the possible prevention of cancer through the use of synthetic drugs could become an important area of cancer research.

In October the NCI announced its intention to sponsor clinical tests of another possible anticancer agent—one far more controversial than any the institute has ever tested. Laetrile, a substance derived from apricot pits, has not yet been recognized by medical authorities as a cure for cancer. It was scheduled, however, to be used in the treatment of 300 patients with advanced cancers that had not responded to conventional therapy. NCI director Arthur Upton announced that the program would start in January, 1979, last for six months, and involve victims of ten different forms of cancer.

With the announcement of this study, the supporters of laetrile scored their second major victory of 1978. Three months earlier, in July, the U.S. Court of Appeals for the 10th Circuit had ruled that terminal cancer patients were entitled to laetrile injections even though the Food and Drug Administration (FDA) had banned the substance because of lack of scientific evidence that it was either effective or safe. The ruling said that the words "safe" and "effective" have no meaning when applied to terminal cancer patients.

Although the judgment weakened the FDA's ban on the substance, it was still illegal to transport laetrile across state borders for purposes other than those stated in the ruling. Laetrile supporters, however, expressed optimism that the outcome of the proposed NCI study would deal the final blow to the remaining legal restrictions against the use of the controversial substance.

Cancer Risks. U.S. health officials were concerned when cancers associated with exposure to asbestos, a common insulating material, began to show up during 1978, although its widespread use had been banned in 1973 when it was found to cause asbestosis, a debilitating lung disease. The substance had been used extensively in the building of ships for World War II; many workers exposed to it then died during 1978, victims of cancer of the lung, stomach, colon, and rectum. Since it takes thirty years for the cancer to manifest itself, it is not surprising that asbestos-related cancers should have appeared during the 1970's.

Although asbestos was also used in brake linings, home construction materials, and even gravel prior to 1973, most people were not exposed to as heavy a concentration of the carcinogenic substance as the World War II shipyard personnel: The general public does not, therefore, face the same cancer risk. However, in May the NCI took measures to alleviate the anxiety of the shipyard workers by establishing a telephone service through which they could get expert information on the dangers, real and exaggerated, that exist for them.

During 1978 another widely used substance also gained notoriety as a carcinogen. Ethylene dichloride, a colorless, oily liquid used in gasoline additives, dry-cleaning compounds, plastics, and many other familiar products, was tested by the NCI and found to produce cancer in animals. When spokesman Cipriano Cueto announced the results of NCI tests in September he noted that 2,000,000 American workers are exposed to the chemical and 163,000,000 lb. of it are released into the environment every year. He also stated that people who were frequently exposed to the substance did run a high risk of developing cancer. And he said that further tests were scheduled, to determine at precisely what level and duration of exposure cancer might be expected to develop.

Saccharin, the artificial sweetener widely used as a sugar substitute for over seventy years, was officially added in 1978 to the ever-growing list of substances considered carcinogenic. As a result of a definitive study concluded by the National Academy of Sciences during the year, researchers announced in November that saccharin is clearly a cancer-causing agent when ingested by humans. The study did note, however, that saccharin was of low potency when compared with other carcinogens. One important finding of the academy

A masked sanitation worker cleans the streets of New York City's garment district in September, after six area workers were struck by Legionella pneumophila—legionnaires' disease. Water used in air conditioners was at first thought to be harboring the bacteria that cause the disease, but city health inspectors were not successful in pinpointing the source of the short, isolated outbreak. Cases were reported on four continents during 1978, including more than 1000 in the U.S. alone.

Tests concluded during 1978 demonstrated the efficiency of this hand exerciser for patients with rheumatoid arthritis. Invented by doctors from St. Vincent's Hospital and Krewer Research Laboratories in New York, the device can delay crippling hand deformities caused by the progressive and painful disease.

was that even small doses of saccharin, when taken over a long period of time, as is the case with people who have used it since childhood, could increase the U.S. cancer rate by as many as 3000 cases per year. This finding could substantially increase sugar consumption among children. Furthermore, the academy's research found no scientific support for the claim that saccharin is helpful in controlling obesity or diabetes. The academy did not consider whether or not the substance should be banned, but a follow-up report was to be issued in February, 1979, recommending the best government policy for controlling its use.

A New Test for Cystic Fibrosis. An effective test for detecting carriers of cystic fibrosis (CF) or for detecting the condition in a fetus before birth was reported in 1978 by Jan Leslie Breslow and coworkers at the Children's Hospital Medical Center in Boston. The disease, which occurs in one of every 1600 to 2500 births, is a genetic disorder, manifested by an inability to digest food and difficulty in breathing. It is found mostly in Caucasians.

In the test, skin cells from people afflicted with CF were found to be more resistant than normal cells to the cell-killing effects of dexamethasone, a synthetic steroid hormone. Moreover, analysis of amniotic fluid cells (embryonic cells that have sloughed off into the fluid that surrounds a fetus in the womb) from expectant mothers known to be carriers of the disease showed resistance to the test hormone, indicating that the unborn baby was also a victim of CF. On the other hand, amniotic fluid cells from expectant mothers who did not have CF were killed by the test substance—an indication that their babies were normal.

Safe Detection of Sickle-Cell Anemia. In October a safe method for detecting sickle-cell anemia in unborn infants was reported by Yuet Wai Kan of the University of California at San Francisco. Hereditary sickle-cell anemia, which occurs chiefly among Blacks, is characterized by deformed (usually crescent-shaped) hemoglobin, acute abdominal pains, and ulcerations on the legs.

In the new test amniotic fluid is withdrawn from the womb of an expectant mother and fetal cells from the fluid are examined for evidence of the disease. Such evidence can be detected by mapping the sequence of genes in the cells' chromosomes, the DNA strands that carry hereditary information. The sequence is compared with that of someone with the disease, and if it is the same, then the fetus, too, has sickle-cell anemia.

A previous test for detecting the disease, which involved the withdrawal of blood from the uterine membrane that attaches the embryo to the mother, carried a 5 to 10 percent risk of fetal death. The new test, however, has proved to be a safe as well as accurate tool for diagnosing a pernicious disease before the victim's birth. G.W.N.

MENTAL HEALTH
The wide-ranging influences of the home and work environment on mental health became co-

siderably more apparent during 1978. The long-suspected link between emotional stress and numerous physical and behavioral problems was also confirmed by several studies. And after a year of investigation, the White House formally identified improvement of mental health services as a major priority of the administration of President Jimmy Carter.

Life Events and Pathology. Of course current life events exert a powerful influence on an individual's physical and emotional well-being, but a major historical disaster was also found to have had great impact on some individuals. In a report presented in May at the annual meeting of the American Psychiatric Association, researchers told of an "anniversary reaction" among children of Jewish survivors of the Nazi holocaust.

The reaction—found in 80 percent of the thirty children of survivors who were studied at Long Island Jewish–Hillside Medical Center—involved marked emotional problems at an age corresponding to the age at which their parents were interned in concentration camps. Moreover, the children's difficulties often seemed to revolve around fantasies of what their parents did to survive, as well as fantasies of what their parents' persecutors were like, according to Sylvia Axelrod, unit chief of the hospital's inpatient service.

A study of Italian-Americans living in Roseto, Pa., found that they had been adversely affected by something far different from the holocaust. Residents of Roseto had become nationally known in the 1960's for their uncommonly good health: Their heart attack death rate was astoundingly low, and their rates of peptic ulcer, senile dementia, and certain other emotional difficulties were considerably lower than the rates for the rest of the U.S.—and for neighboring towns as well.

However, investigator Stewart Wolf reported in April that since the 1960's, the health of the Rosetans had grown progressively worse, until it had become indistinguishable from that of the rest of the country. Wolf attributed the decline to a generational shift of Rosetans from a close-knit ethnic Italian life-style to a more Americanized way of life, emphasizing the family far less. The erosion of family and community ties that most Americans had experienced over several generations seemed to have happened to Roseto within just a few years, Wolf explained. The result was a decline in overall physical health. "American society emphasizes 'standing on one's own feet' and being independent,' " he said. "We just went too far with it."

The Mental Health Commission. One year and $800,000 worth of investigation and public hearings culminated in May with the report of the President's Commission on Mental Health. With the President's wife, Rosalynn Carter, serving as honorary chairperson, the commission offered 117 recommendations, including one that suggests allocating $50,000,000 per year over a five-year period for the phasing down of large state hospitals and the development of "community-based services" instead. Such services would replace the Community Mental Health Centers concept, started under President John F. Kennedy, with more available and informal urban, suburban, and rural help centers. Earlier, in January, President Carter's budget requests had already reflected the preliminary suggestions of the commission—calling for substantial increases in appropriations for mental health and alcohol and drug research.

Stress. The long-suspected stress-illness link was pinpointed with considerable accuracy in 1978. At a March meeting of the American Psychopathological Association, Johns Hopkins University so-

William Milligan (right) was arrested in Columbus, Ohio, during 1978 and charged with several counts of rape. During his interrogation it became apparent that Milligan, 23, suffered a rare disorder, true multiple personality. Ten "people"—eight of them male, two of them female, ranging in age from 3 to 23—inhabit his body. Several of the personalities are talented artists, and each draws or paints in an entirely different style.

ciologist M. Harvey Brenner detailed the connection between economic trends and such indications of pathology as suicides, admissions to mental hospitals, heart disease, imprisonment, homicide, and cirrhosis of the liver.

However, Brenner reported that according to one study, upswings in illness and antisocial behavior coincided not with downward economic trends, but with short-term upward spurts that frequently followed economic depressions or recessions. The study, which spanned 1900 to 1975, suggests that certain persons hit hard by financial loss in a depression are unable to recover as others do during the overall prosperity period that follows. This phenomenon is so devastating and pronounced, says Brenner, that "there are people who would not have died if they had not also experienced a rapid economic growth period."

And in research results presented at the same meeting, it was reported that the rigors of being an air traffic controller appeared to trigger extreme fluctuations in blood pressure in one third to one half of the 400 controllers involved in the test. Blood pressure shot up significantly for more than half the men on high work load days, reported Robert Rose of the University of Texas Medical Branch at Galveston. And in another study, by Boston University researcher Steven Locke, stressful situations for air traffic controllers apparently triggered deficits in immunity against certain diseases within certain "poor coping" individuals.

Drugs and Alcohol. To help them cope with a variety of stresses—and for a variety of other reasons as well—millions of Americans have turned to drugs and alcohol. But the latest surveys in the U.S. indicate that the use of such mind-altering substances, although still extensive, is holding fairly constant and in some cases is showing signs of declining.

National Institute on Drug Abuse figures reflect a 73 percent decline in prescriptions for barbiturate sleeping pills from 1971 to 1976. Even the most frequently prescribed sleeping pills—nonbarbiturate tranquilizers such as Valium and Librium—have decreased in use since 1974, according to the report, issued in February.

An October report from the Department of Health, Education, and Welfare (HEW) indicated, to a lesser degree, a leveling off of per capita alcohol consumption. However, HEW estimated that 10,000,000 adults are either alcoholics or problem drinkers and that as many as 205,000 deaths each year are alcohol related. In addition, more than 3,000,000 14- to 17-year-old youngsters in the U.S. are considered problem drinkers, according to HEW estimates.   J.P.G.

DENTISTRY

With continued emphasis on prevention and increased productivity, the dental profession during 1978 continued to maintain its long-standing track record of holding dental fee increases to about the same level as the rise in the overall economy. These efforts drew praise from President Carter, who wrote the American Dental Association (ADA) commending the nation's dentists on "the more moderate behavior of dentists' fees." In response, Frank P. Bowyer of Knoxville, Tenn., ADA president, explained that "high speed technology, innovations in the use of dental auxiliaries and other advancements have enabled us to treat more patients in a given day. Because of this we have been able to avoid passing on to the patient much of the inflationary rise in dental office equipment and supplies and wage increases of dental office personnel. Such advances in dental office productivity are essential to our continued progress in fee moderation."

Although the ADA has had reservations about the Carter administration's principles for a national health plan, the organization announced in July that it was encouraged by the President's recognition that "so complex an undertaking deserves an extremely careful and judicious approach." The ADA said it was encouraged by the President's recognition of a need to forge a partnership with the private practice system in providing health care for Americans. "Reference to freedom of choice, financing through multiple sources, including employer-employee contributions, and consumer cost sharing appear to conform to elements of the Association's Guidelines for Dentistry's Participation in a National Health Program," ADA officials said.

Gum Disease. University of Texas dental researchers have suggested that periodontal or gum disease may actually consist of several separate diseases caused by different bacteria which in turn induce different inflammatory cell responses in the gum tissues. Barnet M. Levy and Bruce F. Mackler of Houston reported that their findings are based on the development of a new research tool, a method to isolate inflammatory cells directly from diseased human tissue for therapeutic reasons. At the annual meeting of the International Association for Dental Research in March 1978, they stated that functional studies of these isolated inflammatory cells and of lymphocytes (white cells) from the blood of patients shed new light on how the gum tissues can be destroyed. For instance, lymphocytes can produce an enzyme called collagenase, which destroys the tissue fibers holding the teeth in place.

Fluoride Rinse Cuts Decay. A two-year fluoride

Dentistry took a new turn in 1978 with the introduction of dental services in retail stores, such as this Sears establishment in California. Many stores there and in New York offered complete services to their customers as a low-cost alternative to private-office dentistry—and they were open seven days per week.

treatment study in schools in seventeen communities has proved that a weekly mouth rinse program can be an effective and inexpensive way of reducing caries, according to scientists at the National Institute of Dental Research (NIDR). "We now have a method for partial prevention of caries (decay) that is effective, costs very little, is easily administered and is readily accepted by the public," said James A. Carlos, director of the NIDR's National Caries Program. Preliminary test results, involving 75,000 children, indicated that cavity reduction after two years ranged up to 46 percent. The cost of such a program was estimated at 50¢ per child for each school year.

New Clues to Tooth Decay. Dental scientists may have some new answers to the question of why some individuals escape the misery of dental decay throughout their lives and others are severely affected. "One possible explanation is that the bacteria which reside in the mouths of caries-free people are different from the oral bacteria of caries-active individuals," a research team at the University of Maryland reported to the International Association for Dental Research annual meeting. A newly developed culture technique enables laboratory studies of bacteria thought to

be responsible for tooth decay and gum disease. Preliminary experiments with caries-free and caries-active dental students and caries-active patients at the University of Maryland have shown that the populations of certain oral bacteria are remarkably stable while others fluctuate periodically. Another finding was that the diet, particularly the amount of sugar eaten, correlated with the extent of decay activity of the subjects. The decay-free individuals consumed significantly less sugar per week than the caries-active subjects.

Sealant Protection. Plastic sealant that is well applied can protect a tooth from further deterioration even if some decay is inadvertently left behind, a Temple University dental scientist reported in 1978. Results of a five-year study indicated that "a well-applied pit and fissure sealant polymerized by ultraviolet light will retard or prevent the progression of decay in the teeth of teenaged patients," Robert Going of Philadelphia told the International Association for Dental Research. The study's objective was to determine the viability of bacteria in cavities that had been sealed for five years. The sealant treatment resulted in 89 percent reversal from the caries-active (decayed) state.   J.B.

HONDURAS. Three rightist military leaders ousted moderate Col. Juan Alberto Melgar Castro from the presidency of Honduras in a bloodless coup on Aug. 7, 1978. The overthrow came in the wake of charges of administrative squandering, admitted bribery of officials by North American

banana companies, and allegations that senior military officers were linked with the lucrative traffic in cocaine between South America and the United States. The new president, Gen. Policarpo Paz García, a tough field commander in the Honduras–El Salvador border war of 1969, made no allusions to these circumstances. He promised to carry on the policies of Melgar, including a continuation of discussions with El Salvador over the disputed border and a plan to hold free elections in 1980.

The Paz cabinet, which retained several holdovers from Melgar's government, also included new representatives from the business community, perhaps indicating recognition by Paz of the nation's desperate need for new economic planning to lift it out of its recession. Although the 1978 earnings on bananas were roughly comparable to those in 1977, banana production was down and prospects for 1979 were unfavorable. The Paz government promised to encourage industry and fishing in order to help diversify the heavy dependence on agriculture that has long been traditional in Honduras.

See STATISTICS OF THE WORLD. J.N.G.

HONG KONG. *See* STATISTICS OF THE WORLD.

HUNGARY. On Jan. 6, 1978, after more than three decades in U.S. custody, the 1000-year-old Crown of St. Stephen and other Hungarian coronation regalia were returned to Budapest. In a formal ceremony in the Hungarian capital, U.S. Secretary of State Cyrus Vance handed the jewels, which Hungarians consider a symbol of nationhood, to Antal Apró, president of the Hungarian National Assembly. U.S. President Jimmy Carter's decision to give back the crown, which fell into American hands during World War II, was intended as a gesture of approval toward Hungarian Communist Party First Secretary János Kádár, whose leadership has been described as the least repressive in the Soviet bloc.

The Kádár regime continued to pursue a relatively liberal domestic course throughout 1978. At a meeting of the Communist Party Central Committee in April, party officials agreed to push ahead with economic reforms by phasing out subsidies that kept prices for consumer goods unrealistically low. Price increases were to be gradual, and coupled with increases in wages. At the same time, the 65-year-old Kádár appeared to have chosen a new heir apparent. Politburo member Károly Németh, 56, became the party's second-ranking secretary. He replaced Béla Biszku, who reportedly had been openly critical of economic reform.

Hungarian authorities were concerned by the country's rate of alcoholism. In January a decree restricted the sale of spirits. To discourage drinking still further, the government raised prices of alcoholic beverages by 25 percent in July.

Hungary and the United States concluded a significant new economic accord in March. The agreement called for the removal of trade barriers and a broadening of commerce. Relations between Hungary and Rumania fared less well, as Rumania's alleged repression of its Hungarian minority became a source of increasing concern to the Budapest regime; *see* RUMANIA.

See STATISTICS OF THE WORLD. F.W.

ICELAND. Economic problems and foreign-policy controversy—exemplified by mounting inflation (to a high of 55 percent in mid-August) and left-wing demands for the nation's withdrawal from the North Atlantic Treaty Organization (NATO)—constituted Iceland's most serious challenges during 1978. They also helped bring about a two-month cabinet crisis.

The inflation rate had risen to 32 percent in 1977, with wage increases of 60 percent leading the way. Iceland devalued the króna by 13 percent against the U.S. dollar on Feb. 8, 1978, and by an additional 15 percent on Sept. 4. These devaluations were an attempt to bolster lagging exports, especially of fish and fish products to the United States.

In a political development that proved to be a forerunner of later events, left-wing opposition parties made major gains at the expense of the government coalition parties in municipal elections held on May 28. In Reykjavík the conservative Independence Party lost control of the city council for the first time in fifty years. The losses of the governing party were attributed to unpopular measures introduced to slow inflation, which by election day had reached a rate of 40 percent.

When the general elections were held on June 25, the ruling Independence-Progressive coalition under Prime Minister Geir Hallgrímsson suffered heavy losses and retained a bare 4-seat majority in the 60-seat Althing (parliament). Again, the major issue was inflation. The opposition Social Democrats raised their strength from 5 seats to 14. The Communist-dominated Marxist People's Alliance gained 3 seats, also raising its strength to 14. Hallgrímsson's Independence Party declined in strength from 25 seats to 20. The Progressive Party also lost 5 seats, emerging with 12.

Acknowledging its heavy losses, the cabinet announced on June 26 that it was resigning. The government crisis that followed was ended on Aug. 31 with the formation of a left-wing coalition government. The new prime minister was Ólafur Jóhannesson, leader of the Progressive Party, chosen despite the fact that three other parties exceeded the Progressives in parliamentary strength; the Progressives's partners in the coalition were the Social Democrats and the Marxist People's Alliance. The strongest party, outgoing Prime Minister Hallgrímsson's Independence Party, had no role in the new government.

One of the chief disputes that had delayed the formation of the new government was the People's Alliance demand that Iceland quit NATO. The final compromise, under which three members of the People's Alliance were given cabinet posts, was achieved when the Communist-dominated party agreed to enter the government despite the support of NATO by the other coalition members.

See STATISTICS OF THE WORLD.   L.A.S.

I

IDAHO. See STATISTICS OF THE WORLD.
ILLINOIS. See STATISTICS OF THE WORLD.
INDIANA. See STATISTICS OF THE WORLD.
INDIANS, AMERICAN. In 1978 extensive land claims pressed by American Indian tribes in Rhode Island and Maine were settled by tentative compromises; other similar suits remained in court. A group of demonstrators trekked across the continent to protest legislation sponsored by Western congressmen that would extinguish any further Indian land and resource claims. Tribal status, tribal legal jurisdiction, and mineral leases were also issues.

"The Longest Walk." A group of Indians and sympathizers set out from San Francisco in February on a 2700 mile transcontinental "Longest Walk" to protest the white backlash against recent Indian economic and land claims. The demonstrators, who also wanted to draw attention to Indian culture, reached Washington, D.C., on July 17. Establishing camps on the city outskirts and near the Lincoln Memorial, they conferred with legislators, held news conferences, heard speeches from leaders and supporters, and dispersed peacefully. One of the two dozen Indians who walked all the way said, "Now we have our own legends, like the ones our grandfathers gave us." Dennis Banks, the American Indian Movement leader credited with conceiving the walk, had remained in California; Gov. Edmund G. Brown, Jr., refused in April to extradite him to South Dakota. (Banks was wanted in South Dakota for sentencing on a riot and assault conviction stemming from his group's 1973 occupation of Wounded Knee.)

Land Claims. Indian land-claim suits in fourteen states moved slowly through the courts. The Wampanoag of Massachusetts, who were declared not legally a tribe at key dates in question, lost their suit for 11,000 acres in March. The Narraganset settled for 1800 of 3500 claimed acres in Rhode Island. In the out-of-court Narraganset settlement, signed by President Jimmy Carter in September, half of the relinquished land was state owned and half was to be purchased with $3,500,-00 in federal funds.

In October the Passamaquoddy and Penobscot, who claimed most of the northern half of Maine, came to a tentative settlement with federal and state negotiators. The tribes agreed to accept $27,000,000 in federal payments and an additional $10,000,000, half of it state money, with which to buy 100,000 acres of Maine forestland from fourteen large landowners.

The Zuñi Salt Lake in New Mexico was returned to Zuñi ownership after eighty years, in accordance with a congressional act allowing the gov-

American Indians gather on the steps of the Capitol in Washington, D.C., July 17. They had just completed a five-month "Longest Walk" across the continent to express grievances and commemorate the forced resettlement of Indian tribes in the 19th century.

ernment to purchase sacred lands to hold in trust for Indians.

Tribal Rights and Jurisdiction. In May the U.S. Supreme Court ruled that questions of Indian civil rights must be decided in tribal courts. The case was that of a woman of the Santa Clara Pueblo in New Mexico who challenged the validity of her tribe's law denying tribal membership to her children, who had a non-Santa Clara father. The Supreme Court also ruled that non-Indians may not be tried on criminal charges in tribal courts. Tribal police may arrest non-Indians, but they must be tried in state or federal courts. Forrest J. Gerard, assistant secretary of the interior for Indian affairs, noted that tribal law officers had become increasingly active because neither state nor federal government had been effectively enforcing criminal law on reservations. He asked the Justice Department to fill the void.

The Pasqua Yaqui Indians, who fled the Arizona Territory in the 19th century and lived precariously on the Arizona-Mexico border thereafter without legal status, were finally awarded tribal status by Congress. Signing the bill, President Carter warned that federal recognition of tribes, with its resultant special relationships, should be granted with extreme care.

Water Rights. Assistant Secretary Gerard urged during the year that the President's water-projects policy include a firm commitment to develop Indian water resources, seek federal jurisdiction over adjudication of Indian water rights, and encourage tribal participation in water-resources planning.

Several tribes made progress in fights to preserve or increase vital water supplies. The AkChin reservation south of Phoenix began receiving irrigation water to compensate for a dropping water table (20 ft. per year) which threatened their self-sufficient agricultural community. The San Carlos Apache of Arizona and a corporation of eleven southern California tribes conducted experiments with drip irrigation and development of the jojoba, a desert plant yielding a liquid wax similar to the oil of the sperm whale and thus offering a potential new industry.

Other Resources. The Council of Energy Resources Tribes, a coalition of twenty-five mineral-rich tribes, opened offices in Washington, D.C., and Denver, Colo. Navaho Chairman Peter MacDonald, who served as chairman of the council, complained of leases unfavorable to Indian resource owners.

"An ice cream cone or two tons of Crow coal" could be bought for 35¢, said legal advisers urging the Crow of Montana to renegotiate permits held by four oil and coal companies dating back to

Two college-trained language researchers of the Makah tribe of northwestern Washington State talk with Joseph D. Duffey (center), chairman of the National Endowment for the Humanities. Duffey turned over a $90,000 federal grant to finance a project to preserve the nearly extinct Makah language.

1968. The Interior Department threatened to cancel existing leases. After six months of unsuccessful bargaining for better terms, a federal court found the leases invalid, and the Crow were considering new bids. The Navaho negotiated a coal-mining lease for a 12.5 percent royalty, but rejected a coal gasification plant. The Shiprock Navaho community voted to end a uranium project after a U.S. Geological Survey showed the water supply would be seriously depleted by the mines. A district court issued an injunction against non-Indian commercial fishing in Washington because the state was "evidently unwilling or unable" to protect allocations of salmon awarded to treaty tribes (see FISH AND FISHERIES). On the Klamath and Trinity rivers in California, a new federal rule allowing commercial fishing apparently contributed to a dangerous reduction in the size of the salmon run. On Aug. 28 state officials imposed a moratorium on all but tribal subsistence fishing.   C.C.

INDIA, REPUBLIC OF. While the government of India moved very cautiously in 1978 to bring former Prime Minister Indira Gandhi to trial for assuming emergency powers three years earlier, she succeeded in rebuilding a large following and once again became a major political force.

Politics. The ruling Janata (People's) Party, hastily formed from five widely disparate parties in early 1977, held together during 1978, but only because its leaders were determined to prevent Indira Gandhi from regaining power. Defeated both in the general election of March, 1977, and in her bid to win the presidency of the National Congress Party, she resigned from the party's executive committee in December, 1977, together with seven supporters. They held a rival convention on Jan. 1–2, 1978, at which she was unanimously elected president. Her breakaway party was promptly dubbed Congress-I ("I" for Indira). Meanwhile, the government of Prime Minister Morarji Desai continued to investigate various aspects of her rule during the 1975–77 emergency period. She refused, however, to be questioned by the commissions involved.

In legislative elections held in five states and one territory on Feb. 25, Congress-I won overwhelming victories in the major southern states of Karnataka and Andhra Pradesh. No party won a majority in the other states. The Janata Party was thus effectively reduced to a north Indian party, while the National Congress Party appeared close to eclipse.

Dissension within Janata over Prime Minister Desai's cautious handling of Indira Gandhi came to a head on June 30, when Desai forced the resignation of his most vocal critics, Home Minister Charan Singh and Health Minister Raj Narain. On July 11 the government filed preliminary criminal charges against Indira Gandhi, her son Sanjay, and some of her aides; however, the charges were relatively minor, and the government still refrained from arresting her.

In August, Indira Gandhi launched a nationwide political offensive. Entering a parliamentary by-election in Karnataka, she won easily in November. On Dec. 19, however, parliament voted to expel her and to jail her for the few remaining days of its current session for having used her powers as prime minister to block a parliamentary investigation of her son Sanjay's business dealings in 1975. Released on Dec. 26, she vowed to seek another seat in parliament.

The Economy. For the fourth consecutive year, India enjoyed a good grain harvest, with total output reaching approximately 125,500,000 tons. The rural economy continued to be a leading concern of the government, which budgeted the equivalent of $2 billion for rural development in the fiscal year beginning April 1, compared with $600,000,000 in 1977–78. These plans suffered a setback when record floods swept the Ganges River valley in September and October, killing some 2100 people and inundating over 17 percent of India's cropland.

Thanks to the plentiful grain harvest and a very comfortable foreign exchange situation, which permitted the import of items in short supply, inflation was almost halted. But prices had already

Mr. Desai and Mrs. Gandhi

There were pleasures: He played host to U.S. President Jimmy Carter in January; in June he returned the courtesy by touring the United States. Meanwhile, however, his problems mounted. The austere, 82-year-old prime minister of India, Morarji Desai, survived a no-confidence vote in May, but prolonged squabbling within his Janata Party forced the resignation of two key ministers. And then there was the startling resurgence of his archrival, the autocratic Indira Gandhi, whom Desai had defeated in 1977 on a slogan of "Democracy Over Dictatorship." The Gandhi comeback was briefly sidetracked with her parliamentary expulsion and jailing in December, but Desai could hardly doubt that, freshly martyred, she would be heard from again.

Morarji Desai, troubled prime minister of India.

Indira Gandhi, India's former prime minister, takes a short break from political campaigning for a sip of coconut milk. Although she regained her seat in parliament during the November elections, she was expelled and jailed (for one week) in December.

reached very high levels, with the result that industry was plagued by numerous strikes for higher wages. Industrial production grew by only 4 percent in 1977–78, compared with 10.4 percent in 1976–77. New investment declined markedly, as business confidence was hurt by the government's policy of shifting the manufacture of many items to small rural factories.

One very promising development was the continued growth of oil production from the new offshore Bombay High field in the Arabian Sea. With output from this source already amounting to 80,000 bbl per day, it was hoped that India might achieve self-sufficiency in oil during the 1980's.

Favorable developments in foreign trade and other international transactions (including greatly increased family remittances from Indians working in the Middle East) raised official foreign exchange holdings to a record $7 billion in late 1978.
Foreign Relations. The government devoted much attention to the improvement of India's relations with the major world powers. U.S. President Jimmy Carter was warmly received when he arrived on Jan. 1 for a two-day visit, and Prime Minister Desai paid a return visit to the United States in mid-June. The U.S. agreed to increase its direct aid to India, but some points of irritation remained, most notably the reluctance of the U.S. to

sell enriched uranium for a nuclear power plant at Tarapur, near Bombay, because of India's refusal to comply with U.S. requirements for inspection. Taking advantage of a provision in the pertinent U.S. law, President Carter authorized a shipment of more than seven tons of the nuclear fuel, but he was unable to offer assurances of further shipments.

Although taking steps to limit Russian influence, India at the same time continued to cultivate good relations with the Soviet Union. The two countries reaffirmed their "eternal friendship" and concluded a number of new economic and technical assistance agreements. There was also a gradual relaxation of tensions with the People's Republic of China, although Prime Minister Desai indicated he was not prepared to drop India's claim to 14,000 sq. mi. of Himalayan territory occupied by the Chinese since the early 1960's.

See STATISTICS OF THE WORLD.   W.J.G.

INDONESIA. In 1978 Indonesia remained firmly under the control of President Suharto and the country's military, despite opposition from student groups and Muslim leaders.

A wave of student protest swept the country in January. Unhappy with spiraling prices, government corruption, and restrictions on political activity, the demonstrators called on Suharto to relinquish power. Suharto refused, and the army arrested 500–600 student leaders. At the same time, the government muzzled the press by temporarily banning seven of Djakarta's leading newspapers. The demonstrations continued into February but subsided by March, when the People's Consultative Assembly unanimously elected the 57-year-old former general to his third five-year term as president.

Spurred by foreign criticism the Suharto government released 10,000 political prisoners during 1978 and pledged that another 10,000 would be released in 1979. (Estimates varied as to the total number of political prisoners held in Indonesian jails.) To the astonishment of many Indonesians the government also ordered a new crackdown on corruption in the upper echelons of the bureaucracy.

Perhaps the greatest potential threat to Suharto's rule came from the Muslim opposition, claiming to speak for some 90 percent of all Indonesians. During the year Muslim leaders took an increasingly militant stand against modernization, corruption, and the government's "irreligious use of power."

Indonesia's economy turned in a satisfactory performance in 1978. Over the first ten months inflation ran at only 3 percent, compared to percent in 1977. Rice stocks were at a record high and the country's foreign exchange and balance-of-payments positions were healthy. In November the government devalued its currency, the rupiah, by 33.6 percent. The move was designed to bolster the competitive position of Indonesian industry at home and abroad, even at the risk of touching off a new round of inflation.

A prime topic in Indonesian foreign affairs was the country's relations with the People's Republic of China. In March, China announced that it was prepared to reestablish formal ties with Indonesia, but the Djakarta government—still suspicious of Peking's role in the left-wing coup attempt of 1965—politely rebuffed the overture. Although Foreign Minister Mochtar Kusumaatmadja made a surprise visit to Hanoi in November, Indonesia's relations with the Communist regimes of Southeast Asia were generally cool. As in the past, the keystone of Indonesia's foreign policy was close ties with Japan, the United States, and the other members of the Association of Southeast Asian Nations. *See* INTERNATIONAL CONFERENCES.

See STATISTICS OF THE WORLD. R.J.C.

INSURANCE. The profits picture remained bright for the insurance industry in 1978, although prospects were dimmer for the years 1979 through 1981. During the year, U.S. President Jimmy Carter unveiled his proposal for a comprehensive national health insurance program, and there were several new regulatory developments.

Earnings and Outlook. Property and liability (non-life) insurers continued to enjoy profitable operations in 1978, after earning record underwriting profits of $1.1 billion in 1977. But the rosy picture was clouded by predictions of underwriting losses beginning in 1979, including a forecast by Chase Econometrics that such losses would continue through 1981.

Life insurers enjoyed another year of profit and growth, with more than $2.5 trillion of insurance in force at the beginning of 1978. Earnings during 1977 represented 7 percent of sales, of which about 3 percent was contributed to surplus.

National Health Insurance. In late July, President Carter announced his administration's proposal for comprehensive national health insurance. The plan (which was a set of ten principles, rather than a fully worked-out program) called for providing all Americans with comprehensive health protection, including protection against medical catastrophes. Other important aspects of the plan included freedom of choice for the patient, control of health-care costs through payment methods designed to encourage efficiency and innovation, multiple-source financing of the program, and consumer representation in policy-making processes. The Administration proposed to make extensive use of the resources of the private insurance industry and to contribute no new federal funds until the 1983 fiscal year.

Prospects for adoption of the proposal were dimmed by its failure to win the support of Sen. Edward Kennedy (D, Mass.), the leading advocate of and spokesman for a national health insurance program. Legislative action on the issue was expected in 1979.

Insurance Regulation. The federal government showed new interest in insurance regulation, an area that by tradition and statute has generally been left to the states. In January the Department of Housing and Urban Development (HUD) assumed full control over the National Flood Insurance Program, ending a long-standing partnership with private insurers in providing this protection. The transition was not easy, with widespread dissatisfaction among consumers over delays in the issuance of policies and the payment of claims. HUD also conducted public hearings into the underwriting practices of property and liability insurers, especially their failure to provide fire insurance to homes and businesses in inner city areas ("redlining"). Also in 1978, the Federal Trade Commission began investigating the proposed mergers of several insurance companies.

The Community Housing Law passed by Congress in 1978 required companies belonging to FAIR Plans (property insurance pools) to write property insurance at no higher than standard rates; failure to do so would disqualify such companies from participation in the Riot Reinsurance Program. In a move designed to end the antitrust exemption the industry has enjoyed, Rep. John J. LaFalce (D, N.Y.) introduced four bills to eliminate or substantially restrict the insurance industry's freedom from federal regulation of its interstate operations under the McCarran-Ferguson Act of 1945.

On the state level, New York passed legislation establishing two new insurance facilities: a free zone and a reinsurance exchange. The free zone would permit insurers to write certain large and unusual contracts free of customary restrictions; the zone also would provide tax advantages to companies operating within it. The New York Reinsurance Exchange, a facility similar to Lloyd's of London, was expected to begin operation in 1979.

Several states challenged the rating and underwriting practices of insurers, particularly in the politically sensitive area of private auto-vehicle coverage. Meanwhile, the popularity of state competitive rating laws continued to grow. J.F.M.

INTERNATIONAL CONFERENCES. Many important international conferences were held in 1978. For some of the conferences and organizations

Yugoslav President Tito, a founder of the Third World movement, addresses the opening session of a conference of nonaligned nations in Belgrade on July 25.

not covered below, *see* AFRICA; ARAB LEAGUE; NORTH ATLANTIC TREATY ORGANIZATION; ORGANIZATION FOR ECONOMIC COOPERATION AND DEVELOPMENT; ORGANIZATION OF AMERICAN STATES; ORGANIZATION OF PETROLEUM EXPORTING COUNTRIES; UNITED NATIONS; WARSAW TREATY ORGANIZATION. *See also* articles on the individual countries mentioned.

Conference on Security and Cooperation in Europe. In March the Conference on Security and Cooperation in Europe concluded its session in Belgrade, Yugoslavia. Called to review compliance with the 1975 Helsinki accords on territorial security and human rights in Europe, the conference had dragged on for many months. In session after session, Western delegates charged that the Soviet Union was not living up to the guarantees of human rights contained in the Helsinki pact. The Communist delegates accused the West of using the human rights issue to divert attention from more important matters. Nothing was resolved. In a final communiqué the thirty-five participants did little more than agree to meet in Madrid in 1980 and once again review the consequences of Helsinki.

ASEAN Conferences. The Association of Southeast Asian Nations (ASEAN) met on a number of occasions. In June, the foreign ministers of the five member countries—Indonesia, Malaysia, the Philippines, Singapore, and Thailand—met in Pattaya, Thailand, to consider refugee problems in the region, as well as ties to the Communist regimes in Indochina. The delegates failed to forge a common policy on either issue. In August the ASEAN foreign ministers met with U.S. Secretary of State Cyrus Vance in Washington, D.C., to review the group's political and economic ties with the United States. The most tangible American pledges to emerge from the meetings were to

send trade and investment missions to Southeast Asia and to "pursue actively" the creation of an international fund to stabilize the prices of raw materials.

Other Conferences. At a conference of eighty-seven nonaligned nations (plus numerous observers and guests) held in Belgrade in July, Yugoslav President Tito warned African states not to let their disputes become part of a wider East-West struggle. The warning was generally interpreted as a slap at Soviet and Cuban (as well as Western) policy in the region. Also in July, talks on mutual and balanced force reductions in Europe—known as the East-West talks—recessed in Vienna, after five years of fruitless negotiations. A Soviet proposal to establish equal ceilings on the number of opposing ground forces in Central Europe foundered over differing estimates as to how many troops the Soviet bloc had stationed there.   R.J.C

IOWA. *See* STATISTICS OF THE WORLD.

IRAN. Shah Mohammed Riza Pahlavi of Iran faced the worst crisis of his thirty-seven-year reign in 1978. Protests by Islamic traditionalists against the shah's rapid modernization of Iran gradually escalated into nationwide demonstrations demanding the end of his rule. At the close of 1978, Iran's economy was virtually paralyzed by strikes, and the future of the monarchy appeared most uncertain.

Unrest. Internal order began to break down in January, when policemen opened fire on Muslim religious demonstrators in the holy city of Qum. In succeeding months, mourning processions repeatedly led to new clashes with police or the army, resulting in more deaths, followed by new mourning processions. The incident that dramatically escalated the crisis occurred Aug. 20, when a theater fire set off by arsonists claimed 430 lives

Abadan. The government blamed the fire on Islamic zealots who had burned a number of cinemas across the country during the holy month of Ramadan. Residents of Abadan, however, blamed the shah's secret police, Savak, and demonstrators took to the streets shouting: "Death to the shah." The next major escalation occurred Sept. 8 in Tehran, when army troops fired submachine gun bursts into a crowd of antigovernment demonstrators after the shah had imposed martial law in the major cities. At least fifty-eight persons were killed in that incident—some estimates were much higher. From that point, confrontations between demonstrators and troops took place almost daily. While the demonstrations continued to be organized by Muslim leaders led from exile by Ayatollah Ruhollah Khomeini, the forces demanding the shah's ouster came to represent almost the entire political spectrum. More than 4000 Iranians were believed to have been killed during the 1978 demonstrations, including 1500 in December alone.

Government. As he fought to cling to power, the shah repeatedly shuffled his governments and sought to meet some of the demonstrators' key demands. On Aug. 27 he replaced Prime Minister Jamshid Amouzegar with Jaafar Sharif-Emami, hoping that the latter's close ties with Muslim leaders would end the disturbances. The government also released more than 1100 political prisoners on Oct. 25 to celebrate the shah's birthday. A few days later it was announced that all political prisoners would be released. As these steps failed to halt the rioting, on Nov. 5 the shah replaced Sharif-Emami with a military government headed by Gen. Gholam Riza Azhari, who had been chief of Iran's armed forces since 1971. One of the new government's first actions was to arrest two for-

mer top officials—Amir Abbas Hoveida, prime minister from 1965 to 1977, and Nematollah Nassiri, former head of Savak—on corruption charges. The unrest continued, however, and on Dec. 31 Azhari resigned. At year's end the shah asked a civilian, Shahpur Bakhtiar, a longtime foe who had never been considered a major opposition leader, to form a new government.

The Economy. Iran's economy was crippled in late 1978 when oil exports, which had been expected to bring in more than $22 billion, were cut to a trickle by strikes in the oil fields. By the end of December, oil production was down from its normal daily level of 6,500,000 bbl to less than 300,000 bbl, not nearly enough to meet domestic needs. Even before the oil crisis, the shah had sharply cut back military expenditures to make more money available for pay raises for government workers and housing construction. During the first half of 1978, the government ran up a $5.5 billion deficit, and the figure was expected to be considerably higher for the second half.

Foreign Relations. Much of the anger of Iranian demonstrators was focused on approximately 41,000 Americans living in Iran and working on the shah's prestige projects. Mobs attacked U.S. installations and killed one American petroleum executive, Paul Grimm, in December as thousands of Americans fled the country. In December, President Jimmy Carter expressed continued support for the shah but voiced concern whether the shah could survive. The United States also warned the Soviet Union, whose southern border is the northern border of Iran, not to "interfere in the internal affairs of Iran."

See STATISTICS OF THE WORLD. See also MIDDLE EAST; ORGANIZATION OF PETROLEUM EXPORTING COUNTRIES; RELIGION.   M.R.B.

* happened in oil-rich Iran:
esidents of Tehran stand in
ne to buy kerosene on Dec.
3. The shortage of petroleum
roducts was caused by wide-
read strikes and the con-
uing political struggle.

IRAQ. The government of Iraq appeared to be edging toward a more pragmatic, Western-oriented foreign policy in 1978—probably because of the fact that the Iraqis possess one of the world's largest petroleum reserves. Oil exports were expected to bring Iraq $12 billion in 1978, and Iraqi planners said they hoped to triple current production by 1985. The government continued to maintain close ties with Moscow, although some strains were beginning to show—for example, Iraq executed twenty-one Communists in May for forming secret cells in the armed forces. Officials also showed increasing eagerness to modernize with Western assistance. Declared Information Minister Saad Qasim Hamoodi, "Iraq intends to catch up with the latest technology—whatever the sources may be."

Iraq continued during 1978 to denounce Egyptian President Anwar el-Sadat's peace negotiations with Israel, and an Arab summit conference that condemned the proposed Egyptian-Israeli peace treaty was held in Baghdad in November. More surprisingly, Iraq decided to shelve its long-standing feud with Syria in an effort to strengthen the ranks of Arab states arrayed against Israel. In October, Syrian President Hafez al-Assad visited Baghdad, and the two countries signed a "national charter for joint action" that calls for a "full military union." Iraq did, however, continue to engage in a bloody feud through most of 1978 with the Palestine Liberation Organization (q.v.), and the PLO's military arm, Al Fatah, staged several attacks on Iraqi diplomats and embassies across the world.

See STATISTICS OF THE WORLD. See also ARAB LEAGUE; MIDDLE EAST.　　　　　　　　M.R.B.

IRELAND, NORTHERN. See GREAT BRITAIN.

IRELAND, REPUBLIC OF. The tragic communal strife in Northern Ireland continued during 1978 to be a principal focus of the Republic of Ireland's concern. Economic problems, particularly inflation, also troubled the country, but a change in monetary relations was a hopeful sign.

The Economy. The Fianna Fáil government's 1978 budget, presented to the Dáil (parliament) on Feb. 1, provided for tax cuts, wage restraints, a 10 percent increase in social welfare benefits, and inducements to increase employment and investment. These budget measures were part of a program to raise the industrial growth rate to 7 percent and to reduce inflation from the 13.5 percent rate of 1977. In addition, all residential property taxes were eliminated as of Jan. 1, in a measure that was expected to stimulate the economy.

In what was considered a victory for Prime Minister Jack Lynch's anti-inflation plans, the Irish Congress of Trade Unions voted on March 22 to accept a wage accord limiting raises during 1978 to 8 percent.

The Irish economy, however, was disrupted by several strikes during 1978. Telephone and telex services were crippled by a strike started by post office employees on Feb. 7 and not ended until May 4. Business losses caused by the strike may have been as much as $5,700,000 per day. Ground staff employees of Aer Lingus, the national airline, struck for seven weeks, beginning in March. On May 5 the walkout ended with a settlement providing for a 5 percent raise for clerical workers.

In December, Ireland decided to break its monetary link with Great Britain and instead join seven other Common Market countries in the European Monetary System, scheduled to begin on Jan. 1, 1979. The move was a major change in Ireland's relations with Great Britain and the countries of continental Europe. See EUROPEAN COMMUNITIES.

Other Events. Controversy flared when Prime Minister Lynch reaffirmed in a radio interview on Jan. 8 that his Fianna Fáil Party's eventual aim was to reunite Northern Ireland with the Irish Republic. He urged Great Britain to announce its intention to release Ulster eventually. Lynch's remarks were criticized by the Opposition in Dublin as well as by spokesmen in Belfast and London.

Several police scandals culminated in the dismissal on Jan. 19 of Edmund Garvey, commissioner of police of the Republic of Ireland. No official reason was given for his ouster, but charges of brutality in interrogation had been made.

Tentative plans to build a nuclear power plant near Carnsore Point, about 130 km (81 mi.) south of Dublin, drew protesters to the site for a demonstration in mid-August. The 6000 demonstrators included nuclear-power opponents from several Western European nations.

A Death. Cearbhall O Dalaigh, president of the Republic of Ireland from 1974 to 1976, died at his home in the fishing village of Sneem on March 21 at the age of 67.

See STATISTICS OF THE WORLD. See also GREAT BRITAIN.　　　　　　　　　　　　　　　L.A.S.

ISRAEL. Events in Israel during 1978, the country's first year under a non-Labor government, were dominated by the rise and fall of hopes for peace settlement with Egypt.

Peace Negotiations. A year after Egyptian President Anwar el-Sadat's historic November, 1977, visit to Jerusalem, conclusion of negotiations for peace still seemed elusive. The coalition government of Israel, led by Prime Minister Menachem Begin's Likud Party, devoted a major part of its efforts during 1978 to the negotiations, which

A President of the People

Sephardim (Jews of Mediterranean background) make up a majority of the Israeli population, but Ashkenazic Jews from Eastern Europe have always dominated the country's political life. In April, however, the Knesset elected Itzhak Navon, 57, the nation's fifth president—its first of Sephardic descent (as well as its first native-born). Scholarly and urbane, a political protégé of the late David Ben-Gurion, Navon had been chairman of the Knesset's important Foreign Affairs and Security Committee. Often critical of Prime Minister Menachem Begin's policies, he backed more flexible approaches in peace negotiations. In spite of the mostly ceremonial nature of his new job, Navon said he intended to be a "President who mingles with the people."

Israeli President Itzhak Navon.

were broken off and restarted several times. Expectations reached their highest point after conclusion of the summit conference held at Camp David, Md., in September when Israel, Egypt, and the United States signed two agreements containing a framework for Middle East peace and a framework for a peace treaty between Egypt and Israel.

Although large majorities in the Israeli cabinet and in the Knesset (parliament) supported the Camp David accords, many members of the prime minister's own party were opposed. Eleven of Begin's 18 cabinet members approved, 2 were against, 1 abstained, and 4 did not participate in the voting. In the Knesset, 84 members voted for the agreements, 19 were against, and 17 abstained. Only 29 of Begin's 45-member Likud bloc sup-

ported him. Without support from opposition parties, the Camp David accords would not have been approved.

Opposition focused on requirements for withdrawal of several thousand Israelis from eighteen settlements established in Sinai after 1967, as well as on fears that provisions for autonomy in the West Bank and Gaza in the "Framework for Peace in the Middle East" would lead to establishment of a Palestinian state. Egypt's insistence on linking the peace treaty with a timetable for Israel's withdrawal from the West Bank and Gaza, and on establishment of an autonomous Palestinian government, stymied the peace talks by mid-November, although Begin and Sadat were awarded the Nobel Peace Prize for their efforts. (Sadat sent a representative to Norway for the

Israeli forces ceremoniously hand over a position 5 miles inside the Lebanese border to Lebanese Christian militiamen. In June, after a three-month occupation, the Israelis withdrew all their troops from southern Lebanon.

In Jerusalem on April 26 an organizer of a Peace Now demonstration shows a letter asking Israeli Prime Minister Menachem Begin to offer territorial concessions on the West Bank.

presentation as a hint of his dissatisfaction with the progress of negotiations; Begin accepted in person.) *See* PRIZES AND AWARDS.

U.S. Relations. Difficulties in the negotiations also strained relations with the U.S. when President Jimmy Carter attempted to persuade Begin to move closer to the Egyptian position. Before and after Camp David both Sadat and Begin visited the U.S. for discussions with Carter; Secretary of State Cyrus Vance and other high-level State Department officials made several rounds of visits to Israel and other Middle Eastern countries to find compromises. Tensions with the U.S. also mounted over establishment of new Jewish settlements in the occupied territories, the status of Jerusalem, and the future of the West Bank.

Despite these disagreements Israel's dependence on the U.S. was greater than ever. Officials disclosed that more than $1.5 billion worth of American arms were to be delivered to Israel, not including 15 F-15 and 75 F-16 fighter planes approved as part of Carter's controversial Middle East arms package (and another 20 F-15's promised by Secretary Vance); the planes would be delivered between 1981 and 1985. The $1.5 billion included arms authorized during President Gerald R. Ford's administration. There were also discussions of a ten-year arms program and of American payments for oil imports to make up for the loss of the Sinai petroleum fields under the peace treaty.

Invasion of Lebanon. Israel mounted a large-scale invasion of southern Lebanon during March in retaliation for a terrorist attack by the Palestinian commando organization Al Fatah on an Israeli bus. Thirty-seven Israelis and nine guerrillas were killed in the March 11 terrorist raid, one of several undertaken by groups in the Palestine Liberation

Organization during 1978 to undermine the peace talks. Israel's counterattack three days after the bus raid was its largest military operation into Lebanon. Thousands of Israeli troops sought to "eliminate the fedayeen bases along the border." Within a week all of southern Lebanon up to the Litani River, an area of about 1100 km (425 sq.mi.), was seized. The invasion sparked a series of international crises and several weeks of debate in the United Nations Security Council, and it further strained relations with the U.S. After three months Israel withdrew the last of its troops from Lebanon, although the Israelis turned many strong points over to Lebanese Christian militiamen, rather than to the U.N. Interim Force in Lebanon, thus creating further controversy.

The Economy. Continued high military expenditures undermined efforts by the Likud government to alter the economic structure and end the inflationary spiral. Prices were expected to increase more rapidly than in 1977, when the rise was 35 percent. The Israeli pound continued its decline in value from 11.6¢ in U.S. currency early in 1977 to 5.4¢ by the end of 1978. The balance-of-payments deficit was continuing to increase. Inflationary pressures and the rising cost of living precipitated numerous strikes by teachers, postal workers, communications engineers, civil aviation employees, and radio and television journalists. At various times during 1978 schools were closed, mail service suspended, El Al airlines ceased flying, and radio and television broadcasts were halted.

Domestic Politics. Disagreements over support for Begin's policies within the Democratic Movement for Change (DMC), Israel's third largest party after the 1977 elections, caused it to split in August. Seven of 15 DMC Knesset members formed a new opposition bloc. DMC founder and Deputy Prime Minister Yigael Yadin and 7 Knesset followers remained in Begin's government. Ex-general Meir Amit, one of the 4 DMC cabinet members, resigned his post as minister of transport. Although the DMC split reduced Begin's Knesset support by 8 of the 120 Knesset members, he still retained a parliamentary majority.

Another indication of unrest was the rapid growth of the Peace Now movement, a protest group formed to oppose Jewish settlement in the occupied territories and other Begin policies. In one of the largest political demonstrations ever held in Israel, nearly 100,000 people showed support for Peace Now at a Tel Aviv rally during September, displaying such slogans as "Compromise is not a dirty word."

The first direct election of mayors of Israeli cities occurred in 1978. Previously they were chosen by municipal councils or by the Interior Ministry. Reelection of 67-year-old Teddy Kollek, Jerusalem's mayor since 1965, was the most notable victory. Running as an independent he won 62.4 percent of the combined Arab and Jewish vote. In other elections the Labor Party retained 9 of 13 mayoralties in Israel's largest cities and towns, while Likud showed gains in smaller towns. With the retirement of Ephraim Katzir, the Knesset in April elected a new president, Itzhak Navon, the first native-born Israeli chosen for the post.

See STATISTICS OF THE WORLD. See also ARAB LEAGUE; MIDDLE EAST; PALESTINE LIBERATION ORGANIZATION; and articles on individual countries mentioned.   D.P.

ITALY. The continuing chaos of Italian politics was marked in 1978 by the assassination of a former premier, the resignation of the current premier, the resignation of the president, and the threat of Communist Party entry into the cabinet. **Terrorism.** On March 16 former Premier Aldo Moro, president of the Christian Democratic Party, was abducted in Rome by a dozen terrorists of the Red Brigades after they killed his five guards in a machine-gun ambush. Premier Giulio Andreotti's government rejected pleas from Moro's family and from the captors to negotiate for his release, even after they threatened to execute him unless thirteen imprisoned terrorists then on trial were freed. On May 9, Moro's body, riddled by eleven bullets, was found in a car near his party's headquarters in Rome.

This crime climaxed some 3000 personal attacks since January, 1977, hundreds of them by the Red Brigades, who shot politicians and industrialists in the legs, a practice that came to be known as kneecapping. In June, Renato Curcio, one of the Brigades' founders, and twenty-eight other terrorists were sentenced to up to fifteen years in prison. In late October, Corrado Alunni, the alleged mastermind of the Moro kidnapping, and five other Red Brigades members were sent to prison for crimes committed in 1975, with their trial for the murder of the former premier still to come.

The government proclaimed a "situation of emergency" on March 21 and decreed mandatory life sentences for kidnappers whose captives were slain, thirty-year terms if the victims were not

Italy's First Socialist President
Twin blows—the resignation of Italian President Giovanni Leone amidst corruption charges and the kidnap-murder of Aldo Moro (who had been expected to succeed Leone)—almost ruined Rome's governing Christian Democrats. To preserve their tenuous partnership, the Christian Democrat and Communist parties compromised in naming Socialist Alessandro ("Sandro") Pertini, 81, as Italy's seventh president. Pertini's twenty-year record as an antifascist partisan hero made him one of the most prestigious figures of the Italian Left, admired for his outspoken courage and salty integrity. In an openly leftist acceptance speech in July, the aging but vigorous Pertini admonished the nation's ruling establishment to get moving on social and economic problems neglected during decades of interparty squabbling.

Sandro Pertini, president of Italy.

This photograph of former Italian Premier Aldo Moro holding an April 19 newspaper was circulated by his Red Brigades captors to disprove a report that he had been killed. Three weeks later, however, Moro was dead.

killed, severe penalties for criminals handling ransoms, and extended use of information secured by wiretapping. The parliament ratified this decree and made it law on May 16 by a 522–27 margin. In a national referendum held June 11–12, 77 percent of the voters favored retention of the 1974 Reale Act, which permits strong law-and-order measures.

On May 10, Moro was buried near Rome in a private ceremony directed by his family; in accordance with his wish Christian Democratic leaders were excluded. Interior Minister Francesco Cossiga, an intimate friend of Moro, resigned from the cabinet.

Politics. In the face of extremist violence and the declining economy, Andreotti's Christian Democratic government resigned on Jan. 16. The Communists, Socialists, and Republicans had notified him that he could no longer depend on their benevolent abstention in parliament. Also, they had insisted on Communist participation in the cabinet, a demand which was rejected. The Communists dropped this demand on Feb. 7, allowing Andreotti to form a new minority government, Italy's fortieth cabinet since 1943. It was sworn in

on March 13, thus ending the two-month crisis, Italy's longest.

A compromise was reached with the Communist, Socialist, Social Democratic, and Republican parties whereby the Communists would proffer parliamentary support instead of neutrality for the first time since 1947. In return, the Communists won a pledge of new reforms, including demilitarization of most of the Italian police to allow them to unionize and higher indirect taxes to finance industrial growth. The main effect of these reforms was to postpone a risky national election; the coalition was not considered strong enough to govern the country decisively.

In local and provincial elections on May 14–15, involving 10 percent of the electors, a backlash vote in the wake of Moro's murder gave the Communists a severe setback. They got only 26.5 percent of the vote, down from 35.6 percent in the 1976 election, while the Christian Democrats won 42.5 percent, up from 38.9 percent.

Italy was again jolted on June 15 when President Giovanni Leone resigned amid charges of tax evasion and participation in bribery scandals involving public officials and the Lockheed Aircraft Corp., which he solemnly denied. On July 8, after much maneuvering and sixteen ballots, Socialist Alessandro Pertini, Resistance hero and former chamber speaker, was elected president by the Electoral Assembly. He won with 832 votes, the greatest total ever obtained by a presidential candidate.

Meanwhile, parliament enacted a controversial abortion law on May 18, despite the strong objection of the Roman Catholic Church. It enables a woman over 18 to get an abortion practically on demand if childbirth would "compromise her economic, social, family, or psychological well-being."

The Economy. Chronic strikes by workers in such fields as hospitals, railways, airlines, ferryboats, hotels, restaurants, and the judiciary threatened the continuance of the Christian Democratic–Communist alliance by the end of November. The strikers opposed the government's three-year recovery plan calling for a decrease in public borrowing, promotion of exports, limits on wages, and higher labor efficiency and mobility. Early in the year, unemployment was estimated to be 9 percent.

The lira was stabilized against the dollar, and strict exchange controls diminished the flight of capital. By mid-May inflation was cut to 13 percent, and the balance-of-payments deficit was transformed into an anticipated surplus of $2.5 billion for 1978. Italy intended to repay some $4 billion of its foreign debts during the year. How ever, the government's official aim for a 1978 budget of $28 billion was expected to wind up in a huge deficit.

On Dec. 13, parliament approved Italy's entry into the European Monetary System, which was scheduled to begin operating on Jan. 1, 1979. *See* EUROPEAN COMMUNITIES.

Foreign Affairs. In an effort to forestall Communist Party participation in an Italian cabinet, the United States warned on Jan. 12 that the Communists did not cherish democratic "values and in-

terests." The administration of U.S. President Jimmy Carter also asked Italy and other Western European nations to try to reduce Communist influence.

On July 12, President Pertini appealed to the Soviet Union to respect the human rights of two dissidents then on trial, Anatoly Shcharansky and Aleksandr Ginzburg; *see* UNION OF SOVIET SOCIALIST REPUBLICS.

See STATISTICS OF THE WORLD.   J.N.

IVORY COAST. *See* STATISTICS OF THE WORLD.

J

JAMAICA. Prolonged civil unrest in Jamaica appeared to have ended in 1978, but economic problems continued.

After years of gang warfare in the slums of Kingston, the Jamaican capital, two armed henchmen from Jamaica's rival political parties declared peace in mid-January. The cease-fire was supported by Prime Minister Michael Manley's People's National Party and the opposition Jamaica Labour Party. The cessation of killings, robberies, and other crimes lasted through the year, creating a sense of optimism among Jamaicans.

Manley's austerity program of tight government control, begun in 1977, was continued through 1978 in an effort to solve Jamaica's pressing economic troubles. These included a 30 percent unemployment rate, business bankruptcies, and a serious shortage of currency reserves. The full effect of aid packages from the United States and Canada, granted in 1977, was not expected to be felt until 1980. Also of delayed effect was Jamaica's first economic agreement with the Soviet Union, reached in December, 1977, under which the Soviets would build a cement factory and study water power resources. New loans were obtained in 1978 from the World Bank, for industrial development and the modernization of sugar production, and from Great Britain, for the purchase of British goods. Norway announced plans to prospect for oil in the waters off Jamaica.

See STATISTICS OF THE WORLD.   J.N.G.

JAPAN. On the political scene, 1978 saw a change in Japanese leadership. Although the Liberal-Democratic Party (LDP) remained in power, LDP members elected a new party president and, accordingly, a new prime minister. On the economic front, as in previous years, huge foreign trade surpluses created problems with Japan's

trading partners, and the domestic economy responded slowly to the government's stimuli. And in the world arena, Japan figured prominently in international realignments, most notably signing a historic peace treaty with the People's Republic of China.

Politics. The defeat of Prime Minister Takeo Fukuda in a November primary election for the presidency of the LDP surprised many observers. Although Fukuda's position seemed weak early in the year, his political stock rose significantly with the successful conclusion of a peace treaty with China. Meanwhile, Fukuda's main rival, LDP Secretary-General Masayoshi Ohira, suffered an important setback when his party faction lost the August regional elections on the southern island of Shikoku. Nevertheless, Ohira won easily in the primary balloting held Nov. 27, and Fukuda chose to resign his high office rather than face Ohira in a second round of parliamentary voting, scheduled for December. Ohira, 68, was five years younger than Fukuda, but his rise to power was not expected to mean any major change in foreign or domestic policy. A third candidate, LDP Executive Council Chairman Yasuhiro Nakasone, ran well behind in the primary. His position was weakened when a former official of the Lockheed Aircraft Corp. testified that Nakasone had intervened on behalf of Lockheed in 1972, at a time when the aerospace conglomerate was offering millions of dollars in illicit payments to Japanese government leaders.

The Fukuda administration was embarrassed in late March when violent protests by radicals succeeded in delaying the opening of Tokyo's new international airport. Some 7000 leftists clashed with police, while a small band of radicals seized a control tower and smashed many of its delicate

Followers of Masayoshi Ohira (foreground) had a lot to cheer about. Ohira won the presidency of the Liberal-Democratic Party in a primary election, and then became prime minister of Japan in December, succeeding Takeo Fukuda (extreme right).

instruments. The airport finally opened under heavy guard on May 21.

The issue of resurgent militarism sparked a lively political debate at midyear. In late July, Gen. Hiroomi Kurisu, chairman of the Joint Staff Council, was forced to resign after stating publicly that in times of emergency (such as a surprise attack), the commander of Japan's Self-Defense Forces could take "supralegal" action. Kurisu's defenders noted that present laws prevented Japanese forces from even firing back at an invader without the express approval of the prime minister.

The Economy. As a result of a trade surplus of more than $11 billion in calendar year 1977, a threefold increase over 1976, Japan's foreign exchange reserves soared to nearly $23 billion. Trade with the United States alone showed a surplus of over $8 billion. Exports of four-wheeled vehicles led the way with a gain of 17 percent over 1976. Early in 1978, responding to pressures from the U.S. and Europe to increase imports and reduce its huge trade surpluses, the Fukuda government announced that it would take measures to stimulate domestic demand. The target for real growth in the economy for fiscal 1978 (April, 1978–March, 1979) was set at 7 percent, up from 5.4 percent in fiscal 1977.

In early September the government unveiled a king-sized economic stimulus package totaling about $13 billion. The package included allocations for housing, public works, and emergency imports. Observers expressed concern that even these measures would not be sufficient to maintain growth at the 7 percent level without a cut in personal income taxes, since Japan depends on consumer spending for about half of its gross national product. Nevertheless, the Fukuda government remained adamantly opposed to such a move, because of the large deficit already in the budget.

Japanese ultraleftists, in full battle dress, protest the completion of Tokyo's new international airport at Narita. In late March the radicals had successfully prevented the airport from opening; the demonstration shown here, two months later, was a failure, and the facility opened officially on May 21.

A stopped clock amid the rubble reads 12:24—the precise moment when a mid-afternoon earthquake devastated the town of Kawazu, Shizuoka. Twenty-three people were killed in the earthquake, which struck central Japan on Jan. 14.

Another problem brought on by Japan's huge surplus was the sharp appreciation of the yen, especially against the U.S. dollar. In the latter half of 1978 the official exchange rate for the dollar was a record low of less than 180 yen. (At the beginning of 1977 the rate was 292 yen to the dollar.) The cost of Japanese goods on foreign markets rose correspondingly. This was particularly threatening to small exporting concerns, which did not have the capital to sustain adjustments in the international market.

Statistics released in May indicated that Japan's population had passed 114,000,000 by October, 1977. The annual rate of increase, however, has been slowing since 1975, and in 1977 was a modest 0.94 percent. Japan's gross national product per capita ranked seventeenth in the world in 1977.

Foreign Affairs. On Oct. 23, six years after Japan reopened diplomatic relations with China and more than forty years after the outbreak of the Sino-Japanese War, the two nations ratified a treaty of peace and friendship in Tokyo. Initial agreement on the pact had been reached in Peking in August.

The ten-year accord binds the two countries to settle all disputes peacefully and to oppose he-

gemony in Asia by any power. Despite Japan's denials, the antihegemony clause was widely interpreted as a reference to the Soviet Union, further complicating Japan's already strained relations with Moscow. The Chinese announced their intention to withdraw in 1979 from the defunct Sino-Soviet alliance against Japan. Peking even encouraged Japan to maintain its defense pact with the U.S., since this no longer held anti-Chinese implications but remained a powerful deterrent to Soviet aggression.

The Soviets responded immediately by preempting Japan's efforts to keep Southeast Asian nations nonaligned and open to Japanese commercial overtures. On Nov. 3 the U.S.S.R. signed a friendship treaty with Vietnam which was clearly directed against China and the Chinese-Japanese alliance.

The new pact with China strengthened Tokyo's policy ties with Washington. U.S. President Jimmy Carter had given the proposed alliance his blessing in early May when he conferred with Prime Minister Fukuda. For the most part, however, 1978 was marked by wrangling between Washington and Tokyo over trade and monetary issues.

See STATISTICS OF THE WORLD.   T.L.K.

JORDAN, HASHEMITE KINGDOM OF. In 1978 Jordan's King Hussein found himself facing one of the biggest dilemmas in his twenty-six years on the Hashemite throne. Despite pressure from his longtime ally the United States, he decided to reject the Arab-Israeli peace worked out at Camp David, Md., with its provisions for the West Bank, and moved closer to Arab hard-liners and his former Palestinian guerrilla enemies.

The Peace Process. Hussein caused dismay in Washington, D.C., when he pronounced the Camp David proposals for Jordanian participation in peace negotiations unacceptable "in the present form." U.S. President Jimmy Carter had counted on Hussein's help in diminishing the impression that Egyptian President Anwar el-Sadat was about to make a separate peace with Israel. But Hussein said he did not feel bound by the Camp David accords, since he was not consulted in their formulation. The accords called for a five-year transition period on the Israeli-occupied West Bank, which Jordan had controlled before the 1967 Middle East war. But King Hussein noted that many key questions about the future of the area had been deliberately ignored or only partially addressed. He asked for specifics about the future of Israeli forces on the West Bank, the fate of existing Israeli settlements in the area, and whether Palestinians living as refugees abroad would be allowed to return to the West Bank. He also sought assurances on the return of Arab East

Jerusalem. It quickly became apparent that the Israeli position on most of these issues was not acceptable to Hussein, and at the end of 1978 the prospects for early Jordanian involvement in peace talks with Israel appeared poor.

Arab Relations. In the wake of the Camp David talks, Hussein began to draw away from Egypt's Sadat and to seek improved relations with the Arab hard-liners. Hussein pronounced himself "absolutely shattered" by Sadat's apparent willingness to sign a separate peace treaty with Israel. Since Egypt had apparently withdrawn from the Arab military front against Israel, Jordan moved to strengthen relations with Syria, the most powerful of the remaining Arab confrontation states. Moreover, Hussein welcomed Palestine Liberation Organization leader Yasir Arafat back to Jordan for the first time since 1970–71, when Palestinian guerrillas had tried to topple his monarchy.

U.S. Relations. Hussein's longtime close relationship with the U.S. was severely strained by the Camp David accords. The king declined an invitation from President Carter to visit Washington in mid-October, stating that the timing "was not suitable." The king also expressed concern over whether the U.S. was genuinely committed to an overall Middle East settlement.

The Monarchy. King Hussein took a 26-year-old American woman, Elizabeth (Lisa) Halaby, as his fourth wife in 1978. At their royal wedding in Amman on June 15, the king's bride, daughter of former Pan American airlines executive Najeeb Halaby, took the name of Noor al-Hussein and was made queen of Jordan by her new husband. Hussein's third wife, Queen Alia, had died in a helicopter crash in 1977.

See STATISTICS OF THE WORLD. See also ARAB LEAGUE; MIDDLE EAST.   M.R.B.

K

KANSAS. See STATISTICS OF THE WORLD.
KENTUCKY. See STATISTICS OF THE WORLD.
KENYA. The death of Jomo Kenyatta and the peaceful transfer of power to a new president dominated Kenyan affairs in 1978. On Aug. 22, President Kenyatta died in his sleep while vacationing at Mombasa; he was believed to have been at least 83; see OBITUARIES. Kenyatta had served as the country's chief executive since independence in 1963 and had been the spokesman for an increasingly conservative element among the Kikuyu, an ethnic group that constitutes some 20 percent of Kenya's population.

Daniel Arap Moi, who had once led a rival, non-Kikuyu political party, but who had served as Kenyatta's handpicked vice-president for eleven years, was immediately sworn in as interim president. Under the constitution, Moi was required to call presidential elections within ninety days. However, a faction within the Kikuyu-dominated Kenya African National Union, the country's only political party, succeeded in having Moi selected as the party's lone presidential candidate; on Oct. 10, Moi was formally declared Kenya's second president, without a general election. (In September, Moi had suspended all further allocations of government lands and pledged fairer land distribution. He had also mounted anticorruption drives within the government.)

In party elections which followed on Oct. 28, Moi supporters won all eight key posts and

emerged as the new dominant faction. They had gained general popular support; they had also managed to divest conservative Kikuyus and former Kenyatta supporters of some of their power.

In foreign affairs, the Kenyan government continued to support Ethiopia in its border troubles with Somalia, and Kenya experienced an increase in Somali banditry along its own frontier. In February, Kenya temporarily halted rail shipments to Uganda because of nonpayment of about $1,000,-000 in debts. Although relations later improved, Kenya continued to strengthen its armed forces, partly by purchasing U.S. jet fighters.

See STATISTICS OF THE WORLD. See also AFRICA.   J.T.S.
KHMER REPUBLIC. See CAMBODIA.
KOREA, DEMOCRATIC PEOPLE'S REPUBLIC OF, or NORTH KOREA. Communist North Korea remained rigidly isolated—and economically crippled—in 1978. Apparently in total control of the country, President Kim Il Sung was the subject of a personality cult surpassing even those of Joseph Stalin and Mao Tse-tung.

Politics. Over the year rumors circulated that Kim was in poor health and had been flown to Rumania for treatment. But visitors to P'yŏngyang reported that Kim, 66, seemed in good condition despite a large growth on his neck. The person who figured most prominently in speculation about a successor to Kim was the president's 38-year-old son, Kim Chong Il. In the previous year the younger Kim had been the subject of a personality cult second only to his father's, but during 1978 the son was conspicuously absent from the public eye. His picture was removed from buildings, and his birthday in February passed without the usual observances. According to some reports, Kim Chong Il had been the victim of an assassination attempt that left him severely wounded. Some analysts theorized, on the other hand, that the president—embarrassed by criticism that he was creating a "Communist crown prince"—had removed his son temporarily from public notice.

The Economy. The North Korean economy remained deeply troubled during the year. In the early 1970's the country attempted to modernize quickly by importing huge amounts of technology from the Soviet Union, Japan, and the West. The scheme began to unravel when oil prices rose and demand for North Korea's metal and mineral exports plummeted. By 1978 North Korea owed an estimated $2.5 billion to foreign creditors, who were openly expressing their impatience.

Another major reason for the country's flagging economic performance, according to a study by the U.S. Central Intelligence Agency, was that North Korea was spending about 16 percent of its gross national product on its armed forces (South Korea reportedly spends 5 percent). In 1978 North Korea continued its long-term arms buildup, raising its tank strength to 1950, its fleet of amphibious craft to 90, and its force of armored personnel carriers to 750, far outdistancing South Korea in each category.

Foreign Policy. Over the year North Korea resisted overtures from South Korea to resume direct talks on economic cooperation. President Kim insisted that North Korea would talk only with the U.S., and only after a U.S. troop withdrawal would he negotiate with South Korea on arms limitation and reunification. Both Seoul and Washington rejected this approach, and even some of Kim's Communist allies were disturbed by his inflexibility. In the spring North and South Korean naval vessels engaged in a series of skirmishes, but there was no indication that Kim had plans for a major military strike.

Chinese Premier Hua Kuo-feng visited North Korea in early May. This was Hua's first foreign trip as head of state and the first foreign journey by a Chinese Communist Party chairman in more than two decades. While in P'yŏngyang, Hua backed North Korea's stance on reunification, but no communiqué was issued at the end of the visit—a sign that Kim and Hua may not have seen eye to eye on other issues.

See STATISTICS OF THE WORLD. R.J.C.

KOREA, REPUBLIC OF, *or* **SOUTH KOREA.** South Korea enjoyed a stable and prosperous year in 1978—at a cost. Although public dissent was largely stifled, a sizable antigovernment protest vote was registered in parliamentary elections.

Politics. In July the National Conference for Unification met in Seoul and elected President Park Chung Hee to his fourth six-year term. The choice came as no surprise, since the conference was stacked with Park supporters and no other candidate was nominated. Park received all but one of the 2578 votes cast.

Outwardly the country was tranquil. A number of student demonstrations did take place, however, with the protesters demanding an end to the emergency proclamations under which Park had governed since 1972. A large demonstration was planned for downtown Seoul in October, but it was snuffed out before it started when student leaders were arrested and masses of police appeared in the streets.

In December, Park suffered a sharp rebuke in the voting for the National Assembly when his ruling Democratic Republican Party was outpolled by the combined Opposition. Nevertheless, the government party did win 68 of the 154 contested seats, with 61 going to the New Democratic Party. Since the president then named 77 additional delegates to the 231-member body, as was his right under the 1972 constitution, Park's control of parliament was assured. He subsequently ordered the release of some 4000 political prisoners, including his best-known opponent, Kim Dae Jung.

The Economy. South Korea's dynamic economy roared along at an impressive pace in 1978. Spurred by a continuing export boom, which saw exports reach the $10 billion mark for the second straight year, the economy as a whole grew at an estimated 12.5 percent. So confident were the economic planners in Seoul that they forecast exports of more than $22 billion and a per capita gross national product of $1700 by 1981. The chief drawback to South Korea's outstanding economic performance in 1978 was inflation, which ran at an average rate of over 12 percent.

Foreign Policy. Relations with the United States underwent some painful changes. In late February, President Park permitted businessman Park Tong Sun, then under indictment in the U.S., to fly to Washington, D.C., and testify before Congress on alleged South Korean influence-buying on Capitol Hill. (Park Tong Sun testified under an agreement that promised him immunity from prosecution for previous wrongdoing.) The president refused to allow Congress to question Kim Dong Jo, his former ambassador to Washington,

Two passengers were killed when a South Korean jet flying from Paris to Seoul strayed over Soviet territory; the craft crash-landed on a frozen lake after being fired on by a Russian interceptor. The surviving passengers and crew were then flown to Helsinki. Finally, on April 23, they boarded this plane and completed their journey to Seoul.

on the grounds that Kim had diplomatic immunity.

Of far greater importance to South Koreans than the so-called Koreagate affair was the beginning of the withdrawal of U.S. ground troops. More than 500 troops were flown home in December, the first step in a five-year phased withdrawal of 32,000 American troops. In an attempt to reassure Seoul, U.S. Secretary of Defense Harold Brown visited South Korea in November and restated the U.S. pledge to come to its aid in the event of an attack from the north.

See STATISTICS OF THE WORLD.   R.J.C.

KUWAIT. The new ruler of Kuwait, Sheikh Jaber al-Ahmad al-Sabah, kept his country on a moderate course during 1978, his first year in power. Sheikh Jaber took over as emir of the oil-rich nation at the outset of 1978, following the death on Dec. 31, 1977, of Sheikh Sabah al-Salem al-Sabah, his cousin. One of the first tasks facing the Kuwaiti leader was to resolve political infighting within the ruling al-Sabah family over who would become the new crown prince. The final choice was Sheikh Saad al-Abdullah al-Sabah. On Feb. 8 the new crown prince was also named prime minister. Sheikh Saad and his cabinet took over from an interim caretaker government, appointed in January after the resignation of the old cabinet.

Under the new regime, the year 1978 was largely a time of economic consolidation for Kuwait. Oil revenues, which give the 1,130,000 inhabitants of Kuwait the world's highest per capita income, had declined as a result of the global oil surplus that developed in 1977. A year of squabbling over price-shaving by Kuwait and its Persian Gulf neighbors was finally brought to an end in February, when the Organization of Petroleum Exporting Countries (OPEC) approved moves by Kuwait to cut its oil prices in an effort to keep its share of the overall market. The OPEC decision allowed Kuwait to underprice its heavier varieties of crude oil in relation to those of Saudi Arabia, Iran, and Iraq.

Although Kuwait sought an oil price hike at the June meeting of OPEC to compensate for the decline in the value of the U.S. dollar, the organization did not approve a boost, partly because of the surplus oil on the market at that time. But in December, OPEC approved a 14.5 percent oil price rise for 1979.

Throughout the year Kuwait remained cool to Egyptian President Anwar el-Sadat's peace negotiations with Israel. In December Kuwaiti officials took part in the Arab summit conference in Baghdad that condemned the Egyptian position. The summit also agreed to transfer Arab League headquarters out of Cairo if Egypt went through with plans to sign a separate treaty with Israel. Kuwait was reported to be the leading choice to become the new headquarters country.

See STATISTICS OF THE WORLD. *See also* ARAB LEAGUE; MIDDLE EAST; ORGANIZATION OF PETROLEUM EXPORTING COUNTRIES.   M.R.B

L

LABOR. The big labor stories of 1978 were a string of legislative setbacks for organized labor in the U.S. Congress and a sixteen-week strike by coal miners. Unemployment fell below 6 percent for the first time in four years but inflation rose to 9 percent, raising pressure on unions for more moderate wage demands. Most U.S. railroads were closed down by a brief but economically damaging strike by a railway clerks union. The U.S. Labor Department sued former trustees of an International Brotherhood of Teamsters' pension fund for alleged financial abuses.

Congressional Setbacks. A heavily Democratic Congress, which organized labor helped elect in 1976, refused in 1978 to pass several bills strongly backed by labor forces. Political analysts concluded that organized labor had lost much of its influence as a pressure group. Labor's top legislative priority was passage of a bill revising the National Labor Relations Act to make it easier for unions to organize workers. The bill, passed by the U.S. House of Representatives, was killed in the Senate in June.

Organized labor also failed to win congressional backing for a national health-insurance program and tax-law changes to shift tax burdens from working people to business. Labor leaders won partial victories with the enactment of the Humphrey-Hawkins full-employment bill and an extension of an $11 billion public-jobs program

called the Comprehensive Employment and Training Act (CETA). The full-employment act, adapted from a version cosponsored by the late Sen. Hubert H. Humphrey (D, Minn.) and Rep. Augustus F. Hawkins (D, Calif.), merely stated the government's nonbinding intention to reduce unemployment to 4 percent and inflation to 3 percent by 1983. It offered no new programs to achieve those goals. The CETA extension provided money to create about 660,000 jobs for the unemployed in 1979. CETA created 725,000 jobs in 1978.

President Jimmy Carter signed into law a bill raising from 65 to 70 years the age at which most employees could be forced to retire. The law also abolished the mandatory retirement age for federal workers, who previously had to retire at age 70.

Unemployment and Inflation. Unemployment declined to an average rate of about 6 percent in 1978 from 7 percent in 1977. It was the lowest rate since 1974. In December, 1978, there were 95,900,000 persons employed (compared with 92,589,000 in December, 1977) and 6,010,000 persons unemployed (compared with 6,337,000 in December, 1977). Unemployment among Blacks and other minorities remained high, however. The jobless rate for non-Whites in December was 11.5 percent, more than double the rate for Whites.

While employment improved, inflation worsened. Consumer prices rose 9 percent (compared

A Quiet Man at Labor

If Labor Secretary F. (for Freddie) Ray Marshall is "the invisible man" of the Carter cabinet, it may be because of his deliberately unflamboyant style. Though he toiled around-the-clock during the bitter, 111-day coal strike early in the year, he avoided public posturing. Marshall also worked quietly behind the scenes to help steer the Humphrey-Hawkins full-employment bill to congressional passage in October. Studious even during his impoverished early years (he grew up in a Mississippi orphanage), Marshall plugged on to a PH.D. in economics and to professorships at the universities of Mississippi and Texas. In his sympathies and outlook, the 49-year-old labor secretary meshed well with the President. Or as Marshall himself put it: "I can talk Baptist to Jimmy."

Labor Secretary F. Ray Marshall.

A striking fireman and a National Guardsman keep a tense vigil outside the main fire hall of Memphis, Tenn., on the night of Aug. 14. About 1500 guardsmen were called in to maintain order during a week of strikes by both policemen and firefighters.

with 6.8 percent in 1977). Wage increases also rose 9 percent. President Carter proposed a new program on Oct. 24 to reduce inflation. It included voluntary guidelines that would limit wage and fringe benefit increases to 7 percent a year and hold price increases below their rate of increase during 1976–77. The American Federation of Labor and Congress of Industrial Organizations branded the program unfair to workers. The federation called instead for mandatory wage and price controls.

Coal Strike. Coal miners staged the longest major strike of 1978. About 160,000 members of the United Mine Workers of America (UMW) left their jobs on Dec. 6, 1977, in a contract dispute with the Bituminous Coal Operators Association. The workers stayed off the job for 111 days, returning to work on March 27 after ratifying a new three-year contract. During the strike the miners rejected a proposed contract recommended by UMW President Arnold Miller. When President Carter invoked the Taft-Hartley Act on March 6, few miners returned to work as ordered by the act's provisions, but the pressure finally led to a successful settlement. The government had predicted that a long strike would trigger extensive power shortages and factory closings. Those predictions proved wrong. The strike cut U.S. coal production in half, and shortages arose in such coal-dependent states as Ohio, Indiana, and West Virginia. But large pre-strike stockpiles of coal and increased output at nonunion mines kept most electric utilities running normally.

The two big issues in the strike involved wildcat strikes and health insurance. The industry failed to win the right to fire leaders of wildcat strikes, which plagued Appalachian coalfields in 1977. The UMW was forced to give up an industrywide

health-insurance plan partly administered by union trustees. Under the new contract, each company would set up its own health plan through private insurance carriers. The contract also raised a miner's base wages 31 percent over three years, from $7.80 an hour in 1977 to $10.20 in 1980.

Other Strikes and Settlements. Two thirds of the nation's railroads were struck for four days in September by the Brotherhood of Railway, Airline, and Steamship Clerks (BRAC). The union had been on strike since July against the Norfolk & Western Railway (N&W) in a dispute over job losses caused by automation. BRAC picketed more than fifty other railroads which were giving money to the N&W through a mutual aid pact. The strike ended a day after President Carter issued a sixty-day back-to-work order. BRAC later agreed to stay on the job through the end of 1978.

Wages and job security were the principal issues in a contract dispute beginning in April between the U.S. Postal Service and three unions representing 516,000 postal workers. Although federal law prohibits mail strikes the unions threatened throughout the five months of talks to strike if their demands were not met. The unions never called a strike, although there were a few brief wildcat strikes in New York, New Jersey, and California in July. After workers rejected one proposed contract the dispute was settled in September through binding arbitration. The contract raised wages 21.3 percent over three years and promised lifetime job security to employees hired through July, 1979.

Pressmen at New York City's daily newspapers struck over job security for several months beginning in August. Pilots struck Northwest Airlines for 109 days beginning in May. Strikes also were staged by aerospace workers, insurance agents, paperworkers, and teachers. There was a rash of strikes by municipal employees, most of them coming in the summer months. Firefighters went on strike in Memphis, Tenn.; Louisville, Ky.; and Youngstown, Ohio. Police walked out in Memphis, Cleveland, and Youngstown, and sanitation workers in Philadelphia, New Orleans, and San Antonio. Transit workers staged wildcat strikes in Washington, D.C., and Boston. Labor Department figures showed no unusually high number of strikes during the year, however. Department figures also showed that major wage settlements averaged 7.7 percent in first-year increases during the first nine months of 1978, about the same as in the first nine months of 1977.

Corruption. Several union officials ran into problems with the law in 1978. The Labor Department sued Teamsters President Frank E. Fitzsimmons and sixteen other former trustees of a Chicago-based union pension fund in February to recover millions of dollars allegedly lost because of imprudent loans. The suit accused the ex-trustees of violating a U.S. pension law by making questionable loans involving gambling casinos, racetracks, risky real-estate ventures, and reputed organized crime figures. The suit did not come to trial in 1978.

On June 21, Anthony ("Tony Pro") Provenzano, a longtime Teamsters leader in New Jersey, was sentenced to life in prison for the 1961 murder of a rival union leader. Provenzano had been investigated by federal authorities in connection with the 1975 disappearance of former Teamsters President Jimmy Hoffa. Joseph Tonelli, president of the United Paperworkers International Union, resigned his post after pleading guilty in October to embezzling union funds. Former UMW President

W. A. ("Tony") Boyle was convicted again in the 1969 murders of union rival Joseph Yablonski and Yablonski's wife and daughter. Boyle's first conviction in 1974 was overturned. In June officials of the International Longshoremen's Association and several East Coast shipping company executives were indicted on racketeering charges.

Other Events. On April 28 the National Labor Relations Board and J. P. Stevens & Co. reached an out-of-court settlement of a board suit charging the textile company with extensive U.S. labor-law infractions. The suit was dropped after Stevens agreed not to violate any laws in its twelve-year fight to prevent the Amalgamated Clothing and Textile Workers Union from organizing company employees. In September, General Motors Corp. and the United Auto Workers reached an agreement that would let the union represent workers at GM's new plants in the South.

The Labor Department's Occupational Safety and Health Administration (OSHA) issued tightened regulations to reduce worker exposure to a number of harmful substances found in workplaces, including benzene, lead, and cotton dust (in textile mills). Some of the rules did not go into effect, however, because of delays resulting from industry court challenges. The U.S. Supreme Court ruled on May 23 that OSHA could not make unannounced safety inspections of a workplace without an employer's permission unless the inspector first obtained a search warrant.   O.U.

LABRADOR. See STATISTICS OF THE WORLD.

LAOS. During 1978 Laos continued to undergo a harsh transformation at the hands of its Communist rulers. Real power was held by the neighboring Communist nation of Vietnam, which had 40,000 troops stationed in Laos. Prince Souphanouvong, however, held onto his position as pres-

More than 5000 job seekers line up at the state fairgrounds in Oklahoma City on May 16. They were applying for 2000 jobs in a General Motors assembly plant that was scheduled to begin operations early in 1979.

ident and nominal leader. By his regime's own reckoning, 40,000 people (out of a population of about 3,400,000) remained in the so-called reeducation camps, giving Laos the distinction of having more political prisoners per capita than any other country in the world.

In June the government announced a new agricultural collectivization program. The aim was to improve food production and strengthen control over the countryside. By August, Laotian peasants were said to have formed a total of 700 collectives, but the involuntary program touched off a new exodus across the Mekong River into Thailand. With some 2000 to 4000 people leaving each month, it was estimated that 140,000 Laotians had fled the country between the Communist takeover in 1975 and the end of 1978.

Throughout 1978, armed resistance to the government flared in pockets across the country. Some guerrilla groups, led by former army regulars and Communist defectors, cut off roads, struck at supply depots, and ambushed government patrols. In the northern hill country, Meo tribesmen fiercely resisted government plans to force them out of their ancestral homeland and into agricultural collectives on the lowland plains. The Meos, who call themselves Hmong ("free men"), claimed that their villages were being attacked with napalm, phosphorous bombs, defoliants, and poison gas.

Meanwhile, Laos, with a per capita income that ranked as one of the world's lowest, was close to outright destitution in 1978. In the best of times the country's feeble export earnings had barely paid for the rice that had to be imported to supplement its sagging production. In 1978 this plight was worsened—first by a severe drought, then by one of the worst floods of the century. A shortfall of well over 100,000 tons of grain had to be made up by contributions from the Soviet Union, the Scandinavian countries, the United States, and other donors.

In general, Laotian foreign policy reflected Vietnam's pro-Soviet line. Nevertheless, the People's Republic of China had thousands of people working in the northern provinces of Laos, building roads and other installations. Under the circumstances, the Laotian government kept anti-Chinese rhetoric to a minimum.

See STATISTICS OF THE WORLD.   R.J.C.

LEBANON. The rivalries that had combined to turn Lebanon into a battlefield three years earlier continued to wreak havoc there in 1978. First, Israeli troops invaded in March in an attack on Palestinian guerrilla bases; the Israelis occupied most of southern Lebanon below the Litani River for three months. Then in June, new fighting broke out between the Christian militias and the Arab League peacekeeping force that had been sent to restore order in Lebanon in 1976. Although the level of bloodshed had lessened at year's end, there seemed little hope that any semblance of peacetime normality would soon be restored.

The Israeli Invasion. A Palestinian terrorist attack on a tour bus on the Haifa–Tel Aviv road resulted in the death of 37 Israelis on March 11. This event triggered a massive Israeli invasion of southern Lebanon three days later. Israeli army radio said more than 25,000 Israeli troops, backed by armor and warplanes, were taking part in the operation. The invading forces took control of much of southern Lebanon and claimed to have inflicted heavy casualties on Palestinian guerrilla units. Arab peacekeeping troops—largely Syrian—remained clear of the fighting. On April 11, after driving the Palestinian guerrillas out of the border area, Israeli forces began a phased withdrawal. They turned control of the area over to United Nations peacekeeping troops—the U.N. Interim Force in Lebanon (UNIFIL)—and to Lebanese Christian militiamen. The Israeli army completed its withdrawal from Lebanon on June 13.

Syrian-Christian Fighting. In February, a month before the Israeli invasion, heavy fighting broke out between members of the Lebanese Christian militias and the Arab League peacekeeping force in Lebanon, whose 30,000 troops were primarily Syrian. The goal of the peacekeeping units was to force the Christians to submit to the authority of the central Lebanese government, headed by President Elias Sarkis. This struggle abated during the Israeli invasion, but Syrian forces resumed their efforts in late June, surrounding and shelling Christian strongholds in East Beirut. The heaviest fighting came at the end of September, when Syrian artillery began a nine-day bombardment of East Beirut that resulted in the worst destruction of the Lebanese civil war. Christian leaders reported 800 persons killed and 3000 wounded— most of them civilians—before Syria finally heeded a U.N. Security Council appeal for a cease-fire. The bombardment failed to break the spirit of the Christian militias, however, and new outbreaks of fighting continued through the rest of the year. On Oct. 26 the Arab League agreed to extend the mandate of the Syrian-dominated peacekeeping force for another six months, to May, 1979.

Government. As a result of their inability to bombard the Christian militias into submission, the Syrians' efforts to establish a strong central government in Lebanon made little headway during 1978. President Sarkis at one point threatened to resign over the Syrian tactic of attempting to bring

On March 21 Israeli soldiers look across the Litani River, the northern limit of their invasion of Lebanon. A few hours later, a cease-fire went into effect.

the Christian factions into line by force. He later withdrew his threat. On Dec. 20, in the first cabinet reshuffle in two years, the commander of the Lebanese army, Maj. Gen. Victor Khoury, was named minister of defense to succeed Fuad Butros. Butros remained in the cabinet as deputy prime minister and foreign minister. The appointment of Khoury, a military leader, was widely viewed as a signal that the central government intended to make a major effort to reestablish its authority.

Economic Developments. The continued fighting in Beirut and throughout southern Lebanon frustrated efforts to bring the country's war-ravaged economy back to life. Most of the major Western

A dramatic time-exposure photograph of Beirut on Oct. 1. Rocket- and shellfire caused the worst destruction in three years of Lebanese civil war.

banks that had once had large operations in Beirut remained closed, and little new construction took place. Hopes for at least a partial economic recovery during 1978 were dashed July 27 when the U.S. State Department announced that it was reducing the size of its embassy in Beirut and advised all Americans to leave Lebanon as quickly as possible.

Terrorism and Intrigue. A number of explosions and kidnappings during 1978 added to the general atmosphere of instability.

A bomb explosion Aug. 13 demolished a nine-story building in Beirut in the worst act of sabotage ever to occur in Lebanon; as many as 200 people may have been killed in the explosion. The building had been the headquarters of the pro-Iraqi Palestine Liberation Front, and although the guerrilla leaders publicly accused Israel of involvement, they privately expressed their belief that the explosion was the work of the pro-Syrian Popular Front for the Liberation of Palestine–General Command.

Another incident that caused widespread concern in Lebanon was the disappearance of one of the country's most prominent religious leaders. The Imam Musa Sadr, spiritual leader of nearly 1,000,000 Lebanese Shi'ite Muslims, was last seen in Tripoli, Libya, on Aug. 31. Libyan officials claimed that he took a flight to Rome that night, but authorities in Italy claimed there was no proof the imam had actually left Libya. Lebanese Shi'ites, who charged that Libyan leader Col. Muammar el-Qaddafi had had the imam arrested, staged strikes and protests to demand his release.

See STATISTICS OF THE WORLD. *See also* ARAB LEAGUE; MIDDLE EAST; PALESTINE LIBERATION ORGANIZATION.   M.R.B.

LESOTHO. *See* STATISTICS OF THE WORLD.

LIBERIA. *See* STATISTICS OF THE WORLD.

LIBRARIES. The unprecedented revolt of taxpayers in 1978 against what they considered excessive government spending caused the nation's public libraries to reconsider their programs and budgets.

Reduced Funding. In California the passage in June of Proposition 13 forced a statewide reduction in property taxes. This action resulted in serious financial curtailment for many tax-supported library systems. Libraries lost up to 70 percent of their budgets, forcing them to cut staff, shorten hours, and limit services; some branches were shut down entirely. Alameda County libraries were especially hard hit, losing most of their employees and putting an end to programs for shut-ins, prisoners, the aged, and the Spanish-speaking population. Other libraries began to charge fees or made plans for using volunteers.

As opposition to high taxation spread across the nation, the Library of Congress lost 5 percent of its funding and Philadelphia's library budget was reduced by $2,000,000. The House of Representatives cut the budget of the Comprehensive Employment and Training Act (CETA), which provides free clerical and paraprofessional help, usually from minority groups, to city libraries.

New Funding. Before the Proposition 13 movement caught fire, local and state support plus new forms of federal aid, such as revenue sharing and new public works projects using some CETA employees, continued to stimulate library construction and renovation. In California, revenue sharing provided $419,000 to build and stock the Newport Center Branch Library. In Ohio, the Stark County District Library in Canton received $4,600,000 in public works funds to build a pyramid-shaped library largely fueled by solar energy.

In contrast to taxpayer resistance in other parts of the country, voters in Dallas overwhelmingly supported a $40,000,000 library bond issue. Dallas thereby gained a new main library, a new branch, and four branch library sites. The cost of the main library and its stock was to be met by public works funds, private gifts, and a challenge grant from the National Endowment for the Humanities, as well as by the bond issue.

Thanks to the concerted campaign of a citizens' library committee, voters in Tulsa increased the property tax to cover the rising cost of library maintenance. In New York City the Vincent Astor Foundation offered a $5,000,000 challenge grant to help the financially troubled New York Public Library. Two hundred volunteers from Pennsylvania Teamsters Local 773 saved the Allentown Public Library $40,000 in moving costs by transporting 6000 cartons of books from the old library building to the new building.

New Libraries. The Chicago Public Library system opened the new Illinois Regional Library for the Blind in 1978. Distinctively triangular in shape with undulating windows, it was designed for easy use by the handicapped. The New York State Library moved into a new home in the Cultural Education Center in Albany. The Bridgewater (N.Y.) Free Library completed a new, prefabricated, 1200 sq.ft. building, which cost only $16,000 fully insulated and furnished. Similar prefabricated buildings became the first "outpost libraries" of rural West Virginia. California Polytechnic State University announced plans to construct a five-story, 500,000-volume library, costing $10,630,000, to replace its crowded 1947 building; the new structure was to provide space also for readers, offices, and book repairs.

Other Developments. The National Commission on Libraries and Information Science issued the first draft of a revised plan for state aid to libraries. The new plan calls for a switch from the old method—aid to libraries by category (public, school, and academic)—to "block grant" aid, which would allow each state to use its allotment according to its particular needs.

The Library of Congress announced plans to "freeze" its card catalog in 1980. This means that all titles published after that year would be listed on automated equipment rather than on cards, a procedure that has already been adopted by the New York Public Library and other large systems. In addition, the rules for describing works in the catalog were to be revised. Protests from leading librarians, who felt that these changes, which would also affect Canadian and British libraries, needed more time, resulted in a postponement until 1981.

Meetings. The Canadian Library Association's thirty-third annual conference was held in Edmonton, Alberta, June 15-20, with the theme, "Strategies for Change, Organizing for Growth." The ninety-seventh American Library Association conference, held in Chicago, June 24-30, focused on the theme, "Toward a National Information Policy." The International Federation of Library Associations held its annual meeting in Strebske Pleso, Czechoslovakia, Aug. 28–Sept. 3. The first independent national conference of the Association of College and Research Librarians met in Boston, Nov. 9-11; the association meeting coincided with the International Antiquarian Book Fair.   R.J.S.

LIBYA, officially SOCIALIST PEOPLE'S LIBYAN ARAB JAMAHIRIYAH. Libya continued its efforts during 1978 to use its oil wealth to build President Muammar el-Qaddafi's vision of the "new socialist society."

Internal Affairs. Early in 1978 the Libyan government mounted an assault on whatever private property and wealth remained in the socialized country. Private houses were confiscated under a law banning ownership of more than one building; the next scheduled step was a ban on the accumulation of individual savings. The time-honored way of life of Libya's 2,630,000 people was altered in 1978 in other ways, too: by compulsory education, compulsory military training, and the introduction of women into the work force. The government pressed ahead with its efforts to break down the traditional patterns of rural life, and expected to have the entire nation linked by means of bus service and television by 1980. Under the country's $24 billion development program, financed out of oil revenues, there was

rapid construction of new schools, hospitals, apartment houses, farms, and roads.

However, there was at least one indication of internal opposition to the Qaddafi regime. In March, when two East German officials and nine other persons were killed in a helicopter crash, press reports maintained that the vehicle had been sabotaged by dissident officers who thought that Qaddafi was on board. After the crash it was reported that a number of air force officers had been arrested.

Foreign Affairs. Libya continued to maintain its close ties with the Soviet Union during 1978. A top member of the Libyan government, Abdel Salam Jalloud, traveled to Moscow in February for talks with President Leonid I. Brezhnev and other Soviet leaders. In the summer, however, Jalloud visited Peking, and on Aug. 9, Libya and the People's Republic of China announced that they had agreed to establish full diplomatic relations. The two countries signed pacts covering trade, scientific, economic, and technical cooperation. Also, the United States appeared to be attempting to improve relations with Libya late in the year. On Nov. 30 the government disclosed that it had decided to approve the sale to Libya of 400 high-bed trucks.

On Feb. 6, Chad broke relations with Libya. The neighboring North African country alleged that Libya was providing support for antigovernment guerrillas within Chad and was, moreover, occupying a strip of uranium-rich territory belonging to Chad. Diplomatic relations were resumed on Feb. 20, but later in the year fighting broke out between troops of the French-backed Chadian government and the Muslim rebels who were believed to be supported by Libya. And on June 22, Chad's president, Félix Malloum, charged that thousands of Libyan soldiers were in his country.

Nuclear Potential. Libya's plan to purchase a 300,000 kw nuclear reactor from the Soviet Union became the subject of controversy in late 1978 when a U.S. organization, the Federation of American Scientists, accused Libya of continuing to attempt to obtain nuclear weapons. Jeremy J. Stone, executive director of the federation, said Ahmed Shahata, head of Libya's foreign liaison office, had told him in November that the government was seeking a nuclear capability. (Libya had inquired earlier in the 1970's about the possibility of buying an atomic bomb from China.) The federation called on the Soviet Union to reconsider its plan to supply Libya with a nuclear power plant.

See STATISTICS OF THE WORLD. See also AFRICA; MIDDLE EAST.   M.R.B.

LIECHTENSTEIN. See STATISTICS OF THE WORLD.

LIFE SCIENCES. News events concerning life sciences, more often found in the scientific journals, made their way to the front pages of the world's newspapers during 1978. First, there was the cloning controversy. It centered on a book, *In His Image,* published in April as nonfiction by a highly reputable firm, J. B. Lippincott Co. David M. Rorvik, the book's author, insisted that he had met its central figure, a boy who he claimed was the genetic copy, or clone, of an American millionaire named Max. Prominent scientists immediately labeled the book a fraud, and more than one suit has been filed against the publisher. However, as a result of the widespread discussion of the book, a large segment of the public did learn that mammalian cloning—the asexual production of animal progeny—has yet to be accomplished.

The second widely publicized biological event of the year was authentic. On July 25, in Lancashire, England, a so-called test-tube baby was born—the first human child to have been created outside the mother's womb. *See* HEALTH AND MEDICINE: *Medicine: Louise Joy Brown and Friends.*

BIOLOGY

Recombinant DNA techniques made 1978 another landmark year for genetic engineers. Harvard researchers got bacteria to produce rat insulin, scientists at the City of Hope National Medical Center near Los Angeles went one step further by inducing bacteria to manufacture human insulin, Stanford University biochemists succeeded in transplanting for the first time a func-

tional gene from one mammal species to another, and an international team of researchers developed a test for abnormal genes in human fetuses. These achievements brought the medical and scientific communities closer to solving problems associated with human genetic abnormalities and to the realization of relatively inexpensive means of manufacturing such rare and expensive natural products as human insulin.

Rat Insulin from Bacteria. In 1977 rat genes for insulin were successfully transplanted into bacteria, but the bacteria could not be prompted to produce the insulin. One key step had been taken

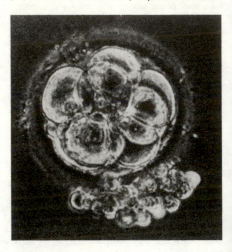

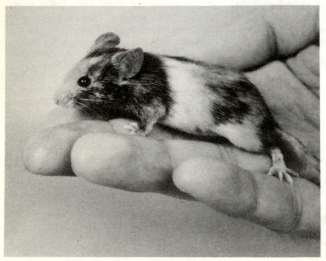

Above: This eight-celled human embryo was formed in vitro. An egg was removed from the mother's body and fertilized with sperm from the father. (The cells at the right originally enveloped the egg.) Implanted in the mother's womb, the embryo would develop into a so-called test-tube baby—like Louise Joy Brown, born July 25 in England. Left: This mouse—yellow-faced, black-eared, and white-bellied—is the result of research performed at Yale University. There, for the first time, scientists had combined three eight-celled embryos— one from black, one from white, and one from yellow parents—then transferred them to a foster mother. Color patterns in such so-called chimeric mice give vital clues to cell movement during embryonic development.

in the process. In 1978 the next step was taken.

Led by Walter Gilbert of Harvard University, a team of researchers working at the Massachusetts Institute of Technology synthesized a rat gene for insulin. Their next challenge was to link this gene to a bacterial gene—but not just any bacterial gene. The scientists were after a gene that was the blueprint of a protein normally excreted from the bacteria cells. In this way the bacteria might be made to excrete rat insulin, which could then be collected and analyzed. The scientists chose a bacterial gene that is the blueprint for a protein called penicillinase, a substance given off by bacteria that breaks down penicillin. The bacterial and rat genes were linked in the bacteria. Proteins given off by this new bacteria culture were analyzed. The researchers discovered that one of them was a hybrid protein, part bacterial penicillinase and part rat insulin. So now a simple way must be found to separate the two parts of the hybrid protein.

Bacteria Produces Human Insulin. The solution to the hybrid protein problem, however, may have significance mainly to interested scientists, since another achievement in 1978 seemed to bring the manufacture of human insulin by bacteria to the threshold of reality. Recombinant DNA researchers Roberto Crea, Tadaaki Hirose, Adam Kraszewski, and Keiichi Itakura of the City of Hope National Medical Center near Los Angeles produced artificial genes for human insulin, in a project sponsored by Genentech, Inc., of San Francisco. These artificial genes were then linked to genes in bacteria. Two groups of bacteria were used. One group produced one part of the human insulin molecule; the other group produced another part; the two parts were harvested and purified. And finally, the two parts were put together chemically to become complete insulin.

Shortly after the success of the City of Hope scientists, a major pharmaceutical company, Eli Lilly and Co., announced an agreement with Genentech to find ways to commercialize the breakthrough. Pilot studies were begun and it was predicted that the large-scale manufacture of human insulin by bacteria would be achieved between 1980 and 1983. This process should eventually provide enough human insulin to supply the needs of diabetics throughout the world. Presently, insulin is derived from other mammals. Such insulin can cause adverse side effects, is in short supply, and is relatively expensive.

Gene Transplant from Mammal to Mammal. Until 1978, gene transplants had been accomplished only between vastly different forms of life, such as human beings and bacteria, rats and bacteria, and yeasts and bacteria. These accomplishments had promised great benefits for human beings as well as an increase in our basic scientific knowledge of how genes work. But the event that both eluded and tantalized scientists was the transplant of a gene from one mammal to another. For if this could be done the possibility of "gene therapy" might be a giant step closer to reality. (Gene therapy would involve the replacement of abnormal genes with normal ones.)

Researchers have been quick to caution that gene therapy for all victims of genetic diseases is still far off. But a stunning success in 1978 brought the day closer. In mid-October Stanford University scientist Paul Berg announced the transplant of a gene between mammals: He and colleagues Richard Mulligan and Bruce Howard had transplanted a rabbit gene to an African green monkey.

The researchers first transplanted the rabbit gene, which directs the manufacture of part of the hemoglobin molecule, into viruses known to infect monkeys. The viruses were then introduced into a culture of monkey cells, where the genetic material from the rabbits became incorporated with that of the monkeys. The monkey cells then produced rabbit hemoglobin. Whether or not the monkey itself could have used the rabbit hemoglobin in its physiological processes remains to be determined. Berg said that the work of his team would later be reported in full detail in a professional journal. Other researchers pointed out that the impact of Berg's success was multifold. It would provide a valuable tool in the "mapping" of mammalian genes—the discovery of their structure and position on chromosomes. These discoveries might, in turn, help in the construction of artificial genes and in the repair or replacement of defective ones. Gene therapy may not be around the corner, but, owing to Berg and his research team, it is somewhat closer.

Lovable When Not Lethal

For eleven years, since their escape from captivity in Brazil, the so-called killer bees from Africa have been the subject of legends, nightmares, and horror films. But the reports of animals and people stung to death by the northward-migrating flying objects were, it seems, exaggerated. In 1978 the U.S. Department of Agriculture released its own 14-minute film, which states that the killer bee, while aggressive, is also quite manageable—in short, "a much maligned insect."

A ban on the export of rhesus monkeys from India to the U.S., announced in the spring, caused an expansion of activities at primate breeding stations such as this one, at Yemassee Primate Center in South Carolina. About 12,000 of the monkeys had been used each year as stand-ins for human subjects in biological and physiological experiments. The Indians apparently objected because a small percentage of the animals were used in military-related testing.

Test for Abnormal Genes. Until Berg's work at Stanford can be translated into a clinical tool to deal with genetic disorders, other approaches to these diseases must be utilized. One such approach is the prenatal diagnoses of inherited abnormalities. In many cases such diagnoses are difficult to make and the procedures can be dangerous to the fetus.

In 1978 a group of researchers using recombinant DNA techniques discovered a way to analyze the structure of genes from fetuses. Such analysis could alert parents and physicians to the presence of a genetic disease in an unborn embryo. A number of options would then be available to the parents and the physician, depending on the kind of genetic disorder discovered and its severity. Stuart H. Orkin of Children's Hospital Medical Center in Boston led the research team, which included members from Harvard and Yale University medical schools and Hacettepe University in Ankara, Turkey. They adopted a trick devel-

oped by recombinant DNA scientists—the use of special enzymes to snip apart genes.

One series of experiments involved the diagnosis of a blood disorder called delta beta-thalassemia. Like sickle-cell anemia, this inherited disease is caused by an abnormal gene that affects hemoglobin synthesis. Usually a blood sample is taken from a fetus to make the diagnosis. This procedure, however, is dangerous to the fetus. A much safer technique is to take a sample of the amniotic fluid, which surrounds the fetus. This fluid, however, generally does not contain red blood cells. In the new method developed by Orkin and his colleagues, the genes in fetal cells floating in the amniotic fluid are studied. These might be skin cells that have been sloughed off; yet, since all body cells carry a full complement of genes, they contain genes for hemoglobin manufacture even though they are not red blood cells. To break apart the genes, the researchers used enzymes—biochemical catalysts; these are the same enzymes used in recombinant DNA work to break apart and rebuild genes. The gene fragments—from both normal and suspect genes—are linked to radioactive substances. The fragments are then photographed and compared. A fetal sample in which gene fragments are shorter or longer than normal, are missing fragments altogether, or are present in reduced amounts indicates the presence of a genetic abnormality. If the function of each fragment is known, then the precise abnormality can be identified. In the case of delta beta-thalassemia, the genetic fragments responsible for the condition are known.

Orkin pointed out that his technique could be applied to many genetic disorders. He suggests that his "gene visualizing" method would be especially useful in some developing countries, where hereditary blood diseases are common and generally go undiagnosed. Cell samples gathered from fetal amniotic fluid in such countries could be sent for analysis to a network of international centers. Although not suggested by Orkin, information revealed by the analysis—together with genetic counseling—could help reduce the incidence of inherited diseases by giving parents of genetically abnormal fetuses the option of electing therapeutic abortions at early stages of pregnancy.   C.P.

BOTANY

In 1978 botanists continued to make progress in three classic areas of research: the extraction of valuable products from plants that were previously regarded as useless, the development of new ways to destroy pests, and the study of nitrogen fixation in leguminous crops.

Plant Products. Several plants previously thought to be of little practical value have been brought to the attention of researchers at the U.S. Department of Agriculture (USDA). Among these weeds, wild plants, and exotic ornamentals are some that may yield valuable products. For example, Indian plantain, guayule, desert milkweed, rabbit brush, and Edison's goldenrod have been found to be rich in natural rubber. It was announced in 1978 that guayule in particular, long regarded as a strong potential source of rubber, might soon receive congressional funding for additional research and development; the major rubber companies (Firestone, Goodrich, Goodyear, and Uniroyal) were already investigating its potential. Other plants (such as ragweed, ironweed, and thistles) were proved to be good sources of gutta (a latex derivative), oils, polyphenols, and protein. These so-called botano-chemicals could replace many petrochemicals and reduce our dependence on imported petroleum. In fact, Russell A. Buchanan of the USDA has invented an extraction process for them because of their potential usefulness.

On another front, researchers at the National Academy of Sciences discovered that the tropical weed *Leucaena* is an extremely productive source of lumber and cattle feed. *Leucaena* thrives on marginal farmland because of a long, moisture-seeking taproot and a symbiotic relationship with nitrogen-fixing bacteria—bacteria that convert atmospheric nitrogen into usable nitrates. The latter property enables the plant actually to enrich the soil.

Control of Pests. For the first time, an insect sex scent, a pheromone, was commercially produced (by the Albany International Corp.) in 1978. It proved effective against the pink bollworm, which attacks cotton. The pheromone is contained in short, sticky plastic fibers that stick to cotton plants. Normally emitted in trace amounts by the female, the pheromone evaporates from the fibers and saturates the air. This saturation confuses the males; in this way they are prevented from locating, tracking, and mating with the females.

During 1978 the USDA increased its research into pesticides comprised of disease organisms that are specific for insects. Three of these insect-specific microbial pathogens appeared to be promising: a bacterial-induced disease specific for caterpillars, a protozoan-induced disease for grasshoppers, and a viral-induced disease for the bollworm and tobacco budworm. Also, a team of researchers at the University of California at Riverside—Graham R. Sterling, Michael B. McKenry, and Ron Mankay—discovered a fungus (*Dactylella oviparasita*) that controls root-knot nematode, which is a highly destructive parasite on certain peach trees.

Viroids, single strands of RNA without a protein coat, are below viruses in simplicity. In West Germany, botanists Heinz Sanger and Hans Gross determined the nucleotide sequence and structure of a viroid that causes a disease of potatoes. The results of their research suggest that, unlike viruses, viroids depend upon existing plant cell metabolism for replication. (Viruses initiate new forms of metabolism for their replication in the plant cell.)

M. T. Stephen Hsia found evidence that biodegradable chemical pesticides may be as toxic as their nondegradable predecessors (DDT, for example). The University of Wisconsin scientist showed during the year that, upon degrading, the herbicide propanil becomes TCAB (3,4,3',4'-tetrachloroazobenzene). This substance, chemically similar to dioxin, a highly toxic material, appears to have mutagenic and carcinogenic properties. So degradation products, as well as the original pesticide, may need to be examined as potential pollutants and health hazards. *See* CHEMISTRY.

Finally, foxing—the yellow brown discoloration of paper in old books—has been shown to be the result of slow germination and retarded growth of fungi. This was indicated in research performed by G. G. Maynell and R. J. Newsam at the University of Kent in England.

In 1973, when it was on the verge of demolition, the New York Botanical Garden conservatory in the Bronx was declared a city landmark. In 1978, after two years of restoration costing in the millions, it reopened. The conservatory has a 90-ft.-high dome and ten interconnecting pavilions—ranging from herb gardens to an American Desert House. Shown here is an interior view of the Fern Forest.

Genetic Engineering. Nitrogen-fixing bacteria on the roots of leguminous crops reduce the need for nitrogenous fertilizers. Researchers Feral O'Gara and K. T. Shanmugam at the University of California at Davis genetically altered some of these bacteria. The result was that the altered clover-specific bacteria were able to use soybean and mungbean as hosts.

On another front, researchers at the University of Washington in Seattle and the State University of Ghent in Belgium worked with a bacteria, *Agrobacterium tumefaciens*, which causes plant tumors. They found that foreign DNA, the component of genes, can hitch a ride with these bacteria and become incorporated into a host plant. Such foreign genes could be used to improve plant yields, nutritional quality, and disease resistance, as well as to add nitrogen-fixing ability. The foreign DNA introduced into the host plant by this bacterial agent has not yet proved itself, but researchers appear confident that this difficulty will be resolved in time. R.P.P.

ZOOLOGY

For zoologists, 1978 was a year to make new discoveries concerning termites, poisonous reptiles, and the symbiotic relationship between an extinct bird and a tree.

Cellulose Digestion in Termites. Termites are a

bane to the homeowner because of their ability to burrow into and eat wood. Yet no known multicellular animal can produce the necessary digestive enzymes to break down cellulose; all must rely on the digestive activities of their internal microorganisms or eat partly decomposed cellulose. Primitive termites have symbiotic flagellate protozoa (protozoa that have tails for swimming) resident in their gut which digest the cellulose ingested by the termite, thereby permitting the animals to utilize the sugars resulting from cellulose breakdown.

One group of advanced termites, the macrotermitines, are notable for their symbiotic relationship with fungi that grow in their nests on structures known as fungus combs. These fungus gardens are prepared by the termites from chewed but undigested plant fragments.

The precise feeding habits of these macrotermitines in nature are not known. They will starve if fed only pure cellulose, such as wood or filter paper; but they will survive for long periods if they are also provided with fragments of fungus comb, including the nodules or spore bodies of the fungus.

In 1978, Michael and Joan Martin of the University of Michigan showed that the fungus-growing termite (*Macrotermes natalensis*) of South Africa possesses an entire set of the enzymes needed to digest cellulose. They found two groups of these enzymes in termite tissues such as the gut membranes and glands. But a third group of enzymes is not found in termite tissue, nor is it found in the gut of termites deprived of fungus combs, or of fungus combs from which the nodules have been removed. The level of all cellulose enzymes is high in the nodules but low in the comb material, and the level of enzyme activity is especially high in termites fed only fungus nodules. These observations show conclusively that fungus-growing termites obtain the essential component of the cellulose enzymes from the fungus nodules and that the material of the fungus combs is not an essential part of their diet. During the evolution of the advanced termites the symbiotic intestinal protozoa have been replaced by a symbiotic fungus external to the termite but internal to their nests.

Antipredatory Toxins. Prey animals have evolved many types of defense mechanisms against predators. One of these is the production of toxic materials. It often occurs in small, slow-moving species; it exists as skin secretions in frogs, toads, and salamanders. These toxins vary from a mild irritant to deadly poisons.

Skin toxins of frogs and toads are well known; less known is that many species of salamanders secrete toxic materials from specialized glands usually found along the upper surface of the animal's back or tail. E. D. Brodie, Jr., of Adelphi University, who studied toxins and other antipredatory adaptations in salamanders for many years, issued a report during 1978. It appears that the glandular secretions of salamanders are not highly potent, but may be considered as noxious irritants that repel the predator. Once subjected to the toxin, a mammalian predator will retreat if presented with another individual of the same species, but it will kill and eat nontoxic species. Many species of toxic salamanders have evolved patterns of bright colors which serve as distinctive recognition signals to warn the experienced predator that a noxious taste will follow if it bites the prey. Brodie also showed that many salamanders have antipredator display postures that expose the characteristic warning colors and place the body surface that contains the granular glands closest to the predator.

In contrast to the mild toxins of salamanders, the skin secretions of the neotropical poison-dart frogs of the family Dendrobatidae are extremely deadly. C. W. Myers of the American Museum of Natural History in New York City and his associates showed that the toxins found in this family are among the most deadly nonprotein poisons, that these toxins differ in the various genera of this family, and that the brilliant color patterns of these frogs serve as warning signals. He described a new species of large size and uniform bright yellow color from Colombia, a frog named *Phyllobates terribilis* because of the frightful toxicity of its skin secretions (batrachotoxin and homobatrachotoxin) and the fear evoked by the warlike people who used them in blowgun darts. This terrible poison-dart frog is the largest member of the Dendrobatidae, almost 2 in. long, and is either uniform yellow or metallic green in color. When disturbed, the frog will escape by hopping away, but it makes no attempt to hide. Indeed, there is little reason for it to hide, because these frogs have almost no predators aside from man. Their bright yellow or green color serves to warn possible predators away from them—and from their deadly poison.

The toxin of *Phyllobates terribilis* is used by the Emberá Indians to poison blowgun darts. The Indians capture the frog, taking care to hold the animal between two leaves. Darts are poisoned by rubbing them several times along the frog's back and then allowing them to air dry. The toxin remains potent for a long time and is far more effective than curare. Finally, it has been estimated that the toxin from a single frog will kill 20,000 mice.

Dodo Dead—Tree Dead. The close symbiotic rela-

The homing pigeon is demonstrating its ability to see ultraviolet (UV) light—an ability not possessed by humans and thought to be absent in other vertebrates as well. In the experiments conducted by Melvin Kreithen (seen here) and Thomas Eisner at Cornell University, UV light was flashed through the window; the bird was then subjected to a mild electric shock. Later, when the UV was flashed alone, the birds exhibited anxiety in anticipation of the shock, indicating that they saw the light.

tionship between numerous pairs of species is well known, be it mutualism, parasitism, predator-prey, or whatever. If one member of the species pair is modified or eliminated, the other member will be affected. In many cases, such as the termites and fungus described above, the two species have developed an obligatory mutualism in which one or both members of the pair absolutely depend on the other for survival.

The dodo, a large flightless terrestrial bird, closely related to the pigeon, was formerly found on the island of Mauritius, in the western Indian

Two tropical fish made news in 1978: an anglerfish (left) and a flashlight fish (right). What appears to be algae-encrusted rock with a fish moored to it is, in reality, the anglerfish. These fish of the Antennariidae family have evolved lures to attract prey. But this Philippine Islands specimen, discovered in a tropical fish store, has gone its peers one better; it has developed as bait an appendage that looks remarkably like a small fish common to the Philippine region. The Atlantic flashlight fish was captured in the Caribbean after not having been seen for seventy years. The fish, Kryptophanaron alfredi, navigates at a depth of more than 500 ft. with the help of a light organ that contains glowing bacteria.

Ocean. Early European sailors hunted it extensively for its meat and it became extinct by 1681. Indeed, the dodo has become the symbol of extinction through the phrase, "dead as a dodo."

With the extinction of the dodo came the near-extinction of a native tree, *Calvaria major*. Only a few large, old, and overmature individuals remain of this once common tree. The age of these individuals is estimated to be over 300 years. Although these remaining trees produce an abundance of apparently fertile seeds, none of them germinate, and there has been no evidence of *Calvaria* seed germination for several hundred years. An answer to this puzzle was provided in 1978 by S. A. Temple of the University of Wisconsin on the basis of reports that dodos fed on large fruits and seeds and possessed a well-developed gizzard that contained large stones used to crush tough food items. He postulated that the dodo fed on the fruit of *Calvaria* and that the grinding action of its gizzard abraded the hard, woody, thick-walled endocarp (seed shell) of the seed. The tree gained an advantage because the dodo dispersed its seeds; the bird profited from the food provided by the fleshy meat of the *Calvaria* fruit. But the

endocarp of the *Calvaria* seed became so thick that the seed could not germinate unless the endocarp was abraded.

Temple germinated *Calvaria* seeds by first feeding them to turkeys, then planting the seed after its passage through the turkey's gizzard. Thus the tree was saved from extinction. The solution to continued survival of *Calvaria* lies in feeding their fruit pits to turkeys or other suitable birds and planting the recovered, abraded pit. Temple's study demonstrates the relationship between pure zoological study and the work of the conservationists. W.J.B.

LITERATURE. What most struck book reviewers as they looked back over 1978 was the strength of biography in the English-speaking world, the vitality of the literary spirit in Eastern Europe, and the signs that a vast new body of creative writers and readers might awaken in the People's Republic of China. As if to dramatize the international character of contemporary literature, the winner of the 1978 Nobel Prize for literature was the Polish-born, Yiddish-writing, widely translated American storyteller Isaac Bashevis Singer. In his acceptance speech at Stockholm, Singer called himself "an entertainer of the spirit," a description that also fit such far-flung literary lights of 1978 as Graham Greene, Jesús Fernández Santos, Patrick Modiano, Natalia Ginzburg, David Malouf, Czeslaw Milosz, Mikhail Emtsev, and Hsia Chih-yen.

AMERICAN

The year's literary production was the usual combination of overpublicized best-sellers and solid

With *Hamlet* You Get Egg Rolls

Once upon a time there was a twelve-volume set of the works of Shakespeare in Chinese translation. But it omitted six of the histories and all of the miscellaneous poetry, and during the Cultural Revolution of the late 1960's it was withdrawn from the bookstores of the People's Republic of China and its author was labeled a reactionary bourgeois. In 1978 the People's Literature Publishing House of Peking brought forth a new, complete, best-selling eleven-volume edition, and William Shakespeare was rehabilitated.

achievements. Thematically, such issues of the 1970's as feminism, political corruption, and the aftereffects of the Vietnam war seemed to have been absorbed into the mainstream of American fiction and nonfiction alike.

Fiction. Perhaps the most interesting novel by a major author was John Updike's *The Coup,* in which the erstwhile explorer of the American suburban bedroom scene turned his attention to Africa. The novel, set in an imagined state called Kush, is told through the eyes of Col. Hakim Félix Ellelloû, the strongman ruler of the country. Another important work was James Jones's posthumous *Whistle,* which completed the World War II trilogy begun by *From Here to Eternity* (1951) and

In the Idiom of Hopeful Humanity

Yiddish was the language of his childhood in the Warsaw ghetto, and Isaac Bashevis Singer made it the language of his writings. Emigrating from Poland in 1935, he arrived in New York City to work as a journalist for the *Jewish Daily Forward,* toiling for years in near-obscurity and near-destitution. It wasn't until the 1950's when his bittersweet stories of life in the shtetls (Jewish communities) of Eastern Europe were translated that he found a wider audience—and critical acclaim. In 1978, at 74, he received the Nobel Prize for literature. Even then he paid tribute to his childhood language. "In a figurative way," the new laureate said in December, "Yiddish is the wise and humble language of us all, the idiom of the frightened and hopeful humanity."

Nobel laureate I. B. Singer.

Novelist James A. Michener, shown standing on the shore of the bay that is the locale of his 1978 best-seller, Chesapeake.

whose work critics likened to that of Chekhov.

Other fiction of note included Barry Hannah's *Airships,* a solid collection of stories with a Southern exposure; Marge Piercy's rich tale of gay sexuality, *The High Cost of Living;* Winston Groom's large-scale Vietnam novel, *Better Times Than These;* Diane Johnson's artfully written and constructed *Lying Low;* John Irving's complex but lively portrait of a literary mind confronting modern life, *The World According to Garp;* and Mary Gordon's promising first novel, *Final Payments,* the tale of a Catholic girl from Queens, N.Y.

Poetry. Adrienne Rich continued to build her reputation as a major poet with *The Dream of a Common Language.* The poetry in this volume transcends the topical interest in feminism and lesbianism to reach for a comprehension of the pain and limited triumph of the human condition. America's favorite guru, Allen Ginsberg, offered a collection of recent work in *Mind Breaths,* which critics viewed as a welcome return from a rhetorical to a personal style. Another well-published poet, David Ignatow, produced *Tread the Dark,* which disappointed some reviewers with its brooding nihilism. A poet of increasing reputation was John Hollander, whose *Spectral Emanations* collected some of his best work of the previous two decades. Novelist Larry Woiwode

A talent "bright and strong" was how one critic praised John Irving, author of the novel The World According to Garp.

The Thin Red Line (1962). *Whistle* follows the same characters from the earlier works and traces their painful readjustment to peacetime life. James A. Michener's best-selling *Chesapeake* was another massive product of that author's technique of combining thoroughly researched historical detail with a colorful narrative about fictional families. This time, Michener labored at recreating four centuries of life on the shores of Chesapeake Bay. Although critics generally rated Mario Puzo's *Fools Die* far below his best-selling *The Godfather* (1969), this saga of Las Vegas was also a commercial success.

Don DeLillo, one of the most consistently inventive and engaging of novelists, manufactured yet another mad plot in *Running Dog,* which describes the search for a pornographic movie made in Hitler's bunker. Hubert Selby, always interesting in a far different manner, sets *Requiem for a Dream* in the Bronx and explores the careers of two junkies who long for a big score. *The Stories of John Cheever* comprised a substantial package by one of the foremost American fiction writers,

An illustration from The Legend of Scarface: A Blackfeet Indian Tale *by Robert San Souci, drawn by his son Daniel San Souci. Their work was cited as one of the ten best illustrated children's books of 1978 by the editors of the New York Times Book Review.*

(*Beyond the Bedroom Wall,* 1975) turned to poetry with *Ebb Tide,* a sporadically successful autobiographical collection.

History and Biography. The most anxiously awaited book of the year was former President Richard M. Nixon's memoirs; however, *RN* turned out to be a disappointing replay of Nixon's familiar defense of his role in the Watergate scandal with little new material. Nixon's political enemy, Robert F. Kennedy, was raised to almost mythical proportions by Arthur M. Schlesinger, Jr., in *Robert Kennedy and His Times,* which favorably portrays the late Senator as the Kennedy most likely to have effected major changes. The reporter who has chronicled so much of American political life, Theodore H. White, turned his attention to himself in a moving autobiography, *In Search of History.*

Literary critic Alfred Kazin's *New York Jew* continued the autobiography begun in *A Walker in the City* (1951) and *Starting Out in the Thirties* (1965). The latest volume tells of Kazin's rise in the New York literary world and his friendships with writers and critics from the 1940's to the 1970's. Another major critic, Malcolm Cowley, also looked back on his life in 1978. His *And I Worked at the Writer's Trade* covers half a century of charitable and perceptive reminiscences about Hemingway, Faulkner, and others. Another figure from this period, the gifted Scribner's editor Max-

well Perkins, is given a full and worthwhile treatment by A. Scott Berg in *Max Perkins: Editor of Genius.*

Three other biographies attempt to plumb the depths of very different men. Maynard Solomon's *Beethoven* was hailed as a major contribution to our understanding of that composer. Deirdre Blair's *Samuel Beckett* offers copious information on the laconic, Irish-born novelist and playwright. And William Manchester appreciates the strengths and weaknesses of a brilliant megalomaniac in *American Caesar: Douglas MacArthur 1880–1964.*

Attitudes behind racism in the United States are examined in Ronald Sanders's *Lost Tribes and Promised Lands,* which traces Christian oppression of Jews and Blacks in Europe, and Robert F. Berkhofer, Jr.'s *The White Man's Indian,* which defines the racist stereotyping of the American Indian. Harrison E. Salisbury provides a richly textured interpretation of the Russian Revolution in *Black Night, White Snow.* And Barbara W. Tuchman depicts Europe during the plague-devastated 14th century in *A Distant Mirror,* a work that, surprisingly, made the best-seller lists.

225

Act III Scene I   A MIDSUMMER NIGHT'S DREAM

A page from The Annotated Shakespeare, *edited by A. L. Rowse. The elegant three-volume set presented the Bard to readers of 1978, offering numerous notes in its broad margins and 4200 illustrations—many of them film and theatrical stills (as here, from the 1935 movie version of* A Midsummer Night's Dream*).*

wall in the great chamber; for Pyramus and
Thisby, says the story, did talk through the
chink of a wall.
    Snout. You can never bring in a wall. What
say you, Bottom?
    Bot. Some man or other must present Wall:
and let him have some plaster, or some loam, or
some rough-cast about him, to signify wall; and
let him hold his fingers thus, and through that
cranny shall Pyramus and Thisby whisper.
    Quin. If that may be, then all is well. Come,
sit down, every mother's son, and rehearse your
parts. Pyramus, you begin: when you have
spoken your speech, enter into that brake: and
so every one according to his cue.

Enter PUCK *behind.*

● *Puck.* What hempen home-spuns have we
        swaggering here,
So near the cradle of the fairy queen?   80
● What, a play toward! I 'll be an auditor;
    An actor too perhaps, if I see cause.
    Quin. Speak, Pyramus. Thisby, stand forth.
    Bot. Thisby, the flowers of odious savours
        sweet,—
    Quin. Odours, odours.
    Bot. —— odours savours sweet:
So hath thy breath, my dearest Thisby dear.
But hark, a voice! stay thou but here awhile,
And by and by I will to thee appear. [*Exit.*
    Puck. A stranger Pyramus than e'er played
here.   [*Exit.* 90
    Flu. Must I speak now?
    Quin. Ay, marry, must you; for you must
understand he goes but to see a noise that he
heard, and is to come again.
    Flu. Most radiant Pyramus, most lily-white of
        hue,
Of colour like the red rose on triumphant brier,
● Most brisky juvenal and eke most lovely Jew,
    As true as truest horse that yet would never
        tire,
● I 'll meet thee, Pyramus, at Ninny's tomb.
    Quin. 'Ninus' tomb,' man: why, you must
not speak that yet; that you answer to Pyramus:
you speak all your part at once, cues and all.
Pyramus enter: your cue is past; it is, 'never
tire.'
    Flu. O,—As true as truest horse, that yet
        would never tire.

Re-enter PUCK, *and* BOTTOM *with an ass's head.*

    Bot. If I were fair, Thisby, I were only thine.
    Quin. O monstrous! O strange! we are
haunted. Pray, masters! fly, masters! Help!
        [*Exeunt Quince, Snug, Flute, Snout, and
                Starveling.*
● *Puck.* I 'll follow you, I 'll lead you about a
        round,
Through bog, through bush, through brake,
        through brier: 110
Sometime a horse I 'll be, sometime a hound,
    A hog, a headless bear, sometime a fire;
And neigh, and bark, and grunt, and roar, and
        burn,
Like horse, hound, hog, bear, fire, at every turn.
                                        [*Exit.*
● *Bot.* Why do they run away? this is a knavery
of them to make me afeard.

79 *hempen home-spuns.* Coarse rustics.

81 *toward.* In progress.

Bottom (James Cagney) and Flute (Joe E. Brown).
From Max Reinhardt's and William Dieterle's film,
USA, 1935

97 *juvenal.* Youth. *eke.* Also.

99 *Ninny.* Ninus founded Nineveh.

Quince: 'O monstrous! O strange! . . .' Engraving from
Hanmer's edition of Shakespeare's works, 1744

109 *round.* Round about.

115 *knavery.* Trick or joke.

253

Garry Wills's *Inventing America* is an instructive analysis of the composition of the Declaration of Independence, and the seemingly annual review of the Alger Hiss-Whittaker Chambers case is provided by Allen Weinstein in *Perjury,* a study which concludes that Hiss was guilty.

Contemporary Affairs. More and more, America was becoming a nation of joggers, and James F. Fixx's *The Complete Book of Running* topped a long list of popular works on the subject. Philosopher and critic Susan Sontag takes a deeper look at our culture in *Illness as Metaphor,* which analyzes tuberculosis and cancer as social metaphors. A more down-to-earth social analysis is employed by Tom Wicker in his collection of essays and reportage, *On Press.* Feminist-related works included Natalie Gittelson's *Dominus,* which ana-

lyzes the impact of feminism on men; Linda Bird Francke's *The Ambivalence of Abortion,* a collection of interviews on that controversial subject; and Selma Fraiberg's *Every Child's Birthright,* which advocates full-time mothering for young children.

An escape from weighty U.S. affairs was provided by Bruce Chatwin, whose *In Patagonia* chronicles a leisurely and interesting tramp through southern South America.

Deaths. Faith Baldwin, Bruce Catton, James Gould Cozzens, Janet Flanner, Phyllis McGinley, Mario Pei, John Hall Wheelock, and Louis Zukofsky died during the year; *see* OBITUARIES. Other deaths included those of historian of the Middle East Philip Hitti (Dec. 24 at 92); biographer Matthew Josephson (March 12 at 79); Russian-born humorist

George Papashvily (March 29 at 80); and novelists James Bassett (Sept. 26 at 65), Josephine Lawrence (Feb. 22 at 88), F. Van Wyck Mason (Aug. 27 at 76), and Earl Thompson (Nov. 9 at 47). S.C.L.

AUSTRALIAN

There was one outstanding novel in an indifferent year for Australian imaginative literature. David Malouf, better known as a poet, published *An Imaginary Life,* about the Roman poet Ovid's last years in exile. The book was widely praised both for its language and style and for its unusually intelligent examination of such themes as the meaning of humanity and civilization.

Nonfiction. A remarkably savage debate raged over eminent historian Manning Clark's book about a hero of Australian literature, *In Search of Henry Lawson.* The work was castigated for alleged historical inaccuracies but praised for its intimate portrayal of the turn-of-the-century wanderer who wrote stories and verse about Australian working life. The year also saw the publication of the fourth volume of Clark's controversial *A History of Australia,* covering the years from the gold discoveries of 1851 to 1888, the centenary of Australia's foundation.

For the first time a complete and up-to-date history of Australian drama became available. Leslie Reese's *The Making of Australian Drama: From the 1830s to the Late 1960s* appeared in a revised edition and was supplemented with a second volume covering the Australian theater boom, *Australian Drama in the 1970s: A Historical and Critical Survey.* Another reference book, G. Wilkes's *A Dictionary of Australian Colloquialisms,* was acclaimed by critics as a scholarly yet enormously enjoyable work.

Poetry. Five established poets, all of whom differed widely in their approach to the reader, published new collections of their work. The best was Geoffrey Lehmann's *Ross's Poems,* a free-verse, segmented long poem that dwells on the past in a rural setting. *Product,* by Robert D. Fitzgerald, one of the grand old men of Australian poetry, is remarkable for its strong traditionalist style. Les Murray's *Ethnic Radio* dazzles with its imagery and vivacious language. The other two volumes were Rosemary Dobson's *Over the Frontier* and David Campbell's *Words with a Black Orpington.*

Awards. The Patrick White award was won by the novelist and playwright Sumner Locke Elliott, whose most recent novel, *Water Under the Bridge* (1977), is set in the Sydney of 1932. The prestigious Miles Franklin award for the best novel of the year went to Ruth Park's *Swords and Crowns and Rings,* a 20th-century fairy tale about a dwarf and his girl.

Two authors whose troubled backgrounds were a powerful motivation for their writing received the main prizes in the National Book Council's annual awards. Helen Garner won first prize with *Monkey Grip,* a novel about heroin addiction, inner-city communal living, and obsessive love. Second prize went to aboriginal author Kevin Gilbert's book *Living Black,* an edited collection of taped interviews with Blacks around Australia. I.K.

CANADIAN

In a period of hiatus before the planned referendum on Québec sovereignty, French-Canadian writers amused themselves with the ambiguities of their national status, while the proficient writers in English produced little that was noteworthy.

Works in French. Jacques Godbout's *Dragon Is-*

On April 4, King Juan Carlos I of Spain gives the Cervantes Literary Award, the most important Spanish-language literary prize, to Cuban writer Alejo Carpentier. The ceremony was held at the University of Alcalá in Madrid.

Popular Brazilian author Jorge Amado, with his grandson. Doña Flor and Her Two Husbands, a movie based on a novel by Amado, played to critical acclaim in the U.S. during the year.

land (translated into English by David Ellis) is a simple political allegory in which a lovely island in the St. Lawrence River is saved from industrialization by the Québec hero, who gets a villainous American industrialist drunk and feeds him to the island dragon. In a less fanciful vein, playwright Michel Tremblay's first novel, *La Grosse Femme d'à Côté Est Enceinte* ("The Fat Woman Next Door Is Pregnant"), scathingly exposes the vicissitudes of life in the poorer sections of Montréal.

Two works by women novelists, Louise Maheux-Forcier's *Appassionata* and Genevieve Amyot's *Journal de l'Année Passée* ("Journal of Last Year") explore their authors' hard-won freedoms. Another woman, Denise Boucher, wrote the most controversial Canadian play of 1978. Her militantly feminist *Les Fées Ont Soif* ("The Fairies Are Thirsty") had a successful run in Montréal in the autumn, but not before Roman Catholic groups attacked it as blasphemous and obtained a temporary legal injunction against its sale in bookstores. The play denounces the church, represented on stage by the Virgin Mary, for its part in the subjugation of women.

René Lévesque, the premier of Québec, produced *La Passion du Québec,* a small book tracing the evolution of modern Québec and attempting to clarify his and his party's ideal of Québec independence. Lévesque himself is one of the subjects of Don and Vera Murray's *De Bourassa à Lévesque* ("From Bourassa to Lévesque"), a thoughtful study of Québec politics.

Works in English. English Canadian literature maintained a high standard; many well-known authors produced new works which, although not of their usual perception, continued to reveal a sound proficiency. Two works are of note.

Peter Newman's *Bronfman Dynasty: The Rothschilds of the New World* deals with the rise of a multibillion-dollar Canadian-based liquor business. In part a tribute to the free enterprise system, yet raising the larger issues implicit where such economic power is involved, the book is essentially what Newman intended: a clinical portrayal of how power can be exercised, diffused hoarded, and abused, all within one family.

A major literary event was the return of Leonard Cohen with *Death of a Lady's Man*. Here the writer-balladeer found a means to accommodate his poetic needs with his intellectual wit by in venting a persona who comments ironically or the verse.   B.M.P

CHILDREN'S LITERATURE
It was a less than exciting year in children's boo publishing, but a few good books found a wid audience. Nobel Prize-winner Isaac Bashevi Singer delivered a memorable tribute to childre as readers, saying in part: "They still believe i good, the family, angels, devils, witches, goblin logic, clarity, punctuation, and other such obsc lete stuff."

Fiction. Paula Fox's *The Little Swineherd and Otl*

er Tales has both originality and style. The tales are mostly animal fables revealing the hazards and absurdity of routinized living, unrelenting pessimism, or the scientific method when misapplied. *Bel Ria* by Sheila Burnford was reviewed as a children's book but was published as an adult novel—a procedure often followed for high-caliber animal stories. The focus in *Bel Ria* is the life of a gypsy show dog struggling to survive during World War II.

The Deadly Mandrake, by Larry Callen, explores the fascinating superstition surrounding that weed—thought to spread an evil force through any region in which it is allowed to grow. While the rural characters in the story are shown as gullible, the author also depicts the loyalty, common sense, and neighborliness of a southern community. Callen's use of colloquial language adds charm and authenticity.

More conventional novels for the 9-to-12 age group included *Tawny* by Chas Carner and *Searching for Shona* by Margaret J. Anderson. The first features a boy with a keen sensitivity toward a wounded deer. By means of flashbacks we also come to know the hero's deceased twin, a key member of his tragedy-stricken family. Shona's story involves two girls who switch identities in a crowded Edinburgh railway station during World War II.

A short book for those who delight in slapstick is Russell Hoban's *The Twenty-Elephant Restaurant,* in which one wobbly table results not only in the construction of a new table, but in the construction of an entire restaurant and the employment of elephants to run it.

Childhood is a time of imagining success, while cringing at the thought of failure. In *The Skates of Uncle Richard,* by Carol Fenner, a 9-year-old black girl longs to excel as an ice skater, and her struggle with self-doubt is faithfully represented.

Picture Books and Folktales. Few exceptional folktale collections were published in 1978, but there was an abundance of single tales designed as picture books. One such book was *Rum Pum Pum,* retold by Maggie Duff and illustrated by José Aruego and Ariane Dewey. Another example was *The Bearskinner,* with a text by the brothers Grimm and drawings by Felix Hoffmann. The sketches for this book were left unfinished at the time of Hoffmann's death, but they are exceptional in the dynamic quality of their draftsmanship.

Appelard and Liverwurst (story by Mercer Mayer, illustrations by Steven Kellogg) is a situation comedy in which a baby rhinoceros is commandeered to plow the fields of a destitute farmer. Arnold Lobel's *Grasshopper on the Road* contains

six fables, all whimsical commentaries on human nature. For the youngest preschooler, Frank Asch's *Turtle Tale* presents the misadventures of one who does everything by trial and error.

Poetry. The black American community is represented in Nikki Grimes's *Something on My Mind,* a series of free-verse impressions of children in the city. Tom Feelings's portraits of black youngsters form an indispensable part of the book. *Life Hungers to Abound,* compiled by Helen Plotz, offers selections on the subject of the family, ranging from the Bible to the works of W. H. Auden, Robert Hayden, and May Sarton. The collection is geared for teenage readers.

Nonfiction. An informative work on Tutankhamen, *Behind the Sealed Door,* by Irene and Laurence Swinburne, chronicles the opening of the Egyptian pharaoh's tomb. It also contains on-the-spot as well as contemporary photographs. Nina Leen, a fine nature photographer, combines a brief text with many close-up views in *Snakes.* Jamake Highwater's *Many Smokes, Many Moons* is a valuable summary of American Indian history and culture, emphasizing works of art.

An etching by the author was featured on the jacket cover of Günter Grass's 1978 novel. The Flounder, an English translation of the German Der Butt (1977), is about cooking, women, and the history of Danzig.

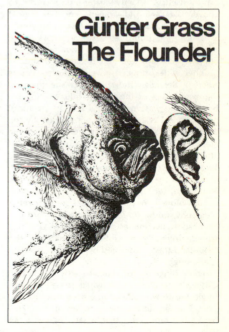

Günter Grass
The Flounder

People. Prizewinners of the year included Katherine Paterson, recipient of the Newbery award for the novel *Bridge to Terabithia;* illustrator Peter Spier, winner of the Caldecott medal for his drawings in *Noah's Ark;* and Judith and Herbert Kohl, recipients of the National Book Award for children's books for *The View from the Oak: The Private Worlds of Other Creatures* (illustrated by Robert Bayless).

Don Freeman, illustrator and author of children's books, died Feb. 1 at 69. Sydney Taylor, author of a series about the immigrant "All-of-a-Kind Family," died Feb. 12 at 73. And Jay Williams, who wrote the Danny Dunn science fiction series and other books, died July 12 at 64.   D.Mac.

ENGLISH

The English literary scene in 1978 was marked by three good novels by well-known writers and a great deal of reminiscence about the early part of the 20th century.

Fiction. Novelist Graham Greene, at the age of 74, produced *The Human Factor,* a characteristically sardonic but sympathetic study of the mixed motives of a double agent in the British intelligence service. Iris Murdoch was a popular winner of the Booker Prize for Fiction (increased in 1978 to £10,000) for her novel, *The Sea, The Sea.* Here her interest in the way people try to change the world through their willpower found a perfect story to express itself: An elderly theater producer tries to convert a 60-year-old woman, who has almost forgotten him, back into the lost love of his youth. Kingsley Amis published *Jake's Thing,* a satire about a university teacher who undertakes modern psychotherapy to restore his sexual desire.

Other widely noticed novels included *Young Adolf,* by Beryl Bainbridge, in which she imagines the experiences of the young Hitler visiting his brother who was, in historical fact, in Liverpool before World War I; *The Cement Garden,* by the young writer Ian McEwan, a strange idyll of some children who bury their mother's body in cement after she has died; and A. S. Byatt's ambitious *The Virgin in the Garden,* a study of a rather bookish but passionate family in Yorkshire in the 1950's.

Nonfiction. The nonfictional prose of the year was notably more literary than political or historical. A biography, *Rudyard Kipling,* by the late Lord Birkenhead excited interest as being a book commissioned originally by Kipling's daughter in the 1940's and then suppressed by her wish because she thought it too critical. A candid, well-researched biography of Thomas Hardy was Robert Gittings's *The Older Hardy,* which some reviewers found too unsympathetic to a great novelist and poet. The second volume appeared of P. N. Furbank's biography of a slightly later figure: *E. M.*

Forster, Vol. 2: Polycrates' Ring was hailed as the completion to a thorough and masterful work. John Pearson studied a literary family that first became famous in the 1920's, the Sitwells—Osbert, Edith, and Sacheverell—whose work and eccentricities he describes in a collective biography called *Façades.*

Two more volumes of previously unpublished writings by Virginia Woolf made a deep impression. These were the second volume of her *Diary,* edited by Anne Olivier Bell, and the fifth volume of her *Letters,* subtitled *A Reflection of the Other Person,* edited by Nigel Nicolson and Joanne Trautmann. The prodigious energy and vivacity of Virginia Woolf were what particularly struck readers. Writings by two vigorous characters of earlier ages also appeared: *Born to Opposition,* volume eight of Lord Byron's letters and journals; and *Boswell: Laird of Auchinleck,* James Boswell's diary of a gloomy Scottish period of his life.

An Edwardian politician, Lloyd George, was the subject of one of the best political biographies of the year, *Lloyd George, The People's Champion,* which is the second volume of a work by John Grigg. Of living politicians, former Conservative cabinet minister Reginald Maudling wrote the best received *Memoirs* of the year.

Poetry and Drama. D. J. Enright's volume of witty variations on the Adam and Eve story, *Paradise Illustrated,* and Ted Hughes's apocalyptic *Cave Birds* were the most accomplished poetry collections. Among plays of the year, Harold Pinter surprised his public with a naturalistic story of adultery called *Betrayal,* while Alan Ayckbourn scored a triumph with his comedy about a local arts festival, *Ten Times Table.* Simon Gray's *The Rear Column* portrays Victorian adventurers in Africa; Tom Stoppard's *Night and Day* is about white journalists in a modern African dictatorship.

A major new edition of Shakespeare's works appeared in 1978. *The Annotated Shakespeare,* in three volumes edited by A. L. Rowse, was acclaimed for its exhaustive and erudite notes, introductions, and illustrative material.

Deaths. F. R. Leavis, Paul Scott, and Sylvia Townsend Warner died during the year; *see* OBITUARIES. The Scottish poet Hugh MacDiarmid died Sept. 9 at 86.   D.M

FOREIGN

Political studies from France, experimentation from Spain, traditional works from Italy, and humor from Latin America highlighted the foreign offerings in a year darkened by continued literary repression in Eastern Europe. Many world-famous authors, notably Mario Vargas Llosa, Günter Grass, Peter Handke, and Amos Oz, published English translations of important recent works.

French. In France one of the more provocative best-sellers of the year was Alain Peyrefitte's *La Maladie Française* ("The French Disease"), in which the author casts a jaundiced look at French economic and cultural institutions. Another literary sensation was caused by *La Révolution de 1980* ("The Revolution of 1980"), by Philippe de Commines (the pseudonym of journalist André Bercoff). This novel predicts a French political crisis that is only solved when a socialist economist assumes dictatorial powers and imposes reforms.

The world-renowned critic, Roland Barthes, published a series of puzzling reflections on love and language entitled *Fragments d'un Discours Amoureaux* ("Fragments from a Love-filled Discourse"). A beautiful bilingual edition of Saint-John Perse's new poems, *Chant pour un Equinoxe—Song for an Equinox,* also appeared during the year, as did a new volume of another well-known French poet, Guillevic. His book, *Du Domaine* ("Of a Place"), is a curiously stark evocation of the simplest things found in nature.

The seventh novel of 33-year-old Patrick Modiano, *La Rue des Boutiques Obscures* ("The Street of Dark Shops"), was considered among his best and won the Prix Goncourt. It tells of an unemployed detective in search of his own forgotten past. The milieu is familiar to Modiano readers: dark streets and shady characters in Nazi-occupied Paris.

Spanish. In Spain one of the most interesting experimental novels of the year was Jesús Fernández Santos's *La Que No Tiene Nombre* ("The Nameless One"), a recreation of a medieval Spanish romance. Three works by contemporary Latin American masters became available in English translation in 1978: Mario Vargas Llosa's *Captain Pantoja and the Special Service,* Julio Cortázar's *Manual for Manuel,* and Gabriel García Márquez's *Innocent Erendira and Other Stories.* Vargas Llosa's novel is a comic masterpiece about a Peruvian army officer's recruitment of prostitutes. *Manual for Manuel,* a novel about Latin American plotter-pranksters in Paris, is also written with a light touch. García Márquez's book contains a vivid short novel in the imaginative style of his *One Hundred Years of Solitude* (1967).

Another interesting Spanish-language novel, G. Cabrera Infante's *View of Dawn in the Tropics,* was also translated into English. Cabrera Infante, a Cuban writer, traces his country's history from the earliest times to the present through a series of vivid portraits and vignettes.

Literary news from at least one Latin American country—Chile—remained discouraging. The worldwide association of writers, PEN Club International, expelled the Chilean chapter from the

Robert Presky, Halo Wines, and Richard Frank (left to right) in a festive scene from Ödön von Horvath's Tales from the Vienna Woods. *The neglected play by the 20th-century Austrian writer, a hit in London during the previous season, was presented twice in the U.S. in 1978: by the Arena Stage in Washington, D.C., seen here, and by the Yale Repertory Theatre in New Haven, Conn.*

organization, charging that the Chilean PEN was "a political arm of a totalitarian government."

Italian. One of Italy's best living novelists, Natalia Ginzburg, published a new novel, *Famiglia* ("Family"), a somber account of a middle-aged man coming to terms with his imminent death. Nobel Prize laureate Eugenio Montale struck a more hopeful note in a new volume of poems, *Quaderno di Quattro Anni.* In these poems, written between 1973 and 1977, Montale tried to "catch through the temporal event a glimpse of the timeless." Another giant of Italian literature, Alberto Moravia, completed a new work in 1978. Entitled *The Interior Life,* the novel is about an Italian woman's participation in the student uprisings of the late 1960's. Yet another contemporary Italian novelist, Giorgio Bassani, rejoiced over the fact that his famous novel, *The Garden of the Finzi-Continis,* was being retranslated into English. The author claimed that the "music is better" in the new English version.

German. Once again a number of East German writers came under attack during the year. Some, like Stefan Heym and Christa Wolf, were banned from a literary congress. Others yielded to pressure and left East Germany. Heym, a former U.S. citizen who returned to his native Germany in the early 1950's to live in East Berlin, had his novel *Five Days in June* published in English in 1978. It concerns a 1953 East German workers' uprising.

Meanwhile, works by Günter Grass and Peter

LITERATURE

Israeli novelist Amos Oz visited the U.S. in May to see his book The Hill of Evil Counsel *published in English translation. After a lecture tour, he returned to his home, a kibbutz near Jerusalem.*

Handke, two of the best-known novelists of the German-speaking world, also came out in English during the year. Handke's *The Left-Handed Woman* is a slim novel that concentrates on a suburban housewife's sudden identity crisis, while Grass's epic novel, *The Flounder,* deals with male-female relationships and the art of eating through the ages. One of the most eagerly awaited publishing events of the year—both in Germany and the U.S.—was the appearance of *Cosima Wagner's Diaries.* The *Diaries* reveal fascinating details about Cosima's life with the great composer Richard Wagner, who was first her lover, then her husband.

Russian. As in previous years, most of the notable Russian books were written by émigré authors, although at least one noteworthy work from within the Soviet Union was authorized for foreign publication: Mikhail Emtsev and Eremei Parnov's science fiction thriller, *World Soul,* which is about the consequences of the indiscriminate use of a device that enables people to read each other's thoughts. Throughout the Soviet Union cultural officials and private citizens alike celebrated the 150th anniversary of the birth of Leo Tolstoy. The occasion was marked in the U.S. by the publication in two volumes of *Tolstoy's Letters* (edited and translated by R. F. Christian).

One of the most gifted Russian émigré poets, Joseph Brodsky, published two collections of poems, *Konets prekrasnoy epokhi* ("The End of a Fine Epoch"), comprising a selection of poems written before he left his native country, and

Chast' rechi ("A Part of Speech"), containing work done since his emigration in 1972. Another well-known Russian poet, the Soviet resident Andrei Voznesensky, visited the U.S. during the year and read his poems before enthusiastic audiences across the country. Gripping Gulag tales—accounts of imprisonment during the Stalin era—were also published during the year. Victor Muravin's *The Diary of Vikenty Angarov* and Lev Kopelev's *To Be Preserved Forever* were judged to be compelling narratives, though lacking the generalizing and evocative power of Aleksandr Solzhenitsyn's work, *The Gulag Archipelago,* vol. 3.

Eastern European. The Polish poet Czeslaw Milosz, a U.S. resident since the 1940's, won the $10,000 Neustadt International Prize for Literature, and a volume of his poetry and a collection of his essays were published during the year. The main theme of his prose work, *The Emperor of the Earth,* is the problem of evil; his book of poems, *Bells in Winter,* examines man's eternal quest for fulfillment.

The lot of Czech writers did not improve during the year. The government began to confiscate mimeographed copies of literary works which it had previously allowed to circulate among silenced writers. Novelist Jiri Grusa was arrested in June for reproducing his novel *The Questionnaire* by means of this underground operation, which is known as the "padlock press."

Other East European writers fared better. For example, one of the most successful Hungarian plays of recent years, István Örkény's *Catsplay,* the tragicomic story of two elderly sisters, was produced in New York City and called by drama critic John Simon the "best new play of the season."

Other Literatures. For the first time in many years modern Chinese works attracted attention in the West. *The Coldest Winter in Peking* by Hsia Chih-yen was a new novel from inside China that has a great deal to say about contemporary Chinese mores, although it was written in the style of the traditional Chinese novel. An indication of the cultural thaw in China was the publication, for the first time, of translations of such modern American works as *Catcher in the Rye* and *Love Story.* Chinese editions of Shakespeare and other classic Western authors went on sale in Peking bookstores. In the fall, wall posters appeared bearing fresh and diverse political statements and skillful poems.

Two Israeli novelists became better known in the English-speaking world with the appearance of their works in translation. Amos Oz's *The Hill of Evil Counsel* is a sensitive evocation of life in Jerusalem just before the founding of Israel. A. B.

Yehoshua's *The Lover* is a subtle novel about a love affair as seen from various perspectives. A product of a relatively obscure literature—Turkish novelist Yashar Kemal's *The Undying Grass*—also made literary news. The new work by the outstanding Turkish writer highlights the paradoxes of contemporary Turkish society.

Deaths. French philosopher Étienne Gilson, Swedish author Harry Martinson, and Italian novelist Ignazio Silone died during the year; *see* OBITUARIES. Other deaths included those of Spanish scholar-diplomat Salvador de Madariaga (Dec. 14 at 92), Portuguese poet and critic Jorge de Sena (in June at 58), Chinese writer and leading Communist cultural figure Kuo Mo-jo (June 12 at 86), and émigré Bulgarian writer Georgi Markov (Sept. 11 at 49), whose death in London was ruled a murder.   A.E.&I.S.

LOUISIANA. *See* STATISTICS OF THE WORLD.

LUXEMBOURG. Economic troubles continued to cloud Luxembourg's horizon in 1978. Banking and steel had been the major supports of the economy, but banking was the only healthy support. After record earnings in 1977, the banking sector continued to make gains throughout 1978 and to provide revenue for government plans to improve the economy.

Although Luxembourg unemployment remained small in 1978—not much over 1000, or less than 1 percent—many of the country's workers were employed in the declining steel industry, and steel operations provided about half of Luxembourg's gross national product.

The European Community Commission has agreed to aid Luxembourg in restructuring its aging steel industry and in making it competitive. One major undertaking was to be the construction of one large blast furnace to replace seven old ones for the giant Arbed steel complex; another was the offer of commission aid for the acquisition of other new equipment.

The coalition government of Prime Minister Gaston Thorn indicated that it intended to use the 1979 budget to accomplish various goals. These included promotion of employment and reduction of the gaps between the highest and lowest incomes. Cuts in income taxes were being planned for the lower and middle income groups. The government planned to increase public spending by 6.3 percent for these purposes, and a 1 billion franc deficit was anticipated.

Finally, a new infantry company was added to the Luxembourg army in 1978. The country's military strength was thus increased by 13 percent—to a total of 630 men.

See STATISTICS OF THE WORLD.   L.A.S.

M

MAINE. *See* STATISTICS OF THE WORLD.

MALAGASY REPUBLIC. *See* STATISTICS OF THE WORLD.

MALAWI. *See* STATISTICS OF THE WORLD.

MALAYSIA. The political life of Malaysia was tranquil in 1978, and the nation's economy was healthy, but the year was clouded by the question of Vietnamese refugees. Malaysia had adopted a humane policy toward the refugees (many of them ethnic Chinese), who were fleeing the repressive rule of a Communist government. All the refugees were placed in camps until they could be resettled in other countries. But as the number of Vietnamese in the transit camps swelled to more than 45,000 late in 1978, the government in Kuala Lumpur came under strong domestic pressure to discourage further arrivals.

Under a tough new policy, refugee boats deemed seaworthy were refused entry into Malaysian ports. Within weeks, hundreds of the so-called boat people drowned when their vessels capsized after being turned away from Malaysia. Then, in November, the freighter *Hai Hong* dropped anchor off Port Klang. The ship was jammed with Vietnamese, but the Malaysians refused to let them come ashore, claiming that these were not true refugees, since each one had paid $2000 in gold for the passage. After weeks of haggling with United Nations officials—and in response to a world outcry over the fate of the *Hai Hong*—Malaysia finally permitted the Vietnamese to debark. The action was taken, however, only after Canada, West Germany, France, and the United States agreed to accept the entire boatload for resettlement.

Malaysia, the only functioning parliamentary democracy in Southeast Asia, went to the polls in July. The issues were chiefly ethnic, centering on the ruling National Front's stated policy of favoring Malays against ethnic Chinese in matters such as college entry, civil service jobs, and business activity. Under the leadership of Prime Minister

233

Vietnamese refugees, beached at Kuala Trengganu, signal their distress to watching Malaysians. Thousands of these "boat people" passed through Malaysian transit camps in 1978, but this particular boatload of refugees was not allowed to come ashore.

Datuk Hussein bin Onn, the National Front coalition swept to victory, winning 132 seats in the 154-member parliament and capturing all ten state assemblies that were contested.

The Malaysian economy continued to expand rapidly in 1978, despite a drought early in the year that reduced agricultural output. Sluggish demand for Malaysia's primary products in the industrialized world narrowed the nation's trade surplus. But strong domestic demand and an active investment picture led to an estimated 7 percent overall growth in the economy.

In foreign affairs, Malaysia continued to emphasize its ties with the Association of Southeast Asian Nations, the regional alliance of non-Communist states. In November, China's Deputy Premier Teng Hsiao-ping made a goodwill visit to Kuala Lumpur. But Teng's visit was less than a success, since he irritated his hosts by refusing to renounce support for Malaysia's underground Communist Party.

See STATISTICS OF THE WORLD.   R.J.C.

MALDIVES. *See* STATISTICS OF THE WORLD.

MALI. *See* STATISTICS OF THE WORLD. *See also* AFRICA.

MALTA. The strategically situated Mediterranean island republic of Malta spent 1978 preparing for a new era. British troops, remnants of the colonial past, began a withdrawal that was scheduled to be completed by March, 1979. Despite the impending loss of revenue from spending by military personnel and rents for bases, Prime Minister Dominic Mintoff expressed confidence that he would be able to keep the tiny country afloat economically.

Although he controlled only 34 of the 65 seats in parliament, Mintoff ruled the island with a firm—some said authoritarian—hand. A controversial new education law, which placed complete control of the University of Malta's financial and academic affairs in government hands, led to a resignation of a member of the Commission for Higher Education in June. Earlier, there had been a two-day teachers' strike over holiday policy, continuing the theme of discontent among professionals expressed in the 1977 doctors' strike.

In search of assistance to offset the loss of revenue from military bases, Mintoff continued to cultivate the People's Republic of China and the radical Arab state of Libya. In July, Libyan strongman Mu'ammar el-Qaddafi visited Malta and promised Mintoff arms, military training facilities, and economic aid after the British withdrawal. In August, a Libyan team flew to the island to set up a helicopter base, and a Chinese mission arrived to discuss joint projects. The Chinese already were financing a number of industrial schemes on the island, including a large ship-repair dock.

Mintoff also appealed to Italy and France for assistance. When neither Western country responded to his satisfaction, Mintoff assailed them in a speech before parliament in September. Negotiations with Italy and France, he declared, were at an end.

See STATISTICS OF THE WORLD.   R.J.C.

MANITOBA. *See* STATISTICS OF THE WORLD.

MANUFACTURING INDUSTRIES. Uncertainty marked the end of 1978 as climbing interest rates, growing inflation, and U.S. President Jimmy Carter's program of voluntary wage-price guideline made manufacturing companies cautious about the future. Nevertheless, positive signs tended to offset the negative. New factory orders increased at a rate consistent with an expanding economy, while factory utilization, which grew steadily throughout the year, was higher in October than at any time since 1974. Orders for machine tools, always an indication of manufacturers' plans to expand capacity or increase productivity, were at record levels in October, with industry backlogs 59 percent above those of a year earlier.

Steel. The steel industry rebounded from its poor showing in 1977. For the first nine months of 1978, raw steel production was well ahead of 1977, as were shipments. Company earnings in the third quarter improved sharply from the depressed levels of the prior year. Initially wary of President Carter's anti-inflation program, the industry, led by U.S. Steel, raised prices on a number of high-volume products. The increases, scheduled to take effect on Jan. 1, 1979, were well within the federal price guidelines.

Steel output reached 101,140,000 tons through September, with domestic mills operating at about 86 percent of capacity. Production was 6.6 percent ahead of 1977, when the mills' average

The largest blast furnace in the Western Hemisphere—at Sparrows Point, Md., near Baltimore—began start-up testing late in 1978. The new facility, which cost the Bethlehem Steel Corp. about $200,000,000 to build, is computer-operated and equipped with the latest pollution-control technology.

utilization rate was only 79 percent. Shipments totaled 73,370,000 tons of finished steel, 5.4 percent ahead of 1977.

Earnings for major steel companies reflected the increase in production and shipments. U.S. Steel reported a jump in earnings of 252 percent over the first nine months of 1977. Bethlehem posted a profit of $64,700,000, compared with a loss of $477,000,000 during the first nine months of 1977. For the same period, Armco's net profit rose 90 percent, Allegheny Ludlum's 59 percent, National's 300 percent, and Republic's more than 100 percent.

In a major move Jones & Laughlin and Youngstown Sheet and Tube, the seventh and eighth largest steel companies in the United States, agreed to merge, creating the third largest company in the industry. The Justice Department approved the merger, and the Federal Trade Commission declined to review it. The price tag for the merger was put at $166,000,000.

Producers remained troubled by the continued sharp rise in imports. For the first ten months of 1978, 17,750,000 tons of steel were imported, up 16 percent from the same period in 1977. It was expected that November and December imports would bring the 1978 total above the 19,300,000 tons imported in 1977.

Some companies, concerned about the high level of imports, complained that the government's trigger-price system, which went into effect in February, did not inhibit imports the way it was supposed to. (Under the system, developed by the U.S. Treasury Department, importers cannot bring in steel at prices below certain levels without running the risk of "triggering" a departmental investigation of whether the steel is being sold at unfairly low prices.) However, other steel executives contended that the trigger system strengthened the industry's ability to raise prices yet still compete successfully against imported steel. For example, although U.S. Steel raised its prices by 3.2 percent as of Jan. 1, 1979, the "trigger price" on imports was scheduled to rise by 7 percent on that same date. *See also* MINERALS AND METALS.

Paper. Strikes were a major factor in the paper industry in 1978. As of mid-October, about 8 percent of total paper capacity and 5 percent of total paperboard capacity were idled by strikes. The American Paper Institute reported that total production for the first nine months amounted to 47,900,000 tons, 2.5 percent over the corresponding 1977 figures. Estimated production for all of 1978 was 63,600,000 tons, compared with 61,700,000 tons in 1977.

Pollution abatement continued to be one of the

235

industry's costliest items of expenditure. Companies spent $443,000,000 for these purposes in 1977 and another $338,000,000 in 1978. Of the 1978 total, $190,000,000 was spent for water-pollution control, $115,000,000 for air-pollution abatement, and $33,000,000 for solid-waste equipment.

Textiles. Through September textile mills shipped products valued at close to $45 billion, about 8 percent above the same period in 1977. Significant for the 1979 outlook was the fact that unfilled orders were up 17 percent for the twelve-month period ending September, 1978. Nevertheless, the American Textile Manufacturers Institute (ATMI) voiced concern at the continued growth of imports. ATMI reported that imports into the U.S. were growing at three times the rate of the domestic market, and that nearly one out of every five garments sold in the U.S. had been manufactured overseas.

ATMI also pointed out the extent to which textile and apparel imports contributed to the huge U.S. trade deficit. According to the institute the 1978 apparel trade deficit may have reached $5.2 billion. Statistics also revealed that in the first nine

Inventor Donald E. Lipfert found a new way to put spring in his step—a cushioning material called Prequal. Useful in shoes as well as chairs, bicycle seats, mattresses, and hospital bedding, Prequal uses a system of plastic levers to distribute weight evenly.

months of 1978, an average of 328,000 American textile and apparel workers were unemployed or on short time.

Electrical and Electronics Industries. Although the U.S. electrical industry enjoyed a banner year, the National Electrical Manufacturers Association (NEMA) reported that the growth of imports outstripped the growth of exports. Total industry shipments were an estimated $85.1 billion, up 7.4 percent over 1977. Exports increased by 18 percent from $10.3 billion in 1977 to an estimated $12.2 billion in 1978, but imports were up 21 percent to $10.3 billion. NEMA noted that the largest trade surplus was with underdeveloped nations, and that U.S. trade in electrical goods ran a substantial deficit with the industrialized nations and with such developing countries as South Korea and Taiwan.

As 1978 drew to a close, Stanford Ovshinsky, a scientist-inventor who rose to prominence ten years ago when he introduced a new class of low-cost electronic materials, reported that he had developed a practical method to convert sunlight into electricity cheaply enough for the average house to employ. He claimed that sheets of solar cells for roofs could be ready in five years, and that they would provide electricity for twenty years at an amortized cost of about 5¢ a kw hour. (The cost of electricity in 1978 ranged from 2¢ to 9¢ a kw hour.) Ovshinsky's solar-cell material is an

alloy of silicon, fluorine, and a small amount of hydrogen that is made by starting with silicon tetrafluoride. *See also* TECHNOLOGY.

Rubber. The rubber industry showed little growth in 1978. The Rubber Manufacturers Association reported that the total of new rubber available through August was 2,230,000 metric tons, down from 2,270,000 metric tons for the same period in 1977. Of the 1978 total, about 23 percent was natural rubber, and the remainder synthetic. Tire shipments increased from 20,900,000 during the first nine months of 1977 to 22,600,000 during the same period in 1978. Goodyear Tire & Rubber Co., the giant of the industry, estimated that in 1978, for the first time in history, radial tires would account for half of all auto tire shipments from U.S. companies.

The most significant development in the rubber industry was the agreement by Firestone Tire & Rubber Co. to recall up to 9,000,000 Firestone 500 steel-belted radial tires. The recall stemmed from a determination by the National Highway Traffic Safety Administration that the Firestone 500 had a "safety-related defect," which had led to thousands of tire failures. Under an agreement reached with the federal government, Firestone was to replace, free of charge, every such tire manufactured between Sept. 1, 1975, and May 1, 1976, and still on the road. It was estimated that the recall would take at least a year to complete. The agreement, which could cost Firestone an estimated $100,000,000, was believed to be the most expensive such settlement ever reached. As 1978 came to an end, Firestone was exploring merger possibilities with the Borg-Warner Co., a leading producer of automotive goods and other items.   S.O.

MARYLAND. *See* STATISTICS OF THE WORLD.
MASSACHUSETTS. *See* STATISTICS OF THE WORLD.
MAURITANIA. *See* STATISTICS OF THE WORLD. *See also* AFRICA.
MAURITIUS. *See* STATISTICS OF THE WORLD.
MEXICO. New oil discoveries in 1978, combined with greater political stability, gave Mexico hope that its oil riches might solve some of its staggering economic problems. Another discovery, that of a vast Aztec temple beneath the streets of Mexico City, reminded the nation of its rich and remarkable history; *see* ARCHEOLOGY.

The Economy. The government announced in early November the discovery of a vast petroleum field in the Chicontepec area south of the Gulf Coast port of Tampico in the states of Tamaulipas and Veracruz. The field is estimated to contain at least 100 billion bbl of high-grade crude oil which, in addition to already proven and estimated reserves, gives Mexico a total potential supply of more than 300 billion bbl, more than double the proven reserves of Saudi Arabia.

It was not yet known how much of the new find could actually be profitably extracted with present-day technology; some authorities suggested about half. Jorge Díaz Serrano, head of Petróleos Mexicanos (Pemex), the state-owned oil corporation, said that the relatively nonporous ground would require the drilling of many small-production wells—approximately 16,000 in thirteen years, each to produce 100 to 200 bbl per day.

Whatever it produces, the Chicontepec find clearly makes Mexico the leading oil power in the Western Hemisphere and a rival of Middle Eastern producers. Although not a member of the Organization of Petroleum Exporting Countries, Mexico promised not to undersell OPEC prices. However, Mexican President José López Portillo stated on Nov. 2 that Mexico would not join OPEC or participate in any future OPEC-sponsored oil boycotts. López Portillo visited Tokyo during the year and negotiated a $1.1 billion loan from Japanese banks in order to improve Mexican oil technology and transportation. At the same time he announced plans to develop the Pacific coast port of Salina Cruz, so that shipments of crude oil to Japan would not have to go through the Panama Canal.

It would doubtless take all of Mexico's rising income from petroleum sales—and a great deal more—to solve its severe economic problems. Although during fiscal year 1978 the country began to recover from its 1976–77 recession, inflation was estimated at more than 17 percent for the first half of the year, and only half the work force was reported to be fully employed. Many jobless Mexicans continued to enter the United States illegally, in search of work. President López Portillo, in his annual report to the nation on Sept. 1, announced plans to provide more full-time jobs. And in November the new oil finds helped to restore Mexico's international credit rating; its whopping $26 billion foreign debt was slightly reduced.

Domestic Affairs. López Portillo's more open policy toward dissidents led to greater political stability. In May the government legalized the Communist Party, for the first time in forty years, together with two smaller parties, the left-wing Socialist Workers Party and the conservative Mexican Democratic Party. Thus a total of six opposition parties would be eligible to compete against the long-entrenched Institutional Revolutionary Party in the July, 1979, congressional elections. At the same time the size of the lower house of Congress was increased by 100 seats to a total of 400 seats. On Sept. 28 the government granted amnesty to prisoners charged with political crimes. The decree was understood to affect more than 1000 people in prison or exile, but there were no clear records of how many had actually been released by the end of the year.

The government worked toward other reforms as well. Scores of prominent officials were charged with corruption, many of them for illegal financial transactions. The government made agreements with more than two thirds of the state governors that within two years all illegal large landholdings would be broken up and all land claims would be settled. One such claim was that made by 600 peasants who occupied 4500 acres in Oaxaca in October on the premise that the land had traditionally been communal property.

Violence continued to trouble the country on other fronts. A number of strikes by workers who wanted to form trade unions independent of the state-controlled Confederation of Mexican Workers were broken up by soldiers and police. Communist terrorists claimed responsibility for the kidnapping and death in August of Hugo Margain Charles, 35-year-old son of the Mexican ambassador to the U.S.

Foreign Affairs. Mexican-U.S. relations were generally friendly. U.S. Vice-President Walter F. Mondale and Secretary of State Cyrus R. Vance visited Mexico in January and May, respectively, to debate common problems, and lower-level discussions continued throughout the year. No solution was reached, however, on how to control the illegal flow of Mexican migrant laborers to the U.S., which announced plans to build two steel-mesh fences at favorite crossing places to keep them out; see CIVIL RIGHTS AND CIVIL LIBERTIES; UNITED STATES OF AMERICA. Nor was there agreement on the price of Mexican natural gas; Mexico demanded payment at a rate considerably above that which the U.S. offered domestic producers. On his trip to the Far East Oct. 30–Nov. 4, President López Portillo visited not only Japan but also the People's Republic of China and the Philippines for top-level conferences.

See STATISTICS OF THE WORLD. J.N.G.

MICHIGAN. See STATISTICS OF THE WORLD.

An Aztec monolith, dating from the 15th century, was unearthed in Mexico City in the spring. Here it comes under the scrutiny of the president of Mexico, José López Portillo (third from left).

MIDDLE EAST

So near and yet so far—that was the status of the Egypt-Israel peace agreement in 1978. Hopes rose dramatically in September after the Camp David (Md.) summit; by December a treaty seemed as remote as ever. Meanwhile, for Iran and Lebanon and several other Arab countries peace was only a word in the dictionary.

By the end of 1978, possibilities of peace in the Middle East seemed, in the words of an American official involved in the negotiations between Israel and Egypt, "so close . . . and yet so far away." The framework for a settlement had been agreed on in September at Camp David, in summit meetings involving the U.S., Israeli, and Egyptian heads of government. The major obstacle to the achievement of peace was disagreement over linking the treaty between Egypt and Israel with a comprehensive Middle East settlement. That attainment of Arab-Israeli peace would not ensure regional political and social stability, however, was frequently demonstrated during 1978 by violent unrest in Iran, Yemen, and Lebanon and by continuing inter-Arab quarrels.

Egyptian-Israeli Peace. Hopes for a peace settlement between Egypt and Israel rose and fell frequently from the time of Egyptian President Anwar el-Sadat's historic visit to Jerusalem in November, 1977, until the end of 1978. After enthusiastic and optimistic beginnings in Cairo and Jerusalem, the negotiations were broken off in January, 1978, when Sadat recalled his delegation from the meetings of the Israeli-Egyptian political committee then being held in Jerusalem. Charges and countercharges were hurled back and forth between the two countries, setting the tone for relations during the months ahead. The substantive issues in dispute were the future status of Sinai and Israel's position there. Would Israel be permitted to maintain a military or civilian presence? Would the eighteen Jewish settlements established in Sinai since 1967 have to be evacuated?

Rescue of the negotiations from complete collapse became a major objective of U.S. foreign policy during 1978; President Jimmy Carter devoted more time to this effort than to any other international issue. Only his personal intervention prevented a break in relations, as the differences of opinion that resulted in bitter clashes between President Sadat and Prime Minister Menachem Begin were overcome by Carter's diplomacy. In August, after months of high-level shuttle diplomacy by U.S. and other diplomats to Egypt, Israel, Jordan, Syria, and Saudi Arabia, Carter announced that he would convene a Middle East summit conference at "great political risk" to himself.

The twelve-day meeting at the Presidential retreat in Camp David during September was unprecedented in terms of both the procedures followed and the environment. Presidents Carter and Sadat and Prime Minister Begin were accompanied by their principal aides and advisers, including foreign and defense ministers and high-ranking military, security, and legal officials. The parleys seemed about to fail when Carter announced, only a few hours before the meetings were scheduled to terminate, that an overall agreement on the principles of peace had been achieved.

The Camp David accords were signed by leaders of the three countries at the White House in Washington, D.C., on Sept. 17. The discussions had resulted in two framework agreements, one for an Israeli-Egyptian treaty, the other for a comprehensive Middle East peace to include autonomy for the Palestinian residents of the West Bank and Gaza.

In "The Framework for the Conclusion of a Peace Treaty between Egypt and Israel" the two former enemies undertook to sign an agreement within three months of the White House announcement and to establish normal diplomatic, economic, and cultural relations. Full Egyptian sovereignty would be restored in Sinai, and Israeli armed forces would withdraw from the area after the signing of the peace treaty. The right of free passage through the Suez Canal would be assured for Israeli ships, and the Straits of Tiran and the Gulf of 'Aqaba would be open to all nations for free navigation. Economic boycotts and barriers to the free movement of goods and people would

239

Photographs of exiled religious leader Ayatollah Ruhollah Khomeini are carried through the streets of Tehran. The Sept. 5 demonstration was one of hundreds of nation-wide protests against the autocratic shah of Iran.

be terminated. An international highway was to be constructed between the Sinai and Jordan near Elath, with guaranteed free passage by Egypt and Jordan. Military forces would be limited on both sides of the Israeli-Egyptian frontier. In certain areas United Nations forces would be stationed and early warning stations established to ensure compliance with the agreement. Terms of the peace treaty were to be implemented between two and three years after it was signed.

"The Framework of Peace in the Middle East" emphasized that: "The solution from the negotiations must . . . recognize the legitimate rights of the Palestinian people and their just requirements." Acceptance of this principle was a major concession by Begin. The agreement provided for a five-year transitional period during which full autonomy would be provided to the inhabitants of the West Bank and Gaza, and the Israeli military government and civilian administration would withdraw into specified security locations. Jordan would be invited to join Egypt, Israel, and the self-governing authority in carrying out the agreement. The final status of the West Bank and Gaza would be negotiated no later than three years after the beginning of the transitional period. Principles and provisions of the agreements would apply to peace treaties to be signed in the future between Israel and its other Arab neighbors.

In the three months after Camp David, talks between Egypt and Israel were continued in Washington and elsewhere. A peace treaty was drafted incorporating the principles of the framework agreements, but conclusion of negotiations was blocked by disagreement over linking the Egyptian-Israeli accord with the future of Gaza and the West Bank. Egypt insisted that there would have to be a timetable for establishing an autonomous government in the occupied areas before conclusion of peace; Israel refused to agree on specified dates for carrying out the West Bank–Gaza agreement and objected to linking it with the Egyptian treaty. By the end of the year negotiations were stymied, awaiting resolution of this disagreement.

Arab Divisiveness. Opposition to Sadat's unilateral initiative was widespread throughout the Arab world. A summit conference was held during November in Baghdad, Iraq, with representatives of all twenty-one Arab League member countries except Egypt in attendance. A communiqué was issued stating that the Camp David accords contradicted previous Arab summit resolutions and the charter of the Arab League. The four-day meeting did not specify what action would be taken against Sadat if he signed a peace agreement, but there were reports of secret resolutions providing for economic sanctions if Egypt concluded the treaty with Israel. Arab League Secretary-General Mahmoud Riad threatened to move his headquarters from Cairo to another Arab capital if Egypt did not heed the Baghdad warning.

The Arab summit resolutions were muted in their criticism of Sadat, reflecting the influence of moderate Arab countries such as Saudi Arabia and Morocco, although the "steadfastness states," Iraq, Libya, Algeria, Syria, and the People's Democratic Republic of Yemen (South Yemen), joined by the Palestine Liberation Organization (PLO), demanded much harsher action. Sadat abruptly turned away an Arab delegation sent with an Iraqi offer of $5 billion a year for ten years if he rejected the Camp David agreements.

While Sadat's peace initiative polarized the Arab world into two blocs—the "steadfastness states" on the one hand and the countries which either supported Egypt or maintained a diplomatic reserve toward it on the other—it became the basis for a Syrian-Iraqi rapprochement in October. The two Ba'athist socialist regimes seemed to suspend the bitter ideological feud that had made them enemies for nearly a decade. Assassinations and bombings of each other's offices ceased, the border between the two countries was reopened, and air communications were reestablished. Iraq offered to send troops to help Syria defend the Golan Heights, and plans for a military union were proclaimed. Joint Syrian-Iraqi committees began talks on economic issues, such as division of the Euphrates River waters, oil transit rights, transport, trade, and communications. However, by the end of 1978 these goodwill gestures had not yet produced any tangible economic, political, or military results.

The War in Lebanon. Fighting in Lebanon was intensified as a result of political disputes over the new peace efforts. The PLO stepped up its guerrilla actions. In March the PLO affiliate Al Fatah attacked a bus on the Haifa–Tel Aviv road; 37 Israelis and 9 PLO guerrillas died. In response, Israel launched the largest military operation its forces had ever undertaken into Lebanon three days later. Thousands of troops stormed across Israel's northern border to wipe out Palestinian Arab guerrilla bases and other installations in southern Lebanon. Within a week Israel had occupied all of Lebanon up to the Litani River, an area of some 1100 sq.km (425 sq.mi.).

Fighting between Israel and Palestinians continued until March 28, when both sides accepted a U.N. cease-fire. U.N. Security Council resolutions called for a halt in the fighting, immediate withdrawal of Israeli forces, and restoration of effective authority by the Lebanese government. The Security Council also established the U.N. Interim Force in Lebanon (UNIFIL) to monitor Israel's withdrawal and to help the Lebanese authorities restore peace and security.

Clashing military units in Lebanon during 1978 included Palestinian commandos from several organizations, Israeli army troops, Lebanese government forces, UNIFIL, several different Lebanese Christian militia units, and units from Syria and several other Arab League countries. Fighting and bombing involving diverse armed groups continued in southern Lebanon throughout the year, long after the arrival of UNIFIL in late March and the departure of the last Israeli ground forces in June.

Elsewhere in Lebanon major battles continued between the Christian militia and Syrian units for control of strategic zones in Beirut. By the end of the year several thousand more Lebanese were killed, tens of thousands wounded, and more than a quarter of a million new refugees created. Nearly half the population of Lebanon had become refugees during the fighting in 1978 and in the civil war of the previous five years.

Turmoil in Iran. Years of political, social, and economic unrest in Iran came to a head during 1978, exploding in violent demonstrations and massive strikes which threatened the regime of Shah Mohammed Riza Pahlavi. Only the Iranian army seemed to maintain loyalty to and confidence in the shah. In opposition were diverse groups with

Salem Rubayi Ali (left) was the president of South Yemen until June, when an envoy from his country assassinated the president of neighboring North Yemen. Rubayi Ali was executed and replaced in office by Ali Nasser Mohammed (right), but real power was said to remain in the hands of ultraleftist political leader Abdel Fattah Ismail (center).

no apparent common goal other than to end the monarch's authoritarian rule. The Opposition differed over whether to terminate the monarchy, remove the shah, or limit his authority.

Iran's Shi'ite Muslim clergy strenuously opposed reforms introduced under the shah's modernization program. They were particularly incensed by the seizure of lands belonging to Muslim religious foundations, by greater freedom for women, and by relaxation of orthodox Islamic controls. Leaders of Iran's largest political party, the National Front, were supported by university students and intellectuals opposed to government suppression of political freedom and the arrest and imprisonment of hundreds of students, writers, and academicians. Bazaar merchants feared many of the government's steps to transform and modernize the country's economic system. Trade unions struck for higher wages they felt were required by a spiraling inflation rate; they also demanded expulsion of more than 100,000 foreigners who had begun flocking to Iran in 1973 when the increase in oil prices accelerated the pace of development. All of these groups demanded an end to the corruption and nepotism that pervaded the shah's government.

Weeks of demonstrations and fruitless efforts by the armed forces to suppress them resulted in hundreds of casualties, which only sparked new demonstrations. After a strike by oil workers in October and November undermined petroleum production and seriously threatened the government's main source of revenue, the shah called for the resignation of the civilian prime minister, who had held office only since August; he established military rule with an eleven-member cabinet headed by the armed services chief of staff. Acknowledging that there were irregularities in government, the shah announced that ". . . after the military government, freedom and the constitution will be freely reimplemented. . . ."

The announcement was followed by the arrest of many high-ranking officials, including a former prime minister and the chief of Savak, Iran's national security agency responsible for apprehending dissidents. Many civil servants were imprisoned for corruption and misuse of funds. These measures failed to convince opposition groups to join a coalition and their protests continued. In December attempts were made to form a new civilian government.

Elsewhere in the region there were many other manifestations of political unrest. In June the president of the Arab Republic of Yemen (North Yemen) was killed by a bomb carried by an envoy from South Yemen; within two days the president of South Yemen was executed and replaced by a strongly pro-Soviet regime. Tensions continued to mount between Morocco and Algeria over the former Spanish Sahara; in Algeria the death of President Houari Boumédienne raised uncertainty about the future of his country. In Tunisia strikes and demonstrations by labor groups and political opponents of the government threatened the stability of a regime that had been outstanding in the Arab world for its democratic orientation and political freedom.

See AFRICA; ARAB LEAGUE; PALESTINE LIBERATION ORGANIZATION; UNITED NATIONS; and articles on individual countries mentioned. D.P.

MILITARY AND NAVAL AFFAIRS. Wars in Africa and Lebanon and a daring paratroop rescue of Europeans trapped by fighting in Zaire were among the leading military events of 1978. Egypt and Israel made major strides toward peace in the Middle East, and the United States and the Soviet Union worked to slow down the arms race. Less than a year after canceling the B-1 bomber program, U.S. President Jimmy Carter touched off new controversy by deferring deployment of the neutron warhead and opposing construction of a new nuclear aircraft carrier.

Wars and Near-Wars. In the first European rescue operation in Zaire since 1964, a force of 1500 Belgian and French Foreign Legion troops parachuted into the mining town of Kolwezi on May 19 to

Reprinted from issue of June 12, 1978, of "U.S. News & World Report." © 1978, U.S. News & World Report, Inc.

In Race With East— Where West Leads and Lags

In military strength, Warsaw Pact countries have an edge

Warsaw Pact
945,000 troops
4,075 planes
20,500 main battle tanks

NATO
630,000 troops
2,350 planes
7,000 main battle tanks

BUT—in population and wealth, NATO nations outstrip Russia and her allies

NATO
558,870,000 total population
$6,040 gross national product per person

Warsaw Pact
363,530,000 total population
$2,780 gross national product per person

Source: Institute for Strategic Studies, World Bank

A Jones Boy Heads the Joint Chiefs

The Presidential nomination in April of Air Force Gen. David Charles Jones, 57, as chairman of the Joint Chiefs of Staff came as a surprise to Jones himself. "I didn't seek the office," admitted the general, who is tall, quiet, and not given to politicking. Jones, who assumed his new post in June, was born in South Dakota, grew up in Minot, N.Dak., and quit school to become a flying cadet in World War II. He served in a variety of combat and staff assignments and earned a reputation as an able manager. Unlike his immediate predecessor, the late Gen. George S. Brown, Jones studiously avoids off-the-cuff opinions that might cause his superiors embarrassment. Or as one Pentagon observer put it: "He won't give the Administration any heartburn."

Gen. David C. Jones.

rescue several thousand Europeans trapped by fighting in Shaba region between loyalist Zairian troops and guerrilla forces. After several days of heavy fighting, the paratroopers repelled the invaders and evacuated 2500 European nationals. The dramatic rescue mission, launched after widespread reports of massacres of Europeans in the province, was supported by the U.S., which provided transport aircraft and support personnel to assist in the airlift. The U.S. charged that Cuban troops were involved in training the rebel troops from base camps in Zambia and Angola and urged that all Cuban soldiers be withdrawn from Africa.

After more than eight months of heavy combat, a shaky peace was restored to the Ogaden region of Ethiopia in March. The war had begun in mid-1977 when nationalist guerrillas invaded Ethiopia in an attempt to reclaim the disputed Ogaden for Somalia, which later sent government troops to fight alongside the guerrillas. In January, 1978, after six months of occupation of the Ogaden by Somalia, Ethiopia launched a counterattack, heavily supported by Cuban and Soviet troops and equipment. By mid-March the Somalis had been driven out of the Ogaden and hostilities, except for guerrilla activity, were terminated. Fighting continued in Eritrea, however, and by the end of the year secessionist fighters had been pushed out of their major strongholds and forced to fall back on guerrilla tactics.

The bitter guerrilla war in Rhodesia continued between black nationalists and the white minority government of Prime Minister Ian Smith. Despite the agreement on majority rule reached by Smith and three influential black leaders in February, the Patriotic Front headed by Joshua Nkomo and Robert Mugabe stepped up its efforts to topple Smith's government through military force. As the proposal by Great Britain and the U.S. to bring about majority rule floundered, fighting between the rebels and government forces intensified. Several massacres of Whites occurred during the year; after a Rhodesian airliner was shot down by a heat-seeking missile fired by guerrilla troops Sept. 3, several survivors of the crash were shot. The incident prompted massive retaliatory raids against rebel camps in Mozambique and Zambia by the Rhodesian army.

Mideast Breakthrough. After three decades of bitterness and warfare, giant strides were made toward peace in the Middle East. After twelve days of intensive negotiations with President Carter at Camp David, Md., Egyptian President Anwar el-Sadat and Israeli Prime Minister Menachem Begin signed separate agreements Sept. 17 committing each side to a bilateral peace treaty and a framework for resolving differences on such volatile issues as the future of the West Bank, Israeli settlements in occupied Sinai, and the status of East Jerusalem. Both leaders were awarded the Nobel Peace Prize in October for their statesmanship. Despite heightened prospects for Mideast peace, however, the situation in Lebanon remained tense, with sporadic fighting throughout the year between Syrian troops and Christian militiamen. Heavier clashes in September prompted international calls for a negotiated settlement.

In retaliation for a terrorist attack on the Haifa–Tel Aviv road that killed thirty-seven civilians,

Israel launched a massive invasion of southern Lebanon March 14. More than 25,000 troops took part in the operation, designed to destroy Palestinian base camps and crush the terrorists. After several days of heavy fighting, the Israelis had established a buffer zone about 10 km (6 mi.) into Lebanon and captured several Palestinian strongholds. When the United Nations created a peacekeeping force, Israel withdrew its troops but pledged future incursions if terrorist attacks continued.

Commando Attack. In a tragic reprise of the 1977 West German commando assault against terrorists holding a German airliner in Somalia, Egyptian commandos stormed a hijacked Cypriot airliner at Larnaca airport in Cyprus Feb. 19. The Egyptians were intercepted by Cypriot troops and fifteen commandos were killed in the fighting. The incident strained relations between the two countries, and Egypt severed relations with Cyprus three days after the abortive raid. The Egyptians were attempting to avenge the murder of a prominent Egyptian journalist by the same terrorists who had hijacked the airliner.

Military Governments. A military junta overthrew the government in Afghanistan April 27. President Mohammad Daud Khan and most of his principal advisers were killed or executed during the fighting. The new government was headed by a Revolutionary Council controlled by the armed forces but headed by Noor Mohammad Taraki, a civilian activist. The new government was overwhelmingly sympathetic to the Soviet Union, which quickly moved to recognize it and which reportedly abetted the takeover.

The military government of Gen. Muhammad

Zia ul-Haq remained firmly in power in Pakistan, after toppling the government of Zulfikar Ali Bhutto and dissolving the National Assembly in early 1977. Zia was proclaimed president in September but pledged that elections for a new assembly would be called in 1979.

After a series of strikes led by Muslim fundamentalists and student activists shut down the oil fields and caused massive rioting throughout Iran, Shah Mohammed Riza Pahlavi replaced his government with a military administration. In November the shah named the armed forces chief of staff, Gholam Riza Azhari, as the new prime minister in a desperate effort to restore order and avert a takeover by reactionary opponents of his regime.

Arms Race. The U.S. and the U.S.S.R. intensified efforts to extend the 1974 Vladivostok accords on strategic arms limitations, and by late 1978 only a handful of differences stood in the way of a new SALT treaty. Nevertheless, both sides proceeded with research and development on a variety of new or improved strategic systems. Construction continued on the U.S.S. Ohio, first of the Navy's Trident ballistic missile submarines, and development and testing proceeded on cruise missiles, the Trident missile, and the M-X, a land-based mobile intercontinental ballistic missile (ICBM) to be deployed in concrete-lined trenches several miles long to enhance survivability from a nuclear strike. The excessive cost of the M-X program prompted Pentagon planners to consider alternate proposals. One new concept, known as Multiple Aim Point (MAP), envisioned the covert transfer of each M-X missile among twenty underground silos, complicating Soviet efforts to locate

The first five women assigned to sea duty board the U.S. Navy repair ship Vulcan on Nov. 1. All ensigns, they are (from left to right) Jo Anne Carlton, Elizabeth Bree, Mary Carroll, Linda Day, and Linda Crockett.

and destroy the entire M-X force in a first-strike attack.

The Soviets began testing a fifth generation of ICBMs, neared completion of the prototype for a new long-range heavy bomber, began deploying more sophisticated and accurate submarine-launched missiles, and stepped up development of antisatellite interceptor programs.

After several months of internal debate, the Carter administration triggered a furor within the defense establishment by deciding April 7 to defer production of a neutron weapon. President Carter ordered the Defense Department to accelerate modernization of Lance missiles and artillery shells to accept the neutron warhead but declared that a production decision would be ultimately influenced by the Soviet Union's willingness to show restraint in the nuclear arms race. Defense hard-liners condemned the decision, the Russians declared it provocative and damaging to the SALT negotiations, and some of America's allies in Western Europe were openly critical of what appeared to be a reversal of U.S. policy on the weapon; see NORTH ATLANTIC TREATY ORGANIZATION. The Senate voted funding of neutron weapon components by a 68–1 margin in September.

First approved by former President Gerald R. Ford, the neutron bomb would produce twice as much radiation as conventional nuclear weapons but only a fraction of the blast, heat, and fallout, thus severely reducing the widespread destruction of buildings and property while killing just as many people. Despite his reluctance to order full production of the warhead in hopes of gaining some leverage in the SALT talks, Carter took a tentative step toward production in October by ordering the additional modernization of some Lance missile components.

Two studies released in 1978 concluded that the U.S. retained military superiority over the Soviet Union. A Pentagon survey issued March 6 rated the U.S. superior in ballistic missiles, heavy bombers, carrier-based aircraft, combat aircraft, air-to-surface missiles, and antisubmarine technology. The Soviets were rated superior in surface ships, antiship missiles, tanks, and surface-to-air missiles. An Arms Control and Disarmament Agency study released Aug. 29 reported that U.S. nuclear strength remained superior to that of the Soviets but that the advantage was declining and the two countries could become "essentially equal" by the mid-1980's. A Central Intelligence Agency report in June estimated that military spending by the Soviet government was expected to increase at an annual rate of 4 to 5 percent for the foreseeable future.

Arms Sales. An Arms Control and Disarmament Agency report disclosed in July that the nations of the world spent nearly $400 billion on armaments during 1976. The Soviet Union topped the list, spending more than $120 billion, followed by the U.S. at $87 billion. Although President Carter pledged to reduce the amount of U.S. arms sales abroad and imposed an $8.6 billion limit on sales to nonaligned countries in February, U.S. arms sales nevertheless increased during 1978. The Carter administration announced Feb. 14 that it intended to sell $4.8 billion worth of sophisticated jet aircraft to Egypt, Israel, and Saudi Arabia. The most controversial aspect of the package deal was the plan to sell Saudi Arabia sixty advanced F-15 supersonic jet fighters. This plan was criticized by Israel and U.S. Jewish groups for setting a dangerous precedent. After bitter debate the Senate approved the sale May 15. In a move with major diplomatic implications, the U.S. agreed to sell scientific equipment with some military applicability to the People's Republic of China. In a related sale the U.S. agreed to sell forty-eight lightweight F-5 jet planes to Taiwan in November but refused to sell the more sophisticated F-4 Phantom jets to the Nationalist Chinese.

U.S. Military Strength. Despite campaign pledges by President Carter that the defense budget would be reduced, U.S. military expenditures continued to rise. Congress approved a fiscal 1979 budget for the Defense Department of $117.2 billion, $2.1 billion less than the Pentagon had sought but $5.9 billion more than the previous year. The Navy received the largest share of the budget, $39.9 billion; the Air Force, $34.1 billion; and the Army, $30.3 billion. The budget maintained a military establishment of 16 Army and 3 Marine divisions, 26 Air Force tactical wings, 28

A Little Child Shall Lead

He was wounded in the battle of Guadalcanal in World War II, but when the U.S. Navy learned that he had lied about his age when he enlisted he was summarily separated from the service and stripped of his medals. Thirty-six years later, in June, 1978, Calvin Graham was finally issued an honorable discharge, and his medals were returned. Upon admission to a veterans hospital in Texas, where he was to be treated for arthritis and diabetes, Graham recalled what it had been like to fight in the Pacific—at the age of 12.

On May 2, five days after a military coup brought down the Afghan government, flower-bedecked tanks remain parked in the principal intersections of Kabul, the capital city.

Navy and Marine air wings, and a Navy fleet of 465 vessels.

The Carter administration pledged to maintain military readiness while at the same time eliminating waste and mismanagement and reducing the size of the defense establishment. The Pentagon announced tentative plans to close or reduce more than 100 military bases in 1979 at a savings of more than $330,000,000 annually. Inevitably, however, defense spending was expected to keep rising to record levels. Secretary of Defense Harold Brown disclosed to the House Armed Services Committee in February that U.S. military outlays would have to increase by more than $56 billion over the next five years simply to keep pace with a steady buildup of Soviet military power. Under Pentagon projections the military budget was expected to expand to more than $172 billion by 1983.

The Carter defense budget reversed the trend of the previous Administration of increasingly heavy spending for strategic weaponry, placing emphasis instead on improving conventional forces in Western Europe and earmarking large spending increases for tanks, tactical aircraft, and missiles.

In personnel developments the Pentagon asked Congress to repeal legal bans against women in combat in March, arguing that growing personnel shortages and equal rights considerations dictated a change in the law. In October the Navy ended 200 years of tradition by assigning women to sea duty aboard twenty-one noncombatant ships. The Army began paying bonuses for reserve and National Guard reenlistments in an effort to reverse a massive decline in reserve strength.

In April President Carter announced that he would withdraw fewer forces from South Korea

during 1978 than had been scheduled. The plan to remove all ground forces from the country was running into problems because Congress, concerned about the Korean influence-buying scandals, had not approved an $800,000,000 arms package for South Korea that was intended to offset the troop withdrawal.

Naval Affairs. The two naval superpowers, the U.S. and the U.S.S.R., continued to duel for worldwide naval supremacy in 1978, with most impartial analysts believing the Soviets were clinging to a slight edge in naval power. U.S. officials claimed the Navy was fully capable of achieving its strategic mission but would fall behind the Soviets without additional fleet modernization. Adm. James L. Holloway 3rd, chief of naval operations, told Congress in March that "if current trends are allowed to continue, the balance of maritime superiority could tip substantially in favor of the Soviets in ten years." In his annual posture statement, Gen. George S. Brown, chairman of the Joint Chiefs of Staff, placed Soviet fleet strength at 62 ballistic missile submarines, 195 attack and cruise missile submarines, 1 Kiev-class aircraft carrier, and 232 cruisers, destroyers, and frigates. By contrast, U.S. fleet strength included 41 ballistic missile submarines, 78 attack submarines, 13 aircraft carriers, 160 cruisers, destroyers, and frigates, and 63 amphibious warfare ships. Construction continued during the year on several new major combatant ships, including a third nuclear carrier. Ships joining the fleet or being commissioned in 1978 included the U.S.S. *Arkansas* and the U.S.S. *Mississippi*, both guided missile cruisers.

Although an aggressive fleet modernization program began reversing the decline in U.S. combatant ships, budget constraints forced the Pentagon to order a drastic curtailment in the Navy's shipbuilding program in March. The previous Administration's plan to build 156 warships by 1983 was slashed; the new plan envisioned construction of 70 ships and modernizing 13 others. The scaled-down plan was bitterly fought by Navy brass and sea-power advocates in Congress, who have been pressing for a 600-ship Navy by the mid-1980's. The Navy suffered another setback Aug. 17 when President Carter vetoed the defense authorization bill, objecting to $2 billion earmarked for a fifth nuclear-powered aircraft carrier Carter viewed as superfluous. The veto was subsequently sustained by Congress and funds for the carrier were deleted from the budget.

See articles on individual countries mentioned. T.D.

MINERALS AND METALS. Air, land, and water pollution problems continued to be a major target for technological development in the minerals and metals industry in 1978.

New Copper-Smelting Technique. In a major effort to overcome air-pollution problems associated with an existing copper-smelting technique, the Kennecott Copper Corp. introduced a new smelting process at its Salt Lake City plant. Under the new system, which took four years to implement, 86 percent of the sulfur present in the ore is captured as a gas and converted to sulfuric acid, compared to only 55 percent by the former process. Construction of a 366 m (1200 ft.) stack, the tallest in the West, helped ensure that what little sulfur gas is eventually emitted to the atmosphere complies with stringent air-pollution regulations. The emission-control project, the first of its kind and magnitude in the copper industry, cost over $280,000,000.

Computer-Controlled Blast Furnace. Another effort to reduce environmental problems associated with the production of a major metal was completed late in 1978, when the Bethlehem Steel Corp. began start-up testing of a new iron-making blast furnace at its Sparrows Point plant near Baltimore. The new blast furnace was the largest in the Western Hemisphere and the first of its kind in the United States. Capable of producing 8000 tons of iron a day, the unit replaced four old furnaces at Sparrows Point. The new furnace is belt fed and computer controlled, operates at high pressures, and has four tap holes that permit nearly continuous removal of both iron and slag. Moreover, it is equipped with facilities to control emissions on the casting floor. Only the Japanese steel industry has larger blast furnaces in operation.

Resource-Recovery Projects. Throughout 1978, increased attention was paid to solving the land-pollution problems associated with the disposal of millions of tons of municipal refuse generated in the U.S. each year. The principal objective was to recover mineral and energy values by separating out the combustible materials in the refuse and converting them into a form of fuel that could then be burned as a supplement to other fuels. Also reclaimed in many such resource-recovery programs were aluminum and the magnetic ferrous metals. By the end of 1978, about 11,000 tons of refuse were being processed daily throughout the U.S.; facilities under construction would allow the processing of another 16,000 tons. The total of 27,000 tons would amount to about 7 percent of the total refuse discarded by Americans each day.

Nickel and Cobalt from Laterite. The U.S. Bureau

Underground mining may cause long-term damage to the environment, according to a report released in September by the U.S. Geological Survey. This photograph shows the surface scars left by the collapse of an abandoned underground mine near Sheridan, Wyo.

of Mines has devised a new way to recover nickel and cobalt from laterite minerals found in the Oregon-California area. If tests are successful, the technique could add these deposits to the nation's mineral reserve. The new method also promises to be more energy-conserving and less degrading to the environment than traditional smelting-refining processes. The process selectively recovers nickel and cobalt, and possibly chromium and copper, by heating the laterite to between 550° and 650°C. (1000–1200° F.) in carbon monoxide. The minerals are then leached in a solution of ammonia compounds, and the leach liquid is treated with organic solvents to extract and separate the metals into acid solutions. Final recovery of the metals is by electrolysis. Domestic production of nickel and cobalt would be highly desirable, since the U.S. now imports about 70 percent of the nickel it needs, and almost 98 percent of the cobalt.

Mineral Production. The value of nonfuel mineral production in the U.S. was an estimated $19 billion in 1978, exceeding the 1977 value by 13 percent. Output of both metals and nonmetals increased about $1 billion each.

In the metals area, aluminum production was estimated at 4,800,000 tons, valued at $5 billion. Copper metal production was about the same as in 1977, 1,500,000 tons, valued at about $2 billion. Domestic production of iron ore—about 80,500,000 tons—was up 41 percent, reflecting a return to normal operating conditions following lengthy strikes at most mines during 1977. Gold production amounted to 970,000 oz., valued at $187,000,000. Gold prices ranged from a low of $166.20 per troy oz. to a high of $243.05. Mine production of silver was 38,000,000 oz., valued at $205,000,000. The average price of silver, $5.40 per troy oz., was about 78¢ above that of 1977.

In nonmetals, production of phosphate rock was about 49,000,000 metric tons, valued at $900,000,000. Sand and gravel production was 937,000,000 tons, valued at about $2 billion. Crushed stone output was 997,000,000 tons, valued at a record $2.6 billion. Cement production increased almost 6 percent to 83,200,000 tons.

See also ENERGY. K.B.H.

MINNESOTA. *See* STATISTICS OF THE WORLD.

MISSISSIPPI. *See* STATISTICS OF THE WORLD.

MISSOURI. *See* STATISTICS OF THE WORLD.

MONACO. *See* STATISTICS OF THE WORLD. *See also* PEOPLE IN THE NEWS.

MONGOLIAN PEOPLE'S REPUBLIC. *See* STATISTICS OF THE WORLD.

MONTANA. *See* STATISTICS OF THE WORLD.

MOROCCO. Again in 1978, Morocco continued to appear to be one of the most stable and trou-

ble-free countries in North Africa. But King Hassan II did find himself increasingly tied down in his battle against the Polisario guerrillas in the Western (or Spanish) Sahara.

The Western Sahara. The three-year-old attempt by Morocco and Mauritania to divide up the former Spanish colony known as the Western Sahara took a new turn in 1978. Mauritania decided in effect to withdraw from the double struggle against the Polisario, the Sahara's nationalist guerrillas. The new Mauritanian military government withdrew its army from the fighting, leaving Morocco to battle the Algerian-backed Polisario forces on its own. Fears that the situation might erupt into open war between Morocco and Algeria abated somewhat in late December with the death of Algerian President Houari Boumédienne, who had been a strong supporter of the Polisario rebels. King Hassan sent a message extending a "fraternal hand" to the new Algerian leadership in hopes of defusing tension over the Western Sahara.

Arab Policy. King Hassan continued to walk a diplomatic tightrope in 1978. Long one of the staunchest allies of Egyptian President Anwar el-Sadat, the Moroccan king nevertheless refused to give an unqualified endorsement to the September Camp David (Md.) accords, which provide a framework for peace between Egypt and Israel. Hassan said a Middle East settlement would be impossible "without the participation of Jordan, the support of Saudi Arabia and the largest possible number of Arab countries, particularly the Palestinians."

African Policy. In June Morocco agreed once again to contribute soldiers to a peacekeeping effort in Zaire's Shaba region. Some 1500 Moroccan troops, who had performed a similar peacekeeping mission in Shaba in 1977, were flown back into the province on June 4 to replace the French Foreign Legionnaires and Belgian troops who had aided Zaire in repelling Katangan rebels based in Angola.

U.S. Relations. King Hassan, long a close friend of the United States, postponed a visit to Washington, D.C., early in the year in response to a U.S. congressional ban on the sale of additional F-5 jets to Morocco unless the government agreed they would not be used in the Western Sahara. In November, Hassan finally flew to the U.S. for talks with President Jimmy Carter. A spokesman for the Carter administration said the U.S. and Morocco were negotiating a nuclear cooperation agreement, including construction of a uranium extraction plant. Before leaving Washington, King Hassan warmly praised the Administration's foreign policy.

On Sept. 30 the U.S. abandoned its last military base in Africa. In a low-key ceremony, the remainder of the American-run communication bases centered at Kénitra, 25 miles north of the capital of Rabat, were handed over to Morocco. The base at Kénitra and two neighboring bases, under nominal Moroccan command since 1965, had served as major U.S. intelligence listening posts and communications centers during the 1950's.

See STATISTICS OF THE WORLD. *See also* AFRICA; MIDDLE EAST. M.R.B.

MOTION PICTURES. It cost more to make films and to see films in 1978. The average price tag of a feature-length motion picture passed the $5,000,000 mark, and ticket prices rose nearly 5 percent. Yet Americans spent more at the box office than ever before, extending a film-industry boom that has continued almost uninterrupted since late 1976.

Admissions to the approximately 17,000 theaters

and drive-ins in the United States numbered substantially higher than those of 1977, bringing in total (U.S.) box-office receipts of $2.75 billion, an increase of some 16 percent. As usual in recent years, the top five films of any given week accounted for one third to one half the money taken in, enabling a handful of blockbusters to dominate the overall financial picture. More than 75 percent of the year's films were aimed at viewers between 18 and 35 years of age, qualifying for PG (parental guidance suggested) or R (restricted) ratings; about 17 percent carried the family-film G rating and the remaining 8 percent were rated X (adults only). Independent producers further strengthened their hold on territory once dominated by the major studios, accounting for 65 percent of the 220 films that began production during the year, while the studios continued their tendency toward financing fewer and ever more expensive movies. Promotion costs also climbed. Warner Bros. expected to spend up to $10,000,000 advertising its film *Superman,* which was released in late December.

Studio Problems. Some of the year's most widely publicized dramas took place offscreen. David Begelman, head of Columbia Pictures' motion-

An updated Land of Oz features a graffiti-bedecked urban playground in The Wiz. The extravagant 1978 musical version of the classic children's story stars Diana Ross under Sidney Lumet's direction.

picture and television divisions, had been suspended from his post and subsequently reinstated late in 1977 after being charged with embezzling some $40,000 from the studio with bogus checks made out to Columbia associates (including actor Cliff Robertson, who pressed the matter with the authorities and in the media). Begelman resigned from Columbia in February, but the controversy flared again in March when it was reported that he had contracted with the studio to act as a highly paid producer and consultant. The Begelman affair was formally resolved in June, when a California court heard his plea of no contest to a count of grand larceny, fined him $5000, and put him on three years' probation; but various government agencies had launched probes into the movie industry by then—prompted by the Begelman scandal, and by less sensational controversies involving profit-skimming allegations against certain studios and charges that dealings between film companies and television networks had violated antitrust standards. Peripatetic studio executive Daniel Melnick was named to succeed Begelman at Columbia, and company President Alan J. Hirschfeld—blaming his ouster on his opposition to Begelman's reinstatement in 1977—was fired by Columbia Pictures Industries, Inc., Columbia's parent organization. Meanwhile, investor Kirk Kerkorian initiated a move to purchase a substantial block of Columbia Pictures Industries stock, amid speculation that his existing holdings at MGM—controlling some 48 percent of that studio's shares—could prompt federal review of the transaction under antitrust statutes.

In another studio shake-up, five top executives of United Artists Corp. resigned in January after a running battle with Transamerica, UA's parent organization, and formed the new Orion Pictures Corp. Also in 1978, legal and legislative battles stepped up in the matter of blind bidding, a practice that requires exhibitors to bid on new films that they have not yet seen. This practice allegedly results in limited exhibitor control over their own theaters and in higher ticket prices. Twentieth Century-Fox paid some $43,000 in fines and grand-jury costs for block booking, after allegedly refusing to rent prints of the top-grossing Star Wars unless exhibitors would rent the less-acclaimed The Other Side of Midnight as well. Further litigation over this illegal practice was expected in New England early in 1979, with the possibility that another decision against Fox might lead to additional suits by exhibitors in Minneapolis and elsewhere.

That's Entertainment. Light entertainment films attracted the largest audiences during 1978, drawing away from the popularity enjoyed in recent years by action-adventure themes and science fiction. Foul Play, starring Goldie Hawn and television personality Chevy Chase, and Death on the Nile, with an all-star cast headed by Peter Ustinov, achieved major success with their amusingly offbeat treatment of "whodunit" plots. Actors Warren Beatty and Buck Henry codirected Heaven Can Wait, a vastly popular fantasy based on the 1941 film Here Comes Mr. Jordan. Less sophisticated comedies that drew surprisingly favorable reviews and heavy attendance were Animal House, a satire of college life during the John F. Kennedy era presented by National Lampoon magazine, and Up in Smoke, a comedy about marijuana smoking starring the comedians Cheech and Chong.

Musicals made a large impact throughout 1978. Grease, based on the Broadway show about high-school students of the 1950's, became one of the year's top money-makers. The Wiz, Sidney Lumet's $23,000,000 adaptation of another long-running Broadway hit, drew large audiences despite mixed reviews following its release late in the year. Rock-music personalities of the 1950's and 1960's were the centerpieces of such nostalgic films as American Hot Wax, The Buddy Holly Story, I Wanna Hold Your Hand, The Last Waltz, and the expensive failure Sgt. Pepper's Lonely Hearts Club Band.

Other films designed for lightweight entertainment included sequels to two earlier hits, Jaws 2 and Damien—Omen 2, both of which missed the stunning impact of the originals, yet became major box-office hits. Superman attracted huge crowds—according to its producers, the biggest Christmas week business in movie history—with impressive special effects and a cast headed by Marlon Brando, Gene Hackman, and newcomer Christopher Reeve. The year's most successful animated features were based on popular books with mythological overtones: The Lord of the Rings, filmed by Ralph Bakshi, and Watership Down, directed by Martin Rosen. In the science-fiction genre, such tradition-attacking efforts as The Incredible Melting Man and Capricorn One received a weak reception. By contrast, The Fury and Coma proved both weird and popular. Films aimed primarily at children during the year included The Cat from Outer Space, a Walt Disney production, and new entries in three popular series: Revenge of the Pink Panther, The Bad News Bears Go to Japan, and The Magic of Lassie.

Drama. Several films examined the history and consequences of the war in Vietnam. The Boys in Company C, directed by Sidney J. Furie, transplants a conventional war-movie plot to Southeast Asia, while Who'll Stop the Rain presents

251

After this poster advertising Warren Beatty's Heaven Can Wait *appeared in the Los Angeles and New York* Times *in March, 60,000 people wrote in to ask for copies. Advertising budgets for films skyrocketed during 1978.*

filmmaker Karel Reisz's bleak vision of moral decay on both sides of the Pacific Ocean. In Hal Ashby's *Coming Home,* Jon Voight plays a paraplegic veteran whose love affair with a volunteer nurse (Jane Fonda) awakens her conscience but destroys her soldier-husband (Bruce Dern). *The Deer Hunter* opened in December, in special engagements designed to qualify it for 1978 critical awards. Michael Cimino directed the drama, a brutal portrait of war and its terrors, which features Robert De Niro, John Savage, Christopher Walken, and the late John Cazale.

Other serious films focused on issues as varied as a young American's torturous experience in a Turkish prison (*Midnight Express*) and discontent and conflict among working-class men (*Blue Collar*), the first film to be directed by screenwriter Paul Schrader. Feminist themes surfaced in *An Unmarried Woman* and *Girl Friends,* two films studying women at different ends of the socioeconomic spectrum. In *Pretty Baby* French director Louis Malle offered a controversial portrait of a child prostitute in New Orleans, while Terrence Malick's visually striking *Days of Heaven* also

turned to the American past for its symbolic tale of a love triangle ending in tragedy. Italian family life in New York City is the subject of *Bloodbrothers* and *Nunzio. A Wedding,* Robert Altman's epic comedy-drama about the marriage of a nouveau-riche bride and a groom from an old-money family, presents forty-eight characters crammed into a single setting on a single afternoon. In his first purely dramatic film, Woody Allen impressed most reviewers and moviegoers with *Interiors.* Allen wrote and directed the picture but chose not to join the accomplished cast that included Diane Keaton, Geraldine Page, Maureen Stapleton, E. G. Marshall, Sam Waterston, and Marybeth Hurt.

Among the year's disappointments was Alan J. Pakula's serious Western, *Comes a Horseman,* about a land baron (Jason Robards) and an impoverished woman (Jane Fonda) trying to maintain their own values in the changing West after World War II. Sylvester Stallone, star of the hugely popular *Rocky,* proved less magnetic in both *F.I.S.T.,* where he plays a union boss, and *Paradise Alley,* his own story of three brothers who use professional wrestling as an escape from poverty. A crime drama, *Straight Time,* attracted limited attention despite superb performances by Dustin Hoffman, Gary Busey, and Harry Dean Stanton. Violence specialist Sam Peckinpah failed to further his reputation with *Convoy,* about a band of renegade truck drivers.

Imports. A wide variety of imported films had successful American engagements in 1978. A French offering, Jean-Charles Tacchella's *Blue Country,* takes a bemused look at the differences between urban and rural folkways. Spain, a country whose films rarely reach screens in the U.S., was represented by the savage drama *Furtivos,* and Brazil by the dark comedy *Doña Flor and Her Two Husbands.* Among other acclaimed imports were the French *Cat and Mouse,* the Italian *Bread and Chocolate,* and the Russian *A Slave of Love.* Reflecting a resurgence in the Australian film industry, several films from that country were picked up for U.S. distribution during 1979, including Peter Weir's *The Last Wave,* which opened to strong reviews in December. For the first time, a fiction film from the People's Republic of China was shown commercially in the U.S.—*Lin Tse-Hsu,* also called *The Opium War.* Two celebrated European filmmakers failed to win praise from critics and audiences with dramas spoken in English: Ingmar Bergman (*The Serpent's Egg*) and Lina Wertmuller (*The End of the World in Our Usual Bed in a Night Full of Rain*). But Bergman recouped with a profoundly sensitive drama in Swedish, *Autumn Sonata,* starring Liv Ullmann

An unheralded motion picture scored a surprising word-of-mouth success during the year. Midnight Express *tells the story of Billy Hayes (right), a young New Yorker who spent several harrowing years in a Turkish prison; actor Brad Davis (left) appears in the film as Billy.*

and Ingrid Bergman. Claude Chabrol's impressive *Violette Nozière* stars Isabelle Huppert as a young woman who poisons her parents, and Eric Rohmer's *Perceval le Gallois* retells a medieval romance in a highly stylized setting.

The Oscars. The Academy of Motion Picture Arts

Her Parents? They're in Show Biz.

In all the flurry of excitement and publicity over the June wedding of Princess Caroline of Monaco, it took *Variety,* which is known as the bible of show business, to put the affair in proper perspective. The weekly publication noted in its "Marriages" column that the bride's mother was "former film actress Grace Kelly," and it identified her father as "casino operator Rainier Grimaldi."

and Sciences presented its awards for 1977 in Los Angeles on April 3. Woody Allen's most popular comedy to date, *Annie Hall,* received most of the major Oscars, winning awards for best picture, best actress (Diane Keaton), best director (Allen), and best screenplay (Allen and Marshall Brickman). Richard Dreyfuss was selected as best actor for his performance as a brash young thespian in *The Goodbye Girl,* with Jason Robards winning as best supporting actor for *Julia.* Vanessa Redgrave won as best supporting actress for her portrayal of the title role in *Julia,* a nomination that was protested by some militant Jewish organizations who objected to her financing of a politically oriented film entitled *The Palestinians.* The controversy thickened when the British actress used her thank-you speech to reiterate her views and screenwriter Paddy Chayevsky felt obliged to re-

---

Mickey at 50

His features filled out a bit over a half century, but his falsetto voice never changed from the day in 1928 that he made his movie debut for Walt Disney. His starring role in *Steamboat Willie,* history's first cartoon "talkie," made Mickey Mouse a celebrity, recognized and beloved the world over. In all he made more than 100 shorts and feature films; with the coming of television, he was ready with the Mickey Mouse Club, the most successful children's program TV ever had. Although semiretired, Mickey was still busy in 1978, greeting millions of guests at Disney theme parks in California and Florida. In November, as the highlight of his coast-to-coast 50th birthday celebration, Washington hostess Amy Carter gave him a party at the White House.

Mickey at home.

ply to her statement. The award for best foreign-language film went to *Madame Rosa,* which stars Simone Signoret as an aging Parisian who looks after the children of prostitutes.

Deaths. Deaths in the motion picture world during 1978 included those of Philip Ahn, Edgar Bergen, Charles Boyer, Dan Dailey, Claude Dauphin, Louis De Rochemont, Leo Genn, Jack Oakie, Mark Robson, Robert Shaw, Jack L. Warner, Chill Wills, and Gig Young; *see* OBITUARIES. Others who died included actress Jean Acker, first wife of Rudolph Valentino (Aug. 16 at 85); screenwriter Claude Binyon (Feb. 14 at 72); stuntman Joe Bonomo (March 28 at 76); John R. Bray, inventor of the animated cartoon (Oct. 10 at 99); actress Sally Eilers (Jan. 5 at 69); actor Oscar Homolka (Jan. 27 at 79); actress Maggie McNamara (Feb. 18 at 48); and Argentine director Leopoldo Torre-Nilsson (Sept. 8 at 54).   D.S.

MOUNTAINEERING. Climbers were active in 1978, challenging—not always successfully—some of the world's highest mountains.

Himalayan Climbs. Perhaps the most unusual climb was that of Annapurna 1 (8078 m/26,504 ft.) by a team of women led by Arlene Blum. Vera Komarkova, Irene Miller, and two Sherpa guides were the first to reach the summit, on Oct. 15. The ascent was the highest ever for a women's team. Two days later two members of the same team, Vera Watson and Alison Chadwick-Onyskiewicz, were killed in a fall; they had been trying to scale

Two accomplished mountain climbers hold a press conference in San Francisco in November. Arlene Blum (left) led the expedition that scaled Annapurna 1 in the Himalayas, the highest climb ever for a women's team; Irene Miller was one of the first two women to reach the summit.

the summit without the aid of Sherpa climbers.

It was reported that on May 8 the team of Reinhold Messner and P. Habeler reached the summit of Mt. Everest (8848 m/29,028 ft.) without oxygen, another record. In October a joint expedition of four Frenchmen (including former Minister of Sports and Culture Pierre Mazeaud) and three Germans also scaled the world's loftiest peak. The summit of Nanda Devi (7817 m/25,645 ft.) was reached on June 21 by David Hambly, W. Fryeberger, Bruce Byers, Steve Casebolt, and Glen Brudero, all from Seattle. On May 10 the team of Nov Kamel and Kiel Landvedt of Switzerland reached the summit of Makalu (8470 m/27,790 ft.) in Nepal.

Other Ascents. There were two assaults on K2, or Mt. Godwin Austen (8611 m/28,250 ft.), in Pakistan's Karakoram Range. Bad luck dogged the British K2 attempt when Nick Estcourt was killed in an avalanche on June 12. The first Americans to reach the summit were Jim Wickwire and Lou Richert on Sept. 8. This expedition, which included two women, was headed by Jim Whittaker of Seattle, who had led an unsuccessful attempt on K2 in 1975.

A Sierra Club group climbed Communism Peak (7495 m/24,590 ft.), the highest mountain in the Soviet Union. Members of this group, together with a Russian climber, also scaled the "Peak of the Four," another challenging summit in the Russian Pamirs.

There were several notable North American climbs. These included the Emperor Face on Mt. Robson in British Columbia; the west ridge of Mt. Logan in the Yukon; Middle Cathedral Rock (a new speed record) in Yosemite; and the north face of Mt. Huntington, the southeast ridge of Mt. Foraker, and Mt. Denison (Katmai National Monument), all in Alaska.

A Death. In August, Switzerland's best-known climber, Jean Juge, 70, died of exposure after reaching the summit of the Matterhorn (4477 m/ 14,688 ft.). Juge, a former president of the International Alpine Association, was unable to descend the mountain because of fierce rain and snow.   S.A.K.

MOZAMBIQUE. Elections had been held in late 1977, so in 1978 Mozambique focused its attention on the economy, hoping to regain pre-independence economic levels by 1981. Since 1975, when independence was achieved, the Front for the Liberation of Mozambique (Frelimo) government of President Samora Machel had tried to concentrate on reviving agricultural production and rebuilding transportation and communication systems. Floods on the lower Zambezi River, in late March, left at least 250,000 people homeless, and destroyed vital corn, cotton, and sugar crops. A massive resettlement program was instituted to move villagers to higher ground. In April, in an effort to improve internal communications and the movement of goods to the cities, the Ministry of Industry and Trade was divided into three new ministries: industry and energy, internal trade, and external trade.

For the most part, the Frelimo government continued to be strongly supported by the general public. Some opposition existed, however, mainly among tribal groups and elements who had lost power following independence. In April, Machel responded to such opposition by replacing 4 of the country's 10 provincial governors.

Throughout 1978 Mozambique continued to press the West for a stron er stand on white-dominated Rhodesia. During the year Rhodesian forces staged more than 300 raids against Zimbabwe nationalists based in Mozambique, including two series of major raids in October and November. (Zimbabwe is the black nationalist name for Rhodesia.) Heavy border fighting prompted the government to allocate more than one quarter of its 1978 budget to defense and security.

See STATISTICS OF THE WORLD. *See also* AFRICA. J.T.S.

MUSIC. The year 1978 was marked by anniversary celebrations throughout the musical world. A number of major orchestras welcomed new conductors, opera companies mounted striking productions of new and seldom-performed works, and big business supported ever-increasing amounts of televised music.

Celebrations. Russian-born pianist Vladimir Horowitz celebrated the 50th anniversary of his American debut by performing Rachmaninoff's Third Piano Concerto with the New York Philharmonic at Carnegie Hall in New York City in January. A benefit for the Philharmonic, it was Horowitz's first appearance with an orchestra in twenty-five years. In February he gave a concert at the White House, in Washington, D.C.; in September he again played the Rachmaninoff with the Philharmonic, this time at Avery Fisher Hall, New York City. The February and September concerts were both televised live.

Other celebrants were Arthur Fiedler, conductor for 50 years of free summer "Pops" concerts on the Boston Esplanade, and Kurt Herbert Adler, music director for 25 years of the San Francisco Opera. Conductor and composer Leonard Bernstein was greeted on his 60th birthday with a nationwide telecast of a concert at Wolf Trap Farm Park near Washington, D.C. Composer Elliott Carter's 70th birthday was honored by numerous concerts and the presentation of New York City's Handel medal. Another 70th birthday—that of Olivier Messiaen—was the motivation for many performances of the French composer's orchestral works, often with his wife Yvonne Loriod as piano soloist.

In celebration of the 150th anniversary of Franz Schubert's death, the American Symphony Orchestra presented an ambitious Schubert festival in New York City in June. In November the Detroit Symphony played Schubert works, both well known and unfamiliar, including a concert ver-

Nathaniel, Meet Elmar

The two young virtuosos had never met until they bumped into each other in a Moscow hotel corridor in June. They were there for the prestigious quadrennial Tchaikovsky Competition, from which each came away with a gold medal—the first Americans to do so in twenty years. Nathaniel Rosen, a 30-year-old Californian and member of the Pittsburgh Symphony, won first prize in the cello competition. Elmar Oliveira, 28, a native of Connecticut, won one of the two first prizes awarded to violinists (the other went to a Russian).

Cellist Nathaniel Rosen (left) and violinist Elmar Oliveira.

Benjamin Britten's opera Billy Budd, *based on Herman Melville's tragic tale of the British navy, was produced in 1978 in both San Francisco and New York City. Here, in the Metropolitan Opera production, Richard Stilwell as Billy (left, on platform) is about to be hanged.*

sion of the opera *Alfonso and Estrella*. André Watts paid his own tribute to Schubert during an extended tour of solo piano and chamber music recitals.

Orchestras and Conductors. In one of the important orchestra appointments of 1978, Neville Marriner, head of the Academy of St. Martin-in-the-Fields chamber orchestra, London, became director of the Minnesota Symphony. Klaus Tennstedt, former director of the State Orchestra of Schwerin, East Germany, was named the Minnesota orchestra's principal guest conductor. Rumanian-born Sergiu Comissiona became head of the American Symphony Orchestra, and in the fall Zubin Mehta took full control of the New York Philharmonic. Mehta's former orchestra, the Los Angeles Philharmonic, greeted its new Italian director, Carlo Maria Giulini, with four special pre-season performances of Beethoven's Ninth Symphony.

The director of the National Symphony, Soviet émigré Mstislav Rostropovich, took the unprecedented step of joining the musicians' picket line in Washington, D.C., in the fall when they struck for higher wages. Another Soviet musician, Kirill Kondrashin, who had been conductor of the Moscow Philharmonic, announced after a guest engagement in the Netherlands that he had decided to stay in the West. Seiji Ozawa, director of the Boston Symphony, received a surprising invitation to spend eight days teaching and conducting in the People's Republic of China. In June Ozawa became the first director of a Western orchestra to lead mainland Chinese musicians since the beginning of the Communist regime.

The most acclaimed of the many orchestras that visited the United States in 1978 was the Concertgebouw of Amsterdam, under Bernard Haitink. The Dutch musicians offered a Beethoven cycle, including all the symphonies and, with Vladimir Ashkenazy as soloist, the piano concertos. A notable 1978 premiere was that of the British composer Peter Maxwell Davies's Symphony, heard in both London and New York City.

Opera. The major operatic event of 1978 was the first performance of composer Krzysztof Penderecki's *Paradise Lost* by the Chicago Lyric Opera. It was the first major European opera to be given an American world premiere since 1921, when Sergei Prokofiev's *Love for Three Oranges* was first presented in Chicago. Critics took note of the production's dark, domed set and somewhat static staging, and of the heavy, conservative score suggestive of Wagner and Alban Berg.

Also new to American audiences was Scottish composer Thea Musgrave's eloquently emotional *Mary, Queen of Scots,* presented in Norfolk by the Virginia Opera Association. Two operatic versions of the lurid and violent 17th-century English play *The Duchess of Malfi* received American premieres during the summer. British composer Stephen Oliver's dissonant version was presented by the Santa Fe Opera, and American composer Stephen Douglas Burton's neo-Romantic version was staged at Wolf Trap.

Forgotten operas were given a fresh airing in Boston, where Sarah Caldwell mounted Verdi's *Stiffelio,* with Anna Moffo, and in San Diego, where Tito Capobianco produced Ambroise Thomas's *Hamlet,* with Sherrill Milnes. The Spoleto Festival, in Charleston, S.C., revived Samuel Barber's *Vanessa,* with Johanna Meier in the title role. Benjamin Britten's *Billy Budd,* based on Herman Melville's classic short novel, was given two successful productions. Accordin. to the critics, Dale Duesing as the good Billy dominated the San Francisco Opera production, while at the Metropolitan in New York City, James Morris as the evil Claggart seemed perhaps more compelling.

Opera singers made news. Soprano Lucine Amara, a twenty-seven-year veteran, announced that she was suing the Metropolitan on the basis of age discrimination. Tenor James McCracken, another eminent member of the Met roster, walked off the job when the company replaced the scheduled telecast of Wagner's *Tannhäuser,* a new production in which he sang the lead, with

Verdi's *Otello*—with Jon Vickers in what was one of McCracken's favorite roles. Italian tenor Luciano Pavarotti became the first singer to have a full-length recital televised live from the Met. Finally, it was announced in December that soprano Beverly Sills, who had already stated that she planned to retire from singing in 1979, was to become director of the New York City Opera after the 1978–79 season. She would replace Julius Rudel, who had held the post since 1957 but had resigned in order to be able to spend more time conducting.

Competitions and Awards. Americans dominated the International Tchaikovsky Competition, held every four years in Moscow. Cellist Nathaniel Rosen won a gold medal; the only two previous American first-place winners were pianist Van Cliburn (1958) and soprano Jane Marsh (1966). Another American, violinist Elmar Oliveira, shared his gold medal with a Soviet contestant. Flutist Carol Wincenc was the winner of the first U.S. flute competition, sponsored by the Walter W. Naumburg Foundation. And Lila Acheson Wallace, a member of the family that publishes the *Reader's Digest,* gave $3,000,000 to the Juilliard School in New York City to develop a program to train American conductors.

Deaths. Among the notable musical figures who died in 1978 were Mexican composer Carlos Chávez, Soviet composer Aram Khachaturian, German-born conductor William Steinberg, and one of the first black composers of serious music, William Grant Still; *see* OBITUARIES. Other deaths included those of Marshall Bartholomew, longtime director of the Yale Glee Club (April 16 at 93);

Seventy-three-year-old pianist Vladimir Horowitz acknowledges the adoration of his fans. He had just performed Rachmaninoff's Third Concerto with the New York Philharmonic at Avery Fisher Hall in New York City. The Sept. 24 concert was telecast live internationally.

NAMIBIA

Russian-born basso Alexander Kipnis (May 14 at 87); Russian-born composer Nicolas Nabokov (April 6 at 75); German operatic producer Guen-

ther Rennert (July 31 at 67); Hungarian composer Tibor Serly (Oct. 8 at 76); and Italian baritone Carlo Tagliabue (April 5 at 80). T.E.

N

NAMIBIA. *See* SOUTH-WEST AFRICA.
NAURU. *See* STATISTICS OF THE WORLD.
NEBRASKA. *See* STATISTICS OF THE WORLD.
NEGROES IN THE UNITED STATES. The mood of Blacks in 1978 was one of cautious hope. There had been less resistance to busing for school integration, and a Gallup Poll revealed that 77 percent of Americans said that they would vote for a Black as President, a considerable increase over the 47 percent who said so in 1963. In the case of Allan P. Bakke, the U.S. Supreme Court ruled against racial quotas in school admissions policies. Reaction to the Supreme Court decision was mixed, but black leaders were unanimous in denouncing President Jimmy Carter's failure to press for new urban-aid and employment programs.
Affirmative Action. If Blacks in 1978 were aware of a lessening outward resistance to racial equality as a goal, they were equally aware that progress toward reaching that goal was stubbornly slow. Affirmative action programs of special assistance to disadvantaged minorities, labeled reverse discrimination by their opponents, faced many challenges, including that of review by the courts. The U.S. Supreme Court took up this issue in the case of Allan P. Bakke, a white California medical school applicant who claimed he was unfairly denied the chance to compete for one of sixteen places reserved for minority applicants in a class of one hundred. In ruling in favor of Bakke, the

Edward W. Brooke of Massachusetts, the nation's only black Senator, concedes defeat. He was unseated by U.S. Representative Paul E. Tsongas (D, Mass.) in the Nov. 7 election.

High Court banned strict racial quotas but upheld the use of race as a factor in admissions policies. The National Association for the Advancement of Colored People (NAACP), meeting in July at its annual convention just after the decision was handed down, called it a victory for civil rights and for voluntary affirmative action. But adminis-

Black leaders hold a somber news conference on June 2 in the wake of the Supreme Court decision in the Bakke case. From left: National Urban League President Vernon E. Jordan, Jr., NAACP Executive Director Benjamin L. Hooks, and the Reverend Jesse Jackson of PUSH.

258

trators and officials concerned with increasing minority enrollment in professional schools feared that the Bakke decision might discourage black applicants.

Economic Conditions. Affirmative action programs were not confined to school admissions; they embraced the job market as well, an area of vital concern to Blacks. In July the U.S. Supreme Court upheld a government decree ordering the American Telephone and Telegraph Co. to hire more Blacks and women. Black unemployment remained twice as high as that of Whites, however, reaching 34.3 percent as of Nov. 1 among black teenagers. Despairing of finding work, many Blacks turned to military service, making up 31 percent of the young Army enlistees during the first three months of the year. Blacks who had jobs were still paid less than Whites in 1978. Data released in October by the Bureau of Labor Statistics showed that the average income of Blacks was about 80 percent that of Whites, a gap that has remained constant since 1973.

In housing, as in employment, Blacks faced familiar problems. There were some efforts to enforce the fair housing laws. The Federal Home Loan Department issued regulations barring its member firms from refusing to make loans on properties in predominantly black neighborhoods. But a nationwide study published in the spring by the Department of Housing and Urban Development showed that Blacks faced discrimination 29 percent of the time in trying to rent new homes and 22 percent of the time in trying to buy them. The plight of impoverished and welfare-dependent Blacks was heightened by the nationwide movement to cut taxes, which generally meant cutting social programs designed to help the poor and needy.

A national urban-aid program was proposed in the spring by President Carter. But urban aid and welfare reform were dropped from consideration in the summer as Congress became preoccupied with energy and tax bills and inflation became the top Administration priority. The subordination of programs that might help Blacks was a source of increasing bitterness among black leaders during the year. In December twelve spokesmen, headed by National Urban League President Vernon E. Jordan, Jr., told Carter they were "deeply distressed" by the trend and warned of urban unrest.

Political Scene. The Congressional Black Caucus, consisting of the sixteen Blacks in the U.S. House of Representatives, led the successful movement to pass a constitutional amendment giving full congressional representation to the predominantly black District of Columbia. The prospects of ratification by thirty-eight states, however,

Retired concert and opera singer Marian Anderson receives a congressional gold medal for services to the nation from President Jimmy Carter at a White House ceremony in October. Thirty-nine years before, Miss Anderson had been banned from singing at Constitution Hall because of her race.

were uncertain. In foreign affairs the Black Caucus maintained its special interest in Africa, meeting on six occasions with African heads of state. In the November congressional elections the only black senator, Edward W. Brooke of Massachusetts, was defeated in his bid for reelection. Two prominent black members of the House, Yvonne B. Burke (D, Calif.) and Barbara Jordan (D, Texas), did not run for reelection; the first-named was defeated in her bid to become California's attorney general.

Persons of Note. Terence A. Todman, a veteran of sixteen years in the State Department, was appointed ambassador to Spain. Joseph Freeman, Jr., of Granger, Utah, was ordained into the priesthood of the Mormon Church, thus ending a 148-year Mormon policy of excluding Blacks from that office. The Pulitzer Prize in fiction was awarded to James Alan McPherson for *Elbow Room,* a collection of short stories. Muhammad Ali defeated Leon Spinks in a September return match, becoming the first boxer to capture the heavyweight championship three times; Spinks had defeated Ali in February.

A dispute erupted in November that involved two well-known black leaders. James Farmer, a founder of the Congress of Racial Equality (CORE), charged that CORE director Roy Innis

259

was damaging the civil rights group by "pursuing a course of violence, corruption, and compromise." Farmer and three CORE officers accused Innis of planning to assassinate a dissident member. They filed suit to oust him from his leadership posts.

Deaths. Lyman Bostock, Jim Gilliam, Daniel James, Ralph H. Metcalfe, and William Grant Still died during the year; see OBITUARIES. Other deaths were those of gospel singer and composer Alex Bradford (Feb. 9 at 51) and art teacher and painter Alma W. Thomas (Feb. 24 at 86).   B.Q.

NEPAL. See STATISTICS OF THE WORLD.

NETHERLANDS, THE. The new government of the Netherlands, elected in late 1977, faced serious economic problems during 1978. Controversy over nuclear policy resulted in the resignation of the minister of defense.

Domestic Affairs. In his inaugural address, delivered on Jan. 16, Prime Minister Andreas van Agt told the Dutch parliament that his coalition government would reduce public spending as part of its war on inflation. He said workers would have to forgo big raises but promised to continue many of the welfare programs of the former Socialist government.

Prime Minister van Agt's Christian Democratic Party scored gains in March 29 elections for provincial councillors. The party won 35.1 percent of the vote in Holland's eleven provinces. The country's largest party, the Labor Party, was 1 percent below the Christian Democrats.

Nuclear Policy. Defense Minister Roelof Kruisinga told parliament Feb. 24 that the Dutch government would try to keep the neutron bomb from being deployed in Europe. His assertion contradicted an earlier statement by Foreign Minister Christoph van der Klaauw that the government would not take a stand on the issue but should let it become a bargaining point in negotiations between the North Atlantic Treaty Organization (NATO) and the Warsaw Pact. Other cabinet members supported van der Klaauw; Kruisinga resigned on March 4.

Four days later, on March 8, the lower house of parliament voted to oppose production of the neutron bomb. Prime Minister van Agt, however, argued that this resolution conflicted with his government's stand that NATO members should not take positions on the issue until they had discussed it with other members of the alliance.

Two days of public protests took place in Amsterdam March 18–19 against the neutron bomb. A discussion forum on March 18 included participants from twenty-eight nations. The protests concluded on March 19 with a march in which 40,000 to 50,000 people participated. More than

From 40,000 to 50,000 Netherlanders gathered to march through Amsterdam on March 19. They were protesting the possible production and deployment of the neutron bomb.

1,000,000 persons were said to have signed a petition against the neutron bomb.

On another nuclear issue, more than 25,000 demonstrators—about 5000 of them from West Germany—marched in the town of Almelo on March 4. They were protesting a British-West German-Dutch plan to expand the atomic energy plant there by adding a facility for the manufacture of enriched uranium fuels for export to Brazil. On June 30 parliament approved such sales to Brazil even though it was felt that the negotiated safeguards against use of the fuel in weapons were not strong enough. Great Britain and West Germany had said that they would proceed with the project anyway, whether or not the Dutch participated.

See STATISTICS OF THE WORLD.   L.A.S.

NEVADA. See STATISTICS OF THE WORLD.

NEW BRUNSWICK. See STATISTICS OF THE WORLD.

NEWFOUNDLAND. See STATISTICS OF THE WORLD.

NEW HAMPSHIRE. See STATISTICS OF THE WORLD.

NEW JERSEY. See STATISTICS OF THE WORLD.

NEW MEXICO. See STATISTICS OF THE WORLD.

NEW YORK. See STATISTICS OF THE WORLD.

NEW ZEALAND. During 1978, New Zealand wa in the grip of a severe economic crisis. When na tional elections were held in November, vote penalized the government of Prime Minister Rob

New Zealander Naomi James waves in celebration on June 8, her husband Rob at her side. She had just completed a solo round-the-world yacht voyage in the record time of 272 days. (And on Jan. 1, 1979, Queen Elizabeth II made her a Dame of the British Empire.)

ert Muldoon by shaving its parliamentary majority.

Politics and the Economy. The country's economic ills were an inheritance from the past. One cause was Great Britain's entry into the European Economic Community (EEC) in 1973, which had deprived New Zealand of a traditional customer for its farm products. To cope with high inflation and an adverse balance of payments, Muldoon's National Party government deliberately set out to lower New Zealand's living standard. Conservative fiscal policies cut inflation somewhat, but unemployment soared to more than 30,000, a forty-year record.

Muldoon seemed confident as election day approached. In June he announced a new budget with tax cuts to stimulate the economy. He also projected the image of an aggressive, can-do leader. By contrast, political observers believed that Labor Party leader Wallace Rowling seemed too moderate and low-key.

On election day, however, citizens took out their economic frustrations on Muldoon. When the votes were all counted, the National Party margin in parliament had dropped from 21 to 8. National held 50 seats, Labor 41, and the Social Credit Party 1. Labor actually won more popular votes than National, and if it had not been for recent changes in electoral boundaries, Muldoon's government would have gone down to defeat. Experts predicted that the election results would complicate Muldoon's attempt to restore the economy to health.

Foreign Relations. Throughout the year the government conducted a vigorous campaign for freer world trade. The matter was discussed in May when U.S. Vice-President Walter Mondale visited New Zealand; in June the United States raised its quota for beef imports. In October, Muldoon sought help from visiting West German President Walter Scheel. He hoped that West Germany would back New Zealand's effort to sell its agricultural produce to EEC nations.

In attempting to win trade concessions from Japan, Muldoon had a high card to play. On April 1, New Zealand's 200-mi.-wide offshore fishing grounds were declared off limits except by special permission. Muldoon made it clear that the price of such permission was Tokyo's promise of easier access for New Zealand exports in the Japanese market. On May 23, Muldoon announced that Japan had made several concessions on trade. After protracted negotiations, a fishing accord was signed in August by the two governments. New Zealand was expected to gain additional trade concessions from Japan in 1979.

See STATISTICS OF THE WORLD.   F.W.

NICARAGUA. Throughout 1978 President Anastasio Somoza Debayle used military force against his striking and rebellious countrymen in a struggle for control of Nicaragua.

Politics. The assassination on Jan. 10 of Pedro Joaquín Chamorro Cardenal, editor and longtime government critic, touched off a string of antigovernment riots, strikes, and guerrilla attacks that disrupted Nicaragua throughout the year. Opposition groups ranging from business leaders to Sandinista National Liberation Front guerrillas formed the Broad Opposition Front (FAO) in July. All demanded the resignation of Somoza, whose family has ruled Nicaragua since the 1930's. The labor force staged nationwide strikes in January and August; guerrillas attacked army posts, threw bombs, and on Aug. 22 seized the National Palace

Nicaraguans flee as black smoke billows over Estelí. In September the town was the scene of fierce fighting between government troops and guerrillas.

in Managua, taking some 1500 hostages. Other guerrillas, joined by students and other groups of youths, set up barricades in León, Masaya, and other towns.

Somoza made some concessions but refused to resign until 1981, when his present term is scheduled to expire. Claiming that the only alternative to his rule would be Marxism under the Sandinistas and refusing to admit the possibility of a coalition government, he used National Guard troops, backed by tanks and planes, to crush the rebels. Several towns were nearly destroyed in September battles, and more than 1000 people died. The United States, which had formerly supported Somoza, in late September pressed him to accept mediation by a team from the U.S., Guatemala, and the Dominican Republic. On Nov. 30, Somoza did agree to hold a general plebiscite on the formation of a constituent assembly, as proposed by the mediators. In early December he agreed to end martial law, relax censorship, and release all political prisoners. But at the end of the month, despite strong warnings from Washington, he once again rejected the U.S. plan for international supervision of a plebiscite. At the end of the year, Somoza had doubled the National Guard, and the FAO was preparing for continued violence.

The Economy. Nicaragua's civil war left the economy a shambles. Many of the rich removed their funds and themselves from the country. Defaults on loans increased and peasants refused to harvest coffee and cotton, the major cash crops. Minimal tax collections and postponement of an International Monetary Fund loan left the government near bankruptcy.

See STATISTICS OF THE WORLD.   J.N.G.

NIGER. See STATISTICS OF THE WORLD.

NIGERIA. A government austerity plan and moves to return to civilian rule dominated Nigerian affairs in 1978. When Nigeria's oil output fell from 2,100,000 bbl per day in 1977 to between 1,500,000 and 1,600,000 in 1978, oil income and government tax revenues also plummeted. At the same time massive imports led to a dramatic increase in the country's balance-of-payments deficit.

The government responded to the economic problems in March by cutting spending by 10 percent and increasing corporate taxes by 5 percent. It also banned a variety of luxury and consumer imports and intensified efforts to channel investment into local production. During the summer a second $1 billion loan from European and U.S. banks was arranged. Efforts to put a lid on wages led to a number of minor strikes. And in April, when the government decided to raise school fees, university and secondary school students rioted throughout Nigeria. At least twelve persons were killed and hundreds arrested before the police and army were able to control the situation; three universities were closed indefinitely.

Despite these difficulties, the military government remained committed to returning power to civilians by October, 1979. Throughout the year high-ranking administrators were gradually returned to their military duties. In June the constituent assembly, which had been deliberating on the proposed new constitution, adjourned indefinitely; a draft constitution was prepared for the approval of the ruling Supreme Military Council. In July civilian deputies were appointed for the nineteen state governors. On Sept. 21, Lt. Gen. Olusegun Obasanjo, Nigeria's head of state, ended the state of emergency and the twelve-year ban on political parties. Three organizations were mobilizing political support by year's end: the United Party of Nigeria, the Nigerian People's Party, and the National Party of Nigeria.

In foreign affairs, Nigeria was active in mediating the Ethiopia-Somalia war and in pressing for an end to white rule in southern Africa. Foreign companies with operations in both Nigeria and South Africa were put on notice that they would have to close their Nigerian operations if they increased their investments in South Africa. U.S President Jimmy Carter's visit to Lagos March 31–April 2 symbolized a significant improvement in relations between the United States and Nige ria. But Obasanjo pressed Carter for a stronger American role in ending apartheid.

See STATISTICS OF THE WORLD. See also AFRICA.　　　　　　　　　　　　　　　　J.T.S.

NORTH ATLANTIC TREATY ORGANIZATION,
abbreviated NATO. In 1978 the NATO political and military alliance, under the leadership of Secretary-General Joseph Luns of the Netherlands and Gen. Alexander M. Haig, Jr., supreme military commander, concentrated on upgrading its military strength to keep pace with forces of the Warsaw Treaty Organization (q.v.).

U.S. Pledge. The United States sought to reassure Europe of its unswerving commitment to the alliance. During a visit to NATO headquarters in Brussels on Jan. 6, President Jimmy Carter pledged that NATO would remain the heart of U.S. foreign policy, that he intended to increase U.S. defense expenditures in support of NATO, and that more than 8000 additional American troops would be stationed in Europe by 1979. The U.S. backed up the rhetoric by beefing up its tactical air units in Germany and Great Britain and by developing a plan for massive, rapid reinforcement of U.S. military strength in Western Europe. The proposal, presented to NATO defense ministers in May, would double existing stockpiles of U.S. equipment in Europe and airlift the equivalent of five U.S. divisions and sixty squadrons of warplanes to Europe within two weeks.

Neutron-Bomb Controversy. Despite these renewed pledges of cooperation, relations between the U.S. and its NATO allies were strained for the second straight year over the controversial neutron, or "enhanced-radiation," nuclear warhead. Carter's April 7 decision to defer production of the nuclear warhead caught most NATO members largely by surprise. After heavy U.S. pressure in 1977 for public statements of support for the warhead from Western leaders, it was generally assumed that Carter would approve production. His decision reportedly was prompted by anger over the reluctance of some alliance members, such as West German Chancellor Helmut Schmidt, to give unqualified public approval to eventual deployment of the weapon in Europe. Though NATO defense ministers went along with the decision at an April 18 meeting of the Nuclear Planning Group, some officials were known to be privately critical of Carter's action.

Embargo Ended. The long-simmering feud between NATO members Greece and Turkey over the status of Cyprus eased somewhat. Although several rounds of bilateral talks failed to resolve the political dispute, Turkey's threat to leave the alliance was averted in July and August when the U.S. Senate and House of Representatives voted narrowly to lift the embargo against shipment of arms to Turkey, in effect since the 1974 Turkish invasion of Cyprus. President Carter, reversing his previous position, had warned that NATO's southern flank would be imperiled without the support of Turkey.

East-West Balance. In its annual assessment of the worldwide military balance, the London-based International Institute for Strategic Studies issued a somewhat pessimistic appraisal of NATO military readiness. In its Sept. 1 report the institute concluded that while NATO's strength "still appears to make military aggression seem unattractive," a military buildup by Warsaw Pact forces was outpacing NATO defense improvements and contributing to a growing edge for the East. The report noted that the Warsaw Pact had added to its 2-1

Landing on a highway to deliver 160 U.S. soldiers to their temporary quarters near Stuttgart, a West German army transport plane takes part in "Autumn Forge." NATO's 1978 war games involved some 323,000 troops.

U.S. President Jimmy Carter takes the rostrum to welcome NATO members to Washington's Kennedy Center on May 30.

margin in tanks and had deployed nearly 2000 more nuclear missiles, although U.S. nuclear missiles in Europe were considerably more accurate and had more warheads.

Military Developments. At a NATO summit in Washington May 30–31, heads of government endorsed a far-reaching defense plan to upgrade the alliance's military preparedness. The unprecedented plan, to be implemented over ten to fifteen years, would be financed by a 3 percent increase in defense outlays by each NATO member. It was estimated that the first phase of the modernization would cost from $60 billion to $80 billion by 1983, with roughly half that sum to be furnished by the U.S.

In an effort to encourage more weapons standardization between NATO members, the U.S. decided Jan. 31 to equip the new XM-1 main battle tank with a 120-mm West German gun. In September, Great Britain announced that it would build its own tank for the late 1980's, thus ending hopes that the NATO countries could develop a standardized tank.

In NATO's annual series of military exercises, code-named Autumn Forge, more than 323,000 troops from NATO armies participated in maneuvers from Norway to the Mediterranean from early September through November. More than 13,000 U.S. troops were airlifted from bases in the U.S. for the war games. At least thirteen soldiers and five civilians were reported to have lost their lives in the maneuvers.

Negotiations on mutual and balanced force reductions in Europe between NATO and Warsaw Pact representatives ended their fifth year in Vienna in October with little apparent progress.

See MILITARY AND NAVAL AFFAIRS and articles on individual countries.   T.D.

NORTH CAROLINA. *See* STATISTICS OF THE WORLD.
NORTH DAKOTA. *See* STATISTICS OF THE WORLD.
NORTHWEST TERRITORIES. *See* STATISTICS OF THE WORLD.

NORWAY. Austerity measures were imposed in Norway during 1978 to counteract economic woes exemplified by declining exports, increasing deficits in the international balance of payments, rising inflation, and a threatened increase in unemployment.

Domestic Affairs. The economy was troubled by declining markets for Norway's traditional products, especially ships, and by slow production of undersea oil. Despite action by the coalition government of Prime Minister Odvar Nordli to hold down prices and curb wage increases, the inflation rate had been at about 9 percent in 1977. Moreover, the trade deficit had risen from $2.22 billion in 1976 to $3.42 billion in 1977. Government moves in 1978 to counter the economic setbacks included the imposition of austerity measures on Jan. 28 and 29 to hold down spending, an 8 percent devaluation of the krone on Feb. 10, and a price freeze announced on Feb. 12. As inflation increased and the foreign debt deepened, the government on Sept. 15 imposed a new freeze on wages and prices until 1980. The austerity budget for 1979 was presented to the *Storting* (parliament) on Oct. 5. Growth of the gross national product in the nonoil and nonshipping sectors was anticipated at a disappointingly low 0.5 percent, and the unemployment rate, then 1.3 percent, was expected to double.

Data made public on May 12 showed that temporarily, at least, the economic problems were not affecting the average Norwegian. Per capita income in Norway had reached $7770, making it the fifth highest among the twenty-four industrialized Western nations, according to the Organization for Economic Cooperation and Development (The United States was ranked fourth.)

Foreign Affairs. Relations between Norway and the Soviet Union underwent strains during the latter half of 1978. Soviet vessels repeatedly halted while traversing Norwegian territorial waters in the Svalbard area instead of continuing through without pause as international law required.

Although the U.S.S.R. and other nations had been given rights to conduct economic and scientific activities in the Svalbard area, which comprises the Norwegian-owned Spitsbergen island group and Bear Island, foreign military activity there was prohibited. The U.S.S.R., however, was reported to have deployed radar equipment and built a landing strip at Barentsburg during the summer; and the Norwegian Foreign Ministry charged on Sept. 28 that the Russians had also erected a satellite tracking station there.

On Aug. 28 a Soviet TU-16 military reconnaissance plane crashed after an alleged illegal flight over Hopen, an island southeast of Spitsbergen. The Soviet Union refused to admit that it had lost a plane there until the Norwegians returned the bodies of the plane's seven crewmen. A Soviet note accused Norway of an "unfriendly act" in deciding to open the plane's flight recorder and transcribe its contents.

See STATISTICS OF THE WORLD.　　　L.A.S.

NOVA SCOTIA. See STATISTICS OF THE WORLD.

O

OBITUARIES. Each entry below contains the name and, wherever possible, date and place of birth and death of a notable person who died in 1978. It also contains a brief description of the accomplishments and the events that contributed to making each person notable.

AHN, Philip. American actor, b. Los Angeles, March 29, 1911, d. there Feb. 28. He appeared in dozens of films, most notably as an Oriental villain in the war films of the 1940's and 1950's. He was also seen as "The Master" in the *Kung Fu* television series (1973–75).

ALLEN, James Browning. U.S. Senator, b. Gadsden, Ala., Dec. 28, 1912, d. Foley, June 1. A conservative Democrat, he was elected to the Senate in 1968; he quickly built a reputation as a master parliamentarian, adept at using the filibuster. He had previously served as a member of the state legislature and as lieutenant governor of Alabama.

ANDERSON, Heartley ("Hunk"). American football coach, b. Tamrack, Mich., 1898?, d. West Palm Beach, Fla., April 24. He was a member of the celebrated Notre Dame football teams of 1918–21. Later he played professionally with the Chicago Bears and served as a coach for six universities and two professional teams.

ASCOLI, Max. Italian-born American journalist, b. Ferrara, Italy, June 25, 1898, d. New York City, Jan. 1. He was publisher and editor of the prestigious weekly magazine *The Reporter* (1949–68). A faculty member of the New School for Social Research (1933–50), he wrote several books on political science.

BALDWIN, Faith. American author, b. New Rochelle, N.Y., Oct. 1, 1893, d. Norwalk, Conn., March 19. In her fifty-year career she produced more than eighty books. Most of them were romantic novels featuring glamorous, rich, highly

Actor Philip Ahn, portrayer of Oriental villains and sages, in a 1974 photograph.

Author Faith Baldwin at work on one of her popular novels in the 1940's.

OBITUARIES

moral characters; they had no literary pretensions but were immensely popular, especially during the Great Depression.

BERGEN, Edgar. American performer, b. Chicago, Feb. 16, 1903, d. Las Vegas, Nev., Sept. 30. Probably the world's best-known ventriloquist, he began his career in vaudeville in the early 1920's, first appeared on radio in 1936, and by 1938 was the most popular performer on the air. He made several films, both as a straight actor and as a ventriloquist, and he achieved success in nightclubs and in frequent appearances on television. With him died Charlie McCarthy, Mortimer Snerd, and Effie Klinker, who were far more than wood and cloth dummies to their millions of fans.

BEST, Charles Herbert. American-born Canadian physiologist, b. West Pembroke, Maine, Feb. 27, 1899, d. Toronto, March 31. In 1921 he isolated the hormone insulin (used in the treatment of diabetes) with Frederick G. Banting of the University of Toronto. Banting was awarded a share of the 1923 Nobel Prize in medicine and physiology for this work; he divided his prize money with Best.

BETZ, Carl. American actor, b. Pittsburgh, March 9, 1921, d. Los Angeles, Jan. 18. He played the father in the long-running television series *The Donna Reed Show;* later he played the title role in *Judd for the Defense.* He also appeared on Broadway and in several films.

BOLIN, Wesley. Governor of Arizona, b. Butler, Mo., July 1, 1908, d. Phoenix, March 4. A Democrat, he succeeded to the governorship in November, 1977, when his predecessor Raul Castro resigned. Bolin had served as Arizona's secretary of state since 1948.

BOSTOCK, Lyman. American baseball player, b. Birmingham, Ala., Nov. 22, 1950, d. Gary, Ind., Sept. 24. In four seasons as an outfielder for the Minnesota Twins (1975–77) and California Angels (1978), he rose to stardom with a career batting average of .312. His 1978 salary was reportedly one of the highest in baseball. He died after being shot by a man who was apparently aiming for another passenger in the car in which Bostock was riding.

BOUMÉDIENNE, Houari. President of Algeria, b. Mohammad Ben Brahim Boukharouba (reputedly on Aug. 23 in Guelma, sometime between 1925 and 1932), d. Algiers, Dec. 27. He seized power in a bloodless coup in June, 1965, and retained the presidency until his death. An influential leader of the world's developing countries, he was particularly strong in Arab councils. In spite of the autocracy of his rule, Boumédienne is credited with having brought political stability and economic progress to Algeria.

Ventriloquist Edgar Bergen reacts to a wisecracking Charlie McCarthy in a mid-career publicity photograph.

Algerian President Houari Boumédienne in 1975.

BOYER, Charles. French actor, b. Figeac, Aug. 28, 1899, d. Scottsdale, Ariz., Aug. 26. With the film *Algiers* (1938), he became a major star, regarded as the epitome of the romantic, charming French lover. His major films included *Mayerling* (1937), *Gaslight* (1944), *Fanny* (1961), and *Barefoot in the Park* (1967). He was nominated four times for Academy Awards. He proved his versatility and skill by also appearing successfully on the stage in

French actor Charles Boyer in a 1939 Hollywood publicity photograph.

Country-music star Mother Maybelle Carter plays the autoharp in a 1975 Grand Ole Opry show.

the United States, in such plays as *Don Juan in Hell* (1951) and *Kind Sir* (1953), as well as in two television series, *Four Star Playhouse* and *The Rogues*. His wife, the British actress Pat Paterson, died two days before he did, and his death was apparently a suicide.

BREL, Jacques. Belgian singer and composer, b. Brussels, April 8, 1929, d. Bobigny, France, Oct. 9. He was one of the most popular entertainers of the French-speaking world, a performer in cabarets and in concert halls, an actor, a recording artist, and a composer of dramatic ballads. His work became popular in the U.S. with the theatrical review based on his songs, *Jacques Brel Is Alive and Well and Living in Paris* (1968).

BROWN, George Scratchley. American Air Force officer, b. Montclair, N.J., Aug. 17, 1918, d. Washington, D.C., Dec. 5. As chairman of the Joint Chiefs of Staff from 1974 until his retirement in July, 1978, he was constantly under fire for his outspoken remarks directed at racial, national, and legislative groups. He was a four-star Air Force general who had served in Europe during World War II, the Korean War, and the war in Vietnam.

BRUGNON, Jacques ("Toto"). French tennis player, b. Paris, May 11, 1895, d. there March 20. With Jean Borotra, Henri Cochet, and René Lacoste (all still alive in 1978), he formed the so-called four musketeers. They dominated tennis for a decade, winning six singles and four doubles titles at Wimbledon between 1922 and 1931.

CARTER, ("Mother") Maybelle. American country musician, b. Nickelsville, Va., May 10, 1909, d. Nashville, Oct. 23. She began her performing career in 1926 with the Carter Family; in 1969 they became the first group named to the Country Music Hall of Fame. After 1941 she appeared with her three daughters as Mother Maybelle and the Carter Sisters. She made more than 250 recordings, and her style of guitar playing influenced all the country musicians who followed her. She was also an autoharpist and composer.

CATTON, Bruce. American historian, b. Petoskey, Mich., Oct. 9, 1899, d. Frankfort, Mich., Aug. 28. For his book *A Stillness at Appomattox* (1953), he won both the Pulitzer Prize and the National Book Award. He wrote several other books on the American Civil War, highly regarded by critics and readers alike.

CHÁVEZ, Carlos. Mexican composer and conductor, b. Mexico City, June 13, 1899, d. there Aug. 2. Probably the best-known figure in the history of Mexican music, he wrote much highly regarded symphonic music, founded and conducted (1928–49) the Symphony Orchestra of Mexico, and guest-conducted most of the world's leading orchestras. He was also an influential educator as head of the National Conservatory of Mexico (1928–34).

CHIRICO, Giorgio de. Italian painter, b. Vólos, Greece, July 10, 1888, d. Rome, Nov. 20. One of the half-dozen most important painters of the 20th century, he influenced the two generations

OBITUARIES

Italian painter Giorgio de Chirico points to his self-portrait in 17th-century costume in this 1959 photograph.

Educator James B. Conant testifies at a congressional hearing in 1945.

of artists who followed him. During the years 1910–20 he produced his best-known works, a series of "metaphysical" oils, fantastic visions of deserted cities haunted by spectral classical elements.

CLAY, Lucius DuBignon. American Army officer, b. Marietta, Ga., April 23, 1897, d. Cape Cod, Mass., April 16. During World War II he served as director of materiel, commander of the Normandy sector in France, and deputy director of the war mobilization office. Later he was military governor of Germany and commander of U.S. armed forces in Europe, with the rank of full general. He achieved his greatest fame as director of the Berlin airlift (1948–49).

CONANT, James Bryant. American educator, diplomat, and chemist, b. Dorchester, Mass., March 26, 1893, d. Hanover, N.H., Feb. 11. A man of greatly diversified accomplishment, he taught chemistry and conducted important research at Harvard University for two decades, served as president of that institution from 1933 to 1953, and helped direct the American atomic energy program during World War II. He also was U.S. high commissioner for Germany (1953–55) and U.S. ambassador to West Germany (1955–57). He wrote several influential books on secondary education.

COX, Billy. American baseball player, b. Newport, Pa., Aug. 19, 1919, d. Harrisburg, March 31. He played third base for the Brooklyn Dodgers from 1948 until 1954. A brilliant fielder, he had previously played for the Pittsburgh Pirates. He was with the Baltimore Orioles in 1955, retiring at the end of the season.

COZZENS, James Gould. American author, b. Chicago, Aug. 19, 1903, d. Stuart, Fla., Aug. 9. His thirteen novels included *S.S. San Pedro* (1930); *The Just and the Unjust* (1942); the highly praised *Guard of Honor,* which won the 1949 Pulitzer Prize for fiction; and the immensely popular *By Love Possessed* (1957).

CRANE, Bob Edward. American actor, b. Waterbury, Conn., July 13, 1928, d. Scottsdale, Ariz., June 29. A former disc jockey, he became a television star playing the glib Col. Hogan in *Hogan's Heroes,* originally telecast from 1965 to 1971. His other series were *The Donna Reed Show* and *The Bob Crane Show.* His death was attributed to a beating.

CULLY, Zara, in full, ZARA CULLY BROWN. American actress, b. Worcester, Mass., 1890?, d. Los Angeles, Feb. 28. A veteran of many television and motion picture appearances, she was playing the role of Mother Jefferson in the television series *The Jeffersons* at the time of her death.

DAILEY, Dan. American actor, b. New York City, 1914, d. Los Angeles, Oct. 15. Tall and gangling, he began his career as a teenager, singing and dancing in Broadway chorus lines and in burlesque. He appeared in dozens of films in the 1940's and 1950's; he was nominated for an Academy Award in 1948 for his performance in *When My Baby Smiles at Me.* He also starred on television in *The Governor and J.J.* (1969–71).

DALY, James Firman. American actor, b. Wisconsin Rapids, Wis., Oct. 23, 1918, d. Nyack, N.Y., July 3. An actor for fifty years, he played leading roles on the Broadway stage and in motion pictures. He also appeared in more than 600 television programs, most notably as the star of two series, *Foreign Intrigue* and *Medical Center.*

Actor-dancer Dan Dailey in a scene from When My Baby Smiles at Me.

DALY, Lar. American political activist, b. Gary, Ind., Jan. 22, 1912, d. Evergreen Park, Ill., April 18. During a political life of forty years he ran for a long list of offices, including the U.S. Senate (six times), the Presidency, and the mayoralty of Chicago; he never won a race. A conservative individualist, he often challenged Republican regulars under the banner "America First." When not campaigning in his Uncle Sam costume, he manufactured bar stools.

DAUPHIN, Claude. French actor, b. Claude Legrand in Corbeil, Aug. 19, 1903, d. Paris, Nov. 16. He appeared in some eighty films, including *Casque d'Or* (1952) and *Madame Rosa* (1976) in French and *Little Boy Lost* (1953) and *Barbarella* (1968) in English. He also played leading roles on the stages of important theaters in Paris, London, and New York City.

DE ROCHEMONT, Louis Charles. American motion picture producer, b. Chelsea, Mass., Jan. 13, 1899, d. near Newington, N.H., Dec. 23. He was highly regarded as a producer of documentary films and of fiction films based on fact. Among his best-known productions were the "March of Time" series of shorts (1934-43), *The House on 92nd Street* (1945), *Lost Boundaries* (1949), and *Martin Luther* (1953).

DU VIGNEAUD, Vincent. American biochemist, b. Chicago, May 18, 1901, d. White Plains, N.Y., Dec. 11. In 1946 he led an international scientific team at Cornell University Medical College that succeeded in synthesizing penicillin. He was awarded the 1955 Nobel Prize in chemistry for his synthesis of two pituitary hormones.

EAMES, Charles. American designer, b. St. Louis, June 17, 1907, d. there Aug. 21. He was an architect, decorator, filmmaker, landscape designer, toymaker, photographer, and educator, often working in collaboration with his wife, Ray Kaiser Eames. He achieved his greatest celebrity as a furniture designer, particularly of the "Eames chair," a molded, form-fitting object designed to be mass-produced from wood or fiberglass.

ELLIS, Don. American jazz musician, b. Los Angeles, July 25, 1934, d. North Hollywood, Calif., Dec. 17. He was a trumpet soloist with symphony orchestras, conductor of a big band, and composer of scores for television commercials and series and such films as *The French Connection* (1971). He was noted for his experiments in combining jazz and classical forms, electronic instrumentation, and unusual time signatures.

ETTING, Ruth. American singer, b. David City, Nebr., Nov. 23, 1897, d. Colorado Springs, Colo., Sept. 24. She began singing in her distinctively clear and lilting soprano in the theaters and radio stations of Chicago in 1922. Later she starred in several editions of the Ziegfeld Follies and in other musical shows on Broadway and appeared in films, both features and short subjects. In the 1930's, because of her success on records and radio, she was often called the most popular singer in the U.S. In 1955 her life story was filmed as *Love Me or Leave Me*.

FIELDS, Totie. American comedian, b. Sophie Feldman in Hartford, Conn., May 7, 1930, d. Las

Comedian Totie Fields, photographed in 1976.

269

Vegas, Nev., Aug. 2. A beloved performer in night-clubs and on television from the early 1960's, she capitalized on her excessive weight, garrulous-ness, and raucous, rasping voice.

FILIPIAK, Cardinal Boleslaw. Polish Roman Catholic prelate, b. Osniszecewko, Sept. 1, 1901, d. Poznan, Oct. 12. He was dean of the Roman Rota, the highest judiciary authority of the Vatican curia, from 1967 until 1976. He was raised to the cardinalate in 1976.

FLANNER, Janet. American journalist, b. Indianapolis, March 13, 1892, d. New York City, Nov. 7. Under the pen name Genêt she wrote the "Letter from Paris" feature of *The New Yorker* magazine for some thirty years. Those pieces and her other articles were collected in several books; she also made notable translations of works by the French novelist Colette.

FONTAINE, Frank. American comedian, b. Cambridge, Mass., April 19, 1920, d. Spokane, Wash., Aug. 4. A veteran of supper clubs, Army service shows, big-band appearances, radio comedies, and small roles in Hollywood films, he won brief national fame on television in the early 1960's. He played the character Crazy Guggenheim, the not-too-bright crony of Jackie Gleason's long-suffering Joe the Bartender.

FRICK, Ford Christopher. American journalist and baseball executive, b. near Wawaka, Ind., Dec. 19, 1894, d. Bronxville, N.Y., April 8. A radio and newspaper journalist, he became president of baseball's National League in 1934. From 1951 until 1965 he served as commissioner of baseball.

FRINGS, Cardinal Joseph. West German Roman Catholic prelate, b. Neuss, Feb. 6, 1887, d. Cologne, Dec. 17. As archbishop of Cologne (1942–69), he was noted for his defiance of the Nazis during World War II. Raised to the cardinalate in 1946, he was a leader of the progressive wing at Vatican Council II.

GEER, Will. American actor, b. Frankfort, Ind., March 9, 1902, d. Los Angeles, April 22. His sixty-year career included performances in every show business medium. He was playing the grandfather in the television series *The Waltons* at the time of his death. A noted raconteur, Shakespearean scholar, botanist, and folksinger as well as an actor, he was blacklisted for several years during the 1950's and 1960's because of alleged Communist sympathies.

GELLER, Bruce. American television producer, b. New York City, Oct. 13, 1930, d. near Santa Barbara, Calif., May 21. He conceived, produced, and frequently wrote for such television series as *Mission Impossible* and *Mannix*. He also wrote for the stage and for the motion picture screen. He was killed in the crash of a private plane.

Will Geer in costume for his role as Grandpa Walton in the television series The Waltons.

Infielder Jim "Junior" Gilliam in his playing days with the Dodgers.

GENN, Leo John. British actor, b. London, Aug. 9, 1905, d. there Jan. 26. In 1930, as a struggling young barrister, he began acting professionally. During his career he appeared in more than two dozen films, fifty plays, and a score of television dramas. He was nominated for a 1951 Academy Award for his performance in *Quo Vadis?* He made other notable appearances on the screen in *Henry V* (1946), *The Snake Pit* (1948), and *Moby Dick* (1956).

GILLIAM, Jim ("Junior"). American baseball player, b. Nashville, Oct. 17, 1928, d. Los Angeles,

Oct. 9. He joined the Brooklyn (later Los Angeles) Dodgers in 1953 and was named Rookie of the Year. During his fourteen seasons as a second and third baseman he batted .265 and played in seven World Series. He remained with the Dodgers as a coach until his death from the effects of a stroke.

GILSON, Étienne Henry. French philosopher, b. Paris, June 13, 1884, d. Cravant, Sept. 19. He was the oldest living member of the French Academy, to which he had been elected in 1946. His lectures and books on St. Thomas Aquinas, St. Augustine, and others earned him a worldwide reputation as an authority on medieval philosophy.

GÖDEL, Kurt. Austrian-born American mathematician, b. Brünn, Austria-Hungary (now Brno, Czechoslovakia), April 28, 1906, d. Princeton, N.J., Jan. 14. Often called the world's leading contemporary logician, he formulated Gödel's Proof in 1931 at the University of Vienna. This theorem, difficult for the layman to grasp, concerns the unprovability of axioms within a branch of mathematics; it had an immeasurable effect on mathematics and logic.

GOFF, Norris. American entertainer, b. Cove, Ark., May 30, 1906, d. Palm Desert, Calif., June 7. As Abner, half of the rural comedy team of Lum and Abner, he was a major star of radio from 1931 until 1955. The team (Lum was played by Chester Lauck) also appeared in five motion pictures.

GORDON, Joseph Lowell ("Flash"). American baseball player and manager, b. Los Angeles, Feb. 18, 1915, d. Sacramento, April 14. At second base for the New York Yankees (1938–46), he was a sensational hitter and fielder, nine times a league all-star and once (1942) the most valuable player. He also played (1947–50) for the Cleveland Indians, and he managed (1958–69) the Indians, the Detroit Tigers, the Kansas City Athletics, and the Kansas City Royals.

GORDON, Max. American theatrical producer, b. Mechel Salpeter in New York City, June 28, 1892, d. there Nov. 2. During his forty-year career he produced many of the major Broadway hits. These included *The Women* (1936), *My Sister Eileen* (1940), *Born Yesterday* (1946), and *The Solid Gold Cadillac* (1952).

GOUDSMIT, Samuel Abraham. Dutch-born American physicist, b. The Hague, July 11, 1902, d. Reno, Nev., Dec. 4. In 1925 he and his University of Leyden colleague George E. Uhlenbeck made the seminal discovery that electrons spin. During World War II he directed the Allied effort to discover whether there was a German atom bomb project.

GRACIAS, Cardinal Valerian. Indian Roman Catholic prelate, b. Karachi, Oct. 23, 1900, d. Bombay, Sept. 11. He was named archbishop of Bom-

Physicist Samuel A. Goudsmit at his desk at the Brookhaven National Laboratory (1962).

bay in 1950. Three years later he became the first Indian-born cardinal.

GRANT, Duncan James Corrowr. British artist, b. Rothiemurchus, Scotland, Jan. 21, 1885, d. Aldermaston, England, May 10. A founder of the Bloomsbury Group of British intellectuals influential during the first quarter of the 20th century, he was noted not only as an easel painter but also as an interior decorator and theatrical designer.

GRONCHI, Giovanni. Italian statesman, b. Pontedera, Sept. 10, 1887, d. Rome, Oct. 17. He was president of Italy from 1955 until 1962. Previously he had been a founder of the Christian Democratic Party (1943) and had served as speaker of the Chamber of Deputies (1948–55).

HAINES, Jesse Joseph. American baseball player, b. Clayton, Ohio, July 22, 1893, d. Columbus, Aug. 5. A star pitcher for the St. Louis Cardinals for eighteen seasons (1920–38), he was elected to the baseball Hall of Fame in 1970.

HUMPHREY, Hubert Horatio. U.S. Senator from Minnesota, b. Wallace, S.Dak., May 27, 1911, d. Waverly, Minn., Jan. 13. An energetic, ebullient orator, he first attracted national attention as mayor of Minneapolis (1945–48) and as a strong civil rights advocate at the 1948 Democratic national convention. He served five terms as a U.S. Senator (1949–65; 1971–78) and, under President Lyndon B. Johnson, one term as the thirty-eighth Vice-President of the U.S. (1965–69). In 1968 he was himself narrowly defeated for the Presidency by Richard M. Nixon. Humphrey was an indefatigable champion of such liberal causes as civil rights, anti-poverty legislation, and arms control. He was

Hubert H. Humphrey, U.S. Vice-President from 1965 to 1969.

a founder of the Democratic-Farmer-Labor Party of Minnesota and of Americans for Democratic Action. He was an effective Senator, serving as party whip and as floor manager for many important bills.

JAMES, Daniel ("Chappie"), Jr. American military leader, b. Pensacola, Fla., Feb. 11, 1920, d. Colorado Springs, Colo., Feb. 25. A much-decorated jet fighter pilot in Korea and Vietnam, he served as commander of the North American Air Defense Command from 1975 until his retirement in 1978, shortly before his death. He was the first Black to attain the rank of four-star general.

JOHN PAUL I, original name ALBINO LUCIANI. Pope of the Roman Catholic Church, b. Forno di Canale, Italy (renamed Canale D'Agordo in 1964), Oct. 12, 1912, d. Vatican City, Sept. 28. His thirty-four-day reign was one of the shortest in the history of the papacy. But during that time "the smiling pope" made a strong impression on the world as a simple, direct man of the people. Ordained in 1935, he taught at and directed the seminary at Belluno until 1958, when he was named bishop of Vittorio Veneto. In 1969 he was appointed patriarch of Venice, and in 1973 he was elevated to the cardinalate.

KARSAVINA, Tamara. Russian-born British dancer, b. St. Petersburg, March 10, 1885, d. London, May 26. She was the prima ballerina of Sergei Diaghilev's legendary Ballets Russes, the principal partner of Waslav Nijinsky, and the versatile creator of leading roles in such modern classics as *Petrouchka, The Spectre of the Rose, Les Sylphides,* and *Firebird.* She retired from dancing in 1933, but continued to teach.

KENNY, Bill. American popular singer, b. Philadelphia, 1922?, d. Vancouver, British Columbia,

Russian ballerina Tamara Karsavina in costume for a performance of Petrouchka in 1911.

Jomo Kenyatta, president of Kenya, in a 1973 photograph.

March 23. He was the last surviving member of the Ink Spots, a vocal quartet popular in the 1930's and 1940's. He joined the group in 1939, the year in which they recorded their first big hit, "If I Didn't Care," featuring Kenny's high tenor lead.

KENYATTA, Jomo. President of Kenya, b. Ichaweri, a Kikuyu village near Nairobi, British East

272

Africa, sometime between 1890 and 1896; baptized in 1914 as Johnstone Kamau; d. Mombasa, Aug. 22. He first attracted attention as a tribal spokesman in the 1920's. In 1931 he began a sixteen-year residence in Europe. Returning to Africa in 1946, he spearheaded the drive for Kenyan independence. From 1952 until 1961 he was imprisoned by the British as an alleged leader of the Mau Mau terrorists. In 1963 he was named prime minister of the newly independent Kenya; in 1964 he became president of the newly formed Republic of Kenya. As president he protected Western political and economic interests and opposed Soviet influence in Africa.

KENYON, Dame Kathleen Mary. British archeologist, b. Jan. 5, 1906, d. Wrexham, Wales, Aug. 24. She made notable discoveries in Jerusalem and Jericho in the 1950's and 1960's, including work that proved Jericho to be the oldest known town. She was made a Dame Commander of the Order of the British Empire in 1973.

KHACHATURIAN, Aram Ilich. Soviet composer, b. Tiflis (now Tbilisi), June 6, 1903, d. Moscow, May 1. His "Saber Dance," an excerpt from his score for the ballet *Gayne* (1942), became a hit tune in the U.S. in the early 1950's. He was a prolific composer of melodic, nationalistic concertos, film and ballet scores, chamber music, and symphonies.

KULAKOV, Fyodor Davydovich. Soviet official, b. near Kursk, Feb. 4, 1918, d. Moscow, July 16. An agriculture expert, he had been national party secretary for agriculture since 1965 and a member of the ruling Politburo since 1971. He was widely regarded as a possible successor to Soviet Communist Party chief Leonid I. Brezhnev.

LEAR, William Powell. American industrialist and inventor, b. Hannibal, Mo., June 26, 1902, d. Reno, Nev., May 14. Founder of the Lear Jet Corp., which he sold in 1967, he received 150 patents, including those for the first practical automobile radio, the eight-track stereo cartridge, and an automatic pilot for aircraft.

LEAVIS, F(rank) R(aymond). British literary critic, b. Cambridge, England, July 14, 1895, d. there April 14. His provocative, uncompromising attacks on what he considered uncivilized writing made him one of the most influential of contemporary English literary critics. He was the guiding spirit of the magazine *Scrutiny* (1932-53).

LEIBOWITZ, Samuel S. Rumanian-born American attorney and jurist, b. Iași, Rumania, Aug. 14, 1893, d. New York City, Jan. 11. He became one of the best-known criminal lawyers of his time through his eloquent defense of several Prohibition-era gangsters and of the so-called Scottsboro boys, nine Blacks accused of raping two white

Attorney Samuel S. Leibowitz pleads for the Scottsboro boys at their 1932 trial in Alabama.

women in 1931. Later he served as judge on the New York State Supreme Court.

LINDNER, Richard. German-born American painter, b. Hamburg, Nov. 11, 1901, d. New York City, April 16. His work, exclusively monumental paintings of huge, predatory women, first became popular among critics and patrons alike in the 1960's.

MacARTHUR, John Donald. American billionaire, b. Pittston, Pa., March 6, 1897, d. West Palm Beach, Fla., Jan. 6. He built his fortune, reportedly one of the largest in the U.S., on his insurance company, Bankers Life and Casualty Corp. He also had vast real estate holdings in Florida and New York City and interests in many banks and oil and textile companies.

MALLOWAN, Sir Max Edgar Lucien. British archeologist, b. London, May 6, 1904, d. Wallingford, Aug. 19. Noted for his excavations of ancient Middle Eastern sites, he was knighted in 1968. He was married to the writer Dame Agatha Christie from 1930 until her death in 1976.

MARAIS, Josef. Original surname Pessach. South African-born American folksinger, b. Sir Lowry's Pass, Nov. 17, 1905, d. Los Angeles, April 27. With his wife Miranda he came to prominence in the folk music vogue of the post-World War II era. Specializing in songs of the South African veldt, they continued to perform and record until 1974.

MARTINSON, Harry Edmund. Swedish author, b. Jämshög, May 6, 1904, d. Stockholm, Feb. 11. He shared the 1974 Nobel Prize for literature with Eyvind Johnson. Of his novels and poetry, largely unknown outside of Sweden, *Aniara* (1956), an epic poem about a space voyage, achieved the most renown.

McCARTHY, Joseph Victor. American baseball manager, b. Philadelphia, April 21, 1887, d. Buffalo, Jan. 13. He led the New York Yankees for

Joe McCarthy, manager of the New York Yankees, at the 1943 World Series in St. Louis.

A 1970 photograph of anthropologist Margaret Mead.

Golda Meir in 1962, when she was Israeli foreign minister.

sixteen seasons (1931–46), during which they won eight American League pennants and seven World Series titles. He became manager of the Boston Red Sox in 1948 and retired in 1950. In 1957 he was elected to the baseball Hall of Fame.

McGINLEY, Phyllis. American poet, b. Ontario, Oreg., March 21, 1905, d. New York City, Feb. 22. She received a Pulitzer Prize for *Times Three* (1960), one of the many collections of her light but trenchant verse about suburban life in the U.S.

MEAD, Margaret. American anthropologist, b. Philadelphia, Dec. 16, 1901, d. New York City, Nov. 15. Beginning with the publication of her first study of the sexual mores of primitive tribes, *Coming of Age in Samoa* (1928), she brought cultural anthropology to the attention of millions of people. A highly visible and articulate advocate of feminism, ecology, mental health, racial equality, and peace, she wrote twenty-three books, delivered hundreds of speeches, and was frequently heard and seen on radio and television.

MEIR, Golda Mabovich. Israeli political leader, b. Kiev, Russia, May 3, 1898, d. Jerusalem, Dec. 8. At the age of eight, she and her family emigrated to Milwaukee, where she became an active Zionist. In 1921 she went to live in Palestine. As a leader of the Jewish labor movement there, she helped to found the state of Israel (1948) and became prime minister in 1969. She held firmly to the reins of government until after the Arab-Israeli conflict of October, 1973, when insoluble problems within the Labor Party caused her to resign in 1974. She remained active, however, respected and listened to by friend and foe alike.

MENZIES, Sir Robert Gordon. Australian statesman, b. Jeparit, Victoria, Dec. 20, 1894, d. Melbourne, May 14. As prime minister of Australia (1939–41; 1949–66), he led the country from colonial status to prominence as a world power. A brilliant conservative politician, he was the leader first of the United Australian Party and, from 1944, of the Liberal Party. He was knighted in 1963.

MESSEL, Oliver. British theatrical designer, b. London, Jan. 13, 1904, d. Barbados, July 13. From the early 1930's until the mid-1960's he was the leading designer of settings for the British theater. He also designed for the ballet and opera.

MESSERSCHMITT, Willy. German aircraft designer and industrialist, b. Frankfurt, June 26, 1896, d. Munich, Sept. 15. He set up his own aircraft manufacturing company in 1923. His ME-109 single-engine fighter plane was the workhorse of the German air force during World War II. He also produced an effective twin-engine bomber, the ME-110, and the world's first jet fighter, the ME-262. In the late 1950's he again began to produce aircraft in West Germany.

METCALF, Lee. U.S. Senator from Montana, b. Stevensville, Mont., Jan. 28, 1911, d. Helena, Jan. 12. A liberal Democrat, he served in the U.S. House of Representatives from 1953 through 1960, when he was first elected to the Senate.

METCALFE, Ralph Harold. U.S. Representative, b. Atlanta, May 30, 1910, d. Chicago, Oct. 10. First elected to Congress in 1970, he had been active in Democratic Party politics in Chicago since 1952. He was also a world-class sprinter, a medal winner in two Olympic Games (1932: silver medal, 100 m, and bronze medal, 200 m; 1936: gold medal, 400 m relay, and silver medal, 100 m dash).

MIKOYAN, Anastas Ivanovich. Soviet political leader, b. Sanain (now in the Armenian SSR), Nov. 25, 1895, death announced Moscow, Oct. 22. He stayed in favor and wielded influence longer than any other figure in the history of the Soviet Union. Under the Communist leaders Lenin, Stalin, Malenkov, Khrushchev, and Brezhnev, he held a variety of posts, including trade chief (for twenty-five years), president, and first deputy premier. He remained on the Central Committee of the Communist Party until 1976.

MONTOYA, Joseph Manuel. American legislator, b. Penablanca, N.Mex., Sept. 24, 1915, d. Washington, D.C., June 5. A liberal Democrat, he served as U.S. Senator from New Mexico from 1965 through 1976. He was a member of the Senate Watergate committee in 1973–74.

MOON, Keith. British rock 'n' roll musician, b. Wembley, Aug. 23, 1947, d. there Sept. 7. As the drummer for the Who rock 'n' roll group for fifteen years, he was noted for his wild antics both on stage and off. He played Uncle Ernie in the film version of the Who's opera, *Tommy* (1975). His death was attributed to an overdose of drugs.

MORO, Aldo. Italian statesman, b. Maglie, Sept. 23, 1916, death announced Rome, May 9. He was permier of Italy five times and, as head of the Christian Democratic Party, the leading candidate for the presidency. A professor of criminal law, he also served as foreign minister and as head of several other ministries during his thirty-year career in public life. Kidnapped by the terrorist Red Brigades on March 16, he was allegedly murdered on May 8.

Soviet leader Anastas I. Mikoyan as he appeared in a 1958 American television interview.

British rock musician Keith Moon performs with the Who in 1968.

NIKODIM, title of BORIS GEORGIYEVICH ROTOV. Russian Orthodox prelate, b. Frolovo, Oct. 16, 1929, d. Vatican City, Sept. 5. Consecrated an archbishop in 1961, he was the metropolitan of Leningrad and Novgorod. An ardent ecumenicist, he was a president of the World Council of Churches and had represented his church at Vatican Council II. He died during an audience with Pope John Paul I, who administered the last rites.

NILSSON, Gunnar. Swedish racing car driver, b. 1949?, d. London, Oct. 20. In 1977, before he retired because of cancer, he was ranked eighth in the Formula I world championship standings.

NOBILE, Umberto. Italian aviator, b. Lauro, Jan. 21, 1885, d. Rome, July 29. His May 12, 1926, flight over the North Pole in the dirigible *Norge* was not a first: An American team in an airplane had preceded him by three days. Nobile's second polar exploration, in 1928, ended in the loss of seventeen lives, for which he was blamed. Not until after the close of World War II was his name cleared and his rank as a general in the Italian air force restored.

NOBLE, Ray. British composer and conductor, b. Brighton, England, 1907, d. London, April 3. He achieved fame in the U.S. during the 1930's and 1940's, first from his jazz recordings, later from his conducting at the Rainbow Room in New York City, and finally as a band leader and comic on various popular radio programs. His songs include "Goodnight, Sweetheart" and "The Very Thought of You."

OAKIE, Jack, professional name of Lewis Delaney Offield. American actor, b. Sedalia, Mo., Nov. 12, 1903, d. Northridge, Calif., Jan. 23. He appeared in more than 100 films, most often as a moon-faced, not very bright college student. His first major role was in *The Fleet's In* (1928), with Clara Bow; he played Napolini in Charlie Chaplin's *The Great Dictator* (1940). His last film was *Lover Come Back* (1962).

PAUL VI, original name GIOVANNI BATISTA MONTINI. Pope of the Roman Catholic Church, b. Concesio, Italy, Sept. 26, 1897, d. Vatican City, Aug. 6. A quiet, intellectual man, he was regarded as both a dedicated doctrinal conservative and a liberal champion of world peace, human rights, and ecumenism. He served in the Vatican secretariat of state from 1933 until 1952, was consecrated archbishop of Milan in 1954, and was made a cardinal in 1958. He succeeded Pope John XXIII in 1963. Among the highlights of his reign was the conclusion of Vatican Council II. His proclamations upheld the church's bans on priestly marriages, the use of artificial means of birth control, and the ordination of women. He also held unprecedented meetings with representatives of the Greek Orthodox, Coptic Orthodox, and Anglican churches, and traveled widely.

PEI, Mario Andrew. Italian-born American linguist, b. Rome, Feb. 16, 1901, d. Glen Ridge, N.J., March 2. His book *The Story of Language* (1949) first brought him widespread recognition as a scholar who had a remarkable ability to make technical linguistics interesting for the average reader. He wrote several other books and taught romance languages at Columbia University for thirty-three years.

PETERSON, Ronnie. Swedish racing car driver, b. Örebro, February 14, 1944, d. Milan, Italy, Sept. 10. In his twelve years of racing, he started in 123 Grand Prix races and won 10 of them; this gave him eighth place on the list of all-time winners. He was fatally injured in a crash at the start of the Italian Grand Prix, held at Monza.

PRIMA, Louis. American jazz musician, b. New Orleans, Dec. 7, 1912, d. there Aug. 24. He was a composer, trumpet player, band leader, and, in his distinctive gravel voice, a singer. In the 1930's he started playing in jazz clubs and led a big band, and in the 1950's he achieved his greatest fame with such records as "Old Black Magic," featuring his wife, singer Keely Smith. He appeared in Las Vegas lounges in the 1960's and 1970's.

RAY, Joie. American athlete, b. Kankakee, Ill., April 13, 1894, d. Benton Harbor, Mich., May 13. He amassed nearly 1000 medals in his career as a long-distance runner. In the 1920's he held both the indoor and outdoor records for the one-mile run, and he competed in three Olympic Games (1920, 1924, 1928).

ROBSON, Mark. Canadian-born American motion picture director, b. Montréal, Dec. 4, 1913, d. London, June 20. He first attracted attention as the director of the serious-minded, low-budget *Champion* and *Home of the Brave* (both 1949). Later he created such popular successes as *Peyton Place* (1957), *Valley of the Dolls* (1967), and *Earthquake* (1974). He died after collapsing on the location set of his latest directorial effort, *Avalanche Express.*

ROCKEFELLER, John D(avison) 3rd. American philanthropist, b. New York City, March 21, 1906, d. Mount Pleasant, N.Y., July 10. The eldest and least known of the five millionaire sons of the oil magnate John D. Rockefller, Jr., he was chairman of the Rockefeller Foundation for many years. He devoted his life to supporting the arts and population planning. He was killed in an automobile accident.

Philanthropist John D. Rockefeller 3rd in 1971.

ROCKWELL, George L. American comedian, b. Providence, R.I., 1888?, d. Brunswick, Maine, March 3. As the pseudoscientist "Dr. Rockwell" he appeared prominently in vaudeville and in Broadway reviews from the 1920's to the 1940's. He was also a popular radio entertainer, a columnist, and a cartoonist.

ROCKWELL, Norman. American illustrator, b. New York City, Feb. 3, 1894, d. Stockbridge, Mass., Nov. 8. Through his magazine covers (especially those for the *Saturday Evening Post*) and his widely distributed World War II posters, he became probably the best-known and certainly the best-loved American painter. Art critics, however, derided his cheerful, folksy work as sentimental and superficial.

ROSENBERG, Harold. American art critic and author, b. New York City, Feb. 2, 1906, d. The Springs, N.Y., July 11. An author of several books and innumerable magazine pieces as well as an educator and consultant, he was art critic of *The New Yorker* magazine from 1967 until his death. He coined the phrase "action painting" for the work of the abstract expressionist painters whose work he greatly admired.

RUBICAM, Raymond. American advertising executive, b. Brooklyn, N.Y., June 16, 1892, d. Scottsdale, Ariz., May 8. With the late John Orr Young he founded Young & Rubicam in 1923; their agency became one of the largest in the world. He wrote seminal advertising copy and introduced marketing research into the advertising business.

A late photograph of artist Norman Rockwell sketching.

SCOTT, Paul Mark. British author, b. near London, March 25, 1920, d. there March 1. His four novels about British India, known collectively as *The Raj Quartet* (1966–75), brought him considerable popularity both in England and abroad. He also wrote several other novels as well as plays and poetry.

SHAW, Robert. British actor and author, b. Westhoughton, England, Aug. 9, 1927, d. Tourmakeady, Ireland, Aug. 27. He was a successful actor on stage and in films for thirty years; he was also the author of five novels and three plays, including *The Man in the Glass Booth,* an international success. He appeared memorably in such movies as *From Russia With Love* (1964), *A Man for all Seasons* (1966), *The Sting* (1973), and *Jaws* (1975).

SIEGBAHN, (Karl) Manne (Georg). Swedish physicist, b. Örebro, Dec. 3, 1886, d. Stockholm, Sept. 25. He was awarded the 1924 Nobel Prize in physics for his work in high precision X-ray spectroscopy at the University of Uppsala. Later he headed the Swedish nuclear research program as director of the Nobel Institute for Physics of the Royal Academy of Sciences.

SILONE, Ignazio, pen name of SECONDO TRANQUILLI. Italian author, b. Pescina, May 1, 1900, d. Geneva, Switzerland, Aug. 22. He was a founder of the Communist Party of Italy in 1921, but broke with the party in 1930 and went into exile in Switzerland the following year. His two most highly regarded books were strongly antifascist: *Pane e Vino* (1937), popular in English translation as *Bread and Wine* (1936); and *Fontamara* (1934).

SMITH, W. Eugene. American photographer, b. Wichita, Kans., Dec. 30, 1918, d. Tucson, Ariz., Oct. 15. He first won wide recognition with his World War II combat photography, which appeared in *Life* magazine. In 1975 his photographs for *Minamata: Life Sacred and Profane* were widely praised for their dramatic depiction of the effects of chemical poisoning on a Japanese village.

STEINBERG, William. German-born American conductor, b. Hans Wilhelm Steinberg in Cologne, Aug. 1, 1899, d. New York City, May 16. He served as musical director of the Pittsburgh Symphony (for twenty-four years), the London Philharmonic, and the Boston Symphony, and as principal guest conductor of the New York Philharmonic. Critics lauded his efficient, calm, responsive performances.

STILL, William Grant. American composer, b. Woodville, Miss., May 11, 1895, d. Los Angeles, Dec. 3. A highly regarded musical pioneer, he established firsts for a serious black composer when

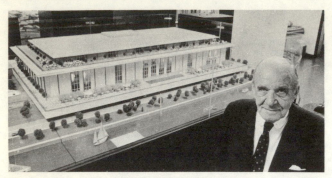

Heavyweight boxing champion Gene Tunney in the 1920's.

he conducted the Los Angeles Philharmonic (1936) and when his opera *Troubled Land* was produced by the New York City Opera (1949). His *Afro-American Symphony* (1931) is regarded as the first symphonic treatment of black music. He composed other symphonies and operas, as well as ballets and a string quartet, all of them melodious and stylistically conservative.

STONE, Edward Durell. American architect, b. Fayetteville, Ark., March 9, 1902, d. New York City, Aug. 6. His career began with the designing of the interiors of Radio City Music Hall in New York City (1931–33). His other early works, including the Museum of Modern Art in New York City (1937), were in the austere international style. With the American embassy in New Delhi, India (1958), he switched to his better known, more romantic later style, often featuring lacy concrete grillwork. Among his many other influential works were the El Panama Hotel, Panamá (1964); the General Motors Building, New York City (1968); and the Kennedy Center, Washington, D.C. (1971).

SWENSON, Karl. American actor, b. New York City, July 23, 1908, d. Torrington, Conn., Oct. 8. He was a leading performer in the heyday of radio serials and he appeared on Broadway and in many films. But he was best known for his appearances as Lars Hanson, the mill owner in the television series *Little House on the Prairie*.

TRIN NHU KHUE, Cardinal Joseph Marie. Vietnamese Roman Catholic prelate, b. Trang Duc, Dec. 11, 1899, d. Hanoi, Nov. 27. Named the first Vietnamese Roman Catholic bishop in 1950, he was imprisoned 1959–60 and barred from leaving the country until his elevation to the cardinalate in 1976.

TUNNEY, James Joseph ("Gene"). American boxer, b. New York City, May 25, 1898, d. Greenwich, Conn., Nov. 8. He won the world heavyweight championship from Jack Dempsey in 1926; he defeated Dempsey again in the famous "long

count" bout of 1927 and retired the following year. Thereafter he was a successful corporation executive and bank official, noted for his encyclopedic knowledge of the works of William Shakespeare.

VENUTI, Joe. Jazz violinist, b. either in Italy or the U.S. between 1896 and 1904; d. Seattle, Wash., Aug. 14. He probably began as a classical performer in Philadelphia; in the 1920's he reputedly joined the Jean Goldkette jazz orchestra in Detroit. He was the most successful jazz violinist of the pre-World War II era; in the late 1960's he made a comeback, as public interest in jazz revived.

WALLENDA, Karl. German-born circus performer, b. Magdeburg, 1904, d. San Juan, Puerto Rico, March 22. His death in a fall from the high

On March 22, circus performer Karl Wallenda struggles to regain his footing on a tightrope stretched 150 ft. above a street in San Juan, Puerto Rico. He fell to his death.

Motion-picture tycoon Jack L. Warner at work in the early 1960's.

wire was the last tragedy to strike the "Great Wallendas," as his troupe was known. A circus performer since childhood, he devised his famous seven-man pyramid in 1947. In 1962 his son-in-law and his nephew were killed during the act, and his adopted son was paralyzed; in 1972 another nephew was killed.

WARNER, Jack L(eonard). Canadian-born American motion picture producer, b. London, Ontario, Aug. 2, 1892, d. Los Angeles, Sept. 9. With his three older brothers (Harry, d. 1958; Albert, d. 1967; Samuel, d. 1927), he began producing films in 1912. In 1923, Warner Bros. Pictures was incorporated in Hollywood; in 1927 they released the epoch-making talkie *The Jazz Singer*. During the decades that followed they produced hundreds of successful films and dozens of classics. Among the stars they developed were Bette Davis, Humphrey Bogart, Edward G. Robinson, Paul Muni, Dick Powell, and Ruby Keeler. Jack L. Warner served variously as head of production, president, and chairman of the board; in 1959 he was given the Irving G. Thalberg Award of the Motion Picture Academy for production excellence.

WARNER, Sylvia Townsend. British author, b. Harrow (now part of London), England, Dec. 6, 1893, d. Dorset, England, May 1. A successful novelist, short-story writer, poet, and biographer, she first gained a large audience with *Lolly Willowes* (1926), a novel. Her thirty books and the many stories she wrote for *The New Yorker* magazine are admired for their quiet grace and wit.

WHEELOCK, John Hall. American poet, b. Far Rockaway, N.Y., Sept. 9, 1886, d. New York City, March 22. His first book of poetry was published in 1911, his last in 1978. His traditionally oriented verse usually celebrated nature, life, and joy. He was also an influential editor in chief at Scribners, the publishing house with which he was associated from 1911 to 1957.

WHITEHEAD, Edward. British naval officer and industrialist, b. Aldershot, England, May 16, 1908, d. Petersfield, England, April 16. As chairman and spokesman for Schweppes (U.S.A.) Ltd. (1953-71), he became familiar to American television audiences in commercials stressing his product's "Schweppervescence."

WILLS, Chill. American actor, b. Seagoville, Texas, July 18, 1902, d. Encino, Calif., Dec. 15. Although he appeared in hundreds of films, he achieved his greatest fame as the voice of Francis the mule in the popular series (1950-56). The raspy-voiced, lanky performer was seen in such classics as *Meet Me in St. Louis* (1944), *The Yearling* (1946), and *Giant* (1956).

WOOD, Peggy. American actress, b. Brooklyn, N.Y., Feb. 9, 1892, d. Stamford, Conn., March 18. She appeared (1910-59) in more than seventy Broadway productions, ranging from musical comedy to classic drama. She starred on television as the Norwegian matriarch of *I Remember Mama* (1949-57). The last of her rare film appearances was in *The Sound of Music* (1965).

YOUNG, Gig. American actor, b. Byron Ellsworth Barr, St. Cloud, Minn., Nov. 4, 1917, d. New York City, Oct. 19. He appeared in more than fifty films, including *The Gay Sisters* (1942), in which he played a character named Gig Young, and *They Shoot Horses, Don't They?* (1969), for which he won a best-supporting-actor Academy Award. He also appeared on Broadway and in theatrical tours. His death was attributed to a self-inflicted

Actor Jack Oakie as Napolini in Charlie Chaplin's film *The Great Dictator (1940).*

German-born William Steinberg was the conductor of the Pittsburgh Symphony for twenty-four years.

Daniel ("Chappie") James, Jr., here a lieutenant general, was a four-star general at the time of his death.

Robert Shaw—British actor, novelist, and playwright—as he appeared in The Deep *(1977).*

The unique gravel-toned voice of Chill Wills was well known to several generations of filmgoers.

Umberto Nobile, photographed at the time of his famous dirigible flight over the North Pole.

An early photograph of Carlos Chávez, dean of Mexican composer-conductors.

A dapper Commander Edward Whitehead, president of Schweppes, Ltd., off on a promotion tour.

Actor Gig Young in his Oscar-winning role as the dance-marathon MC in They Shoot Horses, Don't They? (1969).

In her heyday, former Ziegfeld Follies star Ruth Etting was known as the most popular singer on the radio.

gunshot wound; the simultaneous death of his fifth wife, 31-year-old Ruth Hannelore Schmidt, was called a murder.

YU PIN, Cardinal Paul. Chinese Roman Catholic prelate, b. Lan Si-Sien, April 13, 1901, d. Vatican City, Aug. 15. A dedicated anti-Communist, he was named archbishop of Nanking in 1946. He fled China for the U.S. in 1949, settled in Taiwan in 1960, and became a cardinal in 1969.

ZUKOFSKY, Louis. American poet, b. New York City, Jan. 23, 1904, d. Port Jefferson, N.Y., May 12. An objectivist, greatly admired by critics and his fellow poets, he also wrote works of fiction and criticism.

OHIO. *See* STATISTICS OF THE WORLD.
OKLAHOMA. *See* STATISTICS OF THE WORLD.
OMAN. *See* STATISTICS OF THE WORLD. *See also* MIDDLE EAST.
ONTARIO. *See* STATISTICS OF THE WORLD.
OREGON. *See* STATISTICS OF THE WORLD.
ORGANIZATION FOR ECONOMIC COOPERATION AND DEVELOPMENT, abbreviated OECD. Inflation, the uncertain health of the U.S. dollar, and oil prices occupied the attention of the twenty-four-member OECD in 1978.

On oil prices, at least, events in 1978 illustrated some of the perils of economic forecasting, one of the OECD's major activities. An OECD staff paper released in November predicted that in 1978 and 1979 the balance of payments (current accounts) for all OECD members collectively would be near equilibrium for the first time since the huge oil-price rises of 1973. The developed countries had a combined payments deficit of $30 billion in 1977; by 1979, said the OECD staff, they might even show a small surplus. In particular, the U.S. payments deficit would drop from about $18 billion in 1978 to $8 billion in 1979. However, these predictions came before the Organization of Petroleum Exporting Countries announced a new round of oil price hikes in December. These increases were expected to raise the U.S. payments deficit to $11 billion in 1979, and to add $19 billion to OECD members' aggregate oil bill. Developed countries could expect to earn back about half that amount through increased sales of goods to the oil exporters, the OECD forecasters said.

The rise in oil prices also caused the OECD to revise its estimate of U.S. inflation in 1979 from 7 percent up to 7.4 percent. Rates of 3.3 percent for West Germany and 4.5 percent for Japan were also forecast. This sharp differential in inflation rates between the United States and its leading foreign-trade competitors could lead to increased pressure on the U.S. dollar against the mark and the yen in 1979. In July, an OECD report on the

American economy had urged the U.S. to dampen economic growth (and, if necessary, increase unemployment) in order to curb inflation and strengthen the dollar on currency markets.   G.H.

ORGANIZATION OF AMERICAN STATES, abbreviated OAS. In 1978, for the third consecutive year, the OAS was primarily concerned with the issue of human rights in Latin America.

At its eighth general assembly, held in Washington, D.C., in June, the OAS issued its strongest statements to date in regard to human rights. A seventy-page special report was issued, accusing Uruguay of gross violations of such rights; in its annual report the organization detailed similar offenses by Chile and Paraguay. Some progress in reducing such violations was also noted. The organization's concern for human rights was encouraged by U.S. President Jimmy Carter in an address to the assembly on June 21. Delegates from four member countries—Colombia, Costa Rica, Mexico, and Venezuela—also spotlighted the issue.

A majority of member countries accepted resolutions urging Uruguay, Paraguay, and Chile to end abuses. The resolution approving the annual report was passed with 21 favorable votes, with Argentina, Brazil, and Uruguay abstaining; Chile abstained from voting on the section referring to Chilean policy. Resolutions on Uruguay and Paraguay were approved by 16 states with 1 negative vote and 8 abstentions.

OAS investigative panels were refused entry into Uruguay, but they were admitted to several other countries. A panel visiting Haiti in August concluded that there had been marked improvement in the Haitian government's regard for human rights but urged President Jean-Claude Du-

On July 18 in Washington, D.C., the signature of Fabian Alexis Redhead (center), ambassador from Grenada to the OAS, brings into effect the American Convention on Human Rights. Redhead is flanked by U.S. Ambassador Gale McGee (left) and OAS Secretary-General Alejandro Orfila.

valier to do even more. In October, OAS observers visiting Nicaragua called on President Anastasio Somoza Debayle to curb his National Guard, which they accused of murdering scores of unarmed civilians in the wake of the August–September rebellion; *see* NICARAGUA.

In July, Grenada became the eleventh OAS member to ratify the American Convention on Human Rights, which was drawn up in 1969. Eight nations had ratified it before the first of the year, and Panama and El Salvador had provided ratification in June. With the ratification by Grenada, the convention was brought into force for all of the signatory powers. (Eight other nations, including the United States, have signed but not ratified it.) The convention establishes a new Inter-American Court of Human Rights, with seven judges to be elected by the OAS general assembly.

Secretary-General Alejandro Orfila of Argentina noted in September that the OAS was acting decisively on the human rights issue. But he emphasized that there was still a great need to work for economic improvements, specifically for greater access to U.S. markets for Latin American goods and stabilization of world commodity prices.

See STATISTICS OF THE WORLD.   J.N.G.

ORGANIZATION OF PETROLEUM EXPORTING COUNTRIES, abbreviated OPEC. Again in 1978, OPEC cracked the whip. And just as in 1973–74, when OPEC raised prices fourfold, the world's oil consumers shuddered.

Meeting in Abu Dhabi. In December the OPEC oil ministers convened in Abu Dhabi, in the Union of Arab Emirates. The price of Saudi Arabian light crude, which is used as a benchmark to set the prices of other grades of oil, had remained frozen at $12.70 since mid-1977. In the meantime, worldwide inflation and the loss in value of the U.S. dollar—the currency in which OPEC members are paid for their oil—had reduced OPEC revenues significantly. A price rise clearly was in the cards. The only question was: How much?

The oil consumers were convinced that the increase would be moderate. At an OPEC meeting in Geneva in June, the price "doves," Saudi Arabia and Iran, were in control. During the summer, Saudi Arabia, the single most influential member of OPEC, decisively rejected the idea of indexing the dollar price of oil to a basket of other currencies, a plan favored by the OPEC price "hawks," such as Algeria and Libya. With Saudi Arabia leading the way, it was hoped, OPEC would settle for a maximum overall price rise of 10 percent, to be imposed in stages during 1979.

As it turned out, the ministers agreed at the Abu Dhabi meeting to a substantial overall increase of 14.5 percent by the end of 1979. The quarterly increases, beginning on Jan. 1, 1979, were expected to bring the price of light Arabian crude to $14.54 a barrel by the end of the year. For Americans, the decision would mean a 3¢ rise per gallon for products ranging from fuel oil to gasoline. The U.S. bill for imported oil was expected to rise by $6 billion annually, to an estimated $51 billion, thus fattening an already swollen trade deficit and further damaging the dollar.

World Reaction. Alfred E. Kahn, director of U.S. President Jimmy Carter's anti-inflation campaign, said he was "terribly disappointed." The President himself could only "regret" OPEC's decision and ask—without any hope at all—for a reconsideration.

Dismay over the size of the increase came from both industrialized and developing nations. The Japanese, who import 99 percent of their oil, predicted dire consequences. In Bern, a Swiss government spokesman said the more expensive oil would jeopardize economic growth, monetary

Sheikh Manae Said al-Oteiba, oil minister of the Union of Arab Emirates, joins the folk dancing in Abu Dhabi on Dec. 17. An OPEC conference, of which he was president, had just decided to raise the price of oil by 14.5 percent during 1979.

stability, and the fight against inflation. India's petroleum minister, H. Nandan Bahuguna, believed the developing world would be hardest hit by the move. "It is not good news for us in India," he commented.

Saudi oil minister Sheikh Ahmed Zaki al-Yamani insisted that he was not happy with the size of the increase, but he argued that market conditions had largely dictated the rise. The earlier worldwide glut of oil, caused by conservation as well as by the opening up of new sources in Alaska, the North Sea, and Mexico, had been absorbed by rising demand. The political turmoil that swept Iran in the latter part of the year sharply cut production there, further tightening the oil market. Yamani believed, however, that there would not be another price hike at the end of 1979.   R.J.C.

P

PAKISTAN. Political tensions ran high in Pakistan in early 1978, as Zulfikar Ali Bhutto, the country's leader from 1971 to 1977, stood trial for murder. (The charges involved the 1974 ambush of a political opponent in which the latter's father was killed.) On March 18 a five-judge panel of the Lahore High Court found Bhutto and four codefendants guilty and sentenced them to be hanged. The verdict touched off demonstrations by members of Bhutto's still-powerful Pakistan People's Party and also brought a wave of appeals from many foreign governments, including major donors of aid to Pakistan. Bhutto appealed the sentence to the Supreme Court on March 25, and the court began hearing his case in May.

Gen. Muhammad Zia ul-Haq, who led the coup which overthrew Bhutto in July, 1977, continued to rule Pakistan by martial law. In January he established a council of advisers consisting of bureaucrats and military men, but on July 5 he converted this body to a cabinet and brought seven anti-Bhutto politicians into it. On Aug. 23, Gen. Zia swore in a new cabinet consisting mainly of politicians. Gen. Zia assumed the presidency in September, succeeding Chaudhri Fazal Elahi, whose five-year term expired in August.

The economy, previously in the doldrums, showed some signs of revival. Industrial production rose about 5 percent in the fiscal year ended June 30, 1978, compared with 2 percent in 1976–77. The government moved to give a wider role to the private sector (reversing Bhutto's socialistic policies), and the mood of the business community was described as the best in years. Exports rose somewhat during 1978, and there was a huge increase in family remittances from Pakistanis employed abroad. But Pakistan continued to run a large balance-of-payments deficit and was heavily dependent on foreign aid.

See STATISTICS OF THE WORLD.   W.J.G.

PALESTINE LIBERATION ORGANIZATION, abbreviated PLO. Internecine conflict among its diverse factions and a return to a militant political stance characterized the activity of the PLO during 1978. **Internal Conflict.** Disagreements between moderates affiliated with the organization's chairman, Yasir Arafat, and members of the so-called rejection front factions erupted in recurrent gunfights, assassinations, and bombings of each other's headquarters during the year. The rejectionists disputed hints by Arafat that the Palestinians would agree to a compromise establishing a state in only part of their homeland.

Several small rejectionist factions based in Iraq attacked PLO representatives associated with the moderate line. In January, Said Hammami, PLO representative in London, was killed by members of the Black September faction. A counterattack on the Paris Iraqi embassy, resulting in the deaths of French police and embassy officials during August, was believed to be revenge for Hammami's death. Within the next few days the violence spread to Karachi, Islamabad, and Beirut, where pro-Iraqi Palestinians and PLO representatives engaged in gunfights and further attacks on each other's offices, including one bombing that demolished a headquarters building and reportedly killed hundreds of people.

Several dozen casualties resulted from clashes in refugee camps in Lebanon between pro-Iraqi factions and members of Al Fatah, the largest PLO group, headed by Arafat.

Anti-Sadat Moves. Opposition by all PLO groups to Egyptian President Anwar el-Sadat's peace initiatives led to reconciliation attempts by some of the non-Iraqi rejectionists.

Although Arafat had seemed prepared to enter into Middle East peace negotiations during 1977, he adamantly opposed Sadat's unilateral efforts. From the time of Sadat's Jerusalem visit in No-

PLO leader Yasir Arafat and Maj. Gen. Emmanuel Erskine, supreme commander of the United Nations forces in Lebanon, meet in Beirut March 28. Arafat's decision to accept the presence of the U.N. forces was criticized and rejected by several PLO factions.

vember, 1977, through the September meetings at Camp David, Md., and the subsequent peace treaty negotiations in Washington, D.C., all organizations affiliated with the PLO charged Egypt with betrayal. The PLO joined the so-called steadfastness states at the Baghdad conference in November in calling for punitive action against Sadat.

Relations between the PLO and Egypt seriously deteriorated in February when Sadat charged the organization with responsibility for the assassination in Cyprus of Yousef el-Sebai, a leading Egyptian political figure, journalist, and personal friend. In mid-March, after a Fatah attack on a bus in which 37 Israelis and 9 commandos were killed, Sadat for the first time publicly criticized a Palestinian action against Israel.

Continued Fighting. The Fatah terrorist raid precipitated within days a massive Israeli invasion of southern Lebanon. Fighting between Israeli troops and various Palestinian commando groups continued until the end of March, when Arafat agreed to a United Nations cease-fire, supervised by the U.N. Interim Force in Lebanon (UNIFIL). Nevertheless, fighting continued throughout the year between Palestinians and the Christian militia, which demanded the removal of all PLO forces from Lebanon.

Sporadic terrorist attacks by PLO groups on Israelis culminated on Nov. 19, the first anniversary of Sadat's Jerusalem visit, in a series of bombings and attempted bombings at several places in Israel. Demonstrations by Palestinian youths in the West Bank against the peace talks erupted periodically during 1978 with support and backing from the PLO.

Year-end Developments. In December a PLO offi-

cial in Paris said that his organization was prepared to give de facto recognition to Israel and to cease hostile acts against it if a Palestinian state could be created on the West Bank and in the Gaza Strip. Two days later, however, Palestinian guerrillas fired rockets at an Israeli town in retaliation for Israeli air attacks on their positions. These were the first overt military actions in at least three months, and it appeared that the Palestinian guerrillas were renewing their military efforts.

See ARAB LEAGUE; MIDDLE EAST; and articles on individual countries mentioned. D.P.

PANAMA. Ratification of two new Panama Canal treaties and the inauguration of a new president were the political high points of 1978 in Panama. **Politics.** On June 16 in the city of Panamá, after fourteen years of negotiation, Panamanian head of government Brig. Gen. Omar Torrijos Herrera and U.S. President Jimmy Carter exchanged instruments of ratification of two new treaties governing the future of the Panama Canal. They replaced the original document of 1903, which gave the United States perpetual control of the waterway it had built. The first treaty granted ownership of the canal to Panama in the year 2000 and guaranteed its subsequent neutrality, with the reservation that the U.S. could send in troops if operations were disturbed. The second provided for the gradual takeover of the canal's operations and defense by Panama, with a modified reservation that U.S. troops protecting the canal were not to intervene in Panama's internal affairs.

Debate on the treaties had been intense in both countries. Panamanians generally objected to the reservations; in the U.S. many people felt that the treaties gave away sovereign U.S. territory. Torrijos

Arnulfo Arias, three-times-deposed president of Panama (1941, 1951, 1968), arrives in Panamá from Miami on June 10. Returning after almost ten years in exile, Arias was greeted by a crowd of more than 2500 enthusiastic supporters.

The new president of Panama, 38-year-old Arístides Royo (left), is sworn into office by Victor Corrales Nunez, president of the National Assembly. The ceremony took place on Oct. 11.

strongly supported the treaties in hopes that they would bolster his sagging popularity.

Torrijos, who had ruled Panama since 1968 when a military coup had ousted President Arnulfo Arias Madrid, faced another challenge when the former president returned from exile on June 10. Arias was wildly cheered by the people as he rejected the treaties as a setback to Panamanian sovereignty and accused the Torrijos government of treason. In October, Torrijos gave up his political office, as provided by the 1972 constitution. On his recommendation the National Assembly elected Education Minister Arístides Royo, a 38-year-old lawyer, to serve as president, at the same time increasing his powers. In December it was reported that Torrijos had virtually disappeared from public view, leaving the government in the hands of young technocrats, but he retained command of the National Guard and thus ultimate authority.

The Economy. Panama continued in deep economic recession. Unemployment, with a national average of 12 percent, reached 15 percent in the city of Panamá and 22 percent in Colón. The rate of inflation stood at 11 percent. Only Panama's new income from canal tolls was expected to improve the situation.

See STATISTICS OF THE WORLD.   J.N.G.

PAPUA NEW GUINEA. See STATISTICS OF THE WORLD.

PARAGUAY. Gen. Alfredo Stroessner was reelected to a sixth term as president of Paraguay on Feb. 12, 1978. In office since a bloodless military coup in 1954, he had ruled longer than any other Latin American dictator. (The man whom Stroessner overthrew, Federico Chaves, died in Asunción on April 24; he was 97.) As usual, Stroessner won easily, with more than 89 percent of the vote. Opposition leaders had had little opportunity to publicize their views; signs proclaiming "Peace, work, well-being with Stroessner" were plastered throughout the capital, while those advertising opposition candidates were quickly removed by public works crews. The Opposition could not hold rallies because gatherings of more than three people had been declared illegal. Carlos Pastore, a leader of the opposition Liberal Party, was expelled from the country for organizing opposition elements.

Stroessner originally agreed, under pressure from the United States, to allow the Organization of American States (OAS) to investigate alleged violations of human rights in Paraguay. But in July, when the OAS called on Paraguay to eliminate such abuses, the government denied them. On July 7, when opposition leader Domingo Laino of the Authentic Radical Liberal Party returned from testifying against the Stroessner government before the OAS meeting in Washington, D.C., he was arrested. He was subsequently released, but kept under surveillance.

On the economic front, foreign trade grew rapidly. A deficiency in exports was made up by capital inflow in connection with joint hydroelectric projects between Paraguay and Argentina and Brazil.

See STATISTICS OF THE WORLD.   J.N.G.

PENNSYLVANIA. See STATISTICS OF THE WORLD.

PEOPLE IN THE NEWS

The news in 1978 was made not only by people (three men in a balloon, one man with a dogsled), but by objects (a group of flesh-colored statues, a prescription for drugs) and by places (the wedding palace in Moscow, the Gator Bowl in Florida).

When everything has been said, the subject that still interests people the most is other people. Again in 1978 the headlines chronicled human achievements and failures, joys and sorrows, courage or tragedy. On the following pages is a sampling of the names that made news during the year. Detailed individual biographies of some of the year's more significant figures appear at the end of the article.

Proximity to Presidential power inevitably attracts attention. This principle applied most especially to White House aide **Hamilton Jordan,** who continued to have his problems with the capital's gossip columnists in 1978. Among his well-chronicled escapades was an episode in February in which Jordan (who had separated from his wife, **Nancy**) was supposed to have spat on a woman in a trendy Washington (D.C.) bar. The White House promptly marshaled a thirty-three-page rebuttal denying that the incident had occurred. This unprecedented response, among other things, signaled that Jordan's standing as chief political strategist and the "strong right arm of Carter" remained unimpaired in Presidential eyes.

Another aide and longtime chum of **President Jimmy Carter** fared less well. **Peter G. Bourne,** the White House adviser on health and drug issues, was himself linked to a police investigation into a drug prescription that bore a fictitious name. The British-born physician admitted he wrote the prescription for a White House staff member but insisted he inserted the made-up name solely to protect the staffer's privacy. The resulting publicity forced Bourne's resignation, although he was spared legal prosecution on the grounds that his act did not constitute criminal intent.

The tangled financial affairs of former Budget Director **Thomas Bertram ("Bert") Lance** continued to claim the attention of government investigators and the press. Lance settled two Securities and Exchange Commission complaints against him in the spring by neither admitting nor denying any improprieties but by promising to discontinue the practices under question. In October,

White House political adviser Hamilton Jordan was often in the news in 1978. Here he is trying out his backhand at a benefit celebrity tennis tournament in Arlington, Va., in February.

Peter G. Bourne, White House health adviser, was forced to resign in July when it was disclosed that he had written a fraudulent drug prescription for an aide, falsifying her name. Bourne then raised eyebrows by charging that there was a "high incidence" of marijuana use among White House staff members.

287

Henry Winkler, who as Arthur Fonzarelli ("The Fonz") was one of the most popular television performers of 1978, married Stacey Weitzman in New York City on May 5.

Debra Glenn (left), a 19-year-old university student, married singer Donny Osmond, 20, in Salt Lake City on May 8. Here the bride and groom celebrate with Donny's sister Marie and actor Dirk Benedict—who attracted considerable attention on his own part during the year, as a star of television's Battlestar Galactica.

David and Julie Eisenhower show off their new baby girl as they leave the hospital in San Clemente, Calif. Jennie, born Aug. 15, was the first grandchild of former President Richard M. Nixon.

A radiant Betty Ford shows off her new face in October, three weeks after she underwent cosmetic surgery. The 60-year-old wife of former President Gerald R. Ford was presenting an award from the American National Theatre and Academy to actor-dancer Fred Astaire (left).

during a grand jury investigation of Lance's banking activities in Georgia and bank loans to the Carter peanut business, the President's younger brother, **Billy Carter,** invoked the Fifth Amendment "a few times." At year's end, a Justice Department probe of Lance was still under way.

The President's second son, **Chip Carter,** 28, and his wife, **Caron,** 27, separated in November after five years of marriage; they had one son. Family confidants said that while Chip enjoyed the White House limelight, Caron found it uncomfortable. In December Chip's brother, **John Carter,** 1, and his wife, **Judy,** 28, presented **Jimmy** and **Rosalynn Carter** with their third grandchild and first granddaughter; her name: **Sarah Rosemary.**

Richard and **Pat Nixon** also became grandparents. In August **Julie Nixon Eisenhower** and husband **David** became the parents of the Nixons' first grandchild, a girl. Young **Jennie Eisenhower** has a unique distinction: A great-grandfather on her paternal side and a grandfather on her maternal side were both U.S. Presidents.

Former First Lady **Betty Ford** entered the U.S. Naval Hospital at Long Beach, Calif., in April for treatment of drug dependence induced by arthritic pains. Later she also forthrightly told of her problem with alcohol. In September, apparently fully recovered, she made news again by undergoing cosmetic surgery. "I'm 60," she explained, "and I wanted a new face to go along with my beautiful new life."

Gerald and Betty **Ford**'s only daughter, **Susan,** 21, was making a new life for herself as well. A freelance photographer, she announced her engagement in October to **Charles Frederick Vance,** 37, a Secret Service agent. They met in 1977 when Vance was assigned to guard the Ford family. By coincidence, **Patricia Hearst,** 24, the kidnapped newspaper heiress who was later convicted of taking part in a San Francisco bank robbery, announced her engagement to her bodyguard, San Francisco policeman **Bernard Shaw,** 30. Shaw had moonlighted on the Hearst security detail while Patty was out on bail. Returned to prison in May when her appeals were exhausted, she hoped for a Presidential commutation of her seven-year sen-

Having lost an appeal of her 1976 bank robbery conviction, newspaper heiress Patricia Hearst arrives at the federal prison in Pleasanton, Calif., on May 15 to resume serving a seven-year term. She is accompanied by her bodyguard and fiancé, Bernard Shaw.

tence so that she would be free in time for a wedding on Valentine's Day, 1979.

Two royal weddings in June caught the fancy of much of the world. A brief Muslim ceremony in Amman, Jordan, united **King Hussein,** 42, with his American-born fourth wife **Elizabeth (Lisa) Halaby,** 26. The bride, a graduate of Princeton and the daughter of former Pan Am president Najeeb Halaby, would henceforth be addressed as **Queen Noor al-Hussein** ("Light of Hussein"). Both civil and religious ceremonies were held to celebrate the marriage of **Princess Caroline** of Monaco, 21, to commoner **Philippe Junot,** 38, a self-described merchant banker who is the son of a deputy mayor of Paris. The ruling Grimaldis, **Prince Rainier** and **Princess Grace,** were said to be less than enthralled with Junot's bon vivant past, but Their Serene Highnesses acknowledged: "We wish above all for her happiness."

A ceremony at Moscow's state wedding palace in August was determinedly proletarian (fee: about $2.15) although the bride was **Christina Onassis,** 27, heiress to a $500,000,000 Greek shipping empire founded by her late father, **Aristotle Onassis.** Christina was wed to **Sergei Kauzov,** 37, once connected with the Soviet merchant marine. "I'm very adaptable," insisted Christina, who was twice previously married and divorced, but few were convinced that this restless, strong-willed woman was cut out to be a Moscow housewife.

On the other side of the marital ledger, there

On Aug. 1, Greek shipping heiress Christina Onassis accepts a wedding band from Sergei Kauzov, an unemployed Soviet citizen, at their surprise marriage in Moscow. The bride later returned to Greece alone, sparking rumors of a divorce.

Lord Snowden and his new bride, the Countess of Snowden. Antony Armstrong-Jones and the former Lucy Lindsay-Hogg were photographed in London after their civil marriage ceremony on Dec. 15. Snowden had ended his eighteen-year marriage to Princess Margaret seven months earlier.

were several notable divorces. Great Britain's **Princess Margaret** and her husband, **Antony Armstrong-Jones (Lord Snowden),** formally dissolved their union after eighteen years of marriage and two years of legal separation. Theirs was the first open split involving an immediate member of the British royal family since Henry VIII divorced Anne of Cleves in 1540. Margaret's friendship with **Roddy Llewellyn,** an aspiring rock singer who, at 30, was seventeen years her junior, provoked criticism from the British Parliament, press, and public. Snowden, an accomplished photographer, was remarried in December to television researcher **Lucy Lindsay-Hogg,** 37. They had met four years earlier in Australia when they worked together on a BBC documentary film.

The divorce of Alabama's Gov. **George Wallace** and his second wife, **Cornelia,** became final, ironically, on their seventh wedding anniversary. Confined to a wheelchair since an assassination attempt in 1972, Wallace, the onetime arch segregationist and four-time Presidential candidate, decided against running for a Senate seat in May. That, in effect, spelled the finish to his active political career.

Trouble came in many forms during the year. For **David W. Marston,** a 35-year-old U.S. attorney in Philadelphia and a Republican, it took the form of a discharge from his office in January. Marston's firing caused the Carter administration considerable embarrassment, since he was in th

Arkady N. Shevchenko, United Nations Under Secretary-General, at a U.N. meeting shortly before his defection to the U.S. in April. Shevchenko, the highest-ranking Soviet diplomat ever to defect, celebrated his new freedom by spending $40,000 on a woman from a Washington, D.C., escort service.

midst of an investigation of Democratic politicians—including Pennsylvania Congressmen **Joshua Eilberg** and **Daniel Flood,** both of whom were later indicted. The Administration also had some difficulty reconciling Marston's fate with Carter's earlier pledge to appoint federal judges and prosecutors on the basis of merit, not politics. Marston later made a run for the GOP nomination in Pennsylvania's gubernatorial election but wound up a distant fourth in the May primary.

When United Nations Under Secretary-General **Arkady Shevchenko,** the highest-ranking Soviet in the U.N. Secretariat, received a summons from Moscow early in the year to return home, his response was to drop out of sight. Later, through his lawyer, he announced that he was defecting to the West, owing to "differences with my government." Speculations that Shevchenko was talking to the Central Intelligence Agency were fanned in October when a certain **Judith Taylor Chavez,** employed by a Washington "escort service," alleged that Shevchenko had plied her with $40,000 in cash and gifts. The mysterious Russian emerged from hiding just long enough to explain that the money came from his U.N. severance pay and to denounce the affair as a "squalid little episode."

For a young sheikh from Saudi Arabia, the problem was a matter of taste. His California neighbors were aghast when **Sheikh Mohammad al-Fassi,** 23, and his 19-year-old wife, **Dena,** had their Beverly Hills mansion painted a pale lime green and decorated the grounds with plastic plants and skin-toned statues. To set the neighbors at ease, the sheikh's father had them over for a housewarming in June. But the neighbors' reactions to such improvements as a bathroom deco-

rated with pornographic posters went unrecorded.

Over 33 seasons, the last 28 of them at Ohio State, coach **Woody Hayes** led his teams to 205 victories, the fourth best record in college football history. But Woody also suffered 61 defeats (plus 10 ties), none of them gladly. The tantrum-prone coach usually took out his anger at reporters, cameramen, game officials, and yard markers, but at the Gator Bowl in Florida in December he punched an opposing Clemson player. Living legend or not, Hayes was fired one day later.

Other athletic greats made no-less emotional but far more decorous exits. All over the National Basketball Association circuit, there were tearful farewells for Boston forward **John ("Hondo") Havlicek,** 37, who thrilled the fans with his race-horse style of play. Over 16 seasons, he appeared in a league-record 1270 games, pumped in 26,395 points (third best ever), and recorded 6114 assists (sixth best). In his emotional finale at the Boston Garden in April, his green Number 17 jersey was permanently retired and placed on display alongside those of other former Celtic stars.

Hockey's two most famous "Bobbys" hung up their skates within a week of each other in October and November. **Bobby Hull,** 39, who played 14 seasons with the Chicago Black Hawks of the National Hockey League and 6 with the Winnipeg Jets of the World Hockey Association, posted a combined 1012 goal total that was the second highest in hockey history. He was three times the NHL's scoring champ and twice the most valuable player in the two leagues. Also a retiree was **Bobby Orr,** who all but revolutionized rink strategy as a rushing defenseman for the Boston Bruins, the first at his position ever to lead the league in scoring. He was also the NHL's most valuable player three times and an eight-time all star. Despite two courageous attempts at a comeback with the Black Hawks, Orr, at the age of 30, yielded to a game-ravaged knee.

Leg problems also ended the racing career of **Forego,** three times named horse of the year. The 8-year-old gelding was one of the most versatile thoroughbreds of all times, able to win running long races or short and under a variety of weights and track conditions. Forego's career winnings of $1,938,957 were second only to those collected by **Kelso.**

In the category of sentimental comebacks, however, the return of 39-year-old pitcher **Jim Bouton** was one for the memory. After an absence from the big leagues of eight years (spent as a successful author and television sports reporter), Bouton had long since lost the fastball that made him a 21-game winner for the New York Yankees

PEOPLE IN THE NEWS

On July 26, Pete Rose of the Cincinnati Reds acknowledges the cheers of the crowd after setting a new National League modern record for consecutive games with base hits. Rose set another record in December, when he became the highest paid athlete in history.

For individual heroics, however, the baseball season belonged to Cincinnati Reds third baseman **Pete Rose.** During a six-week stretch of the season, he kept alive a hitting streak that passed Tommy Holmes's "modern" National League record of 37 games (set in 1945) and George Sisler's American League mark of 41 (1922), finally tying Willie Keeler's pre-1900 National League record of 44. Rose's string ran out a dozen games short of **Joe DiMaggio**'s all-time major-league record of 56, but Rose's market value as a postseason free agent soared. The Philadelphia Phillies ultimately won the spirited bidding for his services with a contract estimated to be worth $3,200,000 to $3,500,000 over four years. For the moment at least, the star nicknamed "Charlie Hustle" reigned as America's highest-paid team athlete.

Money and earnings were not the main concerns of balloonists **Ben Abruzzo, Max Anderson,** and **Larry Newman.** Following in the "footsteps of Lindbergh," more or less, the trio from Albuquerque, N.Mex., lifted off silently from Presque Isle, Maine, on Aug. 11. More than 137 hr. and 3233 mi. later, they landed in a wheat field about 60 mi.

On Aug. 17 three American adventurers touch down about 60 mi. outside Paris, completing the first successful transatlantic crossing in a manned balloon. It took Ben Abruzzo, Max Anderson, and Larry Newman six days to make the 3233 mi. trip in the helium-filled "Double Eagle II."

in 1963 (plus 18 more wins and 2 World Series victories in 1964). But in the pursuit of a personal dream, his hopes resting on an unpredictable knuckleball, Bouton worked his way back through an assortment of minor-league clubs until September, when he was given a chance to pitch for the Atlanta Braves. To the cheers of fans and the sneers of some opposing players, he posted a credible 1–1 won-lost mark to prove to his satisfaction that "I belong here." He then re-retired from baseball to return to television broadcasting.

Group-comeback-of-the-year honor went to the 1978 Yankees, although at midseason the team seemed bent on self-destruction. First, excitable manager **Billy Martin** suspended temperamental star outfielder **Reggie Jackson** for bunting against orders. Then, Martin made unkind remarks about feisty owner **George Steinbrenner,** resulting in Martin's weeping resignation. He was replaced by unflappable pitching coach **Bob Lemon.** But a week later Steinbrenner announced that Martin would return to manage the Yankees in 1980. Despite all the confusion, the Yanks pulled from 14 games back to tie Boston at the end of the season, then won the playoff, defeated Kansas City for the American League pennant, and finally triumphed over the Los Angeles Dodgers in the World Series.

292

northwest of Paris. Enroute they had braved high-altitude cold and dizzying plunges toward the ocean, but they succeeded where at least seventeen previous attempts at transatlantic balloon crossing had failed. The only casualty was their eleven-story-tall helium balloon, named "Double Eagle II," which was nearly torn apart by souvenir hunters after the intrepid trio had landed.

Open-ocean marathon swimmers also endured pain and exhaustion but achieved far less happy results. The most publicized of their attempts was that of 28-year-old **Diana Nyad.** She attempted to swim from Cuba to Florida in August. But high seas and waves created by her own shark-protection cage, jellyfish attacks, and faulty navigation by her crew (which had her swimming in circles) all conspired against her. She was in the water for more than 41 hr., but she covered only about half the necessary distance. On the same August day, 46-year-old **Stella Taylor** fell short by only some 10 mi. in her attempt to swim from the Bahamas to Florida. In a repeat attempt in October, she set a new endurance record of 51 hr. in the water but was again frustrated by adverse currents about 20 mi. from her goal. "I won't try this again this

Indiana State University student Kurt Thomas practices for the World Gymnastics Championships, held in October at Strasbourg, France. Thomas won a gold medal in floor exercises while leading the U.S. men's team to its best performance—fourth place—in the nineteen-year history of the event.

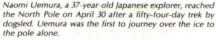

Naomi Uemura, a 37-year-old Japanese explorer, reached the North Pole on April 30 after a fifty-four-day trek by dogsled. Uemura was the first to journey over the ice to the pole alone.

way," said Taylor, a former nun. "Maybe next time from the Keys to the Bahamas."

As a lonely traveler, Japan's **Naomi Uemura** could hardly be topped. On April 30 the veteran explorer completed history's first solo run to the North Pole, crossing 600 mi. of ice floes by dogsled in 54 days. Then, airlifted to the northernmost tip of Greenland, he became the first to trek the 1875 mi. to Greenland's southernmost tip. Uemura had previously sledded 7500 mi. from Greenland to Alaska and had made solo conquests of the highest peaks on four continents. Why always alone? "I hate testing myself in front of others," he explained.

On the tennis court, a newcomer to watch was a slim, lanky (6-ft.-tall) Maryland high school student named **Pam Shriver.** At 16 and in her first year in top-level tennis competition, Pam became the youngest player ever to advance to the finals of the prestigious U.S. Open Tournament (at which point she lost to **Chris Evert**). In gymnastics, one of the finest young performers in recent memory was Indiana State University senior **Kurt Thomas,** 22, who won a gold medal in the floor exercise at the World Gymnastics Championships in October. The creator of a whirling maneuver

World chess champion Anatoly Karpov faces challenger Viktor Korchnoi during their grueling, three-month-long match in Baguio, the Philippines. In the psychological duel—that almost became an ideological duel—the Soviet champion, an icy-nerved "chess robot," outlasted the temperamental Korchnoi, a Soviet defector, to retain his crown. The final score on Oct. 17 was 6 wins to 5, with 21 draws.

It was Steve Martin's year. The popular comedian appeared frequently on television—with Johnny Carson, on Saturday Night Live, and on his own special. He also made the cover of Newsweek magazine. And he received a Grammy award (above) for his album Let's Get Small.

on the pommel horse called the "Thomas flair," he headed a talented contingent of gymnasts who, for the first time in a half century, provided a ray of hope for medal-winning performances by Americans in that sport at future Olympic Games.

Finally, the title of fastest finisher of the year could well have gone to **Darrel McHargue,** 24. On the last day of the year, the Oklahoma-born California jockey booted home three winners at Santa Anita, boosting the winnings of his mounts to a record $6,188,353 in 1978, or exactly $36,603 more than the previous high, set by **Steve Cauthen** in 1977. To add to McHargue's laurels, he was chosen jockey of the year.

ALI, MUHAMMAD

World Boxing Association heavyweight champion, born Jan. 18, 1942, in Louisville, Ky. Nearing the end of his eventful ring career, Ali fought only twice in 1978, but both bouts were memorable. In February an Ali noticeably slowed by age lost a split decision to Leon Spinks (see below) in Las Vegas. Yet seven months later, in a tactical if not artistic masterpiece, he regained his title in a unanimous decision over Spinks in New Orleans. Ali thus became the first fighter in history to win the heavyweight championship three times.

In or out of the ring his record earnings (more than $50,000,000 over his career) and irrepressible personality kept him among the world's most readily recognized faces. During a visit to the Soviet Union in June, he and Soviet President Leonid I. Brezhnev spent 35 minutes exchanging verbal bouquets. Ali often talked of being weary of the ring but refused any outright announcement of retirement. Alternatives included acting (he was at work late in the year on a movie called Freedom Road being filmed in Mississippi).

BAKER, HOWARD H(ENRY), JR.

Minority leader of the U.S. Senate, born Nov. 15, 1925, in Huntsville, Tenn. Although a consistent Republican critic of the Democratic Administration, Baker supported the Panama Canal treaties and was instrumental in getting the Senate to ratify them in March and April. His stance nettled GOP conservatives, and he needed a solid win in his bid for reelection to a third term as Senator from Tennessee to keep alive his rumored 1980 Presidential hopes. In November he turned back Democratic challenger Jane Eskind with nearly 60 percent of the vote, approximately the victory margin he had expected.

A law graduate of the University of Tennessee and the son of a seven-term Congressman, he became the first popularly elected Republican Senator in his state's history in 1967. Reelected in 1972, he assumed the minority leadership. He gained national prominence during the Watergate inves-

Senators Howard H. Baker, Jr. (R, Tenn.; left), and Robert C. Byrd (D, W.Va.) confer before a roll-call vote. Rivals on the Senate floor, the two party leaders cooperated on several foreign policy issues during the year.

tigations, in which he was an early critic of the Nixon administration. Baker's Senate record pegged him as "a classical moderate" whose style was less flamboyant but steadier than that of the late Sen. Everett M. Dirksen of Illinois, Baker's father-in-law and a predecessor as minority leader.

BEGIN, MENACHEM

Prime Minister of Israel and co-winner of the 1978 Nobel Peace Prize, born July 31, 1913, in Brest Litovsk (now Brest), Russia. His tenacious reluctance to give up occupied territories without full assurances of peace and security for Israel elicited both admiration and exasperation. It led to strains in Israeli relations with its primary ally, the United States, over such issues as Israeli settlements in Sinai and on the West Bank of the Jordan River. Begin's meeting in Washington, D.C., with Jimmy Carter in March was termed by the President a "failure." Israeli-Egyptian peace negotiations continued on a roller-coaster path until Begin and Egyptian President Anwar el-Sadat (see below), assisted by Carter's tireless mediation, reached the basis for a draft accord at the historic Camp David, Md., summit in September. The initial euphoria, however, gave way to a renewed stalemate, punctuated by Jerusalem's complaint of a Carter administration tilt toward Cairo.

In December, Begin traveled to Oslo, Norway, to accept the Nobel Peace Prize that he shared with Sadat and pledged his continued efforts for peace in the Middle East. Despite a history of heart problems and a brief hospitalization in late September for fatigue, doctors announced the prime minister's health "excellent."

BELL, GRIFFIN B(OYETTE)

U.S. Attorney General, born Oct. 31, 1918, in Americus, Ga. Dealing with difficult issues left over from an earlier era, Bell walked a political tightrope during 1978 while drawing fire from both liberals and conservatives. In January the attorney general was criticized for firing Republican U.S. Attorney David Marston of Philadelphia, who was then investigating corruption charges against Pennsylvania Democrats. In April the Justice Department indicted three former high officials of the Federal Bureau of Investigation (FBI) on charges connected with illegal break-ins and searches conducted during the early 1970's. But Bell's refusal in July to surrender files on FBI informers led to his being cited for contempt of court by a federal district judge in New York City—the first such incident in history involving a chief U.S. law officer (a higher court stayed the citation, pending appeal).

Known for his practicality and candor, Bell still preferred to be addressed as "Judge," reflecting his fifteen-year service on the bench of the Georgia Court of Appeals. He was credited with innovative reforms in his reorganization of the Justice Department.

Attorney General Griffin B. Bell in a casual moment at the Department of Justice.

PEOPLE IN THE NEWS

BREZHNEV, LEONID I(LYICH)
President of the Presidium of the Supreme Soviet and General Secretary of the Soviet Communist Party, born Dec. 19, 1906, in Kamenskoye. A cooling of East-West relations contributed to the delay in completing a pact limiting strategic arms in 1978 and the postponement of his anticipated visit to the U.S. For his part, Brezhnev defended Soviet involvement in the affairs of African nations, objected to U.S. criticism of the trials of Soviet dissidents, and warned the North Atlantic Treaty Organization against deployment of the high-radiation neutron bomb, which he said the Soviets had tested but never produced. His worries over Sino-Soviet relations were underscored by a Siberian tour in March. He warned the West "not to play the China card" against Moscow and expressed fear of an anti-Soviet Sino-U.S. alliance. In greeting many visiting U.S. political and business leaders in Moscow, he argued for stronger trade ties and "most favored nation" status for the U.S.S.R.

Brezhnev's unsteady demeanor during a visit to West Germany in May renewed speculations of his failing health. In November he announced a record 1978 grain harvest but lashed out at Soviet farm managers for "inefficiencies."

BROWN, HAROLD
U.S. Secretary of Defense, born Sept. 19, 1927, in New York City. His annual defense posture statement to Congress in January urged stepped-up defense spending to keep pace with Soviet military efforts. Brown also assured Asian allies that the U.S. would "maintain and strengthen" its military commitments in their area. In December he was reported to be working on recommendations for mobile basing of intercontinental ballistic missiles to make the missiles less vulnerable to an enemy first strike.

The first scientist to serve as civilian head of the Pentagon, Brown was a prodigy who graduated from high school at 15 and earned a PH.D. in physics from Columbia University at 21 (in 1949). Much of his career had been in the defense establishment, including stints as Pentagon research chief (1961–65) and Air Force secretary (1965–69). Described as "neither a hawk nor dove, but a pragmatist with a world view" (he was a longtime proponent of arms control), Brown was president of the California Institute of Technology prior to joining the cabinet in January, 1977.

BRZEZINSKI, ZBIGNIEW
National security adviser to the President of the U.S., born March 28, 1928, in Warsaw, Poland. He became more prominent in 1978 as the U.S. took a foreign policy course that he helped to chart— away from the Soviet Union and toward improved relations with the People's Republic of China. Early in the year his warning that agreement on a strategic arms limitation treaty could be set back by Soviet adventurism in Africa appeared at odds with the position of Secretary of State Cyrus R. Vance (see below), who advocated no linkage between the two developments. Brzezinski's position reinforced his image as a hard-liner toward the Soviets, a charge he refuted as an "oversimplification." In any event, the leaders of China clearly viewed him in that light on his five-day Asian visit in May, during which he stopped in Tokyo and Seoul as well as Peking. Brzezinski set forth the view that a "strong and secure China" served U.S. interests, and was cred-

Zbigniew Brzezinski poses with touring Chinese sailors on the Great Wall of China in May. By Dec. 15, Brzezinski's private contacts had brought about a historic agreement to establish full U.S.-Chinese diplomatic ties.

Secretary of Defense Harold Brown, shown reviewing a West German honor guard, urged a buildup of NATO forces in Europe.

296

PEOPLE IN THE NEWS

ited with the final secret negotiations that led to agreement in December on formal diplomatic recognition between Washington and Peking.

BYRD, ROBERT C(ARLYLE)

Senate majority leader, born Nov. 20, 1917, in North Wilkesboro, N.C. The skillful leadership of the Democratic Senator from West Virginia was a key in Senate approval of the Panama Canal treaties in March and April and of Middle Eastern warplane sales in May. A flurry of preadjournment legislative activity under Byrd's direction also brought passage of Administration-sponsored energy policy and civil service reform bills.

An orphan reared in bleak poverty by an uncle in West Virginia, Byrd learned early to fend for himself. His gifts as a Baptist lay preacher and fiddler brought him local fame and took him first into West Virginia politics, then to the U.S. Congress in 1952. Elected a U.S. Senator in 1958, he became majority leader in 1977. He went to Washington with the reputation of being a rustic—even racist—conservative but moved steadily over the years toward the political middle. Sober in manner and intensely dedicated to his job, he stood as a defender of the Senate's power and independence. Of his relations with the Carter White House, he said: "I am the President's friend, but not his man."

CALIFANO, JOSEPH A(NTHONY), JR.

U.S. Secretary of Health, Education, and Welfare (HEW), born May 15, 1931, in New York City. A hard-driving lawyer and longtime social activist, he was said to have been at "the fulcrum of almost every major domestic policy issue" during 1978.

In January Califano, himself a reformed smoker, announced a government antismoking campaign aimed at breaking the habit among an estimated 53,000,000 Americans. Proposals included a smoking ban on airliners and in public areas of government buildings, a hike in tobacco taxes, and more

Joseph A. Califano, Jr., secretary of health, education, and welfare, briefs newsmen on the Administration's national health insurance plan in July.

British Prime Minister James Callaghan defends his economic policy at a Labour Party conference in Blackpool in October.

stringent labeling requirements. The failure of these proposals to become law, as well as continuing federal subsidies to tobacco farmers, made some antismoking lobbyists scornful of Califano's campaign. Other key issues before him during the year included plans for welfare reform and a national health insurance program. In December HEW issued guidelines forbidding sex discrimination in intercollegiate athletics. Despite the inherently controversial nature of his job, Califano's relations with the White House were termed "solid."

CALLAGHAN, (LEONARD) JAMES

Prime Minister of Great Britain, born March 27, 1912, in Portsmouth. His minority Labour government was hard pressed to remain in power through 1978. Britain's small but pivotal Liberal Party delegation in the House of Commons announced that after July it would end its pact to support Labour in votes of confidence. Callaghan survived such a vote in June, although the margin, 287 to 282, was the narrowest since he took office. With the help of small Scottish and Welsh nationalist parties, Callaghan's Labourites won two more close votes of confidence in November and December. Opposition attacks were aimed at the government's economic measures, designed to stimulate the economy and still hold inflation below 10 percent. Callaghan's call to limit wage boosts to 5 percent was denounced even by his own party at Labour's annual Blackpool Conference in October. The prime minister, however, confounded those who expected general elections in the autumn by postponing the vote until 1979.

297

PEOPLE IN THE NEWS

Described as "solid if cautious" and usually unflappable, "Sunny Jim" Callaghan first entered Parliament in 1945. He served in a variety of cabinet posts before rising to prime minister on the sudden resignation of Harold Wilson in 1976.

CARTER, JAMES EARL, JR.
See PRESIDENT OF THE UNITED STATES.

FORD, GERALD R(UDOLPH)
Former President of the U.S., born July 14, 1913, in Omaha, Nebr. The Fords moved into their new golf course home at Rancho Mirage, near Palm Springs, Calif., early in 1978. But the head of the household was often on the road, speaking at Republican fund raisers, lecturing on campuses, and making television appearances. During the fall election campaign, he stumped through thirty states on behalf of GOP candidates. Although sharply critical of Carter administration economic policies, the former President threw the weight of his prestige behind Carter by supporting the Panama Canal treaties, the lifting of the embargo on arms sales to Turkey, and the extension of formal diplomatic recognition to the People's Republic of China. His hectic public schedule inevitably fueled speculation that he hoped to make another run for the Presidency in 1980.

GISCARD D'ESTAING, VALÉRY
President of France, born Feb. 2, 1926, in Koblenz in the then French-occupied Rhineland. Although theoretically aloof from France's national legislative elections in March, he nonetheless emerged as the big winner. His ruling Center-Right Union of French Democrats turned back the challenge of a shaky Socialist-Communist coalition and, at the

French President Valéry Giscard d'Estaing and his wife emerge from a polling place after voting in national elections on March 12.

298

same time, reduced pressures from the Gaullist Right. Giscard also enjoyed close personal ties with West German Chancellor Helmut Schmidt (see below). Together, the leaders of Western Europe's two strongest economic powers took the lead in formulating a new monetary system for the European Communities.

At the midpoint of his seven-year presidential term, Giscard was viewed by many as the most stable and durable leader within the Western alliance. One manifestation of his leadership was his rapid reaction in dealing with African problems. In May, with Belgian and U.S. cooperation, he dispatched French Foreign Legionnaires on a dramatic mission to Zaire to rescue foreigners trapped during an invasion of Shaba region by secessionists based in Angola. His travels during the year took him to Spain, Portugal, the Ivory Coast, West Germany, and Brazil, and he played host to a visiting U.S. President Jimmy Carter in January.

HARRIS, PATRICIA R(OBERTS)
U.S. Secretary of Housing and Urban Development (HUD), born May 31, 1924, in Mattoon, Ill. She was the first black woman to head HUD and the only Black in the 1978 cabinet. She directed an interagency group that formulated the Administration's $2.6 billion National Urban Policy proposed by the President in March. In April HUD announced a $400,000,000 program to promote private construction projects in economically distressed cities.

The daughter of a Pullman car waiter, Harris said she always reacted "furiously" to discrimination. An honor graduate of Howard University (1945) and the George Washington University Law School (1960), she was the first black woman to serve as a U.S. ambassador (to Luxembourg in 1965-67). Although criticized for her lack of experience in urban affairs at the time of her cabinet appointment in January, 1977, the secretary emerged as an outspoken advocate for urban minorities and a vigorous defender of HUD's jurisdictions.

HUA KUO-FENG
Chairman of the Chinese Communist Party and Premier of the People's Republic of China, born about 1920 in Shansi Province. Although he held the top posts in party and government, Hua often gave the impression in 1978 of being a leader-in training.

Hua's first-ever trip abroad in May—to neighboring North Korea—seemed as much designed to acclimate him to foreign travel as for conducting diplomatic business. A longer trip followed in August to Rumania, Yugoslavia, and Iran, during which Hua launched verbal attacks against th

Seated on the papal throne, John Paul II listens intently during an audience for cardinals at the Vatican on Oct. 18, two days after his election.

Soviet Union. The travels of Hua enhanced his leadership stature, but his relationship with his nominal subordinate, First Deputy Premier Teng Hsiao-ping (see below), remained a puzzle. Peking wall posters blossomed late in the year with startling criticism of the late Chairman Mao Tse-tung, which some observers interpreted as criticism of Hua as Mao's chosen successor. But Hua's appearance in an unprecedented news conference in December to announce the agreement to establish formal diplomatic relations with the U.S. served as a sign of unity in China's leadership. Seventeen years younger than Teng, Hua probably had time enough to emerge as China's leader in fact as well as in titles. Meanwhile, a few details about the chairman's personal life emerged during the year. According to official Chinese press reports, his real name was Su Chu and he had a wife and four children.

JOHN PAUL II

Pope of the Roman Catholic Church, born May 18, 1920, in Wadowice, Poland. The death of Pope Paul VI in August followed by the death of his successor, Pope John Paul I, in September (see OBITUARIES) shocked the world. But sadness gave way to surprise when Poland's Cardinal Karol Vojtyła, archbishop of Cracow, ascended the papal throne in October as Pope John Paul II. He became the first non-Italian Pope since 1522, the first from Poland or any other Eastern European nation, and the first from a country under a Communist government. In the first months of his reign, John Paul II impressed many with the warmth of his personality (often expressed in a joyous plunging into crowds to greet the faithful) and his vigor (favorite sports: skiing and canoeing). Already a widely traveled man—and fluent in seven languages—he planned to continue traveling extensively as pope.

In his youth a laborer in a stone quarry and a chemical factory worker, he risked his life in the Polish resistance movement during the Nazi occupation in World War II and prepared for the priesthood at a clandestinely operated seminary. Ordained in 1946, he taught ethics at the Catholic University of Lublin and moved up the ranks of the church, receiving a cardinal's red hat in 1967. A resilient foe of Communism, he was regarded as a conservative on theological issues.

KREPS, JUANITA M(ORRIS)

U.S. Secretary of Commerce, born Jan. 11, 1921, in Lynch, Ky. Facing a widening U.S. trade deficit in April, President Jimmy Carter appointed Juanita Kreps to head a special task force seeking ways to promote exports. Adopting its recommendations, the President announced in September a plan aimed at increasing export financing assistance while reducing regulatory restrictions. Kreps personally headed trade missions to Japan in October and to India in November. One of the most outspoken commerce secretaries in recent memory, she warned against the use of trade sanctions to pry concessions from the Soviets on human rights issues.

Juanita Kreps was the first woman and first practicing economist to serve in the commerce post, and she was given high marks for revitalizing a cabinet department that had been regarded as semimoribund. A 1942 graduate of Berea College with a PH.D. from Duke University (1948), she was vice-president of Duke prior to her 1977 Washington appointment.

MILLER, G(EORGE) WILLIAM

Chairman of the Federal Reserve Board, born March 9, 1925, in Sepulpa, Okla. His appointment to succeed "Fed" Chairman Arthur F. Burns was marred by charges that while Miller was head of Textron, Inc. (1960–77), the industrial conglomerate paid $2,900,000 to foreign officials to expedite helicopter sales. Miller, however, insisted the payments had been sales commissions, not bribes. The Senate confirmed him by voice vote in March. He called for a national energy policy and joined the Treasury Department in efforts to defend the value of the U.S. dollar abroad. Although a credit tightening policy drove interest rates to near-record heights, Miller argued that recession would not inevitably result.

A graduate of the U.S. Coast Guard Academy and a line officer in World War II, Miller took top honors in his law class at the University of Califor-

G. William Miller testifies at a Senate hearing on Feb. 28 after his nomination to head the Federal Reserve Board.

Spokesman, troubleshooter, and political adviser were among the roles played by Vice-President Walter F. Mondale for the Carter administration. His 1978 assignments included meeting with Indian Prime Minister Morarji Desai.

nia at Berkeley (1952). He earned a social activist's reputation in the 1960's as a member of President John F. Kennedy's Committee on Equal Employment Opportunities. Unassuming ("Hi, I'm Bill Miller") and briskly efficient, he seemed somewhat less independent and more the team player than his predecessor at the Fed.

MONDALE, WALTER F(REDERICK)

Vice-President of the U.S., born Jan. 5, 1928, in Ceylon, Minn. During the Arab-Israeli-U.S. Camp David summit in September, while President Jimmy Carter was absent from the Oval Office for two weeks, Mondale served as the hub of executive branch operations. Among other 1978 assignments, the Vice-President was dispatched in January on a "listen and learn" tour of the Western

states (where the Carter ticket ran poorly in 1976); he visited Southeast Asia and the Middle East later in the year. The death of Minnesota Sen. Hubert H. Humphrey in January (*see* OBITUARIES) was a personal as well as a political loss for Mondale. Another blow, Democratic defeats for the Minnesota governorship and both Senate seats in November, weakened Mondale's political base. Although he discreetly turned back speculations, many still regarded "Fritz" Mondale as well placed to head his party's ticket in 1984.

NIXON, RICHARD M(ILHOUS)

Former President of the U.S., born Jan. 9, 1913, in Yorba Linda, Calif. The year marked his full return to the public's eye.

In January he made his first trip back to Washington, D.C., since his 1974 resignation to attend the funeral of Sen. Hubert H. Humphrey. *RN—the Memoirs of Richard Nixon* was published in April and remained on national best-seller lists for three months. Nixon's confidence appeared to blossom on an outing in July to Hyden, Ky., to dedicate a recreation center and on visits to Texas and Mississippi in the fall. Traveling to Western Europe in late November, he was greeted warmly in France but got a mixed reception in England. "I have retired from politics, but I have not retired from life," he told a politely applauding crowd inside the Oxford University Union, while a throng of hecklers outside chanted "No more Nixon." He issued his own summary of the Watergate debacle that made him the first U.S. President to resign from office: "I screwed up. I paid the price."

Richard M. Nixon autographs a copy of his newly published memoirs in London, Ky., in July. The former President was cheered by thousands as he attended a dedication ceremony for a recreational complex in nearby Hyden.

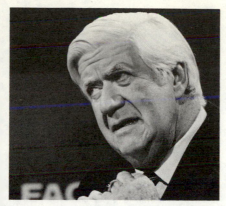

Speaker of the House Thomas P. O'Neill, Jr. (D, Mass.), prepares for a television interview in January.

O'NEILL, THOMAS P(HILIP), JR.

Speaker of the U.S. House of Representatives, born Dec. 9, 1912, in Cambridge, Mass. An experienced and well-liked political leader, he gained much of the credit for the Democratic-sponsored legislation passed during the year and claimed to have taught President Jimmy Carter some effective lessons in the art of dealing with Congress. But Carter-O'Neill relations were not always friendly. The White House was stung by the Speaker's wrath in August at the ousting of Robert T. Griffin, number two man at the General Services Administration (GSA) and an old friend of O'Neill's. As the firing, a result of GSA hierarchical jostling, threatened an open breach, the White House reassigned Griffin to mollify the Speaker. In July, O'Neill himself was absolved of charges related to the South Korean influence-peddling scandal.

Educated at Boston College and long known by his nickname "Tip," O'Neill was first elected to the Massachusetts state legislature in 1936. He arrived in Washington in 1952 by winning the House seat vacated by a Senate-bound John F. Kennedy. Elected Speaker in 1976, O'Neill generally cooperated with the administration in shepherding Carter programs through Congress, despite well-publicized aversions to some members of the Carter staff. He was easily reelected in November to his fourteenth House term and was renamed Speaker by the Democratic caucus.

RHODES, JOHN J(ACOB)

Minority leader of the U.S. House of Representatives, born Sept. 18, 1916, in Council Grove, Kans. As a spokesman for the Republican Party, the Arizona Congressman maintained a running critique of Carter administration policies. In January he rebutted the President's State of the Union address and budget message, offering an alternative proposal of a 10 percent tax cut each year for three years. He took the White House to task for linking jet sales to Egypt and Saudi Arabia with sales to Israel. During the fall election campaign, he joined a traveling group of Republican leaders speaking on behalf of large tax reductions. Rhodes himself was easily reelected to a fourteenth term in November.

A graduate of Kansas State University and Harvard Law School (1941), Rhodes was stationed in Arizona with the Air Corps during World War II. He stayed on to become the first Republican in Arizona's history to be elected to the U.S. House of Representatives (1952). Known over the years as a "master of procedure," John J. Rhodes succeeded Gerald R. Ford as House GOP leader in 1973.

SADAT, ANWAR EL-

President of the Arab Republic of Egypt and co-winner of the 1978 Nobel Peace Prize, born Dec. 25, 1918, in Talah Moniufiya. Even more than the other participants, he placed his political prestige on the line with the September Camp David accords on an Arab-Israeli peace settlement. Although Sadat seemed to have the backing of Egypt's war-weary population, those tentative agreements touched off heated debate within his government and led to a severing of ties between Cairo and several hard-line Arab states. The agreements added to his growing international reputation as a statesman. In the U.S., polls showed him to be the most admired foreign leader. In his Nobel message, he again cited guarantees of Palestinian self-rule as a necessary part of any actual Egyptian-Israeli peace treaty. His decision not to go to Norway in December to accept the award in person—as did co-winner Menachem Begin (see above)—reflected Sadat's displeasure with the stalemated negotiations.

At home in Egypt a referendum in May providing Sadat with a mandate to limit political opposition passed by a claimed 98.29 percent of the vote. Yet his efforts to restructure Egyptian political life through a newly created National Democratic Party left Egypt with, in effect, no opposition at all.

SCHMIDT, HELMUT H(EINRICH) W(ALDEMAR)

Chancellor of the Federal Republic of Germany, born Dec. 23, 1918, in Hamburg. His ruling coalition of Social Democrats and Free Democrats foiled opposition challenges in a series of regional votes, including a crucial state election in Hesse in October. That success and his stewardship over Europe's strongest national economy greatly reduced chances that Schmidt might face

Chancellor Helmut Schmidt of West Germany (left) and Prime Minister Pierre Elliott Trudeau of Canada enjoy a conversation during a break at the July economic summit in Bonn, West Germany.

rude political shocks prior to the normal expiration of his term in 1980.

In foreign relations, Schmidt continued to demonstrate his seeming inability to warm up to U.S. President Jimmy Carter. In February the U.S. was rebuffed in its efforts to persuade Schmidt to pump up the West German economy as a means of taking pressure off the U.S. dollar. And Carter's decision in April to put off production of the neutron bomb left Schmidt in the political lurch. The chancellor, on the other hand, forged a close working relationship with French President Valéry Giscard d'Estaing (see above). In September they took the lead in shaping a unified monetary system among the nine-member European Communities.

SPINKS, LEON
World heavyweight boxing champion (Feb. 15–Sept. 15, 1978), born July 11, 1953, in St. Louis. For seven giddy months Spinks, a rank novice to the professional ring, held the most coveted title in boxing. With youthful strength and a brawling fighting style, he outlasted veteran Muhammad Ali (see above) in a February bout in Las Vegas. But in a September return match in New Orleans, a superbly prepared Ali gave Spinks a boxing lesson to regain the title (as recognized by the World Boxing Association).

Although a product of poverty and a broken home, Spinks demonstrated enduring loyalties to family and friends. He dropped out of school in the tenth grade to enlist in the Marine Corps and gained his first ring notices with the Camp Lejeune (N.C.) boxing team. At Montréal in 1976, he

and his younger brother Michael, a promising middleweight, became the first pair of siblings ever to win gold medals at the same Olympic Games. Turning professional soon afterward, Leon Spinks had only seven bouts prior to his startling Las Vegas upset. His immaturity showed in frequent scrapes with the law during the year, mostly involving traffic offenses. But with his burning drive "to be somebody," the former champion had high prospects of becoming a future champion as well.

TENG HSIAO-PING
Vice-Chairman of the Chinese Communist Party and First Deputy Premier of the People's Republic of China, born in 1904 in Kuang-an, Szechwan Province. Teng's official ranking placed him below Chairman Hua Kuo-feng (see above) in Peking's ruling hierarchy. But there was hardly any question that the doughty Teng, twice previously purged and rehabilitated, was the mainspring of an astonishing transformation in China in the post-Mao era. With hopes of raising China to the first rank of world powers by the year 2000, Teng promulgated the "Four Modernizations," a program for across-the-board improvements in Chinese agriculture, industry, science, and defense.

Pursuing China's new outward-reaching foreign policy (in almost every direction except the Soviet Union and Vietnam), Teng visited a half-dozen Asian nations during the year. The high point of his travels came in August when he was on hand in Tokyo to witness the signing of a historic, ten-year treaty of peace and friendship between China and Japan. He was also a key figure in the improvement in U.S.-Chinese relations that led to a December agreement on formal diplomatic recognition. Significantly, it was Teng, not Hua, who was slated to visit Washington, D.C., early in 1979.

TRUDEAU, PIERRE ELLIOTT
Prime Minister of Canada, born Oct. 18, 1919, in Montréal, Québec. He had come to power in 196 on a platform of national unity, and ten years late the threat of national dissolution was still Trudeau's main political problem. In March, during speech in New York City, he conceded that Québec separatism was a factor in depressing the Canadian economy. Inflation and unemployment rates both climbed past 8.5 percent during the year, while the value of the Canadian dollar in international trade dropped to its lowest level since 1933. Trudeau's decision to postpone general elections until 1979 turned out to be a wise one in light of the drubbing his ruling Liberal took in fifteen by-elections in October. When December Gallup Poll showed his party slipping further behind, the prime minister responded combatively: "I can lose, but I never do."

Adm. Stansfield Turner, director of the Central Intelligence Agency, was praised for his broadened supervision of U.S. intelligence-gathering activities during 1978.

Between diplomatic missions, Secretary of State Cyrus R. Vance enjoys an unusual moment of relaxation in his State Department offices.

TURNER, STANSFIELD

Director of the U.S. Central Intelligence Agency (CIA), born Dec. 1, 1923, in Chicago. In January a White House executive order expanded Turner's role in coordinating intelligence-gathering activities to include "full and exclusive" budgetary authority over all U.S. intelligence agencies. But the order also banned certain types of covert operations (assassination plots and medical experimentation, among others) that had brought discredit on the CIA in the past. Although widely credited with steering the CIA back onto a steadier course, Turner nonetheless drew some fire from the President himself in November—notably for the agency's failure to predict and warn of the turmoil in Iran.

By coincidence, Turner was a member of the same Amherst College class as the new director of the FBI, William H. Webster. And in 1943 Turner transferred to the Naval Academy class that included Midshipman Jimmy Carter (the two, however, hardly knew each other at Annapolis). Turner went on to become a Rhodes scholar and then rose through the Navy ranks to full admiral, serving with distinction in a variety of combat, staff, and command postings. He was appointed CIA director early in 1977.

VANCE, CYRUS R(OBERTS)

U.S. Secretary of State, born March 27, 1917, in Clarksburg, W.Va. It was a year of almost-though-not-quite in Vance's two major areas of foreign policy concern. The Carter administration's target date for an Israeli-Egyptian peace agreement—Dec. 17—passed unmet, despite Vance's intensive efforts to break the impasse through shuttle diplomacy. And the year ended without the signing of a pact with the Soviet Union putting limits on both nations' nuclear-armed missiles and bombers. In both instances, however, substantial progress brought high hopes of settlement in 1979.

As the lowest keyed and least impetuous member of the U.S. foreign policy triumvirate of Carter, Vance, and Zbigniew Brzezinski (see above), Vance advocated a more patient line in U.S. dealings with foreign nations in general and the Soviet Union in particular. "I have a great deal of fun," Vance said of his job in a *Time* magazine interview, although he found the need to travel 100,000-plus miles each year "quite burdensome." How long would he keep up his hectic pace? "One term," he replied, "is all I can take."

YOUNG, ANDREW J(ACKSON), JR.

U.S. Ambassador to the United Nations, born March 12, 1932, in New Orleans. His penchant for undiplomatic remarks continued to embroil Young in controversy during the year.

As one who consistently argued against direct U.S. military involvement in Africa, the ambassador appeared to be at odds with his own government on the significance of Cuban intervention in African affairs. In May he publicly contradicted President Jimmy Carter by asserting that congressional restraints did not hinder the conduct of U.S. foreign policy. In July, on the eve of the trials of two Soviet dissidents in Moscow, Young told a French Socialist newspaper that U.S. jails held "hundreds—perhaps even thousands—of people I would call political prisoners." The statement

303

undercut U.S. efforts to pressure the Kremlin into halting the trials and earned for Young sharp rebukes from the White House and State Department. He agreed "it was a mistake," and a move to impeach him was shelved in the House. Despite the flaps, President Carter, a longtime friend and ally in Georgia politics, defended Young as "a very valuable asset to our country," particularly in his efforts to open up communications between the U.S. and Third World nations.   D.C.

PERU. A staggering economy caused a series of strikes and violent demonstrations in Peru in 1978.

Election of a new 100-member constituent assembly to draft a constitution that would return Peru to civilian rule in 1980 was scheduled for May but did not take place until June 18. The winning party, in the first election since the military government took over in 1968, was the moderate American Popular Revolutionary Alliance, founded and led by 83-year-old Victor Raúl Haya de la Torre; Haya was also elected president of the assembly. The rightist Popular Christian Party was next, followed by the more extreme leftist groups. Meanwhile, President Francisco Morales Bermúdez resigned his army commission but made it clear that the armed forces would not relinquish power.

Spending more, especially on arms, than it took in, the military government realized early in 1978 that it could not meet payments on a foreign debt totaling $8.2 billion. The International Monetary Fund (IMF) and foreign banks refused to extend credit unless the government adopted an austerity program. Accordingly, in mid-May, the government drastically cut expenses, laying off workers and ending subsidies on consumer goods. Prices rose sharply on bread and milk and imported gasoline and cooking oil.

The populace, battling 80 percent inflation, responded with riots, looting, and a general strike in late May. Teachers struck from May to late July, and copper miners struck in August and September, causing an estimated loss of $2,000,000 a day. Civil servants and others walked out in September. The government arrested leftist labor leaders and closed the universities. Martial law was imposed from May 20 to June 8, and a partial state of emergency was declared in August. In November the IMF and the foreign banks finally agreed to refinance Peru's foreign loans. But with agriculture stagnant, unemployment rising, and the population increasing, Peru's economic struggle seemed far from over.

See STATISTICS OF THE WORLD.   J.N.G.

PETS. The recognition of a new breed of hound, the growing popularity of psittacine bird species and purebred cats, and heightened activity in the rabbit market excited the interest of pet fanciers in 1978.

A Short and Nasty Life

In 1977 a black-and-white rabbit named Harvey made headlines as the world's first attack bunny. Somebody had abused him when he was just an impressionable kit, and ever afterward he tended to bite anyone who came near. So the ASPCA used him in a national campaign against animal abuse. Until March, that is, when Harvey, age 3, died of an ear infection. It was typical of the cantankerous Harvey that, as an ASPCA official noted, "he picked Easter to kick off."

Birds. Bird sales soared during 1978, with psittacine species of all types leading the way. The relatively expensive psittacine birds, such as cockatoos and macaws, sold especially well. The Australian psittacines popularly known as grass parakeets (genus *Neophema*) grew in favor, as did some of the Amazon parrots (genus *Amazona*). Budgerigars (or "budgies") continued to dominate the hook-bill bird market in sales volume; cockatiels and lovebirds also maintained their popularity. The demand for good canaries held steady, despite record prices.

Dogs. The trend among first-time purchasers to buy canine breeds traditionally regarded as guard dogs tapered off somewhat during 1978, although interest remained high in large dogs as a group. The year's most noteworthy development among purebred dogs was the recognition given the Ibizan hound, a breed originating in Spain, by the American Kennel Club. The breed was approved for dog-show exhibition in the hound group as of Jan. 1, 1979.

New York City revised its public health code effective Aug. 1, 1978, to mandate fines of up to $100 for dog owners who fail to clean up after their pets. Observers noted a sharp rise in sales of "pooper scoopers" and an immediate improvement in the cleanliness of city streets. Compliance lagged later in the year, however, and there was an increase in the number of dogs abandoned by their owners.

PHILIPPINES, REPUBLIC OF THE

A satirical view of New York City's canine cleanup law from cartoonist Oliphant of the Washington Star/Los Angeles Times syndicate.

THE LATEST FROM FUN CITY: NEW YORK CITY DOG-SCOOPING LAWS ARE NOW IN EFFECT.

The Ibizan hound was recognized as a breed by the American Kennel Club in 1978. This handsome specimen is Amberlithe Simbel, owned by Sharon Schoffstall and Nancy Kilgore Koppel of Baltimore.

Tropical Fish. The tropical-fish field continued to decline in 1978. Unrest in the areas surrounding Lakes Malawi and Tanganyika in Africa, sources of the specialty fishes that have become important revenue producers in recent years, curtailed the importation of new species. Pet dealers also noticed at least a relative decline in the number of young people (especially boys) interested in keeping fish as a hobby.

Other Pets. The trade in small mammals such as gerbils, hamsters, and guinea pigs remained at 1977 levels. The rabbit field, however, showed heightened activity in all three rabbit specialty areas—fancy, meat, and fur.

The popularity of purebred cats grew during 1978, and so did the trend toward showing these animals at exhibitions sanctioned by national cat associations. Cat breeders and cat lovers were successful in heightening public awareness of such lesser-known breeds as the Somali, Rex, and Balinese.

Land hermit crabs were offered by more retail pet outlets than ever before, but the reptile and amphibian market was hurt by import restrictions.　　　　N.P.

PHILIPPINES, REPUBLIC OF THE. Six years after he proclaimed martial law and assumed authoritarian powers, President Ferdinand E. Marcos continued in 1978 to rule the Philippines with a firm hand.

Politics. As Marcos had promised, a general election was held on April 7 to choose an "interim" National Assembly. Marcos permitted his longtime foe, former Sen. Benigno Aquino, Jr., to run for the assembly from prison as head of the Laban (Fight) Party. The Laban Party ran an unexpectedly strong campaign, playing on popular hostility to martial law, corruption, and the personal wealth of the Marcos family. The official results, however, gave the president's New Society movement 152 of the 165 elective seats in the 200-member body. Of the remaining 35 seats, 20 went to cabinet members and 1 to Marcos himself.

Opposition leaders charged the government with ballot-box stuffing, intimidation, and fraud. Following a protest demonstration in Manila, more than 500 people were arrested. Curbs on freedom of speech, lifted during the forty-five-day election campaign, were reimposed. Local elections were postponed indefinitely.

The assembly, the first national legislature in six years, convened on June 12. Its official purpose was to prepare the way for elections to a permanent parliament. But the interim assembly had little power. As president, Marcos could veto any law. As prime minister (a post he assumed at the opening session), he named the cabinet, which could prevent any bill of national importance from coming to a vote. Moreover, Marcos retained the right to rule by decree, if he deemed it necessary.

305

Former Sen. Benigno Aquino, Jr., casts his ballot in Philippine legislative elections in April. While serving his sixth year in a prison camp because of antigovernment activities, Aquino led the political opposition to President Ferdinand E. Marcos and ran (unsuccessfully) for the national assembly.

Martial law remained in effect, although Marcos promised that military tribunals would be ended. In June, in another conciliatory move, Marcos granted amnesty to hundreds of political prisoners, although not to Aquino.

The president's wife, Imelda Marcos, gained new power in 1978. In addition to keeping her job as governor-general of metropolitan Manila, she won a seat in the assembly and was named by her husband to a new cabinet post—minister for ecology and human settlements, a position that empowered her to supervise the development of the country's towns and cities. Talk persisted that Marcos would choose her as deputy prime minister, thereby placing her in line to succeed him at some future time.

Opposition. After the April election, the most vocal opposition to the Marcos government came from sectors of the Roman Catholic Church. Radical priests preached in the villages against police brutality and social inequality. In Manila, Cardinal Jaime Sin openly questioned the fairness of the April election and called for the release of Aquino.

Muslim insurgents in the southern provinces continued their long fight for autonomy, while a Maoist rebellion in northern Luzon also remained alive. The two-front fighting tied up much of the Philippine army and proved a costly drain on the national treasury.

Economic and Foreign Affairs. A growth rate of around 6 percent was healthy enough, but exports—chiefly sugar and copper—earned far less than anticipated, forcing the government to borrow heavily to finance development programs. On the positive side, foreign investment was up 50 percent after a two-year lull.

U.S.-Philippine relations, stormy in recent years, took a few surprising turns in 1978. Marcos began by accusing Washington of financing opposition candidates in the April election. And after U.S. Vice-President Walter F. Mondale visited Manila in May and rebuked Marcos for violations of human rights, the Philippine president charged the United States with "moral imperialism." In late December, however, the two countries announced a new accord that would guarantee the U.S. "unhampered" use of its military bases in the Philippines in return for $500,000,000 in economic aid over the next five years.

See STATISTICS OF THE WORLD.   R.J.C.

PHOTOGRAPHY. In 1978 photographers and photography fans noted the return of *Life* magazine to newsstands, six years after it had ceased regular publication. The year also saw the introduction by Polaroid Corp. of a new automatic focusing system and the announcement of a surprising verdict in a major antitrust suit against the Eastman Kodak Co. Other important events of 1978 included a controversial exhibition at New York's Museum of Modern Art and the death of W. Eugene Smith, one of the world's best-known photojournalists.

The Return of *Life*. In a move that had been eagerly awaited by photojournalists, Time, Inc., the giant publisher, resumed publication of *Life* magazine in October. Founded in 1936 as a weekly newsmagazine, *Life* had been an instant success with its blend of on-the-spot news photographs and essays by outstanding photojournalists. At its peak, in 1969, the magazine had a circulation of 8,500,000. However, in the face of rising postage costs and increased competition from television, its circulation had dropped steadily, and in 1972 it had ceased regular publication, although ten occasional special issues had been published subsequently.

The new version of *Life*, which was to be published monthly, retained the large format, emphasis on photographs, and extensive use of color reproductions that had marked the original magazine. Time, Inc., planned to sell the magazine pri-

In 1912 Baron Adolphe de Meyer photographed the legendary Russian dancer Waslaw Nijinsky in one of his most celebrated choreographic works, The Afternoon of a Faun. De Meyer, a Frenchman who died in 1946 at the age of 77, put together an album of thirty of these photographs; only four copies of the album survived into the 1970's. In 1978 an American, Richard Benson, himself a photographer, made a new album of the thirty original photos, to which he added three others that had been found in the Dance Collection of the New York Public Library. The thirty-three studies, reproduced by hand in the palladium process on translucent paper, were not only bound into an album, they were also put on display at the Washburn Gallery in New York City during the year. The evocative portrait above gives some idea of what de Meyer wanted to achieve in his photographs, that is, a sense of being present at a performance of the ballet.

PHOTOGRAPHY

W. Eugene Smith, holding his portrait of Albert Schweitzer. Smith, a highly respected master of the photoessay, concerned about his subjects and dedicated to his art, died in 1978. He had photographed the humanitarian for Life magazine in 1954.

marily through retail outlets, such as supermarkets and newsstands, rather than by subscription. The first issue of the new *Life* included features on Antarctica, ballooning, and the shah of Iran. It had a circulation of 700,000.

It was also announced in 1978 that *Look,* a pho-

Alfred Stieglitz's arresting 1918 photograph of Georgia O'Keeffe is one of hundreds he took of the painter both before and during their marriage. O'Keeffe selected a number of them for an exhibit of Stieglitz's work, which opened at the Metropolitan Museum of Art in New York City in November.

tographic weekly similar to *Life,* which had been published from 1937 to 1971, would reappear in early 1979; *see* PUBLISHING.

New Technology. Polaroid's new automatic focusing system, introduced in April on special models of the SX-70 and Pronto! cameras, determines focus distance by measuring sound waves. When the shutter release button is pushed in, a transducer built into the front of the camera emits an inaudible sound wave (called a "chirp"). An electronic clock measures the amount of time that it takes for the chirp to bounce back from the object to the camera, and a servomotor adjusts the focus of the lens accordingly. An advantage of Polaroid's system over automatic focusing systems that had been announced earlier is that, because it uses sound to measure distance, it can operate in very low light. *See* TECHNOLOGY.

Antitrust Case Settled and Appealed. On Jan. 21 a jury in New York City found the Eastman Kodak Co., long dominant in the photographic industry, guilty of violating federal antitrust laws by monopolizing the manufacture, sale, and processing of goods for the amateur photography market. The verdict in the landmark case—the first successful antitrust action against a major industry leader in twenty years—was the result of a suit brought in 1973 by Berkey Photo Inc., a smaller New York City firm that makes cameras and processes film. On March 22 the jury in the case awarded Berkey damages of $37,600,000. This amount was later reduced to about $27,000,000 by Judge Marvin E. Frankel in a seventy-nine-page decision. The damages were then raised to $81,000,000, plus several million dollars in court fees, in accordance with federal antitrust laws.

Photojournalist Eve Arnold caught the 1950's film star Marilyn Monroe dancing with her husband, playwright Arthur Miller, in this example from Flashback! The 50's. The book, a collection of 113 of Arnold's nostalgic photographs, was published by Knopf in 1978.

Polaroid marketed two self-focusing cameras—with their own battery-powered sonar systems—in 1978: the SX-70 Sonar OneStep (top) and the Pronto! Sonar OneStep. The principal difference between the two is that the SX-70 has a built-in preview stage, enabling the photographer to see through a view-finding system how the picture will actually look.

Judge Frankel also ruled that Kodak must supply independent photo processing companies with any information about new or modified products that it might give to its own color-print processing operation. Kodak must also make available color-print paper without the Kodak name printed on the back, as it has been in the past.

Kodak appealed the decision on Sept. 1, and the complex case was expected to be settled finally sometime in 1979. Although Kodak was expected to retain its overwhelming importance in the photographic field, no matter what the outcome, the decision was expected to lead to similar challenges to Kodak from other photographic manufacturers.

Exhibitions. "Mirrors and Windows," an exhibition shown during the summer at the Museum of Modern Art in New York City, was an ambitious attempt to provide a survey of American photography since 1960. Organized by John Szarkowski, director of the museum's Department of Photography, the exhibition included nearly 200 photographs by 101 photographers. Szarkowski's central argument was that contemporary photographers were no longer concerned with documenting public events. He claimed that they could be divided into two main groups: those who used photography as a means of self-expression, and those who used it realistically to explore the world. The

exhibition sparked a heated critical debate, as many photographers called Szarkowski's position overly simplistic.

New York City's Metropolitan Museum of Art held a spring exhibition of photographs from the collection of Alfred Stieglitz, who in the early 20th century introduced photography to the American public as art. Works in the Stieglitz collection ranged from Edward Steichen's autochrome portrait of Stieglitz himself to Arnold Genthe's record of the San Francisco earthquake of 1906, and from Ansel Adams's quiet landscapes to Paul Strand's geometric close-up of an iris flower. In the fall the Metropolitan mounted a retrospective exhibition of the work of the photographer Richard Avedon. Critics noted the sophisticated treatment of his early subjects, most of whom were elegant beauties; his later works have more often been portraits of notables.

Deaths. W. Eugene Smith, a noted photoessayist for *Life,* died in 1978; *see* OBITUARIES. Other major figures in the world of photography who died during the year were Victor Hasselblad, the Swedish inventor of the cameras that bear his name (Aug. 6 at 72); and two American photographers: Consuelo Kanaga, whose favorite subjects were poor families (Feb. 28 at 84); and Frederick Kent Truslow, photographer of wildlife (Aug. 19 at 75). C.H.

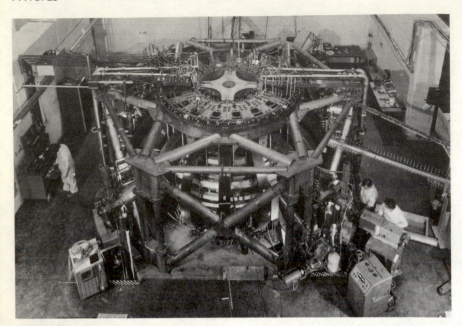

This giant tokamak at Princeton's Plasma Physics Laboratory is known as the PLT—the Princeton Large Torus. Within the tokamak, a doughnut-shaped reactor that uses magnetic coils to keep the superhot plasma confined, a record 60,000,000° C. was achieved.

PHYSICS. During 1978 a well-publicized development in plasma research appeared to bring physicists somewhat closer to harnessing the awesome energy of thermonuclear reactions. The year also witnessed the development of a laser beam with a life span of less than one trillionth of a second, providing scientists with the most accurate clock yet for measuring other short-lived physical phenomona.

Princeton's Tokamak. In July a significant step in extracting usable power from a nuclear fusion reactor was taken by a group of Princeton University scientists working under the sponsorship of the U.S. Department of Energy. At the Plasma Physics Laboratory, Director Melvin B. Gottlieb and colleagues Wolfgang Stodiek, Harold Eubank, and Harold P. Furth not only heated hydrogen-deuterium plasma to a record 60,000,000° C., but also started a fusion reaction that produced 1 percent of the energy it used. Previous reactions had generated only about 0.01 percent of the energy they had taken in.

The scientists reached the record temperature by introducing a 2-megawatt beam of deuterium atoms into the hydrogen-filled chamber of the Princeton Large Torus (PLT), a descendant of the tokamak reactor designed by the Russians in 1968. To confine the superheated plasma safely within the PLT's doughnut-shaped reaction chamber, the inside wall of the chamber was lined with an electromagnetic force. This force repelled the charged particles of the plasma and thus prevented them from melting the reactor's metal walls.

Although its temperature was high enough to get the reaction started, the plasma was not sufficiently concentrated to sustain the fusion process for more than 15 thousandths of a second—too short a period to release appreciable energy. Nonetheless, the physicists were confident that they were one step further along in their quest for a self-sustaining fusion reaction that would produce more energy than it uses. According to the Department of Energy, however, that goal is going to take at least fifty more years to reach.

Metallic Xenon. In mid-November, Cornell University researchers headed by Arthur L. Ruoff announced that they had created a metallic form of a highly nonreactive inert gas, xenon.

Using a special diamond anvil, they subjected a tiny sample of the gas to an unprecedented pressure of 320 kilobars—320,000 times the pressure of the atmosphere at sea level. The scientists discovered that the sample had reached metallic form when it started to conduct electricity as freely as stainless steel. Other scientists had previously suc-

---

---

ceeded in converting xenon to liquid and solid states, but they had failed to produce the highly conductive metallic form.

Although the researchers see no potential uses for their discovery at this time, the creation of metallic xenon is a significant step toward the production of metallic hydrogen, a superconductor even in liquid form. Power lines using this form of hydrogen could, for instance, transmit electricity over great distances with almost no energy losses.

Acoustic Microscope. In August two Stanford University scientists, Calvin Quate and Victor Jipson, announced success in their development of an acoustic microscope. This device has the ability to send sound of extremely short wavelengths below the surface of objects, revealing microscopic details of internal structure.

Until this breakthrough, other scientists had failed to find a means of generating sound waves short enough to use in microscopic investigations. In order to transmit high-resolution images of extremely small objects, a microscope must use sound or light waves no longer than one half the length of the object being magnified. After numerous attempts the Stanford researchers finally developed a system to generate sound waves with a frequency of 3 gigahertz (3 billion cycles per second). The wavelength of sound generated at this frequency is just 520 nanometers (520 billionths of a meter, or approximately 20 millionths of an inch). The scientists also discovered that some of these waves can penetrate as deep as 1 or 2 microns (approximately 40 to 80 millionths of an inch) below the surface of a sample and give sharp images of its internal structure. In other words, they could look into as well as at the sample. The acoustic microscope should thus prove an invaluable tool in biomedical research and microcircuit technology.

Bullets of Light. On Aug. 11, Jean Claude Diels and his associates at the University of Southern California (USC) reported that they had generated the shortest laser light pulses ever produced. Using a thin stream of dye and a special set of mirrors, the USC scientists produced a laser pulse with a life span of 0.17 picoseconds (0.17 trillionths of a second). The shortest previous pulse had a life span of 0.3 picoseconds.

The laser pulses generated by Diels and his colleagues can best be described as speeding bullets of light. They can be used not only to measure the time spans of other physical phenomena, such as split-second chemical reactions, but also to carry communications signals.

Deaths. Samuel Goudsmit, Dutch-born American physicist who was a codiscoverer of the electron's spin, died in December; *see* OBITUARIES. Edward O. Salant, a researcher at Brookhaven National Laboratory and professor of physics at Vanderbilt University, died Sept. 13 at 78.   M.J.C.

POLAND. The election of a Polish pope was the emotional highpoint of 1978 for Poland; *see* PEO-

A happy farmer near Karol Wojtyła's hometown learns that the Polish cardinal will reign as Pope John Paul II.

PLE IN THE NEWS; RELIGION. Although the Roman Catholic Church had come under attack from the Communist government for more than three decades, four fifths of all Poles still regarded themselves as Catholics. The choice of Cardinal Karol Wojtyła as the first non-Italian pope in four centuries aroused feelings of intense nationalist pride among Poles. It also seemed likely to add to the political worries of Communist Party leader Edward Gierek.

Church and State. Poles were both stunned and elated in October when word came from Vatican City that Cardinal Wojtyła had been elected. The day Wojtyła was invested as Pope John Paul II, virtually the entire Polish nation watched the event on television.

Communist Party chief Gierek dispatched an immediate telegram of congratulations to the pope. It expressed "great satisfaction" at his election, while carefully avoiding any endorsement of religion. There was no question, however, that a Polish pope posed new problems for Gierek. For one thing, Wojtyła was an outspoken anti-Communist. In addition, the church was already a focus for dissent in Poland.

Since taking over as Communist secretary in 1970, Gierek had attempted to improve relations between church and state in order to defuse feelings of public discontent. His campaign had met with only limited success, however. In one of their sharpest challenges yet to the government, Polish bishops issued a pastoral letter in September that called for abolition of censorship and criticized state persecution of those who have "the courage to express their opinions on public matters."

Political Dissidents. Political activists also challenged the government. The Social Self-Defense Committee, originally called the Workers' Defense Committee, continued to operate, though its leaders were periodically arrested. More than two dozen underground journals were published on a regular basis. And in 1978 university professors began to organize so-called flying universities to give informal talks on political and historical topics not discussed in state classrooms.

The Economy. High import costs and food shortages plagued the country. To maintain stable food prices, the government spent one third of its budget on subsidies. Western economists believed that Poland needed thoroughgoing economic reform, but Gierek preferred traditional Communist policies. At a Communist Party conference in January, he attempted to placate consumers by promising there would be no sudden price increases and by pledging even higher subsidies to stimulate production.

Foreign Affairs. Polish foreign policy was closely coordinated with that of the Soviet Union. Gierek made an April visit to Moscow to talk with President Leonid Brezhnev, and again conferred with him in August in the Crimea. The closeness of the two nations was dramatized in June, when a Polish officer joined a Russian cosmonaut for a week in space aboard a Soviet Soyuz 30; see SPACE EXPLORATION.

French President Valéry Giscard d'Estaing journeyed to Warsaw in September. Economic cooperation was the chief topic of his talks with Gierek.

See STATISTICS OF THE WORLD.   F.W.

POPULAR MUSIC. The year 1978 will be remembered as the year that disco music came of age. Disco, music specifically designed for dancing, had been growing in popularity since the introduction of two energetic dances, the Hustle and the Bump, in the early 1970's, but no one had foreseen that such a phenomenal burst of accept-

On Aug. 21, country music queen Dolly Parton becomes the queen of Gotham. With her platinum record ("Here You Come Again") and her entertainer-of-the-year award (from the Country Music Association), it was only natural that the voluptuous singer-songwriter should also receive a key to the city of New York. She responded with a thirty-minute concert on the steps of City Hall.

God Bless You, Irving Berlin

Born Israel Baline, the child of Jewish refugees from Russia, he grew up in the dreary tenements of New York City's Lower East Side. His formal schooling amounted to only two years and he never did learn to read music. But no matter—Irving Berlin's gift as a tunesmith and his irrepressible optimism couldn't be denied. From "Alexander's Ragtime Band" to "White Christmas," from "Easter Parade" to "God Bless America," his was a torrential outpouring of songs, nearly 1000 in all, that kept millions singing and singing and. . . . He turned 90 in May, and a birthday message from the White House expressed appropriate appreciation by declaring: "God bless Irving Berlin."

Irving Berlin in the 1920's.

ance would occur before the end of the decade. It happened not just overnight but in the even shorter space of eighty-five minutes, the length of time it took audiences to watch the 1977 film *Saturday Night Fever*, with its star John Travolta moving to the disco sounds of the Bee Gees singing "Stayin' Alive" and "Night Fever" and Yvonne Elliman doing "If I Can't Have You."

Disco-oriented releases dominated the record charts for nearly 26 of the 52 weeks of the year, with A Taste of Honey's "Boogie Oogie Oogie"

The New York Times *called him "the hottest male singer in the land." And Billy Joel had three albums—the latest of which was "52nd Street"—that sold well over 1,000,000 copies each during 1978.*

In 1978 the Swedish group known as ABBA—their name is an acronym of the first names of the four members— became the largest selling band in the history of recorded music. Left to right: Benny Andersson, Anni-Frid Lyngstad, Agnetha Faltskog, and Bjorn Ulvaeus, whose lush, "easy listening" sound has made them famous all over the world.

(Capitol), Donna Summer's "MacArthur Park" (Casablanca), and Chic's "Le Freak" (Atlantic) among the leaders. Everyone wanted to get in on what the Italians were calling "travoltismo." Rod Stewart cut a disco single, RCA put out a disco version of a Dolly Parton country number, and even the great composers of classical music became disco contributors as Beethoven's "Turkish March" became "Love in a Turkish Bath" and Weber's "Invitation to the Dance" was restyled as "Fancy Feet." Radio stations throughout the country turned to all-disco formats following the example of WKTU-FM, New York City, which went from a 1.4 percent share of audience as a soft-rock station to an 11.3 percent share as a disco station, making it the number-one station in the number-one market.

Riding the crest of the disco phenomenon and contributing greatly to it was the British-born Gibb family. The three older brothers—Barry, Maurice, and Robin, known as the Bee Gees—

composed much of the music for *Saturday Night Fever* and brought musical legitimacy to a form that had not previously been taken seriously by many observers of the popular music scene. Joining them as a new solo superstar was their younger brother, Andy Gibb, whose songs "Shadow Dancing" and "Love is Thicker than Water" were major best-sellers. Among them, the members of the Gibb family performed five of the top ten records of 1978 and wrote two others of the top fifteen.

Other Trends and Events. Rock music remained strong in 1978. But "punk rock," one of the more highly publicized movements of 1977, appeared to be running aground. The most notorious advocates of this lyrically violent and frequently hostile approach to rock, the Sex Pistols from England, did initiate a brief U.S. tour but broke apart when the most prominent member, Johnny Rotten, left the group. Another Sex Pistol, Sid Vicious, was arrested and charged with the murder of a girl friend. And late in the year Rotten, under the name John Lydon, released a recording with a new group, Public Image, Ltd.

The most successful personal appearance tour of 1978 was made by the Rolling Stones; it culminated in a performance before more than 80,000 fans in the New Orleans Superdome. For a single performance, however, nothing surpassed the estimated 200,000 people who gathered at a World War II air base in southern England on July 15 for a daylong open-air concert featuring Bob Dylan, Eric Clapton, and Joan Armatrading. Other particularly successful concert appearances were those of Neil Young, Bruce Springsteen, and Billy Joel. Country music singer Willie Nelson was honored with a White House engagement in September.

The Newport Jazz Festival, which had been moved to New York City several years previously, celebrated its 25th anniversary in 1978. Concerts were held at a variety of sites, ranging from Carnegie Hall and the Roseland ballroom to Greenwich Village and the Staten Island ferry. On July 1, the festival became a street fair, with groups playing on platforms along 52nd Street, the mecca for jazz in the 1930's and 1940's.

Recordings. The popular music record industry experienced its best year ever in 1978 with sales in excess of $3.5 billion. Some of the dollar increase in sales could be attributed to the raising of list prices to $7.98 and in some cases $8.98, but overall it was the fantastic selling power of the top records that created the surge. The sound track album from *Saturday Night Fever* (RSO) sold 15,000,000 copies domestically (landing in one out of every eight American homes) and another 13,000,000 copies internationally—the equivalent of 28 Platinum records, the industry standard for records achieving sales of 1,000,000 or more. Not far behind in domestic sales was the sound track album from *Grease* (also RSO). By the end of the year the dollar sales from the two sound tracks were running neck and neck with the enormous box-office grosses of the films themselves.

Other best-selling albums of the year included Billy Joel's "The Stranger" and "52nd Street" (both Columbia); a highly praised new album from the Rolling Stones called "Some Girls" (Rolling Stones); the best jazz-instrumental record of the year, Chuck Mangione's "Feels So Good" (A&M); and exciting releases by two "new wave" rock groups from New York, Talking Heads and Blondie. The consensus choice of critics, disc jockeys, and other popular music aficionados as top single record of the year was Andy Gibb's "Shadow Dancing" (RSO). *Billboard* magazine named Gibb and Linda Ronstadt the top male and female vocalists of the year.

One noteworthy trend in 1978 was the popularity of duet recordings. Led by John Travolta and Olivia Newton-John singing "You're the One I Want" and "Summer Nights" (RSO), the duos included Barbra Streisand and Neil Diamond with "You Don't Bring Me Flowers" (Columbia), Johnny Mathis and Deniece Williams with "Too

Much, Too Little, Too Late" (Columbia), Kenny Loggins and Stevie Nicks with "Whenever I Call You Friend" (Columbia), and Roberta Flack and Donny Hathaway with "The Closer I Get to You" (Atlantic).

Pictures and Pirates. One of the innovations of the year was the commercial distribution of picture disks, a promotional gimmick in which multicolored artwork is printed directly onto the record. The process is expensive (list price for the records approached $15) and the type of vinyl used produces inferior sound quality, but the novelty value attracted the interest of a number of companies. Even more extravagantly, MCA Canada issued a special pressing of Neil Diamond's "20 Golden Greats," which was in fact a 24-karat gold-plated record retailing for $85.

The problem of piracy in the recording industry was dramatized in early December when 300 agents from the Federal Bureau of Investigation made simultaneous raids at twenty-nine locations in five states and seized millions of dollars worth of illegal product and the equipment used in its manufacture. Originally begun as the bootlegging of live performances and unauthorized duplication on private labels of legitimate recordings, piracy in 1978 was extended to the highly profitable counterfeiting of major recordings, including artwork, album sleeves, and packaging. Unlike earlier efforts that were usually sold through gas stations, variety stores, and other offbeat outlets, these new and seemingly genuine disks made their way into regular record shops and department stores and were also shipped abroad in quantity.

Country Music. In October, at the twelfth annual Country Music Association awards show, voluptuous Dolly Parton was named country music's entertainer of the year. Her album "Here You Come Again" (RCA) had sold over 1,000,000 copies, spurred on by her frequent promotional appearances on various television shows. The Kendalls won the award for the single of the year, "Heaven's Just a Sin Away" (Ovation). The Oak Ridge Boys, a gospel group that had switched to country, were named vocal group of the year, displacing the Statler Brothers (who had won the honor for six consecutive years). The most consistently successful country recording stars of 1978, however, were Waylon Jennings and Willie Nelson. Their album "Waylon and Willie" (RCA) led the charts for 18 weeks, then yielded first to Willie's "Stardust" album (Columbia) for the following 13 weeks and later to Waylon's "I've Always Been Crazy" (RCA) for another 6 weeks. Finally, at the end of the year, Willie had a new album at the top—"Willie and Family Live" (Columbia).

PORTUGAL

Deaths. Among those who died during the year were Jacques Brel, Mother Maybelle Carter, Bill Kenny, Josef Marais, Keith Moon, Ray Noble, Louis Prima, and Joe Venuti; see OBITUARIES. Other notable deaths included those of country entertainer Johnny Bond (June 12 at 63); leading British pop singer Sandy Denny (April 26 at 30); Claude François, one of France's most popular singers (March 11 at 39); Gregory Herbert, member of Blood, Sweat and Tears (Jan. 31 at 30); Terry Kath of the group Chicago (Jan. 23 at 31); conductor Enoch Light (July 31 at 71); Dorothy Shay, "the Park Avenue Hillbilly" (Oct. 22 at 57); country singer Mel Street (Oct. 21 at 43); cool jazz pianist Lennie Tristano (Nov. 18 at 59); and composer-pianist Mabel Wayne (June 19 at 86).   W.P.P.

PORTUGAL. There were two changes of government in Portugal during 1978. No significant progress was made in solving the country's chronic economic and social problems, however.

Government and Politics. The Socialist government of Mário Soares fell in December of 1977 as the Opposition reacted against his austerity program, but he was able to form a new government on Jan. 19, 1978, in cooperation with the conservative Social Democratic Center, by taking three members of their party into his new cabinet. Their 41 votes added to the Socialists' 102 gave Soares a majority in the 263-seat National Assembly.

The problems that caused his previous downfall continued to haunt Soares. The austerity programs demanded by the International Monetary Fund had to be approved or the IMF would supply no loans to shore up Portugal's economy. The budget approved in April incorporated some austerity measures, such as a rise in the sales tax from 12 percent to 30 percent, but further measures remained to be worked out between government and IMF representatives. In addition, the government had been unable to return to their private owners the lands taken over during the 1975 radical reforms. Much of those lands was held by farm cooperatives dominated by Communists and other radicals, and Soares did not want to use force to dislodge them.

For months the Center Democrats carried on a campaign against Soares. They wanted him to dismiss Agriculture Minister Luís Saias and to allot more government credits to farmers in the north where the Center Democrats were strong. They accused Soares of favoring the southern Communist-dominated farmers.

Soares rejected their demands, and on July 24 the Center Democrats withdrew their three ministers from the cabinet, ending the fragile coalition that had enabled Soares to govern for six months.

Three days later President António Ramalho Eanes called a meeting of Portugal's watchdog Revolutionary Council and after consultation with it dismissed the government. Soares agreed to continue as a caretaker prime minister.

On Aug. 9, President Eanes named Alfredo Nobre da Costa as the new prime minister. Da Costa, 55, an industrialist and engineer who had been minister of industry in Soares's cabinet, was designated prime minister by the president without consultation with the political leaders. Da Costa assembled a cabinet of independent tech-

On a Portuguese Merry-Go-Round
With Portugal's parliament near paralysis, President António Ramalho Eanes decided to try something different. In August he asked a political independent, Alfredo Nobre da Costa, 55, an industrial engineer known for his skills as a manager, to form a new government. But the "transitional prime minister" failed to break the parliamentary deadlock, and after only two months Eanes was forced to try again. This time he tapped Carlos Alberto Mota Pinto, a respected 42-year-old law professor, who put together Lisbon's tenth government since 1974.

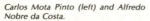

Carlos Mota Pinto (left) and Alfredo Nobre da Costa.

nicians, intended as a transition government to hold power until the next elections.

On Sept. 7, da Costa presented his cabinet and legislative program before the National Assembly. He said that he did not seek power, was not aligned with any party, and did not fear popular or political pressure. He proposed the same economic austerity programs that Soares had advocated. He would debate his program for five days; if approved he would govern until elections were held; if defeated he would resign.

On Sept. 14 the National Assembly voted down da Costa's program. He resigned after seventeen days in office but continued in office as a caretaker.

President Eanes waited until Sept. 26 to consult with political leaders, giving them a week to agree on a solution of the government crisis. But the leaders failed to agree, blaming each other for the situation. In the meantime, da Costa's temporary government had accelerated the return of expropriated lands, enforcing laws approved by parliament in 1977. On Oct. 16, however, the land-return effort was suspended after resistance by farmers, aided by workers, that left scores injured.

On Oct. 25, President Eanes designated Carlos Alberto Mota Pinto as prime minister and asked him to form a government. Mota Pinto, 42, a law professor at the University of Coimbra, had been Social Democratic parliamentary leader until he left the party. Although he remained an independent, he was expected to receive the support of the Socialists and Center Democrats.

It took him a month to assemble a cabinet, in which he incorporated three ministers from the da Costa government, including Minister of Agriculture Apolinario Vaz Portugal, disliked by the radicals because of his land policies. Mota Pinto's cabinet was composed of politically independent technicians, not very different from the one it replaced. On Nov. 22 the prime minister swore in his cabinet and submitted his program to the National Assembly.

The Economy. Portugal's economy showed little improvement in 1978. The foreign trade deficit reached $2.73 billion in 1977 and was expected to be worse in 1978. Inflation was so high (27 percent in the first quarter) that workers' real wages were declining. The austerity program recommended by the IMF, with $800,000,000 in loans contingent on it, could not be fully implemented because no political party was strong enough to push it through. Nevertheless, in March the United States agreed to lend $300,000,000 to the Bank of Portugal whether the IMF was satisfied or not. The first $100,000,000 was released in October.

Foreign Relations. Portugal normalized relations with the former Portuguese colony of Angola. President Eanes went to Guinea-Bissau, another former colony, in June, and there he met with Agostinho Neto, president of Angola. The two chiefs of state signed a general accord of cooperation on June 26, to be elaborated in bilateral treaties, mostly relating to air and sea transportation, the training of Angolans in Portugal, and the recruiting of Portuguese technicians to work in Angola. They also discussed the repatriation of Angolans who had fled to Portugal at the time of independence and the return of Portuguese property expropriated by Angola. Angolan refugees reportedly began returning home from Portugal in August.

President Valéry Giscard d'Estaing of France visited Lisbon in July. He announced a $100,000,000 loan to Portugal and discussed the country's possible admission to the European Community.

See STATISTICS OF THE WORLD. A.R.

PRESIDENT OF THE UNITED STATES. Jimmy Carter, thirty-ninth President of the United States, was born Oct. 1, 1924, in Plains, Ga. During his second year in office, President Carter found his sea legs after a troubled first year. He began 1978 in dire straits, widely accused in political and media circles of lacking competence in his job. Serenely confident in his own abilities, however, Carter reversed his political slide with a series of midcourse corrections. He ordered more centralized control of the government by a strengthened White House staff and husbanded his own resources more efficiently, paring his list of priorities to a more manageable scale. He grew more persuasive and more willing to assert his authority with Congress, winning several major legislative victories. And in a diplomatic triumph that seemed to demolish the competence question, he personally negotiated a framework for peace in the Middle East between the leaders of Egypt and Israel in September.

Mideast Triumph. When Mideast peace talks began degenerating in midyear, Carter placed his personal prestige squarely on the line by inviting Egyptian President Anwar el-Sadat and Israeli Prime Minister Menachem Begin to a summit meeting at the Presidential retreat at Camp David, Md., in September. It was viewed as a desperate gamble to restore momentum to the peace talks and arrest Carter's own sagging political fortunes. After thirteen grueling days of intense personal diplomacy, Carter persuaded both leaders to agree to a framework for a peace treaty that was to be spelled out in later talks. Egyptian-Israeli negotiations then bogged down; full agreement was not reached by the end of the year, much to Car-

Israeli Prime Minister Mena-chem Begin, U.S. President Jimmy Carter, and Egyptian President Anwar el-Sadat (left to right) take time out from their summit negotiations at Camp David, Md., on Sept. 10. A guide explained the Civil War battlefield at Gettysburg, Pa., to the three heads of government.

ter's frustration. Nevertheless, the Camp David summit was a singular political triumph for the President. Shortly before the summit the Gallup Poll recorded his approval rating at 39 percent, a level lower than those of his five predecessors at comparable periods during their Presidencies. After the summit, however, Carter's Gallup approval rating soared to 56 percent; it leveled off to 50 percent in December—showing that half of the American people felt he was doing a good job.

Congress and Politics. After a difficult first year, during which Carter was repeatedly faulted for lack of consultation, the President's fortunes on Capitol Hill improved markedly in 1978. He com-

bined a willingness to cooperate with congressional leaders with a resolve to challenge the legislative branch on carefully selected issues. The result was a perceptible rise in Presidential clout. In virtually unprecedented actions, Carter vetoed public works and defense authorization bills that he regarded as wasteful, and was sustained on both counts. He used the veto four times during the 1978 congressional session without being overridden, and pocket-vetoed thirteen more bills after Congress adjourned on Oct. 15. Congress gave Carter major victories by passing legislation reforming the civil service and deregulating the airline industry. After more than a year of haggling and compromise, a national energy policy was finally signed into law on Nov. 9. Other Administration initiatives were less successful; *see* Congress of the United States.

After exhaustive lobbying campaigns by the administration, Congress gave Carter three critical foreign policy victories. The Senate ratified treaties returning control of the U.S. Canal Zone to the Republic of Panama by the year 2000 and approved the controversial sale of jet fighters to Egypt and Saudi Arabia, a decision defended by Carter as crucial to Mideast peace efforts. The four-year embargo on U.S. military aid to Turkey was lifted by Congress at Carter's urging; although he had favored the embargo as a Presidential candidate, Carter argued that its continuation would severely jeopardize the security of the Western alliance.

Staff Changes. Concerned by negative ratings in public opinion polls and a widespread perception that his administration was lacking in competence, Carter summoned his cabinet and senior advisers to Camp David in the spring for several soul-searching meetings. One result was a decision by Carter to keep a tighter rein on his cabinet officers, overseeing their personnel decisions and clearing all policy pronouncements before release. To provide for stron, er coordination of policymaking, Carter added several aides to his senior staff. The most notable appointments were those of veteran Democratic Party leader Anne Wexler as assistant for public liaison and former campaign advertising manager Gerald Rafshoon

as director of communications. Wexler improved relations with Washington lobbyists and power brokers, and Rafshoon undertook to remake the Presidential image into one of toughness and decisiveness.

Foreign Affairs. The Carter administration continued to pursue an activist foreign policy on a variety of fronts. Quiet contacts with the People's Republic of China led to a dramatic December announcement by Carter that full diplomatic relations between the U.S. and China would be established on Jan. 1, 1979. The breakthrough was regarded as a major accomplishment for the President. But he was criticized for agreeing to cut diplomatic and military ties with Taiwan and for not consulting with Congress. Carter sought to normalize relations with such previous adversaries as North Vietnam and Cuba, but his displeasure over Cuban involvement in African wars slowed a warming trend toward President Fidel Castro's regime. While U.S. efforts to mediate explosive conflicts in southern Africa were failing, Carter's attempts to help resolve the Mideast conflict were proving more fruitful. He set new ceilings on the sale of American arms to nonaligned countries and adhered to his controversial policy of publicly criticizing alleged human rights violations in the Soviet Union and elsewhere.

Carter pressed the Russians for an accord in the prolonged negotiations for a second Strategic Arms Limitation Treaty (SALT II) to replace the pact signed in 1972. Intensive negotiating sessions during the year narrowed the differences signifi-

Democratic Party activist Anne Wexler, appointed April 19 as a top political adviser to President Jimmy Carter. The former associate publisher of Rolling Stone magazine proved effective in marshaling support for the President's policies among Congressmen and lobbyists.

cantly and by December a SALT II treaty appeared within reach.

To underscore his foreign affairs credentials, Carter made four overseas trips. As the year began he was midway through a nine-day visit to Poland, Iran, India, Saudi Arabia, Egypt, France, and Belgium. Emphasizing his interest in the Third World, Carter visited Venezuela, Brazil, Nigeria, and Liberia between March 28 and April 4. He flew to Panama in June to sign the canal treaties and attended an economic summit in Bonn, West Germany, in July.

Inflation Fight. As the rate of inflation began edging toward double-digit figures and many economists were forecasting a recession in 1979, Carter made inflation his chief domestic priority. He abandoned a largely rhetorical approach in favor of sterner remedies. He remained steadfastly opposed to wage and price controls but unveiled a stringent anti-inflation plan in a televised address to the nation Oct. 24. He requested compliance with voluntary limits of 7 percent on wage increases and 5.75 percent on price increases. Violators of the guidelines were to be discouraged through a variety of government sanctions, in-

cluding the denial of federal contracts. Economist Alfred E. Kahn was appointed to explain and administer the program as chairman of the Council on Wage and Price Stability. Carter also limited raises for government workers to 5.5 percent, placed a partial freeze on government hiring, and pledged to reduce the fiscal-1980 federal budget deficit to less than $30 billion. On Nov. 1 he announced several bold fiscal and monetary maneuvers designed to support the dollar in foreign currency markets.

To dramatize his determination to bring inflation under control within two years, Carter pledged deep cuts in federal spending. He warned that the budget for fiscal year 1980 would be "very, very tight" and would contain virtually no funding for new programs. Planned cutbacks in social programs underscored a growing awareness of a President considerably more conservative than in 1976, when, running for the office, he had angered many liberal elements within the Democratic Party. At the party's midterm issues conference in December, 40 percent of the delegates supported a proposal to urge Carter not to cut the budget for social services. Flying to Memphis to address the discontented conferees, the President reaffirmed his commitment to traditional Democratic Party ideals and pledged that his politics of austerity would be applied fairly to all special interest groups.   T.D.

A vacationing President waves to photographers as he and his family run the Tappan Falls rapids of Idaho's Salmon River. The Carters were on a three-day August raft trip.

PRINCE EDWARD ISLAND. *See* STATISTICS OF THE WORLD.

PRIZES AND AWARDS. The following is a selected listing of prizes awarded during 1978 and the names of the persons who received them. For awards given in specific fields, see the appropriate subject entry, such as LITERATURE; MOTION PICTURES.

NOBEL PRIZES

Six U.S. citizens and two heads of government were among the winners of the 1978 Nobel prizes, announced in October. The winners were as follows.

Chemistry. For "his contribution to the understanding of biological energy transfer through the formulation of the chemiosmotic theory":

Mitchell, Peter (1920–), British researcher in chemistry. Director of research at the Glynn Research Laboratories in Cornwall, England, since 1964, he was previously connected with Cambridge University and the University of Edinburgh. His explanation of the process by which nutrition is transformed into energy in living cells was first proposed in 1961.

Economics. For "his pioneering research into the decision-making process within economic organizations":

Simon, Herbert A. (1916–), American social scientist. He became a professor at Carnegie-Mellon University in Pittsburgh in 1949, teaching administration, psychology, and, later, computer science. His original research, carried on in the late 1940's and 1950's, challenged simple classical assumptions and formed the basis for modern business economics and administrative research.

Literature. For his "impassioned narrative art which, with roots in a Polish-Jewish cultural tradition, brings universal human conditions to life":

Singer, Isaac Bashevis (1904–), Polish-born Yiddish-language writer, U.S. citizen. His novels and short stories, widely circulated in English translation, portray the world of Eastern European Jews which he left in 1935. Among the best known are *Satan in Goray* (1935), *The Manor* (1967), and *The Estate* (1969). *See* LITERATURE.

Peace Prize. Given "not only to honor actions already performed in the service of peace, but also to encourage further efforts" toward the final achievement of a treaty between Egypt and Israel:

Begin, Menachem, prime minister of Israel. *See* biography at PEOPLE IN THE NEWS.

Sadat, Anwar el-, president of Egypt. *See* biography at PEOPLE IN THE NEWS.

Physics. The Nobel Prize in physics was given to two Americans and a Soviet scientist for unrelated achievements:

Kapitza, Peter Leonidovich (1894–), Soviet physicist. A fellow at Cambridge University from

Prime Minister Menachem Begin of Israel (center) receives his half of the 1978 Nobel Peace Prize in Oslo, Norway, on Dec. 10. Looking on is Sayed Ahmed Marei, a stand-in for Begin's co-winner, Anwar el-Sadat, president of Egypt. Sadat, dissatisfied with the progress of the Arab-Israeli peace negotiations, had chosen to stay at home.

For this photograph, which shows Anthony Kiritsis holding Richard Hall hostage in Indianapolis on Feb. 10, 1977, Jim Schweiker of UPI won the 1978 Pulitzer Prize in spot news photography. Later, however, it was determined that the picture had actually been taken by Schweiker's free-lance colleague and protégé John W. Blair. So the $1000 prize money was reawarded—to Blair.

1925 to 1936 and director of the Institute for Physical Problems of the U.S.S.R. Academy of Sciences from 1935 to 1946 and from 1955 to the present, he was under house arrest during the Stalin era for refusing to work on nuclear weapons. He was cited for his work in magnetism and the physics of supercold temperatures.

Penzias, Arno A. (1933–), American radio astronomer and physicist. Head of the Radio Physics Research Department at Bell Laboratories since 1974 and visiting professor at Princeton University since 1972, he received the prize for his 1965 discovery of heat left over from the "big bang" that is believed to have been the beginning of the universe.

Wilson, Robert W. (1936–), American radio astronomer. Associated with Bell Laboratories since 1963, he was codiscoverer with Penzias of the heat of creation.

Physiology or Medicine. For the discovery of "restriction enzymes" and their application in the study of genetics:

Arber, Werner (1929–), Swiss microbiologist. A professor at the University of Basel in Switzerland since 1971, he had previously been associated with the University of Southern California and the University of California at Berkeley. He was honored for discovering "restriction enzymes," which can sever DNA molecules.

Nathans, Daniel (1928–), American microbiologist and molecular biologist. Professor of microbiology at Johns Hopkins University since 1967, he won the prize for his use of restriction enzymes to make precise studies of the DNA of a virus.

Smith, Hamilton O. (1931–), American specialist in microbial genetics. A professor of microbiology at the Johns Hopkins University medical school since 1973, he was the first to establish that restric-

tion enzymes cut DNA molecules at specific locations along their length.

PULITZER PRIZES

The 1978 Pulitzer prizes were announced on April 17. A gold public service medal was awarded to the Philadelphia *Inquirer* for investigative reporting on police abuses; Richard Lee Strout of the *Christian Science Monitor* and the *New Republic* received a special citation for distinguished commentary; and E. B. White received a special citation for his literary work, including his contributions to *The New Yorker* magazine and such books as *Stuart Little* (1945) and *Charlotte's Web* (1952). For the first time a single newspaper, the New York *Times,* won three journalism awards.

Biography. Walter Jackson Bate, *Samuel Johnson* (Bate's second Pulitzer).

Commentary. William Safire of the New York *Times* for columns on the Bert Lance affair.

Criticism. Walter Kerr of the New York *Times.*

Drama. Donald L. Coburn for *The Gin Game.*

Editorial Cartooning. Jeffrey K. MacNelly of the Richmond *News Leader* (he also won in 1972).

Editorial Writing. Meg Greenfield of the Washington *Post.*

Fiction. James Alan McPherson, *Elbow Room.*

General Nonfiction. Carl Sagan, *The Dragons of Eden.*

History. Alfred D. Chandler, Jr., *The Visible Hand: The Managerial Revolution in American Business.*

Music. Michael Colgrass, *Déjà Vu for Percussion Quartet and Orchestra.*

Photography, Feature. J. Ross Baughman of the Associated Press.

Photography, Spot News. John W. Blair, freelance.

Poetry. Howard Nemerov, *Collected Poems.*

Public Service. William K. Marimow and Jonatha

Neumann of the Philadelphia *Inquirer* for a series on police brutality and corruption.

Reporting, General Local. Richard Whitt of the Louisville (Ky.) *Courier-Journal* for coverage of the May, 1977, Beverly Hills Supper Club fire and investigative reporting on unenforced fire laws.

Reporting, International. Henry Kamm of the New York *Times* for reports on the Indochinese refugees known as the boat people.

Reporting, National. Gaylord Shaw of the Los Angeles *Times* for investigative articles on unsafe dams.

Reporting, Special Local. Anthony R. Dolan of the Stamford (Conn.) *Advocate* for a series on municipal corruption.

OTHER PRIZES AND AWARDS

Among the many other prizes and awards distributed during 1978, the following were notable.

Academy of American Poets. Walt Whitman Award to Karen Snow.

American Academy and Institute of Arts and Letters. The Gold Medal for History to Barbara W. Tuchman; the Gold Medal for the Short Story to Peter Taylor; the $4000 Richard and Hinda Rosenthal Award in Literature to Douglas Day; the $4000 Rosenthal Award in Art to Clifford Ross; the Award for Distinguished Service to the Arts to U.S. Rep. John Brademas (D, Ind.); awards of $3000 in literature to Renata Adler, William Arrowsmith, Lerone Bennett, Jr., Terrence Des Pres, Leslie Epstein, Michael Herr, Murray Kempton, Alison Lurie, Toni Morrison, and Page Smith; awards of $3000 in art to William Dole, Daniel Maloney, Herman Maril, Richard McDermott Miller, Sara Roszak, Reuben Tam, and Ulfert Wilke; awards of $3000 in music to Wallace Berry, Curtis O. B. Curtis-Smith, Elie Siegmeister, and Richard Swift. The Morton Dauwen Zabel Award of $2500 to Joan Didion; the Marjorie Peabody Waite Award of $2500 for a composer to Dane Rudhyar.

Association of American Publishers, National Book Awards. Award in contemporary thought to Gloria Emerson, in fiction to Mary Lee Settle, in translation to Richard and Clara Winston, in biography to Walter Jackson Bate, in poetry to Howard Nemerov, in children's literature to Judith and Herbert Kohl, in history to David McCullough. A special Achievement Medal to S. J. Perelman.

Bancroft Prizes for American History. Awards of $4000 to Alfred D. Chandler, Jr., and Morton J. Horwitz.

Bristol-Myers Award for Cancer Research. Award of $25,000 to James Miller and Elizabeth Miller.

Ernest Hemingway Foundation. Award of $6000 for a first book to Darcy O'Brien, *A Way of Life, Like Any Other.*

Special Gold Medal Authorized by Congress. To Marian Anderson for promotion of the arts and efforts on behalf of the brotherhood of man. *See* illustration at NEGROES IN THE UNITED STATES.

Theodore Weicker Memorial Award. Award of $10,000 by American Society of Pharmacology and Experimental Therapeutics to Ernest Bueding.

Vetlesen Prize. Award of $50,000 in Earth Sciences to J. Tuzo Wilson. L.A.S.

PUBLISHING. The publishing industry enjoyed another good year in 1978. Book sales showed substantial increases, magazine advertising revenues set new records, and daily newspaper circulation maintained its recent upward trend. Rising postal rates were again an issue during the year, and the trend toward concentration of ownership in book and newspaper publishing caused continuing controversy.

Postal Rates. Sharply increased postal rates brought protests and warnings from all segments of the U.S. publishing industry. Publishers of books, magazines, and newspapers asked Congress to help roll back the latest round of increases by exerting pressure on the U.S. Postal Service. New rate schedules approved in May increased the cost of second-class mail (magazines and newspapers) by 30 percent. Special-rate

Life *magazine resumed monthly publication in October after a six-year absence. Photos of balloons, icebergs, puppies, and celebrities were enlisted in an effort to recapture the picture newsmagazine's old preeminence.*

fourth-class mail (books) went up 60 percent, more than any other category. The cost for mailing a typical two-pound book jumped from 41¢ to 66¢ and was scheduled to rise to 81¢ in July, 1979. The same book could have been mailed for 18¢ in 1970.

Escalating postal rates prompted some publishers to bypass the post office and experiment with alternative means of delivering books, magazines, and newspapers. In a statement to the U.S. Postal Rate Commission, the Association of American Publishers warned that publishers were being forced to consider cheaper ways of delivering books, including the large-scale use of private delivery systems.

Mergers and Takeovers. Two of the nation's leading independent publishing houses—Charles Scribner's Sons and Atheneum Publishers—agreed to join forces in August. According to Charles Scribner, Jr., and Alfred Knopf, Jr., chairmen of the two companies, the merger was intended to preserve the editorial independence of the firms and avoid any possible takeover by a conglomerate. Scribner's and Atheneum would continue to operate as separate divisions of a newly formed third company: The Scribner Book Companies. In another important merger, Harper & Row acquired the J. B. Lippincott Co., uniting two of the oldest publishing houses in the country. Following the acquisition, Lippincott announced that it would reduce its staff by about 30 percent and would close its Philadelphia office, consolidating all the division's activities in New York City.

Three publishers specializing in children's books were taken over by bigger firms. Parnassus Press, based in Emeryville, Calif., was acquired by Houghton Mifflin; Platt & Munk (publishers of the perennial children's favorite, *The Little Engine That Could*) was purchased by Grosset & Dunlap; and Parents' Magazine Enterprises, which ran Parents' Magazine Press, was bought by a West German publishing firm, Gruner + Jahr.

Following a yearlong investigation, the U.S. Department of Justice filed a complaint against CBS Inc., asking that its 1976 acquisition of Fawcett Publications, Inc., be judged a violation of the Clayton Antitrust Act. CBS was already involved in the mass-market paperback business with its Popular Library when it acquired Fawcett, also a publisher of mass-market paperbacks. The Justice Department suit demanded that CBS divest itself of Fawcett and be enjoined from acquiring any other mass-market paperback firm.

Houghton Mifflin, one of the last major book publishers not yet scooped up by a larger corporation, maintained its independence by rebuffing

a takeover attempt by Western Pacific Industries, which had purchased 10.2 percent of the publishing firm's stock. News of the conglomerate's interest in the independent Boston publisher had caused several prominent Houghton Mifflin authors to issue statements of concern. Following further protests by the Authors Guild, Western Pacific agreed to sell all its shares back to the publishing house.

Congress, meanwhile, continued to investigate the long-term trend toward conglomerate takeovers of publishing houses. The Antitrust and Monopoly Subcommittee of the Senate Judiciary Committee, headed by Sen. Edward M. Kennedy (D, Mass.), began a series of hearings on book publishing mergers and acquisitions. Similar hearings were initiated in the House of Representatives.

Everest House, announced as a major new publishing venture, was launched in New York City to issue general hardcover trade books. Funded by the International Cultural Foundation, an offshoot of the California-based World Wide Church of God, and capitalized at $2,500,000, the new firm became one of the largest publishing start-ups since the founding of Atheneum in 1959.

Magazine cover pictures of John Travolta were not unusual in 1978, but this one was. The popular star of the film Saturday Night Fever was the first man to appear on the cover of McCall's in the magazine's 102-year history.

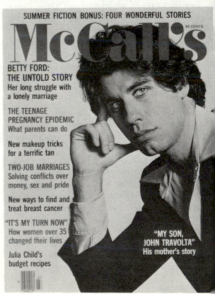

Book Sales. A new record for paperback reprint rights was established when New American Library paid $2,550,000 for Mario Puzo's best-selling 1978 novel, *Fools Die*, published in hardcover by G. P. Putnam's Sons. The record was almost equaled later in the year when Fawcett Books paid $2,250,000 for the paperback rights to *Linda Goodman's Love Signs*, a book on astrology that was published in hardcover by Harper & Row. Other best-selling fiction of 1978 included *Chesapeake* by James A. Michener (Random House); *War and Remembrance* by Herman Wouk (Little, Brown); *Evergreen* by Belva Plain (Delacorte); *Second Generation* by Howard Fast (Houghton Mifflin); *Scruples* by Judith Krantz (Crown); *Bloodline* by Sidney Sheldon (Morrow); *The Human Factor* by Graham Greene (Simon & Schuster); and *The Women's Room* by Marilyn French (Summit Books).

Nonfiction best-sellers published during the year included *The Complete Book of Running* by James F. Fixx (Random House); *Mommie Dearest* by Christina Crawford (Morrow); *A Distant Mirror: The Fourteenth Century* by Barbara W. Tuchman (Knopf); *If Life Is a Bowl of Cherries—What Am I Doing in the Pits?* by Erma Bombeck (McGraw-Hill); *Gnomes* by Wil Huygen, illustrated by Rien Poortvliet (Harry N. Abrams); *The Country Diary of an Edwardian Lady* by Edith Holden (Holt); *Pulling Your Own Strings* by Wayne W. Dyer (Funk & Wagnalls); *My Mother/My Self* by Nancy Friday (Delacorte); and *The Amityville Horror* by Jay Anson (Prentice-Hall).

The 1976 best-seller *Roots* involved author Alex Haley in two plagiarism suits in 1978. In December, Haley settled one suit out of court by conceding that his fictionalized account of his African ancestry contained material taken inadvertently from the 1967 novel *The African*, by Harold Courlander. An undisclosed amount of money was paid to Courlander and his publisher, Crown. A similar suit, alleging similarities amounting to plagiarism between *Roots* and Margaret Walker's 1966 novel *Jubilee*, was dismissed by a New York City judge in September.

In its annual roundup of industry sales figures, the Association of American Publishers reported that book sales reached a total of $4.6 billion in 1977, an increase of 10 percent over the year before.

Periodicals. *Life* magazine, which suspended regular weekly publication in 1972, returned to the newsstands in October as a monthly. Founded in 1936 (when it sold for a dime), *Life* became magazine publishing's most successful venture before it succumbed to changing tastes and advertising competition from television. While many magazines had shrunk in size in recent years, the new *Life*, priced at $1.50 a copy, retained its big-page format. The first issue contained fifty-six advertising pages worth $848,568—a record amount for any magazine's debut.

Life returned amid indications that the picture magazine might be making a general comeback. Daniel Filipacchi, the French publisher of *Paris-Match*, announced plans to revive *Look* magazine as a weekly early in 1979. The new *Look* would be published in New York City.

The number of new magazines started in 1978 showed a substantial increase over the previous year, according to figures reported by *Folio: The Magazine for Magazine Management*. In 1978, 314 new publications were started, as against 272 in 1977. Among the newcomers were *Omni*, the latest venture of publisher Bob Guccione (*Penthouse* and *Viva*), which was billed as "the first magazine of the space age" and would print both science fiction and science fact; *Self*, a monthly women's magazine devoted to "physical and emotional fitness," published by Peter G. Kiamandis of Condé Nast Publications; and an American version of the French fashion magazine *Mode*, scheduled to appear ten times a year with a cover price of $2.95.

A growing segment of the U.S. population, women with full- or part-time jobs, was the target of several new magazines. McCall's put out *Working Mother* in a successful test issue in September. Family Circle countered with two test issues of *Women Who Work*. Both were scheduled for regular publication in 1979, when they would compete with *Working Woman*, which first appeared in 1976 and increased its circulation to 300,000 by heavy promotion in 1978.

Among the year's magazine failures was the biweekly *New Times*, which began publication in 1973 during the Watergate investigation. Under editor Jonathan Z. Larsen, the magazine had specialized in hard-hitting investigative articles. Publisher George A. Hirsch attributed the magazine's demise to declining reader interest in "investigative reporting, social issues or public affairs." As an indication of shifting reader concerns, Hirsch pointed to the instant success of his new magazine, *The Runner*, which premiered in October.

Other magazine losses included *American Home*, published since 1929, which succumbed to a $5,000,000 deficit and was absorbed by *Redbook*; *WomenSports*, which claimed a circulation of 200,000 but had lost money since being founded in 1974 by tennis star Billie Jean King and her husband; and R. R. Bowker Company's *Bookviews*, launched in 1977 as a mass-audience literary magazine. Also folding were Bob Guccione's

PUBLISHING

Rupert Murdoch, publisher of the New York Post, *watches as the Oct. 5 edition of his newspaper rolls off the presses after a fifty-six-day shutdown caused by striking pressmen. By settling independently with the pressmen, the* Post *scooped New York City's other two dailies, which remained off the stands until Nov. 6.*

Viva, a monthly that began in 1973 as a women's counterpart to the sex-oriented *Penthouse* but met with distributor problems and failed to find its market; and *More,* a small but respected journalism review. The crudely explicit sex magazine *Hustler* survived despite several traumas. The religious conversion of its publisher, Larry Flynt, influenced its content in ways that puzzled its readership. And in March, Flynt himself was shot and left partially paralyzed by an unknown gunman in Lawrence, Ga., where the publisher had been testifying at his own obscenity trial.

Magazine advertising revenues again set new records in 1978. The Publishers Information Bureau reported that ad revenues for the first eleven months of 1978 totaled $2.2 billion—an increase of 20 percent over the same period in 1977 and an all-time high.

Newspapers. The Washington *Star,* the only evening daily in the nation's capital, was purchased by Time, Inc., for $20,000,000 plus the assumption of an additional $8,000,000 in debts. Acquisition of the newspaper placed Time, Inc., in direct competition in Washington, D.C., with the Washington Post Co., which owns the city's only morning newspaper and *Newsweek* magazine. The 125-year-old *Star,* once the dominant newspaper in Washington, had a 1978 daily circulation of 349,000, compared to the *Post's* 541,000.

The Gannett Co., the largest of the chains in number of newspapers owned, expanded its holdings again in 1978. In January, Gannett, based in Rochester, N.Y., purchased two Wilmington, Del., dailies from E. I. du Pont de Nemours. In May, Gannett announced plans to buy Combined Communications Corp., and would thereby acquire two more metropolitan dailies—the Cincinnati *Enquirer* and the Oakland *Tribune*—plus 1. radio and 7 television stations. Completion of the deal would raise the chain's nationwide ownership to 81 newspapers with a combined circulation of about 3,400,000—second only to the Knight-Ridder chain, which owned newspapers in thirty-two of the larger cities.

The latest Gannett acquisitions focused renewed attention on the continuing trend toward

326

concentration of ownership in the newspaper field. In 1978, chain publishers controlled 72 percent of the country's daily newspaper circulation. Rep. Morris K. Udall (D, Ariz.) called the Gannett acquisitions "an alarming development . . . a case of a whale swallowing a whale." With seventy-two other members of the House of Representatives, Udall introduced legislation aimed at checking the trend toward concentration by reducing inheritance burdens on independent publishers.

The U.S. Supreme Court addressed the issue of media conglomeration in a June ruling that banned thenceforth the acquisition of radio or television stations by newspapers in the same community. Existing combinations of newspapers and broadcasting outlets were allowed to continue. In another decision that startled the publishing world, the Supreme Court ruled that police armed with a warrant could make unannounced raids on newsrooms in search of criminal evidence. The case involved the Stanford University *Daily,* a student newspaper that had sued police after a 1971 raid. During 1978 the High Court and lower courts generally upheld criminal defendants' rights rather than reporters' rights to freedom of information when the two conflicted; *see* CIVIL RIGHTS AND CIVIL LIBERTIES; SUPREME COURT OF THE UNITED STATES.

The Chicago *Daily News,* that city's last afternoon daily, ceased publication in March after 102 years. Since 1959, when it was purchased by Field Enterprises (owners of Chicago's morning *Sun-Times*), the *News,* like many other evening dailies, had lost readers to the suburbs and television. The loss of the *News* left Chicago with two dailies— the *Sun-Times* and its morning rival, the Chicago *Tribune.*

In another newspaper failure, the New York *Trib,* a morning tabloid, folded in April after three months of publication. Leonard Saffir, the paper's founder, had aimed for a first-year circulation of 200,000, but when the *Trib* shut down, its paid circulation was below 40,000. Saffir and his backers had invested $5,000,000 in the *Trib,* the first major morning paper introduced in Manhattan since 1924.

New York's three major dailies—the *Daily News,* the *Times,* and the afternoon *Post*—lost an estimated $150,000,000 in advertising and circulation revenues during a three-month-long strike by pressmen and other newspaper employees that began on Aug. 9. The key issue concerned manning levels in the pressrooms. The settlement allowed the publishers to reduce pressroom manning through attrition and also guaranteed jobs through 1984 for the 1508 pressmen involved. Halfway through the strike, the *Post* resumed

publication after publisher Rupert Murdoch broke with his fellow publishers and reached a separate agreement with the unions.

In another major newspaper labor dispute, the St. Louis *Post-Dispatch* and the St. Louis *Globe-Democrat* were shut down in November by striking pressmen. At year's end, the pressmen had approved a new three-year contract and related unions were expected to come to terms soon. Meanwhile, in Great Britain, the London *Times* suspended publication on Nov. 30 for what was expected to be a lengthy period of negotiation with sixty-five labor bargaining units. The *Times* management announced that the paper and its supplements would not reappear until all employees agreed to end strikes and slowdowns and accept new technology and manning schedules.

The New York *Times* settled a sex discrimination suit out of court by agreeing to pay female employees nearly $350,000 and promising to hire and promote substantial numbers of women. Among the women promoted was Le Anne Schreiber, who at 33 became the first woman sports editor in the history of the *Times.*

New York Times *reporter Myron A. Farber talks to reporters on Oct. 12 before entering prison in Bergen County, N.J. Farber was jailed for forty days for refusing to turn over his notes on a murder case. Behind Farber is* Times *executive editor A. M. Rosenthal.*

In its annual statistical roundup, the 1978 edition of *Editor & Publisher International Year Book* reported that daily newspaper circulation continued its upward trend in 1977 for the second year in a row, after three years of recession-induced losses. Total daily circulation increased to 61,495,-140, a gain of slightly below 1 percent over the year before and the highest circulation figure since 1974. The number of daily newspapers in the U.S. decreased, however, from 1762 in 1976 to 1753 in 1977.

Deaths. In 1978 the publishing world lost Max Ascoli, Janet Flanner, and many authors; *see* OBITUARIES; *see also* LITERATURE. Other deaths included those of George W. Bliss, investigative reporter for the Chicago *Tribune* (Sept. 11 at 60); Hal Borland, who wrote seasonal nature editorials for the New York *Times* for thirty-five years (Feb. 22 at 77); Price Day, editor in chief of the Baltimore *Sun* (Dec. 9 at 71); John Fischer, editor in chief of *Harper's Magazine* (Aug. 18 at 68); Robert Harrison, former publisher of *Confidential* magazine (Feb. 17 at 73); Stephen E. Kelly, former publisher of *The Saturday Evening Post* (April 6 at 58); sports cartoonist Willard Mullin (Dec. 21 at 76); French newspaper publisher Jean Prouvost (Oct. 17 at 93); British newspaper publisher Viscount Rothermere (Esmond Cecil Harmsworth; July 12 at 80); Victor Weybright, publisher of the paperback New American Library (Nov. 3 at 75); and veteran New York *Times* reporters Clayton Knowles (Jan. 4 at 69), Thomas Mullaney (Oct. 21 at 56), and James P. Roach (March 16 at 70).   R.F.

PUERTO RICO. The long standing debate on the island's future status—independence, statehood, or continued commonwealth association with the United States—continued to dominate the Puerto Rican political scene in 1978.

Politics. Gov. Carlos Romero Barceló, head of the pro-statehood New Progressive Party, announced in February that, if reelected in 1980, he would call for a plebiscite on Puerto Rico's future. He claimed that the island's status as a commonwealth was "in limbo," giving it neither the benefits of full association with the U.S., as statehood would, nor the advantages of complete independence. Using the same argument, two small political parties—the Puerto Rican Independence Party and the Socialist Party—urged severing U.S. ties.

On July 3–4 two advocates of Puerto Rican independence briefly held captive the Chilean consul in San Juan, Ramon Gonzalez Ruiz, and another Chilean national, in the first political kidnapping in the history of Puerto Rico. They demanded release of four Puerto Rican nationalists imprisoned in the U.S. and cancellation of the U.S.-oriented July 4 parade, but surrendered to

This store in San Juan is owned by a "Neorican," a Puerto Rican who once lived in New York City. During 1978 many such returnees reversed the migration pattern of a generation ago.

police and Federal Bureau of Investigation officers after seventeen hours. Most Puerto Rican nationalist agitation had previously taken place in the U.S., at the hands of the Armed Forces of National Liberation for Puerto Rico (FALN). In late May the FALN claimed responsibility for small fires at three airports in the New York City area and for a bomb explosion at the Justice Department building in Washington, D.C.

Political observers regarded the election on Oct. 24 for twenty-two delegates to the U.S. Democratic Party midterm convention (held in Nashville, Tenn., in December) as a test of pro-statehood sentiment. The traditional proponent of continued commonwealth status, the Popular Democratic Party (PDP), had been dominant in island politics until the election of Romero Barceló in 1976. In 1978 a split in the PDP between party regulars and a new group favoring statehood put the commonwealth cause in jeopardy. Former Gov. Rafael Hernández-Colón stepped down as party chairman in July; he was succeeded by the senate minority leader, Miguel Hernández Agosto, a commonwealth advocate. About the same time the 80-year-old former Gov. Luis Muñoz Marín, the grand old man of Puerto Rican politics, ended his eight-year retirement to campaign against statehood. The PDP called for a boycott of the election, but more than 360,000 voters turned out, although political machinations had left the pro-statehood candidates virtually unchallenged. The large turnout was regarded as an affirmation of continued strong ties with the U.S.

In late August and early September advocates of all three options took part in the annual United Nations debate on whether Puerto Rico is in fact a colony of the U.S. (It had been removed from the U.N. Decolonization Committee's list in 1963.) A resolution was sponsored by Cuba and Iraq calling for Puerto Rican self-determination; on Sept. 12 the decolonization committee voted 10 to 0, with 12 abstentions, in favor of the resolution. The policy of the U.S. government was restated by President Jimmy Carter on July 25: Any change in the status of Puerto Rico would have to be initiated by the Puerto Rican electorate.

The Economy. In January Romero Barceló announced his long-awaited industrial incentive program. By ending the 100 percent tax exemption on companies with annual incomes above $100,000 and instituting a set of lower exemptions, he claimed that more industry would be developed and Puerto Rico would lose its "commonwealth mentality." In May the governor unveiled a series of television commercials extolling the island's industrial potential and its tourism; they were later broadcast in six major U.S. cities. Also in May the U.S. Commission on Human Rights urged the Carter administration to create an interagency coordinating committee to study the effects of federal aid to Puerto Rican communities on the island and the mainland. The commission maintained that their special needs had long been neglected.

See STATISTICS OF THE WORLD.   J.N.G.

Q

QATAR. *See* STATISTICS OF THE WORLD.

QUÉBEC. *See* STATISTICS OF THE WORLD.

R

RADIO AND TELEVISION BROADCASTING. Issues concerning child viewers and deregulation of television and radio dominated news of the broadcasting media in 1978. NBC-TV's program scuttling in November and affiliate switches were among the more startling events of a startling year, which began with the defection of Fred Silverman—who had started in the business at CBS—from ABC to NBC.

Television Influence Dispute. Television "incitement" was on trial in San Francisco, where the mother of Olivia Niemi had sued NBC-TV in 1974 for $11,000,000, claiming the telecast of a rape scene in the television film *Born Innocent* had provoked a similar attack on her 9-year-old daughter three days later. A California Superior Court judge had dismissed the case on First Amendment grounds. The State Court of Appeals then reversed this ruling, and on April 24 the Supreme Court of the United States cleared the way for a jury trial. Finally, on Aug. 8, a judge ruled that the plaintiff could not prove "intent" on the part of the network to incite a similar attack in real life, and the case was again dismissed.

From the Supreme Court, radio stations learned "seven dirty words" that are not to be broadcast when children are likely to be listening. The Federal Communications Commission (FCC) had reprimanded a radio station for playing a George Carlin comedy record at 2 P.M., when children were in the audience. The owners of the radio station—WBAI-FM in New York City—challenged the FCC in the U.S. Court of Appeals for the District of Columbia and won their case. On July 3, the Supreme Court reversed the lower court and affirmed the FCC ruling, finding the seven words spoken by Carlin to be obscene. However, FCC Chairman Charles Ferris assured broadcasters that the ruling would be interpreted very narrowly.

The FCC also reopened its long-dormant inquiry into the relationship between television and young people, with the major consideration being how to define "children's" programming. The commission decided to review proposals that would ban all advertising that is directed toward children under 8 years of age or that appears in programs with audiences having a "significant proportion" of children.

Operation Prime Time challenged the networks in May with a 4-hour, $3,600,000 production. Patricia Neal and Andrew Stevens played mother and son in The Bastard, *which was called* The Kent Family Chronicles *by 10 of the 93 stations that showed it.*

The Federal Trade Commission, meanwhile, proposed a ban on television advertising for sugared products—notably cereals—unless they are "balanced" by nutritional and dental messages paid for by sponsors. Hearings on the proposed ban were scheduled to start in early 1979.

Government and Broadcasting. FCC actions during 1978, particularly regarding license renewals—a million-dollar matter—portended keener dedication to the public interest and consumers' rights. Licensees felt less complacent. To help Blacks acquire television and radio stations, the FCC said it would issue "tax certificates" to licensees selling to black groups and would permit "distressed sales" (without renewal hearings) to minorities. Moreover, the National Association of Broadcasters formed a minority-ownership task force, hoping to raise $30,000,000 to help Blacks acquire stations. The most active citizens' groups in this area have been the National Black Media Coalition and the United Church of Christ.

CBS received the most severe, if indirect, penalty ever given a network by the government when CBS-owned KNXT in Los Angeles was granted only a one-year license renewal (the normal term is three years) because of the network's involvement in what it called "winner take all"

tennis tournaments. The series, *The Heavyweight Championship of Tennis,* was telecast from 1975 to 1978. After CBS had proclaimed that losers of matches received nothing, the FCC learned that substantial advance guarantees were provided to all participants. CBS Broadcast Group President Gene Jankowski took the unusual step of apologizing to the public on the air.

A controversial bill favoring "market forces" rather than regulation was introduced early in the year by Rep. Lionel Van Deerlin (D, Calif.) and Louis Frey, Jr. (R, Fla.) to "rewrite" the Communications Act of 1934; the co-sponsors said a totally new act was needed to cut red tape and to reflect new technologies. The new bill proposed a less powerful regulatory commission than the FCC, elimination of regular review of licenses, and discontinuance of the equal-time or "fairness" doctrine (except for local elections). Following lengthy hearings, Van Deerlin planned to introduce a revised bill early in 1979.

The Office of Telecommunications Policy of the White House was abolished in 1978. In its place the National Telecommunications and Information Administration was established within the Department of Commerce. The new office combines former broadcast functions of the White House and of the Commerce Department.

Television and radio made inroads into the parliaments of three countries during the year. Experimental live radio broadcasts of the proceedings of the U.S. House of Representatives turned out to be less than enthralling, as did regular air coverage in England of House of Commons oratory. Canada, however, had inaugurated five-day-a-week television coverage of its parliament in October, 1977. In 1978 the ratings were good. Said the House clerk: "We can't meet the demand for videotapes."

Affiliates and Defections. The switch from NBC to ABC by influential midwestern stations KSTP-TV (Minneapolis-St. Paul) and WRTV (Indianapolis) left indelible handwriting on the walls for NBC in 1978.

In the realm of network-affiliate rivalry, ABC had another heartening year, matching NBC and CBS in substations for the first time in twenty-five years. In May twelve "apostate" station owners from NBC and CBS attended their first convention as new, profit-minded children of ABC. As an executive of Knight-Ridder Newspapers, Inc., put it: "We decided to go with the guys who were more aggressive and professional. . . ." Since 1976 ABC had lured 17 stations away from CBS and 9 from NBC. Observers noted that networks need affiliates not only to attract national advertisers but for tie-ins with good local news shows.

Battlestar Galactica, *the most expensive television series ever made, began its regular Sunday night run in the fall. Lorne Greene lent his dignified presence to a starring role, that of the leader of a group of space wanderers.*

On the creative side, a group of independent and affiliate stations banded together in 1978 to form Operation Prime Time. They presented a $3,600,000, 4-hour miniseries, *The Bastard* (called *The Kent Family Chronicles* on ten stations), in an attempt to challenge the three major networks in prime time. The series was seen on ninety-three stations in May and was remarkably successful.

Network Programming. It was a year of specials, biographical dramas, and a winsome creature named Mork.

Following the January, 1977, success of *Roots* on ABC-TV—repeated in its September, 1978, rerun—the networks continued to rely heavily on miniseries and prime-time specials. Both CBS and NBC continued to lose ground to ABC as the evening ratings leader, and ABC took over from CBS in November as all-day "most-watched" television network.

During 1978 television programmers favored instant replays of celebrities' lives. Among the biographies aired were those of the young Judy Garland, comics Bud Abbott and Lou Costello, television reporter Betty Rollin, and athlete Ron LeFlore. Many more such programs were scheduled for 1979. The most conspicuous movie derivative of the year was ABC's *Battlestar Galactica,* a big-budget, hardware-heavy weekly series in the mode of *Star Wars,* more notable for special effects than for characterization. Also on an epic scale was NBC's maxi-miniseries *Centennial,* a 25-hour-long saga of a fictional Colorado town. Based on James Michener's novel, it was sched-

uled to run into 1979. Much attention was also focused on NBC's *Holocaust,* a miniseries of well-intentioned, well-acted dramas about the Nazi pogrom, which was shown on four consecutive nights in April.

ABC's powerful Tuesday night lineup of *Happy Days, Laverne & Shirley, Three's Company,* and *Taxi* (new in 1978) continued to lead the way among regularly scheduled programs. The season's new hit series was ABC's *Mork & Mindy,* which featured the many-voiced talents of Robin Williams as an unflappable alien houseguest on earth. The Williams show and *Taxi* were the only new programs to rate consistently in the top ten. The critics found a few new series to admire, including *The Paper Chase,* set in a law school, and the comedy *WKRP in Cincinnati,* both on CBS.

Many new shows were added to the schedule in the fall of 1978. Precious few of them were destined to survive into 1979. In what the New York *Times* described as the "most dramatic midseason" changes ever made by a network, NBC in late November canceled half its weekly series—including all the new shows that started in September. (One of the casualties was *The Waverly Wonders,* starring Joe Namath as a basketball coach.) The drastic moves by Fred Silverman, new NBC president and ex-programming head at both

One of the most talked about of the year's many mini-series was Holocaust. Seen on four consecutive nights in April, the drama depicted Germany in the 1930's and 1940's. Here, Meryl Streep as Inga Weiss tries to reach the outstretched hand of her concentration camp-bound husband Karl, played by James Woods.

CBS and ABC, confounded many in the industry. NBC moved to eight hours weekly of movies and specials, along with fifteen new programs, mostly comedies. Silverman made it clear that NBC would not emphasize sex and violence in order to gain a larger audience, and took an indirect swipe at permissive ABC programming, most of which had gone on the air when he was president of ABC Entertainment. (One of his first moves at NBC had been to place a cinema verité medical series, Lifeline, in a Thursday night prime-time slot. "You've got to take chances," he explained.)

CBS got a boost in late November when its news show 60 Minutes (seen on Sunday nights), which had consistently rated in the top ten, actually reached number one. With "anchorperson" having become a part of the language, ABC News and Sports President Roone Arledge repackaged newscast stalwarts as "news desks," with more emphasis on personalized reporting outside the studio. In 1978 the newspersons on all three networks remained aloof from the folksy personal style common to newscasters at local stations across the U.S.

CBS made less dramatic changes in its prime-time schedule for January, 1979, than did NBC, adding 5 new shows; ABC added only 2. CBS also changed the time periods of 7 holdover programs, and NBC did a lot of similar shifting—both networks jockeying to stem the ABC surge. In December some 20 new "limited series"—rather than single pilots—were announced as trial balloons for the networks.

Public, Cable, and "Superstation" Television. Public broadcasting had a good—and more public—year in 1978. The Public Broadcasting Service (PBS) audience was twice as large as it had been five years previously, and by the end of the year it had become the only network to link its stations, 270 of them, by relay satellite—a boon to nationwide live coverage. Eager for federal funding, public stations anticipated opening meetings and audits to the public and community advisory boards in 1979, to court a "less affluent" viewership. Congress passed a five-year appropriations bill which contained increased funding.

A former FCC chairman, Newton Minow, became chairman of PBS in 1978, and ex-Michigan State University President Robben W. Fleming was elected chairman of the Corporation for Public Broadcasting, through which federal funds for broadcasting are channeled. The two chairmen promised to end the bickering that has existed between the two organizations and strive for a united front in dealings with the FCC, Congress, the White House, and the public.

PBS programming for 1978 was perhaps the most enterprising it had been in its nine-year history. To lure more of the public from commercial station viewing, PBS offered more recent movies (along with classics), live White House concerts, and such controversial documentaries as *California Reich*, about West Coast neo-Nazis—which some PBS affiliates refused to carry. The solid appeal of *Masterpiece Theatre* continued; the well-received dramatization of Thomas Hardy's *The Mayor of Casterbridge* was the forty-fourth production to be imported from literature- and period-wise British television sources.

For the cable television networks, 1978 was a year of progress. Deregulatory impetus intensified

in Congress and at the FCC. Subscribers signed up by the thousands, principally because of pay-cable offerings of new films, concerts, and special sports events not shown on commercial stations. Major pay-cable entrepreneurs included the Time, Inc., subsidiary Home Box Office, Viacom's Showtime, and Madison Square Garden Productions.

From coast to coast, "super" television stations, such as WTGG (Atlanta), KTVU (San Francisco), and WGN-TV (Chicago), proliferated. Relaxed FCC rules governing so-called distant signals, or stations brought into a market far beyond normal coverage area, allowed these stations to broadcast their far-reaching signals.

CB and Commercial Radio. After two poor years, the citizens-band (CB) radio industry showed signs of recovery. During the first three months of the year the FCC granted almost 1,000,000 CB licenses. But many fewer companies were competing for the customer's dollar. At the height of the

The greatest personal success of the fall television season was achieved by a rubber-faced, multivoiced young clown. Robin Williams could well afford to grin as his show, Mork & Mindy, *climbed in the ratings.*

When Jane Cahill Pfeiffer was elected to the chairperson-ship of NBC in the fall, she became the highest ranked woman in the history of radio and television broadcasting. The former IBM vice-president also became a director of RCA Corp.

boom in 1975–76, more than 125 companies were selling the radios; by the spring of 1978 only about 60 companies remained and predictions were that no more than 25 would survive and flourish. In 1978 only 40-channel radios could be sold, according to a new FCC regulation; these sets were far too sophisticated for many companies to produce.

Commercial radio's story in 1978 was one of deregulation. The disputed congressional broadcast bill (see above) would remove nearly all government regulations for radio. Failing that, the FCC was prepared to take many steps on its own. Every member of the commission spoke out for radio deregulation, and Chairman Ferris announced his intention to take some concrete steps early in 1979, steps that would not require congressional approval.

In December the commission tentatively approved a plan to add 125 new AM radio stations to serve small-town (and nighttime) America. Previously the commission had favored the so-called clear-channel superstations to service those areas.

If given final approval, the plan would widen station-owning competition and spur waveband power for minorities (making ultra-high-frequency reception comparable to very-high-frequency reception).

People. Joining Fred Silverman (who moved from ABC to NBC in January) in the many major network personnel changes of 1978 was Jane Cahill Pfeiffer. Silverman picked her to become chairperson of NBC—and the top female executive in broadcasting. Pfeiffer, 45, was a former vice-president of IBM. Her duties at NBC (she would also be a director of RCA Corp.) were to include employee relations and government and legal affairs. In another ERA-oriented move, it was announced that the name of attorney Anne Jones, appointed to the FCC by U.S. President Jimmy Carter, would go to the Senate for confirmation in January, 1979.

In other top echelon moves, Anthony Thomopoulos replaced Silverman as ABC Entertainment president; Washington CBS Bureau Vice-President William Leonard was tapped to succeed Richard Salant as president of CBS News in April, 1979; and Lester Crystal replaced Richard Wald as NBC News president. Wald moved to ABC News as senior vice-president under Roone Arledge. In July, W. Allen Wallis resigned his chairmanship of the Corporation for Public Broadcasting "for personal reasons." Eager to get out of daily news and into documentaries, anchorman Harry Reasoner left ABC and Barbara Walters in July for a slot on *CBS Reports.*

Deaths. Among the radio and television personalities who died during 1978 were Carl Betz, Bob Crane, Zara Cully, James Daly, Totie Fields, Frank Fontaine, Will Geer, and Karl Swenson; *see* OBITUARIES. Other notable deaths included those of early television personality Wendy Barrie (Feb. 2 at 65); Myrtle Vail Damerel, "Myrt" of the radio serial *Myrt and Marge* (Sept. 18 at 90); raconteur Walter Kiernan (Jan. 8 at 75); Bret Morrison, voice of *The Shadow* (Sept. 25 at 66); all-night talk show pioneer Long John Nebel (April 10 at 66); and Bruce Geller, 47, writer-producer who conceived *Mission Impossible* and *Mannix,* and Stephen Gentry, 37, ABC-TV West Coast programming chief, who were killed in an airplane crash (May 21). D.N.

RECORDINGS. The year 1978 was one of consolidation rather than innovation for the classical record industry. Most companies concentrated on repeating standard works rather than venturing in new directions. Even the year's most notable commemorative event, the 150th anniversary of the death of Franz Schubert, was not marked by any effort to record his many obscure and neglected works. The one major Schubert release of the year

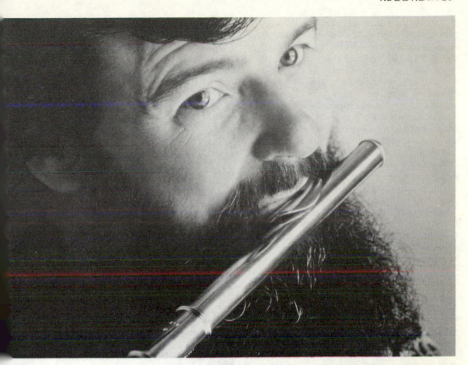

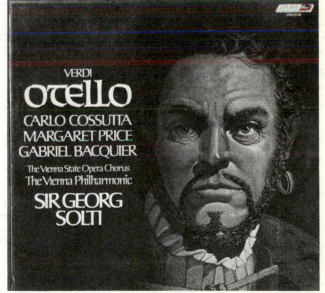

Irish-born James Galway, widely acclaimed solo flutist, made several recordings for RCA in 1978. He also toured the U.S. in concert.

Carlo Cossutta as the tragic Moor stares from the cover of the London album of Otello. Sir Georg Solti conducted the Vienna State Opera Chorus and the Vienna Philharmonic in one of the two recordings of the Verdi work made in 1978.

was a five-record Angel album devoted to all eight of his symphonies plus the *Rosamunde* incidental music, played by the Berlin Philharmonic Orchestra under Herbert von Karajan.

Symphonic Cycles. In orchestral music, the most notable trend was toward substantial packages containing all or most of a composer's works played by a single conductor and orchestra. Von Karajan was particularly active in this regard; in addition to his Schubert cycle he also recorded the complete symphonies of Beethoven and Brahms (each for the third time) with the Berlin Philharmonic for Deutsche Grammophon. For Angel, East German conductor Klaus Tennstedt and the London Philharmonic launched a complete Mahler cycle with their recording of his First Symphony. In London, Iranian-born conductor Loris Tjeknavorian led the National Philharmonic Orchestra through the complete orchestral music of Aleksandr Borodin for RCA. Another important RCA release was the last six symphonies of Mozart played by Jean-François Paillard and the English Chamber Orchestra.

From Vanguard came a four-record collection of the symphonies of Jean Sibelius by the Utah Symphony led by Maurice Abravanel. Especially notable was "A Baroque Festival," a three-record album of works by Vivaldi, Bach, Handel, Corelli, and others, performed by Neville Marriner and the Academy of St. Martin-in-the-Fields chamber orchestra for Argo.

Opera. As is often the case, some of the more adventurous recording enterprises of the year were operatic. First recordings were made of Mozart's *Mitridate, Rè di Ponto* (DG), composed at the age of 14; French composer Henri Rabaud's *Marouf* (Peters), dating from 1914; and Manuel de Falla's *Atlántida* (Angel), completed after his death in 1946 by Ernesto Halffter.

Among other rarely performed operas, three of the most notable recorded during the year were Mozart's next-to-last opera, *La Clemenza di Tito*, with Colin Davis conducting a cast including Janet Baker, Stuart Burrows, and Frederica von Stade (Philips); Verdi's early *I Due Foscari* with Lamberto Gardelli conducting and the leads sung by Katia Ricciarelli, José Carreras, and Piero Cappuccilli (Philips); and Rimski-Korsakov's *The Snow Maiden*, sung in Russian with a Moscow cast headed by soprano Irina Arkhipova (Melodiya/ Columbia).

Columbia described its four-record set of Ambroise Thomas's *Mignon* as the first full-length recording of that opera. Its cast includes Marilyn Horne in the title role with Ruth Welting, Alain Vanzo, and Frederica von Stade. Antonio de Almeida conducted. For RCA, Raymond Leppard

Austrian-born conductor Herbert von Karajan leads the Berlin Philharmonic Orchestra in a 1978 recording session. They performed Schubert symphonies to commemorate the 150th anniversary of the composer's death.

conducted the first recording in several years of Henry Purcell's masterpiece, *Dido and Aeneas*, with Tatiana Troyanos and Richard Stilwell.

In some respects the year's most unusual operatic recording was the Philips album of Gaetano Donizetti's familiar *Lucia di Lammermoor*, with Montserrat Caballé. Conductor Jesús López Cobos, preparing a new edition of the score for the Ricordi publishing house, went back to the original to discover that the composer intended the work to be performed as a dramatic entity rather than a coloratura showpiece. The recording accordingly dispenses with many of the traditional vocal ornaments and shows the opera as a work of stronger musico-dramatic fiber than it appears in previous versions.

The year's end produced two competing recordings of Verdi's *Otello*. The RCA set, directed by James Levine, had the stronger cast, with Placido Domingo in the title role; but the London set, by Georg Solti, with Carlo Cossutta as the tragic Moor, had superior sound. Neither quite fulfilled the need for a definitive recording of this masterful work.

Chamber and Solo Instrumental Music. In 1978 a continuing series of the complete string quartets of Haydn by the Aeolian Quartet, on the London Treasury budget label, reached volume five. An interesting novelty was the first recording ever made of a Trio for Violin, Cello, and Piano in D minor by Fanny Mendelssohn, the older sister of Felix Mendelssohn. She was an accomplished composer, most of whose works are still in manuscript. This recording, made by the Camerata Canada for Crystal, shows her to have had both talent and taste.

Noteworthy among the pianists who were recorded in 1978 was Russian-born Vladimir Horowitz. His performance of Rachmaninoff's Concerto No. 3 was recorded live by RCA at Carnegie Hall in New York City on Jan. 8, the 50th anniversary of Horowitz's debut in the United States. The orchestra was the New York Philharmonic under Eugene Ormandy. For Columbia, Glenn Gould performed a collection of seldom-heard Sibelius pieces. The artistry of the late Bruce Hungerford was beautifully represented by Beethoven sonatas

numbers 9, 10, and 18 (Vanguard). One of the most talked-about piano recordings was a Columbia release devoted to Hungarian-born Ervin Nyiregyházi, a spectacular virtuoso of the 1920's who dropped out of sight until he was rediscovered in 1974 playing at a fund-raising recital in a San Francisco church. At the age of 75 he was rehabilitated musically for many listeners by his recording of a Liszt recital for IPA/Desmar and another for Columbia. Among other instrumentalists, Irish-born flutist James Galway won great approbation for several RCA releases, French musician Marcel André was praised for a series of trumpet recordings (RCA), and Soviet-born cellist Mstislav Rostropovich and the Melos Quartet received critical acclaim for their performance of Schubert's String Quintet in C major (DG).

One major recording project came to an end during the year, while another was forging ahead. New World Records, funded by the Rockefeller Foundation to produce a hundred-record "Anthology of American Music," issued its final release. Telefunken Records reached approximately

Hungarian-born virtuoso Ervin Nyiregyházi, who had not played for several decades, returned to the notice of the musical world with his 1978 recordings of Liszt.

RED CROSS

the one-third point in its schedule for enregistering the complete cantatas of Bach in authentic baroque style. The series reached Cantata No. 72 during the year out of a planned total of 215. At the present rate of progress, the project would be completed just before the year 2000.

See also Music.   H.K.

RED CROSS. The 150th anniversary of the birth of Jean Henri Dunant, founder of the Red Cross movement and one of the first recipients of the Nobel Peace Prize, was May 8, 1978. One of the commemorative events was a round-table meeting in Geneva of nine international institutions that had also won the Nobel Prize. The purpose of the meeting, convened by the International Committee of the Red Cross (ICRC) and the League of Red Cross Societies (LORCS), both former Nobel winners, was "to discuss how each organization contributes to peace and how to overcome obstacles to the promotion of peace."

War Relief. Peace, however, proved to be very elusive in 1978, with conflicts in the Middle East, Central America, and Africa requiring humanitarian action by the ICRC in behalf of displaced persons, refugees, those who were wounded or sick, prisoners of war, and political detainees.

Renewed fighting in Lebanon during March brought massive humanitarian problems comparable to those at the height of the civil war in 1975–76. Out of 250,000 displaced persons, only 50,000 were able to return to their homes in southern Lebanon by May. The ICRC treated the wounded, distributed thousands of tons of food and medical supplies valued at millions of dollars, carried out its prisoner protection role on both sides, and operated a tracing and family message service.

The outbreak of civil strife during the summer in Nicaragua caused the ICRC to spend over $1,000,000 for local purchase of food, medicine, and clothing for victims there and for refugees who fled to neighboring Costa Rica and Honduras.

In Africa, ICRC relief for victims of the conflict in Rhodesia included delivery of ambulances, hospital beds, blankets, sheets, tents, and medical supplies. Because of increasing warfare in a dozen African countries, the ICRC made appeals for money to maintain its sixty-five delegates on the continent and for respect of the Geneva Conventions by parties to the conflicts.

American Red Cross. At its February, 1978, meeting, the Board of Governors restructured the management of Red Cross blood services by establishing a nine-member standing Blood Service Committee and by endorsing the appointment of a vice-president whose sole responsibility would

A doctor and a nurse treat patients at an improvised Red Cross medical center at Sairine, Lebanon, in April. The Lebanese civil war was one of the many conflicts during which the Red Cross was called upon for aid in 1978.

be to supervise the fifty-seven regional blood centers. These centers collected a new record of over 5,000,000 units of blood from volunteer donors during the fiscal year 1977–78.

Blizzards disrupted life in the U.S. Midwest and Northeast in January and early February. At the request of Red Cross disaster workers in Cincinnati, 60,000 lb. of food supplies were airlifted there and distributed to snowbound families in twenty counties in Indiana, Kentucky, and Ohio. When snowstorms buried Boston, Providence, and other New England cities, emergency mass care assistance in Red Cross shelters was given to thousands of stranded people.

Sept. 17, 1978, marked the 50th anniversary of the Certificate of Merit, the highest American Red Cross safety award. It is presented to individuals who have saved or sustained a human life using skills and knowledge learned in a Red Cross first aid, small craft, or water safety training program. Since its inception in 1928, more than 6000 persons have received the award. The recipients have ranged from an 8-year-old boy who saved a 3-year-old from drowning to a 79-year-old man who ran up two flights of stairs and resuscitated an 80-year-old heart attack victim.

See also Accidents and Disasters; and separate articles on countries mentioned.

RELIGION

Religious figures were often in the headlines. The Roman Catholic Church had three successive popes, an exiled Shi'ite leader provoked riots in Iran, and a commune established by a Protestant cult in Guyana was wiped out in a stunning tragedy.

The year 1978 was the first in modern times in which the world's most prominent office of religious leadership, the papacy of the Roman Catholic Church, was filled by three different men.

CHRISTIANITY

Pope Paul VI died on Aug. 6; Pope John Paul I was elected on Aug. 26; Pope John Paul II was installed on Oct. 22.

Roman Catholic Affairs. Paul VI died at the age of 80, weeks after marking the completion of the fifteenth year of his pontificate and days after the tenth anniversary of his birth control encyclical *Humanae Vitae* ("Of Human Life"). That reaffirmation of the church's opposition to artificial contraception in 1968 was the most memorable event of Paul's reign to the general public. However, he also had an immense impact on internal church affairs. He completed Vatican Council II (1962–65) begun by John XXIII, promulgated all of its decrees, and led the subsequent implementation of its work. He tentatively applied the new concept of "collegiality" (power-sharing) in the hierarchy by establishing a Synod of Bishops to meet at the Vatican every few years to advise the pope. In 1969 he approved a new text for the Mass, replacing that fixed by the 16th-century Council of Trent, and presided over its translation for most liturgical use into vernacular (common) languages instead of the traditional Latin; it was introduced in the United States in 1970. Following the council, he also took dramatic initiatives in social justice and world peace and in relations with other Christian bodies, with Jews and other non-Christians, and with Communist regimes. Paul also internationalized the papacy as never before, traveling personally to Israel, India, the U.S., Turkey, Colombia, Uganda, and numerous sites in an Asian-Oceanian tour, in addition to travels in Italy and Western Europe. He brought an unprecedented number of non-Italians into high Vatican positions and introduced fixed terms of office and other reforms in the Curia (Vatican administration). Most significant in the election of his successors was his expansion of the size of

and of non-Italian and non-European representation in the Sacred College of Cardinals and his decree that cardinals age 80 and over could not join in the conclave that elects a pope. Thus, the body of electors that met at his death in August consisted of only 26 Italians and 30 other Europeans out of a total of 115 eligible (4 did not vote, for various reasons). Non-Europeans held a slight majority for the first time since cardinals acquired exclusive power to elect the pope in the 12th century.

In a surprisingly short conclave of one day—Aug. 26—the cardinals elected a relatively unknown figure, Albino Luciani, 65, the patriarch of Venice. He took the unusual double name of John Paul I in honor of his two predecessors. Luciani's election was interpreted as a reaction against the Vatican bureaucracy; the better-known candidates had worked in the Curia or the papal diplomatic corps, and Luciani was conspicuous for never having done so. His church career was limited to northeastern Italy, where he was briefly a parish priest, then a teacher of theology and canon law, vicar general of the Belluno diocese, bishop of Vittorio Veneto (1958–69), and patriarch of Venice (1969–78). He became a cardinal in 1973.

The most important act of John Paul I's reign was his decision not to have a traditional "coronation" ceremony in which he would be crowned with the papal tiara. Instead he scheduled a Mass (Sept. 3) to mark his installation as "supreme pastor" (not supreme pontiff). John Paul's friendly, humble, and down-to-earth personality, made familiar by wide media coverage, had an unusually strong and positive impact on the world.

In policy terms, Luciani's election signified commitment to the Vatican II mainstream, rejecting both liberal interpretations and the anti-council protest led by right-wing French Archbishop Marcel Lefebvre; a warm pastoral style in the papacy, under a pope with ample grass-roots experience; and opposition to compromise with Communism in Italy. He continued Paul's attempts to

Thousands of Roman Catholics welcome their second new pope of the year as John Paul II visits the shrine of St. Francis of Assisi in November. The former Polish cardinal visited the shrines of both patron saints of Italy—St. Francis and St. Catherine of Siena (in Rome).

negotiate toward church freedom in Eastern Europe.

When John Paul I died of a heart attack after only thirty-four days in office, shock swept the Catholic world. In their second conclave of the year, in October, the cardinals made a historic decision, electing as pope the archbishop of Cracow, Poland, Cardinal Karol Wojtyła. Taking his short-lived predecessor's name, John Paul II, he was installed on Oct. 22. The choice broke many conventions. No non-Italian had been elected since 1522 (Adrian VI). At 58, he was the youngest pope elected since 1846 (Pius IX). He was also the first pope from a Communist nation, the first from Eastern Europe, and the first from Poland, a devoutly Catholic land in which more than 90 percent of the people are church members.

Whatever their policy similarities, the two John Pauls were very different in background. John Paul II was a world traveler, able to speak six languages, including fluent English, and was a noted

intellectual and expert in modern philosophy, specializing in phenomenology. He was an actor, drama producer, and writer of plays and poems in his youth and an active outdoorsman as an adult. He worked in a stone quarry and a chemical factory during the Nazi occupation of Poland, acquiring more direct knowledge of the life of the workers than was available to previous popes. Wojtyła went to ordinary secondary school and university, rather than "minor seminary," and had a normal social life before turning to studies at an illegal underground seminary in 1942.

Wojtyła earned a doctorate at Rome's Angelicum University and another at Cracow's Jagiellonian University, where he taught philosophy and ethics, later moving to the Catholic University of Lublin. He was appointed an auxiliary bishop of Cracow in 1958, and became, in effect, the archbishop in 1962, receiving the actual title two years later. He was named a cardinal in 1967. Although his entire career, like that of his predecessor, was spent outside the Vatican, Wojtyła was more prominent at Vatican II and had been more active in Vatican meetings since that time.

By the best-informed press accounts, the cardinals turned to a non-Italian pope in the second day and eighth ballot of the conclave because of a stalemate between two Italians, one an archcon-

This Cardinal's Not for the Cardinals

Fans of the Boston Red Sox baseball team come from all walks of life, the ecclesiastical as well as the secular. And they are noted for their loyalty, both at home—where they established a major-league attendance record in 1978—and on the road, no matter how far from home they may be. One fan, Boston's Cardinal Humberto Madeiros, was in Rome choosing a pope during the 1978 stretch drive. Hurrying from an important Vatican meeting, he asked for the latest score and was told his team had won. It is recorded that His Eminence thereupon uttered, with gratitude and humility, these appropriate words: *"Deo gratias!"*

1,000,000 persons over six weeks. After the exhibition, scientific tests were begun in an attempt to determine the age and authenticity of the shroud. In December the Vatican and the Italian government reached final agreement on a revision of their 1929 concordat. The most important change, now that Catholicism was no longer considered the state religion, was the end to compulsory religious instruction in public schools.

In the U.S., the Catholic Theological Society of America published a report of its research team on the women's issue that stated that traditional arguments do not "present any serious grounds to justify the exclusion of women from ordination to pastoral office." This report conflicted with a Vatican decree issued in 1977.

Eastern Orthodoxy. A conference of theologians at the Greek Orthodox seminary in Massachusetts discussed progress toward an international Great Council of Orthodox Bishops, which would be Orthodoxy's equivalent of Vatican II. The last ecumenical council recognized by Orthodoxy had been held in 787. The autonomous national

servative, considered more comfortable with the pre-Vatican II church, and the second a moderate Vatican official who had served Paul VI for many years. When supporters of each of these two showed enough strength to stop the other, and when no other Italian emerged, the electors coalesced around Wojtyła because of his outstanding personal qualities.

In his first months, John Paul II became a popular figure among his newly adopted Italian flock, plunging into crowds to greet people. At the Vatican, he reappointed most top officials, after a slight delay, but gave hints of important innovations to come.

After John Paul I's death, the Latin American Bishops' Conference postponed its once-a-decade meeting to early 1979. The gathering was expected to produce a confrontation between political liberals and conservatives and, in anticipation of this, the bishops of Brazil took a decidedly activist stance on social and economic justice at their April meeting. As reported by the U.S. Catholic Mission Council in July, some 850 priests in a number of Latin American nations had been jailed or murdered by right-wing vigilantes. In Africa, eighty-one representative bishops held their fifth assembly, at which they issued a protest against meddling by foreign powers and denounced infringements of human rights on the part of unspecified African regimes.

The church in Italy suffered defeat when parliament passed a law allowing virtual abortion on demand, after five years of opposition by the bishops. Meanwhile, the "shroud of Turin" was on display in that Italian city, drawing more than

Pope Paul VI (left) and his successor John Paul I, photographed in 1976; at the time, John Paul was Cardinal Albino Luciani, patriarch of Venice. Both prelates died in 1978.

RELIGION

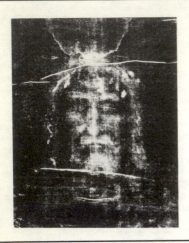

The Face of Christ?

The 14-foot swath of ancient linen bears the ghostly image of a man who had been beaten, crowned with thorns, and crucified. For centuries many Christians believed it to be the burial shroud of Jesus Christ, but how the near-photographic image was impressed onto the cloth remained a mystery. From Aug. 26 to Oct. 8, to mark the 400th anniversary of its arrival in Turin, Italy, the Holy Shroud was placed on public display for the first time in forty-five years, and tens of thousands of the faithful—and the curious—filed through San Giovanni Cathedral to see the cherished relic. In addition, a team of U.S. scientists received permission for a closer look. Using space-age technology, they began tests to determine the shroud's authenticity, once and for all.

A portion of the shroud of Turin, seen in the official negative print.

churches had laid the groundwork for such a council, speakers reported, but final arrangements and the council itself were years away.

The responsibility for convoking such a council remained with the "first among equals" of the hierarchy, the ecumenical patriarch of Constantinople (İstanbul). Political difficulties in its home country, Turkey, limited the patriarchate in carrying out that responsibility. Supporters of the patriarch complained of harassment of Hellenic Christians by the Turks, but in March the patriarch's representatives won some relief. Premier Bülent Ecevit agreed that his government would remove a tax on church properties and rescind travel restrictions on the Orthodox clergy. In addition, churches were allowed to make repairs on their buildings.

In Greece, leaders of the Orthodox Church expressed discontent with their position in the World Council of Churches. They said that the council had refused to recognize some of the representatives appointed by the Orthodox and had ceased publishing Orthodox views on matters of doctrine. Archbishop Seraphim of Athens said in May that his church was considering withdrawing from active participation in the council and assuming observer status similar to that of the Roman Catholic Church.

In the U.S., the Greek Orthodox Archdiocese of North and South America approved a new charter of church organization. Under it, nine new dioceses were formed, each headed by a bishop. The archbishop, formerly the supreme head of the church, would share authority with a Synod of Bishops, composed of all diocesan heads. Individual bishops would also assume functions previously carried out only by the archbishop. In effect, the dioceses in the U.S. assumed the form of

The Reverend Mary Michael Simpson, a canon of New York City's Episcopal Cathedral of St. John the Divine, stands before Westminster Abbey in London in April. She had just become the first ordained woman to preach in the venerable abbey.

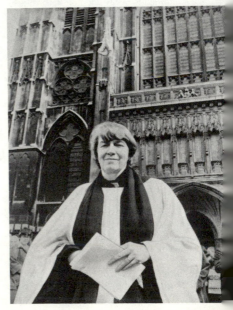

a national church. The reorganization was begun in September.

Protestantism and Anglicanism. The issue of ordination of women continued to capture attention in the Anglican Communion. The bishops of the world held the 11th Lambeth Conference at the University of Kent, Canterbury, England, July 22–Aug. 13. Of twenty-five autonomous Anglican churches, those in the U.S., Canada, New Zealand, and Hong Kong had admitted women to the priesthood, and those in some other nations had indicated readiness to do so. The conference, however, voted down a five-year moratorium on more women priests and then approved a compromise statement by a vote of 316-37 (17 abstaining). This statement took no stand for or against women priests and asked for mutual tolerance between member churches on the two sides. The bishops recommended that women exercise their ministry only where the bishop, priests, and parish authorities agreed. In two separate resolutions, Lambeth recommended that no women be consecrated as bishops without consultation with primates of other nations and "overwhelming support" by the national church and diocese concerned, lest the bishop's office become a cause of disunity, and that all member churches open the third order, that of deacon, to women.

In advance of Lambeth, the international Anglican-Orthodox Joint Doctrinal Commission held a special session in Athens and stated that women priests had brought this ecumenical dialogue "to a point of acute crisis." The Orthodox participants said continued approval of women would have "a decisively negative effect" on mutual recognition of clergy and would "drastically" change the dialogue itself. The Orthodox stated that today's church is "bound to remain faithful to the example of our Lord, to the testimony of Scripture, and the constant and unvarying practice of the Church," which reveals the ban on women as "the will of God." Roman Catholic observers at Lambeth also indicated ecumenical problems, and after the decision the Vatican daily *L'Osservatore Romano* stated that Lambeth had acted "at the cost of greater distance from the Roman Church," terming this "an extremely serious step."

In November the General Synod of the Church of England voted decisively against authorizing women priests. Bishops and lay delegates voted in favor, but priest-delegates, who also had to approve as a body, voted against, 94-149. This could delay change until at least the mid-1980's.

The small schism in the U.S. Episcopal Church over the issue was formalized in Denver in January with the consecration of the first four bishops of a breakaway denomination. The consecrations

The towering nave of Liverpool's Cathedral Church of Christ, praised as "one of the great buildings of the world." Completed after seventy-four years in construction, the church was dedicated by Queen Elizabeth II of Great Britain in November.

were performed by retired Episcopal Bishop Albert Chambers and a Philippine Independent Church bishop, but the regularity (though not technical validity) of the act was challenged because the customary three bishops did not participate. The new body constituted itself in October as the Anglican Catholic Church. Fourteen Episcopal bishops filed charges against Chambers that would have led to a church trial, but withdrew the action after the Episcopal House of Bishops censured Chambers "in the strongest terms" and also denounced bishops who had ordained women priests before the church had approved the change and ordered a study of whether to expel them.

In another Anglican development, the Church of England synod rejected a proposal that in some cases a divorced person should be allowed to remarry under church auspices while his previous spouse is alive. Archbishop of Canterbury Donald Coggan opposed liberalization, but a majority of bishops favored it.

In the U.S., the United Presbyterian Church became the nation's first major denomination to consider allowing subunits to ordain a "self-affirming practicing homosexual Christian," including one open to or actually involved in "full companionship or partnership with a person of the same sex." The liberal policy, proposed by an official national task force after a two-year study, was defeated by a margin of 10 to 1 or more at the church's General Assembly at San Diego in May. Reflecting grass-roots conservatism and the influence of the Evangelical wing, the assembly also declared that sexual practices should occur only within heterosexual marriage, opposing the so-called new morality on sex that assembly delegates came close to endorsing in 1970. The United Church of Christ published a study guide on sex-'ual issues that took a tolerant stance on homosexual behavior, leading to the first conservative caucus within that denomination. The United Methodist Church saw a New York City bishop reappoint an openly acknowledged and active

On the eve of Sukkoth, Oct. 15, Jews in Washington, D.C, demonstrate their concern for Jews imprisoned in the Soviet Union. Pictures of the prisoners line the walls of a sukkah (booth) erected in Lafayette Square opposite the White House.

homosexual to his parish; a church trial could result. Meanwhile a Methodist seminary in suburban Chicago refused to readmit two openly homosexual students.

Two of the three major U.S. Lutheran bodies published a joint *Lutheran Book of Worship* with liturgy and hymns. A third body, the Lutheran Church–Missouri Synod, withdrew from sponsorship of the interdenominational volume and issued a critique of it.

America's Evangelical Protestant movement continued to attract media attention. The Christian Booksellers Association reported that member stores had gross 1977 revenues of $600,000,-000. Bill Bright's Campus Crusade for Christ pursued an effort to raise $1 billion for world evangelism by 1982. Oral Roberts, despite opposition from an Oklahoma advisory board, won approval for a medical center in Tulsa at an eventual cost of $100,000,000. Another television preacher, Pat Robertson of the "700 Club," opened the first component of a university in Virginia affiliated with his Christian Broadcasting Network.

Billy Graham, the evangelist, added Poland to the long list of nations in which he had preached and released the first full public financial accounting for his association. It showed a 1977 income of $38,400,000, larger than the national program budget of most entire denominations. (It excluded Graham Crusades, which were financed by local church committees.) In a poll of thirty-five expert journalists, the liberal *Christian Century* found that Graham was considered by far the most influential U.S. religious personality. (The runners-up, in order: author and University of Chicago historian Martin Marty; President Jimmy Carter; Rabbi Marc Tanenbaum of the American Jewish Committee; President Theodore Hesburgh of the University of Notre Dame; Oral Roberts; Bill Bright; black activist Jesse Jackson; singer and antihomosexual crusader Anita Bryant; and the United Presbyterians' chief executive, attorney William P. Thompson.)

More than one-hundred Evangelical scholars from several nations produced the *New International Version,* the latest of the translations of the Bible in contemporary English. The New Testament portion was first issued in 1973.

Ecumenism. Although the World Council of Churches (WCC), in a campaign against racism, had been making grants to violence-oriented black liberation groups in Africa since 1970, a 1978 grant of $85,000 to Rhodesia's Patriotic Front renewed the church controversy over the program. The grant came as Rhodesia's new interracial regime struggled to take hold. Paradoxically, two of its four leaders were clergy in WCC churches

Ayatollah Ruhollah Khomeini, twice exiled—from Iran in 1963 and from Iraq in 1978—took refuge in France as Shi'ite demonstrations raged against the Iranian government. He was prominent among leaders of the religious movement opposing Shah Mohammed Riza Pahlavi.

whose black nationalist parties had formerly received aid. The WCC defended the grant, saying that the Rhodesian internal settlement left the white minority in effective control. Member denominations were worried about apparent endorsement of political violence, particularly because Patriotic Front guerrillas were charged with murdering forty missionaries and making other attacks on noncombatants. The Salvation Army suspended its membership in the WCC as a result of the grant.

The All Africa Conference of Churches (AACC) issued a condemnation of foreign intervention in African affairs. It also suffered an internal struggle that ended in an extended leave for its general secretary, Canon Burgess Carr, one of Africa's most outspoken churchmen. On the eve of the opening of new AACC headquarters in Nairobi, Carr sought to pull the organization out of Kenya because of a dispute with the government that

included charges of personal misconduct against Carr.

Two statements were released in September as a result of international Lutheran-Catholic talks. A joint statement on the Eucharist was issued at the end of the month; earlier, the churches had announced the end of their discussions on the infallibility of the pope, in which they reached no agreement.

In U.S. ecumenism, the bishops of the United Methodist Church met in Atlanta with the bishops of three black denominations, the African Methodist Episcopal, African Methodist Episcopal

Zion, and Christian Methodist Episcopal churches. Future talks and possible long-range union remained in prospect.

The National Council of Churches issued a report on the nation's women clergy, said to number an estimated 10,470, or 4 percent of the clergy in the 76 denominations that ordain members of both sexes. The United Church of Christ and Christian Church (Disciples of Christ) had the largest number, but nearly two thirds of the total were found in smaller Pentecostal and Holiness denominations. The council also lobbied against the defeated Packwood-Moynihan bill, which would have given a federal tax credit to families paying tuition to private grade and high schools. The U.S. Catholic Conference favored the bill.

JUDAISM

In April the Reform branch of Judaism in the U.S. released the latest component of its revised liturgy, the High Holy Day services, under the title *Gates of Repentance*. The rites are contemporary but show the growing use of traditional materials in liberal Judaism.

The Jewish Publication Society of Philadelphia issued *Nevi'im* (*The Prophets*), the second of three sections of its modern Bible in English translation. The first volume, *The Torah,* was released in 1962, and the final section, *Ketubim* (*The Writings*), was due in the 1980's. When complete, this translation would supplant the society's English Bible of 1917.

Jewish interest groups were disturbed when conservatives, having won the town council election in Oberammergau, West Germany, decided to continue use of the 1860 text of the famous Passion Play. Jewish and Christian groups had lobbied for an older text because of alleged anti-Semitism in the 1860 version. The council promised text reforms before the next performances in 1980.

In Israel, Orthodox religious parties that were part of the ruling coalition won their long-desired "antimissionary law," which decreed fines, or up to five years in prison, for using any "material inducement" to foster religious conversion. The loosely worded law was aimed at Christian missions. In a U.S. counterpart to the same problem, President Carter's sister, "memory healer" Ruth Carter Stapleton, declined an invitation to speak to a "Jewish Christian" organization on Long Is-

Sikhs fought among themselves in New Delhi, India, in November. Here, orthodox Sikhs trying to prevent a meeting of a small Sikh faction clash with police; the fracas left 3 dead and about 100 injured.

On Nov. 6, the heir to the throne of Thailand (left) assumes his traditional religious duties in the Temple of the Emerald Buddha in Bangkok; his father Bhumibol Adulyadej is at his side. Wearing the robe of a Buddhist monk, Prince Vajiralongkorn observed a fifteen-day period of begging in the streets, all contact with women forbidden.

land (N.Y.) after protests from Jewish organizations opposed its style of conversion activity.

The Orthodox monopoly over religious education in Israel was slightly diminished in May. The government granted full recognition to a religious school sponsored by a Conservative synagogue whose congregation numbered many American Jews. The previous government policy was to support only Orthodox teachings in its government-financed religious schools. Some commentators saw the action as a recognition of the growing demand for religious diversity in Israel.

Above all else, Jews were intent throughout 1978 upon negotiations for peace in the Middle East (q.v.).

ISLAM

In a dramatic example of tensions that afflict all secularizing and modernizing Muslim nations, Iran (q.v.) faced a severe outburst of political rioting against the reign of Shah Mohammed Riza Pahlavi. Most of Iran's population follows the larger of the two forms of Shi'ism, which broke from orthodox Islam centuries ago over a question of leadership succession and retains distinct beliefs. Fierce rioting resulted in 1963 when the mullahs (religious authorities) opposed the shah for appropriating religious landholdings and giving women the vote and other privileges. In the 1978 troubles, religious leaders based in the holy city of Qum were joined in an unlikely alliance with the dissident Left and youths. To placate religious conservatives, short-term Prime Minister Jaafar Sharif-Emami restored the old Islamic calendar, shut gambling casinos, and abolished the women's affairs post in the government. The Opposition was directed from exile by the Ayatollah (a title of high learning) Ruhollah Khomeini, 78, a Shi'ite leader who was expelled from Iran after the 1963 riots. Demonstrations against the shah escalated during the year and were particularly heated in December during the annual period of mourning.

Right-wing Muslim nationalism was a force in other nations. Indonesia, for example, arrested more than forty leaders of the fanatical Komando Jihad movement, which seeks to overthrow the regime in favor of an officially Muslim state. One leader was sentenced to life imprisonment.

The Muslim population of Europe continued to grow as a result of immigration. A new mosque opened in London and another was planned in Rome. An immigration study in France showed

The first black Mormon priest stands with his wife in Salt Lake City in June. Joseph Freeman, Jr., a telephone repairman, was the first Black to be ordained after the Mormons announced the revelation that changed their 148-year-old policy of racial discrimination.

that Islam, claiming 2,000,000 adherents, had passed Protestantism and Judaism to become the second largest faith in France (the first is Roman Catholicism).

The shift to Islamic orthodoxy by America's Black Muslims, renamed the World Community of Al-Islam in the West, produced a schism that became noticeable outside the movement. The leader of the main group, Wallace D. Muhammad (whose father, Elijah Muhammad, founded the organization), announced that he would become a full-time evangelist, and handed control over to ten imams.

HINDUISM

Despite official elimination of the caste system in India, it remained ingrained in the religious culture. Riots and several deaths resulted when the government of impoverished Bihar State ordered a type of "affirmative action" plan, guaranteeing 26 percent of government civil service jobs for those from the backward castes that are numerous in population and just above the lowest group, the *Harijans* ("untouchables"). Since *Harijans* were previously granted 24 percent of the jobs, this meant that each of the higher castes would get a minority of the positions.

In a related event, leaders of the Protestant and Catholic minorities met to denounce the fact that if *Harijans* convert from Hinduism to Christianity they are denied these job quotas and other spe-

cial benefits. The rationale for the policy was that Christianity recognizes no caste distinctions, and therefore government help is no longer required.

NEWER FAITHS

On June 9 the Church of Jesus Christ of Latter-day Saints, with more than 4,000,000 members worldwide, announced a historic change in policy. At headquarters in Salt Lake City, the First Presidency (President Spencer W. Kimball and his two counselors) declared that the Mormon priesthood would henceforth be open to those of black African ancestry. In Mormonism, which has no clergy, most young teenagers enter the priesthood, the basis for all church officeholding. The leaders announced that after much prayer in the Mormon Temple, God "has heard our prayers, and by revelation has confirmed that the long-promised day has come when every faithful, worthy man in the Church may receive the holy priesthood."

The racial distinction in Mormonism had been a major embarrassment for the church. Some observers linked the revelation with the scheduled opening of the first temple in Brazil four months later; in that racially mixed land it would have been difficult to tell which people were racially eligible for priesthood and subsequent temple rites. The missionary-minded Mormons had been expanding overseas, and the revelation opened the way to begin work in black Africa, though there was no immediate plan to do so.

The racial prohibition was believed to date back to the sons of Adam, and to be taught in the "Book of Abraham" within the *Pearl of Great Price,* one of three scriptures issued by the prophet Joseph Smith and not accepted by non-Mormons. The key verse states that Canaanites (interpreted to mean Africans) are "cursed as to the priesthood." This was why only a direct revelation from God could alter the policy. Related doctrinal questions remain unanswered.

In an August statement the Mormon First Presidency reaffirmed its opposition to the Equal Rights Amendment to the U.S. Constitution, which it considered a threat to sexual morality, the family, and the legal protection of women.

The *Yearbook* of the U.S.-based Jehovah's Witnesses revealed that the number of active members in the U.S. had dropped by 2.6 percent, to 530,374, in 1977. The worldwide total also dropped slightly. It was the first decrease since World War II in an organization whose members spend much of their time seeking new converts and in which steady growth had been routine. The *Yearbook* also showed a precipitous drop in baptisms of new converts during the preceding two years. Leaders attributed the decreases to reporting problems in local groups. Some observers speculated, however, that it was related to the fact that the current world system was not abolished in 1975, as Watch Tower publications had previously suggested.

In the Worldwide Church of God, led by the aged prophet Herbert W. Armstrong, another schism erupted when Armstrong banished his son and designated successor, radio and television preacher Garner Ted Armstrong. He said that his son had opposed his policies and undermined his regime. The son, mysteriously banished once before, established a new denomination in Texas, and control of the church after the eventual death of the father was thrown into question.

One of the worst religious atrocities of modern times occurred in Guyana in November. Rep. Leo J. Ryan (D, Calif.), who was investigating complaints about the People's Temple and its leader Reverend Jim Jones, was murdered along with four others on Nov. 18. More than 900 temple followers, including some 260 children, died in the bizarre ritual that followed, an orgy of suicide-murder-infanticide that defied all attempts at rational analysis. Jones, an Indiana clergyman who emphasized interracial harmony and social justice to outsiders, had moved to California in 1965. He was a mayoral appointee in San Francisco before 1977, when complaints about the inside workings of his movement led him and many of his disciples to establish Jonestown, their Guyana commune. The Jonestown incident provoked extensive examinations of cult behavior, as well as a move in Congress to reexamine national policies in regard to religious tolerance.

OTHER ISSUES

Interreligious tensions over abortion persisted in the U.S. A broad religious coalition filed a brief in the pending Brooklyn (N.Y.) federal court case of *McRae vs. Califano,* contending that laws to limit welfare funding for abortions constituted an "establishment of religion," forbidden by the First Amendment. The theory was that the laws are based on a particular religious view of the human fetus, especially the Catholic one, and thus the laws prefer those religions that forbid abortion over those which do not. It was asserted that the laws also inhibit "free exercise of religion" by women on public aid whose beliefs require them to abort. The laws in question had been supported by antiabortion groups representing the views not only of Catholics, but also those of conservative Protestants, Orthodox Jews, Eastern Orthodox, and Mormons. Those filing the controversial brief included the United Presbyterian Church, agencies of the United Methodist Church, United Church of Christ, Christian Church (Disciples of Christ), and the synagogue unions of Reform and Conservative Judaism, as well as nine other organizations. The brief was filed after Secretary of Health, Education, and Welfare Joseph Califano, Jr., issued (Jan. 26) a set of guidelines for federal funding in cases of abortion, as required by congressional legislation passed in December, 1977. As the year 1978 came to an end, a decision had not yet been reached in the McRae case.

In Vitro Fertilization. Moral theologians debated the implications of another biomedical matter,

The Reverend Jim Jones, founder of the People's Temple, sits surrounded by his family in a 1976 portrait. His death and the deaths of more than 900 of his followers shocked the world in 1978.

the birth of the first baby conceived outside the womb, the so-called test tube baby; see HEALTH AND MEDICINE; LIFE SCIENCES. To official Catholicism, in vitro fertilization interferes with nature, as does artificial insemination by a husband or donor. Others asked whether sufficient transplant work had been done first on subhuman species. Paul Ramsey of Princeton University, a Protestant expert on biomedical ethics, wrote in the *Hastings Center Report* that early experiments were immoral because the chance of risk was too high for the subject, that is, for the child-to-be, who could give no consent for the experiment. Ramsey also objected to all trends toward conscious "manu-

facture" of children, noting that one of the experimenters had proposed selection of a child's sex before implantation.

Deaths. For many noted religious leaders who died in 1978, see OBITUARIES. Among others who died during the year were Abdel Halim Mahmoud, the Grand Sheikh of Al-Azhar Mosque and University in Cairo since 1973, perhaps the best-known scholar and religious authority in Islam, in Cairo, Oct. 17, at 68; and Anders Nygren, Swedish Lutheran theologian and bishop of Lund, the first president of the Lutheran World Federation (1947–52), in Lund, Oct. 20, at 87.

See also PEOPLE IN THE NEWS. R.N.O.

REPUBLICAN PARTY. In 1978, Republican Party candidates in the United States made tax cutting their motto and pursued a new, less ambitious electoral strategy that gained modest success in November. In Congress, the GOP sided with Democratic President Jimmy Carter on some important fiscal and foreign-policy votes. Party Presidential contenders for 1980 began to raise money, make plans, and challenge the Democrats on defense and inflation issues.

Republicans in Congress. Outnumbered almost two to one in both houses of Congress, Republicans nevertheless exerted considerable influence on legislation passed in 1978. Under Senate minority leader Howard H. Baker, Jr., of Tennessee and House minority leader John J. Rhodes of Ari-

zona, the Republicans kept up a steady barrage of criticism of Carter's policies and performance. They demanded production of the neutron bomb and other new weapons systems. They called Carter's fiscal-year 1979 budget a "time bomb," and argued that the government caused inflation by overspending and could cure it by cutting back. GOP pressure, inflation fears, and the public mood of frugality combined to keep strict limits on Administration spending programs.

Republicans sided with President Carter on many key votes. Sixteen Republican Senators voted to ratify the treaties ceding the Panama Canal to Panama by the year 2000 and guaranteeing its neutrality thereafter, giving the treaties their one-vote margin of victory. A 26–11 majority of

Senator Henry Kissinger?
During 1978 private citizen Henry Kissinger was somewhat less visible than he had been during his days of shuttle diplomacy. Of course the former secretary of state was occupied with his memoirs, of which he was said to have reached Volume 2. But he still got around, hobnobbing with world leaders, commenting on foreign affairs on TV, lecturing, and acting as consultant to business leaders. Most intriguing of all was his emergence as a fast-quipping star attraction at GOP fund-raising dinners during the fall election campaigns. That inevitably spawned rumors that he was practicing for a run for the U.S. Senate, in the event New York's Republican veteran Jacob Javits should choose to step down in 1980. True? Kissinger didn't say "yes." He also didn't say "no."

Henry A. Kissinger.

Former U.S. President Gerald R. Ford (left) and former California Gov. Ronald Reagan (right) give advice to Texas gubernatorial candidate Bill Clements at an August fund-raising affair. It worked; Clements won in November.

Republican Senators again supported Carter in a May vote authorizing the sale of military aircraft to Israel, Egypt, and Saudi Arabia. Near the end of the congressional session in October, Carter acknowledged his debt by inviting thirty Republican congressmen to a White House breakfast and thanking them personally.

A New National Strategy. Members of the Republican National Committee (RNC) debated changes in the party's strategy at January meetings in Washington, D.C. In 1976 the Republicans had set out to defeat many of the younger Democratic incumbents in Congress but had failed to increase their minorities. It was decided that in 1978 the GOP would lower its sights and concentrate on ousting a smaller number of older incumbents regarded as weak in providing services to constituents. Special efforts were also made to gain control of more state legislatures to prevent Democratic majorities from gerrymandering congressional districts after the 1980 census.

At the same January meetings, RNC Chairman William E. Brock argued that the party could and should make a stronger appeal to black voters. Black civil rights activist Jesse Jackson, the meeting's keynote speaker, said that Blacks would vote Republican if the party came up with attractive programs in such areas as employment, education, and health care.

An early sign that the Republican attitude toward Blacks might actually be changing appeared in August, when GOP leaders supported a constitutional amendment granting full congressional representation to the District of Columbia. The District, about 75 percent black in popula-

tion, would be entitled to two Senators and one or two Representatives if thirty-eight states ratified the amendment. Senate Republicans split 19 to 19 on the vote.

Riding the Tax Revolt. As it became clear that people across the nation were rebelling against high property and income taxes, the Republicans decided to base their congressional election campaign on a tax plan that would far outcut the Democrats. The Kemp-Roth bill, sponsored by Rep. Jack F. Kemp (R, N.Y.) and Sen. William V. Roth, Jr. (R, Del.), proposed to reduce everyone's federal income taxes 33 percent over a three-year period. In September fifty GOP leaders crossed the country speaking at shopping centers, commuter stations, and backyards in a "tax blitz" for Kemp-Roth. Few large crowds appeared and the bill was voted down twice in Congress, but the venture provided a platform for party spokesmen and garnered much free television advertising.

Party Candidates for 1980. The field was wide open for the 1980 Republican Presidential nomination, and several probable candidates emerged. Former President Gerald R. Ford spoke widely and pounded away on the inflation issue during the year. Both Ford and former Secretary of State Henry A. Kissinger supported ratification of the Panama Canal treaties. Ronald Reagan, former governor of California and Ford's opponent for

Thad Cochran and his wife Rose celebrate his election to the U.S. Senate in November. Cochran won handily, to become the first Republican Senator from Mississippi in one-hundred years.

the 1976 nomination, said in September that he would probably run again. The best financed and perhaps the best organized of the potential candidates, Reagan was active as a leader of the conservative opposition to the canal treaties and a promoter of the Kemp-Roth bill. Former Texas Gov. John B. Connally, Jr., was also exploring his 1980 prospects. Among GOP moderates, former Central Intelligence Agency director George Bush was often mentioned as a possible candidate, as were Sen. Baker of Tennessee and Gov. James R. Thompson of Illinois.

In August, Rep. Philip M. Crane (R, Ill.), the photogenic young president of the American Conservative Union, became the first Republican to announce his Presidential candidacy. Insiders regarded him as a stalking horse for Ronald Reagan. Another long shot for 1980 was Jack Kemp, cosponsor of the Kemp-Roth bill and a popular GOP after-dinner speaker.

Elections. Fund raising for the November elections was generally successful. In addition to the efforts of individual candidates and those of conservative direct-mail fund raiser Richard A. Viguerie, party campaign groups collected and distributed about $20,000,000 on behalf of Republican candidates—far more than the Democrats and

twice as much as the GOP in 1976. In the election results the Republicans exceeded their hopes by picking up three Senate seats to trim the Democratic majority to 59–41. The most notable Republican victories came in Minnesota, where the floundering Democratic–Farmer-Labor Party lost its traditional control of both Senate seats, and in Mississippi, which sent a Republican to the Senate for the first time since Reconstruction. Gains in the House were marginal: 11 more Republicans were elected for a total of 158 to the Democrats' 277. Perhaps most important for party prospects in 1980 and thereafter, 6 more Republican governors and about 275 more Republican state legislators were elected.

See also CONGRESS OF THE UNITED STATES; ELECTIONS. W.M.H.

RHODE ISLAND. *See* STATISTICS OF THE WORLD.

RHODESIA. Prime Minister Ian Smith's gamble to get the best possible deal for white settlers in Rhodesia and to retain his white-controlled army through a settlement with black nationalists appeared to fail in 1978.

Transition Government Established. In December, 1977, Smith's white regime met with the three major black nationalist leaders within Rhodesia— Bishop Abel Muzorewa, Rev. Ndabaningi Sithole, and Chief Jeremiah Chirau—to negotiate an "internal solution" for transferring power to the country's black majority. None of the black leaders had an army. The two nationalists who did— Joshua Nkomo and Robert Mugabe, the co-leaders of the Patriotic Front—were excluded from the talks and continued their guerrilla war from sanctuaries in Mozambique and Zambia.

On Feb. 15, Smith announced that an agreement had been reached on a formula for black rule. The talks had been deadlocked over the question of white minority representation and safeguards; the compromise called for 20 white members in the 100-seat parliament to be elected by Whites alone, with 8 other Whites elected by black and white voters on a common roll. The Whites would thus have a veto over any attempt to annul constitutional guarantees of their rights. The agreement was rejected by the Patriotic Front and condemned by the United States and Great Britain. Instead, they all called for discussion of an Anglo-American plan which required Smith to turn power over to Britain in a transitional period that would culminate in United Nations-supervised elections and a front-dominated army.

However, on March 3, with administrative details resolved, the internal settlement was signed; eighteen days later Muzorewa, Sithole, and Chirau were sworn in as co-leaders with Smith in an Executive Council, which was to have overall con-

In Washington, D.C., on Oct. 9, Ndabaningi Sithole (left) and Ian Smith of Rhodesia's four-member Executive Council hold a news conference. Their one-week visit to the U.S. was first canceled—Smith was denied a visa—then reluctantly approved by the State Department.

trol of Rhodesia. Black and white administrators were to run the government jointly. The War Council, directly responsible for controlling the war effort, was transformed into the Joint Operations Center but remained under Smith's sole command.

Later Events. An intense Anglo-American effort to get the new interim government to meet with front leaders failed. Large-scale guerrilla attacks began in March, followed in April by raids by government troops on rebel bases in Mozambique and Zambia. Government efforts to neutral-

The Bishop as Politician
Rhodesia's "internal solution" toward eventual black-majority rule would founder without the participation of Bishop Abel Muzorewa, 53. Of the three black leaders who joined Prime Minister Ian Smith to form a "transitional government," Muzorewa was the only one with demonstrable popular support. The Methodist churchman, who received part of his education in the United States, won a United Nations Human Rights Award in 1975, although he was prevented from accepting it in person when a then hostile Smith regime lifted his passport. Were he to become the first black leader of Rhodesia—or Zimbabwe—the courageous but politically inexperienced Muzorewa would still face, in all probability, a stern challenge from guerrilla forces operating from bases in exile.

Bishop Abel Muzorewa of Rhodesia.

353

ize the guerrillas—for example, by establishing "free entry zones" on the borders for guerrillas who wanted to return in peace—failed. By August there were gun battles in Salisbury, the Rhodesian capital. In September an Air Rhodesia plane with fifty-six persons aboard was shot down; some of the survivors were slain (by guerrillas, according to the government). Martial law was declared in parts of the country on Sept. 10.

White morale appeared to weaken under the strain of the continued embargo, a crumbling economy, a $1,000,000 per day war effort, and more and more attacks on isolated white farmers. Throughout the year white emigration increased. At the same time, Blacks were becoming increasingly disillusioned with their failure to do away with racial discrimination and to attain parity in running the government. In March, Smith had called for the enrollment of 3,000,000 black and 85,000 white, mixed race, and Asian voters to participate in December parliamentary elections. Parliament, in turn, would select a thirty-seat senate, and, by the end of the year, the two houses would select a president; finally, on Dec. 31, Rhodesia was to become Zimbabwe, under black rule.

The Smith timetable collapsed, however, under Patriotic Front pressure. Smith was permitted an October visit to the U.S. to win support; in November he announced a postponement of elections until April, 1979. Although Smith had met secretly with Nkomo in August, in October Rhodesian forces carried out four days of bombings against the rebel leader's bases in Zambia. The front denounced the raids and demanded the government follow an agenda that the rebels had worked out earlier in the year with Anglo-American negotiators. Guerrilla raids were immediately stepped up, and martial law was extended in response. The government was dealt a serious setback on Dec. 11, when guerrillas attacked an oil-storage depot and destroyed about 20,000,000 gal. of fuel. At year's end, the Smith government was still in power, but its rule appeared more tenuous than ever, and the fate of the white minority appeared less certain.

Deaths. Two of Rhodesia's leading white politicians died during 1978. Clifford W. Dupont, president of the country from 1970 to 1976, died June 28 at 72. His successor, John J. Wrathall, died Aug. 30 at 65.

See STATISTICS OF THE WORLD. *See also* AFRICA.   J.T.S.

RUMANIA. Rumania made President Nicolae Ceauşescu's sixtieth birthday on Jan. 26 a day of national celebration. For most of 1978, however, the Rumanian leader faced thorny domestic problems.

Chinese Premier Hua Kuo-feng (left) and Rumanian President Nicolae Ceauşescu enjoy a folk dancing exhibition in the streets of Bucharest. Hua's trip to Rumania in August marked the first official visit to a European capital by a Chinese Communist head of state.

Politics and Economics. Rumania's large Hungarian minority was a source of concern for the Ceauşescu regime. In 1977, Gyula Illyes, a distinguished Hungarian poet, made a passionate protest against Rumania's treatment of its 1,700,000 Hungarian citizens. In January, 1978, word leaked to the West that a similar complaint had been made to the Bucharest government by Karoly Kiraly, a former high official of the Rumanian Communist Party. Kiraly, of Hungarian extraction, charged that Hungarians were discriminated against in employment and education.

Ceauşescu's response was repressive. There were reports that secret police had been ordered to keep close watch on the Hungarian community. Kiraly told Western newsmen that Rumanian officials threatened him with arrest if he did not withdraw his protest, and he subsequently lost his job as a factory manager. In a speech made during June, Ceauşescu took a hard line on the minority problem. Among other things, he warned the Hungarian government not to interfere in Rumanian affairs.

On the economic front, Ceauşescu continued to push for rapid development. In March, however, he ordered officials to begin decentralizing economic management and to offer increased incentives to workers. To make certain the new policy was carried out, Ceauşescu conducted an extensive reshuffle of the government and the Communist Party that same month.

A further shake-up was undertaken in late summer, following the defection to the West of a high-ranking security expert, Gen. Ion Pacepa. In the wake of Pacepa's flight, Ceauşescu fired Interior Minister Teodor Coman and had at least a dozen other security men arrested.

Foreign Affairs. Rumania's effort to assert its independence of the Soviet Union took much of Ceauşescu's attention. He visited Washington, D.C., in April to strengthen his ties with the United States. The following month, Ceauşescu traveled to Asia for state visits to the People's Republic of China, Vietnam, Laos, Cambodia, and North Korea. In June he became the first Warsaw Pact leader to be a guest of Great Britain's Queen Elizabeth II at Buckingham Palace.

The Soviet Union maintained pressure on Ceauşescu to keep Rumania in line. Moscow was especially disturbed when the Rumanians played host in August to China's Chairman Hua Kuo-feng. Ceauşescu made a gesture of independence in November when he publicly announced that Rumania, unlike its fellow Warsaw Pact members, would not honor Soviet demands to increase military spending.

See STATISTICS OF THE WORLD.   F.W.

RWANDA. *See* STATISTICS OF THE WORLD.

S

SAHARA, SPANISH or WESTERN. *See* AFRICA; MIDDLE EAST; MOROCCO.

SAMOA. *See* STATISTICS OF THE WORLD.

SAN MARINO. *See* STATISTICS OF THE WORLD.

SÃO TOMÉ AND PRÍNCIPE. *See* STATISTICS OF THE WORLD.

SASKATCHEWAN. *See* STATISTICS OF THE WORLD.

SAUDI ARABIA. The close relationship that had developed between Saudi Arabia and the United States was subjected to unexpected strains in 1978. First the Saudis decided late in the year to line up with the opponents of a proposed Egyptian-Israeli peace treaty; then they went along with a decision by the Organization of Petroleum Exporting Countries (q.v.), or OPEC, to hike oil prices by 14.5 percent during 1979.

Oil Policy. Before the 1978 OPEC meeting in December, the Saudis—who had successfully blocked any oil price increase in 1977 and earlier in 1978—indicated that they favored a boost of less than 10 percent. Saudi Arabia had also increased its production to an estimated 10,000,000 bbl per day to prevent an oil shortage from developing as a result of the chaos in Iran. Therefore, Western oil experts were caught by surprise when Saudi Arabia, instead of using its influence as the world's largest petroleum producer to hold the price line, went along with the 14.5 percent hike sought by other exporting countries.

One explanation for the Saudi decision might well lie in the fact that the Saudi government found itself in late 1978 in a temporary cash bind. Earlier in the year, the Saudis, as a result of a worldwide oil surplus, were producing only about 7,000,000 bbl per day—well below the 8,500,000 bbl daily production needed to keep the government's budget balanced. The Saudis cashed in some short-term bank notes in May, and in early summer the council of ministers ordered a 10 percent cut in budget expenditures.

SAUDI ARABIA

U.S. Secretary of Defense Harold Brown visits King Khalid of Saudi Arabia in a Cleveland hospital on Oct. 13. The king, who had had complicated heart surgery ten days earlier, was the biggest purchaser of U.S. arms during 1978.

Economic Developments. Despite the cash squeeze, the long-term Saudi economic position remained bright. Official statistics released in September showed that the country had $26 billion in foreign exchange reserves. In recognition of the emergence of Saudi Arabia as a major economic power, the International Monetary Fund decided in September to give the Saudis their own seat and their own executive director on the IMF executive board.

Nevertheless, Saudi Arabia was finding it difficult to keep pace with its ambitious development schedule. In early 1978 bottlenecks in transportation and communications were reported to be slowing economic development considerably. A shortage of skilled management and labor continued to be a problem as well.

Foreign Policy. Growing Soviet influence in the Middle East was a serious concern to the conservative Saudis during 1978. The U.S.S.R. increased its involvement in Ethiopia and the People's Democratic Republic of Yemen and maintained its influence in Iraq. In addition, the instability in Iran worried the Saudis. As a result, Saudi Arabia was greatly relieved in May when the U.S. Senate approved the sale of sixty F-15's, the most advanced and expensive U.S. fighter plane, to their country. Saudi Arabia was the biggest customer for U.S. arms and military construction projects during 1978, spending an estimated $4.9 billion.

Saudi law, which is based on the Koran and forbids all use of alcoholic beverages, created some problems in the international arena in 1978. Two British workers were publicly whipped in May for making illegal alcohol, creating a public outcry in Great Britain. The official British response was muted, however, in part because

seven other British subjects were being held by the Saudis for similar offenses at the time.

The major surprise of 1978 in Saudi foreign policy was the government's decision not to support Egyptian President Anwar el-Sadat's plan to sign a peace treaty with Israel. Saudi support was eagerly sought by Sadat, whose country's economy relies heavily on Saudi aid. The Saudi government initially maintained a cautious silence after the Camp David, Md., summit accords were announced in September, and Secretary of State Cyrus R. Vance was sent to Riyadh to explain the agreement and seek Saudi backing. But the Saudi government declined to endorse Sadat's move, and in November Saudi Arabia lined up with the hard-liners at an Arab summit meeting in Baghdad in denouncing the proposed peace treaty.

See STATISTICS OF THE WORLD. *See also* ARAB LEAGUE; MIDDLE EAST. M.R.B

SENEGAL. *See* STATISTICS OF THE WORLD. *See also* AFRICA.

SEYCHELLES. *See* STATISTICS OF THE WORLD.

SIERRA LEONE. *See* STATISTICS OF THE WORLD; *see also* AFRICA.

SINGAPORE, REPUBLIC OF. Under Prime Minister Lee Kuan Yew, Singapore continued to prosper in 1978. Despite a surge in rice prices, inflation was moderate by world standards. The balance of payments was comfortably in surplus, thanks to steady inflow of foreign capital. Gross domestic product grew by 8.5 percent in the first half of 1978, a rate that was expected to last through the rest of the year.

Singapore's problems were largely those of success. Lee warned his countrymen against letting their "rugged society" go soft. He fought against protectionist sentiment abroad and its threat

Singapore's exports. He also argued against the International Monetary Fund's proposal to classify Singapore as a developed country—a step that would cost the country preferential status for its exports in the industrialized world.

Like other members of the Association of Southeast Asian Nations, Singapore was courted by the contending Communist powers of Asia. Vietnam's Premier Pham Van Dong visited in October; Deputy Premier Teng Hsiao-ping of the People's Republic of China came in November. Lee, always distrustful of the Communists, treated both visitors politely but warily.

See STATISTICS OF THE WORLD.   R.J.C.

SOCIAL SECURITY. The Social Security Administration got a new commissioner in 1978: Stanford G. Ross, 48, a tax lawyer who had been chairman of the Advisory Council on Social Security. Congress enacted no major changes in the Social Security Act, but proposals to reform the system were the subject of study and discussion both inside and outside government during the year.

Studies of the System. The quadrennial Advisory Council on Social Security—required under the law to review the status of social security programs—was named early in 1978. The council held the first public hearing in its history to obtain the views of witnesses on such matters as the use of general revenues in financing the programs, the treatment of women, changes in the beneficiaries' earnings test, and improvements in disability benefits. The council was to submit its report by Oct. 1, 1979.

The 1977 amendments to the Social Security Act required the Secretary of Health, Education, and Welfare (HEW) to study and report on the feasibility of social security coverage for workers not now covered—chiefly employees of federal, state, and local governments and of nonprofit organizations. The Universal Social Security Coverage Study, set up by HEW Secretary Joseph A. Califano, Jr., conducted public hearings in 1978 to explore the possibility of such coverage and to discuss the issues involved. Private citizens, representatives of interested organizations, and public officials expressed their views at meetings throughout the country. The group's report was due by Dec. 20, 1979.

OASDI Benefits. Under the old-age, survivors, and disability insurance (OASDI) program, cash benefits of $7.8 billion were paid in September, 1978, to 34,400,000 persons. The average monthly benefit received by retired workers was $261; for workers just coming on the rolls, the average was $280. Disabled workers received $287, on the average; new disabled-worker beneficiaries were awarded an average of $328.

A cost-of-living increase of 6.5 percent in social security benefits became effective in June, 1978. Checks mailed in July were the first to reflect the increase.

Changes for 1979. Several changes resulting from the 1977 amendments were to take effect in January, 1979. The maximum earnings base for taxing and benefit-computation purposes was lifted to $22,900. The contribution rate for employers and employees in 1979 and 1980 was raised to 6.13 percent of covered earnings (for the self-employed, it remained at 8.10 percent). The annual exempt amount under the beneficiaries' earnings test in 1979 was $4500 for beneficiaries aged 65–71 and $3480 for those under age 65.

Medicare. In Medicare's twelfth year of operation (September, 1977–October, 1978) about $6 billion from the hospital insurance trust fund went for hospital and related benefits. Some 26,468,300 aged or disabled persons were enrolled for these benefits as of Jan. 1, 1978. Following the annual review of program costs, the hospital deductible (the amount paid by the beneficiary before reimbursement occurs) was raised to $160 for the first 60 days and to $40 a day for the 61st–90th days; for the 60-day lifetime reserve after 90 days are used, the deductible was raised to $80 per day. For care in a skilled-nursing facility after the first 20 days, the beneficiary pays $20 daily, up to his 100th day in the facility.

Under Medicare's supplementary medical insurance program, 25,679,000 aged or disabled persons were enrolled as of Jan. 1, 1978, and were voluntarily paying premiums ($8.20 monthly to July, 1979, $8.70 thereafter) for medical care coverage. About 40,457,000 bills were approved and payments totaling $8.3 billion were reimbursed from January to July, 1978.

Other Programs. Under the supplemental security income program, payments totaling $550,016,000 went to 4,231,500 aged, blind, and disabled individuals in September, 1978. Payment levels were raised in mid-1978 to $189.40 for individuals and to $284.10 for couples.

Under the federal-state program of aid to families with dependent children, a total of $895,100,-000 went to 10,449,081 persons in July, 1978. Payments averaged $257 per family and $86 per recipient.

SOLOMON ISLANDS. See STATISTICS OF THE WORLD. See also COMMONWEALTH OF NATIONS.

SOMALIA. The war with Ethiopia, which began in 1977 with Somali triumphs, ended in 1978 with a resounding defeat. The Somali offensive, which had swept through most of Ethiopia's Ogaden region, ground to a halt in December, 1977. Faced with entrenched Ethiopian forces bolstered by So-

SOMALIA

Muhammad Siad Barre, president of Somalia, announces a total military mobilization against Ethiopia on Feb. 13. More than 100,000 Somali citizens gathered to hear the president's declaration of war.

viet arms and Soviet and Cuban advisers, Somalia's President Muhammad Siad Barre called for arms and aid from the West. The United States rejected the plea in January, but indicated that it would not be displeased if others acceded to the request. Iran, Saudi Arabia, and Egypt did supply arms, and West German funds were used to purchase additional weapons and munitions.

New arms and a full-scale mobilization proved ineffective, however, in stopping the Ethiopian offensive that washed over the Somali forces in February. By March, the remnants of the Somali military in the Ogaden were withdrawn across the border. With Egypt and Sudan pledging troops and with the U.S. committed to reconsidering its refusal to furnish arms if the Ethiopians crossed the Somali border, a quasi-cease-fire was declared in March.

Siad Barre's handling of the war, entrance into which had been opposed by many in the military, further embittered the dissatisfied men at arms,

358

and it was reported that some eighty senior officers were executed for criticizing his leadership (although the report was officially denied). On April 9 a small group of officers, troops, and police attempted a coup, but it was quickly crushed by loyal troops. In the subsequent trial, which ended in September, 17 officers were sentenced to death and 36 others to prison.

Immediately after the abortive coup, Siad Barre visited the People's Republic of China. The Chinese agreed to take over aid projects abandoned by the Soviets. In June, Siad Barre visited Western Europe to secure arms to rebuild the military. The U.S. as well as Great Britain and West Germany indicated that they would provide only economic aid. However, efforts among conservative Middle East states proved more successful, and by the summer Somali guerrillas were again clashing with Ethiopian troops in the Ogaden. In July, after Ethiopia rejected an Organization of African Unity peace plan, the entire Somali military establishment appeared to be rallying behind Siad Barre. In December, Ethiopian bombing raids on towns in Somalia were reported, as well as Ethiopian troop concentrations near the border. Somali officials charged that Ethiopia was planning an invasion, but observers noted that Ethiopia's actions may only have been a response to Somalia's continued support for insurgents in the Ogaden.

See STATISTICS OF THE WORLD. See also AFRICA.   J.T.S.

SOUTH AFRICA, REPUBLIC OF. Political and financial controversy rocked the government of Prime Minister John Vorster of South Africa in 1978 and led to a shift in personnel, if not policy, for the National Party regime.

Political Scandal. Early in the year, opposition newspapers began to investigate rumors that special government funds, estimated to range as high as $20,000,000 per year, were being used to manipulate the domestic and foreign press. Despite the government's silence and its later attempts to cover up the affair, enough was revealed to force the establishment of a parliamentary committee and a three-member judicial investigative commission. The judicial report, issued in early December, absolved Vorster as well as other leading officials. At the height of the scandal during the summer, however, key officials at the Department of Information had been forced to resign; the department was abolished on June 15. Cornelius Mulder, who had served as minister of information and who was considered a possible successor to Vorster, was held responsible for the manipulation scheme and resigned as minister of plural relations (black administration) in November.

Color Him Tough

In their choice of Pieter Willem Botha, 62, as the new prime minister, South Africa's ruling National Party in effect signaled "no retreat" on the harsh racial policies of his recently resigned predecessor, John Vorster. As defense minister (a portfolio he retained), Botha had gained the nickname "Piet Wapans" ("Pete Weapons") for boosting arms spending fourfold in five years (to more than $2 billion annually). Immersed in politics since his law school days, Botha had shown on occasion some flexibility on minor racial questions. But his elevation to the top post in September was taken to mean that the Pretoria government intended to maintain its hard-line stand on apartheid even at the risk of incurring international trade sanctions.

Prime Minister Pieter Botha of South Africa.

Vorster's health appeared to suffer under the strain of the investigation. State President Nicolaas Diederichs had died in August at the age of 74, and Vorster stepped down as prime minister on Sept. 20 and assumed the largely ceremonial role of president. (On the same day he rejected a United Nations plan for establishing independence in South-West Africa.) Defense Minister Pieter W. Botha, who was also absolved of any role in the scandal, succeeded Vorster as prime minister. Botha appeared willing to moderate the country's tough domestic policies slightly but was not expected to make any changes in foreign policy.

Racial Policies. Government attempts to divide the country's black, colored (mixed-race), and Asian majority suffered a setback in January when Zulu, Colored, and Indian leaders called for a common strategy against apartheid. In March they formed an interracial party, the South African Black Alliance, under the leadership of Gatsha Buthelezi, the chief minister of the KwaZulu homeland. Despite opposition from young urban Blacks, many of whom regarded him as a government puppet, Buthelezi appeared to be filling the vacuum created by the suppression of the black consciousness movement in 1977 and the death in February of Robert Sobukwe, the country's leading black nationalist leader. On the government's part, in March, thirteen black activists were released after five months in preventive detention. In June urban Blacks finally were allowed to hold ninety-nine-year leases on their homes—but not on the land under them. The regulations requiring all Blacks to carry passbooks were also relaxed. In November, Andries P. Traurnicht, a conservative on racial issues, was elected National Party leader in Transvaal Province; his election was seen as a challenge to the relatively moderate racial policies of Prime Minister Botha.

Foreign Affairs. As South Africa's resistance to turning South-West Africa (q.v.) over to black rule and as its continued support of white rule in Rhodesia became more apparent, foreign resistance to its policies multiplied. Private groups pressed for an end to investment in South Africa. In August the Swedish government called for an end to South African investment, and the U.S. government began to monitor strictly the export of arms and strategic technology. Transkei, a country whose independence was recognized only by South Africa, which had created it, broke off diplomatic relations with the South African regime in April. At year's end, U.S. State Department sources announced that South Africa had agreed to a U.N. plan for the establishment of South-West African independence, a plan it had earlier rejected.

See STATISTICS OF THE WORLD. See also AFRICA; UNITED NATIONS.　　　　　　　　　J.T.S.

SOUTH CAROLINA. See STATISTICS OF THE WORLD.
SOUTH DAKOTA. See STATISTICS OF THE WORLD.
SOUTH-WEST AFRICA, also known as NAMIBIA. The Republic of South Africa has controlled the mineral-rich desert territory of South-West Africa since 1915, first through military occupation, after 1920 as the administrator of a League of Nations mandate, and, after 1966, in defiance of the United Nations.

Throughout 1978 the United States, Great Britain, France, West Germany, and Canada worked to devise an independence plan that would be acceptable to African nationalists and the U.N., on the one hand, and the Republic of South Africa, on the other. In 1977 the five Western powers had devised a formula calling for a phased reduction of South African troops in South-West Africa from an estimated 25,000 to 1500, an end of fighting with nationalist forces led by the South-West Africa People's Organization (SWAPO), and U.N.-administered elections which would lead to a transitional government and independence. Although the South African government rejected the severe troop reductions, it did begin to dismantle the territory's apartheid laws.

After declaring that it would go ahead with its own plan for independence by the end of 1978, South Africa came under intense pressure to accept the Western plan. Pretoria did agree to the plan on April 25, but, after South African troops attacked SWAPO bases in southern Angola, the nationalists broke off negotiations. Angola and Zambia pressed SWAPO leaders to accept the Western proposals; they did so on July 12. In August a fifty-member U.N. team visited South-West Africa to lay the groundwork for a supervised transition to black rule. Although both sides accepted key provisions of the plan, South Africa refused to agree to a Security Council resolution calling for the early "reintegration" of the city of Walvis Bay into South-West Africa. (South Africa earlier had separated this deep-water port from South-West Africa and claimed sovereignty over it.)

On Sept. 20 South Africa declared it would go ahead unilaterally with elections for a constituent assembly in defiance of the U.N. After intense negotiations, South Africa declared that although the elections would be held, they would not preclude later U.N.-supervised elections. SWAPO boycotted the elections, held Dec. 4–8, and attempted to disrupt them. By and large, these attempts at disruption failed, and South-West Africans allied to the Democratic Turnhalle Alliance, the South African protégé party, won most contests. The assembly opened on Dec. 20 and soon agreed to U.N.-supervised elections—but only on condition that the U.N. withdraw its recognition of SWAPO as sole representative of the territory. At the end of the year, the South African government also accepted the plan for U.N.-supervised transition to independence, according to U.S. sources, raising hopes that Pretoria had abandoned its effort to maintain white domination.

See STATISTICS OF THE WORLD. See also AFRICA. J.T.S.

SPACE EXPLORATION. During 1978 the Soviet Union established new duration records for manned spaceflight. Meanwhile, the U.S. National Aeronautics and Space Administration (NASA) launched twenty applications and scientific research satellites and continued to develop the space shuttle.

Manned Spaceflight. By early December, seven months after their 6-ton space capsule had docked with the 19-ton Salyut 6 space station, Soyuz 29 Commander Vladimir Kovalenok and Flight Engineer Aleksandr Ivanchenkov had brought the total number of hours logged by Soviet cosmonauts in space to 27,283, surpassing the American astronauts' cumulative total of 22,504 hr. A few months earlier the same team of cosmonauts had broken another record—the duration

Soviet cosmonauts Vladimir Kovalenok (left) and Aleksandr Ivanchenkov, photographed on Nov. 2 after their return to earth aboard Soyuz 31. The two men had established a new space endurance record, having been in orbit aboard the space station Salyut 6 for approximately 4½ months.

Pioneer-Venus II is checked by NASA employees before being encapsulated in the Atlas Centaur rocket that launched it into space on Aug. 8. When it neared the planet Venus in early December, the spacecraft separated into five probes, each aimed at a different part of the Venusian surface. Scientists were then provided with a wealth of data on the composition and characteristics of the cloud-shrouded planet.

Intense sunspot activity caused the massive space station Skylab to lose altitude in 1978, leading to predictions that it would soon fall to earth. The photograph here was made by U.S. astronauts in 1973.

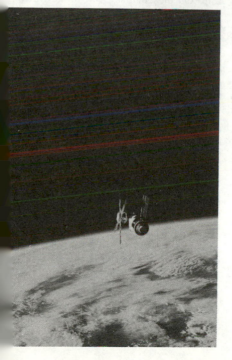

record for manned spaceflight, established by Yuri Romanenko and Georgi Grechko. Romanenko and Grechko had spent 96 days 10 hr. aboard Salyut 6 before they returned to earth in March.

Salyut 6, which had been launched in September, 1977, was also visited in 1978 by the first space travelers from countries other than the U.S.S.R. or the United States. Aboard Soyuz 28, sent to the space station on March 3, was Czechoslovak air force pilot Vladimir Remek. Four months later, on June 27, Polish astronomer Miroslaw Hermaszewski was a member of the crew of the Soyuz 30 rendezvous flight. And finally, on Aug. 26, Sigmund Jahn, an East German, went to Salyut 6 aboard Soyuz 31.

In 1978 four unmanned spacecraft also journeyed to Salyut 6, supplying two successive crews with the food, fuel, and new equipment needed to keep the space station functioning. The first of these supply craft, Progress I, was launched on Jan. 20; guided by ground controllers, it rendezvoused a few days later with the orbiter. The three later shuttles allowed the space station to continue to operate through the end of the year. Western scientists noted that with such shuttling of crews and supplies the Russians could keep Salyut 6 operating indefinitely.

Although the U.S. had not conducted a manned

spaceflight since the joint Apollo-Soyuz mission in July, 1975, NASA continued its efforts in 1978 to prepare the manned space shuttle mission for its first test flight, scheduled for late 1979. In January the space agency selected from 8079 applicants 35 candidates for the shuttle program. Fifteen will be trained as pilot-astronauts and 20 as mission specialists—shuttle personnel who will have a variety of scientific and engineering responsibilities. Six women, 3 Blacks, and 1 Japanese-American were included among the 35 candidates.

Planetary Missions. Two spacecraft targeted for Venus—Pioneer-Venus I and II—were launched on May 20 and Aug. 8, respectively. On Dec. 4 Venus I began its scheduled eight-month orbit of the planet, to collect data on its upper atmosphere and to map its cloud-shrouded surface. Five days later the fine probes of Venus II reached the planet, making qualitative and quantitative analyses of the Venusian atmosphere before landing.

Two Soviet spacecraft also studied Venus in 1978—Veñera XII, which landed on Dec. 21; and Veñera XI, which landed on Dec. 25. The data obtained from all four missions were, however, contradictory and surprising; see EARTH AND PLANETARY SCIENCES.

Scientific Satellites. During 1978 NASA launched a variety of research satellites to aid scientists studying terrestrial, as well as cosmic phenomena. In January the space administration, in cooperation with the European Space Agency (ESA), sent the International Ultraviolet Explorer (IUE) into orbit above the equator. Traveling as fast as the earth rotates and thus remaining constantly at the same point above the earth, or geostationary, the IUE will obtain data on ultraviolet emissions from a variety of stellar sources. In July NASA launched the International Sun Earth Explorer (ISEE-3). Orbiting at a point between the earth and sun where it would travel at the same velocity as the earth around the sun, ISEE-3 will obtain data on the solar wind (the energetic stream of ions emitted by the sun). In October NASA launched the High Energy Astronomical Observatory (HEAO-2). This satellite is equipped with an X-ray-sensitive telescope that will map such celestial sources of high-energy radiation as black holes—those dense, collapsed stars that are invisible to optical telescopes.

Although most of the research satellites launched in 1978 were designed for the study of celestial events, some of them will probe a variety of more earth-related phenomena. In July, NASA orbited United Kingdom 6 (UK-6), an ESA satellite that will investigate the earth's magnetosphere (the region of the earth's atmosphere that is controlled by its magnetic field). The earth's magne-

tosphere was also the object of study for EXOS-A and EXOS-B, two satellites launched by Japan (in February and September, respectively). With these two satellites, and the ISS-B, the Ionosphere Sounding Satellite (also launched in February), Japanese scientists were able to begin in 1978 an in-depth program of study of the earth's upper atmosphere.

Applications Satellites. During 1978 many applications satellites were sent aloft to collect data on weather and natural resources as well as to establish communications and reconnaissance networks.

In May the U.S. launched two of these satellites: a Geostationary Orbiting Earth Satellite (GOES-3) to monitor the environment and Seasat-1 to study the oceans. Three months later NASA launched Nimbus-7 to test advanced sensors for use in monitoring weather pollution and studying the oceans. Seasat-1, which was initially successful, eventually lost internal power and became inactive.

In 1978 NASA also launched into geostationary orbit a number of communications satellites for American domestic corporations, for the ESA, and for Japan, all on a cost-reimbursable basis. Included were three Intelsat-IV A's for the Comsat Corp. and the Comstar-C for the RCA Corp.; NATO-III-C for the North Atlantic Treaty Organization (NATO); and developmental communications satellites for the ESA and Japan. In January the U.S. Postal Service announced plans to test an international message service in cooperation with the Communications Satellite Corp. A field trial for a demonstration of the feasibility of this "electronic mail" service was scheduled to take place in 1979.

One dramatic application of a satellite occurred in 1978. When Japanese explorer Naomi Uemura made his solo trek to the North Pole and across Greenland in the spring (see PEOPLE IN THE NEWS), he carried a 10 kg (22 lb.) beacon transmitter. Signals were sent from his dogsled to the Nimbus-3 satellite, which relayed them to NASA's Greenbelt (Md.) center. There on a large-scale map his progress was noted within an accuracy of 1-2 km (0.6-1.2 mi.).

The Sky Is Falling. In January, Cosmos 954, a Soviet satellite powered by a nuclear reactor, reentered the earth's atmosphere. Its disintegration caused radioactive debris to shower throughout a large area of western Canada. No one was hurt by the falling debris, but the U.S.S.R. agreed to participate in a United Nations study to determine what safety measures must be taken in the launching of satellites that employ nuclear power.

The possibility that Skylab, a 77-ton satellite

SPAIN

launched by NASA in 1973, may also reenter the atmosphere caused further concern. Although in June NASA scientists made efforts to prevent the craft from losing altitude, they later predicted that the satellite will fall to earth sometime in 1979 or 1980. Spokesmen for the space agency emphasized, however, that there is small likelihood that the satellite will fall on land.   F.C.D.III

SPAIN. Despite continuing political violence and a faltering economy, Spain in 1978 succeeded in putting a new democratic constitution into effect, thus becoming a constitutional monarchy under Juan Carlos I.

The New Constitution. A constitutional commission composed of members of the political parties represented in the Cortes (parliament) had been charged with the task of drafting a constitution to replace the legal code under which Spain had been governed for nearly forty years by the dictator Francisco Franco.

Lengthy discussions and revisions produced a draft text that was approved by the Chamber of Deputies in July and by the Senate in October. The final text was approved simultaneously by both houses on Oct. 31; the vote was 325–6 with 14 abstentions in the lower house and 226–5 with 8 abstentions in the Senate. The constitution was submitted to popular referendum and approved by 88 percent of those voting on Dec. 6. However, the voter turnout was surprisingly low, and support for the new constitution was particularly weak in the Basque region. Juan Carlos "sanctioned" the constitution on Dec. 27 and pledged that he would remain above politics.

Under the new constitution, the cabinet is responsible to the Chamber of Deputies, the lower house of the two-chamber Cortes. Church and state are separate, but the state is to "keep in mind the religious beliefs of Spanish society," and Roman Catholic church schools continue to be state subsidized. The constitution guarantees some degree of autonomy to ethnic regions, such as Catalonia and the Basque provinces.

The new constitution also guarantees freedom of expression, abolishes the death penalty, lowers the voting age from 21 to 18, and recognizes the right to strike.

Other Political Developments. The small Popular Socialist Party merged with the largest opposition party, the Socialist Workers' Party, led by Felipe González, who said his party should no longer be identified as Marxist. At the ninth congress of the Communist Party, held in Madrid April 19–23, the Leninist label was dropped from the party statutes, and party leader Santiago Carrillo criticized the international policies of the Soviet Union and praised the democratic process.

Premier Adolfo Suárez González of the Union of the Democratic Center was required by the new constitution to call for a vote of confidence or a general election within thirty days. On Dec. 29, the first day on which such action was legally possible, Suárez announced that a general election would be held on March 1, 1979. Premier Suárez, who hoped to strengthen his moderate party's rule, said that he had acted immediately to avoid a period of uncertainty.

Terrorism. Political violence plagued Spain throughout 1978, especially in the Basque region, where the separatist organization ETA was far from satisfied with the degree of autonomy offered the Basques by the central government. ETA was held responsible for dozens of assassinations during 1978, most of the victims either policemen or members of the Civil Guard. In January and February a wave of bombings swept not only the Basque provinces, but also Catalonia and the Canary Islands, where separatists were also active. Murders continued throughout the year and increased as the December constitutional referendum approached. Between Sept. 1 and Nov. 28, gunmen killed 18 policemen and 10 other persons.

A left-wing group known as the First of October Anti-Fascist Resistance Group, or GRAPO, reportedly killed a number of prominent persons, including Spain's director general of prisons and several high-ranking military officers.

The Economy and Foreign Relations. The Spanish economy was sluggish in 1978. Prices rose approximately 17 percent, down from 26 percent in 1977. Unemployment increased, however, and ran at about 7 percent. Industrial production lagged, and the steel and shipbuilding industries were restructured in August in an effort to reduce their losses. Other sectors of the economy did well, however; 1978 was a good year for agriculture and the tourist trade.

In September, Premier Suárez visited Cuba. It was the first visit to that country by a Western European leader since 1959, when President Fidel Castro came to power. King Juan Carlos and Queen Sofía went to the People's Republic of China in June to sign treaties of friendship and cooperation. On the way home, the Spanish royal mission stopped in Iran to sign similar accords. Later in June President Valéry Giscard d'Estaing visited Madrid; this was the first such visit by a French head of state in forty years. Giscard expressed his country's support of Spain's application for membership in the European Economic Community, of which France is a prominent member; see EUROPEAN COMMUNITIES.

See STATISTICS OF THE WORLD.   A.R.

SPORTS

There were two triple-crown winners: Affirmed, with Steve Cauthen up, won the Kentucky Derby, the Preakness, and the Belmont Stakes; Muhammad Ali won the world heavyweight boxing championship for the third time. Perhaps the most dedicated sportspersons of the year were the joggers; 11,400 of them showed up to run in the New York City Marathon.

More people watched more athletes earn more money in 1978 than ever before.

There was record attendance in many sports—40,600,000 in major-league baseball, 34,200,000 in college football, 29,100,000 in college basketball, 4,900,000 in North American professional soccer.

There were record earnings in thoroughbred racing ($901,541 by Affirmed), harness racing ($703,260 by Abercrombie), men's golf ($362,429 by Tom Watson), women's golf ($189,813 by Nancy Lopez), bowling ($134,500 by Mark Roth), and professional skiing ($92,883 by Andre Arnold).

Muhammad Ali earned $6,750,000 for two fights. Pete Rose signed a four-year baseball contract for $800,000 per year. Prize money exceeded

$10,000,000 in tennis and neared $14,000,000 in golf and $3,000,000 in bowling.

The year's most successful athletes included Ron Guidry and Jim Rice in baseball, Tom Watson in golf, Mario Andretti in auto racing, Guy Lafleur in ice hockey, Eric Heiden in speed skating, and Henry Rono in track and field. The leading women included Lopez in golf, Chris Evert and Martina Navratilova in tennis, and Tracy Caulkins in swimming.

The most exciting team was baseball's New York Yankees, who rallied from season-long turmoil and won their second straight World Series. The most exciting rivalry was the Affirmed-Alydar battle for thoroughbred racing's triple crown (Affirmed won all three races).

AUTO RACING

Mario Andretti of Nazareth, Pa., Al Unser of Albuquerque, N.Mex., and Cale Yarborough of Timmonsville, S.C., won major auto racing titles in

With his wife at his side, Mario Andretti receives the Italian Grand Prix winner's trophy. His victory at Monza on Sept. 10 clinched the 1978 world driving championship for the American master.

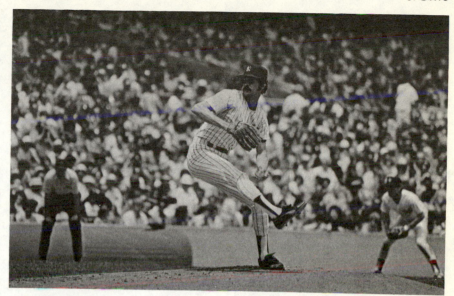

Yankee left-hander Ron Guidry caps a sensational year by pitching a winner against the Los Angeles Dodgers during the World Series. Third baseman Graig Nettles (right), with several sensational fielding plays, ensured Guidry's win in this, the third game of the series.

1978. Andretti and Unser were 38 years old, Yarborough 37.

Andretti became world driving champion, the first American to win that title since Phil Hill in 1961. The championship was decided in a series of 16 Grand Prix races, mostly in Europe, for Formula One cars. Andretti won 6 races in an English Lotus-Cosworth and Carlos Reutteman of Argentina won 4 in an Italian Ferrari, including both races in the United States. Ronnie Peterson of Sweden, Andretti's teammate, was fatally injured in the Italian Grand Prix Sept. 10 at Monza.

Unser won all three 500-mi. races for Indy-type cars—the Indianapolis 500, May 28; the Schaefer 500, June 25 at Long Pond, Pa.; and the California 500, Sept. 3 at Ontario, Calif. His Lola-Cosworth qualified fifth, tenth, and seventh for the three races. Tom Sneva of Spokane, Wash., and Danny Ongais of Costa Mesa, Calif., had faster cars, but they did not always survive the rigors of the long races. Sneva was the year's series champion.

The $1,145,225 Indianapolis 500 was the richest race ever. The best-known European race, the 24 Hours of Le Mans (June 10 and 11 in France), was won by a French Renault Alpine A442 driven by two Frenchmen. It was the first Le Mans victory for Renault, a nationalized company that spent $4,000,000 in three years just to win this race.

Yarborough won the season series of the National Association for Stock Car Auto Racing in an Oldsmobile after having won it the two previous years in a Chevrolet. He won 10 of the 30 races.

Bobby Allison of Hueytown, Ala., won the Daytona 500 Feb. 19 in Daytona Beach, Fla., in a Thunderbird. Strangely, when Allison rode as a passenger in street traffic, he suffered from motion sickness.

BASEBALL

The New York Yankees made baseball history in 1978. They became the first team to win the World Series with four straight victories after losing the first two games. The Yankees, after a season of turmoil, won their third straight American League pennant. The Los Angeles Dodgers won their second straight National League pennant, and they were favored over the Yankees in the World Series.

The first two games were played Oct. 10 and 11 in Los Angeles, and the Dodgers won, 11–5 and 4–3. The next three games were played Oct. 13–15 in New York City, and the Yankees won all three, 5–1, 4–3 (in 10 innings), and 12–2. In the sixth game, Oct. 17 in Los Angeles, the Yankees won, 7–2, behind Jim ("Catfish") Hunter, whose pitching career had been saved by a physician's forced manipulation of his ailing shoulder.

The Yankees overcame obstacles all season. Bickering continued among Billy Martin, the man-

NATIONAL LEAGUE				
Eastern Division	W	L	Pct.	GB
Philadelphia Phillies	90	72	.556	—
Pittsburgh Pirates.............	88	73	.547	1½
Chicago Cubs.................	79	83	.488	11
Montréal Expos...............	76	86	.469	14
St. Louis Cardinals............	69	93	.426	21
New York Mets...............	66	96	.407	24
Western Division				
Los Angeles Dodgers.........	95	67	.586	—
Cincinnati Reds...............	92	69	.571	2½
San Francisco Giants.........	89	73	.549	6
San Diego Padres	84	78	.519	11
Houston Astros...............	74	88	.457	21
Atlanta Braves	69	93	.426	26

AMERICAN LEAGUE				
Eastern Division	W	L	Pct.	GB
New York Yankees..........	100	63	.613	—
Boston Red Sox	99	64	.607	1
Milwaukee Brewers	93	69	.574	6½
Baltimore Orioles	90	71	.559	9
Detroit Tigers	86	76	.531	13½
Cleveland Indians	69	90	.434	29
Toronto Blue Jays	59	102	.336	40
Western Division				
Kansas City Royals	92	70	.568	—
California Angels.............	87	75	.537	5
Texas Rangers	87	75	.537	5
Minnesota Twins.............	73	89	.451	19
Chicago White Sox	71	90	.441	20½
Oakland A's.................	69	93	.426	23
Seattle Mariners	56	104	.350	35

PENNANT PLAYOFFS

National League—Los Angeles defeated Philadelphia, 3 games to 1

American League—New York defeated Kansas City, 3 games to 1

WORLD SERIES

New York Yankees defeated Los Angeles, 4 games to 2

In the National League West, the Cincinnati Reds failed because of inadequate pitching. The San Francisco Giants' unexpected challenge fell short. The Dodgers won despite a porous infield. The Dodgers averaged more than 41,000 spectators per home game, and their season home attendance of 3,347,845 was the highest in history. Major-league attendance of 40,636,886 was a record, too.

In the National League East, the Philadelphia Phillies had erratic hitting. The Pittsburgh Pirates had good hitting, especially from Dave Parker, the National League batting champion with .334. But the Phillies, with better pitching, won their third straight division title.

In the pennant playoffs, the Yankees beat the Royals, 3 games to 1, and the Dodgers defeated the Phillies, also in four games.

The Yankees won the World Series because of better hitting, fielding, and pitching. The best Yankee hitters were shortstop Bucky Dent, voted the most valuable player in the series; and Brian Doyle, the substitute second baseman. While the Dodgers hurt themselves with poor fielding, Graig Nettles of the Yankees made sensational plays game after game at third base. The Yankees also received strong relief pitching from Rich Gossage.

The year's best pitcher was Ron Guidry of the Yankees, who won the playoff game from the Red Sox and the third game of the World Series. His regular-season won-lost record of 25-3 produced a winning percentage of .893, the highest in history for a 20-game winner.

The best hitter was Jim Rice of Boston, the major-league leader in runs batted in (139), home runs (46), hits (213), total bases (406), and slugging percentage (.600). Rice and Parker won their league's most-valuable-player awards. The Cy Young Awards for pitchers went to Gaylord Perry of the San Diego Padres and Guidry.

Pete Rose of Cincinnati hit safely in 44 straight games, a National League modern record. After the season, the 37-year-old Rose became a free agent and signed with Philadelphia for $800,000 a year for four years, the highest salary in baseball history.

Rod Carew of the Minnesota Twins hit .333 and won his seventh American League batting title.

Larry Hisle of the Milwaukee Brewers, whose $3,100,000 contract was the highest of 1977 free agents, had a good season. Lyman Bostock of the Angels, whose free-agent contract totaled $2,700,-000, was shot to death a week before the season ended by the estranged husband of a woman who was in a car with Bostock; *see* OBITUARIES.

The baseball Hall of Fame in Cooperstown, N.Y., inducted Eddie Mathews, a former Braves

ager; George Steinbrenner, the principal owner; and Reggie Jackson, the slugging outfielder. Jackson was suspended for five days for bunting when Martin had ordered him to swing. When Jackson returned, Martin lashed out at Steinbrenner and Jackson and then resigned. Incredibly, the Yankees rehired Martin to manage in 1980, although many people doubted he would actually return.

On June 30 the Chicago White Sox, in last place in the American League West, fired their manager, Bob Lemon. When Martin left the Yankees on July 24, Lemon replaced him. The Yankees, 10½ games behind the Boston Red Sox then (they had been 14 games behind on July 19), closed in. When the regular season ended Oct. 1, the Yankees and Red Sox were tied for first place in the American League East. In a one-game playoff the next day, the Yankees won, 5-4.

In the American League West, the California Angels and Texas Rangers spent millions of dollars on free agents. The Kansas City Royals, who spent nothing, had better pitching and won the division title.

On March 27, Kentucky's Jack Givens goes up for a basket, sparking his team's victory over Duke in the NCAA final. Givens, who scored 41 points, was named the most valuable player of the championship series.

third baseman; the late Addie Joss, a former Indians pitcher; and the late Larry MacPhail, a former executive and innovator.

BASKETBALL

A violent one-punch fight marred the 1977–78 professional basketball season. The puncher was Kermit Washington of the Los Angeles Lakers. The victim was Rudy Tomjanovich of the Houston Rockets.

The incident happened during a game on Dec. 12, 1977, in Los Angeles. After Washington and Kevin Kunnert of Houston had bumped and pushed under a backboard, Washington punched Kunnert and floored him. Kunnert's teammates,

---

NATIONAL BASKETBALL ASSOCIATION 1977–78 Regular Season

EASTERN CONFERENCE

Atlantic Division	W	L	Pct.	GB
Philadelphia 76ers	55	27	.671	—
New York Knickerbockers	43	39	.524	12
Boston Celtics	32	50	.390	23
Buffalo Braves	27	55	.329	28
New Jersey Nets	24	58	.293	31

Central Division				
San Antonio Spurs	52	30	.634	—
Washington Bullets	44	38	.537	8
Cleveland Cavaliers	43	39	.524	9
Atlanta Hawks	41	41	.500	11
New Orleans Jazz	39	43	.476	13
Houston Rockets	28	54	.342	24

WESTERN CONFERENCE

Midwest Division	W	L	Pct.	GB
Denver Nuggets	48	34	.585	—
Milwaukee Bucks	44	38	.537	4
Chicago Bulls	40	42	.488	8
Detroit Pistons	38	44	.463	10
Kansas City Kings	31	51	.373	17
Indiana Pacers	31	51	.373	17

Pacific Division	W	L	Pct.	GB
Portland Trail Blazers	58	24	.707	—
Phoenix Suns	49	33	.598	9
Seattle SuperSonics	47	35	.573	11
Los Angeles Lakers	45	37	.549	13
Golden State Warriors	43	39	.524	15

PLAYOFFS

First Round
Washington defeated Atlanta, 2 games to 0
New York defeated Cleveland, 2 games to 0
Seattle defeated Los Angeles, 2 games to 1
Milwaukee defeated Phoenix, 2 games to 0

Conference Semifinals
Washington defeated San Antonio, 4 games to 2
Philadelphia defeated New York, 4 games to 0
Seattle defeated Portland, 4 games to 2
Denver defeated Milwaukee, 4 games to 3

Conference Finals
Washington defeated Philadelphia, 4 games to 2
Seattle defeated Denver, 4 games to 2

Championship Finals
Washington defeated Seattle, 4 games to 3

including Tomjanovich, rushed to his side. Washington, apparently thinking Tomjanovich was about to punch him, punched Tomjanovich and knocked him down.

Tomjanovich's jaw was broken in two places. His nose was broken. He had a concussion. His face was badly bruised and required surgery. He spent two weeks in a hospital and did not play again that season.

Lawrence O'Brien, the National Basketball Association (NBA) commissioner, suspended Washington for sixty days and fined him $10,000. Two weeks later, the Lakers traded Washington to the Boston Celtics, and after the season the Celtics traded him to the San Diego Clippers (formerly the Buffalo Braves).

On Oct. 18, 1978, in the Lakers' opening game, their celebrated center, Kareem Abdul-Jabbar, punched Kent Benson of the Milwaukee Bucks. The punch broke Abdul-Jabbar's right hand, and he could not play for almost seven weeks. O'Brien fined him $5000.

The Washington Bullets won the NBA championship by beating the Seattle SuperSonics, 105–99, June 9 at Seattle in the seventh game of the playoff finals. The Sonics had a 5–17 won-lost record when Lenny Wilkens replaced Bob Hopkins as coach Nov. 30. After that, their regular-season record was 42–18.

The regular season's most valuable player was Bill Walton, the Portland Trail Blazers center. Walton, who had foot injuries all season, broke an ankle in the playoffs. His leg was still in a cast when the 1978–79 season began.

The college champions were the University of Kentucky men and the UCLA women. Kentucky beat Duke, 94–88, in the National Collegiate Athletic Association final March 27 in St. Louis. UCLA defeated Maryland, 90–74, in the Association of Intercollegiate Athletics for Women final March 25 in Los Angeles.

BOATING

Bill Muncey of La Mesa, Calif., the most successful driver in unlimited hydroplane history, enjoyed an almost perfect year in 1978. He won 6 of the 7 races with his boat, *Atlas Van Lines,* and became national champion for the sixth time. His supercharged Rolls-Royce airplane engine generated 4500 revolutions per minute, and his boat qualified for one race at a record speed of 132.353 mph.

Fifty-five-year-old Betty Cook of Newport Beach, Calif., won the national offshore series. These boats reached speeds of 95 mph from twin engines that exceeded 600 horsepower each.

In yachting, Ted Turner of Atlanta spent the summer winning races with *Tenacious,* his 61-ft.

sloop. In 1977, Turner, sailing the 12-Meter sloop *Courageous,* won the America's Cup, the sport's major prize. In 1978 six foreign yacht clubs (two Australian, two French, one Swedish, one English) issued challenges for the next America's Cup races, to be held in 1980.

BOWLING

Mark Roth of North Arlington, N.J., led the Professional Bowlers Association tour in 1978 for the second consecutive year. The 26-year-old right-hander won 8 of the 35 tournaments and earned $134,500, both records.

Earl Anthony of Walnut Creek, Calif., a 40-year-old left-hander, won 2 tournaments, raising his career record to 30. Although he suffered a heart attack June 20, Anthony competed Aug. 24–27 in the Waukegan (Ill.) Open and finished third.

The purses for the men's tour reached almost $3,000,000, the highest ever. The women set a record of $600,000 in 17 tournaments.

The stars of the women's tour, conducted by

Mark Roth—winner of eight tournaments in the Professional Bowlers Association tour—shows the power and concentration that brought him over $134,000 in prize money in 1978. He was named bowler of the year.

the new Womens Professional Bowlers Association, included Virginia Norton, Vesma Grinfelds, Donna Adamek, and Pat Costello, all Californians. Costello set a women's three-game record of 298–266–299, total 863.

BOXING

Muhammad Ali of Chicago, the world heavyweight champion most of the time since 1964, lost and regained the title in 1978. He ended the year almost 37 years old and declining to say if he would fight again.

Ali lost the title to Leon Spinks of St. Louis on a 15-round decision Feb. 15 in Las Vegas. It was an astounding upset because Spinks, once a frail child with low blood pressure, had fought professionally for only a year.

The World Boxing Council (WBC), which governed the sport in most countries, lifted the title from Spinks March 18 when he refused to make his first defense against Ken Norton of San Diego, the leading challenger. The WBC recognized Norton as champion, but on June 9 in Las Vegas, Larry Holmes of Easton, Pa., who had dropped out of

In Las Vegas on June 9 challenger Larry Holmes (right) follows through after landing a right to the head of Ken Norton. Holmes took the WBC heavyweight title from Norton in a 15-round split decision.

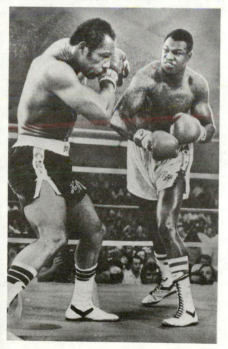

school in the seventh grade, outpointed Norton and took his title. Holmes won his first defense, knocking out Alfredo Evangelista of Spain in 7 rounds Nov. 10 in Las Vegas.

Meanwhile, the World Boxing Association (WBA) continued to recognize Spinks and sanctioned the Spinks-Ali return bout Sept. 15 in New Orleans. Ali trained harder for this bout and won a one-sided decision, although his timing and skills had eroded. Because Spinks was confused and did not seem to know what to do, Ali became the WBA champion and the first man to win boxing's most prized title three times.

Ali earned $3,500,000 from the first Spinks fight and $3,250,000 for the second. The return bout attracted the largest gross gate in boxing history ($4,806,675) and the largest television audience (34,800,000 homes) in sports history.

The light-heavyweight champions were Mike Rossman (WBA) of Turnersville, N.J., and Marvin Johnson (WBC) of Indianapolis. Roberto Duran of Panama was undisputed lightweight champion for the sixth straight year.

FOOTBALL

The Pittsburgh Steelers won the 1978 professional football championship by winning Super Bowl XIII. The University of Alabama and the University of Southern California shared the college title, which was decided in the ballot box rather than on the playing field.

Professional. The 28 teams in the National Football League (NFL) played their longest season ever—16 games rather than the usual 14. The season was distinguished by its problems, especially in the officiating. Although a seventh game official was added, games were won and lost almost weekly on questionable calls.

The officials, who received $325 to $800 plus expenses per regular-season game, were generally business executives or educators who officiated only part-time. An angry Coach Bud Grant of the Minnesota Vikings said: "Officials are the only amateurs in this sport. Everyone else is a pro."

The playoffs were watered down by the addition of two wild-card teams. A weak division produced a playoff team (Minnesota) with only an 8-7-1 won-lost-tied record. A new rule all but legalized holding. Even cheerleaders attracted unfavorable criticism, mainly by posing for *Playboy* magazine.

Many changes, including the longer season, longer playoffs, and new holding rule, were designed to create more games with more scoring for television viewers. It was the first year of the $656,000,000, four-year contracts between the NFL and the three national networks. During the year each team collected about $5,500,000 from televi-

NATIONAL FOOTBALL LEAGUE

AMERICAN CONFERENCE

Eastern Division	W	L	T
New England Patriots	11	5	0
*Miami Dolphins	11	5	0
New York Jets	8	8	0
Buffalo Bills	5	11	0
Baltimore Colts	5	11	0

Central Division	W	L	T
Pittsburgh Steelers	14	2	0
*Houston Oilers	10	6	0
Cleveland Browns	8	8	0
Cincinnati Bengals	4	12	0

Western Division	W	L	T
Denver Broncos	10	6	0
Oakland Raiders	9	7	0
San Diego Chargers	9	7	0
Seattle Seahawks	9	7	0
Kansas City Chiefs	4	12	0

NATIONAL CONFERENCE

Eastern Division	W	L	T
Dallas Cowboys	12	4	0
*Philadelphia Eagles	9	7	0
Washington Redskins	8	8	0
St. Louis Cardinals	6	10	0
New York Giants	6	10	0

Central Division	W	L	T
Minnesota Vikings	8	7	1
Green Bay Packers	8	7	1
Detroit Lions	7	9	0
Chicago Bears	7	9	0
Tampa Bay Buccaneers	5	11	0

Western Division	W	L	T
Los Angeles Rams	12	4	0
*Atlanta Falcons	9	7	0
New Orleans Saints	7	9	0
San Francisco 49ers	2	14	0

AMERICAN CONFERENCE PLAYOFFS
*Wild-Card Round
Houston 17, Miami 9

First Round
Pittsburgh 33, Denver 10
Houston 31, New England 14

Championship
Pittsburgh 34, Houston 5

NATIONAL CONFERENCE PLAYOFFS
*Wild-Card Round
Atlanta 14, Philadelphia 13

First Round
Dallas 27, Atlanta 20
Los Angeles 34, Minnesota 10

Championship
Dallas 28, Los Angeles 0

SUPER BOWL
Pittsburgh 35, Dallas 31

sion, more than it took in from gate receipts.

The Pittsburgh Steelers (14-2), Dallas Cowboys (12-4), and Los Angeles Rams (12-4) had the best regular-season records, and they reached the conference finals with the Houston Oilers (10-6), a wild-card team. Houston got that far because Dan Pastorini, one of the many quarterbacks injured during the longer season, played despite multiple injuries, including cracked ribs.

The conference championship games were played Jan. 7, 1979. Dallas beat Los Angeles, 28-0, at Los Angeles, scoring four second-half touchdowns after three pass interceptions and a Rams fumble. Pittsburgh routed Houston, 34-5, in a freezing rain at Pittsburgh as the Oilers suffered five interceptions and four lost fumbles.

Dallas and Pittsburgh were the two strongest teams at the end of the regular season, Dallas winning its last six games and Pittsburgh its last five. Dallas led its conference in total offense and rushing, and its quarterback, Roger Staubach, led in passing. Pittsburgh led the league in scoring defense and ranked second to Dallas in rushing defense.

The Super Bowl was played Jan. 21 in the Orange Bowl at Miami. Pittsburgh won, 35-31, in the highest scoring game in bowl history. Terry Bradshaw, the Steelers quarterback, was named the game's most valuable player. He set Super Bowl records with four touchdown passes and 318 yd. passing.

It was an insecure year for head coaches. Before the season, 10 of the 28 teams named new head coaches, and three more changes were made in the first month of the season.

Nine of the 10 teams that began with new coaches did not reach the playoffs. Los Angeles was the exception, and its case was unusual. Chuck Knox, who had coached the Rams for five years, quit after the 1977 season to coach the Buffalo Bills. The Rams replaced him with George Allen, who had coached the Washington Redskins. After the first two preseason games, both losses, the Rams fired Allen, saying he had tried to control the front office. Ray Malavasi, the Rams defensive coordinator, replaced Allen, and the Rams began winning again.

The Canadian Football League's most successful team was the Edmonton Eskimos, a frequent runner-up. Edmonton upset the Montréal Alouettes, 20-13, on Nov. 26 in the Grey Cup championship game at Toronto. Marv Levy, who had coached Montréal to the title in 1977, left after that season to coach the Kansas City Chiefs of the NFL.

College. The unofficial college football champion of 1978 was not crowned until 1979, and even then there was disagreement.

When the regular season ended in early December, the Associated Press panel of writers and broadcasters and the United Press International board of coaches ranked the same teams on top—Penn State first, Alabama second, Southern California third, and Oklahoma fourth.

Penn State was the only major team undefeated and untied. The others had lost once—Alabama to Southern California, Southern California to Arizona State, and Oklahoma to Nebraska.

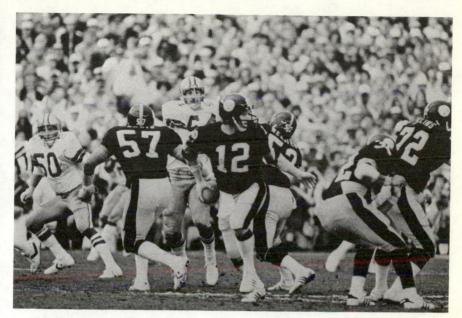

Well protected by his teammates, Pittsburgh Steelers quarterback Terry Bradshaw looks for a downfield receiver during Super Bowl XIII. Bradshaw threw four touchdown passes in the Steelers 35–31 victory over the Dallas Cowboys in the last game of the 1978 professional season, played Jan. 21, 1979, in the Orange Bowl in Miami.

On New Year's Day, 1979, Penn State could have assured itself of the title by beating Alabama in the Sugar Bowl at New Orleans. Instead, Alabama won, 14–7.

Later that day, Southern California defeated Michigan, 17–10, on a disputed touchdown in the Rose Bowl at Pasadena, Calif., and Oklahoma subdued Nebraska, 31–24, in the Orange Bowl at Miami. That set the stage for the electors to choose a national champion.

Alabama was picked by the Associated Press, the National Football Foundation and Hall of Fame, and the Football Writers Association of America. United Press International named Southern California narrowly over Alabama.

Alabama's national championship was its fifth under its 65-year-old coach, Paul ("Bear") Bryant. The season ended differently for Woody Hayes of Ohio State, another 65-year-old coach who had turned out two national champions. Late in Clemson's 17–15 victory over Ohio State in the Gator Bowl Dec. 29 at Jacksonville, Fla., Hayes punched a Clemson player who had just intercepted a pass. The next morning, Ohio State fired the always-volatile Hayes, after twenty-eight years and a 205–61–10 record.

GOLF

Since its beginning in 1952, the women's professional golf tour had existed in the shadow of the richer, more prestigious men's tour. In 1978 the women made a huge stride forward because of one charismatic newcomer, 21-year-old Nancy Lopez of Roswell, N.Mex.

In her first full year on the Ladies' Professional Golf Association (LPGA) tour, Lopez won 9 of the 38 tournaments, 5 in a row. She earned $189,813, the most in the history of women's professional golf, and from July, 1977, to July, 1978, she earned $161,235—the most ever by a rookie golfer, male or female.

Lopez became the best putter on the tour, and she drove longer than anyone except JoAnne Carner. Her swing was unorthodox, with a huge loop on the backswing, but she said with her usual smile: "Heck, Arnold Palmer's swing is not good."

Lopez won the LPGA championship and tied for ninth in the U.S. Open, won by Hollis Stacy for the second straight year. Lopez became a favorite of the galleries and her colleagues. As Jane Blalock, a leading pro, said: "All the publicity and acclaim she gets has focused so much attention on all of us."

Tom Watson and Jack Nicklaus enjoyed good years among the men. Watson won five tourna-

Nancy With the Laughing Face
Rookie golf pro Nancy Lopez, 21, was always easy to spot. She was the one with the looping swing and the big, big smile. Although virtually self-taught (she learned by tagging after her garage-owner father on the public links of Roswell, N.Mex.), she set several records in her first year on the Ladies' Professional Golf Association tour: She won nine tournaments, including an unprecedented five in a row; her winnings came to $161,235, tops ever for a rookie, male or female; and she was selected both LPGA rookie *and* golfer-of-the-year. Meanwhile she found time to become engaged to sportscaster Tim Melton (he interviewed her and it was love at first sight). So why shouldn't Nancy Lopez have smiled a lot during 1978?

Golfer Nancy Lopez.

ments—Tucson, Bing Crosby, Byron Nelson, Hall of Fame, and Napa—on the Professional Golfers Association (PGA) tour. He won $362,429, a record, and led in earnings for the second straight year. In the major tournaments, he tied for second in the Masters and PGA championship, tied for sixth in the U.S. Open, and tied for thirteenth in the British Open.

Nicklaus won his third British Open, Gary Player of South Africa his third Masters, Andy North his first U.S. Open, and John Mahaffey his first PGA championship.

Nicklaus also won the Inverrary and Philadelphia tournaments, giving him 66 career victories on the PGA tour and 17 overseas. His career earnings exceeded $3,500,000, a record. His worst moment came when he took a 79 in the PGA championship, prompting him to say: "For a while, I wasn't sure the ball was round."

HARNESS RACING
Financial records tumbled in harness racing in 1978. Abercrombie, a 3-year-old pacer, earned $703,260, breaking the one-year record of $584,450 in 1977 by Green Speed. The Meadowlands in East Rutherford, N.J., held a $560,000 pace for 3 year olds and a $481,250 pace for 2 year olds, the sport's richest races ever.

Falcon Almahurst was syndicated for breeding for $3,600,000, tying the record for a pacer. Green Speed was syndicated for $3,200,000, a record for a trotter. Sonsam's syndication price of $3,000,000 was the highest ever for a 2-year-old harness or thoroughbred horse.

Abercrombie, who cost $9500 as a yearling, was voted harness horse of the year. He won 22 races,

including the Messenger, in 33 starts. In every victory he paced the mile in two minutes or faster.

Speedy Somolli, the trotter of the year, won the Hambletonian, the Yonkers Trot, and $362,404. Herve Filion of Angers, Québec, with 377 winners, gained his tenth North American driving title.

HORSE RACING
The major battles in thoroughbred racing in 1978 were Affirmed versus Alydar in the triple-crown races and Affirmed versus Seattle Slew and Exceller in the horse-of-the-year voting. Affirmed won both battles.

Affirmed, owned by Harbor View Farm and ridden by Steve Cauthen, swept the triple-crown series for 3 year olds—the $239,400 Kentucky Derby May 6 at Louisville, the $188,700 Preakness May 20 at Baltimore, and the $184,300 Belmont Stakes June 10 at Elmont, N.Y. His respective margins were 1½ lengths, a neck, and a head, and each time Alydar ran second. The Affirmed-Alydar stretch duels in the Preakness and Belmont Stakes were memorable.

Seattle Slew, the 1977 triple-crown champion, missed much of 1978 because of illness. In late-season races at Belmont Park, Seattle Slew beat Affirmed in the $300,000 Marlboro Cup Sept. 16 and Exceller in the $163,000 Woodward Sept. 30. He lost by a nose to Exceller in the $321,800 Jockey Club Gold Cup Oct. 14.

Affirmed, with 8 victories and 2 seconds in 11 races, was voted horse of the year. His earnings of $901,541 broke Secretariat's one-year record of $860,404 in 1973. Exceller earned $879,790 during the year, winning 7 of 10 races.

At year's end Seattle Slew was retired for breed-

Affirmed by a Nose

Thoroughbred racing had rarely seen two 3-year-old colts so evenly matched, and their rivalry at the Kentucky Derby, Pimlico, and Belmont Stakes left railbirds gasping. Three times, Affirmed, with teenage jockey sensation Steve Cauthen aboard, pulled out stretch-run victories over gallant-but-luckless Alydar. Later Affirmed's Triple Crown triumph was marred somewhat when the Florida-bred chestnut colt, without Cauthen, lost twice to Seattle Slew, the previous year's Triple Crown champ. But Affirmed's owner Lou Wolfson found consolation in his horse's record single-season earnings of $901,541. The sting of losing to Slew was also assuaged in the Eclipse Award voting in December, when Affirmed edged out Slew in the horse-of-the-year polling—by a nose, of course.

Affirmed, with Steve Cauthen up, wins the Derby.

ing after a record syndication of $12,000,000. Affirmed was being syndicated for $14,400,000 for stud duty starting in 1980.

Darrel McHargue broke Steve Cauthen's record for money earned by a jockey in one year. McHargue's mounts earned $6,188,353, surpassing Cauthen's 1977 total of $6,151,750.

ICE HOCKEY

The Montréal Canadiens had the fastest forwards, toughest defensemen, and best goaltending in the National Hockey League (NHL) 1977–78 season. So it was not surprising that they achieved the best regular-season record of the eighteen teams and then won the Stanley Cup playoffs for the third consecutive year.

Guy Lafleur, a Canadien right wing, won his third straight scoring title and second straight most-valuable-player award. Larry Robinson, a Canadien defenseman, was voted most valuable player in the playoffs, and he and Lafleur tied as

Guy Lafleur led the Montréal Canadiens to victory over the Boston Bruins in the 1978 Stanley Cup championship series. Lafleur, the National Hockey League's leading scorer for the third straight year, was also its most valuable player—for the second year in a row.

NATIONAL HOCKEY LEAGUE
1977–78 Regular Season

PRINCE OF WALES CONFERENCE

Norris Division	W	L	T	Pts.
Montréal Canadiens	59	10	11	129
Detroit Red Wings	32	34	14	78
Los Angeles Kings	31	34	15	77
Pittsburgh Penguins	25	37	18	68
Washington Capitals	17	49	14	48

Adams Division	W	L	T	Pts.
Boston Bruins	51	18	11	113
Buffalo Sabres	44	19	17	105
Toronto Maple Leafs	41	29	10	92
Cleveland Barons	22	45	13	57

CLARENCE CAMPBELL CONFERENCE

Patrick Division	W	L	T	Pts.
New York Islanders	48	17	15	111
Philadelphia Flyers	45	20	15	105
Atlanta Flames	34	27	19	87
New York Rangers	30	37	13	73

Smythe Division	W	L	T	Pts.
Chicago Black Hawks	32	29	19	83
Colorado Rockies	19	40	21	59
Vancouver Canucks	20	43	17	57
St. Louis Blues	20	47	13	53
Minnesota North Stars	18	53	9	45

STANLEY CUP PLAYOFFS
First Round
Philadelphia defeated Colorado, 2 games to 0
Buffalo defeated New York Rangers, 2 games to 1
Toronto defeated Los Angeles, 2 games to 0
Detroit defeated Atlanta, 2 games to 0

Second Round
Montréal defeated Detroit, 4 games to 1
Boston defeated Chicago, 4 games to 0
Toronto defeated New York Islanders, 4 games to 3
Philadelphia defeated Buffalo, 4 games to 1

Semifinal Round
Montréal defeated Toronto, 4 games to 0
Boston defeated Philadelphia, 4 games to 1

Championship Finals
Montréal defeated Boston, 4 games to 2

WORLD HOCKEY ASSOCIATION
1977–78 Regular Season

	W	L	T	Pts.
Winnipeg Jets	50	28	2	102
New England Whalers	44	31	5	93
Houston Aeros	42	34	4	88
Québec Nordiques	40	37	3	83
Edmonton Oilers	38	39	3	79
Birmingham Bulls	36	41	3	75
Cincinnati Stingers	35	42	3	73
Indianapolis Racers	24	51	5	53
*Soviet All-Stars	3	4	1	7
*Czechoslovakia	1	6	1	3

*Games against these teams count in standing.

WORLD CUP PLAYOFFS
First Round
Winnipeg defeated Birmingham, 4 games to 1
New England defeated Edmonton, 4 games to 1
Québec defeated Houston, 4 games to 2

Semifinal Round
New England defeated Québec, 4 games to 1
Winnipeg, bye

Championship Finals
Winnipeg defeated New England, 4 games to 0

the leading playoff scorers. Ken Dryden of the Canadiens had the best goals-against record of any NHL goalie.

The Canadiens started their playoffs by defeating the Detroit Red Wings, 4 games to 1. Next, they swept by the Toronto Maple Leafs in four straight games. In the finals they beat the Boston Bruins, 4 games to 2, and the Bruins cited their two victories as a sign of respectability.

With all their success, the Canadiens played clean, inspired hockey, and members of the other teams not only respected them, they actually liked them. As Don Cherry, the Boston coach, said: "Hating the Canadiens is like hating your mother."

Lafleur and Dryden were voted to the All-Star team with three New York Islanders (defenseman Denis Potvin, center Bryan Trottier, and left wing Clark Gillies) and one Boston Bruin (defenseman Brad Park).

The eight-team World Hockey Association

(WHA) continued to struggle as a rival major league. The Winnipeg Jets were the best team in the regular season, and they swept four games from the New England Whalers in the playoff finals. The most accomplished player was Marc Tardif of the Québec Nordiques, who led the league in scoring, goals, and assists. After the season the WHA tried unsuccessfully to have at least four teams merge with the NHL. In December, 1978, the Indianapolis Racers went out of business.

ICE SKATING

Nineteen-year-old Eric Heiden of Madison, Wis., who swept the world overall, sprint, and junior speed-skating titles in 1977, repeated in 1978. His 18-year-old sister, Beth, won the world women's junior title and barely lost the sprint title to Lyubov Sadchikova of the Soviet Union. (Another Soviet skater, Khalida Vorobyova, beat the world 1500 m record by more than 2 seconds in April; her time was 2 min. 7.18 sec.)

Both Heidens were students at the University of Wisconsin. Their feats were remarkable because the U.S. had only 5000 competitive speed skaters (the Soviet Union had 500,000). The Americans also had only one Olympic-sized rink—in West Allis, Wis., where the Heidens trained.

In figure skating, Charles Tickner of Littleton, Colo., won the men's title in the world championships March 7–11 at Ottawa, Ontario. Linda Fratianne of Northridge, Calif., the 1977 women's champion, finished second to Anett Poetzsch of East Germany. Tickner and Fratianne retained their titles in the U.S. championships Feb. 9–12 at Portland, Oreg.

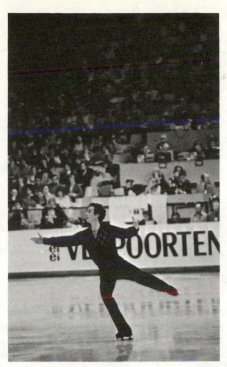

Twenty-five-year-old Charles Tickner of Littleton, Colo., shows the strength of form and style that won him gold medals in both the U.S. and world men's figure skating championships during 1978.

ROWING

East German rowers remained the best in the world. In the 1977 world championships they won 5 of the 8 events for men and 6 of 6 for women. In the 1978 world championships Nov. 1–5 on Lake Karapiro, New Zealand, they won 5 men's and 3 women's events.

The only American medalists were women. The four-oared shell finished second, and Lisa Hanse of Piedmont, Calif., and Elizabeth Hills of Durham, N.H., placed third in double sculls. The best showing by the American men was fourth in coxed fours. In the world lightweight championships Aug. 3–6 at Copenhagen, Denmark, American male scullers won two bronze medals.

Among college eights, Washington was unbeaten until it lost to the Bulgarian national crew in the Grand Challenge Cup final at Henley, England. Syracuse won the Intercollegiate Rowing Association regatta at Syracuse. Harvard surprisingly lost major races to Yale and Navy.

SKIING

Ingemar Stenmark of Sweden, for the third straight year, and Hanni Wenzel of Liechtenstein won the men's and women's World Cup titles in 1978. They had the best overall performances in the two-continent, three-month series.

Phil Mahre of White Pass, Wash., finished second to Stenmark, the highest placing by an American in the World Cup's twelve-year history. Annemarie Proell Moser of Austria, a five-time women's champion, was second to Wenzel.

Stenmark won the slalom and giant slalom in the world championships Jan. 28 through Feb. 5 at Garmisch-Partenkirchen, West Germany. The other winners were Josef Walcher of Austria in men's downhill, Andreas Wenzel (Hanni's younger brother) in men's combined, Moser in women's downhill and combined, Maria Epple of West Germany in women's giant slalom, and Lea Soelkner of Austria in women's slalom. Soelkner was born with her left leg shorter than the right, and physicians had warned that continued skiing could cripple her permanently.

Liechtenstein, with only some 24,000 residents, won 5 of the 24 medals in the world championships. The only American medalist was Pete Patterson of Sun Valley, Idaho, third in the men's combined.

On the professional circuit, Andre Arnold, a newcomer, won the most races (12 of 27) and the most money ($92,883). Ironically, he turned pro only when Austria refused to promote him from its B team.

SOCCER

Argentina, playing before enthusiastic countrymen, won the World Cup for the first time. On June 25, before 75,000 spectators in Buenos Aires and a worldwide television audience of 600,000,-000, Argentina defeated the Netherlands, 3–1, in overtime in the cup final.

Almost every nation in the world played in two years of preliminaries to decide the 14 qualifiers. The qualifiers joined Argentina (the host nation) and West Germany (which in 1974 won the most recent World Cup). The U.S. was eliminated early in the preliminaries.

In first-round games June 1–11, eight teams advanced and eight were eliminated. Second-round games June 14–21 sent Argentina and the Netherlands into the final and Brazil and Italy into the third-place game (Brazil won, 2–1).

Mario Kempes, a high-scoring forward who played in the Spanish League, scored twice for Argentina in the final. Before that, the Argentine star was Ubaldo ("Pato") Fillol, the goalkeeper, who allowed no goals in his three second-round games.

In the U.S., where soccer was trying to gain the public acceptance accorded to baseball and American football, the North American Soccer League expanded to 24 teams (from 18). The Cosmos, playing in East Rutherford, N.J., just across the Hudson River from New York City, won their second straight title. On Aug. 23, in the championship game, they defeated the Tampa Bay (Fla.) Rowdies, 3-1, on their home field before 74,901 spectators.

The Cosmos averaged 47,000 spectators per game, Minnesota 30,000, Seattle 22,000, Tampa Bay 18,000. But partly because of overexpansion, many teams lost money, and average attendance dropped slightly to 13,000.

The league chose Mike Flanagan of the New England Tea Men as player of the year. The Professional Soccer Reporters Association picked Giorgio Chinaglia of the Cosmos and *Soccer Digest* named Franz Beckenbauer of the Cosmos.

SWIMMING

The U.S. dominated the world championships Aug. 19-28 at West Berlin, winning 11 of the 15 events for men and 9 of the 14 for women.

The men's excellence was expected. The women's was surprising because East German women had won most international honors since 1973. But the Americans, who once were the best, ruled again because of an inspired group of teenagers.

Their leader was 15-year-old Tracy Caulkins of Nashville. As the world championships started, she said: "I feel responsible for how we do here." She then won 5 gold medals and 1 silver medal and broke or shared 4 world records. Eighteen-year-old Linda Jezek of Los Altos, Calif., and 14-year-old Cynthia Woodhead of Riverside, Calif., won 3 gold medals each. Among the men, David McCagg of Fort Myers Beach, Fla., won 3 gold medals and Jesse Vassallo of Mission Viejo, Calif., 2 gold and 1 silver.

Caulkins won 7 gold medals in the Amateur Athletic Union's national indoor championships April 5-8 at Austin, Texas, and 7 in the outdoor championships Aug. 2-6 at The Woodlands, Texas. She broke 8 American records in the indoor championships, and when she went to the world championships she had shattered 27 American records in 17 months.

For the year, world records were bettered in 13 of the 15 events for women and 4 of the 16 for men. Tracey Wickham of Australia broke 3 women's records in freestyle.

TENNIS

Tennis in the U.S. underwent a major move in 1978. In ten months the U.S. Tennis Association

Fifteen-year-old Tracy Caulkins, a versatile swimmer from Nashville, led the U.S. women's team to victory in the world championships at West Berlin in August. She won 5 gold medals and broke 3 individual world records.

Nineteen-year-old John McEnroe won both his singles matches against the British to clinch the Davis Cup for the U.S. at Rancho Mirage, Calif., in December.

built a $9,500,000 National Tennis Center in Flushing, N.Y., the site of two World's Fairs. It shifted the U.S. Open there from nearby Forest Hills.

The new facility had a stadium court seating 19,000, a grandstand court seating 6000, 25 other outside courts, and 9 courts indoors. The surface was rubberized asphalt, a thin rubberized coating atop cement. It was hard and fast.

Jimmy Connors of Belleville, Ill., won the U.S. Open title, beating Björn Borg of Sweden, 6–4, 6–2, 6–2, in the final Sept. 10. It was Connors's fifth straight U.S. Open final and his third victory. He won in 1974 on grass and 1976 on a claylike surface. Although the 26-year-old Connors did not play, the U.S. defeated Great Britain 4–1 in the Davis Cup final round at Rancho Mirage, Calif., Dec. 8–10. The victory was achieved mostly by the two smashing singles wins by 19-year-old John McEnroe.

The 22-year-old Borg crushed Connors, 6–2, 6–2, 6–3, in the Wimbledon final on grass July 8 in England. Borg again won the French and Italian Opens on clay, and his endorsements were so lucrative that he became a multimillion-dollar industry unto himself.

Martina Navratilova of Dallas, a Czechoslovak expatriate, made a strong claim for the top ranking among women long held by Chris Evert of Fort Lauderdale, Fla. When Evert took a four-month winter vacation, the 21-year-old Navratilova won 7 straight tournaments and 37 straight matches. Navratilova, no longer troubled by emotional highs and lows, defeated Evert, 2–6, 6–4, 7–5, July 7 for the Wimbledon title.

In the U.S. Open, 16-year-old Pam Shriver of Lutherville, Md., upset Navratilova, 7–6, 7–6, in the semifinals. The 23-year-old Evert, more relaxed than in the past, beat Shriver, 7–5, 6–4, in the Sept. 10 final for her fourth straight U.S. Open title.

The most valuable players in World Team Tennis were Navratilova of the Boston Lobsters during the regular season and Evert of the champion Los Angeles Strings in the playoffs.

TRACK AND FIELD

Henry Rono of Kenya was the only male runner to break a world record in 1978. The 26-year-old

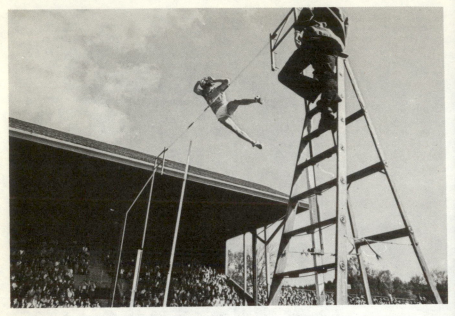

Mike Tully, a senior at the University of California at Los Angeles, broke both the world's outdoor and indoor records in the pole vault during the year. He cleared 18 ft. 8¾ in. outdoors and 18 ft. 5¼ in. indoors.

Rono, a sophomore at Washington State University, bettered 4 records in 12 weeks.

His records were 13 min. 8.4 sec. for 5000 m April 8 at Berkeley, Calif.; 8 min. 5.4 sec. for the 3000 m steeplechase May 12 at Seattle; 27 min. 22.5 sec. for 10,000 m June 11 at Vienna; and 7 min. 32.1 sec. for 3000 m June 27 at Oslo, Norway. No runner had ever held all these records during his career, let alone all at once. As Nick Rose of England, a frequent opponent, said: "Rono is much too good for us."

Franklin Jacobs, a 20-year-old sophomore at Fairleigh Dickinson University, also created excitement. Although Jacobs stood only 5 ft. 8 in., in the Millrose Games Jan. 27 in New York, he high-jumped 7 ft. 7¼ in., a world indoor record. That was 23¼ in. over his head, higher than anyone else had ever achieved. When Jacobs took up high jumping less than two years before, he cleared 6 ft. 1 in. the first day, wearing basketball shoes.

Jacobs's indoor record fell to 19-year-old Vladimir Yashchenko of the U.S.S.R., who jumped 7 ft. 8½ in. March 12 in the European indoor championships at Milan, Italy. Yashchenko raised the world outdoor record to 7 ft. 8 in. June 16 in Tbilisi, U.S.S.R., and he won the European outdoor championship at 7 ft. 6½ in. He thought he could eventually jump 7 ft. 10¼ in.

Mike Tully of UCLA broke both of the world pole-vault records—indoors (18 ft. 5¼ in.) and outdoors (18 ft. 8¾ in.).

Women's world records were broken by Marita Koch of East Germany (22.06 sec. for 200 m and 48.94 for 400 m), Sara Simeoni of Italy (6 ft. 7 in. in the high jump), and Vilma Bardauskiene of Russia (23 ft. 3¼ in. in the long jump).   F.L.

SRI LANKA. *See* CEYLON.

STAMPS, POSTAGE. Many philatelic "firsts" were recorded in 1978, including the first American stamps to be issued outside the United States and Great Britain's first souvenir sheet.

U.S. Issues. The U.S. Postal Service issued twenty-six commemorative stamps and one souvenir sheet containing eight 13¢ stamps. The latter was the controversial CAPEX '78 souvenir sheet, issued on June 10 in Toronto to commemorate the opening of the International Philatelic Exhibition held in that Canadian city. This issue was unique in

Preceding page: Outstanding Stamps of 1978. Top row (left to right): Malta honors Albrecht Dürer; Fiji celebrates Queen Elizabeth II's silver jubilee; St. Kitts–Nevis salutes scouting. Second row: Great Britain's first souvenir sheet. Third row (left to right): Argentina honors the World Cup; Europa issues by Italy and Switzerland; the United Nations salutes its General Assembly. Fourth row (left to right): The U.S. commemorates the bicentenary of its alliance with France; paintings of four U.S. trees; a tribute to photography's impact on the American way of life. Fifth row (left to right): An experimental 13¢ issue; the nondenominated "A" stamp.

two respects: These were the first U.S. postage stamps to be released in a foreign country; moreover, the issue was not placed on sale in the U.S. until Aug. 28, more than two months later. Ironically, when these 13¢ stamps finally became available to Americans, the domestic postal rate had increased to 15¢.

Delays by Congress in establishing a new first-class postal rate did not allow the Postal Service enough time for advance printing of sufficient quantities of a new first-class stamp in the correct denomination. However, in 1975 some 4.8 billion nondenominated stamps, marked only with the letter A and a stylized eagle, had been prepared for possible contingency use and placed in storage. These were released in May to meet the new increased rate until the Postal Service could prepare new 15¢ issues.

Perhaps the most striking change in the physical appearance of U.S. stamps was the 13¢ definitive issued on Jan. 11 portraying an old Indian head penny. This experimental issue was one third smaller in size than the usual definitive stamp (150 stamps per pane instead of 100). It was estimated that if all definitive stamps were printed in this small format, the saving in production costs would amount to millions of dollars annually.

Included in the 1978 output of twelve new definitive issues were six additional values in the continuing Americana series. These were issued in denominations of 8.4¢, 15¢, 16¢, 28¢, 29¢, and $2. The last item represents the first new $2 U.S. postage stamp since the Warren Harding issue released in 1938.

Worldwide Issues. Great Britain, which introduced the world's first adhesive postage stamp in 1840, finally issued its first souvenir sheet of stamps 138 years later, in March, 1978. The sheet contained four stamps depicting outstanding British historic buildings. It sold for an above-face-value premium of 53½p, of which 10p went to a fund for the International Stamp Exhibition to be held in London in 1980.

Highlighting the world's stamp issues in 1978 were the many commemoratives introduced to honor Queen Elizabeth II. Special stamps, mini-sheets, souvenir sheets, and booklets were prepared by all Commonwealth countries, as well as former colonies and other nations, to commemorate her coronation in 1953.

Other notable events that were commemorated by various nations in 1978 included the World Cup soccer matches held in Buenos Aires in June, the 75th anniversary of powered flight by Wilbur and Orville Wright, and the 450th anniversary of the death of the German artist Albrecht Dürer. The 23rd annual Europa issues were also noteworthy. Major stamp exhibitions were held in Canada, Czechoslovakia, Israel, Switzerland, Taiwan, and other countries; these were recognized by special issues of souvenir sheets.

United Nations Issues. The United Nations issued five commemoratives in 1978. In order of release, their subjects were global elimination of smallpox, Namibia, safety in the air (International Civil Aviation Organization), the General Assembly, and technical cooperation among developing countries. The U.N. issued stamps in both U.S. and Swiss currency: U.S. values for use at U.N. headquarters in New York City, Swiss values (centimes and Swiss francs) for use at the U.N. Palais des Nations in Geneva.   J.W.K.

STATE LEGISLATIVE REVIEW. The following is a summary of actions taken by state legislatures meeting in regular or special session during 1978.

Taxes. Tax reductions outnumbered tax increases in 1978. The biggest tax reductions were enacted not by legislatures but by the voters directly. Proposition 13, an initiative approved in June by California voters, rolled property tax rates back to 1 percent of assessed value, rolled assessments back to 1975–76 market values, and limited assessment hikes to 2 percent per year. Similar limits on property or state income taxes were passed in November by voters in eight other states; *see* ELECTIONS.

In 1978 legislative actions, property tax relief was provided by Arizona, Connecticut, Idaho, Iowa, Maryland, and Wisconsin. South Dakota repealed its personal property tax. Income tax relief, through reduced rates or exemptions, credits, and deductions, was offered by Alaska, Arizona, California, Colorado, Hawaii, Idaho, Indiana, Maine, Minnesota, Mississippi, New Mexico, New York, and Vermont. Corporate tax relief was offered by Connecticut, Florida, Maine, and New York. Arizona and Colorado became the first states to in-

Hank Stoppelbein, a 23-year-old waiter, sips a historic *Bloody Mary* at a Charlotte, N.C., restaurant at 8:04 A.M. on Nov. 21—he was the first person to buy a mixed drink legally in the state since 1908. Charlotte's Mecklenburg County and four other localities had voted for mixed-drink sales after the North Carolina legislature approved a local-option liquor law in June.

dex their income tax to inflation.

South Dakota was the only state to raise its sales and use tax in 1978. Rhode Island increased its income tax rates. Gasoline taxes were raised by Iowa, Michigan, Utah, and West Virginia and lowered in Delaware. West Virginia raised its cigarette taxes.

Crime and Justice. Capital punishment was reinstated by new laws in Maryland and Pennsylvania and by voter action in Oregon. Application of the death penalty was expanded by law in South Carolina and by voter action in California. Death penalty bills were vetoed in New York and New Jersey. Idaho became the third state to permit administration of a lethal substance as a means of imposing the death penalty.

Penalties for possession and sale of the drug PCP (phencyclidine hydrochloride), or "angel dust," were increased in California and New York. New laws cracked down on large-scale drug dealers in Maine and Michigan. Nebraska joined 10 other states in making possession of a small amount of marijuana subject to a fine rather than a jail term.

Government. "Sunset" laws, providing for automatic termination of state agencies unless renewed by the legislature, were enacted by Arizona, Kansas, Maryland, South Carolina, and Vermont in 1978. By the end of the year, a total of 29 states had passed such laws. The mandatory

retirement age for public employees was raised to 70 in Arizona, California, Louisiana, Minnesota, and South Dakota. Extensive constitutional revision was approved by voters in Hawaii and Tennessee.

Energy and Environment. Environmental actions included adoption of hazardous waste laws by 8 states to meet federal requirements, resource recovery laws by 7 states, coastal laws by Florida and Georgia, and laws complying with federal strip-mining legislation by Iowa and Kentucky. Hawaii became the first state to enact a comprehensive development plan for the future.

Energy measures included bans on ever-burning gas pilot lights in 3 states, provisions for jointly operated power plants in 3 states, measures to hold down power costs in 10 states, and encouragement of alternative energy systems in 11 states.

Deposits on beverage bottles and cans were required in Connecticut and Iowa, which thus joined 4 other states that had previously enacted such legislation. Delaware said it would impose bottle deposits when its neighboring states imposed them. Bottle deposits lost on the ballot in both Alaska and Nebraska. Antilitter laws passed in 3 states.

Health and Welfare. Abortion funding for poor women was hotly debated in 1978 legislative sessions. Most states opted to follow the federal guidelines, funding abortions only in cases where the woman's life or health is endangered or in cases in which pregnancy is a result of rape or incest. A few states imposed even more restrictive conditions, and only a handful continued to fund most welfare abortions. One of the most comprehensive laws to regulate abortions, modeled after an Akron, Ohio, ordinance, was passed in Louisiana. Both were being tested in court as the year ended.

Measures to control spiraling health costs were enacted in Maine, New Jersey, and Rhode Island. An initiative to control health costs failed on the North Dakota ballot. Mental health reforms were enacted in at least 11 states, including infusions of funds in California and New York.

Controlled use of marijuana for treatment of glaucoma and cancer was legalized in Florida, Illinois, Louisiana, and New Mexico. Use of the drug laetrile for the treatment of cancer became legal in 16 states with the addition of Idaho and Kansas in 1978.

Advertising by doctors and dentists was permitted in Missouri and by dentists in Florida by new laws passed before the Federal Trade Commission ruling ordering the American Medical Association to rescind its advertising ban. Advertising by opti-

---

Look It Up in Your Funk & Wagnalls

William Comer is a member of the Colorado State Senate, a junior high school teacher, and a lover of good grammar. As such he objected to a measure submitted to the state legislature asking for a change in the name of a local community college. Although he got support from good grammar lovers in thirty-three states, Comer lost, and El Paso Community College became Pikes—not Pike's—Peak Community College. A majority of the legislators accepted the fact that usage had long ago determined that Zebulon Pike's discovery was a mountain without an apostrophe.

---

cians was permitted in 4 more states. Substitution of generic for more expensive brand-name drugs was permitted in 6 more states.

A ban on smoking in many public places was enacted in Iowa, which joined 8 other states with similar bans.

Divorce without a lawyer and without an appearance in court was made possible by a new California law. Childless couples married less than two years would qualify for the "do-it-yourself" procedure.

As a result of 1978 enactments, the number of states having penalties for child pornography was increased to more than 30.

Education and Consumer Interests. By the end of the year, minimal competency standards or tests were required in public schools in 35 states, 11 of which required proof of competency for high school graduation. Among those acting in 1978 by law were Connecticut, Kansas, Kentucky, and South Carolina.

Computerized telephone solicitations ("junk" calls) were regulated by law in Alaska and Florida and administratively in California. New laws placed consumers on regulatory boards in Florida, Georgia, and Hawaii. Product liability laws were revised by 5 more states in 1978. No-fault auto insurance laws were revamped by Florida and South Carolina, and skiing-accident liability laws were enacted by New York and Vermont.   E.S.K.

SUDAN. After almost a decade of constant political turmoil, Sudanese President Gaafar Mohammed al-Nimeiry appeared on the verge of restoring harmony to Sudan in 1978. His longtime rival Sadiq al-Mahdi, who had been convicted of plotting to overthrow the Nimeiry government in 1975 and again in 1976, had returned from exile in 1977

and reportedly was attempting to persuade his fanatical Muslim Ansar warriors to return to Sudan from Libya and Ethiopia. Relatively free parliamentary elections were held in February, and opposition candidates won almost half the seats. In April a formal reconciliation was signed between the government and the opposition National Front, a coalition of parties in exile, which thereupon was dissolved.

Since 1969, when he came to power with Communist help, Nimeiry had moved steadily toward the West. He continued to strengthen his ties with the United States and European countries in 1978. On April 4 the administration of U.S. President Jimmy Carter notified Congress of plans to sell twelve F-5 jet fighters to Sudan—the first U.S. combat aircraft to be supplied to that country.

But while Nimeiry appeared to be in good shape politically, his country's economy remained on the verge of bankruptcy. Sudan devalued its currency by 13 percent on June 8 but refused to curtail its development programs as demanded by the International Monetary Fund as a condition of aid. Instead, Sudan appealed to Saudi Arabia for additional financial assistance.

See STATISTICS OF THE WORLD.   M.R.B.

SUPREME COURT OF THE UNITED STATES, THE. The Supreme Court ruled on a variety of issues in 1978, but public preoccupation with one case, *Regents of the University of California vs. Bakke,* tended to overshadow significant developments in the areas of reporters' rights and criminal law.

Membership. There were no changes in the make-up of the Court in 1978, but observers noted that it had become less predictable because several of the justices were showing more independence in their voting patterns. The Court voted unanimously in 36 percent of its decisions in the 1977–78 term, down from 67 percent in the previous term. Chief Justice Warren E. Burger and Associate Justice William H. Rehnquist were the most consistently conservative and Associate Justices William J. Brennan, Jr., and Thurgood Marshall were the most consistently liberal. Remaining in a "shifting center" were Associate Justices Potter Stewart, Byron R. White, Harry A. Blackmun, Lewis F. Powell, Jr., and John Paul Stevens.

The Bakke Case. The most anxiously anticipated and exhaustively interpreted civil rights ruling from the Court in many years came in the "reverse discrimination" case brought by a 38-year-old white engineer, Allan P. Bakke, against the University of California Medical College at Davis. Bakke contended that the school's "special admissions" program, which reserved 16 places for minority applicants in a class of 100, unlawfully operated to exclude him from admission.

In a splintered 4-1-4 decision announced in June, with Justice Powell providing the crucial swing vote, the Court ruled that the special admissions program was illegal because it was racially exclusionary and that Bakke should be admitted, but that flexible affirmative action programs to remedy the effects of past discrimination were permissible.

A critical issue in the Bakke case was the permissibility of affirmative action programs in the absence of a legislative, administrative, or judicial finding of prior discrimination. In an employment case with a potentially greater impact than Bakke, Brian Weber, a white worker in Louisiana, challenged a Kaiser Aluminum & Chemical Corp. job training program that reserved half of its places for minority workers and excluded Whites with higher seniority. There was no acknowledged history of discrimination by Kaiser. The Court was expected to decide the Weber case and clarify its stand on affirmative action in 1979.

Civil Rights. In other civil rights actions in June, the Court opened the way for greater financial recovery by citizens whose rights had been violated. By a 7-2 vote, the justices overruled a 1961 decision and held that municipalities can be sued directly when their official policies or customs deprive citizens of their constitutional rights. Similarly, a 5-4 majority held that federal executive officers are not entitled to absolute immunity from civil damage suits when they deliberately violate citizens' constitutional rights. But in March, the Court held that judges are immune from civil liability even when their actions are erroneous or malicious.

In an important sex discrimination decision, the justices ruled (6-2) that employers cannot require larger pension contributions from women than from men because women generally live longer and thus obtain greater benefits.

In one of the few rulings extending the First Amendment freedom of expression, a 5-4 majority held in a Massachusetts case that corporations may spend unlimited amounts on advertising to disseminate their political views. In two May decisions involving lawyer solicitation of clients, the Court offered (by a 7-1 vote) First Amendment protection to attorneys who give free advice on behalf of politically motivated nonprofit organizations, but denied (8-0) such protection to "ambulance chasers" who seek out clients for their own personal reward.

Reversing a recent trend toward expansion of rights for aliens, the Court in March upheld a New York law requiring U.S. citizenship for state police officers.

Press and Broadcasters' Rights. The communications media came out on the short end of a number of rulings and deplored the Court's failure to protect the newsgathering process. In a stunning 5-3 decision involving the Stanford *Daily* student newspaper, the Court authorized surprise police searches of news offices—or the property of any innocent third party—for the acquisition of criminal evidence. In April the Court ruled (7-2) that broadcasters and record companies could not obtain and release copies of tapes from the administration of President Richard M. Nixon used as evidence in the Watergate cover-up trials before they are made available to the public.

Balanced Judgment
His background—descendant of an old-line Virginia family, successful corporate attorney—was often cited as evidence of his conservative leanings. But in fact Associate Justice Lewis F. Powell, Jr., turned out to be one of the Supreme Court's least predictable members. As in the Bakke decision in June, on which he wrote the majority opinion, Powell often cast the swing vote between Court conservatives and liberals. The scholarly justice, educated at Washington & Lee and Harvard, believes split decisions reflect a strength—and not a weakness—of the Court. He noted that the closeness of the vote in itself was proof that the decision was reached only after "rigorous testing."

Associate Justice Lewis F. Powell, Jr., of the Supreme Court.

A detective studies film seized by police in a court-warranted but unannounced raid on the offices of the Stanford Daily *in Palo Alto, Calif., in 1971. The raid sparked a legal battle that was resolved in June, when the U.S. Supreme Court upheld the legality of surprise searches of newspaper offices and other private property.*

In June the justices unanimously voted to prohibit future single ownership of radio or television stations and newspapers in the same community. And in July the Court ruled (5–4) that the government may regulate radio broadcasting of words that are "patently offensive," though not obscene.

In a single May victory the press secured a unanimous (7–0) decision forbidding a state from imposing criminal penalties for the accurate reporting of confidential judicial disciplinary proceedings.

Criminal Law. In its continuing effort to delineate the proper constitutional circumstances for imposition of the death penalty, a divided Court struck down Ohio's capital punishment law, removing 101 people from the state's death row, because the law failed to allow a judge to consider any potentially mitigating aspect of a defendant's character. The 7–1 ruling was viewed by many, including some of the justices, as a return to 1972, when a slim 5–4 majority found that the death penalty was then so arbitrarily imposed that it violated the Eighth Amendment's ban on cruel and unusual punishment. As a result of the Court's ruling in the Ohio case, many states would have to redraft their capital punishment laws to permit consideration of a wider range of mitigating circumstances.

Ruling in a Georgia case in March, a unanimous Court held that a minimum of six jurors is constitutionally required in criminal trials. And in a 5–4 ruling in December the Court held that automobile passengers cannot—although car owners can—challenge the legality of a police search of a vehicle when criminal evidence is discovered.

See also CIVIL RIGHTS AND CIVIL LIBERTIES.   D.Ca.
SURINAM. *See* STATISTICS OF THE WORLD.
SWAZILAND. *See* STATISTICS OF THE WORLD.
SWEDEN. Disagreement over Swedish nuclear power policy brought about the fall of Prime Minister Thorbjörn Fälldin's coalition government in 1978. Moreover, the Swedish economy was seriously troubled by inflation and diminishing exports during the year.

In the Stockholm Concert Hall on Oct. 10, King Charles XVI Gustavus of Sweden congratulates Isaac Bashevis Singer. The 74-year-old Polish-born American writer received the Nobel Prize for literature in 1978.

Political Affairs. Prime Minister Fälldin resigned on Oct. 5 after failing to settle a dispute over nuclear power. Fälldin's Center Party had opposed the expansion of nuclear power, but the Moderate and Liberal Party members of his coalition supported an increase in the use of such power, to make Sweden less dependent on imported natural fuels.

On the completion of Sweden's seventh and eighth nuclear reactors, Fälldin had negotiated a compromise with the Moderates and Liberals so that the reactors' fueling could be delayed while a study of the safety of storing nuclear wastes in rock formations was completed.

Fälldin's fellow Center Party members rejected the accord. When Fälldin was unable to secure fresh concessions from the Moderates and Liberals, he resigned.

A new premier—Ola Ullsten, leader of the minority Liberal Party—was elected on Oct. 13. The Social Democrats and the Center Party had agreed to abstain from the *Riksdag* (parliament) vote on his appointment, and their abstention prevented the absolute majority needed to keep him from election. The new minority premier's cabinet, chosen on Oct. 18, had 19 members, 6 of whom were women.

Economic Problems. Exports of Swedish manufactured goods to members of the Organization for Economic Cooperation and Development fell by 21.5 percent during 1975–77; rapidly rising wages were largely to blame because they had undercut the competitive position of Swedish products.

The fiscal 1978–79 budget was presented on Jan. 10, with an anticipated deficit of $6.9 billion. One goal of the budget was to reduce the inflation rate from the 13.5 percent of 1977 to 9 percent in 1978. Another goal was to increase the gross national product (GNP) by 0.2 percent. In 1977, in its first decline since World War II, the Swedish GNP had fallen by 2.4 percent.

Data made public by a Swiss bank on July 18 revealed that Sweden had ranked third in GNP per capita income ($9483) among the world's nations in 1977. (Kuwait and Switzerland were first and second.)

In what he described as the "largest planned reorganization ever undertaken in any branch of Swedish industry," Minister of Industry Nils Åsling announced on June 16 government plans to end production at five of Sweden's seven major shipyards by 1981 and to reduce the number of shipyard workers from 21,000 to 12,000. The two remaining shipyards would be the facility in Malmö, where employment would be cut from 5200 to 4100, and the state-owned Uddevalla yard, where employment would decline from 4100 to

2300. Other yards would be shut or converted to other uses requiring fewer workers.

Foreign Affairs. Sweden informed the Soviet ambassador on March 1 of its concern about six nuclear-armed Soviet submarines that had been operating in the Baltic Sea for about a year. Their missiles were described as capable of reaching targets in Western Europe.

Also in March the Soviet Union denied a press report that it had sent trucks filled with electronic equipment through Sweden to gather military intelligence. Vehicles bearing special insignia are permitted to travel through Scandinavia from the Soviet Union to East Germany without undergoing customs inspection.

See STATISTICS OF THE WORLD.   L.A.S.

SWITZERLAND. After years of complaints about alleged linguistic discrimination in the French-speaking Jura district, the Swiss constitution was amended in 1978 to admit the area as a canton, a full-fledged member of the Swiss confederation. In another act that defied a long-standing national tradition, Switzerland joined other countries in an attack on terrorism.

The creation of Jura, Switzerland's twenty-third canton, was approved in a national referendum the weekend of Sept. 23–24. A constitutional amendment, adopted by vote of more than 82 percent of those voting, made possible the creation of the first addition to the Swiss confederation in 130 years. Jura had previously been part of the canton of Bern.

A referendum approved by Swiss voters on Feb. 27 had increased the government's authority to act against inflation and unemployment and to pass laws on foreign trade, public finance, and banking. The electorate, however, voted down a plan to lower retirement ages.

In a referendum on May 28, voters rejected a proposal to prohibit the use of private automobiles on the second Sunday of each month. The plan had been urged as a means of reducing pollution, saving energy, and encouraging greater use of public transportation. Proposals to permit abortions for nonmedical reasons and to authorize daylight saving time were also defeated.

On Dec. 3 voters again rejected a proposal, this time for the creation of a national police force to fight terrorism and guarantee public order. The public was apparently more concerned with preserving the autonomy of the cantons.

According to data made public by a Swiss bank on July 18, Switzerland, with a per capita gross national product (GNP) of $10,010, had the world's second highest GNP in proportion to population in 1977. Only Kuwait had a higher GNP per capita.

A four-nation ministerial meeting was held in Bern on April 8–9 to plan cooperation against terrorism. The four interior ministers—representing Austria, Italy, Switzerland, and West Germany—agreed to set up a hot-line communications system for this purpose. This was the first time Switzerland had taken part in coordinated action against terrorism.

Switzerland was reported on Feb. 1 to have given political asylum to 1055 persons during 1977. Nearly half of them were from Eastern Europe.

See STATISTICS OF THE WORLD.   L.A.S.

SYRIA. The Syrian government continued to be preoccupied in 1978 with its effort to restore order in neighboring Lebanon (q.v.). President Hafez al-Assad also made it clear that he was more adamantly opposed than ever to Egyptian President Anwar el-Sadat's efforts to end the thirty-year-old Arab confrontation with Israel.

The Peace Process. Syria emerged during 1978 as the leading Arab foe of Sadat's Middle East peace efforts. Openly urging Egyptians to overthrow Sadat, Syria denounced the September Camp David (Md.) accords, which made no provision for the return of the Golan Heights, captured by Israel from Syria in the 1967 war. The group organized to oppose Sadat's peace efforts, the "Steadfastness and Confrontation Front" made up of Syria, Algeria, Libya, the People's Democratic Republic of Yemen, and the Palestine Liberation Organization, met in Damascus in late September and designated Syrian President Assad to lead the campaign against the Camp David pact.

Foreign Relations. The biggest surprise of 1978 was Assad's decision to move to end Syria's long-standing ideological feud with Iraq. The two countries, ruled by feuding wings of the socialist Ba'ath Party, had openly sought for years to topple each other's governments. But Assad visited Iraq in late October for the first time since 1973. Relations between Iraq and Syria appeared on the mend, and a closer relationship seemed likely to give new weight to the hard-line Arab bloc opposing peace with Israel.

Syria continued to maintain close ties with the Soviet Union, which like the hard-line Arab states publicly condemned the Camp David peace accords. In February and again in October, Assad visited Moscow for talks with Soviet President Leonid I. Brezhnev and other top leaders. The October talks produced a Soviet pledge of continued support for the Arab states opposing Egypt's peace moves.

Government. Assad was confirmed on Feb. 8 for a second seven-year term in office, and he moved quickly to realign his top civilian and military leadership. On March 27 the speaker of parliament, Mohammed Ali al-Halabi, was named prime minister to succeed Abdel Rahman Khlefawi. Halabi formed a new cabinet on March 30 but retained most of the ministers from the previous one.

The Economy. The Syrian economy continued to slump in 1978. The economic growth rate, which had hit a peak of 14 percent in 1975, was projected to be zero for 1978—a continued slide from the 4 percent rate recorded in 1977. Although a variety of factors contributed to Syria's economic downturn, most economists put the blame on Syria's large, corrupt bureaucracy. Partly as a result of government inefficiency, Syria, potentially a rich agricultural land, was a net importer of food in 1978. Economists also estimated that Syria's industrial capacity, the second largest in the Arab world, was more than 60 percent unused in 1978 because of poor management and planning. The result was that Syria continued to rely heavily on foreign aid, which amounted to about $1 billion in 1978, or almost 20 percent of the country's gross domestic product.

See STATISTICS OF THE WORLD. *See also* ARAB LEAGUE; MIDDLE EAST.   M.R.B

T

TAIWAN, *or* **FORMOSA,** seat of the Republic of China. Taiwan's growing diplomatic isolation was underscored in 1978 by the ratification on Oct. 23 of a peace treaty between Japan and the People's Republic of China, and by the announcement on Dec. 15 that the United States would normalize relations with Peking. Even more damaging than the U.S. withdrawal of recognition from the Republic of China was the U.S. announcement that it was terminating its defense pact with Taiwan at the end of the required one-year notice period and withdrawing all American military personnel.

Angry reaction to the U.S. actions swept across the island. Amid international speculation that Taiwan might seek arms from the Soviet Union or attempt to "go nuclear," the Taipei government

On Dec. 16 President Chiang Ching-kuo of the Republic of China urges his people to keep calm. Shortly after the U.S. announced its intention to abrogate its defense pact with Taiwan and normalize relations with Peking, the Nationalist leader appeared on television, seated under a portrait of his late father, Chiang Kai-shek.

summarily dismissed conciliatory gestures from Peking to initiate diplomatic and trade talks. By the end of 1978, however, it was clear that the U.S.-Taiwan relationship would not change in some important respects: More than sixty economic agreements between the two nations were to remain in effect, and $544,000,000 in U.S. military aid would be delivered as promised.

Early in the year the Kuomintang, the ruling political party, reshuffled its leadership in an attempt to recover from setbacks suffered in the November, 1977, local elections. Although the Kuomintang had won 85 percent of the contested seats in balloting for provincial assemblies, opposition candidates showed surprising gains. Equally surprising was the sharp antigovernment stand taken by some of the new legislators.

On March 21, Taiwan's National Assembly elected Premier Chiang Ching-kuo to a six-year term as president of the Republic of China, replacing Yen Chia-kan, who retired from active political life. Chiang, who was the only candidate, assumed his new title in addition to his posts as chairman of the Kuomintang and commander in

chief of the armed forces. Following his inauguration in May, President Chiang named former Economics Minister Sun Yun-suan to replace him as premier, and appointed Tsiang Yen-si secretary of the Kuomintang.

Data released in 1978 showed that Taiwan's economy continued to grow in 1977. The gross national product reached $19 billion, up more than 8 percent from 1976 (after adjustments for inflation). The government attributed a slight slowdown in the growth rate to protectionism and tight credit abroad, which cut into trade and investment. Per capita income reached $1079, up 11.6 percent over 1976, but wholesale and consumer price inflation cut the real increase in income to under 6 percent.

There was a record trade surplus of $834,000,000 in 1977. During the first six months of 1978, Taiwan accumulated an additional $676,000,000 surplus.

See STATISTICS OF THE WORLD. T.L.K.

TANZANIA. War broke out between Tanzania and Uganda on Oct. 30, 1978, when Uganda invaded the Kagera region, west of Lake Victoria. Ugandan forces pushed as far as the Kagera River, 18 mi. inside Tanzania. Although Tanzania had long furnished a sanctuary for opponents of Uganda's President Idi Amin, the invasion was believed to be a move to divert dissent within Uganda's armed forces. By the end of November, Ugandan forces had withdrawn under Tanzanian military pressure. However, for the remainder of the year, fighting continued at a border skirmish level. News of atrocities in the Kagera fanned public demands in Tanzania that Amin be overthrown.

Tanzania's relations with Kenya, which had reached a low point during the previous year, began to improve in 1978 as both countries felt the impact of their decision to close their borders. In May, Kenya released three Tanzanian ferry boats; in exchange, a variety of light aircraft, trucks, and buses were permitted to return to Kenya. Despite its problems with its immediate neighbors, throughout the year Tanzania, under President Julius K. Nyerere, continued to be at the forefront of the African states demanding an immediate end to white rule in Rhodesia and South-West Africa.

See STATISTICS OF THE WORLD. *See also* AFRICA. J.T.S.

TECHNOLOGY. Miniature digital computers called microprocessors dominated much of the news of technology in 1978, as they found new uses in automobiles, in sophisticated electronic games, and in many other unusual applications. Other significant technological developments included an electronic watch with liquid-crystal "hands" and an instant camera that focuses itself

The handwriting on this pad is being entered directly into a computer. The DATAPAD System recognizes ordinary handwriting and translates it into machine-readable form. It consists of a special pad, a display, and a central processor. A user writes with an ordinary pen or pencil and needs no special skills.

Electronics consultant Thomas LoGiudice screws his Fluro-bulb into an ordinary light outlet. The federal Energy Department has expressed interest in the revolutionary fluorescent bulb, which uses less energy, produces less heat, and lasts longer than an ordinary bulb.

automatically with the help of a built-in sonar system.

The Microprocessor Revolution. A microprocessor is an electronic module about the size of a large postage stamp. Inside is a tiny chip of semi-

conductor material that holds a complex computer circuit. During manufacture the chip can be programmed to perform many different computing and control functions. Greatly improved performance and rapidly falling prices triggered a flood of new applications in 1978.

The General Motors Corp. offered an accessory called a Trip Computer in its 1978 Cadillac Seville that is built around a microprocessor module manufactured by Motorola. At the touch of the buttons on a small keyboard mounted on the car's instrument panel, the computer calculates and displays fuel consumption, estimated time of arrival at destination, average trip speed, time in transit, and other information of use to the driver. It also displays the time of day. The system gets the data it needs to make its computations from sensors installed on the engine and elsewhere on the vehicle. The computer also includes self-diagnostic circuitry that helps pinpoint internal circuit failures, should any develop. When first introduced, the Trip Computer cost $875. The prices of similar systems are expected to drop to much lower levels as the computers gain popularity.

A less visible application of microprocessors in automobiles is the control of engines with a precision that minimizes fuel consumption and exhaust emissions. The first microprocessor control systems were put on the highway late in 1977, but significantly more advanced designs were developed for 1979-model-year cars.

The Ford Motor Co. designed a system that controls ignition timing, engine air-to-fuel ratio, and the rate of exhaust-gas recirculation. It incorporates a microprocessor built by Toshiba, and it was installed on Ford LTD and Mercury Marquis automobiles. The control system is connected to seven sensor devices that monitor such factors as throttle position, engine coolant temperature, and the amount of oxygen in the exhaust gas.

Several General Motors models sold in California were equipped with a control system designed to maintain engine air-to-fuel ratio at the chemically correct level. This means that the relative proportions of air and fuel admitted to the engine are optimum for clean, efficient combustion. Further, because of the chemically correct air-to-fuel ratio, the car's catalytic converter could simultaneously eliminate the three major exhaust pollutants: carbon monoxide, hydrocarbons, and oxides of nitrogen. The control system uses a microprocessor manufactured by Motorola.

An early consumer application of microprocessors was in video games that connect to television sets. In 1978 these familiar electronic toys were joined by some newly developed self-contained, computerized games of surprising complexity and

sophistication. Two of the most popular were Simon, from Milton Bradley Co., and Speak & Spell, made by Texas Instruments.

Simon challenges a player to repeat random sequences of lights and sounds that are generated by the device. The game has four large touch panels; the player must touch the panels in the correct order to duplicate the lights and sounds he sees and hears. Each time the player succeeds, the game generates a longer sequence. When he fails to duplicate the sequence, the machine sounds a somewhat derisive sour note.

Speak & Spell, an educational game for children, incorporates a voice-synthesizer microprocessor that produces the sound of a human voice. It has a vocabulary of more than 200 words. After the device "speaks" a word, the player attempts to spell the word correctly by pushing appropriate keys on a keyboard. The letters appear on a display as they are entered. If the player spells the word correctly, the device voices its approval. If not, the child is urged to try again.

Researchers at Vanderbilt University designed a

In this strip of roadway 50 percent of the asphalt has been replaced by sulfur. Gulf Oil Canada, which developed the mixture and began marketing it in 1978, points out that its sulfur-asphalt doubles road surface strength, increases resistance to climatic changes, and conserves hydrocarbons.

The restored image (below) of the 70-year-old photo above resulted from a process that intensifies images of faded or underexposed negatives. A film or plate is treated with a sulfur isotope in solution; particles of silver in the picture become radioactive; and, when a new print is made, details not formerly visible are revealed. The process, developed at the Marshall Space Flight Center in Alabama, should allow reduction of exposure to medical X rays, with no loss of diagnostic detail.

microprocessor-based system that gives psychological tests for mental alertness. One of the tests flashes a group of numbers on a television screen for a brief period of time. Then a single number appears on the screen, and the person being tested is asked whether or not the number was part of the original group. The system gives and grades the tests without bias. Previously, a skilled person trained in psychology was required to administer such tests.

An engineer at a Canadian firm, Alberta Systems Development Group, incorporated a microprocessor in an audiometer, a device designed for hospital use to test a patient's hearing. The device controls an oscillator circuit that sends tones of varying frequency and volume to the patient's headphones. When the patient hears a tone, he presses a button to signal the microprocessor. The system automatically calculates the patient's hearing ability from his responses and presents the test results graphically in the form of a hearing curve plotted on a piece of paper. The U.S. Elevator Co. developed a microprocessor system that can control a bank of eight elevators. The system, which replaces a roomful of conventional relays and switching devices, fits onto a single printed circuit board 20 cm by 43 cm (8 in. by 17 in.). One of the system's unusual features is that a single two-wire cable links each elevator cab to the controller. Conventional systems use heavy cables with as many as one hundred wires to connect the push-buttons and other switches inside the cab to the controller.

Liquid-Crystal Watch Hands. In 1978, Texas Instruments introduced an electronic wrist watch called the Time Indicator that uses a liquid-crystal display to replicate the appearance of conventional moving hands. Until this development, quartz-controlled electronic timepieces had either a digital display to present the time numerically or moving hands that were driven mechanically.

The face of the new timepiece has 120 separate liquid-crystal segments that are activated by the watch's internal circuitry. The segments are arranged in sixty lines that radiate from the center of the face; each line contains two segments— one long and one short. When both segments in a line are activated, the line becomes the watch's big hand. When only the longer segment is activated, the line becomes the little hand. The first models of the new timepiece cost around $300, but less expensive watches using liquid-crystal hands are expected to become available in 1979.

Focusing a Camera with Sound Waves. Prior to 1978 there had been several attempts, a few of them successful, to develop automatic lens focusing systems based on optical techniques. But in 1978 Polaroid introduced new versions of its SX-70 and Pronto instant cameras that use miniature sonar systems to focus their lenses. (The word *sonar* is an abbreviation for sound navigation and ranging, a technique originally developed to detect submerged objects, such as submarines, underwater.) The heart of the Polaroid system is a transducer assembly, mounted above the lens, which functions both as a transmitter and receiver of ultrasonic sound waves. (A transducer is activated by energy in one form—electricity, for example—and transmits it in another form—such as sound. A telephone receiver is a transducer.)

When the camera's operator presses the shutter button, the transducer broadcasts a brief inaudible "chirp" composed of four ultrasonic frequencies. The sound waves bounce off the subject and are reflected back to the transducer in a few thousandths of a second. An electronic circuit inside the camera measures the round-trip travel time, then uses the measured time to compute the distance to the subject. Finally, the circuit activates a motor that rotates the lens to the correct focus. The entire process takes a small fraction of a second; when it has been completed, the shutter opens to take the picture.

The sonar system is powered by a battery inside the SX-70's film pack. The system can be turned off by photographers who prefer to adjust focus manually. At the end of 1978, many photographic shops were selling the Pronto model with sonar focusing for less than $90. *See* PHOTOGRAPHY.

Underground Electronics. Despite all these obvious innovations, especially in electronics, there appears to have been a decline in the number of patents issued for new inventions during the year. And since patents are taken as an index of our technological creativity, it looked as though we were lagging.

Not so, said spokesmen for the electronics industry. They explained that the industry has been reluctant to patent for several reasons. First, by the time a new patent would be issued, the producer of the patent would in all likelihood have innovated beyond it—rendering it obsolete. Then

there is the matter of proprietary secrets. Patents may help the competition more than they protect the inventor. Especially with regard to an integrated circuit device, the slightest modification of a readily available patent design would give a competitor a completely new device free of any infringement claims.

So the electronics experts came up with a more effective means of protecting their inventions during the year. It is a technique known as "black boxing" or "potting." In this technique they encapsulate the circuit components in epoxy resin, leaving only the terminals protruding. A competitor would have to dissolve the entire unit to get at the circuitry, and he would probably dissolve the circuitry in the process. As one industry executive put it: "The whole field is going underground."   R.Ben.

TENNESSEE. *See* STATISTICS OF THE WORLD.

TEXAS. *See* STATISTICS OF THE WORLD.

THAILAND. Thailand's prime minister, Gen. Kriangsak Chamanand, spent much of 1978 preparing to dismantle the military dictatorship he inherited a year earlier and replace it with an elected civilian government.

Politics. In the early months of 1978, Kriangsak won considerable civilian support when he relaxed martial law and offered an olive branch to organized labor and other relatively liberal elements. The prime minister pledged a new deal for underpaid workers and promised vigorous efforts toward land and tax reform. Despite the opposition of fellow military leaders, Kriangsak also pushed ahead with plans for a new constitution that would lead to parliamentary elections in 1979.

In an effort to control the powerful cliques within the Thai armed forces, Kriangsak reshuffled his cabinet in August. The prime minister himself assumed the post of defense minister, thereby strengthening his control over key military appointments. In October, he named Gen. Prem Tinsulananot to the country's most powerful military post, commander in chief of the army. The surprise appointment of Prem, a strict disciplinarian with few political ties, apparently gave Kriangsak more leverage over his more conservative rivals.

Throughout the summer, factions in the National Assembly, an appointive body dominated by the military, maneuvered behind closed doors over the drafting of the new constitution. The rightists wanted a document that would guarantee their continued dominance. Some young officers wanted a completely democratic constitution modeled after that of the United States. In December a compromise document emerged, pro-

A gift, a garland, and a warm handshake greeted Vietnamese Deputy Premier Nguyen Duy Trinh (left) on his arrival in Bangkok. Thai Prime Minister Kriangsak Chamanand (right) agreed to open diplomatic relations with Hanoi, but stayed neutral in the Vietnam-Cambodia conflict.

viding for an elective lower house and an appointed senate. A key provision gave Kriangsak—rather than Adm. Sa-ngad Chaloryu, the chairman of the military junta that took over Thailand in October, 1977—a commanding voice in making appointments to the upper house.

The Insurgency. Communist insurgents stepped up the pace of their hit-and-run attacks and moved into a number of previously guerrilla-free provinces during the year. A confidential government report revealed that the Communists also had developed a potentially dangerous underground movement of urban guerrillas in Thailand's capital, Bangkok. But stories filtering out of Communist bases along Thailand's borders with Laos and Cambodia told of dissent and demoralization in the guerrilla ranks, in large part because of the conflict between Cambodia and Vietnam, the guerrillas' chief supporters.

Foreign and Economic Policy. In July, Cambodian

Vice Premier Ieng Sary visited Thailand; in September, Vietnamese Premier Pham Van Dong was received in Bangkok. But Thailand, ever wary of its Communist neighbors, adopted a policy of strict neutrality between the Cambodian and Vietnamese antagonists. In early November, Chinese Deputy Premier Teng Hsiao-ping paid a visit to Bangkok, using the opportunity to denounce the Vietnamese and to warn of Soviet designs in Southeast Asia. Treading carefully, Kriangsak played the good host, but he balanced the Teng visit by announcing that he planned to visit the Soviet Union and the U.S. early in 1979.

To the surprise of many observers, 1978 proved to be an excellent year for the Thai economy. Spearheaded by a sharp recovery in agriculture, which had suffered badly during a 1977 drought, the gross national product was expected to grow by more than 8 percent. Thailand's chief economic problems were a nagging inflation and an expanding foreign trade gap.

See STATISTICS OF THE WORLD. R.J.C

THEATER. The theater in 1978 held its recent gains and took some new strides. Broadway, the U.S. commercial theater capital, prospered. Stars performed in many comedies and musicals, but seri ous works were few and far between. The nation-wide professional, noncommercial theater served an ever-growing audience. Peter Zeisler, executive director of the authoritative Theater Communications Group (TCG), described the U.S. theater scene as "the most lively and prolific theater in the world today."

Comedies and Thrillers. Comedies and a couple of comedy melodramas topped the Broadway hit parade. In May, Hugh Leonard's *Da*, the affectionate account of an Irish father-son relationship, moved from Off Broadway to a midtown commercial playhouse; the play won the New York Drama Critics' Circle and Antoinette Perry (or Tony) awards. David Mamet's *The Water Engine*, about a radio station in the 1930's, also moved from Off Broadway to midtown for a very brief run.

Bernard Slade's *Tribute* starred Jack Lemmon as a middle-aged jokester trying to get his life together in the face of a terminal illness. The more socially relevant *First Monday in October*, by Jerome Lawrence and Robert E. Lee, imagines the appointment of the first woman associate justice of the U.S. Supreme Court (Jane Alexander). A conservative, she clashes immediately with the Court's crusty liberal (Henry Fonda). Another of the year's outstanding comedies was *On Golden Pond*, a touching study, by newcomer Ernest Thompson, of a married couple (Tom Aldredge

and Frances Sternhagen) confronting the challenges of old age during a Maine summer. Acclaimed Off Broadway, it was scheduled to move to Broadway early in 1979. Love's old sweet song among senior citizens was dashingly played by Rex Harrison and Claudette Colbert in *The Kingfisher*, a lightweight comedy by England's William Douglas Home.

The year's two Broadway thrillers were *Deathtrap*, Ira Levin's fiendishly complicated melodrama about a writer of whodunits (John Wood), and Paul Giovanni's *The Crucifer of Blood*, which presented Paxton Whitehead as Sherlock Holmes in one of the most scenically spectacular productions of the year.

Musicals. The most successful musical was *Ain't Misbehavin'*, a reprise of songs written and/or recorded by popular musician Thomas "Fats" Waller. Its prizes included the Tony and Critics' Circle awards. *Eubie!* comprised a similar affectionate tribute to a legendary musical figure, nonagenarian Eubie Blake. The songs of Blake and Waller (with words by Noble Sissle and others) provided a lively backward look at the creative contributions of black composers and lyricists.

On the Twentieth Century looked back in another direction. Working from the Hecht-MacArthur-Milholland comedy hit of 1932, librettist-lyricists Betty Comden and Adolph Green and composer Cy Coleman retold the tale of a flam-

Brian Murray (left) is the son and Barnard Hughes is the father in Hugh Leonard's award-winning Irish comedy Da.

THEATER

Ann Reinking kicks high in Dancin', an exuberant and sensual entertainment conceived by choreographer Bob Fosse. Critics and audiences applauded the stunning skill of the dancers; few of them seemed to lament the absence of a story line.

boyant producer (John Cullum) trying to lure back the glamorous star (Judy Kaye) who was once his protégée. Composer-director Elizabeth Swados contributed an unusual entertainment with *Runaways*, whose cast, aged from 11 to 25, delivered the personal histories of urban strays in songs, dances, and soliloquies. *Runaways* was another transfer from Off Broadway to a commercial playhouse.

Three of the year's musicals underlined the unique role of dance in American popular lyric theater. *The American Dance Machine* restaged works of some of the major choreographers (and composers) of the past several decades. Bob Fosse's *Dancin'* was a characteristically dazzling Fosse extravaganza. In Michael Bennett's tenderly sentimental *Ballroom*, taken from a 1973 television special, two middle-aged people (Dorothy

Loudon and Vincent Gardenia) find romance at the Stardust Ballroom. In a decidedly more disreputable vein, *The Best Little Whorehouse in Texas*, by Carol Hall, Larry L. King, and Peter Masterson, concerns itself with the closing of a Texas brothel.

As usual, the year saw the return of several musical hits from the past. *Hello, Dolly!* starred Carol Channing again in the role she created on Broadway in 1964. *Timbuktu!*—a revision rather than a revival—retained the familiar songs of *Kismet* but transferred the locale to 14th-century Africa, spectacularly imagined by director and choreographer Geoffrey Holder. Sammy Davis, Jr., included New York City in the course of a national tour as an Americanized version of the hero Littlechap in Leslie Bricusse and Anthony Newley's *Stop the World, I Want to Get Off*. *Pins and Needles*, an ideological revue of the 1930's with a score by Harold Rome, serenaded Off-Broadway audiences for several months with songs of social significance.

394

One-Man Productions. Along with the more opulent productions, there were several solo shows on and Off Broadway. Most notable was British actor Alec McCowen's recital of St. Mark's Gospel. Other one-man shows by Britons included Donal Donnelly as George Bernard Shaw, and Emlyn Williams impersonating "Saki" (19th-century British short-storywriter H. H. Munro) in *The Playboy of the Weekend World.* An American, Vincent Price, played the Irish author and wit Oscar Wilde in *Diversions and Delights,* and black actor James Earl Jones performed in *Paul Robeson,* a biographical piece about the athlete, singer, and actor that provoked a good deal of controversy.

Off-Broadway Drama. Elsewhere in the Off-Broadway world such established playwrights as Thomas Babe, Sam Shepard, Arthur Kopit, Jay Broad, Lanford Wilson, and Athol Fugard were joined by newcomers Tina Howe, Marsha Norman, Wendy Wasserstein, and Ernest Thompson. An unusual Off-Broadway production was a revival of Bertolt Brecht's *Life of Galileo,* performed in the austere Columbia University lecture hall where Professor Harold Urey first described the discovery of heavy water. *The Biko Inquest,* a harshly realistic documentary by Norman Fenton and Jon Blair, deals with the 1977 thirteen-day hearing on the death of black South African leader Steve Biko while in police custody. At year's end, a revival of *The Diary of Anne Frank,* 1956 Pulitzer and Critics' Circle prizewinner, opened with a cast that included Eli Wallach, his wife Anne Jackson, and their two daughters.

Regional Theater. The widely dispersed, non-profit, professional theatrical organizations of the United States contributed solidly to the theatrical year. A 1978 TCG report found that in the previous season 153 nonprofit groups were operating in 73 cities in 34 states and the District of Columbia. They gave 35,812 performances before audiences totaling 11,100,000. According to TCG spokesmen, the present movement has grown from a nucleus of eight such theaters in 1950.

Theatrical productions across the country

A scene from Zoot Suit, an explosive drama based on Southern California's Mexican-American riots of the 1940's. The highly successful play was commissioned from author Luis Valdez by the Mark Taper Forum of Los Angeles.

showed range and variety. *Getting Out*, which reached Off Broadway via the Actors Theater of Louisville and the Mark Taper Forum of Los Angeles, won Marsha Norman the American Theatre Critics Association award for the best play produced in a regional theater in 1977-78. Eight Atlanta theaters cooperated to present the Atlanta New Play Project. Baltimore's Center Stage became the State Theater of Maryland.

Rumania's Liviu Ciulei staged a well received *Hamlet* for Washington's Arena Stage (as well as productions of Frank Wedekind's *Spring Awakening* and Nikolai Gogol's *The Inspector General* in New York City). From Moscow came Galina Volchek to direct the English-language premiere of Mikhail Roschin's *Echelon* in Houston, and Anatoly Efros to mount his production of Gogol's *Marriage* in Minneapolis.

Alvin Epstein, formerly of the Yale Repertory Theatre, succeeded Michael Langham as artistic director of the Tyrone Guthrie Theatre in Minne-

Nina Vance (left), founder of Houston's Alley Theatre, invited Soviet director Galina Volchek to stage Mikhail Roschin's World War II drama Echelon *at the Texas theater early in the year.*

Evita, *by Tim Rice and Andrew Lloyd Webber, authors of* Jesus Christ Superstar, *was the smash hit of the year in London. Here, Joss Ackland as Juan Perón and Elaine Paige in the title role.*

apolis, launching his first season with Henrik Ibsen's epic, *The Pretenders*. Gregory Mosher, the new artistic director of Chicago's Goodman Theater, presented his own version of the 1941 stage adaptation of Richard Wright's novel, *Native Son*. The Minneapolis Children's Theater assembled thirty-five young actors to present *A Circle Is the Sun*, written by, and expressing the world view of, the young.

After a year's hiatus, the American Shakespeare Theatre in Stratford, Conn., resumed operations. The Shakespeare Festival of Canada celebrated its twenty-fifth anniversary season.

Theater Economics. The generally prosperous state of the commercial theater, caused partly by

rising ticket prices and partly by a 78 percent increase in Broadway attendance over the last five years, was reflected in a midyear survey in *Variety*, the show business weekly. Reporting on the theater season, June 1 to May 31, *Variety* stated that the year 1977-78 was financially the biggest in American history. Broadway box offices took in $100,846,494, an increase of 11 percent over the previous season. Receipts for touring companies totaled $105,696,885, an increase of 28 percent over the previous season.

Institutional theaters, however, notwithstanding their unquestioned cultural value, faced growing financial uncertainties. According to the TCG survey, subsidies from government, corporate, and private donors had not kept pace with mounting costs. TCG found that in a twelve-month period, institutional theater expenses had increased 17.6 percent while grants and contributions had risen by less than 3 percent. More than half the theaters surveyed wound up with deficits averaging $23,715. The report observed that unless the present trend of diminishing subsidies reverses itself, the resulting larger deficits will be detrimental to theaters across the country.

Deaths. Major figures in the theater world who died in 1978 were Charles Boyer, Claude Dauphin, Ruth Etting, Max Gordon, and Oliver Messel; *see* Obituaries. Other notable deaths included those of actress Hortense Alden (April 2 at 76); actress-playwright Ilka Chase (Feb. 15 at 72); British actress Fay Compton (Dec. 12 at 84); actor Thayer David (July 17 at 51); comedienne Charlotte Greenwood (Jan. 18 at 87); actor Irving Jacobson (Dec. 17 at 80); Broadway producer Albert Lewis (April 6 at 93); Micheal MacLiammoir, Irish actor and co-founder of Dublin's Gate Theatre (March 6 at 78); dancer and singer Danny Meehan (March 29 at 47); actress Felicia Montealegre (June 16 at 56); and French-born singer and actress Odette Myrtile (Nov. 18 at 80).   J.B.

TOGO. *See* Statistics of the World.

TONGA. *See* Statistics of the World.

TRANSKEI. *See* Statistics of the World. *See also* South Africa, Republic of.

TRANSPORTATION. Record automobile sales, deregulation of U.S. air service, and the worst oil spill in history were among the major transportation stories of 1978.

AUTOMOBILES

Aided by the continuing boom in sales of vans, the U.S. automobile industry reached record levels, with sales of 15,300,000 cars and trucks during the 1978 model year. Sales of passenger cars alone nearly equaled the record set in 1973. The 1978 performance was even more satisfying to Detroit because U.S. manufacturers increased their share of the automotive market to 85 percent of domestic sales. In the 1977 model year, imports had accounted for 18.3 percent of U.S. sales.

Foreign Manufacturers. Import sales from Japan, the leading exporter, were affected by the rapidly escalating value of the yen compared to the dollar. Toyota, for example, had five price increases in its 1978 model year, with the price of a liftback increasing by $1000 to $4800. Eventually, Toyota dealers felt the competitive pressure and were obliged to offer $200 rebates.

The United States remains the largest market for automotive products in the world, but the weakness of the dollar makes exporting to the U.S. much less attractive than in the past. For this rea-

son, foreign manufacturers have been planning domestic U.S. production of cars that formerly were imported. In 1978, Volkswagen began production of American-built Rabbits at its new plant near New Stanton, Pa. And Honda, a Japanese automaker, agreed to manufacture motorcycles at an Ohio plant, with future car production likely.

Fuel Economy Standard. American manufacturers, who are themselves emphasizing competitive subcompact models, took advantage of the import situation to increase prices. The basic reason that U.S. manufacturers have been shifting toward subcompacts—and educating the American public that smaller is not necessarily cheaper—is the federally mandated fuel-economy standard. In the 1978 model year the major producers had to achieve a fleetwide average of 18 mpg. This means

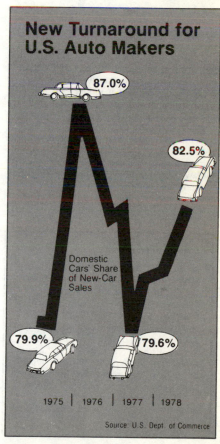

New Turnaround for U.S. Auto Makers

87.0%

82.5%

Domestic Cars' Share of New-Car Sales

79.9%

79.6%

1975 | 1976 | 1977 | 1978

Source: U.S. Dept. of Commerce

James McLernon (right), president of the Volkswagen Manufacturing Corp. of America, hails the first U.S.-built Rabbit to roll off the assembly line. Volkswagen's new plant, located near New Stanton, Pa., began full-scale operations in April.

that for every Cadillac limousine General Motors (GM) sold during the model year, GM also had to sell four subcompacts in order to keep the fleetwide average up to standard.

This was no voluntary program. The federal law specifies that for each tenth of a mile below 18 mpg, a manufacturer may be fined $5 for every car it produced during that model year. For GM, which built approximately 4,500,000 cars in 1978, a fleetwide average of, say, 17.9 mpg could mean a fine of $22,500,000.

As the 1979 model year commenced, with the federal standard going from 18 to 19 mpg, the Ford Motor Co. was hard pressed to comply with the law. Indeed, Ford began imposing stiff premiums on cars equipped with V-8 engines, to discourage customers from buying them. A customer

who insisted on buying this low-mpg engine was often confronted by months of delay for delivery, along with a price hike of up to $400.

Traffic Safety. Chrysler, whose share of the standard-size market has dropped from the traditional 15 percent to less than 5 percent, had a difficult year on the safety front. Its two top-selling models, Aspen and Volare, had to be recalled four times within a few months for safety-related defects. To make matters worse, the front-wheel-drive subcompacts Omni and Horizon, on which Chrysler had based much of its future, received a "not acceptable" rating from the magazine *Consumer Reports.*

A similar pair of subcompact cars, Ford's Pinto and Bobcat, suffered a 35 percent sales drop following publicity about a design flaw in the gas tanks of earlier models. The Pintos and Bobcats sprung massive fuel leaks when involved in rear-end collisions. Ford recalled more than 1,500,000 cars manufactured between 1971 and 1976 to correct the defect.

Even GM subcompacts were not immune. The 1976 and 1977 models of the Chevrolet Chevette had to be recalled to correct a potential gas-tank leakage problem similar to that which afflicted the Pinto and Bobcat.

Also on the safety front, the Firestone Tire & Rubber Co. was forced to recall millions of its "500" steel-belted radial tires—the largest such recall in history. Firestone agreed, under strong government pressure, to replace free up to 9,000,000 of the tires sold since 1975. The cost of the recall was estimated at more than $100,000,000.

See CONSUMER EDUCATION AND PROTECTION.

AVIATION

The U.S. air-transport industry showed extraor-

A Breath of Free Air

In 1977 the New York State legislature banned the pay toilet. In 1978 the Nik-O-Lok Co. of Indianapolis, manufacturers of the device, attempted to regain some of their lost business. Nik-O-Lok installed a new device in some New York State gas stations, forcing drivers to pay a quarter to use the air hose. Hempstead, Long Island, would have none of it. The town board banned the 25¢-a-shot gadget in the belief that "free air is almost a tradition in America." Said the presiding supervisor, "I don't think there is a place in the capitalist system to charge for air."

dinary growth in 1978, when scheduled U.S. airlines flew 280,000,000 passengers, fully 40,000,000 more than in 1977. (In 1958, the year the jet age began, the industry flew only 49,000,000 passengers.) Scheduled airlines also grossed more than $23 billion and earned more than $1 billion in 1978, up from $18 billion and $754,000,000 in 1977.

Strains on the System. The tremendous surge in traffic in 1978 was not accomplished without severe strain. For example, airlines like to have 80 percent of telephone calls for reservations answered within 20 seconds; during the peak summer months, however, waits of half an hour were reported. Access roads to airports were clogged, forcing some passengers to abandon their rental cars and run to catch their flights. Waits for baggage frequently seemed interminable. The industry estimated it wasted 360,000,000 gal. of fuel because of delays.

Perhaps the greatest symbol of the enormous surge in traffic was a "tent city" on London streets, inhabited by passengers waiting to return to the U.S. on Laker Airways, which offered low-cost flights on a first-come, first-served basis. Indeed, the term "standby" came to mean waits of days instead of hours.

Luring the Business Traveler. The heady pace of U.S. economic activity fueled an enormous boom in business travel. Unlike the pleasure traveler, who makes plans far in advance and rarely has to be at a particular destination at any precise time, the business traveler often makes spur-of-the-moment decisions and has specific schedules to meet. The conflict between these two types of travel was exacerbated because of the volume of all traffic during 1978. Business travelers, frequently arriving at the airport at the last minute, found they could not get reservations on the flights they wanted—or, worse, that their seats had been sold to others. They complained that although they were paying full fare, they were getting inferior service.

Consequently, a number of U.S. and foreign airlines established two classes of coach service, either by segregating part of the coach cabin for full-fare passengers or by trying to give them more room and first choice on meals. The experiment did not work smoothly or well. A full airplane continued to be a full airplane, and trying to keep apart two smoking sections and two nonsmoking sections proved to be an administrative nightmare.

Airline Deregulation Act. On Oct. 24, U.S. President Jimmy Carter signed into law the Airline Deregulation Act of 1978. The law calls for the gradual phasing out of the Civil Aeronautics Board (CAB).

According to the provisions of the act, by Jan. 1, 1982, the CAB authority over domestic route assignments and certification will have been terminated, and by Jan. 1, 1983, the CAB will no longer have authority over domestic fares, mergers, acquisitions, and charters. If Congress does not act to save the agency, the CAB will cease to exist as of Jan. 1, 1985.

The intent of the law was to make the airlines more competitive, thereby improving service and reducing fares. However, the immediate effect of the measure was to encourage airlines to protect themselves against competition, either by acquisi-

Adams at the Crossroads

Among the members of the Carter cabinet, the tenure of Transportation Secretary Brock Adams appeared to be the shakiest. He disagreed with the White House on airline deregulation; his department delayed issuing its first comprehensive policy statement until February, 1978—more than a year after he took office. Despite expertise gained as a six-term congressman (D, Wash.) and chairman of the House Budget Committee, Adams, 51, was rarely consulted on key policy questions such as energy. In July the New York *Times* reported that he was "frustrated" and contemplating resignation to return to private law practice or another try at elective office. Adams denied the report, insisting "I still enjoy my job." And indeed, he was still there as the year ended.

Transportation Secretary Brock Adams.

To commemorate the birth of the air age seventy-five years before, 5000 people gathered at Kitty Hawk, N.C., on Dec. 17 to watch a recreation of the Wright brothers' famous flight. Only one thing went wrong—the plane, a replica built and flown by Ken Kellet, barely got off the ground.

tion or merger. For example, Continental and Western agreed to merge in order to meet the threat of competition from United, the largest U.S. air carrier. Two of the so-called regional airlines, North Central Airlines and Southern Airways, announced a proposed merger that would turn the resulting company into a trunk line. And a regional airline, Texas International, tried to acquire control of National, a trunk airline. For its part, National sought to be acquired by Pan Am, an airline that had never before had domestic routes. In short, a law designed to increase competition appeared, late in 1978, to be having the opposite effect.

MASS TRANSIT

For the sixth consecutive year, ridership increased on U.S. mass-transit lines. During the first ten months of 1978, mass-transit systems carried nearly 6.4 billion riders, a 5.5 percent increase over the same period in 1977. The rise came despite two major work stoppages, both in July. The first, in Boston, halted subway, bus, and trolley service for a day; the second, in Washington, D.C., shut down local buses and subways for a week.

Funding and Construction. On Nov. 6, President Carter signed a bill providing $15.6 billion in mass-transit aid through fiscal year 1983. Included in the measure were funds for rapid-transit projects in Baltimore, Boston, Buffalo, Chicago, Detroit, Miami, metropolitan Washington, D.C., and northern New Jersey.

At midyear the Washington subway system had 37 km (23 mi.) open and 56 km (35 mi.) under construction. Service on the Metropolitan Atlanta Rapid Transit Authority subway—a $2.1 billion system fully financed by the federal Urban Mass

Transportation Administration—was scheduled to begin at the close of 1978.

Service for the Handicapped. The Department of Transportation proposed in 1978 that all public transit facilities receiving federal financial assistance—which means, in practice, all such facilities—must be fully accessible to the handicapped and disabled. The cost of putting elevators in existing subway and elevated rail systems and of acquiring "kneeling" buses has been estimated at anywhere between $2 billion and $5 billion. By federal mandate, bus floor levels must be no more than 45.72 cm (18 in.) off the ground as of Oct. 1, 1979.

RAILROADS

In 1978, as in 1977, severe winter weather hampered railroad operations. But in 1978 a coal strike and, later in the year, a shortage of cars and locomotives posed additional problems for U.S. railroads.

Operations. In a sense, the winter of 1978 was even worse than that of 1977. The cold and snow extended farther south, affecting operations over a wider geographic area. To make matters worse, the United Mine Workers (UMW) were in the midst of their four-month strike as the year began. Coal, which is the largest single commodity the railroads haul, almost disappeared from railroads in the Appalachian area organized by the UMW.

In the second quarter, the railroads were put in the difficult position of helping the U.S. recover from the winter slowdown. Because of soaring costs connected with getting their facilities back into shape, eleven of the nation's thirty-seven leading railroads lost money during the first half. But in the late spring and summer, a boom began. Record grain shipments were stimulated by higher prices and rising export demand. The result was a severe shortage of cars (especially boxcars and covered hoppers) and locomotives. By July 1 the backlog of undelivered freight cars on order was equal to a full year's production. Some 120,000 cars had been ordered by the end of 1978, with delivery dates well into 1980. About 1200 new diesel and rebuilt locomotives were delivered (the most since 1974), but even that number proved inadequate.

Another roadblock was the strike during the second half of 1978 by the Brotherhood of Railway, Airline, and Steamship Clerks against the Norfolk & Western Railway, the industry's third largest coal hauler. Sympathy strikes in late September led to a shutdown of 70 percent of all U.S. rail lines. The strikers returned to work under a federal court order on Sept. 29.

Despite these difficulties, the railroad industry handled a record volume in 1978. Expressed in terms of ton-miles (a ton of freight multiplied by the number of miles it travels), the nation's railroads handled approximately 865 billion ton-miles of freight traffic in 1978—4.5 percent more than in 1977, and a new record.

Financial Outlook. According to the Association of American Railroads, the industry earned freight revenues of $21 billion, an all-time high, but nearly all the increase was absorbed by inflation and rising costs. Although a few railroads were highly profitable, the industrywide return on investment—less than 2 percent—was too low to permit most railroads to have access to private capital markets.

In an effort to strengthen themselves, several major railroads sought merger partners in 1978. Of these, the Burlington Northern–St. Louis-San Francisco Railway merger was the closest to winning approval from the Interstate Commerce Commission. The Southern Pacific sought to acquire control of the Seaboard Coast Line Industries; however, the Seaboard agreed late in 1978 to merge with the Chessie System.

Passenger Service. The National Railroad Passenger Corp.—usually known as Amtrak—had a disappointing year. Ridership declined by 1.6 percent to 18,900,000 passengers for the fiscal year ended Sept. 30, 1978. Amtrak's deficit increased from $482,600,000 in fiscal 1977 to $488,500,000 in fiscal 1978, with an even larger deficit forecast for 1979. In December the president of Amtrak, Alan S. Boyd, urged the nation to give up the idea that passenger service can ever be run at a profit.

The Consolidated Rail Corp. (Conrail), which serves the East and Midwest, continued its massive rehabilitation program, the most ambitious in the U.S. During 1978, Congress authorized $1.2 billion for Conrail, in addition to the $2 billion provided under the law establishing the nonprofit corporation in 1976.

SHIPPING

A rate war in maritime shipping and the worst oil spill in history were the leading stories of 1978.

Rate War. The U.S. merchant marine was troubled throughout 1978 by the low-price policies of the Soviet Union and other Eastern bloc countries, whose fleets of modern freighters were growing rapidly. The Soviets in particular were charging between 30 and 40 percent less than the rates set by the shipping conferences to which the merchant marines of most Western nations belong. To help U.S. fleets, Congress approved legislation broadening the powers of the Federal Maritime Commission to suspend rates it found below a just and reasonable level. However, President Carter vetoed the measure. The State Department was known to oppose the bill for fear of retaliation by foreign governments, and the Justice Department was concerned that competition would be diminished.

One large U.S. company, Seatrain Lines, did not

A Chicago train station, normally crowded with commuters, stood empty during a nationwide rail strike in late September. A federal court order put the strikers—and the commuters—back on the tracks.

wait for federal relief. Instead, it instituted sharp rate cuts for that part of the traffic into which the Russians had made their deepest inroads. This action led to comparable cuts by the maritime rate-setting bodies, resulting in a general lowering of rates and shipping company earnings.

Partly because of the unsettled rate structure in 1978, one U.S. flag steamship company, Pacific Far East Lines, entered bankruptcy in June, and a second, States Steamship Co., encountered severe financial difficulties. When Pacific Far East Lines failed, the federal Maritime Administration, which had guaranteed the mortgages on four ships, paid out approximately $100,000,000. Maritime experts estimated that the federal government would lose about $30,000,000 when the ships eventually were sold.

Tankers. Low rates also continued to afflict the world's oil tanker owners. Ever since the Arab oil embargo in the late fall of 1973, worldwide charter rates for tanker voyages had been so low that losses had mounted for most operators. Many orders for new supertankers were canceled in 1978. As a result, two Japanese shipyards went bankrupt and others were under severe financial strain. U.S. shipyards were less affected, because the flow of oil from Alaska kept up demand for smaller tankers that could enter U.S. ports. By law, all oil flowing between one U.S. port and another must be carried on American vessels.

Oil Spill. The worst oil spill in maritime history occurred on March 17, 1978, when the Liberian-registered, American-owned supertanker *Amoco Cadiz*, carrying more than 67,000,000 gal. of crude oil, lost power off the coast of Brittany. The vessel foundered and broke up, polluting some 320 km (200 mi.) of shoreline. What was particularly disturbing about this disaster was that the *Amoco Cadiz* was not what mariners refer to as a rust-bucket; it had been built in 1974 and was well equipped with navigation and safety devices. A defect in the tanker's steering mechanism and some questionable decisions by the captain were blamed for the accident. *See also* ENVIRONMENT.

Cruise Ships. Two passenger ships made news in 1978. The *America,* built before World War II for the high-speed North Atlantic trade, was brought out of retirement for the pleasure cruise business. Health inspectors, the Coast Guard, and disgruntled passengers all gave the vessel such a low rating that the venture collapsed and the ship was sold at public auction. Its postwar-built sister ship, the *United States,* was acquired by a West Coast real estate developer, who announced a two-year, $30,000,000 refurbishing program that would prepare the ship for West Coast–Hawaii cruise operations.   B.W.

TRINIDAD AND TOBAGO. *See* STATISTICS OF THE WORLD.

TUNISIA. Long regarded as a model of stability, Tunisia was jolted in early 1978 by the worst riots since the end of French rule in 1956.

At least 51 persons, and perhaps as many as 200, were killed when a general strike erupted into a bloody confrontation between demonstrators and the army. The 24-hour general strike had been called for Jan. 26 to protest the economic policies of Premier Hedi Nouira, climaxing months of antigovernment agitation by the 650,000-member General Union of Tunisian Workers (UGTT). The UGTT, led by Habib Achour, had contested a five-year pay freeze and also had pressed demands for greater political liberalization. A showdown became inevitable in December, 1977: Nouira fired Interior Minister Tahar Belkhodja, an Achour ally.

In the wake of the rioting, Nouira arrested Achour and made it clear that he would deal firmly with any new outbreaks. On Oct. 10, Achour and seventeen other UGTT officials received prison sentences ranging from six months to ten years. (They had been tried in a political court after a criminal court declared itself incompetent to try them.)

Many political observers felt the riots were a forerunner of the power struggle likely to take place in Tunisia when President Habib Bourguiba is no longer in command. The 75-year-old Bourguiba had handpicked Nouira as his successor, but the premier did not seem to have Bourguiba's popular following.

Some Tunisian officials believed that neighboring Libya was deliberately "destabilizing" the political situation in Tunisia and that Libya's strongman, Muammar el-Qaddafi, was carrying on a vendetta against Bourguiba and Nouira.

See STATISTICS OF THE WORLD. *See also* AFRICA; MIDDLE EAST.   M.R.B.

TURKEY. The worst political violence in Turkey in a decade forced the government to impose martial law in Ankara, İstanbul, and eleven other cities at the end of 1978. The violence capped another year of continued economic and social unrest throughout the country.

Political Instability. Turkey began 1978 in the midst of a government crisis as a result of the Dec. 31, 1977, collapse of conservative Premier Süleyman Demirel's ruling coalition. The leader of the leftist Republican People's Party, Bülent Ecevit, was designated to form a new government on Jan. 1 and was confirmed in office as premier by a confidence vote on Jan. 17. While Ecevit made foreign policy the top concern of his new government, he also sought to deal with the social and economic problems that led to Demirel's downfall.

Policemen and soldiers patrol the streets of İstanbul on Dec. 28. Martial law had been declared in thirteen Turkish cities two days earlier because of widespread violence.

Nevertheless, Turkey's economic situation continued to worsen during 1978. The government devalued the Turkish lira by about 30 percent in March, but the balance of payments situation remained critical. Turkey's 1977 inflation rate of 36.6 percent, the highest in the twenty-four-nation Organization for Economic Cooperation and Development, continued to rise and was estimated to be running about 70 percent by the end of 1978. The government's efforts to deal with Turkey's social problems were also aggravated by an unemployment rate that reached over 20 percent.

The Ecevit government seemed to have little more success than its predecessor in curbing political and religious violence. In December fierce rioting broke out in the city of Maraş between Turkey's dominant Sunni Muslims and the minority Shi'ite Muslims, known in Turkey as Alevis. At least 134 persons were killed and more than 1000 injured in the Maraş fighting, bringing the death toll from religious violence in Turkey to over 1000 for 1978. The Turkish parliament on Dec. 26 endorsed Ecevit's imposition of martial law on thirteen major cities, but the government's handling of the disturbances brought calls from Demirel for Ecevit's resignation. As a result, for Turkey 1978 ended in the same atmosphere of political crisis with which it had begun.

Foreign Relations. Despite Turkey's domestic problems, Ecevit forged ahead with his plan to give top priority during 1978 to foreign affairs. Ecevit, who was premier in 1974 during the Turkish invasion of Cyprus, vowed on taking office to make a major effort to improve relations with Greece. On March 9 he ordered the easing of restrictions on the 15,000 ethnic Greeks living in Turkey. On March 10 he journeyed to Montreux, Switzerland, for a summit meeting with Greek Premier Constantine Karamanlis. Although the summit failed to produce any quick solution of the Cyprus dispute, the U.S. Congress at the end of July voted to end the arms embargo that it had clamped on Turkey in 1974 in reprisal for the Cyprus invasion. *See* CYPRUS.

The U.S. bid to Ecevit may also have been prompted at least in part by concern over the Turkish leader's visit in June to Moscow, where he signed nonaggression, trade, and cultural agreements with representatives of the Soviet Union. Ecevit emphasized that the document would not weaken Turkey's ties with the North Atlantic Treaty Organization, but noted pointedly on a number of occasions that Turkey's value to NATO had been greatly diminished by the U.S. arms embargo. On Sept. 26, U.S. President Jimmy Carter formally lifted the embargo, and on Oct. 4 Turkey announced that it had decided to permit the United States to reopen four strategic intelligence installations used for monitoring Soviet military activities. The Turks had closed the bases in 1975 as a result of the arms embargo.

See STATISTICS OF THE WORLD.   M.R.B.

TUVALU. *See* STATISTICS OF THE WORLD. *See also* COMMONWEALTH OF NATIONS.

U

UGANDA. Growing resistance to President Idi Amin within Uganda's armed forces during 1978 appeared to spark a border war with Tanzania and to mark a new phase in Amin's increasingly erratic rule.

Early in 1978, Amin publicly criticized senior army officers for smuggling coffee into Kenya and for general corruption. Senior officials of the State Research Bureau, Amin's personal secret police, were reassigned, dismissed, or arrested. In the past, similar actions had been disregarded, indeed, condoned in exchange for support of Amin's regime. In April and May, Amin shook up his cabinet, charging corruption and embezzlement. In the process, the president assumed personal responsibility for four important cabinet posts, including foreign affairs. He also established a Uganda news agency in order, he said, "to counter malicious propaganda against Uganda."

After Palestinians and Sudanese Nubians were recruited to discipline the army, mutinies and growing discontent among the officer corps were reported. Perhaps in an attempt to reunify the military, Amin launched an attack against the isolated Tanzanian border on Oct. 30; Ugandan forces penetrated as far as the Kagera River, 18 mi. inside Tanzania. By the end of November, Amin's

troops were withdrawn as Tanzanian forces began to counterattack. Border skirmishes continued through the remainder of the year. Given the haste of the Ugandan withdrawal from Tanzania, it remained unclear whether or not Amin had achieved his presumed goal of once more uniting the armed forces.

In July the United States Senate voted a mandatory ban on trade with Uganda because of its acts of "genocide." (The bill was signed into law on Oct. 10.) Amnesty International estimated that from 50,000 to 300,000 Ugandans had been killed since Amin came to power in 1971. Although the West had been deeply concerned with Amin's actions for several years, increased international attention to human rights—coming on the heels of Amin's unprovoked attack against Tanzania—began to weaken his support within the Organization of African Unity and elsewhere among the developing nations of the world.

See STATISTICS OF THE WORLD. See also AFRICA. J.T.S.

UNION OF ARAB EMIRATES. See STATISTICS OF THE WORLD.

UNION OF SOVIET SOCIALIST REPUBLICS. The Soviet Union's elderly leaders sought to maintain internal stability in 1978 by achieving economic progress and suppressing domestic critics. Internationally, the U.S.S.R. challenged the United States for influence around the world.

Politics. Although he was aging and in ill health, President Leonid Brezhnev continued to be "first among equals" on the Politburo, the Communist Party's highest decision-making body. If anything, Brezhnev's power and influence increased during 1978, especially after the sudden death on July 16 of Politburo member Fyodor Kulakov at the age of 60. Kulakov had been considered a possible successor to Brezhnev, and his death caused the leadership to make changes in top-echelon jobs. At a meeting of the party Central Committee in November, Konstantin Chernenko was promoted to full Politburo membership. First Deputy Premier Kirill Mazurov was dropped from the Politburo, ostensibly for "health reasons." First Deputy Premier Nikolai Tikhonov, 73, and Eduard Shevarnadze, 50, Soviet Georgia party leader, became alternate (nonvoting) Politburo members.

Some Western analysts believed that Brezhnev was positioning Chernenko as his heir. Chernenko had worked closely with Brezhnev since

---

Turtle in the Soup

"Totally untrue, baseless, and nonsensical" screamed a headline in the newspaper *Voice of Uganda* one hot day in August. "Big Daddy" Idi Amin, Uganda's formidable chief of state, had already threatened to shoot anyone spreading the story. And government officials, police, security forces, and local tribal chiefs had held crisis meetings to discuss it. The subject of all this excitement? An "enfundu," a tortoise that thousands of Ugandans believed was on the loose near Kampala, the capital city, not only walking but talking out loud. This story has no ending, except that there were no reports on what the creature had actually said—only that it was "stirring up trouble" for Big Daddy.

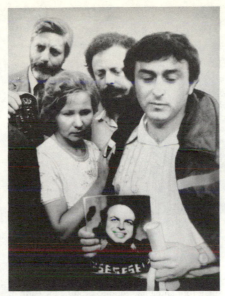

Outside a Moscow courthouse on July 14, Leonid Shcharansky holds a photograph of his brother, Anatoly Shcharansky. The court had just given the Jewish activist a thirteen-year sentence for high treason.

1950, and in 1978 he served as the Soviet president's personal aide. At 67, he was the youngest man to be both a full member of the Politburo and a high-ranking party secretary.

Dissent. The Soviet government pressed its campaign to stamp out political dissent. Members of a small group of activists who attempted to monitor the Soviet human rights record were the target of government repression. One member of this group, physicist Yuri Orlov, was sentenced in May to seven years in a labor camp and five years of domestic exile. In July writer Aleksandr Ginzburg was sentenced to eight years in a harsh "special regime" camp. Ginzburg had administered a fund established by exiled author Aleksandr Solzhenitsyn to help the families of political prisoners. Also in July, Jewish activist Anatoly Shcharansky was convicted of treason and sentenced to thirteen years' imprisonment and hard labor. In August, Aleksandr Podrabinek was given five years' internal exile for collecting and publicizing data on how the Soviet government was using incarceration in insane asylums to punish political dissidents. All these trials were condemned by democratic governments and international human rights organizations throughout the world.

Russian authorities also took steps to punish three dissidents they had allowed to leave the country. In early March the Soviet government stripped Maj. Gen. Pyotr Grigorenko of his citizenship while he was visiting the U.S. for medical treatment. Several days later, renowned cellist and conductor Mstislav Rostropovich and his wife, soprano Galina Vishnevskaya, were also deprived of Soviet citizenship; the couple had been living in the West since 1974.

The Economy. The Soviet grain harvest in 1978 was the largest ever—235,000,000 tons. But economic problems continued to preoccupy the leadership. At the November Central Committee session, Brezhnev delivered a harsh critique of the nation's economic performance. He lashed out at poor management and low productivity. He also called attention to the increasing volume of incomplete construction.

At a parliamentary session that same week, economic planning chief Nikolai Baibakov gave a more detailed report. National income rose 5 percent in 1978, he said, and industrial production also increased about 5 percent. Oil output in 1978 was estimated at 572,500,000 tons and coal at 729,000,000 tons. But while the U.S.S.R. was registering gains, it was falling behind its five-year-plan targets.

Cosmonauts Aleksei Gubarev (top), a Russian, and Vladimir Remek, a Czech, wave good-bye before the March 2 launching of their Soyuz 28 spacecraft. Remek was the first space traveler who was neither Russian nor American.

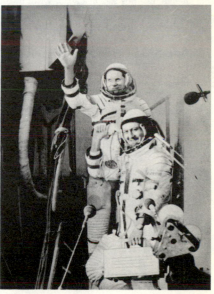

Soviet leader Leonid Brezhnev welcomes Afghan Prime Minister Noor Mohammad Taraki to Moscow in December. The installation of a new left-wing government in Afghanistan represented an important triumph for Brezhnev's foreign policy.

The government announced that the 1979 defense budget would be about $26 billion, the same as in 1978. However, Western intelligence sources said this figure represented only one fourth of actual Russian military spending. Most arms costs, they maintained, were concealed in nonmilitary portions of the budget.

Space Program. An errant Soviet space satellite carrying a nuclear reactor disintegrated over northern Canada in January. The event was the first nuclear-related crisis in space, and it set off an emergency search for radioactive debris. U.S. and Canadian technicians located the remains of the satellite, Cosmos 954, in Canada's Northwest Territories.

In March two Soviet cosmonauts, Lt. Col. Yuri

Moscow correspondents Harold Piper (left) of the Baltimore Sun and Craig R. Whitney of the New York Times. On July 15 the two reporters were found guilty of "crudely" slandering Soviet television in reports they had filed on dissent within the U.S.S.R.

Romanenko and Georgi Grechko, returned to earth after spending a record-breaking ninety-six days in space. Their feat was soon surpassed by another pair of Soviet spacemen, however. Col. Vladimir Kovalenok and Aleksandr Ivanchenkov spent four and a half months orbiting the earth in the Salyut 6 space station, returning safely to the U.S.S.R. on Nov. 2.

As a goodwill gesture to other Soviet bloc nations, the Russians launched cosmonauts from Czechoslovakia, Poland, and East Germany into space during 1978.

See SPACE EXPLORATION.

Foreign Affairs. Seeking to increase its influence around the globe, the Soviet Union scored some notable successes in 1978. In April the Cuban government pledged that it would continue to back Soviet aims in Africa with armed support. Throughout 1978, Cubans and Russians worked together to help black guerrillas against the white regimes of Rhodesia and South Africa. The U.S.S.R. and Cuba also cooperated to help the Ethiopian government battle rebel secessionists. In November, Ethiopian leader Lt. Col. Mengistu Haile Mariam journeyed to Moscow and signed a twenty-year treaty of friendship and cooperation with the Soviets.

In addition, the U.S.S.R. established closer ties with Vietnam and Afghanistan. Concerned about the power of China, Vietnam sought Soviet help, especially for its military campaign against Cambodia, China's ally. Vietnam and the U.S.S.R. signed a twenty-five-year military pact in November. The following month, Moscow reached a twenty-year friendship accord with Afghanistan, where a pro-Soviet regime had been established earlier in the year.

Moscow was greatly disturbed by the People's

Republic of China's campaign to play a more active diplomatic role and to sign up partners for an ambitious domestic modernization program. Tensions between the two nations ran so high that a border clash took place in May. The Soviets officially protested a friendship treaty signed by China and Japan in August, and sharply criticized Premier Hua Kuo-feng's visit to Rumania and Yugoslavia that same month. To counter China, the U.S.S.R. tried to win Warsaw Pact backing for higher arms spending, only to run into Rumanian resistance. The Soviets also registered their displeasure when the U.S. and China announced in December that they would establish full diplomatic relations.

Relations with the U.S. followed a rocky road in 1978. The U.S. government was disturbed by the Soviet presence in Africa and Afghanistan, as well as by the African policy of Cuba, a Soviet ally. The Russian human rights record also came in for criticism from U.S. President Jimmy Carter and other top U.S. officials. Matters were further complicated by Soviet harassment of American journalists and of a prominent American businessman living in Moscow. Two U.S. reporters, Craig Whitney of the New York *Times* and Harold Piper of the Baltimore *Sun,* were fined by Soviet authorities in August for allegedly slandering Soviet television in their articles on Soviet dissidents. Francis Crawford, a representative of the International Harvester Co., was arrested by Soviet police for alleged currency violations; in September he received a five-year suspended sentence and was allowed to leave the U.S.S.R.

Despite these problems, both the U.S. and the Soviet Union gave high priority to the SALT talks and a possible strategic-arms-limitation pact. U.S. Secretary of State Cyrus Vance and Soviet Foreign Minister Andrei Gromyko met on several occasions to hammer out the final details, but no treaty was concluded by the end of the year.

Deaths. Among the prominent Russian-born individuals who died in 1978 were the ballerina Tamara Karsavina, composer Aram Khachaturian, statesman Anastas Mikoyan, and Archbishop Metropolitan Nikodim; *see* OBITUARIES. Mstislav Keldysh, a Latvian-born mathematician who was a pioneer in the Soviet space program, also died in 1978 (June 24 at 67).

See STATISTICS OF THE WORLD.   F.W.

UNITED NATIONS, THE, abbreviated U.N. The year 1978 turned out to be a disappointing one for the world organization. The problems of southern Africa were no closer to solution at the end of 1978 than at the beginning, and the intense Middle East negotiations were conducted outside the U.N. framework.

The perennial problem of Cyprus also eluded solution, despite the efforts of Secretary-General Kurt Waldheim to revitalize the talks between the Greek and Turkish Cypriot communities. The mandate of UNFICYP, the U.N. peace force on the island, was twice renewed, each time for six months.

The U.N. was unable to stop a dangerous new Indochina conflict. In early November the United States complained in a letter to Security Council members not only of "the massive abuse of human rights" in Cambodia but also of "the continuing conflict" between the armed forces of Cambodia and Vietnam and the "possibility of escalation." Cambodian Foreign Minister Ieng Sary, denying the charges of genocide but worried about Vietnamese intentions, invited Secretary-General Waldheim to visit his country.

The U.N. played an advisory role on events in the Western Hemisphere. Costa Rica and other Central American countries affected by the domestic upheaval in Nicaragua alerted both the General Assembly and the Security Council to the dangers of continued rule by President Anastasio Somoza Debayle. In July the Canadians told the General Assembly's Committee on the Peaceful Uses of Outer Space that the cost of cleaning up the radioactive debris left behind when a Cosmos 954 satellite disintegrated over the arctic wilderness amounted to $12,000,000, which they in-

Palestinian guerrillas meet U.N. troops arriving at Tyre in southern Lebanon in late March. Fighting in the region continued throughout most of 1978, despite the presence of the U.N. peacekeeping force.

Actor Paul Newman plays one of the most important roles of his distinguished career in June: U.S. representative to a special U.N. General Assembly session on disarmament. Next to him is Marjorie Craig Benton of Evanston, Ill., an alternate U.S. delegate.

tended to recover from the Soviet Union.

The defection of Under Secretary-General Arkady N. Shevchenko affected U.N. leadership. Shevchenko, the highest-ranking Russian at the U.N., renounced his Soviet citizenship and defected to the U.S. in April. He was forced to resign his U.N. post. In March, Secretary-General Waldheim filled the world body's second most important post by naming Kenneth Dadzie, a Ghanaian diplomat, as director-general for economic development.

Admission of the Solomon Islands and Dominica raised U.N. membership to 151 by the end of the year.

Southern Africa. On the issue of South-West Africa (Namibia), foreign ministers of the U.S., Great Britain, France, West Germany, and Canada submitted proposals in March for the peaceful transfer of power from white to black leadership under U.N. supervision. At first, both South Africa and the main black guerrilla group, the South-West Africa People's Organization (SWAPO), accepted the plan with reservations. But the plan foundered later over South Africa's objections to imple-

mentation proposals made by the secretary-general's special representative for Namibia, Martti Ahtisaari of Finland. Subsequently, South Africa announced that it would conduct elections in the territory. These elections were declared "null and void" by the Security Council on Sept. 29. Nevertheless, the balloting took place in December, despite a threat of sanctions passed by the Security Council on Nov. 13.

Regarding Rhodesia (Zimbabwe), the Security Council faced similar problems. In March the white-ruled regime of Ian Smith agreed to establish a new biracial government. However, this "internal solution" did not comply with the so-called Afro-American plan of transition, which required the participation of both internal and external (guerrilla) forces. The Security Council, on March 14, declared the internal solution "illegal and unacceptable" in a vote of 10-0, with 5 (Western) abstentions. The year ended without any progress toward a U.N.-endorsed settlement.

Meanwhile, the Security Council met repeatedly to discuss the escalating war between the Smith regime and Patriotic Front guerrillas. On Oct. 10 the council recorded its "regret" over the issuance of a visa to Smith permitting him to visit the U.S. The vote was 11-0, with France in favor; the U.S., Britain, West Germany, and Canada abstained.

Middle East. Although Secretary-General Waldheim was kept informed of progress toward an Israeli-Egyptian peace treaty, the Camp David (Md.) negotiations among Israeli Prime Minister Menachem Begin, Egyptian President Anwar el-Sadat, and U.S. President Jimmy Carter were conducted entirely outside the world organization. This trilateral action resulted in the passage of a number of protest resolutions in the General Assembly by great majorities, responding to the complaints of those Arab states that were excluded from the negotiating process. On Nov. 29 the U.N. marked an International Day of Solidarity with the Palestinian People; most Western countries boycotted the project, which included films, photo exhibits, speeches, and declarations, and was undertaken at the initiative of the Palestine Liberation Organization.

U.N. assistance was invoked in the wake of the Israeli invasion of southern Lebanon early in 1978. On March 19 the Security Council set up a new U.N. peacekeeping operation called UNIFIL (U.N. Interim Force in Lebanon), with an authorized troop strength of 6000 troops. (The vote was 12–0, with the U.S.S.R. and Czechoslovakia abstaining and the People's Republic of China not participating.) The U.N. force did secure Israel's withdrawal, but UNIFIL was unable to attain its other objective: the restoration of Lebanon's "effective control" over the area. One reason for the failure was the continued resistance of the Lebanese Christian forces, supplied and supported by Israel. UNIFIL's mandate was extended for another four months on Sept. 18.

The mandates of the U.N. peacekeeping detachments in the Sinai and the Golan Heights were twice extended during 1978 by the agreement of Israel, Egypt, and Syria.

Conferences. Several important special sessions and conferences were held in 1978. Outstanding was the special session on disarmament, held by the General Assembly from May 23 to June 30 in New York City. Four heads of state, 16 prime ministers or vice-presidents, and 49 foreign ministers participated in the session, which passed a declaration and a program of action. The session also opened the Committee on Disarmament to French participation.

The Third U.N. Conference on the Law of the Sea held two sessions in 1978, in the spring in Geneva and in late summer in New York. Neither session produced any agreement on access to marine resources, and another session was scheduled for Geneva in the spring of 1979.

A more successful conference, held in Buenos Aires from Aug. 30 to Sept. 12, dealt with technical cooperation among developing countries. This

A health worker in a UNICEF-aided nursing service weighs a baby at a Solomon Islands clinic. The South Pacific nation, independent since July, became a U.N. member in September.

"TCDC Conference" established a new machinery for closer future cooperation on technological questions.

The General Conference of the U.N. Educational, Scientific, and Cultural Organization (UNESCO), held in Paris in November, was of particular interest to the Western news media. After lengthy debate, the conference ended with a declaration of principles designed to govern the behavior of the media toward the developing countries. Passages recommending state control of the flow of information to and from developing countries were dropped during negotiations.

Associated Activities. The Executive Board of the U.N. International Children's Fund (UNICEF) approved a budget of $226,000,000; the World Health Organization (WHO) passed an aid budget of $183,000,000; and the U.N. Development Program provided for new initiatives costing $322,500,000.

On a less positive note, the U.N. Special Fund, set up in 1974 to help the poorest nations overcome the effects of oil price increases, had to suspend its work on June 22, because contributions had run out.   L.H.

UNITED STATES OF AMERICA

Mass deaths in Jonestown, assassinations in San Francisco, nearly completed strategic arms limitation and Israeli-Egyptian treaties, recognition of Communist China and abandonment of Taiwan, the financial default of the city of Cleveland, the passage of Proposition 13—and through it all, the President's popularity rose and fell like a yo-yo.

For the United States, the year 1978 began with violent storms, a coal miners' strike, unrest among financially pressed farmers, and widespread dissatisfaction with the achievements of President Jimmy Carter. But by June, the miners were back at work, the farmers were harvesting record crops, and Carter had gained a major triumph with Senate ratification of two treaties turning over control of the Panama Canal to Panama by the year 2000. Over the summer, a nationwide movement to cut property taxes gained momentum. The issues of taxes, government spending, and inflation—all of them too high for the voters' comfort—were paramount in the November congressional elections. Democrats, many of them sounding like Republicans in their fiscal conservatism, maintained their majorities in Congress with small losses.

The President himself, although not on the ballot, improved his standing in opinion polls with his September success in getting Egypt and Israel to agree on the outlines of a peace treaty. In actions taken just before the elections, Carter tried to halt inflation and support the slumping dollar in foreign currency markets. And in December he unexpectedly announced the forthcoming establishment of full diplomatic relations with the People's Republic of China. As the year ended, the nation's leaders appeared to be cautious about undertaking new reforms, resigned to a business recession, and fearful of a heightening of the arms race with the Soviet Union. Most Americans hoped only to secure their jobs, savings, and future, and left heroism to another age. If prophets like Soviet expatriate author Aleksandr I. Solzhenitsyn, speaking at Harvard University in June, were heralding "a major turn in history, equal in importance to the turn from the Middle Ages to the Renaissance," the person on the street wanted to know the cost of that turn and would have voted against it in a referendum.

NATIONAL LIFE

In the absence of a national debate, national complaining took the fore, and the favorite topics of 1978 were inflation and taxation. Special interest groups, notably labor and agriculture (qq.v.), had more specific grievances. And conservative, middle-class Americans, perhaps the most indignant group of all in 1978, gained attention and representation in such single-issue movements as the taxpayers' revolt and the antiabortion "right-to-life" cause.

Inflation and Taxation. The rate of inflation hovered around 9 percent, with food prices leading other consumer items at more than 11 percent. On Oct. 24, President Carter went on national television to plead for compliance with a set of voluntary wage and price limits. His anti-inflation plan also called for federal deficit-cutting and spending reductions. A week later the President got the Federal Reserve Bank to raise its interest rates and thus restrain bank lending and reduce the money supply. The dollar responded to these and other measures by ending its yearlong decline in foreign currency markets; stability of the dollar would help stem the rising prices of imports. But the overall problem of inflation, said skeptical economists, was likely to be intractable, and the situation was not helped when the Organization of Petroleum Exporting Countries announced in mid-December that oil prices would rise 14.5 percent by the end of 1979.

Taxation, being a variable function of government, proved more subject to adjustment. A bill passed by Congress in October provided for an $18.7 billion reduction in federal taxes. This was $6 billion less than Carter had requested in January, and about 79 percent of the relief went to the wealthier half of U.S. taxpayers. Most citizens, however, could expect a 6 percent cut in their 1979 taxes—barely enough to offset rises due to inflation and increased social security payments.

High property taxes were the target of a nationwide campaign of homeowners and businessmen. It all started in California, where voters passed Proposition 13 in June. The proposition's limitation on taxes on real property to 1 percent of its

Mr. Tax Revolt

"Never quit," admonished Howard Jarvis in the best try, try again tradition. The 76-year-old retired businessman had indeed tried four times to place tax-cut proposals on the California ballot. Finally Jarvis and his friends collected 1,500,000 signatures to sponsor what became famous as Proposition 13. And in June, California's outraged taxpayers voted nearly 2 to 1 in favor of slashing property taxes by 57 percent. Although the long-term effects of Proposition 13 remained murky, Jarvis expanded his crusade, appearing on national TV and flying 200,000 miles on coast-to-coast speaking tours. Nor did his campaign stop at the water's edge. At year's end he was carrying his message to Great Britain and France.

Howard Jarvis, man of outrage.

assessed value effectively cut California property taxes by 57 percent. The sudden loss of local revenue amounted to about $7 billion, with two thirds of the savings going not to homeowners but to owners of businesses and farmland. Disruptions in school systems and other services were prevented, or at least delayed, by the dispensing of a large state tax surplus. In November many other states adopted similarly drastic property-tax cuts and spending limits; *see* ELECTIONS.

Troubled Cities. The nation's older large cities continued to suffer financial weakness and losses of population and jobs. New York City, where some degree of confidence in municipal government was restored by Mayor Edward I. Koch, still operated with precarious financing. Federal loan guarantees, passed by Congress in July, staved off bankruptcy once again. New Yorkers had to do without their three major newspapers for several months beginning in August because of a strike by press workers. The shortage of reliable news contributed to outbreaks of panic in September, when legionnaires' disease—in one of several flare-ups across the nation—claimed two lives in the city's Garment District. Hundreds more were afraid they had the disease, which in mid-Novem-

Warning the U.S.—and, indeed, all of the West—of a notably widespread "decline in courage," Aleksandr I. Solzhenitsyn delivers the commencement address at Harvard University June 8. The exiled Soviet author-prophet had received an honorary degree earlier in the day.

More than 25,000 San Franciscans came together in City Hall Park in a spontaneous demonstration of grief Nov. 27. Their mayor, George Moscone, and County Supervisor Harvey Milk had been shot to death that morning.

ber finally received a scientific name: Legionella pneumophila.

Cleveland tottered constantly nearer to the verge of fiscal catastrophe and suffered from a cri-

sis of leadership as well. Its embattled young mayor, Dennis J. Kucinich, survived a recall election in August by a mere 236 votes. But he remained at loggerheads with Cleveland business leaders and the city council, which refused to work with him, and the city finally went into default on Dec. 15 when it failed to repay $15,500,000 in loans. It was the first time since the Great Depression of the 1930's that a major American city had defaulted. Major layoffs of city workers were announced,

Troubleshooter

White House organizational charts may have listed Robert Strauss, 59, as special representative for trade negotiations, but that hardly told all of it. In reality he was the Carter administration's all-purpose troubleshooter whose proven persuasiveness was applied during the year to wide-ranging issues from the Panama Canal treaties to the coal strike, from administration efforts to confirm a new Federal Reserve chairman to temporary duty as anti-inflation czar. Strauss, a lawyer-businessman and self-made millionaire from Texas, served as Democratic Party chairman from 1972 to 1976. During that time he took a badly split party and forged a unity that helped carry Jimmy Carter into the White House. Strauss's favorite motto: "It *can* be done."

Administrator-adviser Robert Strauss.

then partially retracted when one bank said it was willing to wait for its money, but the situation was unresolved as the year ended.

Memphis underwent a nightmarish week in mid-August. As thousands of tourists arrived to observe the anniversary of the death of singer Elvis Presley, first the city's policemen, then its firemen went on strike. A brief electrical blackout on the night of Aug. 16 added to the city's perils. But owing in part to patrolling National Guardsmen, arson and looting did not break out as feared, and things were back to normal by the 18th.

Just as residents of San Francisco were comprehending the horror of the People's Temple mass deaths in Guyana (see below), a fresh tragedy struck. On Nov. 27, San Francisco Mayor George Moscone and County Supervisor Harvey Milk were shot to death in their offices in City Hall. Their alleged assailant, Dan White, a 32-year-old former fireman who had tried unsuccessfully to withdraw his Nov. 10 resignation from the Board of Supervisors, surrendered to police 35 minutes after the shootings. He later entered a plea of not guilty by reason of insanity.

Cults. Groups of fervent believers devoted to a Christian minister, Hindu guru, or other powerful leader were a feature of the American religious scene in the 1970's. In November the nation was shocked by reports of mass deaths at a colony of a California-based cult in Guyana. Members of the People's Temple murdered a visiting U.S. Congressman, Rep. Leo J. Ryan (D, Calif.), and four other Americans. Then, by order of their leader, the Reverend Jim Jones, 911 of the cultists were killed or took their own lives by drinking a poisonous liquid. Amid criticism of the State Department for not having foreseen or prevented the tragedy, U.S. troops were sent to airlift the bodies to Dover Air Force Base in Delaware and help to identify them. The operation cost the federal government at least $3,500,000. *See also* GUYANA; RELIGION.

The People's Temple had begun as an idealistic sect and ended as an autocratic cult. Many observers saw a similar corruption at work in Synanon, a communal drug-rehabilitation group founded in 1958 by former salesman Charles Dederich. According to former members, Dederich had grown increasingly dictatorial and hostile to criticism and defection over the years. On Oct. 10, Paul Morantz, a lawyer who had won a court suit charging Synanon with kidnapping and false imprisonment, was bitten by a rattlesnake placed in his Los Angeles mailbox. He recovered. Members of Synanon, including Dederich, were arrested for conspiracy to commit murder.

Severe Weather. The nation's economy and mo-

bility were temporarily crippled by a series of destructive winter storms. First, a blizzard centering on Ohio dumped as much as 80 cm (31 in.) of snow on the Midwest on Jan. 25–26. New York City was still digging out from a Jan. 20 fall of 35 cm (14 in.) when the worst snowstorm in New England history struck on Feb. 5. To the delight of schoolchildren, Boston got 69 cm (27 in.), and a thirty-year high of 45 cm (18 in.) fell on New York City.

Across the continent, heavy rains were putting a violent end to a prolonged drought in California. Three rainfalls in the week ending Feb. 10 caused flooding and mud slides that drowned twenty southern Californians and damaged hundreds of hillside homes. A month later, another heavy rainstorm brought further destructive mud slides.

In July northern Texas suffered a long drought and heat wave. After eighteen consecutive days of temperatures above 38° C. (100° F.), some areas got cruel relief in the form of torrential August rains with flash floods.

Sports and Leisure. The devalued dollar and a sluggish economy did not keep Americans from enjoying ambitious vacations. Airline fares, made more competitive by eased federal regulations, took a nose dive. Round-trip transatlantic tickets could be bought for less than $200, and domestic fares were also reduced. The result was a 16 percent increase in passengers over the summer of

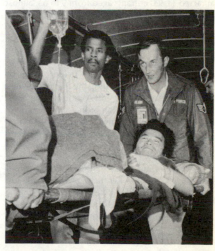

Wounded NBC soundman Steven Sung is carried to a hospital at Andrews Air Force Base, Md., on Nov. 19. Sung was among those attacked near Jonestown, Guyana, allegedly by members of the Reverend Jim Jones's People's Temple cult.

Valdik Enger (left) and a Soviet embassy representative enjoy a respite from Enger's espionage trial at the federal court in Newark on Sept. 29. Enger and another Soviet citizen, Rudolf Chernyayev, were later convicted and each was sentenced to fifty years in prison.

1977. On one July weekend more than 3,000,000 Americans took to the air. Flight paths and airports were dangerously overloaded at peak hours. A dreaded outcome foreseen by many harried traffic controllers occurred on Sept. 25. In the worst air disaster in U.S. history, a jet airliner crashed after being struck by a small plane near San Diego. All 135 people in the planes and at least 13 more on the ground were killed.

Running began to rival swimming and other sports in popularity among Americans in 1978. The New York City Marathon, held on Oct. 22, attracted 11,400 entrants aged from 9 to 63, almost half of them running the 26.2-mi. event for the first time. Police estimated that up to 2,000,000 spectators lined the route. Many had just been spectators, via television, at the baseball World Series, won by the New York Yankees over the Los Angeles Dodgers. The Yankees made history by winning the Series after losing the first two games. In two other televised events, World Boxing Association heavyweight champion Muhammad Ali lost his title to Leon Spinks in a split decision on Feb. 15 and regained it from Spinks in a unanimous decision on Sept. 15. Ali thus became the first person to win the crown three times. Another triple-crown winner was Affirmed, the horse ridden to victory in the Kentucky Derby, Preakness, and Belmont Stakes by jockey Steve Cauthen.

After a long run—or a turn on the newly popular roller skates—the fashionable sportsman of 1978 might steep with his neighbors in a "hot tub," a heated wooden water tank often equipped with seats and whirlpool devices. It was a scene worthy of the brush of illustrator Norman Rockwell, the veteran observer of Americans at leisure who died in November; see OBITUARIES.

GOVERNMENT

In Washington, D.C., the year was marked by a slow improvement in appraisals of President Carter's performance as treaties with Panama were ratified, formal recognition of the People's Republic of China was announced, and other foreign policy and legislative successes were achieved. The U.S. Congress passed a milestone in January with the death of one of its most illustrious members, Sen. Hubert H. Humphrey of Minnesota (see OBITUARIES). Congress went on to sift through much proposed legislation, ending up by passing an energy policy bill and 188 other measures in its last week in October. It also found time in the final rush to restore citizenship to Confederate President Jefferson Davis.

The President and Congress. In his State of the Union address on Jan. 19, the President pronounced the nation "sound." He then proposed a fiscal-1979 budget totaling $500 billion, with few increases beyond those caused in existing programs by inflation. Congress ended up approving outlays of $488 billion. The Senate and House of Representatives balked at much legislation sponsored by the White House, but finally cleared an energy bill—Carter's top legislative priority—in the last hours of the session. This set of taxes and other incentives for reducing the consumption of imported oil gave Carter about half of what he had asked for in 1977 when he called for a "moral equivalent of war" on the energy problem.

Carter also trimmed his original proposals to achieve passage of the $18.7 billion tax-cut bill. In 1978 he showed more willingness to compromise and to negotiate with Congress, and also to defy it. He vetoed four bills during the session without being overridden. Carter's legislative success was due partly to his increasing espousal of fiscal conservatism, which won over Republican Congressmen and was paralleled by national trends evident in the November elections. "We've got a Democratic President singing a Republican song," remarked Sen. Howard H. Baker, Jr. (R, Tenn.). *See also* CONGRESS OF THE UNITED STATES; PRESIDENT OF THE UNITED STATES.

The Panama Canal Treaties. After weeks of lengthy debate, part of it broadcast live on radio, the Senate ratified two treaties with Panama in March and April. The first treaty guaranteed the neutrality of the Panama Canal after Dec. 31, 1999, and stipulated the right of the U.S. to send in troops to keep it open. The second treaty provided for turning over control of the canal to Panama by Dec. 31, 1999. The Senators voted identically on the two crucial roll calls: 68—one more than the two thirds necessary—in favor of ratification, and 32 against.

Constitutional Amendments. Congress gave a boost to the women's rights movement in October by approving a thirty-nine-month extension of the deadline for ratification of the Equal Rights Amendment (ERA). No states ratified the ERA during the year, however. To make it part of the U.S. Constitution, 3 more states, or a total of 38, would have to approve it by June 30, 1982.

Another constitutional amendment, passed by Congress in August, was designed to grant full congressional representation to the District of Columbia. In 1978 the district was larger in population than seven states, but was represented only by a nonvoting delegate in the House. If ratified, the amendment would give the district two Senators and one or two Representatives. New Jersey became the first state to approve it on Sept. 11.

Investigations and Scandals. Results of Justice Department and House ethics committee investigations into South Korean bribery of U.S. legislators made smaller headlines than predicted. No sitting Congressmen were indicted, and the attempt to corrupt and influence the U.S. government during the early 1970's was judged to have been largely a failure. Congressional probes of the assassinations of President John F. Kennedy and civil rights leader Martin Luther King, Jr., produced suggestions that there may have been conspiracies leading to both crimes. The assassinations committee was critical of the efforts of earlier investigators. A number of scandals concerning financial misconduct touched individual Congressmen; *see* CRIME AND LAW ENFORCEMENT.

An incident that came to light in January caused embarrassment and threatened scandal for the Carter administration. David W. Marston, a Republican, was removed as a U.S. attorney in Philadelphia by the Justice Department. It turned out that Marston had been investigating Pennsylvania Democrats, one of whom, Rep. Joshua Eilberg, had phoned Carter in November, 1977, with a request to speed Marston's dismissal. Carter insisted that he had been unaware that Eilberg was under investigation. Despite favorable publicity, Marston came in fourth in a Republican Pennsylvania gubernatorial primary in May. Eilberg was indicted on conflict-of-interest charges in October.

The General Services Administration (GSA),

After bitter debate, the Senate Foreign Relations Committee votes on May 11 on the sale of advanced fighter planes to Egypt, Israel, and Saudi Arabia: Clifford Case (left), New Jersey Republican, and Frank Church (right), Idaho Democrat, vote against the sale; John Sparkman (center), Alabama Democrat, is in favor of it.

which annually dispensed a $5 billion budget providing offices and supplies for the federal government, was accused of massive fraud and mismanagement during the summer. Eighteen persons, including twelve present and former GSA officials, were indicted in September, and hundreds more cases were reportedly being prepared.

Defense. Despite his 1976 campaign promises to cut defense spending, Carter asked for an increased defense budget of $119.3 billion for fiscal 1979. Congress granted an amount just under that. In accordance with agreements among the Western allies to strengthen their forces against a recent Soviet bloc arms buildup, Carter pledged a further 3 percent increase above the inflation-caused rise for fiscal 1980. He was expected to ask for a $10 billion increase. However, some of the President's executive decisions showed skepticism about expensive new weapons systems. He first deferred production of the neutron bomb, a high-radiation explosive designed to kill people but spare equipment and structures, then in October he approved the production of some key components of the weapon. He opposed construction of a $2 billion nuclear aircraft carrier and vetoed a military procurement bill authorizing funds for it.

Pentagon officials and political conservatives warned that the Soviet Union was pulling ahead in the arms race and might soon be in a position to threaten war to gain political ends; see MILITARY AND NAVAL AFFAIRS. At the close of the year, the Defense Department announced plans for a new civil defense program and measures for improving the U.S. capacity to wage limited nuclear wars.

FOREIGN AFFAIRS

It was a year of alarming deterioration in relations with the Soviet Union and successful diplomacy in the Middle East. Full diplomatic recognition of China was announced in December. Relations with the European allies were uneventful, although some Europeans called President Carter's leadership clumsy and unsure. At a seven-nation economic summit in West Germany in July, Carter pledged efforts to cut U.S. oil imports and reduce inflation. Elsewhere, as in Iran, the U.S. generally expressed support for established governments threatened by unrest or instability.

U.S.-Soviet Relations. The two superpowers traded denunciations, expulsions, and spying charges throughout much of the year in what appeared to be a virtual resumption of the cold war. Negotiations for a second strategic arms limitation treaty (SALT II) made slow progress.

In January, Carter warned the Soviets against involvement in the war between Ethiopia and Somalia over the eastern Ethiopian region of Oga-

den. The U.S.S.R., smarting over U.S. criticism of its human rights violations, expelled several U.S. diplomats, and Washington retaliated in kind. Relations took a sharper turn for the worse in May when two Soviet citizens, Valdik Enger and Rudolf Chernyayev, were arrested in New Jersey on spying charges. Their public arraignment and trial angered the Russians, who responded in June by seizing an American businessman, Francis Jay Crawford, and imprisoning him in Moscow for currency violations. During a summer of tension for Americans posted in the Soviet Union, two American tourist guides were expelled, two Moscow-based American reporters were tried and convicted of slander, and U.S. embassy employees were harassed. The July conviction for treason of Soviet dissident leader Anatoly Shcharansky and U.S. protests against his thirteen-year sentence further worsened relations. Official visits, cultural exchanges, and trade agreements were canceled.

The autumn brought a muting of voices. The Soviets released Crawford in September; Enger and Chernyayev were convicted of espionage and sentenced to fifty years each in October, but freed pending appeal or exchange. In December trade talks between the two nations were held as scheduled in Moscow. Meanwhile, Carter announced at a September news conference that the issues dividing the two sides in the SALT talks were now "quite few." A pact was reportedly all but agreed upon by the end of the year.

China. On Dec. 15, President Carter in a surprise move announced that the U.S. and the People's Republic of China would establish full diplomatic relations on Jan. 1, 1979. He also announced that Teng Hsiao-ping, who is thought to be China's real leader, would pay a visit to the U.S. early in 1979. Carter's action drew strong criticism from some Republican leaders because of the termination of diplomatic relations and of the mutual defense treaty with Taiwan, actions usually undertaken with the advice and consent of the Senate. But the Administration responded that Taiwan's security could be maintained through ties that stopped short of full recognition. Taiwan's response was official outrage, and two days of talks in late December failed to resolve any of the differences between the two countries.

The Middle East. The highpoint of the year in U.S. foreign relations occurred in September, when Carter summoned Egyptian President Anwar el-Sadat and Israeli Prime Minister Menachem Begin to a conference at the Presidential retreat at Camp David, Md. During twelve days of informal but intensive talks, Carter persuaded Sadat and Begin to sign agreements on the framework for a peace treaty. The U.S., for its part, agreed to build two

On Jan. 5, Cinda Mastgough of the Radio City Music Hall ballet troupe learns that the famous tourist attraction will close. New Yorkers rallied round, however, and found ways to keep the "showplace of the nation" open—at least through the end of the year.

air bases in southern Israel to replace bases in the Sinai to be abandoned by the Israelis. But talks between Egyptian and Israeli representatives in Washington on an actual treaty became stalemated over such issues as the date for Palestinian self-rule on the West Bank and in Gaza.

Friendship with Egypt and Saudi Arabia was promoted during the year as part of a policy to support moderate Middle Eastern regimes and thus protect U.S. oil supplies. In May the Senate approved the sale of military aircraft to Egypt and Saudi Arabia. Relations with Turkey improved when an arms embargo, imposed after the 1974 Turkish invasion of Cyprus, was lifted by Congress in August.

Africa. The U.S. refused to support the white-led coalition government of Rhodesia and called for negotiations between all parties, including black guerrillas, to end the civil war and turn over power to the black majority. Regarding the civil wars in northern and eastern Ethiopia and in Angola, the U.S. was officially neutral, but protested the presence of Cuban and Soviet advisers among

the Ethiopians and Angolans. In May the U.S. contributed eighteen transport planes to a Belgian-French operation in Zaire to rescue Europeans caught in fighting between secessionists and loyalists.

Latin America. The problem of illegal crossings along the 2000-mi. U.S.-Mexico border came to national attention in October. The Immigration and Naturalization Service, which estimated that millions of Mexicans entered illegally in 1978, announced plans to erect two 6 mi. fences along the border at El Paso, Texas, and San Ysidro, Calif. The fences' original sharp-edged mesh design, called "a serious mistake" by President Carter, was altered after protests by Mexican-Americans and other groups. The issue of the proposed fences was especially sensitive because of charges of discrimination and police abuse against Mexican-Americans in Houston and other southwestern cities; see CIVIL RIGHTS AND CIVIL LIBERTIES.

Some progress in Cuban-U.S. relations was achieved, despite the resumption of U.S. reconnaissance flights over the island to monitor the capabilities of Soviet-made MIG-23 jet fighters deployed there. Cuba began releasing political prisoners in October and promised to ease travel restrictions for Cuban exiles wishing to return for visits. The large Cuban-American community remained predominantly opposed to the regime of President Fidel Castro. In May three anti-Castro Cubans were arrested by the Federal Bureau of Investigation and accused of plotting to kill Orlando Letelier, the former Chilean ambassador to the U.S. who was murdered in Washington, D.C., in 1976.

In Nicaragua, the U.S. urged a plebiscite to determine whether President Anastasio Somoza Debayle should remain in office. Somoza's dictatorial regime was threatened by demonstrations, civil violence, and loss of popular support.

Southeast Asia and Oceania. The U.S. did not take sides in the border war between Vietnam and Cambodia. Relations with Vietnam, not yet normalized, hit a snag in January when a former U.S. Information Agency officer, Roland Humphrey, and Vietnamese student David Truong were arrested on espionage charges. Accused of passing U.S. secrets to Vietnamese agents in France, the pair were convicted by a court in Alexandria, Va., and in July were sentenced to fifteen years each in prison.

In November the U.S. agreed to admit as immigrants increased numbers of Vietnamese refugees who were crowded into ships anchored off Malaysia. Concern for the refugees—mostly ethnic Chinese—grew when two of their overloaded vessels sank with the loss of 330 lives.

Once again the residents of Bikini atoll in the U.S. Trust Territory of the Pacific Islands had to search for a homeland. The islanders had been removed from Bikini in 1946 to allow for U.S. nuclear tests. They were permitted to return to their homes in 1968. But new evidence of lingering radiation was discovered, and in September 139 Bikinians, many resentful and demoralized, were resettled on the island of Kili 500 mi. to the south.   W.M.H.

UNITED STATES OF AMERICA: THE ECONOMY. Economic activity in the United States during 1978 showed notable changes from the 1977 pattern. Although unemployment—a major concern when U.S. President Jimmy Carter first took office—diminished as an economic and political issue, the problem of inflation worsened, and interest rates rose at a pace that threatened the long-lived advance in business activity. Indeed, many economists forecast that ongoing inflation, still higher interest rates, more severe credit restraint by monetary authorities, and a retrenchment on the part of consumers would lead to an economic slowdown or recession in 1979. Nevertheless, at the end of 1978 there was still no visible weakness in the business sector.

Unemployment declined somewhat during 1978, while employment rose by record amounts. At the end of 1977 the unemployment rate was 6.4 percent of the labor force; by the end of 1978 it had declined to 5.9 percent, with some 6,000,000 workers remaining jobless. This total was still rather high for an economy that was in its fourth year of upswing. One explanation was an abnormally large growth in the labor force. During the year the labor force increased by 2,800,000. Employment rose by a very substantial 3,500,000 to almost 96,000,000.

This growth in both the labor force and employment was in part the consequence of the continuing advance in economic activity, which created a demand for new workers. At the same time, inflation and changing social trends also encouraged employment growth. Family budgets were increasingly strained by rising prices. This intensified a trend which had been evident for a quarter of a century—the shift of women from the status of homemaker to that of jobholder. By the end of the year, 41 percent of the labor force consisted of women, and half of all women over the age of 20 were in the job market. The labor force participation rate for the entire population reached a record 64 percent by the end of 1978.

BUSINESS REVIEW

In business, as in other areas of economic activity, the single most compelling problem was inflation. Contrary to most forecasts, the pace of inflation became progressively worse during 1978—a fact which led President Carter and the monetary authorities to change their policies considerably as the year wore on.

The Impact of Inflation. During 1978, consumer

A First at the "Fed"
In its sixty-five-year history, the "Fed"—Federal Reserve System—had never had a woman serve on its seven-member board of governors. That changed in September when Nancy Hays Teeters, 48, was sworn in to fill the seat vacated by former chairman Arthur F. Burns. Her pedigree: educated at Oberlin College and the University of Michigan, a practicing economist, with a prior nine-year stint on the "Fed" staff and service as chief economist for the House Budget Committee. The Indiana-born mother of three is a self-described moderate on economic matters and an unabashedly enthusiastic outdoorswoman. When her new appointment was announced by the White House in August, she and her family were on a Western vacation—rafting down the Colorado River.

Economist Nancy Teeters.

prices rose 9 percent, a substantial increase over the 6.8 percent experienced in 1977. Food prices were the fastest rising of the major items in the family budget; late in 1978, food prices were 11.6 percent higher than a year earlier. The costs of homes, household maintenance, and medical care also rose faster than average. The smallest increase was in apparel. Wholesale prices also rose at an accelerating pace, ensuring that there would be continued inflationary pressure on consumer prices in 1979.

These developments forced the Carter administration to shift its economic focus from fighting unemployment to containing inflation. At the beginning of the year, it was the goal and the expectation of the President's economic advisers that a moderate inflation rate would permit the government to encourage economic growth. Instead, the speedup in price increases altered the character of the business advance, which up to that time had been relatively well balanced.

The Administration's liberal fiscal policies, coupled with an expansion in credit, created not only the fact of inflation but also the general expectation of continued inflation well into the future. This changed consumer buying patterns in an important respect. Heretofore, sudden and large shifts in the inflation rate had turned consumers cautious. In 1978, however, the realization that inflation would likely continue for a long period induced many persons to "buy before prices rose further." People continued to buy "big-ticket items," borrowing heavily to do so. This was particularly evident in the housing market, which witnessed an extraordinary increase in prices for both new and used homes. New home construction remained at an annual rate of 2,100,000 through most of the year, a sharp departure from the usual pattern during the late phase of business recovery. Usually, high interest rates and a shortage of credit cause substantial declines in home building and in the availability of mortgage money. In mid-1978, however, at the first sign of a housing slowdown, savings institutions and commercial banks were permitted to issue six-month savings certificates keyed to the interest rates available on six-month U.S. Treasury bills. This helped these institutions to conserve and expand their holdings and allowed them to supply new funds to the housing industry.

Economic Upswing. The development of the economy proceeded in stair-step fashion, reaching near-boom conditions by the end of 1978. An extraordinarily severe winter was responsible for keeping the real growth in the economy (gross national product adjusted for price changes) almost flat in the first quarter. The economy rebounded vigorously in the second quarter, turned sluggish in the third, and sped up once more during the fall and early winter.

Factory output—one of the most dynamic sectors of the economy, although it accounts for only about one third of national output—registered good gains through most of the year. There was a substantial increase in consumer goods output, buoyed by the resurgent automobile industry. Increases in the production of business equipment were even more dramatic. Industrial production rose slightly more than 6 percent for the whole of 1978.

Inflation added to costs, but it also added considerably to incomes, thereby creating the wherewithal to keep business rolling. Compensation rose at a rate of about 9 percent during the year. This, together with the income generated by the expansion in the number of workers, was largely responsible for boosting personal income during 1978 by more than $190 billion to about $1.8 trillion. Farm income, which had declined sharply from mid-1975 to mid-1977, made a rapid recovery.

Merchandise Trade Deficit. A major negative aspect of the economy was the merchandise trade position of the U.S.—a factor which, along with inflation, was responsible for the decline of the dollar. The 1977 merchandise trade deficit of $27.6 billion contracted somewhat in 1978, but still remained at very high levels. Some reduction in the negative balance occurred in the second half of the year, as the reduced value of the dollar began to encourage exports and restrict the purchase of imports.

Productivity. Productivity, a developing problem in 1977, worsened in 1978. Output per hour rose only 1.5 percent during 1977; through the autumn of 1978, there was no increase at all, thereby contributing to inflationary pressures. Since wage compensation was rising at about 9 percent while productivity was unchanged, labor costs per unit of output rose by more than 9 percent, well above the 6.5 percent recorded in 1977.

Wage-Price Guidelines. In late October, President Carter introduced a modified wage-price program to reduce inflation gradually over a period of several years. The program was supposed to be voluntary, although the Administration let it be known that it would bring pressure on companies not acceding to the guidelines. The program called for targets of 7 percent in wage increases and 5.75 percent in price increases for industrial companies. Additionally, in order to elicit the cooperation of major unions, the Administration introduced a new concept called "real wage insurance." This concept allows a credit against federal income taxes for each point by which consumer prices exceed the target level. The proposal requires congressional approval—approval which seemed less and less likely as the year ended.

FINANCIAL REVIEW

In finance, 1978 was characterized by the creation of debt at an explosive pace. Interest rates rose throughout the year. In particular, short-term interest rates rose extraordinarily fast, in some cases exceeding the record peaks reached during 1974.

The stock market was virtually directionless. Stock prices fluctuated sharply both above and below their levels of December, 1977, but the market as a whole closed out 1978 not far from where it began.

Wall Street. The Dow-Jones average of industrial stocks closed at 805 at year-end, a decline of 3.1 percent from its beginning level. The Standard & Poor's index of 400 industrial stocks registered an increase of 2.4 percent, while the broad composite index of stocks listed on the New York Stock Exchange rose by only 2.1 percent.

Stocks of the smaller companies listed on the American Stock Exchange (ASE) exhibited both more volatility and greater gains than those of the larger American corporations. At its highest point, the ASE index was 38.3 percent higher than at the close of 1977; later the index backtracked, finishing the year with a 17.7 percent increase. A 12.3 percent rise was posted by stocks traded in the over-the-counter market.

At year-end the Dow-Jones index of thirty major industrial companies was 23.5 percent below its peak of 1051.7 (set in November, 1973), although corporate earnings were well above earlier levels. Stock-market prices were conservatively valued by historical standards. During the year the price-earnings ratio of the Dow-Jones stocks ranged from a low of 7.1 to a high of 8.6. This was the lowest valuation since the recession of 1974, and is only one third the price-earning ratio recorded in 1973 for the Dow-Jones industrials.

The Debt Explosion. The use of credit expanded rapidly in all sectors of the economy, with large government borrowing to finance the federal budget deficit accompanied by enormous borrowings of off-budget and government-backed agencies. Total loans and investments of commercial banks reached $966 billion late in 1978, an increase of more than $100 billion over the 1977 level.

Consumers went into debt by record amounts, expanding their debt obligations by $148 billion. About two thirds of the increase represented home mortgages; the balance was consumer credit, mainly in the form of installment loans.

A New "Credit Crunch." As a consequence of a rising economy and inflation, interest rates made a steep climb, accelerating the increase which had begun in the spring of 1977. The prime rate—the rate charged by the major banks to their largest customers—increased fifteen times during the year, rising from 7.75 percent as the year opened to 11.75 percent at the close. This closing rate was only slightly below the record high of 12 percent reached during the "credit crunch" of 1974. Late in the year, six-month Treasury bills were yielding more than 10 percent, a rate not exceeded in this century.

Long-term rates (which are much less volatile than the shorter-dated issues) exhibited much more modest increases, but they started the year from a higher level. The return on U.S. government bonds of ten-year maturity was 9.1 percent at year-end, compared with 7.8 percent twelve months earlier. And long-term corporate bonds, as measured by the Moody's average, rose from 8.6 percent to 9.6 percent.

The rapid increase in interest rates was a reflection of an accelerating inflation imposed on an economy already in the advanced stage of business recovery—the stage that is normally accompanied by increasing interest rates in any event. In this case, however, the rate of inflation intensified the demand for credit, caused a rapid deterioration of the dollar, and forced monetary authorities to apply increasingly more stringent credit restraints. The net effect of these restraints was to encourage interest rates to rise as a matter of public policy, in order to curb speculative excesses and reduce inflation.

This approach had no visible success in curbing inflation. But there were indications that the actions of the Federal Reserve were beginning to have some influence on credit late in the year. Business loans, which had risen rapidly in the first half of the year, lagged somewhat in the second half, with no growth at all in the final two months.

On Nov. 1, in conjunction with the U.S. Treasury Department, the Federal Reserve made a major effort to slow the growth of credit by raising the discount rate—the rate the Fed charges member banks for the temporary use of funds—by a full percentage point to 9.5 percent, a new record. It also increased reserve requirements, a move which reduced the extent to which banks were free to make loans. At the same time, the Treasury set up a multibillion-dollar "swap" arrangement with several European governments to facilitate the purchase of U.S. dollars. This move was designed to halt an accelerating decline in the value of the dollar—a decline which some experts thought might lead to a collapse of the international financial system were it left unchecked.

Federal Reserve Board. In January incoming Federal Reserve Board Chairman G. William Miller, appointed by President Carter to replace Arthur Burns, announced several major goals: cutting inflation, making membership in the Federal Reserve system more attractive, and making it easier for the public to understand economic policy. By the end of the year, none of these objectives had been achieved. Inflation was accelerating, Federal Reserve bank membership declined, and even the financial analysts were confused by federal monetary policy.

The continued erosion in the number of mem-

The price of gasoline—and just about everything else—went up, up, up in 1978. Moreover, another round of oil-price increases late in the year threatened to increase the U.S. trade deficit, further erode the value of the dollar, and fuel domestic inflation.

ber banks had serious implications. One of the Fed's main policy levers is its power to change reserve requirements of member banks—but this power does not extend to state-chartered banks. Any decrease in the number of banks participating in the Federal Reserve System reduces the power of the Fed to free funds for lending during periods of economic distress and to curtail bank loans during periods of overexpansion.

To protect its position, the Federal Reserve Board sent to Congress a request for legislation that would require all federally insured financial institutions with $5,000,000 or more in annual transactions to hold reserves with the central bank. The board also proposed to pay interest on the funds that banks hold on deposit with the Fed. These proposals were received coolly by the congressional banking committees, which began considering an alternative plan that would allow the Fed to charge nonmember banks for its services.

PUBLIC FINANCE

As in each year since 1975, federal spending exceeded revenues, and by a wide margin. This happened despite the fact that expenditures were lower and revenues higher than anticipated. As in 1977, a number of government departments failed to meet their projected spending levels. Shortfalls have occurred in budgeted spending for defense, international affairs, Medicare and Medicaid, public assistance programs, and major construction programs, including environmental protection grants. Increased revenues were attributed to the growth in personal income and business profits, both of which stemmed, in part, from the surprisingly high rate of inflation.

The Deficit Deepens. The federal budget continued to register an abnormally large deficit. In all previous business cycle upswings, the budget deficit narrowed and even disappeared as the economy moved toward a high level of employment. But this did not happen in 1978. On the contrary, the 1978 deficit was larger than in 1977, even though the economy improved substantially during the year.

For the fiscal year ended Sept. 30, 1978, the deficit rose to $48.7 billion from the $45 billion recorded the previous year. Budget receipts rose by $44.2 billion, to $402 billion; outlays rose by $47.9 billion, to $450.7 billion.

The level of federal spending by fiscal 1978 was two-thirds higher than it had been four years earlier. The cumulative deficit for 1975 through 1978 was $218 billion, more than triple the total deficit from 1971 through 1974.

The 1979 Budget. President Carter's initial spending proposal for fiscal 1979 (beginning Oct. 1,

Still in the Driver's Seat
Ambitious, hard-driving Lee (shortened from Lido) Anthony Iococca had risen from trainee to president of the Ford Motor Co. But his thirty-two-year career hit a pothole in July when he was jolted out of his job by board chairman Henry Ford 2nd in a clash that apparently had more to do with personality differences than with policy. Despite a lucrative parting settlement, Iococca conceded that he "really didn't want to retire at 54." As it turned out, he didn't have to. In November he shifted back into high gear, this time as president of the ailing Chrysler Corp., whose losses had totaled nearly $250,000,000 in the first nine months of 1978. His new boss, board chairman John J. Riccardo, said Iococca was recruited to give Chrysler some much needed "firepower."

Motor-man Lee Iococca.

1978) was submitted to Congress in January, 1978. At that time, the President called for expenditures of $500 billion. Total outlays were budgeted to rise by 9.1 percent, compared with the 11.9 percent increase recorded in fiscal 1978. The major increases in planned spending were $13.4 billion (9.2 percent) for income security (largely social security), $9.3 billion (8.8 percent) for national defense, and $8.2 billion (18.7 percent) for interest payments on the national debt. The voters' growing disenchantment with spending and taxing—and the reflection of this mood in Congress—led the Administration to scale down its spending plans by some $12 billion during the year.

The national debt limit was increased by Congress to $798 billion, through the end of March, 1979. Since the federal debt by the end of 1978 was only several billion dollars below that level, it seemed quite likely that Congress would again have to raise the limit by the summer of 1979.

The Carter administration set as its goal a continued contraction in the federal deficit. The anticipated deficit of $37.4 billion for fiscal 1979 was to be followed, according to Administration forecasts, by further reduction to less than $30 billion in fiscal 1980. This entailed considerable scaling down of social programs, since the President had already committed himself to a 3 percent increase in spending for national defense, exclusive of inflation.

TAXATION

At the federal level, Carter administration proposals for tax reduction and tax reform were overhauled by Congress, and the tax bill passed late in

1978 bore little relation to the measure as first submitted. At the state and local levels, what some observers called a tax revolt marched under the banner of "Proposition 13."

Federal Tax Law. In January, President Carter submitted to Congress a major tax-reform bill which was intended to aid low- and middle-income taxpayers and to stimulate the economy. The President's economic advisers believed that without a tax cut the growth rate of the American economy might slow to 3.5 percent in 1979; with a cut, however, the rate was projected at 4.5–5 percent. The tax reduction was also proposed, in part, to overcome the increase in social security payments mandated by Congress in 1977 (*see* SOCIAL SECURITY). Additionally, tax reduction was deemed necessary to compensate for inflation, which, because of the progressive nature of the tax system, was pushing taxpayers into higher income brackets, with higher tax rates, although real incomes were not rising.

Key aspects of the Carter proposal were a $24 billion cut in personal taxes (partially offset by increases of $7 billion, stemming from reforms which would add to revenues) and an $8 billion reduction in business taxes (partially offset by about $2 billion in added revenues). The Administration's tax proposal also sought to replace the existing combination of individual tax exemptions and credits with a single tax-credit allowance of $240 per person, strengthen the minimum tax on exempt income, increase the tax liability of wealthy taxpayers, and limit the attractiveness of tax shelters.

In the course of congressional debate, several additional ideas were raised and discarded. A proposal to allow tax credits for parents with children in elementary and secondary schools and colleges won considerable support in Congress, but was abandoned after President Carter expressed adamant opposition. By a large majority, the Ways and Means Committee of the House of Representatives voted to shift $14.5 billion in general funds to shore up the social security system over a two-year period. The committee had second thoughts about this precedent-making decision, however, and later reversed its vote.

Much altered, the tax bill was passed in October and was scheduled to take effect at the beginning of 1979. The bill provided for federal tax reductions estimated at $18.7 billion during the first year. The measure was generally seen as a departure from previous tax-reform bills, which had granted proportionately greater tax reductions for lower- and middle-income taxpayers than for upper-income groups.

The bill reduced the number of tax brackets, raised the bottom bracket for single persons by $100 to $2300, increased the personal exemption by $250 to $1000, and abandoned the general tax credit previously in effect. Some 4,300,000 taxpayers received a reduction in capital-gains taxes (the President had originally sought a capital-gains-tax increase), and a significant change was made with respect to the sale of a home. Each taxpayer over the age of 55 was permitted a once-in-a-lifetime exclusion from taxes of gains of up to $100,000 on the sale of a home used as a primary residence.

The maximum corporate income tax rate was reduced from 48 to 46 percent, and a special tax credit was introduced to encourage businessmen to hire members of certain underemployed groups, including Vietnam war veterans, handicapped persons, welfare recipients, and convicted felons. Investment tax credits were liberalized to permit not only the acquisition of new equipment but the renovation of rundown industrial and commercial buildings. Restrictions on pension plans and individual retirement accounts were loosened, and the maximum tax credit for political contributions was doubled. The verdict on business "perks" was mixed: The law ended deductions for corporate yachts, hunting lodges, and similar recreational facilities, but left standing the "three-martini lunch," country club dues, and first-class air fares. The general deduction for state and local gasoline taxes was abolished.

The new tax law stated as an objective, but did not mandate, that the growth of federal spending should not exceed 1 percent per year, adjusted for inflation, between fiscal 1979 and fiscal 1983. The intent was to reduce the proportion of national output going to the government to 19.5 percent by fiscal 1983, with the federal budget in balance by 1982.

Proposition 13. One of the most startling and potentially far-reaching tax developments took place in California, with the passage in June of Proposition 13 (also known as the Jarvis-Gann initiative, after its leading sponsors, retired businessmen Howard Jarvis and Paul Gann). By referendum, California voters slashed real estate taxes by 57 percent, or a total of $7 billion. This measure became the centerpiece of the "tax revolt" of 1978 and represented an effort to slow, if not reverse, the rising proportion of income going into tax payments. Leaders of the tax revolt pointed out that federal spending had risen from 18.7 to 22.6 percent of the gross national product (GNP) between 1958 and 1978, and that state and local taxes had increased from 8.7 to 12.4 percent of the GNP since 1960.

Proposition 13 limited property-tax collections by local governments to a base rate of 1 percent of full value at 1975–76 assessments. It also permitted assessments to increase by no more than 2 percent annually, with reassessment allowed only upon resale of the property; required a two-thirds vote of both houses of the California state legislature to levy new taxes aimed at increasing revenue; and provided that local governments must secure approval of two thirds of the voters in order to levy new property taxes. In November, various measures designed to limit taxing or spending were passed by voters in a dozen other states.

Kemp-Roth Amendment. Although it failed to pass Congress, much attention was focused during 1978 on a tax-limitation measure sponsored by Sen. William V. Roth (R, Del.) and Rep. Jack Kemp (R, N.Y.). This so-called Kemp-Roth amendment sought to reduce the range of federal income tax rates from the existing 14–70 percent to 8–50 percent over a three-year period. Supporters estimated that the reduction would return to taxpayers $14.5 billion in 1979 and a cumulative total of $112 billion by 1981. Republicans attempted to make Kemp-Roth a central theme of the fall campaign, with uncertain results.

BANKS AND BANKING

A number of major changes took place in the U.S. banking system, including changes in the laws related to banking. Great strides were made by automatic funds transfer (AFT) systems, in which funds may be transferred electronically from savings to checking accounts. In effect, consumers may now receive interest on their checking accounts, since funds could be converted from savings to checking at the touch of a button. As of

Thousands wait to try their luck at a Resorts International casino on the first day of legalized gambling in Atlantic City, N.J. Gambling fever also struck Wall Street, where trading in Resorts stock (and other casino-related issues) often reached frantic proportions.

Nov. 1, commercial banks were permitted to offer AFT services by the Federal Reserve. The Federal Deposit Insurance Corp. likewise granted permission to the state-chartered banks under its jurisdiction.

Bank Regulation. In an effort to mitigate the problems created by multiple supervision of business enterprises by government agencies, the Office of Management and Budget established a set of guidelines for federal regulators, including the federal bank-regulating agencies. For the first time, these agencies were required to publish a semiannual agenda of all regulations under review or development, and to set up a timetable that would permit a periodic review of current regulations.

Six-Month Certificates. At midyear, savings institutions and commercial banks were permitted to issue six-month certificates of deposits in $10,000 denominations. These certificates were pegged to the interest rate paid on six-month U.S. Treasury bills—a rate that substantially exceeded the interest payable on savings accounts throughout 1978. By the end of the year, the six-month certificates were yielding over 10 percent on an annual basis, nearly double what a savings account could offer. From the bankers' point of view, the certificates were a mixed blessing. Although the high return induced savers to maintain their funds in savings institutions, thereby keeping mortgage money available for homebuilding, the payout rate on the certificates sometimes matched or exceeded state limits on mortgage-loan interest, cutting into bank profits.

New Types of Mortgages. In response to higher interest rates and the sharply rising cost of housing, the Federal Home Loan Bank Board authorized two new mortgage instruments. One, the graduated-payment mortgage, was designed to aid younger families. It permitted lower payments in the early years of the mortgage period, rising to a predetermined level in the later years. The second, the reverse-annuity mortgage, was designed to accommodate older families and was based on the accumulated equity in their homes.

A third type of loan, the variable-rate mortgage, aroused a great deal of controversy in 1978. In a variable-rate mortgage, payments are adjusted up or down depending on prevailing rates of interest. By the end of the year, only California had permitted this type of loan.

Legislation. Late in 1978, Congress passed legislation that affected all financial institutions. The bank regulatory agencies were given new powers to prevent the alleged abuses for which Georgia banker Bert Lance had been forced to resign in 1977 as director of the Office of Management and Budget. Also included in the new law was a financial privacy act which gives individuals the right to be notified of and to challenge federal agency requests for personal bank records. Added to the financial reform bill was the Electronic Funds Transfer Act, which restricts consumer liability for unauthorized use of a bank card to $50.   W.B.F.

UPPER VOLTA. *See* STATISTICS OF THE WORLD. *See also* AFRICA.

URUGUAY. In 1978 the Organization of American States (OAS) pointed to Uruguay, together with Chile and Paraguay, as Latin American countries that had violated human rights. In a seventy-page

424

report issued in June the OAS accused the Uruguayan government of arbitrary arrest, torture, and murder of political prisoners who at that time, according to a New York *Times* estimate, numbered 3000 (the official count was 1500). The military-dominated government, which took control in 1973 when the country was convulsed by a left-wing terrorist movement, the Tupamaros, rejected the condemnation. A military spokesman, Col. Julio Barravino, insisted, "We take pride in being the guiding light in the struggle of our Western Christian civilization against international Marxist sedition." Some prisoners—at least 600—were released during the year; most of those still held were not terrorists but members of the Communist and other banned leftist parties. Although a moderate, Lt. Gen. Gregorio Alvarez, be-

came head of the army in February, the government refused to allow any investigation of rights violations and issued a long rebuttal to the OAS charges. The OAS then rejected Uruguay's invitation to hold its 1978 general assembly in Montevideo.

Thousands of Uruguayans have left the country since 1973, for both political and economic reasons. Average real income has dropped 29 percent in ten years. The situation did improve slightly in 1978, however, with inflation down from 58 to 45 percent and unemployment down from 14 to 12.8 percent. This improvement was the result of higher earnings from cattle exports and greater domestic industrial production.

See STATISTICS OF THE WORLD.   J.N.G.
UTAH. *See* STATISTICS OF THE WORLD.

V

VENEZUELA. A hotly contested presidential election held on Dec. 3, 1978, resulted in a victory for Venezuela's opposition party.

Politics. One of Latin America's few genuine democracies, Venezuela experienced a costly, intense, but peaceful presidential campaign conducted principally by candidates of two Center-Left parties—Luis Piñerúa Ordaz of the incumbent Democratic Action Party (AD) and Luis Herrera Campíns of the opposition Social Christian Party (COPEI). Employing media specialists from the United States as advisers, both sides issued virtually identical platforms, promising to fight inflation, violent crime, the housing crisis, and inadequate public services. Each side accused the other of corruption, but COPEI was particularly aggressive in its attacks on AD.

Political analysts explained that popular expectations, raised by Venezuela's booming oil-based economy, had not been satisfied by the AD government. According to these observers, many Venezuelans felt that the administration of President Carlos Andrés Pérez had spent large sums of money with little obvious effect on the average Venezuelan's standard of living. Also, it was time for a change—the Democratic Action Party had won three out of four elections in recent years. Consequently, Herrera won by a margin unofficially estimated at 200,000 votes out of 5,800,000 votes cast. Third place went to the candidate of the Movement Toward Socialism; the Common Cause Party was fourth, followed by six other mi-

nor parties. The new president announced that he would continue to press for the ousting of the military regime in Nicaragua (q.v.). Continued close relations with the administration of U.S. President Jimmy Carter, who had visited Venezuela in February, were also expected. The inauguration of the new president was scheduled to be held on March 12, 1979.

The Economy. In 1978, after a heady two years of soaring oil prices, Venezuela had to begin to face the prospect of leaner years ahead. The country incurred its first balance-of-payments deficit in a decade. Oil production dropped 27 percent from the 1977 figure of 1,700,000 bbl daily, largely because the needs of Venezuela's principal market, the East Coast of the U.S., were being met more cheaply by Alaskan, Mexican, and Middle Eastern oil. The resulting decline in oil revenues (from $10 billion in 1974 to $5.65 billion in 1978) caused budget cuts, including a reduction in the popular and much needed foreign scholarship program to train young Venezuelans abroad. The government also banned imports of some consumer goods to avoid another trade deficit. Unemployment was a low 5 percent, but the real (unofficial) rate of inflation was estimated to be 20 percent. Observers argued that the most pressing tasks facing the new president would be to brake government spending by consolidating its programs and to channel oil revenues into improved public services.

See STATISTICS OF THE WORLD.   J.N.G.
VERMONT. *See* STATISTICS OF THE WORLD.

VIETNAM, SOCIALIST REPUBLIC OF

VIETNAM, SOCIALIST REPUBLIC OF. During 1978, Vietnam ended its almost total preoccupation with domestic problems and began to flex its muscles on the international scene.

Cambodian Conflict. Militarily, the Vietnamese focused their attention on neighboring Cambodia. Vietnam was supported by the Soviet Union, while Cambodia was backed by the People's Republic of China. As a result, the struggle between the two Southeast Asian Communist countries took on the appearance of a proxy war between Moscow and Peking.

In January, June, and July, the Cambodians beat back Vietnamese offensives. But as the months passed, it became clear that Vietnam was merely biding its time before making another attempt to crush the regime in Phnom Penh. The overall objective was an old one: a Communist "Federation of Indochina" dominated by Vietnam.

When the dry season returned to Cambodia in November, fighting flared once again. In early December, Vietnam announced the formation of the Kampuchean United Front for National Salvation, a signal that a move to topple the Cambodian government and replace it with a pro-Vietnam puppet regime was imminent.

Peking and Moscow. Relations between Vietnam and China went from bad to worse during 1978. Beginning in March, tens of thousands of ethnic Chinese fled from Vietnam into China. Peking accused Hanoi of persecuting Vietnam's Chinese residents, and all through the summer the two sides wrangled over the question. So heated did the dispute become that in August the Vietnamese warned China that they were ready to fight.

Peking, in turn, warned Hanoi against invading Cambodia. But when the Vietnamese finally launched a year-end offensive against Phnom Penh, China—unwilling to risk a confrontation with the Soviet Union—did little more than denounce Vietnam for "towering crimes" and for acting as a surrogate for Moscow in its "expansionist strategic plan."

Hanoi's ties with Moscow were strengthened considerably during 1978. Throughout the year, the Soviets backed Vietnam in the conflict with Cambodia, and in November Moscow and Hanoi signed a treaty of friendship and cooperation. The twenty-five-year pact, the first between the Soviet Union and a Southeast Asian country, provided for increased economic aid and mutual support in the event of military attack.

Non-Communist World. In September and October, Vietnamese Premier Pham Van Dong launched an ambitious regional diplomatic campaign, visiting all five members of the Association of Southeast Asian Nations (ASEAN). Although

Vietnam, preparing to launch a major offensive against Cambodia in the winter, invited a group of international journalists to Ho Chi Minh City (formerly Saigon) in April. Here they interview a Cambodian soldier reportedly captured during a raid in Vietnamese territory.

Dong promised not to support Communist guerrilla activities in their countries, all the members of ASEAN remained wary of Vietnam's attempt to move from hostility to friendship. The Vietnamese also stepped up their attempt to establish commercial and diplomatic ties with the United States. But Washington, suspicious of Hanoi's ambitions in Southeast Asia and unwilling to offend China, remained cool to the overtures.

Domestic Developments. Given the secretive nature of the regime, reports of life in Vietnam were sketchy. However, four French journalists—three of whom had written sympathetically of Hanoi's cause during the Vietnam war—were able to tour the country in 1978. Vietnam, they concluded, was a country marked by harsh misrule, growing political oppression, food shortages, economic mismanagement, and official corruption.

Hanoi continued to seek the economic integration of North and South. The nationalization of all businesses in Ho Chi Minh City (formerly Saigon) was ordered in March, and a single currency, the "unified dong," was created two months later. Hanoi also continued a massive resettlement program that should eventually move 10,000,000 people into so-called New Economic Zones.

See STATISTICS OF THE WORLD.   R.J.C

VIRGINIA. See STATISTICS OF THE WORLD.
VIRGIN ISLANDS. See STATISTICS OF THE WORLD.

WARSAW TREATY ORGANIZATION, former
name of the WARSAW TREATY OF FRIENDSHIP,
COOPERATION, AND MUTUAL ASSISTANCE,
known as the WARSAW PACT. The Warsaw Pact
is a political and military alliance of seven Eastern
European countries led by the Soviet Union.

In November, 1978, the Warsaw Pact held its
first summit conference in two years. Top Communist leaders from Bulgaria, Czechoslovakia,
East Germany, Hungary, Poland, and Rumania
gathered in Moscow to confer with Soviet President Leonid I. Brezhnev. Proceedings were held
in secret, but at the close of two days of meetings
Warsaw Pact spokesmen issued a joint declaration. They called for early completion of a new
strategic arms limitation treaty (SALT) between
the United States and the U.S.S.R. In addition,
they proposed that the five permanent members
of the United Nations Security Council meet formally to discuss nuclear arms curbs. In a separate
statement, the alliance denounced negotiations
between Egypt and Israel (Rumania refused to associate itself with this declaration).

Throughout the year, force-reduction talks between the nations of the Warsaw Pact and the
North Atlantic Treaty Organization (NATO) remained stalemated in Vienna. In June the Warsaw
Pact countries accepted a Western proposal that
each side should cut its forces to 700,000 ground
troops in Central Europe. But NATO spokesmen
said the concession had "questionable" practical
value, since the Warsaw Pact planned to make
cutbacks only from a ground force totaling
805,000 men. Western intelligence sources
claimed the Warsaw Pact actually had an additional 145,000 ground troops in Central Europe
that would not be included in the proposed reductions.

The prestigious International Institute for Strategic Studies, based in London, released its annual
report in September. The institute declared that,
in conventional land arms, the Warsaw Pact was
increasing its advantage over NATO. In tanks, for
example, the Warsaw Pact force consisted of
65,525 against NATO's 25,373.

See NORTH ATLANTIC TREATY ORGANIZATION. F.W.
WASHINGTON. *See* STATISTICS OF THE WORLD.
WESTERN SAMOA. *See* STATISTICS OF THE WORLD.
WEST INDIES. The Caribbean islands presented a
mixed picture in 1978: surprising stability in some
countries, major uncertainty in others.
Dominican Republic. The year's major change oc-

*Surrounded by a phalanx of officers, outgoing Domini-
can President Joaquín Balaguer (left) escorts President-
elect Antonio Guzmán to his swearing-in on Aug. 16.*

curred in the Dominican Republic. There, for the
first time in the country's 134-year history, power
was peacefully transferred to the Opposition after
an election.

The leading opposition candidate for president
in the May 16 election was wealthy 67-year-old
cattle rancher Silvestre Antonio Guzmán Fernández, head of the centrist Dominican Revolutionary Party. The conservative incumbent president,
Joaquín Balaguer, who was backed by the military
and the Reformist Party, had been expected to
win a fourth term, despite rumors of serious illness and charges of corruption. Early returns
showed Guzmán with a commanding lead, so the
Dominican army moved in to stop the ballot
counting. Pro-Balaguer businessmen and Organization of American States (OAS) observers protested; finally the United States—a prime supporter of the Balaguer regime—threatened
economic sanctions and the count was resumed.
Guzmán was officially declared the victor in July.
According to some observers the price for military

acceptance was that the Reformist Party should have a majority in the upper house, thus limiting Guzmán's power. Nevertheless, he acted quickly, retiring or sending into exile unfriendly military officers and promising a moderate government free of corruption. The new president was, however, confronted by a depressed agricultural economy with a $1 billion debt, 16 percent inflation, and unemployment running as high as 40 percent in some areas.

Haiti. The economy of neighboring Haiti, which suffered a severe drought in 1977, improved in 1978. Higher world prices for its principal exports (coffee and bauxite) helped, as did the establishment of new export-oriented manufacturing industries. An 8 percent growth in the economy was estimated for 1978, but the government under President Jean-Claude Duvalier still felt a need for U.S. economic aid. That Haiti had eased its repressive policy toward human rights was reported by an OAS commission after its August visit.

Former British Colonies. Dominica, a Caribbean island with a population of 80,000, had been a British possession for 173 years. In November it became an independent country and a member of the Commonwealth of Nations (q.v.). The neighboring British islands of St. Lucia, St. Vincent, St. Kitts-Nevis, and Antigua discussed their plans to follow suit, opening the prospect of further political fragmentation and economic instability in the Caribbean. The islands of Jamaica (q.v.), Trinidad and Tobago, Barbados, and Grenada had already achieved economically shaky independence.

Robert Bradshaw, prime minister of the associ-

ated state of St. Kitts-Nevis–Anguilla since its formation in 1967 (Anguilla in effect withdrew from the association in 1976), died May 24 at the age of 61. He was succeeded by Paul Southwell, who had been deputy prime minister.

See STATISTICS OF THE WORLD. J.N.G.

WEST VIRGINIA. See STATISTICS OF THE WORLD.

WISCONSIN. See STATISTICS OF THE WORLD.

WOMEN. In 1978, as in previous years, the women's movement focused on the Equal Rights Amendment (ERA) and abortion. Although women made gains in education and athletics, the November election results disappointed political activists.

Equal Rights Amendment. "Equality of rights under the law shall not be denied or abridged . . . on account of sex." So reads the proposed Twenty-Seventh Amendment to the U.S. Constitution, which remained mired in controversy in 1978. When the year began, thirty-five states had ratified the amendment—three short of the number needed for passage. When the year ended, no new states had ratified, but ERA supporters could claim progress on two fronts.

The first tactic of pro-ERA groups was to persuade organizations holding conventions to boycott states that had not ratified the ERA. More than 230 organizations agreed to withhold convention business from nonratifying states; the National Organization for Women estimated that by the end of the year those fifteen states had lost more than $100,000,000 in convention business because of the boycott.

The second successful pro-ERA tactic was the campaign to extend the time for ratification be-

Softer Sell

Sarah Weddington replaced Midge Costanza in late August as the chief White House adviser on women's issues, but the switchover seemed more a change in style than in viewpoint. Costanza was habitually outspoken; not so Weddington. The 33-year-old Weddington, a Texas lawyer and former state legislator, had earned her credentials for competence by winning a landmark 1973 Supreme Court test on liberalizing abortions. General counsel for the Agriculture Department prior to her appointment as Presidential assistant, she was no less determined than her predecessor to marshal Administration support of the Equal Rights Amendment. The difference, as a former colleague noted, was that Weddington "doesn't get people's feathers ruffled while she makes her pitch."

Presidential adviser Sarah Weddington.

yond the original seven-year deadline of March 22, 1979. By votes of 233–189 in the House of Representatives and 60–36 in the Senate, Congress agreed to an extension until June 30, 1982. U.S. President Jimmy Carter signed the congressional resolution, saying he wanted to demonstrate his support for the ERA even though his signature was not legally required.

Elections. The November elections were generally a disappointment to women's rights activists. ERA-related referendums failed to win popular support in Nevada and Florida, and the ranks of women in Congress were thinned. As a result of the elections, the 96th Congress, convening in January, 1979, would find only one woman in the Senate; in the House, there would be just 16 women, a loss of 2 in the 435-member chamber. Four of them were to represent Maryland, the only delegation with as many women as men.

The most significant victory by a woman was the election of Nancy Landon Kassebaum (R, Kans.) to the Senate. She is the first woman ever elected to a full Senate term who was not preceded in Congress by her husband. Jane Eskind, the only other woman running for the Senate in November, lost to incumbent Howard H. Baker, Jr. (R, Tenn.). Sen. Muriel Humphrey (D, Minn.) did not seek reelection, and Sen. Maryon Allen (D, Ala.) lost in the primary; each had been appointed to fill a seat vacated by the death of her husband.

At the state level, advances were made. At the reconvening of the state legislatures in 1979,

women were to hold more than 10 percent of the seats for the first time in U.S. history.

Abortion. The most emotionally charged issue concerning women in 1978 was abortion. All across America, the debate over the morality of abortion was as intense as at any time since 1973, when the practice was legalized. After the Supreme Court ruling of 1977 that even though every woman has the legal right to an abortion, the government is not obligated to pay for it, Congress eliminated federal Medicaid funding for most abortions for the poor. By mid-1978 only seventeen states plus the District of Columbia continued to fund most or all abortions for the poor. Many state legislatures have called for a constitutional convention to draft an amendment that would ban abortion altogether. The National Abortion Rights Action League (NARAL), a "pro-choice" group, alleged in March that fifteen abortion clinics had been bombed, burned, or vandalized during the previous twelve months.

NARAL more than quadrupled its membership in 1978, and the American Civil Liberties Union made abortion rights a top-priority issue. Significant support for the pro-choice movement came with the appointment of Sarah Weddington as White House adviser on women's issues. She had

Senator-elect Nancy Landon Kassebaum (R, Kans.) with her 91-year-old father, Alfred M. Landon, who was the Republican Presidential candidate in 1936. She was the first woman to be elected to the U.S. Senate since 1966.

been past president of NARAL and was the lawyer representing "Jane Roe" in the lawsuits that resulted in the 1973 Supreme Court decision invalidating most state antiabortion laws.

Antiabortion crusaders were cheered by the November elections. The Right to Life movement showed surprising strength in New York State, and a group called Iowans for Life took credit for denying Dick Clark (D, Iowa) a second U.S. Senate term.

Instrumental in the U.S. antiabortion movement has been the money and authority of the Roman Catholic Church. But in Italy, ironically, the Vatican suffered a bitter defeat when parliament legalized elective abortions for most adult women.

Other Developments. In education, women's colleges throughout the United States enjoyed a resurgence. Enrollment at 122 women's colleges increased by 3.4 percent over 1977. And for the first time in history, the elite group of northeastern women's colleges known as the "Seven Sisters" all had female presidents.

In women's sports, swimming and mountain climbing made headlines. Two long-distance swimmers, Diana Nyad and Stella Taylor, shared a common fate: Each challenged the sea and lost. Nyad gave up after swimming more than two thirds of the way from Cuba to Florida. Taylor had almost crossed from the Bahamas to Florida when a change in current forced her to quit. On a more successful note, members of a U.S. women's climbing expedition reached the top of Annapurna 1 in the Himalayas (see MOUNTAINEERING).

Women made new headway in the U.S. armed forces. In May, Margaret A. Brewer became the first female brigadier general in the U.S. Marine Corps. Two months later, Mary Clarke was promoted to major general, the first woman in the history of the U.S. Army to reach that rank.

In a landmark case in Salem, Oreg., John J. Rideout was tried for the first-degree rape of his wife, Greta. What made the case unique was that he was the first man to be charged under a 1977 state law ruling out marriage or cohabitation as a defense against rape. Although the husband was acquitted, women's rights activists saw the fact that the case had been brought—and the constitutionality of the new law upheld—as an advance for the right of women to control their own bodies.

Deaths. Foremost among the women who died in 1978 were former Israeli Prime Minister Golda Meir and anthropologist Margaret Mead (see OBITUARIES). M.W.B.

WYOMING. See STATISTICS OF THE WORLD.

YEMEN ARAB REPUBLIC. Assassinations and coup attempts rocked the Yemen Arab Republic (North Yemen) in 1978.

On June 24, President Ahmed Hussein al-Ghashmi became the second North Yemeni leader to be slain in eight months when a bomb hidden in the briefcase of a visiting diplomat from the People's Democratic Republic of Yemen (South Yemen) exploded. North Yemen immediately severed diplomatic relations with its southern neighbor, and on July 2 the Arab League condemned South Yemen for the "evil crime" of murdering Ghashmi.

According to reports accepted by the Arab League, South Yemen's President Salem Rubayi Ali had telephoned Ghashmi on June 23 and said he wanted to send a personal envoy to San'a to discuss an urgent matter. Ghashmi agreed to receive the envoy, who was shown into his office the next day. As the envoy opened his briefcase, it exploded, killing both him and Ghashmi. The Arab League's reports said that Rubayi Ali's rivals in South Yemen had switched briefcases on the envoy to provide them with a pretext for executing the South Yemeni president forty-eight hours later.

After Ghashmi's death, Lt. Col. Ali Abdullah Saleh assumed the presidency of North Yemen. Four months later, on Oct. 15-16, the new president was the target of a coup attempt. While Saleh was visiting the Red Sea port of Hodeida, four battalions of North Yemen's army and military police attacked the presidential palace in San'a. Saleh returned to San'a after the army's deputy chief of staff, Lt. Col. Abdul Aziz Barkhi, had crushed the uprising. Nine high-ranking army officers were killed during the abortive coup; on Nov. 15 twelve people, including three government officials, were executed for their roles in the uprising.

See STATISTICS OF THE WORLD. See also ARAB LEAGUE. M.R.B.

YEMEN, PEOPLE'S DEMOCRATIC REPUBLIC OF. President Salem Rubayi Ali of the People's Democratic Republic of Yemen (South Yemen) was overthrown and killed June 26, 1978, by rivals within his government who favored a stronger alliance with the Soviet Union. Rubayi Ali and his two aides were executed after a fifteen-hour battle in the capital, Aden, during which the presidential palace was bombed and shelled. The coup took place only forty-eight hours after President Ahmed Hussein al-Ghashmi of the Yemen Arab Republic (North Yemen) was killed by a bomb carried by a South Yemeni envoy. The Arab League subsequently concluded that the North Yemeni assassination had been staged by South Yemeni plotters to give them a pretext for killing Rubayi Ali. Fifteen members of the Arab League voted to suspend relations with South Yemen.

A U.S. diplomatic mission, which had been scheduled to arrive in Aden the day after Rubayi Ali's death to explore the possibility of resuming ties between the two countries, was diverted to another destination. Abdel Fattah Ismail, leader of the force that overthrew Rubayi Ali, was described by U.S. officials as a Marxist ideologue unswervingly loyal to the Soviet Union. Ismail had reportedly grown increasingly alarmed by Rubayi Ali's tentative efforts to achieve a rapprochement with the country's conservative neighbors, North Yemen and Saudi Arabia, as well as with the United States. Ali Nasser Mohammed Hasani, a close ally of Ismail, assumed the presidency after the execution of Rubayi Ali, but Ismail himself was elected president on Dec. 27.

See STATISTICS OF THE WORLD. *See also* ARAB LEAGUE.   M.R.B.

YOUTH ACTIVITIES. No one seemed to mean as much to young people in 1978 as a 24-year-old actor named John Travolta. His performances in three films made his perhaps the most-recognized face in the United States. Meanwhile, college students donned bedsheets and made the toga party a campuswide institution. More seriously, drug counselors and other officials reported that use of a deadly drug nicknamed "angel dust" was on the increase.

Travolta Fever. In 1978, John Travolta became a star. He had had parts in a touring production of *Grease,* the film *Carrie,* and a television series called *Welcome Back, Kotter.* He had starred in his own made-for-television-movie, *The Boy in the Plastic Bubble.* But *Saturday Night Fever,* which became one of the top-grossing films of the 1977-78 season, catapulted him to stardom. *Fever* also nationalized the disco craze, launched the "Travolta look" (vested suits with black shirts), thrust the Bee Gees into the musical limelight, and, to some critics, made a definitive statement about the youth of the 1970's. But most of all, everyone who saw the movie remembered Travolta himself. Reviews noted a presence and a mystique that *Time* magazine said "gives an audience the sense of immediate but always fragile intimacy." Travolta's subsequent film efforts, *Grease* (with Olivia Newton-John) and *Moment by Moment* (with Lily Tomlin), were received more coolly by the critics, but Travolta's stardom was no less assured. *See* FASHION; PUBLISHING.

Animals and Orkans. Another movie sparked the year's liveliest trend. *National Lampoon's Animal House*—a loving, if vulgar, look at the rowdy heyday of fraternity life—reminded thousands of college graduates of the good old days; it also

Inspired by the movie National Lampoon's Animal House, shouts of "Toga! Toga! Toga!" summoned students to toga parties at college campuses all across the country. Here, Columbia University students frolic in New York City.

showed how much things had calmed down recently. The film starred John Belushi, already popular among the young (and their parents) for his broad comic roles on NBC's *Saturday Night Live.*

A highlight of *Animal House* is a hilarious toga party, which seemed to strike a chord with U.S. students. Almost instantly, toga parties sprang up on college campuses like dandelions. Besides the basic toga (a bedsheet tied or wrapped around the body), a successful party also required distinctive touches like garlands of leaves for the head or loosely knotted neckties. Vats of a punch called "Purple Jesus"—grain alcohol and grape juice— were de rigueur, and music always meant "golden oldies." Universal Pictures, which produced *Animal House*, also produced some toga parties, as well as T-shirts, posters, and sundry other items, out of its $4,500,000 promotional budget.

In the fall, youngsters could ape not only a fraternity animal but an Orkan—to wit, Mork from the planet Ork, a lovable extraterrestrial played in the ABC television series *Mork & Mindy* by comedian Robin Williams. Most viewers found Mork's nutty gestures and expressions more fun to imitate than to describe. *See* RADIO AND TELEVISION BROADCASTING.

Homework—A Losing Battle? A survey of 10,000 high school juniors and seniors by the National Assessment of Educational Progress in 1978 indicated that nearly two thirds of them spent less than five hours each week on homework. And teachers throughout the U.S. complained that homework was a lost cause. The reasons cited ran from parental permissiveness to television. Many parents allow their children to set their own rules, according to the teachers. Disadvantaged children must often cope with a turbulent home environment, as well as a lack of authority. More important, however, is the child's unwillingness to let his homework interfere with television. Efforts to make homework assignments more palatable by tying them to television programs met with only limited success.

Angel Dust. Phencyclidine hydrochloride, called PCP within the pharmaceutical industry and known on the street as "hog," "parsley," "flakes," "rocket fuel," or (most commonly) "angel dust," is considered by doctors to be the most dangerous drug to hit the streets since heroin and LSD. In 1978 it could be found almost anywhere in America—from the barrio to the boarding school. In Chicago, angel dust was as easy to get as marijuana or alcohol. It was the drug of choice in the largely white San Fernando Valley and in the black neighborhoods of Baltimore. In fact, its use became so pervasive that the Department of Health, Education, and Welfare and the National Institute on Drug Abuse gathered panels of experts to discuss how best to cope with it.

The Food and Drug Administration classified PCP as a "Schedule II" drug in 1978, placing it in the same category as barbiturates. But experts believe that angel dust is in a category by itself, both pharmacologically and behaviorally. Although deaths from overdose are rare, angel dust can have serious long-term effects on a chronic user.

Fads and Trends. Along with Travolta, Williams, Belushi, and the Bee Gees, entertainers with large youth followings included singer-composers Billy Joel and Bruce Springsteen and comedian Steve Martin. The disco craze roared from the dance floor onto roller skates, as hundreds of skating rinks installed strobe lights and souped-up sound systems. Use of marijuana was up: A University of Michigan study reported that 56 percent of high school seniors surveyed had tried pot and 10 percent used it daily. And there was growing recognition of teenage alcoholism as a pervasive form of drug abuse.

On college campuses, 1978 was one of the most

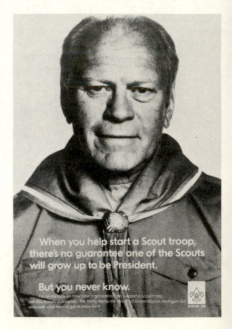

Former U.S. President (and former boy scout) Gerald R. Ford donned a scout uniform during the summer of 1978 to promote scouting in a 30-second television commercial. A host of famous Americans—actors and athletes as well as statesmen—were persuaded to get back into uniform and recite a few words from the boy scout oath.

When you help start a Scout troop, there's no guarantee one of the Scouts will grow up to be President.

But you never know.

politically active years since the riot-torn 1960's. Nuclear power and South Africa's discriminatory racial policies were the principal targets of student discontent.

On the scouting scene, autumn witnessed the launching of a "Stars Are Good Scouts" publicity campaign. Advertisements stressed the fact that notables like former President Gerald R. Ford and baseball star Hank Aaron had been boy scouts. Responding to public sympathy for a cerebral palsy victim who had been denied an eagle scout certificate because he was overage, Scouting USA eliminated age limits for severely handicapped scouts. Finally, for the first time since it was published in 1944, *The Boy Scout Fieldbook* was made available (in a special civilian edition) through bookstores to the public at large. F.V.B.

YUGOSLAVIA. Independence and nonalignment were the policies most heavily stressed in Yugoslavia as President Tito entered his 87th year. Throughout 1978, Tito seemed to be in robust health, but careful preparations were being made for the post-Tito era.

Domestic Affairs. The 11th congress of the League of Yugoslav Communists (Communist Party) was held in June. In both his opening address and closing remarks, President Tito emphasized Yugoslavia's intention to defend its independence against all challenges. The party chose no successor for Tito, but it streamlined its top leadership by reducing membership in the presidium from 48 to 24. Stane Dolanc, at 53 the man whom many observers considered most likely to take over party leadership when Tito dies, was elected secretary-general of the League of Communists at the congress.

Although the Soviet Union did not come in for public attack at the June meeting, Yugoslav authorities continued to guard against Soviet influence inside Yugoslavia. In the spring, a Yugoslav court tried Mileta Perovic, an anti-Tito Communist who had lived in the U.S.S.R. for many years and who had been captured by Yugoslav police under mysterious circumstances. Perovic was charged with seeking Soviet backing for a plot to overthrow the Tito regime. On April 13, he was sentenced to twenty years in prison.

The state of the economy provided grounds for government concern in 1978. Although Yugoslavia was prosperous, it was suffering serious trade imbalances, and 700,000 workers were unemployed.

Foreign Affairs. President Tito strengthened Yugoslavia's foreign ties as a counter to Soviet pressure. In March he journeyed to Washington, D.C., where he was warmly received by U.S. President Jimmy Carter and other top administration officials. In a final communiqué, Carter pledged U.S. support for "the independence, territorial integrity and unity of Yugoslavia." On a stopover in London, Tito received a similar pledge from the British government.

Yugoslavia played host during July to a conference of eighty-seven nonaligned nations. Tito had helped found the nonaligned movement in the early 1960's, and he was considered its senior statesman. He took the occasion to warn visiting diplomats to be wary of foreign intervention in Africa.

Tito's most notable foreign-affairs venture came in August, when he received Chinese Premier Hua Kuo-feng for a state visit. In Belgrade, Hua received a rousing welcome and expressed strong backing for Yugoslavia. He also appeared keenly interested in Yugoslav economic achievements and in the country's system of worker self-management.

Hua's European journey—the first by a Communist Chinese head of state—enraged Moscow, and official Soviet journals denounced it in the strongest terms. In response, President Tito postponed indefinitely an official visit he was to have made to Moscow late in the year.

See STATISTICS OF THE WORLD. F.W.

YUKON TERRITORY. *See* STATISTICS OF THE WORLD.

Z

ZAIRE, REPUBLIC OF. An invasion, similar to the one staged by Shaba rebels a year earlier, once more threatened Zaire's weak economy and the regime of President Mobutu Sese Seko in 1978.

The year opened with reports of urban terrorism in Kinshasa and an uprising in the Idiofa area. Both were put down by the army. On May 11, however, some 2000 secessionists based in Angola invaded Shaba (formerly Katanga) region, swept past border units, and seized Kolwezi, the center of Zaire's mining industry. As in the past, the Zaire army proved ineffectual, and Mobutu was forced to call for foreign military assistance. French Foreign Legionnaires and Belgian troops recaptured Kolwezi and forced the rebels back into Angola, but not before some 136 Whites and

On May 18, one week after Katangan rebels invaded Zaire, burnt out helicopters lie on an airstrip near Kolwezi. The town, an important mining center, had been the focus of heavy fighting between the rebels and French and Belgian troops.

more than 700 Blacks had been killed and the mines disrupted. The French and Belgian troops remained in the province and helped, to some degree, to calm the white technicians who were vital to the mineral industry and who had been key targets in the rebel attack. A force of some 2000 troops from French-speaking African countries replaced the French and Belgian forces in early June. Under Western pressure, the Shaba rebels, who were alleged to have been trained and armed by Cuba, were disarmed in Angola, and Zaire and Angola agreed to improve their relations.

Foreign aid donors met in June to shape a common policy toward Zaire, and Mobutu was urged to institute economic reforms, liberalize his regime, and end corruption. In effect, Zaire agreed to let the International Monetary Fund take control of its economy, and a group of Western nations agreed to supply $1 billion in aid over two years.

On July 17, Angola and Zaire agreed to reopen the Benguela Railway. Crucial for Zaire's exports, the railway had been closed since the outbreak of the Angolan civil war in 1975. In August, Angola's President Agostinho Neto visited Kinshasa and the leaders of the two countries agreed to establish a border commission and to restrict the activities of exiled opposition groups.

See STATISTICS OF THE WORLD. *See also* AFRICA.   J.T.S.

ZAMBIA. In 1978 Zambia's economy, which had appeared near collapse, began to be revived by donations of foreign aid. In the 1960's copper had generated over 90 percent of Zambia's foreign exchange and 50 percent of its government revenues. But as copper prices plummeted, revenues fell from $444,000,000 in 1974 to only $6,500,000 in 1977. In addition, Zambia's opposition to white rule in Rhodesia led to Rhodesian attacks on

guerrilla bases in Zambia, as well as to the closing of landlocked Zambia's main export routes.

To win the confidence of potential aid donors, the government in January announced Zambia's most austere budget since independence. Taxes were raised, and food subsidies were reduced or abolished. The government also devalued the kwacha in March and established price and income policies. These steps, although they led to increased political opposition, also led the International Monetary Fund to provide Zambia with a $305,000,000 standby credit and an immediate loan of $59,500,000 in March. In May, after Zambian President Kenneth D. Kaunda's visits to the United States and Great Britain, the two countries pledged $100,000,000 and $28,700,000 in aid, respectively. And in June the World Bank agreed to provide $1 billion in credits for the improvement or creation of rail lines in Zambia and for lessening the country's dependence on copper.

In October, Zambia reopened the rail line through Rhodesia and South Africa that had been closed for six years. A need for an outlet to the sea to end the country's economic strangulation had come to outweigh its opposition to white rule in Rhodesia, and the inefficiently run Chinese-built railroad through Tanzania had not provided a practical alternative.

Faced with widespread voter discontentment with the economic retrenchment—and with the first national elections since 1973 scheduled for September—the ruling United National Independence Party approved changes in its constitution to ensure that Kaunda would be the only presidential candidate. In the elections that were finally held in mid-December, Kaunda received about 81 percent of the vote, much more than had been expected.

See STATISTICS OF THE WORLD. *See also* AFRICA.   J.T.S.

STATISTICS OF THE WORLD

in the tables on the following pages will be found the latest available statistics on

The section on countries presents the latest information available in early December, 1978. All monetary figures are expressed in United States dollars. The symbol (C) signifies that the country belongs to the Commonwealth of Nations. NA means that the data were not available. * indicates that the category does not apply to the country under discussion. Footnotes at the end of the section contain more specialized information.

Nation Capital	Population	Type of Government	Heads of Government	Currency Value in U.S. Dollars	GNP (000,000)	GNP (per capita)
AFGHANISTAN Kabul	20,340,000 377,715	Republic	President of Revolutionary Council and Prime Minister: Noor Mohammad Taraki	Afghani 0.022	$ 2,300	$ 160
ALBANIA Tiranë	2,620,000 192,000	People's socialist republic	Presidium Chairman: Haxhi Lleshi Chairman, Council of Ministers: Mehmet Shehu	Lek 0.24	1,330	540
ALGERIA Algiers	17,910,000 1,179,000	Republic	President and Prime Minister: Col. Houari Boumédienne	Dinar 0.26	16,060	990
ANGOLA Luanda	6,761,000 480,613	People's republic	President: Agostinho Neto Prime Minister: Lopo do Nascimento	Kwanza 0.025	1,830	271
ARGENTINA Buenos Aires	26,060,000 2,980,000	Federal republic	President: Lt. Gen. Jorge Rafael Videla	Peso 0.0011	39,920	1,550
AUSTRALIA Canberra	14,070,000 166,101	Federal parliamentary state (C)	Governor-General: Sir Zelman Cowen Prime Minister: Malcolm Fraser	Dollar 1.16	83,380	6,100
AUSTRIA Vienna	7,520,000 1,592,800	Federal republic	President: Rudolf Kirchschläger Chancellor: Bruno Kreisky	Schilling 0.071	40,080	5,330
BAHAMAS Nassau	220,000 3,233	Parliamentary state (C)	Governor-General: Sir Milo B. Butler Prime Minister: Lynden O. Pindling	Dollar 1.00	700	3,310
BAHRAIN Manama	270,000 105,400	Emirate	Emir: Isa bin Sulman al-Khalifah Prime Minister: Khalifah bin Sulman al-Khalifah	Dinar 2.58	660	2,410
BANGLADESH Dacca	80,560,000 1,310,972	Republic (C)	President: Maj. Gen. Ziaur Rahman	Taka 0.068	8,470	110
BARBADOS Bridgetown	250,000 88,097	Parliamentary state (C)	Governor-General: Sir Deighton Ward Prime Minister: J.M.G. Adams	Dollar 0.50	380	1,550
BELGIUM Brussels	9,830,000 1,042,052	Constitutional monarchy	King: Baudouin Premier: Paul Vanden Boeynants	Franc 0.033	66,660	6,780

Imports Exports	Revenue Expenditure	Elementary Schools: Teachers Students	Secondary Schools: Teachers Students	Colleges and Universities: Teachers Students
$ 349,000,000	$ 291,913,330	22,093	8,648	1,190
223,000,000	287,706,660	842,560	106,172	12,256
NA	1,878,048,700	22,686	3,990	1,153
NA	1,853,658,500	569,600	102,600	28,668
6,644,000,000	5,341,821,500	70,498	22,605	4,670
5,233,000,000	5,341,821,500	2,785,264	612,301	41,847
625,000,000	791,666,660	12,622	4,723	274
1,227,000,000	791,666,660	516,131	79,055	2,942
4,162,000,000	3,988,842,300	195,997	169,704	45,204
5,651,000,000	4,823,558,300	3,579,304	1,283,056	596,736
12,175,000,000	23,953,886,000	78,390	74,041	19,920
13,002,000,000	27,452,345,000	1,790,050	1,095,691	274,738
14,248,000,000	14,623,447,000	54,922	17,898	10,001
9,808,000,000	16,873,645,000	977,825	361,203	82,600
3,560,000,000	152,155,721	549	657	120
2,879,000,000	156,251,650	34,941	26,030	3,000
2,029,000,000	594,034,370	2,253	834	79
1,822,000,000	630,687,560	44,790	18,601	703
764,000,000	652,528,480	NA	NA	NA
414,000,000	1,250,958,500	8,192,022	2,442,842	183,833
273,000,000	90,786,069	1,561	1,291	179
95,000,000	137,450,240	38,141	26,559	2,064
40,142,000,000[1]	26,218,457,000	48,625	NA	NA
37,457,000,000[1]	30,220,461,000	940,961	945,098	159,652

Nation Capital	Population	Type of Government	Heads of Government	Currency Value in U.S. Dollars	GNP (000,000)	GNP (per capita)
BHUTAN Thimphu	1,232,000 10,000	Limited monarchy	King: Jigme Singye Wangchuk	Ngultrum 0.13	$ 90	$ 70
BOLIVIA Sucre La Paz	5,950,000 63,259 654,713	Republic	President: Gen. David Padilla Arancibia	Peso 0.05	2,280	390
BOPHUTHATSWANA Mmabatho	1,039,000 NA	Republic	President: Chief Lucas Lawrence Manyane Mangope	Rand 1.15	NA	NA
BOTSWANA Gaborone	710,000 36,900	Republic (C)	President: Sir Seretse Khama	Pula 1.21	280	410
BRAZIL Brasília	112,240,000 241,543	Federal republic	President: Gen. Ernesto Geisel	Cruzeiro 0.050	125,570	1,140
BULGARIA Sofia	8,800,000 965,728	People's republic	Chairman, Council of State: Todor Zhivkov Chairman, Council of Ministers: Stanko Todorov	Lev 1.06	20,270	2,310
BURMA Rangoon	31,510,000 2,056,118	Socialist republic	President: U Ne Win Premier: U Maung Maung Kha	Kyat 0.15	3,730	120
BURUNDI Bujumbura	3,970,000 157,100	Republic	President: Lt. Col. Jean-Baptiste Bagaza Premier: Lt. Col. Édouard Nzambimana	Franc 0.011	460	120
CAMBODIA (DEMOCRATIC KAMPUCHEA) Phnom Penh	8,610,000 50,000	People's republic	Presidium Chairman: Khieu Samphan Premier: Pol Pot	NA.	NA	NA
CAMEROON Yaoundé	6,670,000 274,399	Republic	President: Ahmadou Ahidjo Prime Minister: Paul Biya	CFA franc 0.0046	2,240	290
CANADA Ottawa	23,320,000 304,462	Federal parliamentary state (C)	Governor-General: Jules Léger Prime Minister: Pierre Elliott Trudeau	Dollar 0.85	174,120	7,510
CAPE VERDE Praia	310,000 4,054	Republic	President: Aristides M. Pereira Premier: Maj. Pedro Rodrigues Pires	Escudo 0.022	80	260
CENTRAL AFRICAN EMPIRE Bangui	2,610,000 187,000	Constitutional monarchy	Emperor: Bokassa I Prime Minister: Henri Maidou	CFA franc 0.0046	420	230
CEYLON (SRI LANKA) Colombo	13,970,000 618,000	Republic (C)	President: Junius R. Jayewardene Prime Minister: Ranasinghe Premadasa	Rupee 0.064	2,750	200
CHAD N'Djamena	4,200,000 224,000	Republic	President: Gen. Félix Malloum Premier: Hissène Habré	CFA franc 0.0046	510	120
CHILE Santiago	10,660,000 1,759,087	Republic	President: Gen. Augusto Pinochet Ugarte	Peso 0.030	10,980	1,050

438

Imports / Exports	Revenue / Expenditure	Elementary Schools: Teachers / Students	Secondary Schools: Teachers / Students	Colleges and Universities: Teachers / Students
$ NA ....$	5,041,960	382	348	25
NA	5,041,960	16,671	1,523	275
582,000,000	342,045,000	39,835	9,076	NA
713,000,000	399,775,000	912,998	167,486	51,585
NA	82,796,688	4,537	808	NA
NA	82,796,688	288,827	25,047	167
176,287,940	113,740,640	3,921	920	56
113,270,460	167,954,600	125,588	16,275	469
12,204,000,000	14,323,613,000	887,424	156,174	64,479
10,128,000,000	14,323,613,000	19,286,611	1,681,728	954,674
6,329,000,000	10,591,752,000	57,177	24,072	11,619
6,329,000,000	10,565,979,000	1,095,791	320,873	103,662
185,000,000	2,477,332,100	79,653	30,200	3,194
223,000,000	2,572,445,000	3,686,773	1,050,481	81,539
74,000,000	51,382,222	4,209	NA	223
95,000,000	44,701,111	129,597	13,774	1,002
NA	NA	NA	NA	NA
NA	NA	NA	NA	NA
900,000,000	515,090,500	20,803	5,069	408
671,000,000	515,090,500	1,074,021	122,573	7,900
39,561,000,000	32,342,449,000	269,454[2]	[2]	50,000
41,452,000,000	38,586,008,000	2,770,459	2,594,459	613,100
28,887,606	11,012,898	1,346	365	*
1,522,472	11,012,898	56,000	7,874	*
63,000,000[3]	NA	3,329	562	84
82,000,000[3]	93,497,662	221,412	23,895	450
695,000,000	357,602,820	NA	NA	1,860
714,000,000	528,971,720	1,385,001[4]	1,088,089[4]	14,568
116,000,000	68,771,780	NA	NA	65
63,000,000	68,771,780	208,071	13,601	800
2,189,000,000	2,921,816,800	57,164	30,850	11,419
2,190,000,000	2,942,167,300	2,243,274	465,935	149,647

439

Nation / Capital	Population	Type of Government	Heads of Government	Currency Value in U.S. Dollars	GNP (000,000)	GNP (per capita)
CHINA, PEOPLE'S REPUBLIC OF / Peking	865,680,000 / 8,487,000	People's republic	Chairman, Standing Committee of the National People's Congress: Yeh Chien-ying / Premier: Hua Kuo-feng	Yuan 0.58	$ 343,090	$ 410
COLOMBIA / Bogotá	25,050,000 / 3,102,000	Republic	President: Julio César Turbay Ayala	Peso 0.025	15,400	630
COMORO ISLANDS[5] / Moroni	370,000 / 18,300	Republic	President: Ahmed Abdallah / Premier: Abdallah Mohamed	CFA franc 0.0046	60	180
CONGO, REPUBLIC OF / Brazzaville	1,440,000 / 289,700	People's republic	President: Col. Joachim Yhombi Opango / Premier: Maj. Louis Sylvain Goma	CFA franc 0.0046	700	520
COSTA RICA / San José	2,070,000 / 233,691	Republic	President: Rodrigo Carazo Odio	Colón 0.12	2,090	1,040
CUBA / Havana	9,460,000 / 1,861,000	Socialist republic	President and Premier: Gen. Fidel Castro Ruz	Peso 1.35	8,120	860
CYPRUS / Nicosia	640,000 / 147,100	Republic (C)	President: Spyros Kyprianou	Pound 2.76	930	1,480
CZECHOSLOVAKIA / Prague	15,030,000 / 1,175,522	Federal socialist republic	President: Gustáv Husák / Premier: Lubomír Štrougal	Koruna 0.17	57,250	3,840
DAHOMEY (BENIN) / Porto-Novo	3,290,000 / 104,000	People's republic	President: Lt. Col. Mathieu Kérékou	CFA franc 0.0046	430	130
DENMARK / Copenhagen	5,090,000 / 709,300	Constitutional monarchy	Queen: Margaret II / Premier: Anker Jørgensen	Krone 0.19	37,770	7,450
DJIBOUTI / Djibouti	226,000 / 102,000	Republic	President: Hassan Gouled Aptidon / Premier: Barkat Gourad Hamadou	Djibouti franc 0.0054	200	1,940
DOMINICA / Roseau	80,000 / 16,800	Republic (C)	Premier: Patrick R. John	East Caribbean dollar 0.37	NA	NA
DOMINICAN REPUBLIC / Santo Domingo	4,980,000 / 673,470	Republic	President: Silvestre Antonio Guzmán Fernández	Peso 1.00	3,750	780
ECUADOR / Quito	7,560,000 / 599,828	Republic	President: Vice-Admiral Alfredo Poveda Burbano	Sucre 0.037	4,690	640
EGYPT, ARAB REPUBLIC OF / Cairo	38,740,000 / 5,715,000	Republic	President: Anwar el-Sadat / Prime Minister: Mustafa Khalil	Pound 2.54	10,530	280
EL SALVADOR / San Salvador	4,260,000 / 500,000	Republic	President: Gen. Carlos Humberto Romero	Colón 0.40	2,030	490
EQUATORIAL GUINEA / Malabo	320,000 / 19,341	Republic	President: Francisco Macías Nguema	Ekuele 0.014	110	330
ETHIOPIA / Addis Ababa	28,980,000 / 1,242,555	Republic	Chairman, Dirgue: Lt. Col. Mengistu Haile Mariam	Birr 0.48	2,960	100
FIJI / Suva	600,000 / 63,622	Parliamentary state (C)	Governor-General: Ratu Sir George K. Cakobau / Prime Minister: Ratu Sir Kamisese K.T. Mara	Dollar 1.22	670	1,150

Imports / Exports	Revenue / Expenditure	Elementary Schools: Teachers / Students	Secondary Schools: Teachers / Students	Colleges and Universities: Teachers / Students
$ 6,000,000,000	NA	NA	NA	NA
7,200,000,000	NA	150,000,000	45,000,000	1,000,000
1,563,000,000	1,561,254,200	131,211	70,121	21,163
2,302,000,000	1,489,430,500	3,953,242	1,306,275	192,887
22,788,390	13,134,195	849	118	*
7,854,519	13,134,195	34,181	2,586	*
156,000,000³	260,960,470	5,434	2,076	165
182,000,000³	260,960,470	319,101	94,798	3,249
1,006,000,000	444,749,120	10,965	5,266	NA
798,000,000	539,964,990	365,957	116,285	32,928
4,066,000,000	NA	78,451	37,577	5,725
3,573,000,000	NA	1,925,700	613,800	76,900
620,000,000	186,977,640	2,817	3,131	63
318,000,000	169,412,050	74,970	59,956	685
11,149,000,000	43,618,090,000	93,192	25,009	17,367
10,818,000,000	43,584,589,000	1,882,371	444,365	168,310
150,000,000	68,771,780	5,786	1,463	153
46,000,000	68,771,780	279,673	47,259	2,118
13,239,000,000	11,574,982,000	58,012²	²	NA
10,117,000,000	13,695,577,000	567,793	291,141	110,271
NA	NA	268	148	*
NA	51,714,898	9,764	1,994	*
18,444,444	10,561,826	NA	NA	*
10,777,777	11,475,409	17,226	6,887	*
848,000,000	620,300,000	NA	NA	NA
794,000,000	620,300,000	867,592	178,249	50,000
1,440,000,000	504,680,000	NA	NA	NA
1,192,000,000	492,440,000	1,318,475	431,226	170,173
4,808,000,000	13,805,264,000	118,251	78,789	19,300
1,726,000,000	13,805,264,000	4,120,936	2,107,891	419,750
950,000,000	395,040,000	NA	NA	1,275
959,000,000	322,400,000	796,250	59,079	26,692
NA	NA	630	175	*
NA	NA	35,977	6,014	*
349,000,000	562,142,170	NA	6,929	434
330,000,000	636,814,470	959,272	190,922	6,474
306,000,000	146,450,720	4,274	NA	166
173,000,000	203,997,240	134,971	30,545	1,810

Nation Capital	Population	Type of Government	Heads of Government	Currency Value in U.S. Dollars	GNP (000,000)	GNP (per capita)
FINLAND Helsinki	4,740,000 493,000	Republic	President: Urho K. Kekkonen Prime Minister: Kalevi Sorsa	Markka 0.25	$ 26,570	$ 5,620
FRANCE Paris	53,080,000 2,299,830	Republic	President: Valéry Giscard d'Estaing Premier: Raymond Barre	Franc 0.23	346,730	6,550
GABON REPUBLIC Libreville	530,000 169,200	Republic	President: Omar Bongo Premier: Léon Mébiane	CFA franc 0.0046	1,410	2,590
GAMBIA, THE Banjul	550,000 43,883	Republic (C)	President: Sir Dawda K. Jawara	Dalasi 0.49	100	180
GERMAN DEMOCRATIC REPUBLIC (East) Berlin	16,770,000 1,101,123	Socialist republic	Chairman, Council of State: Erich Honecker Chairman, Council of Ministers: Willi Stoph	Mark 0.49	70,880	4,220
GERMANY, FEDERAL REPUBLIC OF Bonn	61,400,000 284,957	Federal republic	President: Walter Scheel Chancellor: Helmut Schmidt	Deutsche Mark 0.52	457,540	7,380
GHANA Accra	10,480,000 716,600	Republic (C)	Chairman, Supreme Military Council: Lt. Gen. Frederick W.K. Akuffo	Cedi 0.36	5,920	580
GREAT BRITAIN London	55,850,000 7,028,200	Limited monarchy (C)	Queen: Elizabeth II Prime Minister: James Callaghan	Pound 1.94	225,150	4,020
GREECE Athens	9,280,000 867,023	Republic	President: Constantine Tsatsos Premier: Constantine Karamanlis	Drachma 0.027	23,600	2,590
GRENADA St. George's	100,000 6,600	Parliamentary state (C)	Governor-General: Sir Leo de Gale Prime Minister: Sir Eric M. Gairy	East Caribbean dollar 0.37	50	420
GUATEMALA Guatemala City	6,440,000 717,322	Republic	President: Gen. Fernando Romeo Lucas García	Quetzal 1.00	4,070	630
GUINEA, REPUBLIC OF Conakry	4,650,000 525,671	Republic	President: Sékou Touré Premier: Lansana Beavogui	Syli 0.049	880	150
GUINEA-BISSAU Bissau	540,000 71,200	Republic	President: Luis de Almeida Cabral Chief State Commissioner: Comdr. João Bernardo Vieira	Peso 0.022	70	140
GUYANA Georgetown	830,000 63,184	Republic (C)	President: Arthur Chung Prime Minister: L.F.S. Burnham	Dollar 0.39	430	540
HAITI Port-au-Prince	4,750,000 475,187	Republic	President: Jean-Claude Duvalier	Gourde 0.20	930	200
HONDURAS Tegucigalpa	2,830,000 270,645	Republic	President: Gen. Policarpo Paz García	Lempira 0.50	1,160	390
HUNGARY Budapest	10,650,000 2,081,696	People's republic	Chairman, Presidential Council: Pál Losonczi Chairman, Council of Ministers: György Lázár	Forint 0.051	24,140	2,280

Imports / Exports	Revenue / Expenditure	Elementary Schools: Teachers / Students	Secondary Schools: Teachers / Students	Colleges and Universities: Teachers / Students
$ 7,603,000,000	$ 8,455,213,200	23,235	36,191	4,420
7,670,000,000	8,734,834,100	406,058	508,774	71,526
70,498,000,000	73,332,837,000	NA	343,084	NA
63,560,000,000	73,916,046,000	4,978,000	5,262,000	777,348
498,000,000[3]	1,087,088,800	2,664	1,016	NA
1,136,000,000[3]	1,087,088,800	128,552	22,542	986
78,000,000	29,275,707	948	347	*
48,000,000	84,061,278	24,617	6,618	*
14,334,000,000	48,995,000,000	158,543[6]	NA	33,570
12,024,000,000	48,803,333,000	2,578,782[6]	460,639	306,783
102,377,000,000	71,336,342,000	269,367	213,494	76,150
119,768,000,000	81,380,522,000	6,819,106	5,442,843	837,079
805,000,000	919,130,430	38,381[4]	22,492[4]	1,103
760,000,000	1,273,304,300	1,157,303[4]	548,924[4]	9,079
63,677,000,000	71,930,627,000	249,191	351,802	NA
57,547,000,000	82,883,552,000	5,965,702	5,143,142	637,086
6,778,000,000	5,643,452,500	30,552	17,624	5,899
2,724,000,000	5,643,480,700	929,906	519,367	97,759
24,518,518	NA	884	198	*
12,222,222	24,208,333	29,795	5,068	*
839,000,000	942,600,000	18,475	7,335	1,664
760,000,000	942,600,000	706,146	135,801	35,600
180,180,100	217,935,000	4,698	2,785	NA
156,472,200	217,935,000	169,132	71,901	1,974
35,142,337	21,382,000	2,415	150	*
5,728,467	20,449,100	84,711	3,046	*
364,000,000	174,743,920	4,077	2,989	231
269,000,000	237,436,700	132,023	67,853	2,307
207,000,000	77,500,000	10,616	4,228	308
127,000,000	77,500,000	488,926	55,213	2,505
580,000,000	415,950,000	13,649	4,007	729
504,000,000	415,950,000	483,210	75,526	12,951
6,522,000,000	19,810,061,000	68,425	14,454	12,233
5,832,000,000	20,005,133,000	1,072,423	373,372	110,528

Nation Capital	Population	Type of Government	Heads of Government	Currency Value in U.S. Dollars	GNP (000,000)	GNP (per capita)
ICELAND Reykjavík	220,000 84,493	Republic	President: Kristján Eldjárn Prime Minister: Ólafur Jóhannesson	Króna 0.0033	$ 1,380	$ 6,100
INDIA New Delhi	625,820,000 301,801	Federal republic (C)	President: Neelam Sanjiva Reddy Prime Minister: Morarji Ranchodji Desai	Rupee 0.12	95,880	150
INDONESIA Djakarta	143,280,000 6,178,500	Republic	President and Prime Minister: Gen. Suharto	Rupiah 0.0016	32,440	240
IRAN Tehran	34,270,000 4,496,159	Constitutional monarchy	Shah: Mohammed Riza Pahlavi Prime Minister: Gen. Gholam Riza Azhari	Rial 0.014	66,250	1,930
IRAQ Baghdad	11,910,000 2,969,000	Republic	President and Prime Minister: Field Marshal Ahmed Hassan al-Bakr	Dinar 3.39	15,940	1,390
IRELAND Dublin	3,190,000 566,034	Republic	President: Patrick J. Hillery Prime Minister: Jack Lynch	Pound 1.94	8,090	2,560
ISRAEL Jerusalem	3,610,000 366,000	Republic	President: Itzhak Navon Prime Minister: Menachem Begin	Pound 0.053	13,980	3,920
ITALY Rome	56,450,000 2,883,996	Republic	President: Alessandro Pertini Premier: Giulio Andreotti	Lira 0.0012	171,250	3,050
IVORY COAST Abidjan	5,150,000 685,800	Republic	President: Félix Houphouët-Boigny	CFA franc 0.0046	4,280	610
JAMAICA Kingston	2,090,000 169,800	Parliamentary state (C)	Governor-General: Florizel A. Glasspole Prime Minister: Michael N. Manley	Dollar 0.62	2,230	1,070
JAPAN Tokyo	113,860,000 8,568,700	Constitutional monarchy	Emperor: Hirohito Prime Minister: Takeo Fukuda	Yen 0.0050	553,140	4,910
JORDAN Amman	2,780,000 691,120	Constitutional monarchy	King: Hussein I Prime Minister: Mudar Badran	Dinar 3.34	1,710	610
KENYA Nairobi	14,340,000 776,000	Republic (C)	President: Daniel Arap Moi	Shilling 0.13	3,280	240
KOREA, DEMOCRATIC PEOPLE'S REPUBLIC OF P'yŏngyang	16,650,000 1,500,000	People's republic	President: Marshal Kim Il Sung Premier: Li Jong Ok	Won 1.02	7,610	470
KOREA, REPUBLIC OF Seoul	36,440,000 7,525,629	Republic	President: Park Chung Hee Premier: Choi Kyu Hah	Won 0.0021	24,050	670
KUWAIT Al Kuwait	1,130,000 78,000	Constitutional emirate	Emir: Sheikh Jaber al-Ahmad al-Sabah Prime Minister: Sheikh Saad al-Abdullah al-Salem al-Sabah	Dinar 3.64	16,480	15,480

Imports / Exports	Revenue / Expenditure	Elementary Schools: Teachers / Students	Secondary Schools: Teachers / Students	Colleges and Universities: Teachers / Students
$ 607,000,000	$ 422,133,180	1,379	2,413	575
513,000,000	418,363,430	26,922	25,028	2,970
6,592,000,000	12,437,878,000	2,055,528	736,053	NA
6,222,000,000	17,586,013,000	84,537,502	8,938,427	2,972,085
6,230,000,000	7,002,409,600	603,327	218,550	NA
10,853,000,000	8,877,590,300	18,232,567	3,361,308	278,200
13,750,000,000	31,052,780,000	152,106	81,855	12,310
24,245,000,000	32,792,281,000	4,468,299	2,183,137	135,354
3,470,000,000	3,437,617,100	68,875	20,098	3,270
9,271,000,000	2,360,252,800	1,765,092	522,904	78,784
5,378,000,000	2,502,894,100	13,060	18,913	4,088
4,396,000,000	2,845,760,900	404,818	270,956	39,928
4,663,000,000	7,959,714,100	31,835	13,384	NA
2,959,000,000	7,959,714,100	578,658	152,384	74,371
47,580,000,000	40,384,685,000	255,267	432,867	43,129
45,063,000,000	52,090,628,000	4,741,650	5,058,303	959,300
1,752,000,000	1,477,851,100	15,358	NA	NA
2,155,000,000	1,380,768,600	672,707	119,482	8,701
861,000,000	736,346,930	11,531	6,125	NA
856,000,000	1,352,248,300	370,200	213,555	10,305
70,660,000,000	128,458,330,000	417,443	511,590	191,551
80,470,000,000	161,541,660,000	10,364,855	10,364,855	2,248,903
1,381,000,000	323,262,830	11,636	8,586	811
249,000,000	794,561,930	402,401	185,700	15,735
1,284,000,000[7]	671,224,240	89,074	12,077	NA
1,213,000,000[7]	904,363,620	2,894,617	289,056	11,351
1,400,000,000	12,794,747,000	100,000[2]	[2]	NA
1,200,000,000	12,794,747,000	1,500,000	1,200,000	300,000
10,810,000,000	5,842,210,700	109,530	88,230	14,255
10,046,000,000	6,296,508,200	5,503,737	3,396,576	325,460
3,327,000,000	8,114,958,900	6,360	9,465	596
9,845,000,000	7,097,465,100	111,820	109,266	8,104

Nation Capital	Population	Type of Government	Heads of Government	Currency Value in U.S. Dollars	GNP (000,000)	GNP (per capita)
LAOS (LAO PEOPLE'S DEMOCRATIC REPUBLIC) Vientiane	3,460,000 176,637	People's republic	President: Prince Souphanouvong Prime Minister: Kaysone Phomvihan	Kip 0.0025	$ 310	$ 90
LEBANON Beirut	3,060,000 474,870	Republic	President: Elias Sarkis Prime Minister: Selim al-Hoss	Pound 0.33	NA	NA
LESOTHO Maseru	1,230,000 14,700	Limited monarchy (C)	King: Moshoeshoe II Prime Minister: Chief Leabua Jonathan	South African rand 1.15	210	170
LIBERIA Monrovia	1,800,000 172,100	Republic	President: William R. Tolbert, Jr.	Dollar 1.00	720	450
LIBYA (SOCIALIST PEOPLE'S LIBYAN ARAB JAMAHIRIYAH) Tripoli	2,630,000 245,000	Socialist republic	Secretary-General, General People's Congress: Col. Muammar el-Qaddafi Chairman, General People's Committee: Abdul Ati al-Obeidi	Dinar 3.38	16,000	6,310
LIECHTENSTEIN Vaduz	24,169 4,620	Constitutional monarchy	Sovereign: Prince Francis Joseph II Chief of Government: Hans Brunhart	Swiss franc 0.58	NA	NA
LUXEMBOURG Luxembourg	360,000 80,000	Constitutional monarchy	Grand Duke: Jean Prime Minister: Gaston Thorn	Franc 0.033	2,330	6,460
MALAGASY REPUBLIC (DEMOCRATIC REPUBLIC OF MADAGASCAR) Antananarivo (Tananarive)	8,520,000 438,800	Socialist republic	President: Lt. Comdr. Didier Ratsiraka Premier: Lt. Col. Désiré Rakotoarijaona	Franc 0.0046	1,870	200
MALAWI Lilongwe	5,530,000 102,924	Republic (C)	President: Hastings Kamuzu Banda	Kwacha 1.21	700	140
MALAYSIA Kuala Lumpur	12,600,000 557,000	Federal constitutional monarchy (C)	Supreme Head of State: Tuanku Yahya Putra Prime Minister: Datuk Hussein bin Onn	Ringgit (Dollar) 0.44	10,900	860
MALDIVES, REPUBLIC OF Male	140,000 17,000	Republic	President and Prime Minister: Amir Ibrahim Nasir	Rupee 0.11	10	110
MALI, REPUBLIC OF Bamako	5,990,000 400,022	Republic	President: Col. Moussa Traoré	Franc 0.0023	590	100
MALTA Valletta	330,000 14,071	Republic (C)	President: Anton Buttigieg Prime Minister: Dominic Mintoff	Pound 2.68	460	1,390
MAURITANIA, ISLAMIC REPUBLIC OF Nouakchott	1,481,000 134,386	Republic	President, Military Committee for National Recovery and Chief of Government: Lt. Col. Moustapha Ould Mohamed Saleck	Ouguiya 0.022	460	340
MAURITIUS Port Louis	880,000 141,343	Parliamentary state (C)	Governor-General: Dayendranath Burrenchobay Prime Minister: Sir Seewoosagur Ramgoolam	Rupee 0.17	600	680
MEXICO Mexico City	64,590,000 8,628,024	Federal republic	President: José López Portillo	Peso 0.044	67,640	1,090

Imports / Exports	Revenue / Expenditure	Elementary Schools: Teachers / Students	Secondary Schools: Teachers / Students	Colleges and Universities: Teachers / Students
$ 65,000,000	$ 32,665,320	7,340	1,104	152
11,000,000	61,740,863	274,067	20,819	828
1,767,815,400	458,496,730	33,245[2]	[2]	2,313
1,105,210,700	680,718,950	497,723	174,711	50,803
135,464,580	33,693,535	4,233	770	130
13,109,475	33,693,535	221,386	17,955	847
464,000,000	190,500,000	3,832	NA	NA
447,000,000	169,700,000	157,821	34,151	2,404
3,212,000,000	6,748,564,100	26,385	14,434	350
9,561,000,000	7,849,763,500	568,781	198,959	12,459
NA	94,363,482	90	80	43
243,886,980	94,190,348	2,122	1,616	1,216
[8]	1,134,659,200	1,711	1,757	137
[8]	1,186,713,100	35,000	22,831	483
285,000,000	NA	18,688	6,030	NA
275,000,000	583,935,400	1,133,013	141,022	11,000
235,000,000	143,729,330	10,735	906	150
195,000,000	153,211,370	663,940	16,703	1,148
4,980,000,000[9]	3,510,548,500	60,248	34,306	2,686
6,545,000,000[9]	3,400,000,000	1,924,775	975,372	35,246
2,449,924	NA	30	66	*
NA	3,261,118	4,411	671	*
145,000,000	107,540,910	9,413	NA	327
67,000,000	119,844,840	253,351	50,773	2,445
513,000,000	239,723,770	1,421	2,498	250
289,000,000	261,061,830	29,834	33,095	1,458
207,000,000	168,295,330	NA	NA	*
157,000,000	168,295,330	58,000	7,050	*
442,000,000	182,358,290	6,008	2,252	99
312,000,000	189,934,990	144,002	69,122	1,203
5,489,000,000	19,669,172,000	255,939	186,498	30,865
4,063,000,000	19,669,172,000	12,600,620	3,137,796	599,920

447

Nation Capital	Population	Type of Government	Heads of Government	Currency Value in U.S. Dollars	GNP (000,000)	GNP (per capita)
MONACO Monaco-Ville	25,000 1,685	Constitutional monarchy	Prince: Rainier III Minister of State: André Saint-Mleux	French franc 0.23	$ NA	$ NA
MONGOLIAN PEOPLE'S REPUBLIC Ulan Bator	1,530,000 334,400	People's republic	Presidium Chairman: Yumzhagiyin Tsedenbal Chairman, Council of Ministers: Jambyn Batmönh	Tugrik 0.33	1,280	860
MOROCCO Rabat	18,240,000 435,510	Constitutional monarchy	King: Hassan II Prime Minister: Ahmed Osman	Dirham 0.25	9,220	540
MOZAMBIQUE Maputo	9,680,000 354,684	People's republic	President: Samora M. Machel	Escudo 0.03	1,600	170
NAURU Yaren	8,000 NA	Republic (C)	President: Hammer DeRoburt	Australian dollar 1.16	NA	NA
NEPAL Kathmandu	13,140,000 171,400	Constitutional monarchy	King: Birendra Bir Bikram Shah Dev Prime Minister: Kirti Nidhi Bista	Rupee 0.083	1,490	120
NETHERLANDS, THE Amsterdam	13,850,000 738,441	Constitutional monarchy	Queen: Juliana Prime Minister: Andreas A.M. van Agt	Guilder 0.48	85,320	6,200
NEW ZEALAND Wellington	3,110,000 138,938	Parliamentary state (C)	Governor-General: Sir Keith Holyoake Prime Minister: Robert D. Muldoon	Dollar 1.06	13,120	4,250
NICARAGUA Managua	2,310,000 313,400	Republic	President: Gen. Anastasio Somoza Debayle	Córdoba 0.14	1,760	750
NIGER, REPUBLIC OF Niamey	4,860,000 130,299	Republic	President, Supreme Military Council: Lt. Col. Seyni Kountché	CFA franc 0.0046	740	160
NIGERIA, FEDERATION OF Lagos	66,630,000 1,060,848	Federal republic (C)	President, Supreme Military Council: Lt. Gen. Olusegun Obasanjo	Naira 1.56	29,320	453
NORWAY Oslo	4,040,000 462,497	Constitutional monarchy	King: Olaf V Prime Minister: Odvar Nordli	Krone 0.20	29,920	7,420
OMAN Muscat	820,000 15,000	Sultanate	Sultan: Qabus bin Said	Rial 2.90	2,130	2,680
PAKISTAN Islamabad	75,280,000 77,318	Federal republic	President and Chief Martial Law Administrator: Muhammad Zia ul-Haq	Rupee 0.10	12,190	170
PANAMA Panamá	1,770,000 415,790	Republic	President: Aristides Royo	Balboa 1.00	2,260	1,310
PAPUA NEW GUINEA Port Moresby	2,910,000 113,449	Parliamentary state (C)	Governor-General: Sir Tore Lokoloko Prime Minister: Michael T. Somare	Kina 1.45	1,400	490
PARAGUAY Asunción	2,810,000 442,000	Republic	President: Gen. Alfredo Stroessner	Guaraní 0.0079	1,680	640
PERU Lima	16,360,000 2,833,609	Republic	President: Gen. Francisco Morales Bermúdez Prime Minister: Gen. Oscar Molina Pallochia	Sol 0.0053	12,610	800

Imports / Exports	Revenue / Expenditure	Elementary Schools: Teachers / Students	Secondary Schools: Teachers / Students	Colleges and Universities: Teachers / Students
$ NA	$ 106,287,010	300[2]	[2]	*
NA	93,444,895	4,929[2]	[2]	*
556,325,300	1,102,409,600	NA	NA	807
249,397,590	1,099,397,500	129,802	184,688	9,861
3,194,000,000	4,018,475,700	NA	NA	1,642
1,300,000,000	5,004,618,900	1,603,872	519,822	45,322
417,000,000	168,656,330	8,345	2,788	326
202,000,000	259,196,640	577,997	54,650	2,621
26,539,280	49,442,715	130[2]		*
84,925,690	28,978,633	1,501[2]	472	*
158,704,000	137,968,000	20,775	11,295	1,516
91,832,000	246,992,000	643,835	262,748	23,504
45,616,000,000	35,105,263,000	52,700	91,193	28,300
43,703,000,000	41,413,596,000	1,453,467	1,283,585	288,026
3,363,000,000	3,950,142,400	21,647	16,251	4,424
3,142,000,000	3,575,118,700	442,082	444,615	66,739
755,000,000	214,389,410	9,223	2,631	1,052
633,000,000	290,207,790	307,567	97,831	20,273
127,000,000	184,462,380	4,273	700	200
134,000,000	184,462,380	159,000	18,835	850
11,306,000,000	11,743,936,000	116,640	20,448	5,019
11,823,000,000	13,202,333,000	4,368,778	544,520	32,971
12,877,000,000	10,196,666,000	19,613	20,454	5,651
8,717,000,000	12,849,629,000	391,079	334,028	66,628
1,101,621,300	2,067,168,500	2,055	208	*
1,320,497,900	2,229,299,300	54,611	1,379	*
2,454,000,000	2,308,790,600	131,400	108,524	5,054
1,152,000,000	2,369,086,600	5,293,504	2,031,799	111,826
840,000,000	346,000,000	13,137	5,667	1,342
237,000,000	370,559,000	343,201	127,806	30,642
567,000,000	532,207,850	NA	NA	NA
723,000,000	536,924,020	255,500	41,100	5,545
308,000,000	173,404,760	15,398	7,201	1,741
279,000,000	173,729,360	452,249	75,424	17,135
1,780,000,000	1,605,838,200	77,448	41,932	11,590
1,304,000,000	2,536,153,900	3,079,307	1,132,071	183,233

Nation Capital	Population	Type of Government	Heads of Government	Currency Value in U.S. Dollars	GNP (000,000)	GNP (per capita)
PHILIPPINES, ... **REPUBLIC OF THE** Manila	45,030,000 1,454,352	Republic	President and Prime Minister: Ferdinand E. Marcos	Peso 0.14	$ 17,810	$ 410
POLAND . . . . Warsaw	34,700,000 1,463,400	People's republic	Chairman, Council of State: Henryk Jabłoński Chairman, Council of Ministers: Piotr Jaroszewicz	Złoty 0.050	98,130	2,860
PORTUGAL . . . . Lisbon	9,730,000 847,300	Republic	President: Gen. António Ramalho Eanes Prime Minister: Carlos Alberto Mota Pinto	Escudo 0.021	16,480	1,690
QATAR . . . . Doha	183,600 130,000	Constitutional emirate	Emir and Prime Minister: Sheikh Khalifa bin Hamad al-Thani	Riyal 0.26	2,390	11,400
RHODESIA . . . . Salisbury	6,740,000 568,000	Unilaterally declared republic	Acting President: Lt. Col. Henry B. Everard Prime Minister: Ian D. Smith	Dollar 1.52	3,560	550
RUMANIA . . . . Bucharest	21,660,000 1,588,592	Socialist republic	President: Nicolae Ceauşescu Chairman, Council of Ministers: Mânea Manescu	Leu 0.20	31,070	1,450
RWANDA . . . . Kigali	4,370,000 89,950	Republic	Head of State and President, Council of Ministers: Maj. Gen. Juvénal Habyalimana	Franc 0.011	480	110
SAN MARINO . . . . San Marino	20,000 4,608	Republic	Co-Regents: Ermenegildo Casperoni I Adriano Reffi I Secretary of State for Foreign Affairs: Giordano Bruno Reffi	Italian lira Vatican City lira 0.0012	NA	NA
SÃO TOMÉ AND . . . . **PRÍNCIPE** São Tomé	80,000 20,000	Republic	President: Manuel Pinto da Costa Premier: Miguel Trouvoada	Escudo 0.028	40	490
SAUDI ARABIA . . . . Riyadh	9,520,000 666,840	Monarchy	King and Prime Minister: Khalid ibn Abdul-Aziz	Riyal 0.30	38,510	4,480
SENEGAL, ... **REPUBLIC OF** Dakar	5,120,000 800,000	Republic	President: Léopold Sédar Senghor Premier: Abdou Diouf	CFA franc 0.0046	1,980	390
SEYCHELLES . . . . Victoria	60,000 14,500	Republic (C)	President: F. Albert René	Rupee 0.15	30	580
SIERRA LEONE . . . . Freetown	3,470,000 274,000	Republic (C)	President: Siaka P. Stevens	Leone 0.99	610	200
SINGAPORE, ... **REPUBLIC OF** Singapore	2,310,000 1,327,500	Republic (C)	President: Benjamin Henry Sheares Prime Minister: Lee Kuan Yew	Dollar 0.46	6,150	2,700
SOLOMON ISLANDS . . . . Honiara	196,823 14,942	Parliamentary state (C)	Governor-General: Baddeley Devesi Prime Minister: Peter Kenilosea	Dollar 1.16	50	250
SOMALIA . . . . Mogadishu	3,350,000 286,000	Republic	President, Supreme Revolutionary Council: Maj. Gen. Muhammad Siad Barre	Shilling 0.16	370	110
SOUTH AFRICA, ... **REPUBLIC OF** Cape Town Pretoria	26,130,000 842,600 634,400	Republic	President: Balthazar J. Vorster Prime Minister: Pieter W. Botha	Rand 1.15	34,850	1,340

Imports Exports	Revenue Expenditure	Elementary Schools: Teachers Students	Secondary Schools: Teachers Students	Colleges and Universities: Teachers Students
$ 4,270,000,000 3,151,000,000	$ 2,821,720,800 3,826,964,700	261,817 8,365,470	72,778 2,254,543	31,783 764,725
14,674,000,000 12,336,000,000	53,207,831,000 53,067,269,000	193,300 4,326,600	101,700 2,648,000	49,900 491,000
4,963,000,000 2,023,000,000	3,993,301,500 3,993,301,500	61,398 1,254,364	30,760 472,413	7,619 73,525
833,830,210 2,211,925,200	2,259,595,900 1,848,232,300	1,252 23,615	829 10,109	69 779
NA NA	978,871,800 1,102,080,600	22,831 885,476	4,494 80,568	229 1,516
6,095,000,000 6,138,000,000	57,002,012,000 57,002,012,000	147,582 3,125,584	46,447 1,015,886	13,662 174,888
114,000,000 92,000,000	78,823,782 63,528,651	8,161 434,150	820 12,520	184 1,069
NA NA	39,053,464 39,053,464	107 1,698	93 1,140	* *
10,501,237 6,568,329	6,097,500 6,097,500	303 10,015	116 2,370	* *
8,694,000,000 38,286,000,000	41,735,897,000 31,737,891,000	35,139 686,108	15,728 222,797	2,133 26,437
576,000,000 461,000,000	667,823,070 667,823,070	8,468 308,526	3,189 79,527	412 8,213
43,774,664 2,622,082	19,213,724 21,229,449	435 9,950	235 4,559	16 142
153,000,000 111,000,000	137,940,890 143,498,160	6,373 205,910	2,596 50,478	335 2,005
10,471,000,000 8,241,000,000	1,443,090,100 1,443,090,100	11,041 306,349	8,393 189,046	1,116 20,734
23,791,417 20,966,865	13,265,460 11,678,140	1,071 28,219	131 2,005	* *
162,000,000 89,000,000	105,957,000 92,613,100	3,481 197,706	1,372 28,857	286 1,845
5,893,000,000 6,158,000,000	8,722,401,100 10,102,345,000	153,000[2] 4,299,570	[2] 992,587	8,128 109,476

Nation Capital	Population	Type of Government	Heads of Government	Currency Value in U.S. Dollars	GNP (000,000)	GNP (per capita)
SPAIN . . . . Madrid	36,350,000 3,870,900	Monarchy	King: Juan Carlos I President, Council of Ministers: Adolfo Suárez González	Peseta 0.14	$ 104,090	$ 2,920
SUDAN, DEMOCRATIC **REPUBLIC OF** Khartoum	16,950,000 333,921	Republic	President and Prime Minister: Maj. Gen. Gaafar Mohammed al-Nimeiry	Pound 2.50	4,610	290
SURINAM . . . . Paramaribo	450,000 151,500	Republic	President: Johan H.E. Ferrier Prime Minister: Henck A.E. Arron	Guilder 0.56	500	1,370
SWAZILAND . . . . Mbabane	510,000 22,262	Monarchy (C)	King: Sobhuza II Prime Minister: Col. Maphevu Dlamini	Lilangeni 1.15	240	470
SWEDEN . . . . Stockholm	8,260,000 661,258	Constitutional monarchy	King: Charles XVI Gustavus Prime Minister: Ola Ullsten	Krona 0.23	71,290	8,670
SWITZERLAND . . . . Bern	6,330,000 146,800	Federal republic	President: Willi Ritschard	Franc 0.58	56,900	8,880
SYRIA . . . . Damascus	7,840,000 1,054,000	Socialist republic	President: Lt. Gen. Hafez al-Assad Prime Minister: Mohammed Ali al-Halabi	Pound 0.25	5,970	780
TAIWAN (FORMOSA) . . . . Taipei	16,678,100 2,089,288	Republic	President: Chiang Ching-kuo Premier: Sun Yun-suan	New Taiwan . . . . . dollar 0.026	17,500	1,070
TANZANIA, UNITED **REPUBLIC OF** Dar es Salaam	16,070,000 517,000	Republic (C)	President: Julius K. Nyerere Prime Minister: Edward M. Sokoine	Shilling 0.13	2,700	180
THAILAND . . . . Bangkok	44,040,000 2,213,522	Constitutional monarchy	King: Bhumibol Adulyadej Prime Minister: Gen. Kriangsak Chamanand	Baht 0.05	16,230	380
TOGO, REPUBLIC OF . . . Lomé	2,350,000 229,400	Republic	President: Gen. Gnassingbe Eyadéma	CFA franc 0.0046	600	260
TONGA . . . . Nuku'alofa	90,000 18,396	Constitutional monarchy (C)	King: Taufa'ahau Tupou IV Prime Minister: Prince Fatafehi Tu'ipelehake	Pa'anga 1.32	40	410
TRANSKEI . . . . Umtata	2,061,000 24,805	Republic	Acting President: Chief Justice G.C.A. Munnik Prime Minister: Chief Kaiser D. Matanzima	Rand 1.15	NA	NA
TRINIDAD AND TOBAGO Port-of-Spain	1,100,000 60,450	Republic (C)	President: Sir Ellis E.I. Clarke Prime Minister: Eric E. Williams	Dollar 0.42	2,450	2,240
TUNISIA . . . . Tunis	6,070,000 550,404	Republic	President: Habib Bourguiba Premier: Hedi Nouira	Dinar 2.42	4,790	840
TURKEY . . . . Ankara	42,130,000 1,701,004	Republic	President: Fahri Korütürk Premier: Bülent Ecevit	Lira 0.040	40,960	990

452

Imports Exports	Revenue Expenditure	Elementary Schools: Teachers Students	Secondary Schools: Teachers Students	Colleges and Universities: Teachers Students
$ 17,846,000,000	$ 12,368,147,000	193,370	79,850	26,565
10,230,000,000	12,182,265,000	6,393,804	1,194,486	461,076
1,060,000,000	1,287,764,400	31,695	13,166	1,420
661,000,000	1,084,720,400	1,169,279	281,839	21,342
266,000,000	349,075,630	4,755	577	113
330,000,000	364,145,650	128,294	7,451	938
154,744,700	80,496,780	NA	1,009	136
151,960,670	86,246,550	92,721	18,350	1,150
19,566,000,000	24,388,650,000	41,150	47,837	NA
18,823,000,000	28,774,304,000	708,896	557,875	121,266
17,979,000,000	5,705,670,900	NA	NA	5,414
17,682,000,000	6,333,865,800	556,885	538,557	64,720
2,672,000,000	4,316,463,200	36,852	25,579	1,312
1,063,000,000	4,316,463,200	1,245,801	482,129	63,031
7,599,000,000	4,478,447,300	64,974	62,392	14,548
8,166,000,000	4,476,736,800	2,341,413	1,539,150	299,414
704,000,000[7]	564,307,830[10]	29,783	3,218	434
501,000,000[7]	915,475,330[10]	1,591,834	63,187	3,064
4,613,000,000	2,356,960,400	270,567	50,220	NA
3,493,000,000	3,302,156,300	6,736,751	1,334,435	81,696
201,000,000	234,597,530	6,080	1,634	236
105,000,000	234,597,530	362,895	64,590	2,353
13,986,000	6,948,700	688	338	11
4,017,600	7,794,716	19,115	11,351	15
NA	156,393,740	7,678	949	*
NA	156,393,740	455,326	33,000	*
1,772,000,000	1,319,541,600	6,471	2,319	NA
2,174,000,000	1,319,541,600	200,095	51,441	2,962
1,825,000,000	1,487,238,900	23,983	8,769	3,089
921,000,000	1,487,238,900	968,436	201,845	23,137
5,694,000,000	10,465,483,000	172,488	53,045	13,778
1,753,000,000	11,468,569,000	5,512,000	1,739,319	218,934

STATISTICS OF THE WORLD

Nation / Capital	Population	Type of Government	Heads of Government	Currency Value in U.S. Dollars	GNP (000,000)	GNP (per capita)
TUVALU Funafuti	6,500 1,300	Parliamentary state (C)	Governor-General: Penitala Fiatau Teo; Prime Minister: Toalipi Lauti	Dollar 1.16	$ NA	$ NA
UGANDA Kampala	12,350,000 542,000	Republic (C)	President: Field Marshal Idi Amin	Shilling 0.13	2,820	240
UNION OF ARAB EMIRATES Abu Dhabi	656,000 150,000	Federal state	President: Sheikh Zaid bin Sultan al-Nahayan; Prime Minister: Sheikh Maktum bin Rashid al-Maktum	Dirham 0.26	9,710	13,990
UNION OF SOVIET SOCIALIST REPUBLICS Moscow	258,930,000 7,819,000	Federal socialist republic	Presidium Chairman: Leonid I. Brezhnev; Chairman, Council of Ministers: Aleksei N. Kosygin	Ruble 1.52	708,170	2,760
UNITED STATES Washington, D.C.	218,059,000 674,000	Federal republic	President: (James Earl) Jimmy Carter (Jr.)	Dollar	1,698,060	7,890
UPPER VOLTA, REPUBLIC OF Ouagadougou	6,320,000 168,607	Republic	President: Gen. Sangoulé Lamizana; Premier: Joseph I. Conombo	CFA franc 0.0046	710	110
URUGUAY Montevideo	2,810,000 1,229,748	Republic	President: Aparicio Méndez	Peso 0.15	3,900	1,390
VENEZUELA Caracas	12,740,000 1,662,627	Federal republic	President: Carlos Andrés Pérez	Bolivar 0.23	31,750	2,570
VIETNAM, SOCIALIST REPUBLIC OF Hanoi	47,870,000 1,443,500	Socialist republic	President: Ton Duc Thang; Premier: Pham Van Dong	Dong 0.46	NA	NA
WESTERN SAMOA Apia	150,000 32,099	Constitutional monarchy (C)	Head of State: Malietoa Tanumafili II; Prime Minister: Tupuola Taisi Efi	Tala 1.35	50	350
YEMEN ARAB REPUBLIC San'a	7,080,000 134,600	Republic	President: Lt. Col. Ali Abdullah Saleh; Prime Minister: Abdul-Aziz Abdul-Ghani	Rial 0.22	1,540	250
YEMEN, PEOPLE'S DEMOCRATIC REPUBLIC OF Aden	1,800,000 264,326	People's republic	Chairman, Presidential Council, and Prime Minister: Ali Nasser Mohammed	Dinar 2.90	480	280
YUGOSLAVIA Belgrade	21,770,000 870,000	Federal socialist republic	President: Marshal Tito; President, Federal Executive Council: Veselin Djuranović	Dinar 0.053	36,170	1,680
ZAIRE, REPUBLIC OF Kinshasa	26,380,000 2,008,352	Republic	President: Gen. Mobutu Sese Seko; First State Commissioner: Mpinga Kasenga	Zaire 1.28	3,510	140
ZAMBIA Lusaka	5,350,000 483,000	Republic (C)	President: Kenneth D. Kaunda; Prime Minister: Daniel Lisulo	Kwacha 1.23	2,200	440

1. Including Luxembourg.
2. Only one figure, for combined elementary and secondary education, is available.
3. Excluding trade with other members of the Customs and Economic Union of Central Africa (Cameroon, Central African Empire, Republic of Congo, Gabon Republic).
4. Figure is for public schools only.
5. Statistical information in this entry pertains to the entire Comoro archipelago. One major island, Mayotte, claimed by the Comoro state, was administered in 1978 as a dependency of France.

Imports Exports	Revenue Expenditure	Elementary Schools: Teachers Students	Secondary Schools: Teachers Students	Colleges and Universities: Teachers Students
$ NA	$ 1,785,766	39	12	°
NA	1,785,766	1,570	250	°
80,000,000[7]	834,523,510	32,490	4,084	617
359,000,000[7]	505,959,260	1,125,817	85,073	5,173
3,331,644,200	2,357,308,300	3,876	1,849	°
8,556,118,500	2,357,308,300	60,742	15,225	°
40,817,000,000	330,294,900,000	2,399,299[2]	[2]	317,152
45,161,000,000	330,026,800,000	35,960,941	10,738,158	4,853,958
156,758,000,000	448,700,000,000	1,167,000[4]	1,020,000[4]	670,000
119,042,000,000	487,500,000,000	29,453,000[4]	14,234,000[4]	11,360,274
145,000,000	98,172,545	2,997	818	166
53,000,000	98,172,545	141,177	16,227	1,067
669,000,000	430,425,000	15,679	13,980	2,149
599,000,000	511,825,000	382,759	141,731	39,927
6,023,000,000	9,038,694,600	75,712	37,232	16,185
9,299,000,000	10,243,123,000	2,333,013	828,495	221,581
831,000,000	4,944,751,300	204,988	108,454	9,642
227,000,000	4,944,751,300	7,403,715	2,915,753	80,323
41,000,000	29,646,370	1,322	NA	NA
13,000,000	25,658,069	32,872	16,571	260
1,040,000,000	339,763,260	6,604	1,345	NA
11,000,000	450,021,920	255,301	24,240	2,408
414,000,000	41,980,312	6,467	1,730	92
249,000,000	75,275,043	196,466	39,696	934
9,634,000,000	5,949,450,500	130,997	30,932	21,448
5,254,000,000	6,506,043,900	2,856,453	939,823	404,273
610,000,000	741,285,600	80,481	14,483	NA
981,000,000	547,038,240	3,538,257	335,203	21,021
670,000,000	575,623,890	18,096	3,202	NA
897,000,000	837,030,500	872,392	73,049	8,403

6. Figure is for ten-year polytechnical high schools.
7. Excluding trade among Kenya, Tanzania, and Uganda.
8. Included in figure for Belgium.
9. Including trade among the states of Malaysia.
10. Excluding Zanzibar.

The material in the following tables is the latest available in early December, 1978. As before, it should be noted that the symbol * indicates that the category is not applicable to the area mentioned, and that NA means that the data were not available. The Office of Territorial Affairs was helpful in supplying some data for the table on Outlying Areas.

State Capital	Population	Per Capita Personal Income	Governor Lieutenant-Governor	Revenue Expenditure	Roads (Miles)	Railways (Miles)
ALABAMA Montgomery	3,742,000 155,658	$ 5,622	George C. Wallace (D) Jere L. Beasley (D)	$ 2,649,994,000 2,593,982,000	86,676	4,534
ALASKA Juneau	403,000 18,705	10,586	Jay S. Hammond (R) Lowell Thomas, Jr. (R)	1,220,263,000 1,028,906,000	9,930	670
ARIZONA Phoenix	2,354,000 679,512	6,509	Bruce E. Babbitt (D) *	1,734,733,000 1,696,911,000	55,746	2,036
ARKANSAS Little Rock	2,186,000 151,649	5,540	David H. Pryor (D) Joe Purcell (D)	1,395,087,000 1,386,550,000	77,451	3,522
CALIFORNIA Sacramento	22,294,000 262,305	7,911	Edmund G. Brown, Jr. (D) Mervyn M. Dymally (D)	20,737,318,000 19,013,777,000	172,841	7,291
COLORADO Denver	2,670,000 479,513	7,160	Richard D. Lamm (D) George L. Brown (D)	2,001,520,000 1,959,284,000	86,106	3,384
CONNECTICUT Hartford	3,099,000 134,957	8,061	Ella T. Grasso (D) Robert K. Killian (D)	2,327,037,000 2,139,424,000	19,044	634
DELAWARE Dover	583,000 22,699	7,697	Pierre S. du Pont 4th (R) James D. McGinnis (D)	638,263,000 620,612,000	5,244	291
DISTRICT OF COLUMBIA *	674,000 *	8,999	Mayor: Walter E. Washington (D)	* *	1,101	30
FLORIDA Tallahassee	8,594,000 84,175	6,684	Reubin O'D. Askew (D) James H. Williams 2nd (D)	4,851,120,000 4,905,515,000	98,094	4,075
GEORGIA Atlanta	5,084,000 425,666	6,014	George D. Busbee (D) Zell Miller (D)	3,180,603,000 3,115,966,000	102,826	5,414
HAWAII Honolulu	897,000 350,000	7,677	George R. Ariyoshi (D) Nelson K. Doi (D)	1,228,873,000 1,352,667,000	3,794	0
IDAHO Boise	878,000 102,915	5,980	John V. Evans (D) William J. Murphy (D)	659,704,000 684,211,000	57,788	2,631
ILLINOIS Springfield	11,243,000 88,221	7,768	James R. Thompson, Jr. (R) David O'Neal (R)	8,166,462,000 8,527,685,000	133,559	10,555
INDIANA Indianapolis	5,374,000 708,867	6,921	Otis R. Bowen (R) Robert D. Orr (R)	3,437,094,000 3,186,557,000	91,662	6,357
IOWA Des Moines	2,896,000 195,405	6,878	Robert D. Ray (R) Arthur A. Neu (R)	2,154,486,000 2,293,244,000	112,460	7,547
KANSAS Topeka	2,348,000 120,196	7,134	Robert F. Bennett (R) Shelby Smith (R)	1,604,009,000 1,590,982,000	134,621	7,514

456

Radio Stations	Television Stations	English-language Daily Newspapers	Public Elementary Schools: Teachers Students	Public Secondary Schools: Teachers Students	Colleges & Universities: Institutions Students
225	26	25	18,400 395,116	19,000 366,764	56 160,377
41	10	7	2,400 50,398	2,100 39,946	9 29,312
102	15	17	16,700 358,889	6,800 154,928	22 181,440
151	13	33	10,500 240,447	11,400 218,331	29 71,071
507	71	125	111,300 2,540,582	76,300 1,748,588	252 1,790,808
137	14	27	14,200 287,613	14,800 274,194	39 153,896
82	10	26	19,300 388,233	15,700 246,767	46 149,268
20	1	3	2,500 57,967	3,700 60,033	10 30,894
20	8	2	3,400 65,616	2,700 54,259	19 83,871
341	41	51	37,500 776,714	36,000 758,856	73 364,204
289	29	37	33,900 663,110	19,700 426,515	67 173,819
36	12	5	4,400 90,299	3,500 82,057	11 47,038
72	11	15	4,600 105,591	4,800 95,842	9 40,250
309	32	88	63,500 1,450,086	47,300 730,238	149 658,655
222	27	79	27,800 585,346	27,400 558,376	64 221,970
174	21	40	15,900 306,345	17,400 282,415	61 126,094
118	14	51	13,600 266,232	11,900 179,893	52 127,671

State Capital	Population	Per Capita Personal Income	Governor Lieutenant-Governor	Revenue Expenditure	Roads (Miles)	Railways (Miles)
KENTUCKY Frankfort	3,498,000 23,150	$ 5,945	Julian M. Carroll (D) Thelma L. Stovall (D)	$ 2,650,503,000 2,577,735,000	69,706	3,517
LOUISIANA Baton Rouge	3,966,000 302,236	5,913	Edwin W. Edwards (D) James E. Fitzmorris, Jr. (D)	3,216,145,000 3,278,254,000	54,814	3,710
MAINE Augusta	1,091,000 20,934	5,734	James B. Longley (Ind.) *	862,847,000 803,719,000	21,670	1,660
MARYLAND Annapolis	4,143,000 32,145	7,572	Marvin Mandel (D) Blair Lee 3rd (D) (acting governor)	3,491,869,000 3,553,955,000	26,113	1,062
MASSACHUSETTS Boston	5,774,000 618,250	7,258	Michael S. Dukakis (D) Thomas P. O'Neill 3rd (D)	4,968,600,000 4,756,516,000	32,867	1,404
MICHIGAN Lansing	9,189,000 126,071	7,619	William G. Milliken (R) James J. Damman (R)	7,891,575,000 7,649,278,000	118,898	5,901
MINNESOTA St. Paul	4,008,000 272,465	7,129	Rudolph G. Perpich (DFL) Alec G. Olson (DFL)	3,867,665,000 3,821,318,000	128,456	7,294
MISSISSIPPI Jackson	2,404,000 188,205	5,030	Charles C. (Cliff) Finch (D) Evelyn Gandy (D)	1,759,384,000 1,738,353,000	67,708	3,432
MISSOURI Jefferson City	4,860,000 35,957	6,654	Joseph P. Teasdale (D) William C. Phelps (R)	2,632,790,000 2,466,856,000	117,223	6,010
MONTANA Helena	785,000 27,348	6,125	Thomas L. Judge (D) Ted Schwinden (D)	669,969,000 667,898,000	77,902	4,862
NEBRASKA Lincoln	1,565,000 164,035	6,720	J. James Exon (D) Gerald T. Whelan (D)	1,044,090,000 998,557,000	96,894	5,360
NEVADA Carson City	660,000 26,590	7,988	Mike O'Callaghan (D) Robert E. Rose (D)	527,434,000 509,765,000	50,068	1,573
NEW HAMPSHIRE Concord	871,000 28,961	6,536	Meldrim Thomson, Jr. (R) *	461,530,000 549,958,000	15,333	751
NEW JERSEY Trenton	7,327,000 99,672	7,994	Brendan T. Byrne (D) *	5,370,256,000 5,452,326,000	33,126	1,676
NEW MEXICO Santa Fe	1,212,000 45,941	5,857	Jerry Apodaca (D) Robert E. Ferguson (D)	1,215,326,000 1,061,998,000	70,858	2,057
NEW YORK Albany	17,748,000 109,196	7,537	Hugh L. Carey (D) Mary Anne Krupsak (D)	18,805,597,000 18,408,079,000	109,419	5,215
NORTH CAROLINA Raleigh	5,577,000 136,883	5,935	James B. Hunt, Jr. (D) James C. Green (D)	4,026,279,000 3,968,161,000	91,187	4,104
NORTH DAKOTA Bismarck	652,000 39,838	6,190	Arthur A. Link (D) Wayne G. Sanstead (D)	677,857,000 627,484,000	106,430	5,060
OHIO Columbus	10,749,000 533,075	7,084	James A. Rhodes (R) Richard F. Celeste (D)	6,061,522,000 6,409,900,000	110,620	7,506
OKLAHOMA Oklahoma City	2,880,000 369,438	6,346	David L. Boren (D) George Nigh (D)	2,110,124,000 1,965,897,000	109,606	4,897
OREGON Salem	2,444,000 79,661	7,007	Robert W. Straub (D) *	1,965,340,000 1,901,338,000	108,278	3,043
PENNSYLVANIA Harrisburg	11,750,000 57,047	7,011	Milton J. Shapp (D) Ernest P. Kline (D)	8,588,406,000 8,947,844,000	116,880	7,837
RHODE ISLAND Providence	935,000 164,989	6,775	J. Joseph Garrahy (D) Thomas R. DiLuglio (D)	850,549,000 803,633,000	5,537	139
SOUTH CAROLINA Columbia	2,918,000 112,779	5,628	James B. Edwards (R) W. Brantley Harvey, Jr. (D)	2,135,404,000 2,143,924,000	61,294	3,033

Radio Stations	Television Stations	English-language Daily Newspapers	Public Elementary Schools: Teachers Students	Public Secondary Schools: Teachers Students	Colleges & Universities: Institutions Students
221	26	27	20,000 441,632	12,300 255,368	38 131,667
170	19	26	23,900 577,452	18,700 261,548	31 153,988
83	12	9	6,900 166,704	4,900 79,064	25 40,125
95	10	13	21,000 421,448	22,600 415,464	52 218,012
155	16	46	30,900 603,204	34,500 561,330	119 376,821
283	34	52	44,900 1,065,004	44,000 971,072	94 481,436
192	18	30	20,400 402,279	24,300 434,141	65 188,871
186	18	25	13,600 277,132	10,800 224,893	45 98,397
223	27	54	24,800 514,997	23,800 450,363	83 221,152
76	13	11	5,300 111,843	3,900 56,889	12 30,730
92	23	19	8,700 161,165	9,000 145,042	29 81,329
40	8	9	3,000 72,651	3,000 70,793	6 31,412
51	7	9	4,800 105,035	4,000 70,461	24 39,319
93	10	27	47,600 890,092	32,600 531,256	65 300,890
96	12	21	6,500 142,872	6,500 139,024	17 54,310
349	41	76	82,200 1,598,667	89,300 1,630,881	287 944,832
328	28	51	38,100 816,645	17,800 365,186	116 255,956
44	13	10	4,500 58,105	3,000 66,980	15 32,241
325	36	96	54,000 1,283,428	52,100 898,551	131 452,811
126	15	54	15,200 320,427	15,000 274,041	44 149,994
130	17	22	13,000 274,570	10,600 198,709	43 141,554
361	35	106	56,800 1,054,040	58,700 1,074,833	179 475,366
27	4	7	5,000 93,579	4,100 73,050	12 63,721
172	19	20	17,700 373,796	11,700 246,927	56 123,779

State Capital	Population	Per Capita Personal Income	Governor Lieutenant-Governor	Revenue Expenditure	Roads (Miles)	Railways (Miles)
SOUTH DAKOTA........ Pierre	690,000..... 11,255	$ 5,957.....	Richard F. Kneip (D)...........$ Harvey Wollman (D)	492,966,000...... 504,903,000	82,426.......	3,352
TENNESSEE .... Nashville	4,357,000..... 430,941	5,785.....	Ray Blanton (D).......... John S. Wilder (D)	2,625,899,000...... 2,552,410,000	81,567.......	3,181
TEXAS............. Austin	13,014,000..... 313,009	6,803....	Dolph Briscoe, Jr. (D)........... William P. Hobby (D)	8,090,170,000...... 7,349,113,000	257,649.......	13,255
UTAH............... Salt Lake City	1,307,000..... 168,667	5,923.....	Scott M. Matheson (D)........... David S. Monson (R)	1,040,213,000...... 1,054,771,000	48,501.......	1,726
VERMONT .... Montpelier	487,000..... 8,180	5,823.....	Richard A. Snelling (R)........... T. Garry Buckley (R)	485,906,000...... 460,936,000	13,909.......	767
VIRGINIA .... Richmond	5,148,000..... 226,639	6,865....	John N. Dalton (R)........... Charles S. Robb (D)	3,576,392,000...... 3,518,413,000	63,430.......	3,848
WASHINGTON......... Olympia	3,774,000..... 27,399	7,528....	Dixy Lee Ray (D)........... John A. Cherberg (D)	3,449,022,000...... 3,345,960,000	84,326.......	4,723
WEST VIRGINIA .... Charleston	1,860,000..... 66,977	5,986.....	John D. Rockefeller 4th (D)........... *	1,552,183,000...... 1,559,346,000	37,244.......	3,460
WISCONSIN......... Madison	4,679,000..... 170,493	6,890....	Martin J. Schreiber (D; acting) ... (vacant)	4,227,293,000...... 4,087,692,000	105,520.......	5,733
WYOMING .... Cheyenne	424,000...... 47,795	7,562....	Ed Herschler (D)............... *	488,464,000...... 402,471,000	32,854.......	1,778

OUTLYING AREAS OF THE U.S

Area Capital	Population	Status	Governor Lieutenant-Governor	Revenue Expenditure	Roads (Miles)	Railways (Miles)
AMERICAN SAMOA .... Pago Pago	30,600 4,700	Unorganized,......... unincorporated territory	Peter T. Coleman.........$ Tufele Li'A	44,813,500.... 44,813,500	94......	0
GUAM .... Agaña	109,089 2,500	Unincorporated........ territory	Ricardo J. Bordallo .... Rudolph G. Sablan	250,528,276.... 204,046,780	230......	0
PANAMA CANAL ZONE ... Balboa Heights (headquarters)	44,000 232	Army-administered ..... territory	Maj. Gen. Harold R. Parfitt.. Col. James H. Tormey	80,850,000.... 82,683,000	144......	48
PUERTO RICO............. San Juan	3,300,000 514,500	Commonwealth....... *	Carlos Romero Barceló .... *	3,074,900,000.... 2,797,200,000	10,456......	60
TRUST TERRITORY **OF THE PACIFIC** **ISLANDS**[1] Capitol Hill, on Saipan Island	123,000 .... NA	U.N. Trust .... Territory	High Commissioner:......... Adrian P. Winkel	78,631,000.... 117,230,800	64......	0
VIRGIN ISLANDS .... Charlotte Amalie	95,650 12,220	Unincorporated........ territory	Juan Luis .... Henry Millin	128,472,514.... 122,860,923	621......	0

1. The Northern Mariana Islands in 1978 were an internally self-governing part of the Trust Territory of the Pacific Islands. The government of the Northern Marianas was headed by Gov. Carlos S. Camacho and Lt.-Gov. Francisco C. Ada. The capital was Susupe, on Saipan Island.

Radio Stations	Television Stations	English-language Daily Newspapers	Public Elementary Schools: Teachers Students	Public Secondary Schools: Teachers Students	Colleges & Universities: Institutions Students
63	19	13	5,300 93,987	3,000 49,643	17 30,982
259	24	34	24,400 541,869	15,700 336,555	67 188,661
513	69	112	75,800 1,516,676	66,600 1,326,166	146 647,840
75	5	5	6,600 173,486	6,300 143,846	14 88,584
47	6	8	3,200 61,557	2,900 41,377	23 29,413
226	22	33	35,400 640,927	25,400 441,257	72 255,969
167	20	23	17,200 395,237	16,500 381,226	48 259,480
111	12	28	10,900 234,174	9,300 167,195	28 80,968
228	27	36	26,300 505,518	24,100 412,345	58 241,164
46	5	10	2,700 48,805	2,700 43,516	8 19,706

Radio Stations	Television Stations	Daily Newspapers	Public Elementary & Secondary School Teachers	Public School Students: Elementary Secondary	Higher Education: Institutions Students
1	1	2	360	7,582 2,144	1 836
7	2	1	1,186	15,652 11,350	1 4,343
1	1	0	370	5,104 3,688	1 1,333
94	11	4	24,761	475,979 212,613	23 100,885
8	3	0	1,703	27,809 6,145	1 831
8	2	3	1,540	15,894 9,677	1 2,122

The material in this table has been prepared with the kind assistance of Statistics Canada, Ottawa. It should be noted that all dollar figures are in Canadian dollars.

Province Capital	Population	Per Capita Personal Income	Premier Lieutenant-Governor	Revenue Expenditure
ALBERTA	1,950,300	$7,722	Peter Lougheed	$5,003,700,000
Edmonton	573,700[1]		Ralph Steinhauer	4,288,000,000
BRITISH COLUMBIA	2,530,200	8,149	William Bennett	4,196,700,000
Victoria	218,300[1]		Henry Bell-Irving	4,266,300,000
MANITOBA	1,032,400	6,886	Sterling Lyon	1,626,700,000
Winnipeg	581,800[1]		Francis L. Jobin	1,795,300,000
NEW BRUNSWICK	695,000	5,560	Richard B. Hatfield	1,136,100,000
Fredericton	45,248		Hédard J. Robichaud	1,231,400,000
NEWFOUNDLAND	568,900	5,048	Frank Moores	1,038,000,000
St. John's	144,300[1]		Gordon A. Winter	1,125,600,000
NORTHWEST TERRITORIES	43,500	6,969[2]	Commissioner:	234,700,000
Yellowknife	8,256		Stuart Hodgson	240,200,000
NOVA SCOTIA	841,900	5,887	John Buchanan	1,312,300,000
Halifax	269,900[1]		Clarence L. Gosse	1,393,100,000
ONTARIO	8,443,800	8,089	William G. Davis	12,950,300,000
Toronto	2,849,000[1]		Pauline E. McGibbon	14,228,200,000
PRINCE EDWARD ISLAND	122,000	4,975	Bennett Campbell	236,800,000
Charlottetown	17,063		Gordon L. Bennett	256,000,000
QUÉBEC	6,285,000	6,897	René Lévesque	13,126,700,000
Québec	545,100[1]		Jean-Pierre Coté	12,982,700,000
SASKATCHEWAN	947,100	6,837	Allan Blakeney	1,629,700,000
Regina	154,600[1]		C. Irwin McIntosh	1,707,400,000
YUKON TERRITORY	21,700	6,969[2]	Commissioner:	82,900,000
Whitehorse	13,311		Arthur Pearson	82,800,000

1. The population given is that of the Census Metropolitan Area of the capital.
2. Figure is the combined average for the Northwest Territories and Yukon Territory.

THE PROVINCES AND TERRITORIES OF CANADA

Roads (Miles)	Railways (Miles)	Originating Radio Stations	Originating Television Stations	Daily Newspapers	Elementary and Secondary Schools: Teachers Enrollment	Post-secondary Education: Institutions Enrollment
108,402	6,082	42	12	8	22,243 450,022	25 49,380
39,890	4,786	66	10	18	27,523 553,861	28 48,020
49,553	4,596	26	6	8	12,313 237,153	15 20,880
14,100	1,664	22	4	6	7,868 163,447	12 12,620
7,838	928	28	7	3	7,767 156,550	7 8,820
1,369	129	13	0	0	660 12,717	0 0
17,564	1,664	27	5	6	10,730 200,624	24 21,260
96,748	9,807	147	27	47	99,048 2,012,985	52 222,850
3,415	254	4	1	3	1,448 27,699	3 2,300
66,975	5,390	106	20	14	68,441 1,318,955	83 213,640
126,277	8,450	29	8	4	11,113 225,525	6 17,340
2,695	58	2	1	0	300 5,380	0 0

KEY TO
SIGNED ARTICLES

Here is a list of contributors to this Yearbook. The initials at the end of an article are those of the author, or authors, of that article.

We would like to thank the following organizations for their kind assistance: American Red Cross; Social Security Administration, U.S. Department of Health, Education, and Welfare.

A.E., AGNES ERDELYI, B.A., M.L.S.
Reference Librarian, Sachem Public Library.

A.J.R., ALLAN J. RISTORI, B.A.
Chairman, Emergency Committee to Save America's Marine Resources.

A.M., ALAN McGOWAN, B.E.
President, Scientists' Institute for Public Information. Trustee and Vice-President, Institute for Environmental Education.

A.R., AGAPITO REY, B.S., M.A., PH.D.
Former Professor of Spanish, University of Arizona. Coauthor of *The Rediscovery of New Mexico* and other books.

A.S., ANDREW SOLTIS, B.A.
Chess Columnist, New York *Post.* First Vice-President, Marshall Chess Club. First prize, New York International Chess Tournament, 1977. International Chess Master, 1974. Author of *The Best Games of Boris Spassky* and other books.

B.M.P., B. M. PARKER, B.A., M.A., PH.D.
Instructor of English, John Abbott College, Québec.

B.Q., BENJAMIN QUARLES, B.A., M.A., PH.D.
Emeritus Professor of History, Morgan State University. Author of *Black Abolitionists* and other books.

B.R., BEA RIEMSCHNEIDER, B.A.
Managing Editor, *Archaeology.* Associate Trustee, American Schools of Oriental Research.

B.W., BRENTON WELLING, B.A.
Associate Editor, *Business Week.*

C.C., CARLOTTA CONNELLY, A.B., M.A.
Consultant, Wattis Hall of Man, California Academy of Sciences. Former Teacher, Bureau of Indian Affairs, Hopi Reservation.

C.H., CHARLES HAGEN, A.B., M.F.A.
Managing Editor, *Afterimage.*

C.P., CARL PROUJAN, B.S.
Former Editorial Director, Science Department, Scholastic Magazines, Inc. Author of *Secrets of the Sea.*

D.C., DANIEL CHU, B.A.
Associate Editor, *People.*

D.Ca., DIANE CAMPER, A.B., M.S.L.
Washington Bureau Correspondent, *Newsweek.*

D.D., DAVE DOOLING.
Science Editor, The Huntsville *Times.*

D.G., DAVID GRAMBS, B.A.
Freelance Writer and Editor. Staff Member, *Penthouse.*

D.J.H., DONALD J. HARVEY, B.A., M.A., PH.D.
Professor of History at Hunter College, City University of New York. Consultant, Rockefeller Foundation Humanities Fellowships. Associate Editor, *Reviews in European History.* Author of *France Since the Revolution.*

D.K., DONALD KENDALL, B.S.
Farm Writer, Associated Press, Washington, D.C.

D.M., DERWENT MAY, M.A.
Literary Editor, *The Listener.* Author of *Dear Parson* and *The Professionals.*

D.Mac., DONNARAE MacCANN, B.A., M.L.S.
Columnist, Wilson Library Bulletin. Coauthor of *The Black American in Books for Children* and *Cultural Conformity in Books for Children.*

D.N., DAWSON NAIL, B.A., M.A.
Vice-President–Executive Editor, *Television Digest, Inc.*

D.P., DON PERETZ, B.A., M.A., PH.D.
Professor of Political Science and Director of the Southwest Asia-North Africa Program, State University of New York at Binghamton. Author of *Middle East Reader* and other books and articles.

D.S., DAVID STERRITT, B.A.
Film Critic, *The Christian Science Monitor.*

E.S.K., ELAINE STUART KNAPP, B.A.
Editor, *Council of State Governments.*

F.C.D. III, FREDERICK C. DURANT III
Assistant Director for Astronautics, National Air and Space Museum, Smithsonian Institution.

F.L., FRANK LITSKY, B.S.
Assistant Sports Editor, New York *Times,* and President, Track Writers Association.

F.V.B., FREDERICK VERNON BOYD, B.A.
Senior Editorial Assistant, *Newsweek.*

F.W., FAY WILLEY, A.B., M.A.
Associate Editor, International Department, *Newsweek.*

G.B.K., GINA B. KOLATA, B.S., M.S.
Staff Writer, Research News Section, *Science.*

G.H., GEOFFREY HORN, B.A., M.A.
Supervising Editor, Funk & Wagnalls Yearbook. Freelance Writer and Editor.

G.W.M., GAIL W. McBRIDE, B.A., M.S. Editor, Medical News Section, *Journal of the American Medical Association.*

H.H., HARVEY HINDEN, B.S. Communications Editor, *Electronics Magazine.*

H.K., HERBERT KUPFERBERG, B.A., M.A., M.S. Senior Editor, *Parade,* and former Music Critic, *The Trib.* Author of *The Mendelssohns* and other books.

H.T.H., HENRY T. HOPKINS, B.A.E., M.A.E. Director, San Francisco Museum of Modern Art.

I.K., I. KEPARS, B.A., A.L.A.A. Chief Reference Librarian, Australian Reference, National Library of Australia. Editor, *Australian Books.*

I.S., IVAN SANDERS, B.A., M.A., PH.D. Associate Professor of English, Suffolk County Community College.

J.A.B., JEAN A. BORGER, B.A. Manager of Officer Services, Bureau of Public Information, American Dental Association.

J.A.R., JANET A. RALOFF, B.S.J., M.S.J. Policy/Technology Editor, *Science News.* Editor, *Energy Research Reports.*

J.B., JOHN BEAUFORT Contributing Drama Critic, *The Christian Science Monitor.* Treasurer, New York Drama Critics' Circle.

J.F.M., JOSEPH F. MANGAN, B.B.A. Assistant Professor, The College of Insurance. Consulting Editor, Werbel Publishing Co.

J.N., JOHN NORMAN, B.A., M.A., PH.D. Professor of History and Government, Pace University. State Factfinder, Connecticut Board of Mediation and Arbitration.

J.N.G., JAMES NELSON GOODSELL, B.A., M.A., PH.D. Latin American Editor, *The Christian Science Monitor.* Author of *The Quest for Change in Latin America.*

J.P.G., JOEL P. GREENBERG, B.S., M.S. Behavioral Sciences Editor, *Science News.*

J.T.D., JOANN TEMPLE DENNETT, B.S., M.S. Manager, Information Services, RDD Consultants. Lecturer in Physics, University of Colorado.

J.T.S., JAMES T. SABIN, B.S., M.A., PH.D. Vice-President, Editorial, Greenwood Press.

J.W.K., JOHN W. KAMPA, B.S. Publishing Consultant. Former Executive Vice-President, Oxford Book Company.

K.B.H., KENNETH B. HIGBIE, B.S. Chief, Division of Solid Wastes, Bureau of Mines, U.S. Department of the Interior.

L.A.S., LESTER A. SOBEL, B.B.A. Editor, Vice-President, Facts On File, Inc. Author of *Russia's Rulers: The Khrushchev Period* and other books.

L.H., LOUIS HALASZ, J.D. United Nations Correspondent, International Feature Service. Lecturer on International Affairs.

M.H., MARION HENDELSON Merchandising and Fashion Consultant to retail stores and manufacturers. Former Lecturer, Merchandising, Laboratory Institute of Merchandising.

M.J.C., MICHAEL J. CUSACK Editor, *Science World,* Scholastic Magazines, Inc.

M.J.L., MARY JANE LAMERS, B.S. News Editor, *Astronomy* magazine.

M.R.B., MILTON R. BENJAMIN, B.A. Deputy Foreign Editor, The Washington *Post.*

M.W.B., MYRNA WEINER BRESKIN, B.A. Editing Manager, McGraw-Hill.

N.P., NEAL PRONEK, B.B.A. Managing Editor, T.F.H. Publications, Inc. Former Managing Editor, *Tropical Fish Hobbyist.*

N.T.G., NANCY TRILLING GOLDNER, B.A. Dance Critic, *The Christian Science Monitor, Dance News,* and *The Nation.*

O.U., OWEN ULLMANN, B.A., M.A. National Labor Correspondent for the Associated Press.

R.B., RONALD BENREY, B.S., M.S. Science Writer. Author of *How to Get the Most from an Electronic Calculator* and other books.

R.F., RUSSELL FREEDMAN, B.A. Freelance Writer and Faculty Member, The New School for Social Research. Author of *Growing Up Wild* and other books.

R.J.C., RAYMOND J. CARROLL, B.A. General Editor and United Nations Correspondent, *Newsweek.*

R.J.S., ROBERT J. SHAW, B.S., B.A., M.S. Freelance Writer. Author of *Libraries: Building for the Future.*

R.N.O., RICHARD N. OSTLING, A.B., M.S.J., M.A. Religion Editor, *Time.* Former President, Religion Newswriters Association. Author of *Secrecy in the Church.*

R.P.P., RAYMOND P. POINCELOT, B.A., PH.D. Assistant Professor of Botany, Biology Department, Fairfield University.

R.W.S., RUTH W. STIDGER, B.A. Editor, *Mining Equipment International.* Coauthor of *Inflation Management* and other books.

S.A.K., SERGE A. KORFF, A.B., M.A., PH.D. Professor Emeritus of Physics, New York University. Former President, New York Academy of Sciences.

S.C.L., STEPHEN C. LEWIS, B.A., M.A., PH.D. Chairman, Humanities Division, Suffolk County Community College. Coauthor of *Focus on the Written Word* and *Student Critic.*

S.C.W., SUSAN CONVERSE WINSLOW, A.B., A.M. Senior Editor, *Funk & Wagnalls New Encyclopedia.*

S.O., SHELDON OSBORN Freelance Writer. Public Relations Accounting Executive.

T.D., THOMAS DEFRANK, B.A., M.A. Correspondent, *Newsweek.*

T.E., THOR ECKERT, JR., B.A. Music Critic, *The Christian Science Monitor.*

T.L.K., THOMAS L. KENNEDY, A.B., M.A., PH.D. Associate Dean of the Graduate School and Professor of History, Washington State University. Author of articles on China.

T.V.S., Thomas V. Szalkiewicz, B.A. Science Editor, McGraw-Hill, Inc.; Holt, Rinehart and Winston.

W.B.F., WILLIAM B. FRANKLIN, B.S., M.S. Editor, *Business Outlook,* and Special Correspondent, *London Economist.* Author of *Current Business Trends* and other books.

W.E.M., WILLIAM E. METCALF, A.B., A.M., PH.D. Curator of Roman and Byzantine Coins, The American Numismatic Society. Adjunct Associate Professor of Art and Archeology, Columbia University.

W.J.B., WALTER J. BOCK, B.S., PH.D. Professor of Evolutionary Biology, Columbia University. Research Associate, American Museum of Natural History. Author of publications on evolution.

W.J.G., WILLIAM J. GILSTRAP, B.A. Former Associate Economist, Chemical Bank.

W.M.H., W. M. HAVIGHURST, B.A. Supervising Editor, Funk & Wagnalls Yearbook. Former Humanities Editor, Cadillac Modern Encyclopedia. Former Editor, American Heritage Dictionary.

W.P., WILLIAM PERRY, B.A., M.A. Music Director, Museum of Modern Art. Executive Producer, *Anyone for Tennyson?* series, PBS.

PICTURE CREDITS

137 Arne Folkedal/San Francisco Ballet
138 *Top:* Martha Swope; *Bottom:* Martha Swope
139 *Top:* Wide World; *Bottom:* Wide World
140 Wide World
143 U.S. Department of the Interior
144 W. A. Cassidy/University of Pittsburgh
145 Hughes/Northern Michigan University
146 Jet Propulsion Laboratory
148 *Top:* CBS Television Network; *Bottom:* Wide World
150 Wide World
151 UPI
153 *All photos:* UPI
154 UPI
156 NASA
158 Bill Ray/Texaco
159 State of Nebraska
160 Steve Northup/New York Times Pictures
161 UPI
162 Wide World
163 Jean Rougeron/Sygma
165 *Left:* Daniel Simon/Liaison; *Right:* Abraham & Straus
166 *Left:* Keystone; *Right:* Johnson Publishing Co./*Ebony Magazine*
167 Wide World
169 *Top:* Brucelle/Sygma; *Bottom:* UPI
170 Wide World
172 Sven Simon/Katherine Young
173 Wide World
174 Wide World
175 Camera Press/Photo Trends
176 Pictorial Parade
177 Photo Trends
178 UPI
182 Pictorial Parade
183 UPI
184 UPI
185 Wide World
186 ® Bel-Art Products 1978/Maddak, Inc.
187 Glen Cumberledge/Columbus *Dispatch* Photo
189 Jim McHugh/Sygma
191 UPI
192 Douglas Wilson/New York Times Pictures
193 Prem Sagar/Photo Trends
194 Wide World
196 Sovfoto
197 Wide World
199 *Top:* Wide World; *Bottom:* Keystone
200 Wide World
201 UPI
202 UPI
204 *Top:* Wide World; *Bottom:* UPI
205 Wide World
208 Wide World
209 Wide World
210 UPI
211 UPI
213 *Top:* UPI; *Bottom:* UPI
216 *Top: Nature* Magazine, London; *Bottom:* Clement L. Markert/Yale University
218 Litton Bionetics, Inc.
220 David Plowden
222 *Top:* New York State College of Agriculture and Life Sciences at Cornell University; *Bottom, Left:* David B. Grobecker/University of Washington; *Bottom, Right:* David Powell/Steinhart Aquarium
223 Keystone
224 *Top:* Antoinette Rhodes; *Bottom:* Shyla Irving/E. P. Dutton
225 From *The Legend of Scarface* by Robert San Souci. Illustration copyright ® 1978 by Daniel San Souci. Used by permission of Doubleday & Co., Inc.
226 Crown Publishers
227 Agencia EFE/Photo Trends
228 Chico Nelson, Editora Abril/Keystone
229 Harcourt, Brace, Jovanovich
231 Joe B. Mann/Arena Stage
232 Herbert Migang
234 Wide World
235 James M. Thresher/The Washington *Post*
236 Hugh Patrick Brown/*Business Week*
238 Francis Stoppelman
240 UPI
241 UPI
242 ® Valtman-Rothco Cartoons
244 Wide World
245 UPI
247 Baldev/Sygma
248 U.S. Department of the Interior
250 Universal Studios
252 Paramount Pictures
253 *Top:* Columbia Pictures; *Bottom:* Pictorial Parade
254 Wide World
255 *Left:* Wide World; *Right:* Wide World
256 Beth Bergman
257 UPI
258 *Top:* UPI; *Bottom:* UPI
259 UPI
260 UPI
261 UPI
262 UPI
263 Wide World
264 UPI
265 *Top:* Pictorial Parade; *Bottom:* Culver Pictures
266 *Top:* Culver Pictures; *Bottom:* UPI
267 *Left:* Culver Pictures; *Right:* Wide World
268 *Top:* Pictorial Parade; *Bottom:* The Granger Collection
269 *Top:* Culver Pictures; *Bottom:* Wide World
270 *Top:* CBS; *Bottom:* Pictorial Parade
271 Brookhaven National Laboratory
272 *Top, Left:* Pictorial Parade; *Top, Right:* Bettmann Archive; *Bottom:* Camerapix/Photo Trends
273 UPI
274 *Top, Left:* Culver Pictures; *Top, Right:* Edward Rice/Photo Trends; *Bottom, Right:* Werner Braun/Photo Trends
275 *Top:* Pictorial Parade; *Bottom:* Brian D. McLaughlin/Globe Photos
276 Photo Trends
277 Culver Pictures
278 *Top:* Ken Spencer/*Newsday*; *Bottom:* Culver Pictures
279 *Left:* UPI; *Right:* Pictorial Parade
280 *Clockwise from Top, Left:* Culver Pictures; Wide World; Wide World; UPI; Pictorial Parade
281 *Clockwise from Top, Left:* Culver Pictures; Bettmann Archive; Culver Pictures; Culver Pictures; Pictorial Parade
282 UPI
283 UPI
285 Wide World
286 *Top:* UPI; *Bottom:* Wide World
287 *Top:* Wide World; *Bottom:* C. Rafshoon/Pictorial Parade
288 *Top:* Pictorial Parade; *Bottom:* Photo Trends
289 *Top:* Wide World; *Middle:* Pictorial Parade; *Bottom:* Wide World
290 *Top:* Keystone; *Bottom:* Kaufman/Sygma
291 Saw Lin/United Nations
292 *Top:* Wide World; *Bottom:* UPI
293 *Top:* Barton Silverman/New York Times Pictures; *Bottom:* UPI
294 *Top:* UPI; *Bottom:* UPI
295 *Top:* Pictorial Parade; *Bottom:* Ken Hawkins/Sygma
296 *Left:* Sven Simon/Katherine Young; *Right:* Liaison
297 *Top:* Keystone; *Bottom:* UPI
298 Jean-Pierre Moutin/Liaison
299 UPI
300 *Top:* Pictorial Parade; *Middle:* Penelope Breese/Liaison; *Bottom:* UPI
301 Wide World
302 Daniel Simon/Liaison
303 *Left:* Jacques Tiziou/Sygma; *Right:* Jim Moore/Liaison
305 *Top:* ® Oliphant, 1978 Washington *Star*/Los Angeles *Times* Syndicate; *Bottom:* N. K. Koppel
306 Wide World
307 Washburn Gallery, New York City
308 *Top:* New York Times Pictures; *Bottom:* Metropolitan Museum of Art, the Alfred Stieglitz Collection
309 *Left:* ® Eve Arnold/Alfred A. Knopf Publishers; *Right:* Polaroid Corp.
310 Princeton University
311 Andanson/Sygma
312 Owen Franken/Sygma
313 *Top:* Wide World; *Bottom:* ® 1978 Ken Regan/Camera 5
314 Jim McHugh/Sygma
316 *Left:* UPI; *Right:* G/S-Photo Trends
318 UPI
319 Wide World
320 UPI
321 UPI

INDEX TO THE 1979 YEARBOOK
EVENTS OF 1978

INTRODUCTION

This Index is a comprehensive listing of persons, organizations, and events that are discussed in the 1979 Yearbook. Entries in **boldface** letters indicate subjects on which the Yearbook has an individual article. Entries in lightface type are to individual references within articles. In either type of entry, the letters a and b refer, respectively, to the left and right column of the page cited. If no letter follows a page number, the reference is to text that is printed across the full width of a page. Only the first significant mention of a subject in a given article has been included in the Index.

In a main entry such as **Australia:** 94a, the number refers to the page on which the article begins. The succeeding lightface page numbers refer to other text discussions in page order of the volume. If, however, as in **Congress of the United States:** 123a; Elections, 152b, another title precedes the second page reference, the discussion is located in the titled subentry in the page location mentioned. In the case of comprehensive articles such as the **United States of America,** reference is made to the page location of the beginning of the article. The discussion of foreign relations of the United States in that article may be augmented by reference to separate articles on the countries and international organizations concerned.

When an Index entry is followed by the abbreviation **illus.,** the reference is to a caption and picture on the page mentioned. If more than one page reference is given in a lightface entry, the first page number provides the most extensive information on that subject.

LIST OF ABBREVIATIONS USED IN THE INDEX

COMECON   Council for Mutual Economic Assistance
NATO   North Atlantic Treaty Organization
OPEC   Organization of Petroleum Exporting Countries

PLO   Palestine Liberation Organization
SALT   strategic arms limitation talks
U.N.   United Nations

UNESCO   U.N. Educational, Scientific, and Cultural Organization
U.S.S.R.   Union of Soviet Socialist Republics

470

Figueiredo, João Baptista da: 100b; **illus.** 101
Fiji: 440
Filbinger, Hans: 173a
Filion, Herve: 372b
Filipiak, Boleslaw: 270a
Fillol, Ubaldo ("Pato"): 375b; **illus.** 88
financial review: 420a
Finland: 167a, 96a, 442
Fischer, Bobby: 110a
Fischer, John: 328a
fish: 305a; **illus.** 222a
Fish and Fisheries: 167b
Fishman, Jack: 146a
Fitzgerald, Robert D.: 227b
Fitzsimmons, Frank E.: 211a
Fixx, James F.: 226a
Flanagan, Mike: 376a
Flanner, Janet: 270a
flashlight fish: **illus.** 222b
Flood, Daniel J.: 133a, 291a
Florida: 380b, 456
fluoride: 188b
Fluro-bulb: **illus.** 388a
Flynt, Larry: 326a
Fontaine, Frank: 270a
Food and Drug Administration: 130b
football: 369b
Ford, Betty: **illus.** 289b
Ford, Gerald R(udolph): 289b, 298a; **illus.** 351b, 432b
Ford, Susan: 289b
Forego: 291b
Formosa. *See* TAIWAN
Fox, Paula: 228b
Fraiberg, Selma: 226b
France: 168b, 157a, 162b, 164a, 298a, 442; Africa, 71a; Communism, 122a; Literature, 231a; Military and Naval Affairs, 243b; Zaire, 433b
Francke, Linda Bird: 226b
François, Claude: 316a
Fraser, Douglas A.: **illus.** 139
Fraser, Malcolm: 94a, 118a
Fratianne, Linda: 374b
Freeman, Don: 230a
Freeman, Joseph, Jr.: 259b; **illus.** 348a
Frick, Ford Christopher: 270a
Frings, Joseph: 270a
Fukuda, Takeo: 203b; **illus.** 112a, 204
Furbank, P. N.: 230a
Furth, Harold P.: 310a

G

Gabon: 69a, 442
Gacy, John Wayne: 134b
Galway, James: **illus.** 335
Gambia, The: 442
gambling: 155a, 211a; **illus.** 424
Gandhi, Indira: 193a; **illus.** 194b
Gandhi, Sanjay: 193b
Gann, Paul: 423b
Gaprindashvili, Nona: 110b
García Márquez, Gabriel: 231a
Gardner, Eliot L.: 98b
Garner, Helen: 227b
"Gasahol": 159b
gasoline: 421a
Gaza Strip: 239b
Geer, Will: 270a
Geisel, Ernesto: 101a; **illus.** 101
Geller, Bruce: 270a, 334b

General Services Administration: 415b
genetics: 26, 183b, 216a
Genn, Leo John: 270b
Gentry, Stephen: 334b
geology and geophysics: 145a
Georgia: 381b, 384b, 456
German Democratic Republic (East Germany): 171a, 375a, 427a, 442; Literature, 231b; Space Exploration, 361b; West Germany, 172b
Germany, Federal Republic of (West Germany): 172b, 164a, 301b, 442; Brazil, 101b; Bulgaria, 102b; Czechoslovakia, 137b; East Germany, 171b; Literature, 231b; New Zealand, 261b; Somalia, 358a
Ghana: 175a, 442
Ghashmi, Ahmed Hussein al-: 430a
Gibb, Andy: 315a
gibberellins: 109a
Gierek, Edward: 312a
Gilbert, Kevin: 227b
Gilbert, Walter: 217a
Gilbert Islands. *See* KIRIBATI
Gilliam, Jim ("Junior"): 270b
Gillies, Clark: 374a
Gilson, Étienne Henry: 271a
Gin Game, The: 322b
Ginsberg, Allen: 224b
Ginzburg, Aleksandr: 203b, 405a
Ginzburg, Natalia: 231b
Giscard d'Estaing, Valéry: 164b, 168b, 174a, 312b, 317b; **illus.** 298a
Gittelson, Natalie: 226a
Gittings, Robert: 230a
Givens, Jack: **illus.** 367
Glistrup, Mogens: 141b
Godbout, Jacques: 227b
Gödel, Kurt: 271a
Goff, Norris: 271a
Golan Heights: 386a, 409a
golf: 371a, 43
Goodall, Jane: 99a
Goodwin, Frederick K.: 98a
Gordon, Joseph Lowell ("Flash"): 271a
Gordon, Mary: 224b
Gordon, Max: 271a
Gossage, Rich: 366b
Gottlieb, Melvin B.: 310a
Goudsmit, Samuel Abraham: 271a
Gracias, Valerian: 271a
Graham, Billy: 344b
Graham, Martha: 139a
Grant, Duncan James Corrowr: 271a
Grass, Günter: 231b; **illus.** 229b
Grasso, Ella: **illus.** 153
Gray, L. Patrick, 3rd: 132a
Gray, Simon: 230b
Great Britain: 175b, 118a, 164a, 297b, 356a, 358b, 442; Ireland, 198b; Military and Naval Affairs, 244b; Rhodesia, 352b
Grechko, Georgi: 361b, 406b
Greece: 178b, 164a, 442; Archeology, 82b; Cyprus, 135b; NATO, 263b; Religion, 342a; Turkey, 403b
Greene, Graham: 230a
Greenfield, Meg: 322b
Greenland: 142a, 362b
Greenwood, Charlotte: 397a
Gregory, Cynthia: **illus.** 138
Grenada: 283a, 428a, 442
Griffin, Robert T.: 301a
Grigg, John: 230b
Grigorenko, Pyotr: 405b

Grimaldi, Rainier and Grace: 253b, 290a
Grimes, Nikki: 229b
Grinfelds, Vesma: 369a
Gromyko, Andrei: 407a; **illus.** 172
Gronchi, Giovanni: 271b
Groom, Winston: 224b
Grüntzig, Andreas: 182b
Grusa, Jiri: 232b
Guam: 460
Guatemala: 179a, 442
Gubarev, Aleksei: **illus.** 405b
Guidry, Ron: 366b; **illus.** 365
Guillevic: 231a
Guinea: 442
Guinea-Bissau: 442
Gulf Oil Canada: 389b
Gur, R. C.: **illus.** 99b
Guyana: 179b, 349a, 413a, 442
Guzmán Fernández, Silvestre Antonio: **illus.** 427b

H

Haig, Alexander M., Jr.: 263a
Haines, Jesse Joseph: 271b
Haiti: 282b, 428a, 442
Halabi, Mohammed Ali, al-: 386b
Halaby, Elizabeth (Lisa): 206b, 290a
Haley, Alex: 325a
Hallgrímsson, Geir: 190b
Hammami, Said: 284b
handball: 43
Handke, Peter: 232a
Hanna, Richard T.: 133a
Hannah, Barry: 224b
Hanse, Lisa: 375a
Hardy, Hugh: 84a
Harmsworth, Esmond Cecil: 328a
harness racing: 372a
Harrington, Robert: 144b
Harris, Patricia R(oberts): 105a, 298b
Harris, William and Emily: 133b
Harrison, Robert: 328a
Hasani, Ali Nasser Mohammed: 431a
Hassan II: 249b
Hasselblad, Victor: 309b
Havlicek, John ("Hondo"): 291b
Hawaii: 380b, 456
Hawkins, Augustus F.: 209b
Haya de la Torre, Victor Raúl: 304a
Hayes, Woody: 291b, 371a
Healey, Denis: 176b
Health and Medicine: 181a, 24, 130b, 195a, 381b
health insurance: 124b
Hearst, Patricia: 133b; **illus.** 289b
heart disease: 182a
Heaven Can Wait: **illus.** 252
Heiden, Beth: 374b
Heiden, Eric: 374b
Helin, Eleanor: 145a
hemoglobin: 109a
Herbert, Gregory: 316a
Hermaszewski, Miroslaw: 361b
Hernández Agosto, Miguel: 328b
Hernández-Colón, Rafael: 328b
Herr, Michael: 323a
Herrera Campíns, Luis: 425a
Hertzler, Barry L.: 110a
Heym, Stefan: 231b
high jumping: 378a
Highwater, Jamake: 229b
Hills, Elizabeth: 375a
Hinduism: 348a
Hirose, Tadaaki: 217a
Hisle, Larry: 366b

Milk, Harvey: 134a, 413a
Miller, Arnold: 210a
Miller, Elizabeth: 323a
Miller, G(eorge) William: 299b, 421a; **illus.** 300a
Miller, Irene: **illus.** 254a
Miller, James: 323a
Miller, Richard McDermott: 323a
Miller, Stephen G.: 82b
Milligan, William: **illus.** 187b
Milosz, Czeslaw: 232b
Minerals and Metals: 248a
mining: **illus.** 248
Minnesota: 380b, 458
Mintoff, Dominic: 234a
missiles: 245b, 264a
Mississippi: 380b, 458
Missouri: 381b, 458
Mitchell, Peter: 321a
Mitterrand, François: **illus.** 187b
Mobutu Sese Seko: 77b, 433a
Modiano, Patrick: 231a
Mohammed, Ali Nasser: **illus.** 241
Moi, Daniel Arap: 72b, 206a; **illus.** 71
Monaco: 253b, 448
Mondale, Walter F.: 95b, 238b, 261a, 306b; **illus.** 123, 300a
Monge, Luis Alberto: 131a
Mongolian People's Republic: 448
Montale, Eugenio: 231b
Montana: 156b, 458
Montealegre, Felicia: 397a
Montini, Giovanni Batista. See PAUL VI
Montoya, Joseph Manuel: 275a
Montréal Canadiens: 373a
Moon, Keith: 275a
Moore, Charles: 83b
Morales Bermúdez, Francisco: 304a
Morantz, Paul: 413a
Moravia, Alberto: 231b
Mork & Mindy: 432a
Mormonism: 259b, 348b
Moro, Aldo: 122b, 201b, 275a; **illus.** 202a
Morocco: 249a, 71b, 240b, 448; Algeria, 77a
Morris (the cat): 68a
Morrison, Bret: 334b
Morrison, Toni: 323a
mortgages: 424a
Moscone, George: 134a, 413a
Moser, Annemarie Proell: 375b
Mota Pinto, Carlos Alberto: 317a; **illus.** 316a
Motion Pictures: 250a
Mountaineering: 254a
MOVE: 134b
Mozambique: 254b, 70a, 172a, 244b, 448
Mugabe, Robert: 244b, 352b
Muhammad, Wallace D.: 348a
Muldoon, Robert: 261a
Mullaney, Thomas: 328a
Mulligan, Richard: 217b
Mullin, Willard: 328a
Muncey, Bill: 368a
Muñoz Marín, Luis: 328b
Muravin, Victor: 232b
Murdoch, Iris: 230a
Murdoch, Rupert: **illus.** 326
Murray, Les: 227b
Music: 255a, 312b, 334b, 432b
Muzorewa, Abel: 352b; **illus.** 353
Mycenaeans: 83a
Myers, C. W.: 221b
Myers, Richard C.: 182b
Myrtle, Odette: 397a

476

N

Nabokov, Nicolas: 258a
Naeye, Richard: 183a
Nagy, Ivan: **illus.** 138
Nakasone, Yasuhiro: 203b
Namibia. See SOUTH-WEST AFRICA
Narraganset Indians: 191a
Nassiri, Nematollah: 197b
Nathans, Daniel: 322a
National Aeronautics and Space Administration: 360b
National Council of Churches: 346a
National Gallery of Art, East Building: 84a, 89a; **illus.** 83
National Highway Traffic Safety Administration: 130a
National Park Service: 162a
national security: 18, 32, 114b
natural gas: 77a, 155b
Nauru: 448
Navaho Indians: 192a
Navon, Itzhak: 201a; **illus.** 199
Navratilova, Martina: 377b
Nazis: 116a
Nebel, Long John: 334b
Nebraska: 159a, 381a, 458
Negroes in the United States: 258a, 330a, 351a; Civil Rights, 114a
Nemerov, Howard: 322b, 323a
Németh, Károly: 190a
Nepal: 448
Netherlands, The: 260a, 164a, 448
Neto, Agostinho: 77a, 317b, 434a; **illus.** 77b
Nettles, Graig: 366b; **illus.** 365
Neumann, Jonathan: 323a
neutron bomb: 245b, 260b, 263a
Nevada: 458
Newbery award: 230a
New Brunswick: 462
Newfoundland: 462
New Hampshire: 154b, 458
Ne Win: 103a
New Jersey: 381a, 424b, 458
Newman, Larry: 292b
Newman, Paul: **illus.** 408
Newman, Peter: 228b
New Mexico: 191a, 380b, 458
Newsam, R. J.: 219b
newspapers: 23, 115a, 134a, 210b, 326a, 383b
New York: 380b, 383b, 398a, 458
New York City: 85a, 124b, 150b, 411a
New York City Ballet: 137a
New York City Marathon: 364, 414a
New York Yankees: 365b, 414a
New Zealand: 260b, 448
Ngouabi, Marien: 122b
Nguyen Duy Trinh: **illus.** 392
Nicaragua: 261b, 283a, 338a, 407b, 417b, 448
Nicklaus, Jack: 371b
Niemi, Olivia: 329a
Niger: 448
Nigeria: 262b, 71b, 174b, 448
Nijinsky, Waslaw: **illus.** 307
Nikodim: 275b
Nilsson, Gunnar: 275b
Nimeiry, Gaafar Mohammed al-: 72a, 382a
nitrites: 130b
Nixon, Richard M(ilhous): 225a, 289a, 383b; **illus.** 300b
Nkomo, Joshua: 244b, 352b
Noah's Ark: 230a
Nobel Prizes: 321a
Nobile, Umberto: 275b
Noble, Ray: 276a

Nordli, Odvar: 264b
North, Andy: 372a
North Atlantic Treaty Organization: 263a; Iceland, 190b; Military and Naval Affairs, 246a; Turkey, 403b; Warsaw Pact, 427a; West Germany, 174b
North Carolina: 458
North Dakota: 381b, 458
Northern Ireland: 177a
Northern Yemen. See YEMEN ARAB REPUBLIC
North Korea. See KOREA, DEMO-CRATIC PEOPLE'S REPUBLIC OF
Northwest Territories: 462
Norton, Ken: **illus.** 369a
Norton, Virginia: 369a
Norway: 264b, 448
Nouira, Hedi: 402b
Nova Scotia: 462
nuclear energy: 29, 96a, 96b, 101b, 155a, 156a, 170b, 215b, 247b, 260a, 310a, 385a
numismatics. See COIN COLLECTING
Nureyev, Rudolf: 138b
nutrition: 43
Nyad, Diana: 293a, 430a
Nyerere, Julius K.: 135b, 387b
Nygren, Anders: 350b
Nyiregyházi, Ervin: **illus.** 337

O

Oakie, Jack: 276a
Obasanjo, Olusegun: 174b, 262b
Obituaries: 265a
Obolensky, Serge: 68b
O'Brien, Darcy: 323a
O'Brien, Lawrence: 368a
oceanography: 146b
O Dalaigh, Cearbhall: 198b
Ogaden region: 70b, 163b, 244a, 357b
O'Gara, Feral: 220a
Ohio: 384b, 458
Ohira, Masayoshi: 203b; **illus.** 204
Ohtake, Masakazu: 145a
oil. See PETROLEUM
oil spills: 162b, 402a
O'Keeffe, Georgia: **illus.** 308
Oklahoma: 458
Oliveira, Elmar: 257b; **illus.** 255
Oman: 448
Onassis, Christina: **illus.** 290a
O'Neill, Thomas P(hilip), Jr.: 140a; **illus.** 301a
Ongais, Danny: 365a
Ontario: 462
opera: 256b, 336a
optics: 120b
orchestras: 256a, 336a
Oregon: 381a, 458
Örek, Osman: 136a
Orfila, Alejandro: 283a
Organization for Economic Cooperation and Development: 282a
Organization of African Unity: 69a, 358b, 404b
Organization of American States: 282b, 13, 88a, 286b, 424b, 427b
Organization of Petroleum Exporting Countries: 283a, 157a, 208b, 237b; Saudi Arabia, 355a; U.S., 410b
Örkény, István: 232b
Orkin, Stuart H.: 218a
Orlov, Yuri: 9, 405a
Orr, Bobby: 291b
Osmani, M.A.G.: 97a

Osmond, Donny and Marie: **illus.** 288
Oswald, Lee Harvey: 132b
Oteiba, Manae Said al-: **illus.** 283
Ovshinsky, Stanford: 236b
Owen, David: 178a
Oz, Amos: 232b; **illus.** 232a
ozone: 146a

P

Pacepa, Ion: 355b
Padilla Arancibia, David: 100b
Pahlavi, Mohammed Riza: 196b, 241b, 347a
Pakistan: 284a, 245b, 448
Palestine Liberation Organization: 284b, 199b, 212b, 240b, 245b; Algeria, 77a; Arab League, 80b; Iraq, 198a; Israel, 200a; Jordan, 206a; U.N., 409a
Paley, Barbara Cushing: 167a
Panama: 285b, 448
Panama Canal treaties: 124b, 285b, 350b, 415a
Panama Canal Zone: 460
Panov, Valery and Galina: 138b
Papandreou, Andreas: 179a
Papashvily, George: 227a
paper: 74a, 235b
Papua New Guinea: 448
Paraguay: 286a, 282b, 448
Park, Brad: 374a
Park, Ruth: 227b
Park Chung Hee: 207b
Parker, Dave: 366b
Park Tong Sun: 133a, 207b
Parnov, Eremei: 232a
Parton, Dolly: 315b; **illus.** 312b
Pasqua Yaqui Indians: 192a
Passamaquoddy Indians: 191b
Passarella, Daniel: **illus.** 88
Passman, Otto E.: 133a
Pastorini, Dan: 370a
Paterson, Katherine: 230a
Patterson, Pete: 375b
Paul VI: 276a, 339a; **illus.** 341b
Paz García, Policarpo: 189b
Peace Prize, Nobel: 199b, 244b, 295a, 301b, 321b
Pearson, John: 230b
Pei, I. M.: 84a, 89a
Pei, Mario Andrew: 276a
Pelli, Cesar: 84a
Pennsylvania: 381a, 458
Penobscot Indians: 191b
Penzias, Arno A.: 322a
People in the News: 287a
People's Temple: 179b, 349a, 413a
Peralta Azurdia, Enrique: 179a
Pereda Asbún, Juan: 100b
Perelman, S. J.: 323a
periodicals: 325a
Perovic, Mileta: 433a
Perry, Gaylord: 366b
Perse, Saint-John: 231a
Pertini, Alessandro: 202b; **illus.** 201
Peru: 304a, 111a, 448
pest control: 219b
pesticides: 109b
Peterson, Esther: 129b
Peterson, Ronnie: 276a, 365a
petroleum: 77a, 155b, 176b, 197b, 208b, 237a, 282a, 283a, 355a, 402a, 410b, 425b
Pets: 304a
Peyrefitte, Alain: 231a
Pfeiffer, Jane Cahill: 334b
Pham Van Dong: 357a, 392b, 426a

Philadelphia: 155a
philately: 378a
Philippines, Republic of the: 305a, 450
Photography: 306b, 391a
physical fitness: 38
Physics: 310a, 157a
Piercy, Marge: 224b
Piltdown hoax: 80a
Piñerúa Ordaz, Luis: 425a
Pinochet Ugarte, Augusto: 111a
Pinter, Harold: 230b
Piper, Harold: 407a; **illus.** 406a
Pittsburgh Steelers: 369b
planetary exploration: 92b, 142a
Player, Gary: 372a
Plotz, Helen: 229b
Pluto: 92b, 142a
Podrabinek, Aleksandr: 405a
Poetzsch, Anett: 374b
Poland: 311b, 299a, 427a, 450; Communism, 122a; Literature, 232b; Space Exploration, 361b
pole vaulting: 378b
Polisario Front. *See* SAHARA, SPANISH OR WESTERN
pollution: 29, 110a, 161a, 235b, 248a, 402a
Pol Pot: 105a
Pomerance, Rafe: **illus.** 139
"Pompeii, A.D. 79": **illus.** 90a
Pope, Virginia: 167a
Popular Music: 312b
Porter, Marina Oswald: **illus.** 132
Portugal: 316a, 164b, 450
post office: 120a, 210b, 323b, 378a
Potvin, Denis: 374a
Powell, Lewis F., Jr.: 382b
Premadasa, Ranasinghe: 108b
Prem Tinsulananot: 391b
Presbyterianism: 343b
President of the United States: 317b
Prima, Louis: 376b
primates: 78b, 98b; **illus.** 218
Prince Edward Island: 462
Prizes and Awards: 321a, 227b, 393a
Proposition 13: 140b, 155a, 214a, 380b, 410b, 423b
Protestantism: 343a
Prouvost, Jean: 328a
Provenzano, Anthony ("Tony Pro"): 211a
Proxmire, William: 38
psychology. *See* BEHAVIORAL SCIENCES
public finance: 421b
Publishing: 323b, 306b
Puerto Rico: 328a, 460
Pulitzer Prizes: 322b
Puzo, Mario: 224a

Q

Qaddafi, Muammar el-: 71a, 214a, 215a, 234b
Qadir, Abdul: 68b
Qatar: 450
Quate, Calvin: 311a
Québec: 106b, 227b, 302b, 462

R

Radio and Television Broadcasting: 329a, 384a; Advertising, 67a
Radio City Music Hall: 417a
Rafshoon, Gerald: 319a; **illus.** 67
Rahman, Ziaur: 97a
railroads: 210b, 400b

Ramsey, Paul: 350a
rape: 430b
Rapu, Sergio: 81b
Rattner, Abraham: 92b
Ray, James Earl: 133a; **illus.** 132
Ray, Joie: 276b
Reagan, Ronald: **illus.** 351b
Recordings: 334b, 315a
recreation. *See* SPORTS
Red Brigades: 122b, 201b
Red Cross: 338a
Redgrave, Vanessa: 253b
Redhead, Fabian Alexis: **illus.** 282b
redlining: 195b
Reese, Leslie: 227a
refugees: 103b, 196a, 233a, 417b; **illus.** 107b, 234
Rehnquist, William H.: 382b
Reid, Rose Marie: 167a
Reinking, Ann: **illus.** 394
Religion: 339a; Guyana, 179b; U.S., 413a
Remek, Vladimir: 137a, 361b; **illus.** 405b
Rennert, Guenther: 258b
Republican Party: 350a, 294b, 298a, 301a; Congress, 123a; Elections, 152b; U.S., 410a
retirement age: 124a, 381b
Rhode Island: 191a, 381a, 458
Rhodes, John J(acob): 301a, 350a
Rhodesia: 352b, 70a, 172a, 244a, 338a, 344b, 408b, 450; Great Britain, 178a; Mozambique, 255a; South Africa, 359b; Tanzania, 387b; U.S., 417a; U.S.S.R., 406b; Zambia, 434a
Riad, Mahmoud: 81a, 240b
Rice, Jim: 366b
Rich, Adrienne: 224b
Rich, Lorimer: 87a
Rideout, John J. and Greta: 430b
Right to Life movement: 430a
Rio de Janeiro: 91b
Rizzo, Frank L.: 155a
Roach, James P.: 328a
Robards, Jason: 253b
Robbins, L. H.: 79a
Roberts, Oral: 344b
Robertson, Pat: 344b
Robinson, Larry: 373b
Robson, Mark: 276b
Rochester, N.Y.: **illus.** 87
Rockefeller, John D(avison), 3rd: 276b
Rockwell, George L.: 277a
Rockwell, Norman: 277a
Roldós, Jaime: 147a
Rolling Stones: 314b
Roman Catholicism: 202b, 299a, 312a, 339a, 430a
Romanenko, Yuri: 361b, 406b
Romero, Carlos Humberto: 155b
Romero Barceló, Carlos: 328a
Rono, Henry: 377b
Ronstadt, Linda: 315a
Rorvik, David M.: 216a
Rose, Pete: 366b; **illus.** 292b
Rose, Robert: 188a
Rosen, Nathaniel: 257b; **illus.** 255
Rosenberg, Harold: 277a
Rosovsky, Henry: 150a
Ross, Clifford: 323a
Ross, Diana: **illus.** 250a
Ross, Stanford G.: 357a
Rossman, Mike: 369b
Rostropovich, Mstislav: 405b
Roszak, Sara: 323a

477